The Prince and the Law, 1200–1600

A CENTENNIAL BOOK

One hundred books
published between 1990 and 1995
bear this special imprint of
the University of California Press.
We have chosen each Centennial Book
as an example of the Press's finest
publishing and bookmaking traditions
as we celebrate the beginning of
our second century.

UNIVERSITY OF CALIFORNIA PRESS

Founded in 1893

The Prince and the Law, 1200–1600

Sovereignty and Rights in the Western Legal Tradition

Kenneth Pennington

UNIVERSITY OF CALIFORNIA PRESS
Berkeley · Los Angeles · Oxford

University of California Press
Berkeley and Los Angeles, California

University of California Press
Oxford, England

Library of Congress Cataloging-in-Publication Data

Pennington, Kenneth.
    The prince and the law, 1200–1600: sovereignty and rights in the
western legal tradition / Kenneth Pennington.
        p.   cm.
    Includes bibliographical references and index.
    ISBN 0–520–07995–7 (alk. paper)
    1. Kings and rulers—History.   2. Prerogatives, Royal—History.
3. Rule of law—History.   4. Monarchy—History.   5. Roman law—
Influence.   I. Title.
K3334.P46   1993   92–40544
340′.11—dc20   CIP

Printed in the United States of America

1   2   3   4   5   6   7   8   9

The paper used in this publication meets the minimum requirements
of American National Standard for Information Sciences—Permanence
of Paper for Printed Library Materials, ANSI Z39.48–1984 ∞

For Marlene

Contents

Acknowledgments

I began writing this book in 1985 during a long sabbatical in Munich. My research was generously supported by the Fulbright Commission, the Gerda Henkel Stiftung, and Syracuse University. During my stay in Munich, Professor Dr. Horst Fuhrmann provided me with a "Sitzplatz" in the Monumenta Germaniae Historica and gave me access to its incomparable library. The staff of the Monumenta was uncommonly helpful, and I owe much to many of the Mitarbeiter who shared their expertise with me on many points. Other European libraries provided materials for this book and generously opened their doors to me. The Bayerische Staatsbibliothek, Munich, the Universitätsbibliotheken in Erlangen, Frankfurt, Heidelberg, Munich, and Würzburg, Stadtbibliothek, Nürnberg, British Library, London, Lambeth Palace Library, London, Bodleian and All Souls College Libraries, Oxford, Cambridge University Library, Bibliothèque nationale and Bibliothèque Mazarine, Paris, Biblioteca Apostolica Vaticana, Biblioteca nazionale, Florence, Biblioteca Laurenziana, Florence, Archivio di Stato, Florence, Archivio di Stato, Pistoia, Nationalbibliothek, Vienna, Landesbibliothek, Kassel, Staatsbibliothek, Augsburg, Stiftsbibliothek, Aschaffenburg, and Staatsbibliothek, Bamberg, all made their manuscripts and their photographic services available to me during my stays. This book would not have been finished without the amiable help of the librarians at these libraries. The Alexander von Humboldt Stiftung supported a second trip to Europe in the summer of 1989, and I gratefully acknowledge, once again, their generosity. At home, where this book was completed, the librarians of Syracuse University responded to my research needs with the same kindness that they have shown me during the last twenty years.

As it matured, many people have read and commented on this book at various stages. Every author owes a great debt to patient colleagues and friends who are willing to struggle with an imperfect text, and my thanks are due to Robert Benson, Stanley Chodorow, Richard Fraher, Richard Helmholz, Joseph Levine, James Powell, Dennis Romano, Brian Tierney, and my students Brendan McManus and Wolfgang Müller. Finally, I must thank the editors at the University of California Press for seeing this work through the press and their copyeditor, Allan Graubard, for his careful, attentive labor.

This book is dedicated to Marlene. Her contribution to this book cannot be found in the text or the footnotes, but not all important things can be found in scholarly monographs.

Abbreviations

JOURNALS AND SERIES

AKKR	*Archiv für katholisches Kirchenrecht*
BMCL	*Bulletin of Medieval Canon Law*
Clm	*Codices latini Monacenses of the Bayerische Staatsbibliothek, Munich*
DA	*Deutsches Archiv für Erforschung des Mittelalters*
DBI	*Dizionario biografico degli Italiani*
DDC	*Dictionnaire de droit canonique*
DMA	*Dictionary of the Middle Ages*
EHR	*English Historical Review*
HZ	*Historische Zeitschrift*
LMA	*Lexikon des Mittelalters*
MGH	*Monumenta Germaniae historica*
MIC	*Monumenta iuris canonici*
MIÖG	*Mitteilungen des Instituts für Österreichische Geschichtsforschung*
NA	*Neues Archiv der Gesellschaft für ältere deutsche Geschichtskunde*
PL	Migne, *Patrologia latina*
QF	*Quellen und Forschungen aus italienischen Archiven und Bibliotheken*

SG   *Studia Gratiana*
TRG   *Tijdschrift voor Rechtsgeschiedenis*
ZRG   *Zeitschrift der Savigny-Stiftung für*
                            Rechtsgeschichte

STANDARD WORKS

Handbuch, ed. Coing: *Handbuch der Quellen und Literatur der*
                          neueren europäischen Privatrechtsgeschichte:
                          1. *Mittelalter (1100–1500)*: *Die gelehrten*
                          Rechte und die Gesetzgebung. Ed. Helmut
                          Coing, München: C. H. Beck'sche Verlags-
                          buchhandlung, 1973
Savigny, *Geschichte*:   Friedrich Carl von Savigny, *Geschichte der*
                          römischen Rechts im Mittelalter. 2d Ed.
                          7 volumes. Berlin: 1834–1851. Reprinted
                          Bad Homburg: 1961
Schulte, *Quellen*:   Johann Friedrich von Schulte, *Die Geschichte*
                          der Quellen und Literatur des canonischen
                          Rechts von Gratian bis auf die Gegenwart.
                          3 Volumes. Stuttgart: 1875–1880. Reprinted
                          Graz: 1956

LEGAL CITATIONS

a.c.   Dictum of Gratian before chapter
Authen.   Novellae or Constitutions of Justinian in their
                              medieval form
C.   Causa (division of the second part of Gratian's
                              Decretum)
c.   chapter
Clem.   Clementines: Constitutions of Clement V
Cod.   Code of Justinian
1 Comp.   Compilatio prima
2 Comp., etc.   Compilatio secunda, etc.
D.   Distinctio (division of the first part of Gratian's
                              Decretum)
De pen.   De penitentia, a section of Gratian's Decretum
Dig.   Digest of Justinian
ff.   Digest of Justinian

Instit.	Institutes of Justinian
l.	lex, law in Justinian's Corpus iuris civilis
p.c.	Dictum of Gratian after chapter
q.	quaestio (division within a causa of Gratian's Decretum)
v.	sub verbo, gloss to a phrase in a law or decretal
VI	Liber Sextus of Boniface VIII
X	Liber Extra or Decretals of Gregory IX

Introduction

In 1987, newspaper columnist Tom Wicker wrote that a former foreign minister of Israel, Abba Eban, preferred that the United States concentrate on new diplomatic initiatives in the Middle East rather than on a "prolonged investigatory ordeal" into the "Iran Affair" that was creating dangerous political storms for the Reagan ship of state. Mr. Eban's suggestion, inveighed Wicker:[1]

> reflects a profound misunderstanding of the rule of law that is at the root of American democracy, and an even greater misreading of democracy's limits. Nothing undermines the rule of law, hence democracy, more than the ability of some temporary government, even for purposes believed good, to set aside law, or distort it, or ignore it.

What worried Mr. Wicker also concerned the medieval jurists, even though they were lamentably ignorant of modern democratic principles. They did dabble in theories of representative government, created doctrines of consent to legislation, and believed in limited government. Through their writing and teaching jurists had created a powerful system of norms and rules derived from natural law, customary law, ancient Roman law, feudal law, and canon law that defined their conception of a properly ordered world.[2] They conceived of law as a re-

---

1. *The International Herald Tribune,* January 5, 1987, p. 4.
2. The best introduction to these ideas is Ennio Cortese's brilliant book, *La norma giuridica: Spunti teorici nel diritto comune classico* (2 volumes; Ius nostrum 6; Milan: 1962–1964).

pository of norms that created an unwritten constitution for society. Modern historians have dubbed this construct "Medieval Constitutionalism." Manlio Bellomo calls their system of thought a "common law" that reigned over medieval and early modern Europe.[3]

Wicker assumed that "rule of law" and "democracy" are tautological—one cannot logically exist without the other. "Rule of law," however, is an equivocal term: It can mean a society regulated by an ordered, just legal system, or it can mean a narrow legal principle.[4] In any case, Wicker is probably right about modern democracies; the "rule of law" is a cornerstone of democratic institutions in the late twentieth century. But a reverential belief in the "rule of law" can and did exist long before Western democracies.

In its earlier lives, "rule of law" was an important element in monarchical and republican (that is, non-monarchical, but not necessarily democratic) governments. When Wicker referred to "rule of law," he wanted to define a government's duty to uphold the rules of the legal system and to maintain the written constitution of the state. The implicit question he posed—could or should a government break the law for the public good?—has been asked regularly by Western thinkers since the twelfth century.

The Middle Ages is a fair trek, in mind and spirit, from the twentieth century. In fact, where twelfth-century jurists had some difficulty even defining law, today the institutions of the state are the primary sources of law. Before the age of legal positivism, however, law could be found in many cupboards: in nature, in the Bible (divine law), in customs of the people, in the law of nations (ius gentium), as well as in the positive law of the prince. Written constitutions bestow great advantages to our age. They define much that was undefined and disputed in earlier legal systems, and they codify the unwritten customs and beliefs of our world.

In the twelfth century, the Roman and canon lawyers, the most important political theorists of the time, confronted an uncharted terrain: the relationship of the prince and the law. Gradually they mapped it, creating metaphorical and visual symbols to represent the prince and his authority. As they plotted the various types of law, they also discovered Wicker's problem: when and under what circumstances could

---

3. For an extended essay on the "ius commune" of the continent, see Manlio Bellomo, *L'Europa del diritto comune* (Rome: 1989).

4. K. Pennington, "Maxims, Legal," DMA 8 (1987) 231–232.

the prince set aside, distort, or ignore the rules of the legal system(s) that he was normally obligated to preserve and uphold?

The first and most basic question the jurists had to answer was this: "who was the prince?" From ancient and early medieval thought, they inherited a vision of a unitary world and a supreme ruler, the Roman emperor. The Romans had Christianized the office of emperor; the early Middle Ages moved his center of authority from Rome to Northern Europe. Even though the empire in its medieval form never achieved the unity that theory described, the rediscovery of Roman law in the eleventh century reinforced its claims of universal power in the twelfth century. In addition, the revival of Roman law did much more than create a jurisprudential doctrine of lordship in Europe. It excited the inconclusive thoughts surrounding the nuclei of monarchy and sent off highly charged ideas in all directions. These ideas, embedded in the dense margins of medieval law books, impacted on medieval governing institutions at every level: the empire, the Church, the national monarchies, principalities, city-states, and local corporations of clerics and laymen. Within a century of this impact, governing institutions just mentioned had all undergone structural changes.[5] Clearly, then, while the revival of learned law was not responsible for all institutional changes in the twelfth century, it was a significant factor.

Out of this medieval reactor emerged two new elements: a juristically defined secular ruler, the emperor, whom the texts of ancient Roman law almost invariably called "princeps" or prince, and a more sharply focused concept of law. Since, however, the medieval emperor did not exercise the comprehensive power and authority of his ancient predecessor, it was inevitable that other rulers would make claims to possess the prerogatives and power of imperial authority—or conversely, that some jurists would claim that their kings could not exercise the same prerogatives as the emperor. By the end of the twelfth century, the jurists had even invented a maxim describing Roman law's impact on the office of kings: "Rex in regno suo imperator est," a king is emperor in his own kingdom.

Before the jurists created the "prince" as a generic term to describe all rulers, they had to come to some understanding of the role of the

5. One could offer an endless bibliography to illustrate this change. An article by Robert L. Benson discusses two examples of the process from the twelfth century: the "renovatio sacri senatus" in the city of Rome after 1143 and the "renovatio sacri imperii" in the twelfth-century empire: "Political 'renovatio': Two models from Roman Antiquity," *Renaissance and Renewal in the Twelfth Century*, ed. R. L. Benson and G. Constable (Cambridge, Mass.: 1982) 339–386.

Roman, Germanic, Christian emperor. His claims of universal rulership impinged not only on the authority of every other monarch's sovereignty but also on the inviolability of the law. By the end of the twelfth century, the jurists conceded that law was not immutable. The emperor, kings, and even city-states could change law. Legislation, however, created problems and posed questions. Must the emperor have cause to introduce new laws? Could he break the law without cause? Could he wrongly deprive a subject of his rights? In the first three chapters I shall explore the evolution of the prince's authority in medieval legal thought.

This book is about power and about rights: the power of the prince and the rights of his subjects. In legal thought these two terms wage almost constant war against each other. The jurists began to write comprehensively about princely power by the end of the twelfth century. At almost the same time, they saw that power without limitations was dangerous and violated their deeply seated beliefs about how the world and society ought to be ordered. In few periods of human history did individuals cling as tenaciously and believe as devoutly in their liberties and privileges as in the Middle Ages. The feudal world encouraged them to think of the world as a set of obligations and prerogatives. A vassal must render his due to his lord, but the lord must steadfastly respect the position of, observe his obligations to, and render justice to his vassals.

In the pages that follow, we shall hear little of the rights of women. Although medieval law did recognize a few rights of women, the story that we shall tell is of male rights, power, and privilege in a male-dominated legal system. Women were not permitted to study or to practice law. Only relatively recently have the fundamental rights that we shall discuss been unreservedly and without exception granted to women.

Like the rule of law, the rights of individuals, men and women, have become shibboleths of late twentieth-century political and legal thought. By treaty and decree, governments have embraced the idea that certain rights are sacred, generally called "natural" or "human" rights, and politicians have declared that only the most callous and amoral regimes ignore them. A cynic might question whether most governments or many politicians would recognize a "right" if it hit them in the face. Nevertheless, human rights have become a political and legal badge of courage in the late twentieth century.

In American law, jurists and the courts have focused on the rights of defendants. Since World War II, the Supreme Court of the United States has created a set of rules governing the treatment of defendants and protecting them from arbitrary treatment by police. William Brennan, a forceful and eloquent proponent of defendants' rights, noted that "the protection of the dignity of the human being and the recognition that every individual has fundamental rights which the government cannot deny him" is the central purpose of the American constitution.[6]

Historians have traced the origins of a doctrine that granted natural rights to all human beings either to John Locke in the seventeenth century or to William Ockham in the late Middle Ages. The question of origins can play an essential role in our understanding of our past. On this point I must pose only one obvious question: Can nondemocratic societies spawn a doctrine of rights? Answering that question with an emphatic yes, Brian Tierney has moved the origins of theories of rights back to the twelfth century. The jurists, he argues, were the first to enunciate a clear doctrine of natural rights.[7]

From chapter 4 on, I shall examine the counterpoint of the prince's power and the rights of litigants in his court. This is a corner of the broader problem of when and where doctrines of rights arose. I shall focus on Justice Brennan's concerns: the rights of defendants before the law—an aspect of what we call in Anglo-American law "due process of law." The jurists juxtaposed the prince's absolute power with the rights of litigants to receive justice. The juxtaposition resulted in an extended discussion of the prince's power and his subjects' rights that stretched over several centuries. That discussion is the heart of this book.

Before I turn to that discussion, I must clarify the term "due process." In modern parlance, "due process" refers to the "course of legal proceedings established by the legal system . . . to protect individual rights."[8] It is, of course, anachronistic to apply the term to medieval

6. Nat Hentoff, "The Constitutionalist," *The New Yorker* (March 12, 1990) 45.

7. Brian Tierney, "Tuck on Rights: Some Medieval Problems." *History of Political Thought* 4 (1983) 429–441; "Villey, Ockham and the Origins of Natural Rights Theories." *The Weightier Matters of the Law: Essays on Law and Religion*. Ed. John White, Jr. and F. S. Alexander. American Academy of Religion Studies in Religion, 51. Atlanta: 1988: 1–31; "Origins of Natural Rights Language: Texts and Contexts, 1150–1250." *History of Political Thought* 10 (1989) 615–646. Tierney surveys modern historical thought on natural rights in these essays and provides extensive bibliographical information.

8. To quote one dictionary's definition; *Webster's New World Dictionary of the American Language* (2d College Edition; 1978).

legal systems—even if it is a medieval coinage.[9] Our concept of due process encompasses far more than the right to have a wrong examined in a court. English legal historians have used "due process" loosely to describe any supposition by medieval lawyers that a case should be judged according to the procedure and laws of the land. This definition is so broad—and in many cases misleading—that it is almost meaningless as a technical term. Every legal system, no matter how primitive, embraces the concept that every litigant should be granted a hearing that conforms to the law of the land or people.[10] I shall use the term in the following pages to describe medieval jurists' treatment of issues that are important elements of our assumptions about due process: the right of a litigant to be summoned, to testify, and to present evidence in court. These rights, which became a part of Western European legal thought only during the thirteenth century, are not part of every legal system.

Finally, in this book I am concerned with the development of a *ius commune*, a common law, in Western Europe during the medieval and early modern periods. When applied to continental legal systems, the term "common law" sounds strange to most English-speaking historians. In the Anglo-Saxon legal world, we speak of common law as being the legal system that evolved in England from the eleventh century to the present. However, the fusion of Roman, canon, and feudal law produced a *ius commune* and a common jurisprudence in Europe between 1100 and 1600.[11] In the pages that follow, we shall see how these three legal systems created new doctrines that became legal tender in each. In this study, I will illustrate how the jurists of Italy, Spain, France, and Germany approached problems informed by a common jurisprudence. Geography and language did not isolate them as modern jurists often are. A common body of law, a common system of legal education, and a common body of literature bound European jurists together. By the year 1300, the two major branches of law in Western Europe, canon and Roman law, were parts of a single intellectual sys-

9. The earliest use of the term is in a statute of Edward III, 28 Edward III, c.3 (1354): "saunz estre mesne en respons par due proces de lei." The phrase is frequently used in the fifteenth century: 4 Henry IV, c.22, "le incumbent ouste sanz due proces." 7 Henry IV, c.4: "sont condempnes a leurs creditours per due proces du loy." 9 Henry V, Statute 1, c.8: "convicta de felonie per due proces de leie."

10. See, for example, Norman Doe, *Fundamental Authority in Late Medieval English Law* (Cambridge Studies in English Legal History; Cambridge: 1990) 27–31, who discusses the Statutes cited in n. 9 without examining what the term might have meant in the fourteenth and fifteenth centuries. See also K. Jurow, "Untimely Thoughts: A Reconsideration of the Origins of Due Process of Law," *American Journal of Legal History* 19 (1975) 265–279.

11. See Bellomo, *L'Europa del diritto comune* 67–89.

tem. Although Romanists, or civilians as they are sometimes called, might distinguish themselves from their canonistic colleagues or vice versa, their rare jibes at one another should not mislead us. They grappled with common problems and solved those problems within the intellectual framework of the *ius commune*. What we may see as "cross-fertilization," they understood as "self-fertilization." The development of Western ideas on the authority of the prince or due process of law was not the work of canon, Roman, or secular jurists, but an intricately choreographed intellectual dance of three partners that lasted more than four centuries. The music ended only with the triumph of national legal systems in the seventeenth century; a finale that not all historians applaud.[12]

12. Ibid., 11–43.

CHAPTER 1

The Emperor Is Lord of the World

The Bolognese Lawyers and Imperial Ideology

Quid autem sit absoluta, vel potius
soluta lege potestas, nemo definiit.
(No one has defined absolute power, or
rather power that has been freed from laws)
—Jean Bodin, *De republica* 1.8

Jean Bodin (1529/30–1596) exaggerated the novelty of his analysis of political power, and historians have exaggerated the novelty of his exaggeration. That Bodin stressed his originality is forgivable; that is an author's prerogative. That historians have accepted his contention without careful scrutiny is less understandable.[1] Bodin went on to write:[2]

> For if we define freed from all laws [as absolute power] no prince anywhere possesses sovereignty (iura maiestatis), since divine law, the law of nature, and the common law of all people, which is established separately from divine and natural law, bind all princes.

1. E.g., Helmut Quaritsch, *Souveränität: Entstehung und Entwicklung des Begriffs in Frankreich und Deutschland vom 13. Jh. bis 1806* (Schriften zur Verfassungsgeschichte, 38; Berlin: 1986) 39–42. Other historians have been much more nuanced in their descriptions of Bodin's thought. See the remarks of Dieter Wyduckel, *Princeps Legibus Solutus: Eine Untersuchung zur frühmodernen Rechts– und Staatslehre* (Schriften zur Verfassungsgeschichte, 30; Berlin: 1979) 151–152. Wyduckel gives a good introductory bibliography on pp. 16–17. See also Wyduckel's *Ius publicum: Grundlagen und Entwicklung des öffentlichen Rechts und der deutschen Staatsrechtswissenschaft* (Schriften zum Öffentlichen Recht, 471; Berlin: 1984) 119–120.

2. *De republica libri sex* (3rd ed. Frankfurt: 1594) 132: "Nam si legibus omnibus solutam definiamus nullus omnino princeps iura maiestatis habere comperiatur, cum omnes teneat lex divina, lex item naturae, tum etiam lex omnium gentium communis, quae a naturae legibus ac divinis divisas habet rationes." The French text differs in several important respects. *Les six livres de la republique* (Paris: 1577) 95: "Vray est, que ces docteurs ne disent point que c'est de puissance absolue, car si nous disons que celuy a puissance absolue, qui n'est point suget aux loix, il ne se trouvera prince au mond souvrain, veu que tous les princes de la terre sonts sugets aux loix de Dieu et de nature et à plusieurs è tous peuples."

Although the terminology was different, the jurists of the twelfth century were the first since late antiquity to pose the question of whether the prince was bound by any laws. Definitions of princely authority in the early Middle Ages were descriptions of rank, legitimacy, prerogatives, or privilege. Those jurists who studied canon law concocted and adopted terms defining power, like "plenitudo potestas," "auctoritas," or "plena potestas," but neither they nor these terms described the prince's relationship to the law nor his right to usurp the legal rights of his subjects.[3]

Prior to the twelfth century, the most interesting list of princely attributes was the so-called *Dictatus papae*. Although this collection of aphorisms was a precocious characterization of papal primacy and jurisdictional supremacy within the Church, it did not define the pope's relationship to the law. The author of the *Dictatus papae* merely observed that the pope could promulgate new laws when necessary.[4] If, however, legend has it right, we must turn to the court of Frederick Barbarossa; the question that Bodin attempted to answer in the *Republic* was posed in an inchoate but recognizable form at Frederick's court and was, most likely, asked by the emperor himself. Two of the most renowned jurists of Roman law in the twelfth century, Bulgarus and Martinus, struggled with the emperor's question. We learn of the question and of their answers only by exploring a set of difficult legal, literary, and historical texts. Although these texts may convey more myth than fact, we have learned that myths may transcend fact but not always truth.

Frederick Barbarossa dominated his age.[5] His empire was the most powerful state of twelfth-century Europe; his court, his chancellors, his

---

3. See Robert L. Benson, "Plenitudo potestatis: Evolution of a Formula from Gregory IV to Gratian," *Collectanea Stephan Kuttner* (SG 14; Bologna: 1967) 195–217, who discusses the terminology and cites the relevant literature. For the term "auctoritas," see Stephan Kuttner, "On 'auctoritas' in the Writing of the Medieval Canonists: The Vocabulary of Gratian," *La notion d'autorité au Moyen Age, Islam, Byzance, Occident*, ed. George Makdisi et al. (Paris: 1982) 69–81 and Jürgen Miethke, "Autorität, I." *Theologische Realenzyklopädie* 5 (1980) 30.

4. *Register Gregors VII.*, ed. Erich Caspar (MGH, Epistolae selectae; Berlin: 1920) no. 7, p. 203: "Quod illi soli licet pro temporis necessitate novas leges condere." No. 18 states that only the pope could rescind the decisions of his predecessors, which is a rough version of the maxim "par in parem imperium non habet." The other versions of the *Dictatus papae* state: "Omni tempore licet ei nova decreta constituere et antiqua (*vel vetera*) temperare." See Hubert Mordek, "*Proprie auctoritates apostolice sedis*: Ein zweiter Dictatus papae Gregors VII.?" DA 28 (1972) 129.

5. Two recent books analyze Frederick's reign from different perspectives: Horst Fuhrmann, *Deutsche Geschichte im hohen Mittelalter* (Göttingen: 1978), translated into English by Timothy Reuter (Cambridge: 1986) and I. S. Robinson, *The Papacy 1073–1198: Continuity and Innovation* (Cambridge Medieval Textbooks; Cambridge: 1990).

poets, and his jurists were the most sophisticated of their time. He also stimulated lugubrious historical prose. Frederick, wrote Gibbon, invaded Lombardy "with the arts of a statesman, the valour of a soldier, and the cruelty of a tyrant. The recent discovery of the Pandects had renewed a science most favourable to despotism, and his venal advocates proclaimed the emperor the absolute master of the lives and properties of his subjects."[6] Gibbon's dark rhetoric contrasts sharply with descriptions of Frederick at the Diet of Roncaglia in November 1158. Rahewin of Freising re-created the pomp of the opening ceremonies in his continuation of Otto of Freising's *Deeds of Frederick Barbarossa.* Young Frederick gave an "oration" to the assembled nobles and clerics that was translated into Italian.[7] He claimed that divine ordinance sanctioned his rule. His imperial duty was to coerce wrongdoers and protect the good.[8] Frederick promised to subject his authority to the law and to preserve each individual's liberties and rights.[9] At this Diet, Frederick continued, he wished to direct his efforts to promulgating laws of peace.[10] Civil law was established by the emperor and confirmed by the customs of the people.[11] When law is reduced to writing, we must

---

The article by H. Appelt, "Die Kaiseridee Friedrich Barbarossas," *Sitzungsberichte der Akademie der Wissenschaften in Wien,* phil.-hist. Klasse 252.4 (Vienna: 1967) is useful.

6. Edward Gibbon, *History of the Decline and Fall of the Roman Empire,* ed. O. Smeaton (New York: n.d.) III 50, quoted by H. Koeppler, "Frederick Barbarossa and the Schools of Bologna: Some Remarks on the 'Authentica Habita,'" EHR 54 (1939) 577–607, at 577.

7. Otto of Freising and Rahewin, *Gesta Friderici I. Imperatoris,* ed. G. Waitz and B. von Simson (MGH, Scriptores rerum Germanicarum in usum scholarum, 46; 3rd ed. Hannover-Berlin: 1912) 236–237; Robert Benson analyzed Frederick's "Oratio" at Roncaglia in 1158 in a paper delivered at Dumbarton Oaks, February, 1985, and still unpublished, in which he demonstrated that the text is a pastiche of quotes from Sallust, Roman law, and Gratian's Decretum. Benson identified the sources of canon and Roman law that I have cited in the notes. See Benson's remarks in "Political 'Renovatio,'" 364–369.

8. Ibid.: "inquieti coherceantur, boni subleventur atque in pacis tranquillitate foveantur." Cf. D.4 c.1, C.23 q.1 c.6.

9. Ibid.: "desideramus potius legittimum tenere imperium et pro conservanda cuique sua libertate et iure." Cf. Instit. 1.1.1.

10. Ibid.: "utrum melius sit patriam armis tutare seu legibus gubernare, altero alterius auxilio indigente, bellorum motibus propitia divinitate sedatis, ad leges pacis negotia transferamus." Instit. pr., Cod. de Iust. Cod. con. pr.

11. Ibid.: "Nostis autem quod iura civilia nostris beneficiis in summum provecta, firmata ac moribus utentium approbata satis habent roboris." D.4 d.p.c.3. On this passage in Gratian, see Luigi de Luca, "L'accettazione popolare della legge canonica nel pensiero di Graziano e dei suoi interpreti," SG 3 (1955) 193–276 and Brian Tierney, "'Only the Truth has Authority': The Problem of 'Reception' in the Decretists and in Johannes de Turrecremata," *Law, Church, and Society: Essays in Honor of Stephan Kuttner* (Philadelphia: 1977) 69–96, especially pp. 74–78. On twelfth-century Romanist views of legislation, see André Gouron, "Coutume contre loi chez les premiers glossateurs," *Renaissance du pouvoir législatif et genèse de l'état,* ed. A. Gouron and A. Rigaudière (Publications de la Société d'Histoire du Droit et des Institutions des anciens pays de Droit écrit 3; Montpellier: 1988) 117–130.

be sure that it is honorable, just, possible, necessary, useful, and suited to the time and place.[12] These precepts are of great importance, Frederick concluded, because after laws have been established, one is not free to judge the laws, but one must judge according to them.[13] If one were to judge Frederick's conception of kingship from this speech that Rahewin preserved, none of his rhetoric could have justified Gibbon's somber reference to Frederick's being "the absolute master of the lives and properties of his subjects."

Afterwards, Hubertus, the archbishop of Milan, rose and delivered an encomium to Frederick's benign rule.[14] Frederick, he declared, did not plan war, but the laws of peace. How Italy had suffered before him! Italians had endured unfair, arrogant, and cruel governments that proscribed the property of the rich without cause; they committed many other crimes as well. We know, he said, directly quoting Roman law, that all the people's authority of making law is vested in you.[15] Your will is law, for what pleases the prince has the force of law, since the people have yielded and granted the prince all their authority and powers. Whatever the emperor has established, decreed, or enjoined is law.[16] Hubertus ended his speech with an impressive piece of legal learning. Quoting a rule of law from the Digest, he stated: It is in accordance with Nature that he should enjoy the benefit of anything who must suffer the unpleasant consequences of that thing. So you who bear the burden of tutelage for all of us ought to rule us all.[17]

Roman law infused the imperial court's rhetoric. When Godfrey of Viterbo, notary and chaplain of the court, composed a poetic panegyric of the emperor's legislative authority, he invoked Hubertus's legal metaphors: The emperor was the living law; he could grant, abrogate, and establish laws.[18] Roman law had created these metaphors, but the

12. Ibid.: "Sive ergo ius nostrum sive vestrum in scriptum redigatur, in eius constitutione considerandum est, ut [sit] honestum, iustum, possibile, necessarium, utile, loco temporique conveniens." Cf. Dig. 1.1.6.1, D.4 d.p.c.2, D.4 c.2.

13. Ibid.: "quia cum leges institutae fuerint, non erit liberum iudicari de eis, sed oportebit iudicare secundum ipsas." Cf. D.4 d.p.c.2.

14. Ibid., 237–239.

15. Ibid.: "Scias itaque omne ius populi in condendis legibus tibi concessum." Cf. Dig. 1.4.1.

16. Ibid.: "Tua voluntas ius est, sicut dicitur: Quod principi placuit, legis habet vigorem, cum populus ei et in eum omne suum imperium et potestatem concessit. Quodcumque enim imperator per epistolam constituerit vel cognoscens decreverit vel edicto preceperit, legem esse constat." Hubertus took his inspiration from either Instit. 1.2.6 or Dig. 1.4.1 (Ulpian).

17. Ibid.: "Profecto secundum naturam est, commoda cuiusque rei eum sequi, quem secuntur incommoda, ut videlicet omnibus debeas imperare, qui omnium nostrum sustines onera tutelae." Dig. 50.17.10. On the importance of the Roman law of tutelage for medieval theories of government, see Walter Ullmann, *Law and Politics in the Middle*

medieval jurists found them exquisitely suited to exalt the authority of their prince. However, despite the rhetoric, these descriptions of imperial legislative power do not transcend those in the *Dictatus papae* nor do they address the issues raised by Bodin. The prince's authority to legislate stands apart from the question of whether he transcends the rights of his subjects.

The reports from Roncaglia may not be true, or, if true, not accurate. We do not know with certainty if Rahewin was at Roncaglia.[19] Historians have suspected that his transcriptions of speeches are far from being precise. Rahewin often borrowed the language of his chronicle from classical sources, and we can never be sure when he was an eyewitness. Although we do not know if he had legal training, we do know that his frequent references to Roman and canon law reflect the importance of jurisprudence in the mid-twelfth century.

Frederick was the first emperor to recognize the importance of Roman law and the jurists for shaping a theory of empire. His aims and interests are reflected in Rahewin's and Otto's descriptions that are redolent of law and replete with references to judicial proceedings at Roncaglia. Although any assembly of this period included political, juridical, and sometimes legislative matters, at Roncaglia all three were considered. According to Rahewin, in the first days of the Diet, the emperor was occupied at his court dispensing justice to the rich and the poor. He also issued legislation governing the feudal relationships in Italy and even summoned the four great doctors of Roman law in Bologna—Martinus, Bulgarus, Jacobus, and Hugo—to aid him with these and other complex questions of law. For the first time since

Ages: An Introduction to the Sources of Medieval Political Ideas (Ithaca, New York: 1975) 49, 58, 70, 205.

18. *Carmen de gestis Friderici* MGH, Scriptores 22.316, line 388. See Laurent Mayali, "Lex animata: Rationalisation du pouvoir politique et science juridique (XIIème-XIVème siècles)," *Renaissance du pouvoir législatif et genèse de l'état*, ed. André Gouron and Albert Rigaudière (Montpellier: 1988) 155–156 and Benson, "Political 'Renovatio,'" 365.

19. See J. B. Gillingham, "Why did Rahewin stop writing the *Gesta Friderici?*" EHR 83 (1968) 294–303; Peter Munz, "Why did Rahewin stop writing the *Gesta Friderici?* A Further Consideration," EHR 84 (1969) 771–779; W. Grundlach, "Zu Rahewin," NA 11 (1886) 569–570; Max Manitius, "Zu Rahewin, Ruotger und Lambert," NA 12 (1887) 361–385; Sigmund Riezler, "Namen und Vaterland des Geschichtsschreibers Rachwin," *Forschungen zur deutschen Geschichte* 18 (1878) 539–540; Henry Simonsfeld, "Bemerkungen zu Rahewin," *Historische Aufsätze dem Andenken an Georg Waitz gewidmet* (Hannover: 1886) 204–227; B. von Simson, "Über die verschiedenen Rezensionen von Ottos und Rahewins Gesta Friderici I." NA 36 (1911) 681–716; Carl Martens, *Ein Beitrag zur Kritik Ragewins* (Greifswald: 1877); Hans Prutz, *Radewins Fortsetzung der Gesta Friderici imperatoris des Otto von Freising, ihre Zusammensetzung und ihr Werth* (Danzig: 1873). Benson, "Political 'Renovatio,'" 365, n. 123.

antiquity, a monarch called upon professors of law to participate in government.

That Frederick Barbarossa took a special interest in the law school at Bologna, issued the authentica, Habita,[20] granting the clerics at Bologna special privileges, and recognized the importance of law for imperial administration and as a justification of his rule should no longer be surprising.[21] In Frederick's chancery, the terminology and metaphors of Roman (and canon) law had begun to shape his legislation.[22]

The new legal learning shaped the laws that Frederick issued at Roncaglia. He promulgated (at least) three laws, later included in the body of medieval Roman law, that were discovered only two decades ago in a Parisian manuscript.[23] These laws touch upon the emperor's rights and prerogatives in Italy. An Italian chronicler, Otto of Morena, wrote that Frederick had called the Four Doctors to him and asked them to describe rights of regalia that were due to him in Lombardy.[24] The results of their consultation must be preserved in the texts of the Parisian manuscript that have the form of decrees issued *proprio motu* (from his initiative) and provide answers to the emperor's question. Two of the laws contain stipulations about the emperor's rights of taxation

20. Edited by Winfried Stelzer, "Zum Scholarenprivileg Friedrich Barbarossas (Authentica 'Habita')," DA (1978) 123–165. Also printed by Koeppler, "Frederick Barbarossa," 606–607; Stelzer dates the decree to the year 1155. See Walter Ullmann, "The Medieval Interpretation of Frederick I's Authentic 'Habita,'" *L'Europa e il diritto romano: Studi in memoria di Paolo Koschaker* (Milan: 1954) I 99–136, reprinted in his *Scholarship and Politics in the Middle Ages* (Variorum Selected Studies Series; London: 1978) and Ingrid Baumgärtner, "'De privilegiis doctorum': Über Gelehrtenstand und Doktorwürde im späten Mittelalter," *Historisches Jahrbuch* 106 (1986) 298–332.

21. On Roman law at Barbarossa's court, see Benson, "Political 'Renovatio,'" 364–369. Peter Munz, *Frederick Barbarossa: A Study in Medieval Politics* (London: 1969) 167–168, especially n. 1, p. 168, seriously underestimates the importance of Roman law for secular governments in the twelfth century (if not its importance for ecclesiastical government). See the corrective remarks of Horst Fuhrmann, *Germany in the High Middle Ages c. 1050–1200* trans. Timothy Reuter (Cambridge: 1986) 147–148 (2d German ed. 1983, p. 164) and Dieter Wyduckel, *Princeps Legibus Solutus* 46. For the importance of legal studies in the development of papal government, see Jürgen Miethke, "Die Kirche und die Universitäten im 13. Jahrhundert," *Schulen und Studium im sozialen Wandel des hohen und späten Mittelalters,* ed. Johannes Fried (Vorträge und Forschungen, 30; Sigmaringen: 1986) 285–320.

22. Heinrich Fichtenau, *Arenga: Spätantike und Mittelalter im Spiegel von Urkundenformeln* (Köln-Wien: 1957) 178.

23. Vittore Colorni, "Le tre leggi perdute di Roncaglia (1158) ritrovate in un manuscritto parigino (Bibl. Nat. Cod. Lat. 4677)," *Scritti in memoria di Antonino Giuffrè* (Milan: 1967): I 111–170; translated into German by Gero Dolezalek, *Die drei verschollenen Gesetze des Reichstages bei Roncaglia wieder aufgefunden in einer Pariser Handschrift (Bibl. Nat. Cod. Lat. 4677)* (Aalen: 1969). See Benson, "Political 'Renovatio,'" 366–368.

24. Otto of Morena, *Historia* 59: "In primis vocavit imperator omnes iam dictos Bononie magistros iussitque eis, quod ipsi indicarent ei in veritate omnia regalia iura, quecumque imperii iure in Longobardia ad ipsum spectarent ac sua esse deberent."

and of having public buildings (palacia et pretoria) in each Italian city where he and his officials could conduct imperial affairs.[25] For the history of political theory, the first law, *Omnis jurisdictio,* is the most interesting.[26]

> The prince possesses all jurisdiction and all coercive power. All judges ought to accept their administration from the prince. They should all swear the oath that is established by law.

The two words used to define the prince's power were Roman and Italian. *Jurisdictio* was a term from Roman law, and *districtus* was Italian. The two are often found together in twelfth-century sources.[27] Roman law dictated that all judges receive their administration from the emperor and stipulated that imperial administrators must swear an oath that they would perform their duties in accordance with the law.[28] Here, then, Frederick's jurists had formulated a concise, succinct definition of imperial power based on Roman precedents.[29]

Although the Bolognese jurists busied themselves with twelfth-century imperial ideology, Frederick himself had an interest in the theory and the practice of power. However, since he did not know law or Latin, we can only speculate what he thought of Roman law and the large, imposing books that preserved Justinian's codification. We can only wonder what vision he conjured when he heard Archbishop Hubertus declare that his will was law at Roncaglia. The jurists, we must remember, dealt with theory and rarely with practice. Their

25. "Palacia et pretoria" were listed as the rights of the imperial rectors in the provinces by the Emperor Anastasius, Cod. 1.40.15(14). See Colorni, *Drei Gesetze* 34–35; Colorni discusses the Roman law precedents for the law on taxation on pp. 36–40. Karl Leyser, "Some Reflections on Twelfth-Century Kings and Kingship," *Medieval Germany and its Neighbors 900–1250* (London: 1982) 247–248, remarks that the laws are an example of the transformation of personal to transpersonal rule. See H. Beumann, "Zur Entwicklung transpersonaler Staatsvorstellungen," *Das Königtum: Seine geistigen und rechtlichen Grundlagen,* ed. T. Mayer (Vorträge und Forschungen 3; Sigmaringen: 1956) 185–224.

26. Colorini, *Drei Gesetze* 26: "Omnis iurisdictio et omnis districtus apud principem est, et omnes iudices a principe administrationem accipere debent, et iusiurandum prestare quale a lege constitutum est."

27. Ibid., 30. The canonists do not seem to have incorporated "districtus" into their terminology of papal power, although the adverb, "districte," is often found in papal decretals of the twelfth century.

28. Ibid., 29; the basis of the oath for magistrates in Roman law is Novel 8, promulgated by Justinian in 535.

29. These three laws would provide evidence to counter Koeppler's view, "Frederick Barbarossa," 587–588, that the jurists "were not employed as creators of imperial policy . . . [theirs] was a subordinate position but a helpful one."

understanding of law was far more sophisticated than Frederick's, and they understood that the prince's will was not completely unfettered. Frederick, perhaps, was not as aware of his limitations. Nevertheless, Frederick and his deeds provided the jurists with ample inspiration to contemplate the authority and rights of the prince.

How did Frederick himself conceive of his office and his status? Unfortunately, outside the laws of Roncaglia, we have very little evidence that would permit us to glimpse his view of the emperor's role. The jurists who may have drafted his legislation offer little guidance. The four doctors wrote only scattered glosses on Justinian's Digest and Code to enlighten us about their conceptions of the imperial office.

Oral traditions dating back to Roncaglia prodded later jurists to consider the authority of the emperor. Invoking the memory of Frederick and his son, Henry VI, they repeated anecdotes that focused on the role of the jurists at Roncaglia. These stories have long been famous for their biographical information; they are also important for the development of political ideas. A careful analysis of each of these anecdotes reveals much about evolving ideas of power and authority in the thirteenth century and something about Frederick's and his jurists' conceptions of imperial authority.

Martinus and Bulgarus, two of the four great twelfth-century doctors of Roman law who took part in the Diet of Roncaglia, are the chief actors of these tales. The two glossators possessed intriguing personalities, and many vignettes circulated about their differences. However, one story captured the attention of many: how Bulgarus lost a horse to Martinus. The jurists retold the anecdote in the lecture halls of Bologna and adapted it for their commentaries. It even had a literary echo. An anonymous author, a novellistà, whom today we would call a writer of short stories, included the tale in a thirteenth-century collection of Italian stories later known as the "Hundred Old Tales."

Although the setting, and perhaps the origin of the story, was Roncaglia, it circulated orally until ca. 1220; it received its first written form in additions made to Otto Morena's chronicle of Frederick Barbarossa's reign and a short notice in Accursius's gloss to Justinian's Codex. Later, Odofredus (ca. 1250), the garrulous Roman lawyer with an inimitable teaching style that shines through dense clusters of legal citations in his commentaries, told a different, but similar story in his lectures, derived, most likely, from a fleeting reference in Azo's *Summa* to the Codex. In the later Middle Ages, many jurists rehearsed the anecdote in their commentaries.[30] These tales raised questions about the authority and status of the emperor in Christian society and, more important, the relationship of the prince and the law. Whether fact or fiction, these stories ask for the first time whether the emperor can transcend law and act arbitrarily in matters touching the rights of others.

The anonymous chronicler who revised Morena's history gave the following account.[31] Frederick was riding on horseback with Bulgarus and Martinus.[32] He asked them whether, according to law, he was the lord of the world.[33] Bulgarus replied that he was not lord over private property. Martinus said that he was the lord of the world. Frederick got off his horse and presented it to Martinus but gave nothing to Bulgarus. Bulgarus lamented Frederick's choice with a series of not-quite-translatable puns: "I lost an equine because I upheld equity, which is not equitable."[34]

We cannot know whether this conversation actually took place as reported. Most scholars think not.[35] Nonetheless, like Salimbene de Adam's stories about Frederick's grandson, Frederick II, if the story is

30. Thomas Diplovatatius, *Liber de claris iuris consultis*, ed. F. Schulz, H. Kantor-wicz, and G. Rabotti (SG 10; Bologna: 1968) 51–52, mentions a third version of the story in his life of Martinus. In this story a certain Frenchman and a certain Johannes were the characters. He also cites a number of jurists who retell the tale.

31. On the revision of Morena's work see Ferdinand Güterbock, "Zur Edition des Geschichtswerks Otto Morenas und seiner Fortsetzer," NA 48 (1930) 116–147.

32. See Savigny, *Geschichte* IV 75–123 (Bulgarus) and 124–140 (Martinus). Bruno Paradisi, "Bulgaro," DBI 15 (Rome: 1972) 47–53. Benson, "Political 'Renovatio,'" 375–376.

33. Robert Holtzmann, "Dominium mundi und Imperium merum: Ein Beitrag zur Geschichte des staufischen Reichsgedankens," *Zeitschrift für Kirchengeschichte* 61 (1942) 191–200.

34. (MGH, Scriptores 18; Hannover: 1863) 607 and Güterbock's edition in MGH Scriptores rerum Germanicarum, Nova Series 7; (Berlin: 1930) 59: "Cum dominus Fredericus imperator semel equitaret super quodam suo palafredo in medio dominorum Bulgari et Martini, exquisivit ab eis utrum de iure esset dominus mundi. Et dominus Bulgarus respondit, quod non erat dominus quantum ad proprietatem. Dominus vero Martinus respondit, quod erat dominus. Et tunc dominus imperator, cum descendisset de palafredo, super quo sedebat, fecit eum presentari dicto domino Martino. Dominus autem Bulgarus hec audiens, dixit hec elegantia verba: amisi equum, quia dixi equum, quod non fuit equum."

35. Ugo Nicolini, *La proprietà, il principe e l'espropriazione per pubblica utilità: Studi sulla dottrina giuridica intermedia* (Pubblicazioni dell'Istituto di Diritto Romano dei Diritti dell'Oriente mediterraneo e di Storia del Diritto, 14; Milan: 1940) 111–115, thinks it improbable that the story has any foundation in fact. He cites (p. 112 n. 2) earlier literature, except for Georg Meyer, *Das Recht der Expropriation* (Leipzig: 1868) 85–90 and 97–113; Otto von Gierke, *Johannes Althusius und die Entwicklung der naturrecht-lichen Staatstheorien: Zugleich ein Beitrag zur Geschichte der Rechtssystematik* (Unter-suchungen zur deutschen Staats- und Rechtsgeschichte, Alte Folge 7; Breslau: 1902; reprinted 6th ed. Aalen: 1968) 268–272. Savigny, *Geschichte* IV 180–183, also discusses the various versions of the story.

not true, it should be. If Martinus and Bulgarus did not hold differing opinions on the extent of the emperor's power, certainly jurists did. A glossed manuscript to the Codex in the Biblioteca Laurenziana contains a gloss signed with "M." that would support Martinus's opinion in the story.[36] Another, unsigned gloss takes Bulgarus's position.[37] This manuscript contains four layers of twelfth-century glosses to the Code by a variety of jurists.[38]

After having looked at the legislation of Roncaglia, we could conclude that Frederick might have asked his question exactly as Otto of Morena's continuator formulated it. In 1157, King Henry II of England had written to the emperor that he placed "our kingdom and everything subject to our rule anywhere at your disposal."[39] After this letter, Frederick might have thought that he was Lord of England; he may well have reflected upon greater prerogatives and claims. Several years later, Frederick's court poet hailed him as "Lord of the World" in rhyme.[40] For us, of course, the anecdote of the horse and of its later adaptations is of interest because it reveals fundamental changes in the lawyers' thoughts about the relationship of the prince to the law at the end of the twelfth and the beginning of the thirteenth centuries.

Part of the story's appeal was its cleverness and ambiguity. Bulgarus's answer presupposed that Frederick was, generally speaking,

36. Florence, Laurenziana, Redi 179, fol. 120r, to Cod. 7.37.3 (Bene a Zenone): "Omnia principis esse intelligantur, ff. de iure fisci, Fiscus [Dig. 49.14.6] Eodem patet in decretis, xxiii. ca. q.viii. Conuenior [C.23 q.8 c.21]." Martinus's laconic formulation is not necessarily a confirmation of his position in the stories. See discussion below.

37. Ibid.: "scilicet fiscalia et patrimonalia, secus in bonis priuatis."

38. Gero Dolezalek, *Verzeichnis der Handschriften zum römischen Recht bis 1600* (Frankfurt: 1972) and *Repertorium manuscriptorum veterum Codicis Iustiniani* (Repertorien zur Frühzeit der gelehrten Rechte; Ius commune, Sonderhefte 23; Frankfurt am Main: 1985) 192–193, dates the manuscript to the first half of the twelfth century. Unfortunately, the manuscript is poorly written and is very difficult to read in places. Much work needs to be done on the manuscripts containing the glosses of the early jurists.

39. *Ottonis et Rahewini Gesta Friderici I. imperatoris*, eds. Georg Waitz and B. von Simson (MGH, Scriptores rerum Germanicarum in usum scholarum 46; 3d ed. Hannover-Leipzig: 1912) 172: "Regnum nostrum . . . vestre committimus potestati." The meaning of this extraordinary gesture has been disputed, see Othmar Hageneder, "Weltherrschaft in Mittelalter," MIÖG 93 (1985) 259 n. 7. Also Robert Holtzmann, "Der Weltherrschaftsgedanke des mittelalterlichen Kaisertums und die Souveränität der europäischen Staaten," HZ 159 (1939) 251–264, at 255. Karl Leyser gives a masterful interpretation of the letter and its influence in "Frederick Barbarossa, Henry II, and the Hand of St. James," *Medieval Germany and its Neighbors* 215–240, originally published in EHR 90 (1975) 481–506. See the remarks of Wolfgang Georgi, *Friedrich Barbarossa und die auswärtigen Mächte: Studien zur Aussenpolitik 1159–1180* (Europäische Hochsculschriften, Reihe 3, Geschichte und Hilfswissenschaften, 442; Frankfurt am Main-Bern-New York-Paris: 1990) 33–41.

40. Heinrich Watenphul and Heinrich Krefeld, eds. *Die Gedichte des Archipoeta* (Heidelberg: 1958) 68, cited by Benson, "Political 'Renovatio,'" 375.

"dominus mundi."[41] He was also determined to point to a limitation
of the emperor's authority over the private property of his subjects. Simply put, Frederick could not exercise arbitrary authority in that realm.
In addition, Bulgarus's answer is somewhat surprising because he did
not address the question put to him in the story, violating a cardinal
principle of the lawyer-client relationship: tell the client only what the
client needs to know. If he had wished to respond to Frederick's question as formulated by Otto of Morena's continuator, he could have
quoted the famous *Lex Rhodia* in which the Emperor Antoninus declared: "Ego orbis terrarum dominus sum, lex autem maris" (I am the
lord of the world and the law of the sea).[42] Or he could have fallen back
on an equally famous phrase in a law of Justinian, *Bene a Zenone*:
"cum omnia principis esse intelligantur" (All things are understood to
be owned by the prince).[43] These would have been perfectly safe answers, capable of being widely interpreted (as in fact the glossators did).

The maxim, "Omnia enim sunt in potestate imperatoris" (All things
are in the power of the emperor), based on the passage in *Bene a
Zenone* and quoted frequently in the thirteenth century,[44] was only
rarely interpreted as meaning that the emperor had dominium over all
property.[45] The jurists preferred to think of the phrase as an acknowledgment of imperial universality *de iure,* but not *de facto.* Much later,
Baldus de Ubaldis resolved the contradiction between imperial claims
and rights by formulating two types of dominium, public and private.
The prince possessed a universal public dominium, but this power did
not give him dominium over the private property of individuals.[46]

41. See Hageneder, "Weltherrschaft" 257–278 for an elegant discussion of this concept and its importance for imperial and papal ideology.

42. Dig. 14.2.9.

43. Cod. 7.37.3 [Bene a Zenone].

44. E.g., Johannes Teutonicus to 3 Comp. 1.6.19 (Venerabilem) v. *in Germanos,* ed.
K. Pennington (Monumenta iuris canonici, Series A, 3.1; Città del Vaticano: 1981) 85.
See Johannes's gloss to C.23 q.8 c.21. D.8 c.1 was also a locus classicus for discussion
of this issue.

45. Nicolini, *Proprietà* 115–126.

46. Baldus, to Proemium of Dig. § Omnem, (Venice: 1493): "nec enim sunt eiusdem
rationis et conditionis ius publicum Cesaris et privatum personarum." See Nicolini, *Proprietà* 123. On Baldus's theories of property, see Joseph Canning, *The Political Thought
of Baldus de Ubaldis* (Cambridge Studies in Medieval Life and Thought 6; Cambridge:
1987) 37, 79–82, and below chapter 3.

47. Azo, *Summa super Codice* to Cod. 3.13 (De iurisdictione omnium iudicum),
Würzburg, Universitätsbibl. M.p.i.f.2, fol. 35r (1st rec.), Bamberg, Staatsbibl. Jur. 24, fol.
36r (with additiones), Jur. 25, fol. 35r (with additiones), Paris, B.N. lat. 4542, fol. 30r:
"An autem hoc merum imperium soli principi competere? Et eum solum habere quidam
dicunt. Diciturque in eo merum, eo quod pure sine alicuius prelatura habet. Set certe
etiam sublimes magistratus habent merum imperium si bona est definitio legis quam diximus. Nam et presides prouinciarum habent ius gladii, ut ff. de offic. presid. Illicitas

Martinus was no fool. If his reply has been reported accurately, it was laconic and sibylline. And whether the words are his or not, they outraged the glossators. "You are the Lord" could mean anything from a rejection of Bulgarus's statement to an acceptance of the emperor's universal jurisdiction (but without rejecting Bulgarus's limitation). Such answers win horses.

Azo alluded to a similar episode in his *Summa super Codice*. Does "merum imperium," he asked, pertain only to the prince? Some say yes. But he observed that "sublimes" and governors of provinces exercise "merum imperium," for they have the power of the sword (that is, they may prosecute major criminal cases). Municipal magistrates do not. Only the prince, he continued, has full or maximum jurisdiction (plena vel plenissima jurisdictio). He concluded with the comment:[47]

> . . . and I say that subliminores[48] potestà exercise merum imperium; although on account of this I lost a horse, but it was not equitable.

At first glance, Azo's question might seem quite different from Barbarossa's. However, one possible meaning of Frederick's question, "Am I the lord of the world?" could be "Do I have supreme jurisdiction (merum imperium) over all other princes and magistrates?" Azo may be answering Frederick's question, but formulating it in more precise language. Exactly how Azo would distinguish between "exalted (subliminores) potestà" and other municipal magistrates cannot be determined. Most likely, he wanted to differentiate those magistrates who occupied lower offices in the city-states of Italy from the potestà who had become a common feature of municipal government by the early thirteenth century.[49]

Perhaps Azo's question can be linked to the law *Omnis jurisdictio*

---

§ Qui universas. Magistratus uero municipales non habent, ut ff. eodem 1. Magistratibus. Plenam ergo uel plenissimam iurisdictionem soli principi competere dico, set merum imperium etiam aliis sublimioribus potestatibus; licet ob hoc amiserim equum, set non fuit equum." The Würzburg text has a crucial variant in the last sentence: "amiserit" instead of "amiserim." This manuscript is the earliest manuscript of Azo's *Summa* known to me and contains the text of his *Summa* before he wrote "additiones." Of the eleven first-recension manuscripts, ten have "amiserim." Only Würzburg reads "amiserit." For a discussion of this problem see below.

48. "Sublimes" means "exalted" in medieval rhetorical usage; see Giles Constable, "The Structure of Medieval Society According to the 'Dictatores' of the Twelfth Century," *Law, Church, and Society: Essays in Honor of Stephan Kuttner*, ed. K. Pennington and R. Somerville (Philadelphia: 1977) 253–267, which does not, however, allow us to decide which group of magistrates Azo has in mind.

49. See John W. Perrin, "Azo, Roman Law, and Sovereign European States," *Post Scripta* (SG 15; Rome: 1972) 87–101.

that Frederick promulgated at Roncaglia. A modern reader might immediately assume that when Frederick stated that the prince possessed all jurisdiction, he implied that other magistrates derived their authority directly from the prince. The medieval reader would not have made the same assumption. As Azo noted in his gloss, he did not think it incongruent to acknowledge that the prince exercised supreme jurisdiction but that other magistrates exercised "merum imperium" too. Azo's gloss might have ultimately had its origins in debates surrounding the meaning of *Omnis jurisdictio*.

In a later, additional gloss to this passage, Azo noted that the Roman people bestowed "imperium merum" on the prince through the Hortensian law. Only the prince may establish what is universally equitable. Nonetheless, he conceded at the end of the addition that municipal magistrates may create a new law, even if they may not, as he had first stated, exercise "merum imperium." [50]

These two stories present interesting differences. In Otto of Morena's chronicle, we cannot be sure what Frederick's original question was. If he asked "Am I the Lord of the world?" meaning "Do I have universal jurisdiction over all kings?" then Bulgarus's answer is odd, to say the least. He certainly could have, in good conscience, conceded primacy of rank to Frederick. If he asked, "Am I the Lord over all things?" meaning "May I alienate the property of my subjects?" then Bulgarus's answer makes perfect sense. He refused to grant that the emperor could arbitrarily take a right away from a subject. [51] Martinus presumed that the prince was "above the law," or, to use a technical term of the jurists, that he was "legibus solutus" (not bound by the law). [52] To transpose the question into Bodin's terms, Martinus would have granted the emperor true sovereignty, unfettered by the law of nations (ius gentium)

50. Azo, additio to Cod. 1.13 v. *soli principi competere dico*, Bamberg, Staatsbibl. Jur. 24, fol. 36r and Jur. 25, fol. 35r, Florence, Laur. Edili 47, fol. 45r, added to the margins of the manuscripts: "cum lege Hortensia populus ei, et in eum omne imperium et omnem potestatem transtulit, ut inst. de iure natur. § Sed quod, et ipse solus statuere generalem equitatem possit, ut C. de leg. et const. l.i. quod innuit iurisdictionis definitio: sic enim dicit equitatis statuende. Concedo tamen quod quilibet magistratus in sua ciuitate ius nouum statuere potest, ut ff. quod quisque iuris in alterum stat. l.i." The printed editions of his *Summa* have the text with the additions included in the text (as is the case in the late manuscripts): Speyer: 1482, Venice: 1489, and Lyon: 1557, repr. Frankfurt a.M.: 1968.

51. Historians have sometimes misinterpreted this story. Cf. the remarks of Helmut G. Walther, *Imperiales Königtum, Konziliarismus und Volkssouveränität: Studien zu den Grenzen des Mittelalterlichen Souveränitätsgedankens* (München: 1976) 82, who would argue that the tale means the jurists in Bologna did not lose sight of the imperial claims to universal dominium.

52. See the study of Wyduckel, *Princeps legibus solutus* 35–62.

with which the jurists had already begun to defend property rights in the twelfth century.

One other point must be made. "Legibus solutus" has a number of quite different meanings; it could define the prince's authority to change, derogate, abrogate, or dispense from positive law—in this sense, it has no "absolutistic" connotations, and every governmental legislative body, whether constitutional or not, is "legibus solutus." Or "legibus solutus" can mean the prince's immunity from prosecution, his authority to transgress or dispense from the normal rules governing the legal system, or his power to transgress the rights of his subjects.[53] If the prince continuously and willfully abused his authority in these latter matters, his behavior becomes tyrannical.

Azo asked two questions, related to but different from those of Otto of Morena. Did the prince alone possess "merum imperium?" and a more subtle query, do magistrates, other than the prince himself, possess "merum imperium" from the offices they hold? Or do they derive all their jurisdiction from the prince?[54] Where does the source of jurisdiction lie? Azo touched upon problems that the jurists were just beginning to recognize at the beginning of the thirteenth century.[55]

In the second and third decades of the thirteenth century, Accursius wrote his Ordinary Gloss to the *Corpus iuris civilis*. Although Accursius knew the story of Bulgarus and Martinus, he gave a more satisfying account than that of Otto of Morena's redactor. Martinus, he wrote, said to the emperor at Roncaglia—he did not know whether from love or fear of Frederick—that the emperor owned all things, even private property.[56] Bulgarus, on the other hand, contradicted Martinus in front of the emperor.[57]

Accursius clearly thought Martinus's position was untenable and presented a series of definitions to illustrate what "omnia principis esse intelligantur" meant. He observed that the emperor was responsible for the protection of the Roman people and that he had jurisdiction over

---

53. These distinctions are too often ignored when historians interpret texts; see e.g., Ernst Schubert, *König und Reich: Studien zur spätmittelalterlichen deutschen Verfassungsgeschichte* (Göttingen: 1979) 120–139.

54. I do not think Azo's words can be interpreted to include kings as being included in the term, "potestates." Cf. Perrin, "Azo, Roman Law" 100–101.

55. Brian Tierney, *Religion, Law, and the Growth of Constitutional Thought 1150–1650* (Cambridge: 1982) 25–53.

56. Accursius to Cod. 7.37.3 (Bene a Zenone) v. *omnia principis*: "etiam quod ad proprietatem ut dicit M. principi apud Roncaliam, timore uel amore. Et pro eo ff. de offic. pret. l. Barbarius, in fine" [Dig. 1.14.3].

57. Ibid.: "Sed Bulga. contra etiam ibidem."

all things—in the same sense as one may say that the boundaries of Roman rule are owned by the Roman people.[58]

Accursius had no interest, however, in expounding the emperor's universality. He concluded his gloss on *Bene a Zenone* by defining "omnia principis esse intelligantur" in a much more restricted sense:[59]

> But more truly, "all things are his," namely property of the imperial treasury and the imperial patrimony, as in the Digest, "res enim fiscales quasi propriae et privatae principis sunt." Consequently the prince does not own my book, and I may initiate legal action to recover it directly; the prince may not.

Accursius limited the meaning of *Bene a Zenone* to the private property of the prince and goods acquired by the fisc (i.e., imperial treasury). A more restrictive reading of the law was not possible. His was not a new idea. Other jurists, writing before Accursius, had restricted the words "cum omnia principis" to the private patrimony of the emperor before his election and to the imperial treasury, that is, said Otto Papiensis, all imperium.[60]

With such varied interpretations, what Bulgarus and Martinus actually thought is difficult to know. We do know that Martinus received much bad press from later jurists. Odofredus, who could turn a knife as skillfully as anyone, wrote acidly: "Martinus was more beloved than Bulgarus because he knew better how to bestow praise."[61] For Martinus's and Bulgarus's part, they discussed the emperor's authority further, if briefly, in their commentaries on the Codex.[62] In this same context, one twelfth-century source, *Dissensiones dominorum*, reports that "some jurists" thought that the emperor could expropriate private property on the basis of the key text in Roman law, *Bene a Zenone*. Martinus and Jacobus, however, interpreted *Bene a Zenone* as meaning

---

58. Accursius, loc. cit.: "Et hic expone ad protectionem uel iurisdictionem. Sic et littora Romani imperii dicuntur populi Romani, ut ff. ne quid in loco publico l. Littora publica" [Dig. 43.8.3].

59. Accursius, loc. cit.: "Vel verius omnia sua sunt, scilicet fiscalia et patrimonialia, ut subiicit, arg. ff. ne quid in loco l.ii § ii. Vnde codex meus non est principis, sed mihi pro eo datur rei vindicatio directa, non principi. Accursius."

60. Cod. 3.37.3 v. *cum omnia principis*, Clm 22, fol. 163r: "Duo sunt imperatoris patrimonia: priuatum que ante (MS conante) habuit quam esset imperator, et fiscale, idest totum imperium, et siue imperium siue sit priuatum, semper tutus est qui erat. ot." Most likely, Otto Papiensis is the author of this gloss. A similar early definition is found in an apparatus in Vienna, N.B. 2267, fol. 165v to Cod. 7.37.3, v. *cum omnia principis esse*: "scilicet tam fiscalia quam patrimonialia, ut supra tetigit; uel dic omnia quantum ad iurisdictionem."

61. Savigny, *Geschichte* IV 179, 187; Cortese, *La norma* I 25.

62. See fnn. 36 and 37 above.

that the emperor could only expropriate property when he did not know it belonged to another.[63] Meijers published a gloss attributed to Martinus that confirms this moderate interpretation of his thought.[64] Cortese has noted that the sources attribute the extreme opinion of Martinus in the story of the horse to Pilius and Albericus.[65] And, according to another gloss published by Meijers, Jacobus and Hugo developed the idea that the emperor could alienate the property of another for the good of the commonweal.[66] This escape clause, "for the public good," plays an important role in the story of the prince's relationship to the law, for it was commonly used to justify actions that were not normally licit.[67]

For the purposes of our story, what Martinus may have thought is less important than the doctrines that later jurists attributed to him. Odofredus incorporated Otto Morena's redactor's tale into his commentary and imaginatively expanded—perhaps, again on the basis of an oral tradition—Azo's cryptic comments. While lecturing on the Digest, he told Azo's story;[68] when discussing the Code, Morena's.[69]

By the middle of the thirteenth century, the original question had become too vague to satisfy the jurists. Odofredus posed it to conform to the language of the day. He asserted that Martinus wanted to prove that the emperor was the "lord of all things owned by individuals" (dominus omnium rerum singularium). In Odofredus's argument, Mar-

---

63. *Dissensiones dominorum sive controversiae veterum iuris Romani interpretum,* ed. Gustav Haenel (Leipzig: 1834; reprinted Aalen: 1964) 57: "Nam quidam dicunt, sive imperator scivit sive ignoravit rem esse alienam, illud obtinere, quod dicit C. de quadrienni praescriptione, l. Bene [Cod. 3.37.3]. Martinus et Iacobus illam legem loqui dicunt cum ignoravit." Cortese, *La norma* I 125.

64. Eduard M. Meijers, *Études d'histoire du droit,* ed. R. Feenstra and H.F.W.D. Fischer (4 volumes; Leiden: 1956–1966) III 221: "Edictum divi Marci quod emptor erat tutus prescriptione quinquennii tunc vendicabat sibi locum, cum fiscus rem alienam vendebat ut suam, ergo et constitutio Zenonis que secundum id edictum loquitur tunc prestabit statim defensionem accipienti cum ut suam fiscus donat vel vendit bona fide credens suam, ne inde iniuriarum nascatur occasio unde iura sumuntur. M." Cortese, *La norma* I 125–128.

65. Cortese, *La norma* I 126.

66. Meijers, *Études* III 221: "Cum autem ut alienam vendit aut donat scienter, nihil agit nisi causa cognita, ut scilicet magnum deprehenderetur rei publice commodum ... Sed si non vertatur commodum rei publice, nec servum alienum potest facere liberum, nec rem alienam transfertur ... Ia. U."

67. Cortese's two volumes explore the importance of this concept and similar phrases: "iusta causa," "causa utilitatis," "communis utilitas," and "causa rei publicae," in medieval legal thought.

68. Odofredus, *Super prima, secunda patre Digesti veteris.* 2 vols. Lyon: 1550–1552, Opera iuridica rariora, 2; reprinted Bologna: 1967–1968 to Dig. 2.1.3, vol. 1, fol. 38r–v.

69. Odofredus, *Lectura ad Codicem.* 2 volumes. Lyon: 1480; Lyon: 1552, reprinted Bologna: 1968–1969 to Cod. 7.37.3 (Bene a Zenone).

tinus cited three laws from the Digest and a passage from the Bible, Samuel 1, 8.11: "It is the right of a king who rules over you to take your sons for his wagons." Although the passage is a striking justification of arbitrary royal authority, during the Middle Ages, Samuel's claim was interpreted as illegitimate, tyrannical power. The Ordinary Gloss to the Bible and the jurists rejected it.[70] Odofredus reported that Bulgarus contradicted Martinus; he also thought Martinus's opinion was incorrect.[71] He gave two reasons, both based on conceptions of property in private law. First, each person had the right to bring suit to defend owned property, and second, the emperor could not be the lord of each person's property, because two people cannot simultaneously have total ownership of an object.[72] Odofredus concluded by citing Accursius's definition of what "omnia sunt principis" meant.[73]

Like Bodin in the sixteenth century, the jurists of the mid-thirteenth century considered a subject's dominium over private property to be a right derived from natural law that was exempt from princely authority, with several exceptions: the prince could expropriate property if he had cause, was pressed by necessity, or could rest his action on the public good. Odofredus's conclusion that each person had the right to defend individual property in court is ultimately based on contemporary ideas about natural law. Odofredus added a further principle taken from Roman private law: two men cannot have complete dominium over the same property.[74]

70. Nicolini, *Proprietà* 118–119.
71. Odofredus to Cod. 7.37.3 (Bene a Zenone) (Lyon: 1480), vol. 1, unfol.: "Tex.: 'cum omnia principis.' Hic uoluit colligere dominus Martinus quod imperator sit dominus omnium rerum singularium. Item pro sua opinione inducit legem que dicit quod imperator potest dare predia nostra militibus ob stipendia, ut ff. de rei uendic. l. Item si uerberatum [Dig. 6.1.15] et ff. de euict. l. Lucius [Dig. 21.2.11] et quia in libro Regum continetur 'Filias nostras,' etc. [Kings 1 8.11] Item pro sua opinione inducit ff. de offic. pretor. l. Barbarius [Dig. 1.14.3] et sic respondit imperatori Frederico seniori, dum esset apud Ronchaliam timore uel amore. Set Bul. dixit contra in eodem loco."
72. Nicolini, *Proprietà* 100, n. 2, points out that Johannes Teutonicus anticipated Odofredus's conclusion: no one could buy his own property, because "meum amplius meum esse non potest," Glossa ordinaria to C.23 q.8 d.p.c.22 v. *emeret*.
73. Odofredus, loc. cit.: "Set dicimus contra, quia cum quis habeat rei uendicationem pro sua re, ut supra de rei uendicat. l. Doce [Cod. 3.32.9]; ergo imperator non habet rei uendicationem cum duo non possunt esse domini unius rei insolidum, ff. commod. l. Si ut certo § Si duobus uehiculum [Dig. 13.6.5.15]. Et intelligebat dominus Bulgarus quod dicitur hic quod 'omnia sunt principis' quo ad protectionem uel iurisdictionem; uel uerius 'omnia sunt principis,' scilicet fiscalia et patrimonialia. Non obstat leges que dicunt quod licet imperatori dare predia nostra militibus ob stipendia, quia uerum est dato nobis pretio, ut supra pro quibus causis serui accip. prem. libert. l.ult. [Cod. 7.13.4]."
74. See Cortese, *La norma* I 131–134. Odofredus to Cod. 1.22(25).6 (Omnes): "sicut imperator non potest auferre dominium rei mee, nec sequelam dominii, scilicet rei uindicationem."

When Odofredus turned to Azo's enigmatic comment in his commentary on the Digest, he took up the issue Azo had raised: did other magistrates hold "merum imperium," or did the prince hold it alone?[75] He recounted the story with his typical love of exaggeration and detail. Emperor Henry VI summoned Azo and Lotharius, who were teaching in Bologna, to settle an affair. As he rode with the two scholars one day, he posed the question: "To whom does 'merum imperium' belong?" "You tell me," Azo arrogantly asked Lotharius, who declared that "merum imperium" belonged to the emperor and to no one else. Lotharius, explained Odofredus, was the better knight, but Azo was more learned in our law (Roman law). Further, as he told his students, Lotharius loved many women and looked on them with pleasure.[76]

Odofredus's story reveals two significant points: his love of a good tale as well as a growing sophistication of political thought in the thirteenth century. In his version, Azo toyed with Lotharius. "You tell me" the answer to the question, demanded Azo. Lotharius confidently declared that "merum imperium" belonged to the emperor and to no one else. Azo responded that the emperor had "merum imperium," but other magistrates possessed it too. "If you have not revoked the jurisdiction of magistrates, others exercise 'merum imperium.'" When Henry returned to the imperial palace, he gave Lotharius a horse and Azo nothing.[77]

---

75. Odofredus, *Lectura super Digesto veteri* (2 volumes, Lyon: 1550–1552; repr. Bologna: 1967–1968), I fol. 38r–38v to Dig. 2.1.3 (Imperium), Florence, Biblioteca nazionale (Grandi formati 39) Magliabecchiano, Cl.xxix.27, fol. 34r: "Sed hic queri consueuit cui competit merum imperium? Et certe nos dicimus quod merum imperium competit principi per excellentiam, et post principem ceteris maioribus magistratibus et clarissimis, quia si presides habent merum imperium, ut supra de offic. procon. et leg. l. Illicitas [Solent *male*] § Qui uniuersas [Dig. 1.18.6.8], multo fortius maiores iudices."

76. Ibid.: "Vnde dominus imperator Henricus pater domini Frederici minoris qui regnabat modo sunt xl. [sexaginta Ed.] anni tunc temporis: dominus Azo et dominus Lotarius docebant in ciuitate ista et imperator uocauit eos ad se pro quodam negocio, et dum [deinde Ed.] una die equitaret cum eis fecit eis talem questionem: 'Signori dicatis mihi cui competit merum imperium.' Dixit Azo domino Lotario, 'Dicatis mihi,' et licet dominus Lotarius esset melior miles, tamen dominus Azo fuit melior in iure nostro, et debetis scire quod dominus Lotarius diligebat multum dominas et libenter eas uidebat, licet postea fuerit factus archiepiscopus Pisanus, et propter eum fuit facta decretalis, extra. de foro compet. c. Si diligenti [X 2.2.12 and 2.26.17]." For the biography of Lotharius, see my article in BMCL 20 (1990) 43–50.

77. Odofredus to Dig. 2.1.3 (ed. et MS cit.): "Et dixit dominus Lotarius ex quo uult dominus Azo quod prius eo dicam, dico quod uobis soli competit merum imperium et non alii. Postea dixit imperator domino Azo, 'Vos quid dicetis?' Dixit dominus Azo in legibus nostris dicitur quod alii iudices habent gladii potestatem, sed uos habetis per excellentiam, tamen et alii iudices habent ut presides prouinciarum, ut supra de offic. presid. l. Illicitas § Qui uniuersas [Dig. 1.18.6.8]; multo fortius alii maiores; ex quo non reuocatis iurisdictionem magistratuum, alii possunt exercere. Quando fuerunt reuersi ad palatium

Is Odofredus's story about Azo's losing a horse true? He taught in the generation following Azo and could have heard anecdotes about his predecessor. If Gero Dolezalek's identification of an early commentary of Odofredus on the Codex is correct, Odofredus heard Azo's lectures.[78] Henry VI might have asked Azo and Lotharius in whom "merum imperium" resided. The question is not improbable. Whether magistrates had rights and powers that were not delegated by the prince was an important issue in secular and, particularly, ecclesiastical government during the thirteenth century.[79]

As previously mentioned, Odofredus was a gifted storyteller. In this light, historians should consider his reports about the history of law in Bologna with skepticism. Savigny, for example, noted that, at the time, three different stories circulated about jurists' losing horses. The two discussed here, and a third told by Albertus Papiensis, were repeated by Diplovatatius, the sixteenth-century historian. Savigny felt intuitively, and quite rightly, that only one story could be true and dismissed Albertus's rendition out of hand. Although a number of different thirteenth-century authors told the story of Bulgarus and Martinus and Odofredus is the *only* source of the Azo-Lotharius tale, Savigny concluded that the meeting between Henry VI, Azo, and Lotharius must be the true version. His reasoning was simple and, at first glance, irrefutable. Azo mentioned losing a horse in his commentary on the Codex.[80] We have no first-person evidence for the story of Bulgarus and Martinus.

Like most things in life, the truth seems to be a little more slippery than Savigny had imagined. The textual tradition of Azo's *Summa* is complicated. Azo composed his *Summa* on the Code and then added "additiones" in the margin. He did the same to his *Summa* on the Institutes.[81] These "additiones" have the character of glosses to particular points of his text and were very quickly incorporated into the text of

dominus imperator misit domino Lotario unum equum et domino Azo nichil. Vnde dominus Azo dicit in summa huius tituli, 'Dico merum imperium competere soli principi per excellentiam, tamen alii possunt exercere merum imperium ut presides prouinciarum, multo fortius maiores iudices per § Qui uniuersas et si propterea i. Propter ista uerba amisit [amisimus Ed.] equum, non tamen fuit equum, quia bene dixi de iure et non dominus Lotarius.' "

78. "The *Lectura Codicis* of Odofredus, recensio I and Jacobus Balduini," *The Two Laws: Studies in Medieval Roman and Canon Law Dedicated to Stephan Kuttner* (Studies in Medieval and Early Modern Canon Law, 1; Washington, D.C.: 1990) 97–120.

79. I have explored this question for ecclesiastical government in *Pope and Bishops: The Papal Monarchy in the Twelfth and Thirteenth Centuries* (Middle Ages; Philadelphia: 1984); see especially pp. 186–195.

80. Savigny, *Geschichte* IV 180–183.

81. I have located three manuscripts with "additiones" added to the margins: Bam-

his *Summa,* most likely not by Azo himself. Most manuscripts and all the printed editions contain this version of his *Summa.* I have seen over forty manuscripts of the *Summa* and have found only eleven that omit all or most of these "additiones."[82] The eleven manuscripts preserve the first stage of the *Summa*'s text. Of the manuscripts preserving the earliest version of Azo's text, the Würzburg manuscript is the oldest and, in my opinion, contains a very reliable text. At the point in question, the Würzburg manuscript reads:[83]

> I say that full and most complete jurisdiction belongs to the prince alone, but "merum imperium" also pertains to other higher magistrates. On account of this he lost a horse, but it was not fair.

If the Würzburg reading is correct, Azo was referring to the story of Bulgarus and Martinus, not to himself. All later manuscripts read "I lost a horse," and from that phrase Odofredus spun his tale of Azo's having lost a horse.

There are other, nontextual, reasons for accepting the reading in the Würzburg manuscript. Azo taught in Bologna until 1220 and would have undoubtedly told the story of how he lost a horse to Lotharius in his lectures. But apart from Odofredus, no one repeated Azo's story. The jurists and popular writers told the story of Bulgarus and Martinus. If Azo did lose a horse, then we must imagine that contemporaries who still had the opportunity to hear Azo's lectures altered his story and changed the names of the characters to Martinus and Bulgarus.[84] This fact is particularly crucial when we consider Accursius's evidence. Accursius had been a student of Azo. If we assume that only one of the stories is probably true, it is highly doubtful that Accursius would have transformed Azo's story that he had heard in his master's lectures into Bulgarus and Martinus's story. Consequently, even without the evidence of the Würzburg manuscript one might have been tempted to emend Azo's text.

Historians and jurists were not the only writers intrigued by the

berg, Staatsbibl. Jur. 24 and 25, Erlangen, Univ. Bibl. 801. The "additiones" are not uniform. Azo (or others) may have added them in stages. Bamberg Jur. 24 contains more additiones than Bamberg Jur. 25.

82. Aschaffenburg, Stiftsbibl. Perg. 15; Florence, Bibl. Laur. Edili 47; Herford, Cathed. Lib. P.5.xiv; Klosterneuburg, Stiftsbibl. 119; Olomouc, Statní Archiv, C.O. 398; Paris, B.N. lat. 4542; Paris, B.N. lat. 4560A; Paris, B.N. n.a. lat. 2376; Seo de Urgel, Bibl. de la Catedral, 2040; Vat. lat. 2312; Würzburg, Univ. Bibl. M.p.j.f.2.

83. Würzburg, Univ. Bibl. M.p.j.f.2, fol. 35r: "Plenam ergo uel plenissimam iurisdictionem soli principi competere dico, set merum imperium etiam aliis sublimioribus potestatibus; licet ob hoc amiserit equum, set non fuit equum."

84. P. Fiorelli, "Azzone," DBI 4 (1962) 774–775.

story. To better illustrate how deeply the new science of jurisprudence penetrated thirteenth-century thought, we can turn to an anonymous storyteller, who had a sophisticated knowledge of law and told the tale of Martinus and Bulgarus in the vernacular. In so doing, he created the most interesting story, both juristically and psychologically.[85] Although this novella was first printed as part of a collection of one hundred novelle,[86] the manuscripts of the collection show that it began as a much smaller collection and evolved into its final form at the end of the thirteenth century.[87] The first rendition of the story, however, most probably dates to the first quarter of the thirteenth century.

The anonymous author began the story as it had always begun. One day Frederick Barbarossa was standing with his two wise jurists, Martinus and Bulgarus. Frederick asked them whether, according to our law, he could take something from his subjects, from whomever he wished, and give it to another, without any other cause than he was the lord and because the law said "what pleases the prince is the law for his subjects." Frederick asked Martinus and Bulgarus to tell him if he could do whatever he wished.[88] The author of this striking tale knew more than a little law. The question was asked in sophisticated terms, particularly his query whether the prince could expropriate the property of his subjects without cause. By the middle of the century, most jurists would have agreed that the prince could take away the rights of his subjects with cause or for the public good.[89] At the conclusion of the tale, Frederick then asked Martinus and Bulgarus directly, if he held this power from the famous texts in Justinian's Institutes and Digest, "Quod principi placuit, legis habet vigorem" (What pleases the prince has the force of law).[90] Frederick wanted to know if this text did not justify his acting arbitrarily, and if not, then why not?

85. *Novellino e conti del Duecento,* ed. Sebastiano Lo Nigro (Classici italiani 4; Torino: 1963) nr. 24, 99–100.

86. *Le ciento novelle antike* (Bologna: 1525).

87. One of the earliest collections is found in Florence, Laurenziana, Gaddiano Reliqui 193, fol. 12r–21r, which contains 32 novelle, corresponding to 23–69, with some omissions, in the printed edition. I have given the text of the story from the Laurenziana manuscript because modern editors have obscured the precise juristic language of the anonymous author in the Florentine manuscript with their modern, "mixed" editions of the text based on this and later manuscripts.

88. Ibid. fol. 12v: "Signori, secondo la nostra legge, posso io ai subditi miei torre a cu' io mi voglio e dare ad un altro, sanz'altra cagione, accio ch'io sono signore e la legge dice che cio che piace al signore e legge intra i subditi suoi. Dite se io lo posso fare poi chi mi piace."

89. See again, in general, Cortese's superb and detailed discussion of these concepts in *Norma,* especially I 97–181.

90. Institutes 1.2.6; Dig. 1.4.1 (Ulpian, in the first book of his Institutes).

Reversing the positions that they had taken in earlier stories, Bulgarus responded:[91] "You may do what you please with the property of your subjects, without any blame."[92]

Martinus dissented: "I do not believe it. The law is most just, and one should justly observe and follow the terms of the law. When you act, you must know why and to whom you grant your favors."[93] Martinus paraphrased another famous text of Roman law in Justinian's Codex, *Digna vox*. The prince should submit himself to the law, for his authority rests on the law.[94]

Because both spoke the truth, Frederick gave Bulgarus a scarlet hat and a palfrey; to Martinus he gave the right to "issue a law from his breast."[95] Again, the author has flaunted his learning: the maxim, "Princeps habet omnia iura in scrinio pectoris,"[96] was a standard definition of the prince's legislative authority in juristic thought. Afterward, the jurists debated to whom Frederick had given the more valuable gift. Some thought that since Bulgarus had praised Frederick, he gave the hat and horse as he would have to a fool who praised him; to Martinus, who loved justice, he gave the right to promulgate a law.[97] The readers of the tale are drawn into the same debate: to whom did Frederick give the more honorable gift? The answer, of course, is uncertain.

In this literary version of the anecdote, Frederick was transformed into an erudite man who could formulate learned questions touching upon his imperial prerogatives and who valued the right of legislation

91. If we assume that the author has carefully maintained Bulgarus as the "uno" and Martinus as the "altro."

92. Jacques de Révigny, *Lectura ad Codicem* (Attributed to Pierre de Bellapertica) (Paris: 1519) to Cod. 7.37.3 also reverses the roles in his commentary.

93. *Ciento novelle* (MS cit.): "Messere, a me non pare; accio che la legge e iustissima; le sue condictioni si vogliono iustissimamente oservare e seguitare. Quando voi toglete, si vuole sapere perche, e a cui date."

94. Cod. 1.14(17).4: "Digna vox maiestate regnantis legibus alligatum se principem profiteri: adeo de auctoritate iuris nostra pendet auctoritas. Et re vera maius imperio est submittere legibus principatum." Brian Tierney has analyzed how contemporary jurists understood this text in "'The Prince is Not Bound by the Laws': Accursius and the Origins of the Modern State," *Comparative Studies in Society and History* 5 (1963) 378–400; also Dieter Wyduckel, *Princeps Legibus Solutus* 130–137.

95. MS cit.: "Perche l'uno savio e l'altro dicea vero e pero dono ad ambendue. Al'uno dono cappello scarlato e pallafreno bianco; e al'altro dono che facesse una legge a suo senno." I cannot agree with Savigny *Geschichte* IV 181, that the author has combined the original story with that describing the genesis of "Sacramenta puberum." The point of the two stories is quite different—here neither jurist wished to persuade Frederick to issue a new law—and his interpretation dismisses the underlying irony in the novella.

96. Based on, ultimately, Cod. 6.23.19.1.

97. MS cit.: "Di questo fue quistione intra savi, a cui avea piu ricchamente donato. Fue tenuto ch'a quelli, ch'avea detto che potea torre come li piacea, si li dono robe e pallafreno, come a iullare, pero che l'avea lodato; a colui che seguitava iustitia, si diede a fare una legge."

more than rich gifts (although there is, perhaps, a touch of irony here; the author may have known very well that not all his readers would prefer the right to legislate to riches). Although fiction, the story is infused with legal learning. One is tempted to conjecture that, like Boccaccio, this anonymous author spent some time studying law and presumed that his audience would understand his legal allusions. The most receptive, and perhaps the intended, audience would have been the same as Odofredus's: a lecture hall of students in Bologna.

Later jurists continued to retell the story, but we shall end our study of it at this point. If we return to Frederick Barbarossa's original question as posed by Otto of Morena's continuator, "Am I the Lord of the World," we can now see that the question was open to a wide range of interpretations. The modern historian of political thought would have undoubtedly answered Frederick's question by focusing on the relationship of the "imperium et regnum" (imperial and royal power), a favorite theme of nineteenth- and twentieth-century historiography. However, the medieval jurists perceived an entirely different set of questions—questions that were, and this point must be stressed, of much more interest to them. They cared not whether the emperor had jurisdiction and authority over other kings and princes, but focused on his power to usurp the rights of his subjects—to subvert the law arbitrarily.

Frederick may have asked, at some time during his reign, whether the emperor and the emperor alone exercised universal jurisdiction. However, with the rise of national monarchies in the twelfth century this question had less and less relevance to law or politics. Modern historians, imbued with twentieth-century theories of sovereignty, have focused on questions of the emperor's and the pope's claims of universality to the exclusion of other issues that had, in fact, more relevance for medieval jurists. They have sometimes assumed, for example, that national states could not be truly sovereign until the jurists had stripped the emperor and the pope of their claims of universal rule. While interesting, the question of "divided sovereignty" was only marginally important to the medieval jurists. Accursius, Odofredus, and their successors explored the prince's relationship to law, the rights of his subjects, and the authority of lesser magistrates. Not one of the writers we have examined wanted to decide whether the emperor was the "de facto" or "de iure" sovereign over the other kings of Europe when discussing the emperor's title of "dominus mundi."

Some modern historians have argued vehemently and vigorously that the "state," in fact, did not exist in medieval juristic thinking because papal and imperial universal claims of sovereignty made the concept of state logically impossible. They ask how a state could exist in a legal system in which every jurist and monarch acknowledged that the pope had the right to judge the subjects of the monarch in matters governed by canon law. A state subjected to this "divided sovereignty," they contend, could exist no more than a rose in a vacuum. Today, of course, at a time when European states are giving up parts of their sovereignty to the central institutions of the Common Market, their definition of what is and what is not a "state" seems hopelessly anachronistic.[98]

Leaving aside modern anachronisms, we must emphasize two principal elements of medieval thought touching upon the emperor's power. First, although the "king was emperor in his own kingdom" (rex imperator in regno suo est) was not an important question in the twelfth and early thirteenth centuries, the maxim becomes a critical issue in the second half of the thirteenth. Second, the maxim can have several different meanings. The most obvious is the literal: every king who is independent of the emperor can exercise the prerogatives of imperial sovereignty within the boundaries of his kingdom. In the long—overlong—debate about the origins and meaning of the maxim, Francesco Calasso made a significant point that historians of political thought have not taken as seriously as they should: he argued that when some jurists used the maxim they did not necessarily mean that a king was independent of the emperor, but only that kings could exercise the same authority within their kingdoms as the emperor. A third possible definition of the maxim is the reverse of Calasso's insight: a king might be independent of the emperor but not have the authority to exercise imperial prerogatives described by Roman law. In other words, the king may be independent of the emperor, but he cannot wield the same authority and exercise the same power as the "prince" of Justinian's *Corpus iuris civilis*. Some French and Italian lawyers of the later thirteenth century, who interpreted the maxim in this last sense, insisted that the king was not "legibus solutus" (only the "prince" could be

98. E.g., Walther, *Imperiales Königtum,* discusses the maxim "rex imperator in regno suo," pp. 65–111, and assumes that every jurist who called the emperor "dominus mundi" advocated universal imperial rule and subjection of kings to that rule. Every jurist who postulated that the king was emperor in his own kingdom was taking a step toward national sovereignty. First, as we have seen, "dominus mundi" had several different meanings for the jurists. Only one of those meanings had anything to do with kings, and it was not important in their thought. Second, the maxim could also be interpreted in at least three ways (see discussion that immediately follows); consequently, Walther and other historians have misinterpreted their texts by not making the same distinctions that the jurists themselves made.

"legibus solutus"). He was bound by the customs of the realm and feudal law.[99] As we shall see in chapter 3, this third possible definition is of crucial importance for understanding a particular strand of juristic thought north of the Alps.

Because this maxim's first meaning shall play an important role in the dispute between the Emperor Henry VII and Robert of Naples,[100] and because the meaning of "Rex imperator in regno suo est" is intimately connected with the concept of the emperor's being "dominus mundi," we shall summarize the early history of the "dominus mundi" in juristic thought.[101]

The jurists began to give general definitions of the emperor's authority in a series of aphoristic glosses at the beginning of the thirteenth century. Somewhat surprisingly, the canon, rather than the Roman lawyers, wrote the first catalogues of imperial powers and prerogatives. We have already seen that the civilians were not inspired by *Bene a Zenone* or other texts of Justinian's codification to expatiate on the authority of the emperor. However, when the canonists glossed *Venerabilem,* Pope Innocent III's famous decretal regulating imperial elections, they gathered together the emperor's prerogatives. Johannes Teutonicus, a German canonist, began this canonistic tradition in his gloss to *Venerabilem:*[102]

> The emperor is over all kings . . . and all nations are under him . . . for he is the lord of the world . . . even the Jews are under him . . . and all provinces are under him . . . unless they can show themselves to be exempt . . . none

99. See below, chapter 3.
100. See chapter 5 below.
101. The best discussion of this maxim and its historiography remains Brian Tierney, "Some Recent Works on the Political Theories of the Medieval Canonists," *Traditio* 10 (1954) 594–625 at 612–619, reprinted in *Church Law and Constitutional Thought in the Middle Ages* (Variorum Collected Studies Series; London: 1979).
102. Johannes Teutonicus, *Apparatus glossarum in Compilationem tertiam,* ed. K. Pennington (MIC, series A, 3.1; Città del Vaticano: 1981) to 3 Comp. 1.6.19 v. *in Germanos,* pp. 84–85: "Est autem imperator iste super omnes reges, ut vii. q.i. In apibus [C.7 q.1 c.41] et omnes nationes sub eo sunt, ut xi. q.i. Volumus [C.11 q.1 c.37]. Ipse enim est dominus mundi, ff. ad leg. Rod. de iac. Domine [Dig. 14.2.9] etiam Iudei sub eo sunt, C. de Iudeis, Iudei [Cod. 1.9(12).8] et omnes prouincie sub eo sunt, ut lxiii. Adrianus [D.63 c.22] nisi aliquis se doceat exemptum, ut xxiii. q.viii. § Ecce [C.23 q.8 p.c. 20]. Nec aliquis regum potuit prescribere exemptionem, cum non habeat in hoc locum prescriptio, infra de prescript. Cum ex officii [3 Comp. 2.17.6 (X 2.26.17)] nec aliquod regnum potuit eximi ab imperio, quia illud esset acefalum, ut xxi. di. Submittitur [D.21 c.8] et esset monstrum sine capite. Immo omnes de capite suo dabunt imperatori tributum, nisi ex hoc sint exempti, ff. de censibus l.ult. [Dig. 50.15.8]. Omnia enim sunt in potestate imperatoris, xxiii. q.viii. Conuenior [C.23 q.8 c.21] C. de quadrien. prescript. Bene [Cod. 7.37.3]." On Teutonicus see K. Pennington, "Johannes Teutonicus," DMA 7 (1986) 121–122.

of the kings can have prescribed an exemption, since prescription has no place in this. . . . A kingdom cannot have been exempted from imperial authority, since it would be without a head . . . and that would be monstrous. Rather all must give the emperor tribute, unless they are exempt. . . . All things are in the power of the emperor.

Johannes quarried Roman and canon law for a set of milestones marking imperial prerogatives. We should note, however, that this list of privileges and prerogatives is similar to the *Dictatus papae* and does not define the emperor's relationship to the law or to the rights of his subjects.

Johannes's gloss to *Venerabilem* was not his last word on the omnipotence of the emperor. He repeated the substance of this gloss in his Ordinary Gloss to the Decretum.[103] In the printed edition, his gloss to the Decretum declared that "the kings of Spain are not under the emperor, for they have plucked their kingdom out of their enemies' jaws."[104] The manuscripts prove, however, that this sentence was a later addition.[105]

In other glosses, Johannes added elements to his eulogy of the emperor. He taught that those who deny that they are under Roman rule cannot own anything.[106] Further, the emperor shall crown all kings.[107] If one did not recognize the Roman emperor as the prince of the whole world, one could not claim hereditary rights or other rights that private persons have under Roman law.[108] His glosses to the Decretum were read and taught in the schools for centuries; his gloss to *Venerabilem* was copied word for word by Bernardus Parmensis into his Ordinary Gloss on the Decretals of Gregory IX.[109] Much later in the thirteenth century, Guilielmus Durantis included the substance of Jo-

103. D.63 c.22 v. *per singulas*.
104. Ibid.: "Obstat quod reges Hispaniae cum non subessent imperio, regnum ab hostium faucibus eruerunt."
105. Clm 14024, fol. 41r and Vat. lat. 1367, fol. 47r omit the sentence; a later hand adds it to the Vatican manuscript.
106. D.63 c.22 v. *per singulas*: "Si enim dicunt se non subesse Romano imperio, per consequens dicunt se non habere aliquid proprii."
107. C.7. q.1 c.41 v. *imperator*: "Arg. quod omnes reges coronabit imperator, ut dixi lxiii. di. Hadrianus [D.63 c.22]." This is an allegation rather than a statement of fact.
108. D.1 c.12 v. *quod nulli*: "Nam imperator est princeps totius mundi, ut vii. q.i. In apibus. Sed in diversis provinciis, diversi reges sub eo constituti sunt, vi. q.iii Scitote et ff. ad legem Rhod. de iac. Qui levendae et l. Deprecatio. Qui ergo non vult esse sub Romano imperio, nec hereditatem habere potest, nec alia quae hic de iure Romano enumerantur."
109. Bernardus Parmensis to X 1.6.34 v. *transtulit in Germanos*. On other canonists and their reaction to Johannes's glosses see Gaines Post, *Studies in Medieval Legal Thought: Public Law and the State, 1100–1322* (Princeton: 1964) 453–493.

hannes's gloss in his great textbook on procedure.[110] Consequently, the canonists' glosses became embedded in the textbooks and would play a major role in the polemics of the fourteenth century defending imperial prerogatives.[111]

Historians, particularly German historians, have been keenly interested in the emperor's title, "dominus mundi," because it adumbrates a unitary theory of a Germanic empire that was one of the great myths of medieval and early modern Europe. Like all myths of real power, it was deeply buried in the consciousness of men like Frederick Barbarossa, and long after the empire was no longer a political force in Western Europe its sometimes baleful influence still captured the imaginations of many in the twentieth century.[112] Other historians, mainly French and Italian, have concentrated on the equally interesting question of when a juridical theory first appeared granting independence from imperial rule to European national states.

Sidney Woolf took a third position. He noted that Bartolus never used the maxim "a king is emperor in his own kingdom" and consigned this omission to Bartolus's being much more concerned with the Italian cities than with kingdoms.[113] Woolf's observation can be expanded. Because most early jurists were not notably concerned to explore the relationship between emperor and kings, the debate over origins and meaning has been quite acrimonious—and slightly beside the point.

The debate has had the salutary effect, however, of clarifying the historical roots of the maxim, "Rex imperator in regno suo est." Although historians have argued about the maxim's French or Italian origins and

110. *Speculum iuris* (Basel: 1574), De appellationibus § 4 (Nunc) II 839.
111. See chapter 5. See also Walther, *Imperiales Königtum* 85–111 and Michael Wilks, *The Problem of Sovereignty in the Later Middle Ages: The Papal Monarchy with Augustinus Triumphus and the Publicists* (Cambridge Studies in Medieval Life and Thought, 9; Cambridge: 1964) 433–451.
112. The literature is enormous. I have already cited the works of Hageneder, "Weltherrschaft" and Holtzmann, "Weltherrschaftsgedanke." Older works can still be read with profit: Friedrich Bock, *Reichsidee und Nationalstaaten vom Untergang des alten Reiches bis zur Kündigung des deutsch-Englischen Bündnisses im Jahre 1341* (München: 1943); Heinrich Finke, *Welt-imperialismus und nationale Regungen im späteren Mittelalter* (Freiburg i. B.: 1916); Helene Wieruszowski, *Vom Weltimperium zum nationalen Königtum: Vergleichende Studien über die publizistischen Kämpfe Kaiser Friedrichs II. und König Philipps des Schönen mit der Kurie* (Historische Zeitschrift, Beiheft 30; München-Berlin: 1933) esp. pp. 141–175. Richard Schlierer, *Weltherrschaftsgedanke und altdeutsches Kaisertum: Eine Untersuchung über die Bedeutung des Weltherrschaftsgedankens für die Staatsidee des deutschen Mittelalters vom 10. bis 12. Jahrhundert* (Tübingen: 1934, 2d. ed. 1968).
113. C.N.S. Woolf, *Bartolus of Sassoferrato* (Cambridge: 1913) 108–109.

its exact meaning,[114] there is no doubt that jurists used it to reconcile the difference between the political realities in thirteenth-century Europe and the ideal description of the emperor in their texts. English canonists, Alanus and Ricardus Anglicus, and a Spaniard, Vincentius Hispanus, articulated unambiguous statements of royal independence from the emperor in the early thirteenth century.[115] Azo cited a version of the maxim in a question he wrote (ca. 1200).[116] By the middle of the thirteenth century the maxim had become a commonplace. Calasso was right to argue that the maxim is not an unambiguous statement of national independence for Europe's kings, but I think that, from early on, the preponderance of evidence points to the jurists' having most often interpreted it as the juristic justification for royal independence from imperial authority.[117] The jurists always defined the maxim as granting kings their independence from the emperor after the middle of the fourteenth century. However, as we shall see, the period from roughly 1270 to 1330 was crucial for the maxim's development. During that time, jurists debated its meaning and, as we shall see in chapter 5, it played

114. Francesco Calasso, *I glossatori e la teoria della sovranità: Studio di diritto comune pubblico* (3d ed. Milan: 1957), explored the meaning of the maxim in the writings of the jurists. He maintained that the maxim had its origins in the writings of the Italian jurists and that it did not mean that the national monarchs were independent of the emperor *de iure*. It meant only that a king had the same authority in his kingdom as the emperor had in the world. Calasso's thesis has not been generally accepted. See the bibliography of his critics that Calasso provides (pp. xviii–xix), and Brian Tierney's analysis in "Some Recent Works."

115. Texts cited by Brian Tierney, "Some Recent Works," 615, 617. Calasso, *Glossatori* 31. See also S. Mochi Onory, *Fonti canonistiche dell'idea moderna dello stato* (Milano: 1951) and Gaines Post, *Studies in Medieval Legal Thought* 453–493, where he reprinted his article on Vincentius.

116. *Die Quaestiones des Azo,* ed. Ernst Landsberg (Freiburg i. B.: 1888) 87: "Item quilibet rex (rex is omitted from 3 of the 5 MSS) hodie videtur eandem potestatem habere in terra sua quam imperator, ergo potuit facere quod sibi placet. Item ratione publicae utilitatis potuit, quia forte hoc fecit ut faceret pacem cum alio. Multa autem licita sunt ratione publicae utilitatis." On Azo's questions, see Peter Weimar, "Die legistische Literatur der Glossatorenzeit," *Handbuch der Quellen und Literatur der neueren europäischen Privatrechtsgeschichte,* I: *Mittelalter,* ed. Helmut Coing (München: 1973) 248. Calasso, *Glossatori* 33–34. Walther, *Imperiales Königtum* 82–83 n. 42, oversimplifies Azo's remarks and takes no account of the significant qualifications Azo placed on any royal claims of independence in the last two sentences. Azo admits that the king (or, as three manuscripts of the work read, an unspecified "prince." See above text) possesses the same powers as the emperor when he acts *for the common good.* He seems to imply that the king's actions are licit because they are in concord with the common good, not because he exercises an independent legislative authority.

117. Calasso, *Glossatori* 39–81. See also Robert Feenstra, "Jean de Blanot et la formule 'Rex Franciae in regno suo princeps est,'" *Etudes d'histoire du droit canonique dédiés à Gabriel Le Bras* (Paris: 1965), II 885–895 and Post, *Studies in Medieval Legal Thought* 471–482.

an important role in one of the most important disputes of the time, the treason trial of Robert of Naples.

This brings us back to the main topic of this chapter: the authority of the prince. "Princeps" was, then, a multicolored cloak whose colors shifted hue and intensity at different times and with different owners. The jurists bestowed the title on the emperor, kings, and city-states. Paradoxically, the title could grant independence, arbitrary authority, and limited power to the bearer. Nevertheless, all these possible meanings were not present in juristic thought in equal proportions. If I may underline the main point of this chapter, when most jurists of the twelfth and thirteenth centuries explained "dominus mundi," they concentrated on the relationship of the prince and the law. Consequently, Calasso and others have overemphasized the importance of the question "was the emperor the universal sovereign of medieval Europe?" The early jurists were not consumed by the problem of whether the emperor exercised *de iure* or *de facto* jurisdiction over kings. By the beginning of the thirteenth century, the jurists played rather than grappled with the idea of universal imperial sovereignty.[118]

Calasso argued that when Frederick Barbarossa asked whether he was "dominus mundi," he wished to know whether he had *de iure* authority over all kings.[119] In fact, we cannot know what Frederick's real or fictional mind was. He might have wanted to know the status of the emperor in classical Roman law. The story of Martinus and Bulgarus suggests that he wished to know whether he might expropriate the property of his subjects. Azo believed that the emperor wanted assurance that he alone possessed "merum imperium." Indeed, although none of the anecdotes asks the question, he may have wondered whether he exercised jurisdiction over Europe's kings. "Am I the Lord

118. See my comments on Johannes Teutonicus's famous gloss in *Pope and Bishops* 30. This is a subjective judgment and not easily proven, but others have come to similar conclusions. See Domenico Maffei, *La donazione di Costantino nei giuristi medievali* (Milan: 1969) 117–125 and "Il giudice testimone e una 'quaestio' di Jacques de Révigny (MS Bon. Coll. Hisp. 82)," TRG 35 (1967) 54–76 at 72, and Feenstra, "Jean de Blanot" 885–895. Feenstra and Maffei argue that the jurists were analyzing the theoretical authority of the emperor as they found it described in their texts; they were not thinking of the Germanic Roman emperor. Some historians, as Walther, *Imperiales Königtum* 65–111, take such statements of the jurists at face value. In the case of Johannes Teutonicus, he never discussed the relationship of kings and the emperor, and he criticized none of Innocent III's decretals touching upon papal prerogatives to interfere in secular and imperial affairs. One cannot describe Johannes as a supporter of universal empire on the basis of his gloss to *Venerabilem* unless one ignores all of his other glosses touching upon issues of church and state.

119. Calasso, *Glossatori* 89.

of the World?" could encompass all of those questions. But, ultimately, speculation about Frederick's original question is fruitless. The important fact is that the jurists explored more difficult terrain that ultimately led to Jean Bodin's question: what were the limits of the prince's power? Could the prince expropriate the property of his subjects? Could the prince act arbitrarily? Did the prince's power have limits? These questions provide a framework for the problems that we shall discuss in the following chapters.

CHAPTER 2

The Prince's Power and Authority 1150–1270

The Contribution of the Canonists

Existens sub Monarcha est potissime liberum.
— Dante, *Monarchia* 1.12

By the beginning of the thirteenth century, the jurists discussed the power of the prince under many different names.[1] They did not restrict themselves to the emperor's or the pope's authority but extended their analysis to kings and magistrates. They began thinking about kingship conceptually rather than concentrating narrowly on the authority of a particular monarch. A sign of this change is that a generic term, "prince" (princeps), surfaced in their commentaries when they explored the terrain of governmental power. Additionally, new institutions and offices appeared and forced the jurists to expand their traditional categories of thought. The governments of Italian city-states, for example, offered them a particularly rich variety of new offices that challenged their ingenuity. One of the most important was that of the *podestà,* a foreigner appointed by a city and granted executive, legislative, and judicial authority over the commune. Since he was an outsider and not tainted by the familial and factional parties within the city, the podestà functioned as an arbiter between factious townspeople. He also took part in the civic rituals of the city-state.[2]

In his *Antiquitates,* Ludovico Muratori published an anonymous

1. For a convenient listing of titles that the jurists attributed to the pope and emperor in the late twelfth and early thirteenth centuries, see P. V. Aimone-Braida, "Titoli attribuiti al papa e all'imperatore nella decretistica," *Apollinaris* 59 (1986) 213–249.

2. G. Hanauer, "Das Berufspodestat im dreizehnten Jahrhundert," MIÖG 23 (1902) 377–426.

tract that applied the legal norms of rulership to the podestà.[3] The manuscript was defective and the tract incomplete, but enough of the text remains to see that its author attempted to write a guide for podestà ruling Italian city-states. Although Muratori dated the work ca. 1222, the evidence does not permit such precision.[4] The author mentions an emperor F., presumably Frederick II, and makes indirect references to his legislation of 1221. The most recent editor of the text concludes that a general date of the late 1220s is likely.[5]

The author knew some academic law, and he filled his text with references to Roman and canon law.[6] He could have been a jurist writing for the general public[7] or he may have been a cleric. He noted rather gracelessly on two occasions that he wrote without rhetorical flourishes because his intended audience was "uneducated or partially educated laymen" who were usually selected as podestà (laici rudes et modice literati).[8] The tract closely resembles contemporary "Mirrors of Princes"[9] and is the earliest medieval guide for magistrates of the Italian city-states. The work bore no title, and Muratori called it "Oculus pastoralis" or "Libellus erudiens futurum rectorem populorum."

The title is not a happy one. The tract begins with a section that might best be labeled a "Liturgical Order," describing the ceremonial rites for installing a podestà to his office, and is followed by an "Ars dictandi," offering the new podestà examples of speeches he should make upon his arrival in the city. The author then gave instructions to the podestà for the management of the law courts and assemblies. Next

3. *Oculus pastoralis sive Libellus erudiens futurum rectorem populorum*, ed. L. Muratori, *Antiquitates Italicae medii aevii sive Dissertationes* (Milan: 1741) IV 95–128.

4. Fritz Hertter, *Die Podestàliteratur Italiens im 12. und 13. Jahrhundert* (Beiträge zur Kulturgeschichte des Mittelalters und der Renaissance, 7. Leipzig-Berlin: 1910), dated the tract to the twelfth century, but on very shaky evidence. He argued that the reference to "imperator F." was diplomatically closer to twelfth-century usage than thirteenth; therefore, F. must be Frederick Barbarossa (p. 24–25). Conclusive, however, is the juristic evidence: "Pro ratione voluntas" would not have been cited nor would the complaints about torture have been included in a twelfth-century tract.

5. Terence O. Tunberg, *Oculus pastoralis* (PhD dissertation, University of Toronto, 1986) 3–17.

6. Tunberg edited the text and cited many, but not all, of the legal references in notes to the edition.

7. Hertter, *Podestàliteratur* 40, took the author's disclaimer at the beginning of his work literally and attributes rhetorical training to him: "Et sodali prece deposco lectores ut parcant insufficientiae et insipientiae meae" is, however, a commonplace disclaimer in such works and should not be taken seriously.

8. The expression may be a commonplace, but the author uses the cliché to define his audience.

9. Wilhelm Berges, *Die Fürstenspiegel des hohen und späten Mittelalters* (MGH, Schriften 2; Stuttgart-Leipzig: 1938) 106.

he presented four examples of funeral elegies that could be given for a podestà, an indigent soldier, a fellow citizen, and a fellow citizen who died abroad.[10] The tract concludes with sections describing the evils of war and depicting the proper deportment of a podestà. Following the section of rhetorical models is an allegorical dialogue, embodying the principles of the *ius commune*, between Justice and a podestà after the completion of his office.[11]

This dialogue best corresponds to the title Muratori gave the entire tract and reveals the author's concern over malfeasance of podestà. Justice began by asking: "I bring you all to the bench, secular podestà. Tell me, why do most of you, although not all, transgress the rules of secular law because of your inane desire of glory? Why, on the contrary, do you not follow the commands of both laws, secular and divine: 'Love justice, ye who judge the world. Do not reap in the field of another.' "[12] Are not the laws and municipal statutes and customs sufficient, she asked? They bind the inhabitants of the land, until you exercise your crass will, especially when you wish to inflict an unlawful punishment, saying "so do I wish, my will is reason."[13] You should remember, Justice continued, that at the end of your term you must answer for your

10. Terence O. Tunberg has published four of the speeches in *Speeches from the Oculus pastoralis edited from Cleveland, Public Library, MS. Wq 7890921M-C37* (Toronto Medieval Latin Texts 19; Toronto: 1990). The Cleveland manuscript is the only known Latin manuscript. The text was translated into Italian during the fifteenth century, at least the manuscript dates from then. Tunberg's edition in his dissertation was preceded by Dora Franceschi's in "Oculus pastoralis pascens officia et continens radium dulcibus pomis suis," *Memorie della Accademia delle scienze di Torino*, Classe di scienze morali, storiche e filologiche, series 4, vol. 11 (1966) 1–74.

11. Muratori noted that the work was bound with Boncompagno's "Liber de obsidione Anconae" and thought that Boncompagno may have been the author of the tract (IV 92). Muratori, *Dissertazione sopra le antichità italiane* (Rome: 1755) III 36 noted another manuscript of the work in Padua. See Tunberg, *Oculus pastoralis* 122–127 for a description of the Cleveland manuscript. Hertter, *Podestàliteratur* 7–43 and Antony Black, *Guilds and Civil Society in European Political Thought from the Twelfth Century to the Present* (London: 1984) 48–49, 57–58, 247, discuss the importance of the tract.

12. *Oculus pastoralis*, ed. Tunberg, 201 (Muratori, 125): "Vos, inquam, convenio, o seculi potestates respondere michi quare, inanis glorie cupidi, tam frequenter, etsi non omnes, mandata legis transgredimini secularis, quin imo precepta conditoris utriusque iuris, tam seculi quam divini dicentis: 'Diligite iustitiam qui iudicatis terram; et nolite falcem in messem mittere alienam' (Deut. 23.25)." Deut. 23.25 was a favorite passage of the jurists and popes. See 3 Comp. 1.6.19 (X 1.6.34) (Venerabilem) and C.6 q.3 c.1. See also the prologue of Bernardus Papiensis to 1 Comp.: "Iuste iudicate filii hominum et nolite iudicare secundum faciem, sed iustum iudicium iudicate, ut ostendatis vos diligere iustitiam, qui iudicatis terram."

13. Ibid.: "Nunc dicatis, 'nonne sufficiunt vobis leges que diversimode puniunt delicta nocentum, et iura municipalia, quibus sese pensato moderamine statuunt quique populi coherceri, ac etiam consuetudines approbate locorum, quibus insuper incole se patiuntur astringi,' nisi quod arbitrio utimini multocies stolido, maxime cum vultis ultionem sumere inconcessam, dicentes: 'Sic volo, sic pro ratione voluntas'?"

deeds publicly within fifty days. And do you not remember your oath to maintain the laws and statutes?[14]

The underlying argument of Justice's complaint touches upon the powers of the podestà. He was chosen from another city and held office for six months or a year. At the end of his term, the podestà's conduct was examined by a special court in which any citizen could bring a complaint. At the beginning of his office a podestà swore an oath to uphold the laws of the city. Because podestà were most vulnerable to accusations of unlawfulness arising from their handling of court cases, they protected themselves from future prosecution by asking jurists to compose consilia (legal opinions or briefs) for important or legally complicated cases. Consequently, from the middle of the thirteenth century, jurists composed consilia in greater and greater numbers.[15] Nonetheless, Justice accused the podestà of subverting the laws they had sworn to uphold.

Jurists occasionally wrote about this problem. Sometime before 1317, in the second recension of his commentary to the Decretals of Gregory IX, Johannes Andreae noted that when a person swore an oath to another, the recipient could remit or relax it. This paralleled the podestà, he continued, who, by swearing to uphold the statutes of the city, are released from their oaths by the "anciani" and "consiliarii" who have the power to promulgate and abrogate the statutes.[16] Nonetheless, other jurists disputed the point.[17] Certainly Justice, one may infer, would have been dubious about the truth of Johannes's claim.

---

14. Ibid.: "Non reminisimini quod, finito officio administrationis vestre, publico destituti regimine, ibidem remanere debetis, ubi gessistis, et illud non privatim in domo vel alibi, sed publice ante ora omnium quos rexistis, et quinquaginta dierum spatio respondere super gestionibus vestris, et damnari graviter de male gistis a vobis per illos, quos gravastis indebite, cum regebatis eosdem? Item estis immemores iuramenti, quod secundum leges et statuta prestatis in initio dominatus et salutis proprie, cuius nemo debet sani capitis oblivisci?"

15. Gunter Gudian, "Die grundlegenden Institutionen der Länder," *Handbuch*, ed. Coing, 438. Hanauer, "Das Berufspodestat" 377–426.

16. Johannes Andreae, *Additiones* to X 2.24.1 v. *Ex administrationis*, Clm 14026, fol. 74r and 15703, fol. 145v: "In superscriptione habes Gregorium iii.; dic in antiqua dicebatur 'omnibus Christianis.' Et nota ex hoc capitulo quod si iurasti mihi facere uel dare uel conseruare aliquid, ego possum tibi remittere iuramentum. Item illud quod cottidie fit per potestates seculares qui iurant seruare statuta ciuitatum, quia anciani et consiliarii qui potestatem habent destruendi et concedendi statuta eis possunt relaxare iuramenta, et sic seruatur de facto et concord. quod dixi supra de testi. cog. c.ult. et infra de censi. Significauit. De hoc dicam infra de spon. c.ii." On Johannes's "Additiones" see my "Johannes Andreae's Additiones to the Decretals of Gregory IX," ZRG, Kanonistische Abteilung 74 (1988) 328–347.

17. Azo thought that a podestà could promulgate new statutes; see above, chapter 1 n. 47.

The podestà's answer to Justice's accusation was forceful. Quoting the opening words of Justinian's Institutes, "Justice is the firm and eternal resolve (voluntas) to render to each his due," [18] he asked whether Justice herself had not established the office of judge with wide-ranging authority. There was so much evil in the world, he pointed out, that new measures are always needed.[19] With your restrictions, you would hinder the punishment of wrongdoers, he complained.[20]

Justice, however, had a bill of particulars. Podestà abused their authority, she claimed, when they handled court cases. Nations are bound by the commands of civil wisdom, and she could not pass over the clamor of the people without endangering the unity and integrity of the world (machina mundialis).[21] The podestà's collective vice was, she continued, the indiscriminate use of torture in judicial proceedings. When proof was lacking, podestà immediately resorted to torture. They did not distinguish, as law distinguishes, under which circumstances, by whom, when, how, and whether in civil or criminal cases, defendants are to be tortured. Torture, Justice maintained, was a flawed method of proof. Some could endure it without ever telling the truth; others would rather lie than undergo the slightest pain. Consequently, the latter must always confess their crimes again, free from the fear of torture, if their confessions were to be valid.[22]

Justice's indictment of torture is one of the earliest from the Middle Ages.[23] Torture had been a part of classical Roman law for cases involv-

18. Inst. 1.1.1 and Dig. 1.1.10.
19. Cf. Augustine, D.50 c.25: "Cogunt enim multas invenire medicinas experimenta morborum."
20. *Oculus pastoralis*, ed. Tunberg 202 (Muratori, 126): "O pia mater et lux nostra, constans et perpetua voluntas, ius suum cuique tribuens, regni mundi domina . . . cur nos ita acerbe tuos increpasti ministros? . . . Tu ipsa ius dicentis officium esse latissimum statuisti, et modo, cum [in] immensum inoleverit iniquitas, acrius solito punienda, et novi morbi novis indigeant medicinis, intendis coharctare licentiam corrigendi nocentes et ampliare carcerandis viam et materiam malis in me debacandi, et nichil aliud erit istud quam annulare, et in contemptum apud pravos quoslibet reducere judicantes."
21. Ibid. 203: "Tantus undique clamor ad me pervenit de excessibus potestatum in subditos, quod illum cum silentio pertransire nequirem, nisi vellem nodos dissolvi machine mundialis, que tegit singulas nationes, nexibus preceptorum civilis sapientie colligatas."
22. Ibid. 204: "Vt cum deficit probatio in delictis, confestim concurritis ad tormenta, non distinguentes, ut iura distinguunt, qui et quales et quando et que precedant indicia, ac quibus ex causis, civilibus an criminalibus, torqueri debeant, nec considerantes quanta talibus questionibus sit fides habenda, et ita non caute proceditis multis horis. Nam plerique in patientia sive duritia tormentorum, taliter ipsa contempnunt, ut exprimi veritas nequeat ab eisdem. Alii autem tanta fugiunt, ut potius in quovis mentiri velint quam brevi mora talia sustinere tormenta [Dig. 48.18.1.23]. Et ideo confessiones reorum sic extorte non habentur a iure pro exploratis facinoribus, nisi postea tuti dudum perseverent in eis."
23. Piero Fiorelli, *La tortura giudiziaria nel diritto comune* (Ius Nostrum 1–2; 2 vols.

ing slaves, treason, or other particularly serious crimes, but had been virtually abandoned in the early Middle Ages. The revival of Roman law had the unfortunate effect of reviving torture as well, and it became a part of judicial procedure in many legal systems during the thirteenth century.[24] The Italian city-states and principalities seem to have used torture and, in some cases, indiscriminately applied it to litigants.

Although the use of torture was restricted by theory and practice, Justice's accusation that the podestà were too quick to use torture must have had a basis in fact. The city-state of Vercelli promulgated a statute (ca. 1241) prohibiting anyone from being tortured unless that person was a notorious criminal or of evil reputation. A later, marginal addition to the statute in a manuscript underlined the commune's prohibition of wholesale torture and specifically forbade the podestà from seeking to circumvent the decree.[25]

Before defendants were tortured, judges had to have great certainty that the accused were guilty—to use the technical term of the time, there must be a strong presumption of guilt (presumptio vehemens).[26] The jurists carefully limited the authority of the judge to torture defendants without cause and without having had a chance to defend themselves. Nonetheless, theory was jettisoned often enough in practice.[27] But, as

---

Milan: 1953–1954) I 1–66, Edward Peters, *Torture* (Oxford: 1985) 40–73. R. Lieberwirth, *Christian Thomasius, über die Folter: Untersuchung zur Geschichte der Folter* (Weimar: 1960), argued that use of torture continued into the early Middle Ages, but his arguments have not been accepted.

24. But not in the twelfth; therefore, Hertter's dating *Oculus pastoralis* to the twelfth is improbable.

25. Leges municipales, II: *Statuta communis Vercellarum*, ed. Giovambattista Adriani, *Historiae Patriae Monumenta* (Augustae Taurinorum: 1876) XVI 1224: "et potestas seu rector communis Vercellarum precise teneatur hoc capitulum attendere et observare et attendi et observari facere. Nec inde possit vel debeat petere recipere vel habere licentiam vel absolutionem vel remissionem consilio [sic] credencie vel arengi vel alio modo vel ingenio. Nec istud capitulum possit mutari vel deleri vel omitti per emendatores statuti vel per aliquam aliam personam. Sed semper precise in statuto communis Vercellarum remaneat. Super quod quilibet potestas seu rector communis Vercell. iurare debeat."

26. Ibid.: "Item statutum est quod nullus homo torqueri debeat seu martyrizari nisi fuerit fur publicus seu latro vel homo male fame." See R. C. Van Caenegem, "Methods of Proof in Western Medieval Law," trans. J. R. Sweeney and D. A. Flanary, *Mededelingen van de Koninklijke Academie voor Wetenschappen, Letteren en Schone Kunsten van Belgi*, Klasse der Letteren 45 (Brussel: 1983) 85–127 at 114. On the meaning of "mala fama" see Francesco Migliorino, *Fama e infamia: Problemi della società medievale nel pensiero giuridico nei secoli XII e XIII* (Catania: 1985) and Edward Peters, "Wounded Names: The Medieval Doctrine of Infamy," *Law in Medieval Life and Thought*, ed. Edward B. King and Susan J. Ridyard (Sewanee: 1990) 43–120.

27. See in particular Ennio Cortese, "Nicolaus de Ursone de Salerno: Un'opera ignota sulle lettere arbitrarie angionine nella tradizione dei trattati sulla tortura." *Per Francesco Calasso: Studi degli allievi* (Rome: 1978) 191–284. I shall discuss the problem of torture and due process in chapter 4.

Justice observed, practice and theory agreed that a person who had confessed under torture must repeat the confession later before the judge, free from torture and the threat of torture.[28]

This eloquent dialogue was an uncompromising condemnation of the arbitrary and tyrannical exercise of power. Podestà must maintain justice, observe the rules of law, and protect the rights of their subjects. Justice quoted a phrase taken from Juvenal's *Satires* (6.223), "est pro ratione voluntas" (his will is held to be reason), to describe the podestà's penchant for putting defendants to the "question" as torture was euphemistically described.[29] The phrase is key to understanding thirteenth-century conceptions of power.

"Pro ratione voluntas" led a double life in the high and late Middle Ages. Jurists used it to describe the new locus of legislative authority: the will of the prince. Popular and polemical writers hurled it against rulers they deemed besotted with their own power.[30] The jurists did not necessarily attribute connotations of unjust power to the phrase. Like a similar term, but one less laden with emotional baggage, "princeps legibus solutus est" (the prince is not bound by the law), "pro ratione voluntas" defined the prince's relationship to the law.[31] Whereas "princeps legibus solutus est" described the prerogative of the prince to promulgate, abrogate, or derogate law, "pro ratione voluntas" placed the prince's will at the center of the legislative process. Law was derived from his will and his will alone. Reason, which had been a guiding principle for evaluating the validity of a law before the emergence of "pro ratione voluntas," was no longer the main touchstone for deciding whether or not a law was just. In response, non-jurists did not react quite as negatively to "princeps legibus solutus est" as they almost in-

---

28. Johannes Fried, "Wille, Freiwilligkeit und Geständnis um 1300: Zur Beurteilung des letzten Templergrossmeisters Jacques de Molay," *Historisches Jahrbuch* 105 (1985) 388–425, at 389–396. Fried observes, quite rightly, that there has been no thorough study of the theory and practice of torture in the Middle Ages.

29. This distinction between a government of law and of will played an important role in Italian political thought describing the city-states; see Charles T. Davis, *Dante's Italy and Other Essays* (Philadelphia: 1984) 227–232, where he discusses Ptolemy of Lucca's thought.

30. Pennington, *Pope and Bishops* 34–37.

31. For the paragraphs that follow see Pennington, *Pope and Bishops* 15–30; Gaines Post, "Vincentius Hispanus, 'Pro ratione voluntas,' and Medieval and Early Modern Theories of Sovereignty," *Traditio* 28 (1972) 159–184; Ernst Kantorowicz, "The Sovereignty of the Artist: A Note on Legal Maxims and Renaissance Theories of Art," *Essays in Honor of Erwin Panofsky*, ed. Millard Meiss (New York: 1961) 267–279; Pennington, "Law, Legislative Authority, and Theories of Government, 1150–1300," *Cambridge History of Medieval Political Thought*, ed. J. H. Burns (Cambridge: 1988) 424–453.

variably did to "pro ratione voluntas." Although they could accept the idea that the law could be and should be changed, they found it much more difficult to assimilate the idea that law could be contrary to reason.

Yet reason had been, and would continue to be, a fundamental principle of law.[32] Custom had held sway in the early Middle Ages. Around 1100, Irnerius defined custom as old, contrary to neither reason nor law, and law that is used frequently in judgments.[33] The people consented to custom. The prince was subject to the law, and his authority to change law was circumscribed by the principle that the people must accept a new law.[34] The presumptions underlying customary law emphasized the immutability of law, its justness, and its reasonableness.

When jurists first distinguished between reason and the will of the prince in the early thirteenth century, they broke profoundly with past patterns of thought. By introducing the prince's will into political discourse, they fashioned an element of a new political language that became "the basis of a new philosophy of law with Marsiglio and [much later with] Hobbes and was the original kernel of the recently dominant theory of legal positivism."[35] Marsiglio of Padua's thought was an important stage of this development, but he was not the first medieval thinker to exalt the will of the prince. The canonist, Laurentius Hispanus, first took that step.

In the early thirteenth century, Pope Innocent III (1198–1216) provided Laurentius with a part of his inspiration. Innocent fostered the exaltation of papal political power and the language of that power in his letters, sermons, and decretals. The popes had always claimed that their authority was different from that of secular rulers. Christ had founded the Church, established its hierarchical structure, and granted its authority. Innocent enhanced the theory of papal monarchy during his pontificate, emphasizing, as had no pope before him, the pope's "plenitudo potestatis" (fullness of power) within the Church. Although the term dated back to the early Church, Innocent found it particularly

---

32. See the excellent chapters in Cortese, *Norma* I 183–338, II 241–293.

33. William Brynteson, "Roman Law and Legislation in the Middle Ages," *Speculum* 41 (1966) 432 n. 57: "si consuetudo sit longa, nec aduersetur rationi uel legi, cuius etiam idoneum argumentum est si frequenter in similibus questionibus iudicatum."

34. See Luigi De Luca, "L'accettazione popolare della legge canonica nel pensiero di Graziano e suoi interpreti," SG 3 (1955) 193–276. Brian Tierney, " 'Only the Truth has Authority': The Problem of 'Reception' in the Decretists and in Johannes de Turrecremata," *Law, Church and Society: Essays in Honor of Stephan Kuttner*, ed. K. Pennington and R. Somerville (Philadelphia: 1977) 69–96.

35. Black, *Guilds and Civil Society* 55.

congenial for describing papal supremacy. He made "plenitudo potestatis" synonymous with papal authority—it frequently described
episcopal or legatine power in the twelfth century—thereby creating an
attractive term defining all types of power that secular rulers would also
adopt to designate their authority.[36]

Innocent added another dimension to "plenitudo potestatis" in his
decretal *Quanto personam*. He made an unprecedented claim in the
decretal by stating that the pope exercised divine authority when he
severed the bond between a bishop and his diocese.[37]

> God, not man, separates a bishop from his church because the Roman pon-
> tiff dissolves the bond between them by divine rather than human authority,
> carefully considering the need and usefulness of each translation. The pope
> has this authority because he does not exercise the office of man, but that
> of the true God on earth.

The canonists were quick to grasp the importance of Innocent's rhetoric
and the implications of his decretal for a new definition of papal authority. They understood that papal power (as royal power) was divinely
ordained. The constitution of the Church was supported by this old
idea. However, to rest monarchical authority on divine ordination was
one thing, indeed a commonplace in medieval political thought;[38] to
claim to share authority with the deity was quite another.

Laurentius Hispanus (ca. 1215), one of the most creative canonists
of his generation, expanded upon Innocent's words when he wrote his
commentary on *Quanto personam*.[39]

---

36. See Pennington, *Pope and Bishops* 43–58, and particularly the bibliography on
43–45, nn. 2–7. Alexis, the papal legate to England, noted that the pope had granted
him "plenitudo potestatis" to decide a court case: "Vnde auctoritate domini pape, qui
nobis super toto negotio ecclesie sancti Andree et in causis decidendis plenitudinem
potestatis commisit," *Papsturkunden in England,* ed. Holtzmann, I, nr. 181, p. 451. By
the thirteenth century, this term of power was reserved for the pope.

37. 3 Comp. 1.5.3 (X 1.7.3) dated 1198. On the circumstances surrounding the
decretal, see *Pope and Bishops* 15–19; 31–33.

38. *Cambridge History of Medieval Political Thought,* ed. J. H. Burns, 33–34, 63,
135–136, 142–143, 171, 214–215, 218, 224–225, 364.

39. Laurentius Hispanus to 3 Comp. 1.5.3 v. *puri hominis,* Admont 55, fol. 110r
and Karlsruhe Aug. XL, fol. 128v: "Vnde et dicitur habere celeste arbitrium, C. de summa
trin. l.i. in fine [Cod. 1.1.1.1] et, o quanta est potestas principis quia etiam naturas rerum
immutat substantialia huius rei applicando alii, arg. C. commun. de leg. l.ii. [Cod. 6.43.2]
et de iustitia potest facere iniquitatem, corrigendo canonem aliquem uel legem, immo in
his que uult, est pro ratione uoluntas, arg. instit. de iure naturali § Set quod principi
[Instit. 1.2.6]. Non est in hoc mundo qui dicat ei, 'Cur hoc facis,' de pen. di.iii § Ex persona [De pen. D.3 d.p.21] Hanc tamen potestatem tenetur ipse utilitati publice confor-
mare, extra. de foro compet. Licet legalis (regalis MSS) [Bern. Comp. Coll. Romana
2.2.6]." On Laurentius see Antonio García y García, *Laurentius Hispanus: Datos biográficos y estudio crítico de sus obras* (Madrid-Rome: 1956); Knut Wolfgang Nörr, "Der

Hence [the pope] is said to have a divine will. . . . O, how great is the power
of the prince; he changes the nature of things by applying the essences of
one thing to another . . . he can make iniquity from justice by correcting
any canon or law, for in these things his will is held to be reason. . . . And
there is no one in this world who would say to him, "Why do you do
this?" . . . He is held, nevertheless, to shape this power to the public good.

The language of the gloss is obscure and the ideas tantalizingly paradoxical. Laurentius wanted his readers to think about the juristic definitions of legislative authority, and he created a successful heuristic de-
vice. Later jurists adopted Laurentius's language and ideas and changed
forever the way in which they discussed the prince's power.[40]

Laurentius meant to provoke and to teach. He proved that the prince
could and had made laws that were unjust and unreasonable. Therefore, reason could not be the measure by which legislation was judged.
Rather, the will of the prince and his will alone was the source of positive law. Earlier jurists had confused the content of law with the source
of law. In this regard, Laurentius was the first jurist in the Western tradition to demonstrate that the attributes of a law had no necessary connection with its source. While earlier canonists had readily conceded
that a law could be annulled if it were not reasonable, Laurentius understood that the will of the prince must be supreme over positive law.[41]
He did not mean that the prince could exercise absolute or arbitrary
authority, and the jurists did not interpret "pro ratione voluntas" to
license tyranny. His definition of legislative authority could be applied
equally well to constitutional or despotic princes.

We should reflect for a moment on the differences between Laurentius's approach to the authority of the prince and that of the Roman
lawyers, previously discussed in chapter 1. The civilians defined two
concepts when they explicated their texts: the emperor as "dominus
mundi" and as "legibus solutus."[42] They discussed the prince's sovereignty, his superiority to the law, and his obligation to submit himself
to the law. They did not ask where the locus of the prince's authority
lay. The Roman jurists may have been held captive by their sources.

Apparat des Laurentius zur Compilatio III." *Traditio* 17 (1961) 542–543. Brendan
McManus, *The Ecclesiology of Laurentius Hispanus (c. 1180–1248) and his Contribution to the Romanization of Canon Law Jurisprudence with an Edition of the "Apparatus
glossarum Laurentii Hispani in Compilationem tertiam"* (PhD dissertation, Syracuse University, 1991).

40. I have explored the meaning of this gloss and the glosses of later canonists in
Pope and Bishops 17–30.

41. Pennington, "Law, Legislative Authority" 427–429.

42. We shall discuss the civilians' interpretation of "legibus solutus" in chapter 3.

The *Corpus iuris civilis* was ancient and unchanging (except for the very few medieval constitutions added to it). Consequently, Roman law did not stimulate the jurists to explore a complete theory of legislation.[43]

Perhaps because they were always conscious of describing the pope, a living legislator, the canonists took the analysis of civilians one step further and examined the source of the law. In contrast to Roman law, canon law was a living legal system, and the canonists quite naturally searched for its heart.

Laurentius did not comment on Innocent III's claim that the pope exercised an authority that transcended human authority. Perhaps he could not perceive how the prince could exercise a greater authority over positive law than he already had. Be that as it may, it was left to one of the most creative jurists of the thirteenth century to draw out the full implications of Innocent's and Laurentius's thought.

Henricus of Segusio, or Hostiensis as he was known after he became cardinal bishop of Ostia, had a remarkably varied career. Born in the small Piedmont town of Susa (Segusio or, as it sometimes appears in the manuscripts, Segusia), he became prior of Antibes ca. 1235, bishop of Sisteron in 1244, archbishop of Embrun in 1250, and cardinal bishop of Ostia in 1262. He went to England in the late 1230s where he was richly beneficed and entrusted with several legations by King Henry III. While on the king's business, he had the honor of drawing Matthew of Paris's xenophobic invective. He taught canon law at Paris in the 1230s, but he did not teach after his election to higher ecclesiastical office. His influence and importance is remarkable because he did not have a long teaching career, had no disciples, and, from 1244 to his death, continuously occupied high ecclesiastical offices. In 1270, he fell ill during the long conclave that eventually elected Pope Gregory X and renounced his right to participate in the election. He drafted his testament in Viterbo on 29th October, 1271, and died there a week later.[44] His com-

---

43. The most complete discussion of medieval theories of legislation and codification remains Sten Gagnér, *Studien zur Ideengeschichte der Gesetzgebung* (Acta Universitatis Upsaliensis, Studia Iuridica Upsaliensia, 1; Stockholm-Uppsala-Göteborg: 1960).

44. Errors of fact—uncritically taken from earlier literature—have marred the biographies by Charles Lefebvre, "Hostiensis," DDC 5 (1953) 1211–1227 and Elisabeth Vodola, "Hostiensis (Henry of Susa)," DMA 6 (1985) 298–299. They have presented dates and relationships as certain that Noël Didier only conjectured cautiously, see Didier, "Henri de Suse: Evêque de Sisteron (1244–1250)," *Revue historique de droit français et étranger* 31 (1953) 244–270; "Henri de Suse en Angleterre (1236?–1244)," *Studi in onore di Vincenzo Arangio-Ruiz nel XLV anno del suo insegnamento* (Napoli: [1953]) II 333–351; and "Henri de Suse, prieur d'Antibes, prévôt de Grasse (1235?–1245)," SG 2 (Bologna: 1954) 595–617. Pennington, "Enrico da Susa, detto l'Ostiense (Hostiensis)," DBI 42 (1993).

prehensive *Lectura* and synthetic *Summa,* along with Pope Innocent IV's *Commentary* on the Decretals, had enormous influence on later writers lasting well into the seventeenth century.

Despite a life of administrative activity, Hostiensis composed three major legal works: a *Summa* on the Decretals (ca. 1253);[45] a *Commentary* on the *Novellae* of Innocent IV (ca. 1253);[46] and an expansive *Lectura* on the Decretals (ca. 1253). He wrote two recensions of his *Lectura.* The first was finished sometime before 1268; the second was completed in the last year of his life.[47]

Hostiensis's pastoral and administrative activities seem to have had a significant influence on his writing. He was more sensitive to and interested in legal questions touching on the structure and constitution of the Church than other canonists of his time. Although he was an uncompromising advocate of papal authority, he was also keenly aware of episcopal rights and prerogatives within the Church. Quoting Baldus de Ubaldis, Diplovatatius noted that Hostiensis defended bishops with faulty knowledge and a worse conscience, and some historians have characterized him as an overzealous defender of the episcopal status.[48] However, modern historians have been misled by Diplovatatius. He quoted Baldus out of context. Baldus had not intended to generalize; he wished only to criticize Hostiensis's opinion in one narrow case. Consequently, we should not draw broad conclusions about Hostiensis's attitude towards bishops from Baldus's remark. Hostiensis did have a strong sense of episcopal collegiality, but this was counterbalanced by an equally firm conviction of papal authority. In the following pages, I shall concentrate on his ideas about papal monarchy and the authority of the pope.[49]

45. Pennington, "A 'Quaestio' of Henricus de Segusio and the Textual Tradition of his 'Summa super decretalibus,'" BMCL 16 (1986) 91–96.

46. Peter-Josef Kessler, "Untersuchungen über die Novellengesetzgebung Papst Innocenz IV." ZRG Kan. Abt. 33 (1944) 65–83.

47. Pennington, "An Earlier Recension of Hostiensis's Lectura to the Decretales," BMCL 17 (1987) 77–90.

48. Thomas Diplovatatius, *De claris iuris consultis,* ed. F. Schulz, H. Kantorowicz, and G. Rabotti (SG 10; Bologna: 1968) 141: "quod Hostiensis in favendo episcopis habuit malam scientiam et peiorem conscientiam." The quotation is taken from a consilium of Baldus: in the vulgate edition book 4, consilium 500. Diplovatatius cited it from the Brescia-Venice tradition, book 2, consilium 166. See Pennington, "The Consilia of Baldus de Ubaldis," 56 (1988) TRG 85–92.

49. Pennington, *Pope and Bishops* 128–129. On Hostiensis's ecclesiology see Clarence Gallagher, *Canon Law and the Christian Community: The Role of Law According to the "Summa aurea" of Cardinal Hostiensis* (Analecta Gregoriana 208; Rome: 1978); P. Fedele, "Primato pontificio ed Episcopato con particolare riferimento alla dottrina dell'Ostiense," *Collectanea Stephan Kuttner* (SG 14.4; Bologna: 1967) 349–367. Tierney

Hostiensis gave papal "plenitudo potestatis" more attention than any other thirteenth-century jurist.[50] John Watt listed 19 references to the term in Hostiensis's *Summa* and 71 in his *Lectura* on the Decretals of Gregory IX and the *Novellae* of Innocent IV.[51] I have found a few additional glosses, but they do not add anything of substance to his thought.[52] "Plenitudo potestatis" encompassed all aspects of papal power, from the pope's supreme authority over the Church to his obligation to care for his Christian flock. As he described the intricacies of papal power in his glosses, Hostiensis also had much to say about law and its relationship to "plenitudo potestatis."

Perhaps it is best to begin with the most unusual feature of Hostiensis's thought. He insisted on the divinity of canon law and underlined the divine nature of papal rule with vigor and forcefulness that had no precedent in earlier canonical jurisprudence.[53] His formulation meant more than the commonplace that all law or political authority was, ultimately, of divine origin, although these medieval platitudes are also found in his work. What distinguishes Hostiensis from his predecessors and contemporaries is his almost compulsive insistence that every aspect of papal authority rested upon divine foundations. Innocent III, of course, had begun this line of thought in *Quanto personam*. Hostiensis embellished Innocent's thought with extravagant rhetoric, whose metaphors, if not substance, greatly influenced later jurists and theologians.

---

and Watt have written a series of articles discussing his thought touching the college of cardinals: Brian Tierney, "Hostiensis and Collegiality," *Proceedings of the Fourth International Congress of Medieval Canon Law*, ed. Stephan Kuttner (MIC, Series C, 5; Città del Vaticano: 1976) 401–409. John A. Watt, "The Constitutional Law of the College of Cardinals: Hostiensis to Johannes Andreae," *Mediaeval Studies* 23 (1971) 127–157 and "Hostiensis on 'Per venerabilem': The Role of the College of Cardinals," *Authority and Power: Studies on Medieval Law and Government Presented to Walter Ullmann*, ed. P. Linehan and B. Tierney (Cambridge: 1980) 99–113. His political theory is discussed by A. Rivera Damas, *Pensamiento politico de Hostiensis: Estudio jurídico-histórico sobre las relaciones entre el Sacerdocio y el Imperio en los escritos de Enrique de Susa* (Zürich: 1964).

50. Melloni, *Innocenzo IV* has analyzed Innocent's political thought. He found few references to "plenitudo potestatis" and few only rudimentary discussions of the terminology of papal power (cf. 146–166). Melloni has highlighted Innocent's forceful definition of God's constitutional design for ecclesiastical authority: "regimen unius personae."

51. John A. Watt, "The Use of the Term 'Plenitudo potestatis' by Hostiensis," *Proceedings of the Second International Congress of Medieval Canon Law*, ed. Stephan Kuttner and J. Joseph Ryan (MIC, Series C, 1; Città del Vaticano: 1965) 161–187 at 178–187.

52. X 1.6.6 v. *et receptus*; X 1.8.3 v. *in quo*; X 1.9.10 v. *extraneum*; X 1.36.1 v. *nostra auctoritate*.

53. The idea is not new with Hostiensis, and Melloni has recently described Innocent IV's thought, *Innocenzo IV*, especially pp. 154–166.

To appreciate the breadth and depth of his innovations, they must be presented in some detail.

In his commentary on Pope Innocent III's *Cum ex illo, Quanto personam,* and *Inter corporalia,* Hostiensis wrote that law has one ultimate source, and all political authority is derived from God.[54] Consequently, all princes exercised authority by divine mandate. The pope, however, had a special status. Drawing upon the same texts that inspired Laurentius Hispanus to create his pathbreaking definition of legislative power, Hostiensis observed that whatever the pope does, he acts on God's authority, because he is the vicar of God and receives his authority from him.[55] In his gloss to *Quanto personam,* he extended his analysis further. Hostiensis called the consistory[56] of the pope and of God the same. Whatever the pope does is licit, as long as the "key does not err." With the exception of sin, whenever he acts "de iure," he almost always acts as God.[57]

The pope exercised divine authority and presided over a consistory that reached from earth to heaven. Pope Innocent III might have paused to catch his breath after reading Hostiensis's commentary. If the pope had divine authority, then his law must be divine as well. Nor did this simple conclusion escape Hostiensis. Canon 27 of the Fourth Lateran Council began "Cum sit ars artium regimen animarum" (Since the science of sciences is the care of souls).[58] The teachers of liberal arts, Hos-

---

54. Hostiensis to X 1.7.1 (Cum ex illo) v. *privilegio,* (Strassbourg: 1512 = S) fol. 84v, (Venice: 1581, repr. Torino: 1963 = V) fol. 81v: "Largo tamen modo omnis potestas a domino Deo est, unde ad Rom. xiii. 'Non est potestas nisi a Deo. Itaque qui resistit potestati,' etc. Ideo dicitur quod utrumque, scilicet sacerdotium et imperium ab eodem emanarunt, in authen. quomodo o. e. in prin. col. i. [Authen. 1.(Nov.6).6.]."

55. Hostiensis to X 1.7.2 (Inter corporalia) v. *dissoluitur,* Oxford, New College 205, fol. 34r, Clm 28152, fol. 49r: "Quia quod fit auctoritate pape, auctoritate Dei fieri intelligitur, et quia uicarius eius est, ut sequitur. Et quia hanc potestatem a Deo habet, ut supra eodem, c.i. in principio et probatur, xxiiii. q.i Quodcumque (C.24 q.1 c.6) et q.iii. Si quis non recto [c.4] et xi. q.iii. Nemo contemnat [C.11 q.3 c.31], extra. d.n. de homicid. Pro humani, lib. vi. [Novellae Innoc. IV = VI 5.4.1]."

56. In his gloss to "Romana," the Novellae of Innocent IV v. *consistorium,* V fol. 21r–22v, Hostiensis defined the papal curia as "consistorium." A bishop's court, he thought, was called "auditorium."

57. Hostiensis to X 1.7.3 (Quanto personam) v. *uicem,* S fol. 87r, V. fol. 84r: "Ergo consistorium Dei et pape unum et idem est censendum, extra. d.n. de appell. Romana, responso i. [VI 2.15.3], quia et locum Dei tenet, infra ut benef. eccles. c. unico § Porro [X 3.12.1] et in ligando et in soluendo ratum est quicquid facit, claue tamen non errante. Sic intelligas xxiiii. q.i. Quodcumque ligaueris [C.24 q.1 c.6], et habuisti simile supra eodem, c.i. responso i. uer. Non enim. Et breuiter excepto peccato quasi omnia de iure potest ut Deus, de pen. di. ii. Charitas [De pen. D.2 c.?], quod dic ut not. infra de concess. preben. Proposuit [X 3.8.4] et de uoto, Magne § i. [X 3.34.7]."

58. Antonio García y García, *Constitutiones Concilii quarti Lateransis* (MIC, Series A, 2; Città del Vaticano: 1981) 72–73. 4 Comp. 1.8.4 (X 1.14.14).

tiensis wrote in a gloss to these words, claim that dialectic is the "ars artium." Grammarians put forward grammar as the foundation of all knowledge, while Roman lawyers assert that only their discipline has a "finis mirabilis" (a glorious end). They are all like gardeners, he concluded, who praise only the leeks from their own plots.[59] The truth is, however, that divine law is the "ars artium" from which human and canon law are not excluded. Civil law is divine because the emperors fashioned the judicial process and rules of litigation by divine inspiration. The emperor is the living law whom the Lord has given to men and to whom He has subjected the law.[60]

Canon law is also divine. You may say, continued Hostiensis, that Roman and canon law are one with theology, and all are necessary for the holy Church of God. Switching to the anthropomorphic metaphor of the Church as a body, he noted that theology functioned as the Church's head, Roman law as its feet. Canon law is the Church's hand, that sometimes leads the head, sometimes the feet.[61]

To this point Hostiensis did not formulate new principles, he just articulated the old with remarkable eloquence. In other glosses, however, he defined all law as being human or divine and developed the idea that canon law is not human; it is divine and is included under theology.[62] His opinion had few precedents. He himself recognized, as we shall see, that canon law could also be defined as human and positive, but in his commentary on canon 27, he insisted on the divinity of canon law. Nevertheless, the rhetoric of his ecclesiology rested on a clearly developed theory of divine canon law. In a gloss to canon 43 of

59. Hostiensis to X 1.14.14 v. *ars artium.* S fol. 114r–114v and V fol. 110r.

60. Ibid.: "Set hec est ueritas: quod ars artium est diuina lex a qua non est excludenda canonica nec humana. Ciuilis enim diuina est, quia imperatores ad actiones diuinitus peruenerunt, C. de prescript. long. temp. l. finali [Cod. 7.33.12], et quia a uiua lege, scilicet imperatore, quem dominus misit hominibus legem animatam in terris, et ei ipsas leges subiecit, ut in authen. de consul. ante finem, col. iiii. [Authen. 4.3 (Nov. 105).2.4]."

61. Ibid.: "De canonica uero lege planum est quod diuina est, ut patet infra de iura. calum. c.i. § Nos utique, ubi de hoc supra de translat. episc. Inter corporalia § Set neque uer. Et quod non est. [X 1.7.2]. Vnde dicas quod iste due leges unum sunt cum theologia, et omnes sunt necessarie ecclesie sancte Dei . . . Dicamus ergo quod in regimine ecclesie sancte Dei theologia locum capitis obtinet, ciuilis locum pedis, canonica uero que quandoque ad caput, quandoque ad pedem ducitur locum manus."

62. Hostiensis to X 2.7.1 (Inherentes) v. *diuine et humane,* S fol. 247r, V fol. 28v, Clm 28152, fol. 171r: "Notatur quod omnis lex in hec duo membra diuiditur, ut hic patet et infra de iureiur. Nimis [X 2.24.30], infra de censi. Peruenit [X 3.39.5], iii. q.v. Quia suspecti [C.3 q.5 c.15], C. de sacrosanct. eccles. Vt inter diuinum. [Cod. 1.2(5).23(20)] Set certum est quod lex canonica non est humana, supra de translat. epsic. c.ii. et iii. [X 1.7.2 and 3]. Ergo est diuina et sub theologica comprehenditur."

the Fourth Lateran Council, he pondered the words "Certain laymen attempt to usurp divine law":[63]

> That is ecclesiastical or canonical. And so it is clear that canon law is divine ... for it is taken from the Bible ... and whatever the pope promulgates as law, God, whose vicar he is, establishes ... who gave the pope the power of interpreting the Bible ... hence his opinion, rather than that of the masters, should be followed in cases of tithes and other doubtful cases ... as in *Gravi*.[64] ... But it seems possible to say the same about civil law, for laws are divinely promulgated through the mouth of princes. ...This is true only indistinctly, for strictly and properly speaking, this is true only of the pope. The pope, not the emperor, is the general vicar of Christ.

This extravagant conception of canon law did not persuade later jurists. In the middle of the fourteenth century, Johannes Andreae objected to Hostiensis's definition. Johannes argued that canon law was human and positive.[65] Later canonists adopted Johannes's opinion, rather than Hostiensis's, although some conceded that canon law might be, in part, divine.

While describing the pope's legislative and judicial prerogatives, Hostiensis did borrow much of his terminology from earlier canonists. He claimed that the pope could make something out of nothing, borrowing a phrase Johannes Teutonicus had invented to define the pope's right to sanction invalid legal decisions or acts.[66] Echoing Huguccio, Laurentius Hispanus, and others he demanded, "we dare not say to

---

63. Hostiensis to X 2.24.30 (Nimis) v. *diuino*, S fol. 364v, V fol. 136v–137r, Clm 28152, fol. 255v: "idest ecclesiastico siue canonico. Et sic patet quod ius canonicum est diuinum et de hoc not. supra de iuram. calum. c.i. § Pretera uer. 'Nos itaque' [X 2.7.1] nam et a diuinis scripturis tractum est, ut patet infra de accus. Qualiter ii., in principio [X 5.1.24] et quicquid iuris promulgat papa, Deus cuius uicarius est intelligitur promulgare, ut patet supra de translat. epis. c.ii. respon. i. uer. 'Non enim,' [X 1.7.2] et qui ei dedit potestatem interpretandi etiam diuinas scripturas, ut patet infra quia fil. sint legit. Per uenerabilem § Rationibus [X 4.17.13] Vnde et interpretationi sue potius standum est circa solutionem decimarum integram et alia dubia quam magistrorum, ut patet in eo quod not. infra de decim. In aliquibus, etiam extra. Graui [VI 3.13.1] et supra de postul. prelat. c.i. § Nec ualet. Set et idem uidetur posse dici de iure ciuili, nam et leges sunt per ora principum diuinitus promulgate, xvi. q.iii. c. finali, C. de prescript. l. finali [Cod. 7.37.3] Set non obstat quia largo modo hoc uerum est, porro stricto modo et proprie loquendo de solo papa hoc uerum est, et quia nec imperator, sicut papa, Christi uicarius est generalis."

64. *Gravi* was a decretal of Gregory IX's that circulated outside of the *Gregoriana*. Hostiensis discussed it in his commentary. For the text of *Gravi* see Pennington, "An Earlier recension of Hostiensis's Lectura," appendix two, 89–90.

65. Johannes Andreae, *Novella* to X 2.7.1 (Venice: 1581; repr. Torino: 1963) II, fol. 46v, nr. 9.

66. Hostiensis to X 1.6.36, 1.10.4, 1.36.8, 3.40.9.

him, why do you do this?"[67] Although these phrases have been misunderstood, they define rather mundane aspects of papal power.[68] But here too Hostiensis ascended to new rhetorical heights. He described the right of the "prince"—and it is significant that Hostiensis began to blur the distinction between the secular and ecclesiastical "prince"—to grant dispensations from positive law, legitimate bastards, and restore "fama" to the infamous as "almost miraculous and contrary to nature."[69] Emphasizing the pope's divine authority, he wrote that the pope was "lord" (dominus) as long as he lived; he could change squares into circles and settle all matters as a lord, excepting violations of faith.[70] Significantly, Hostiensis did not use legal terminology to explain the pope's power to change squares into circles, as earlier canonists had always done, but presented the reader with a generalized "theorem" of papal power that could be called "miraculous."

Historians have argued, rightly I think, that Hostiensis was far from being an advocate of unbridled papal power. In their view, his conception of the Church's constitution was oligarchic rather than autocratic.[71] But, and this should not be seen as paradoxical, he wrapped papal authority in a rich blanket of brightly colored metaphors, which seemed to create a pattern of limitless papal power. He must have thought it natural, given his predilection to clothe papal authority with divine attributes, to endow the pope with the terminology of divine power as well. Just a few years before Hostiensis wrote an earlier version of his *Lectura,* theologians had invented the terms "potestas absoluta et potestas ordinata" to describe God's powers over the universe.

67. Hostiensis to "Rex pacificus," v. *Gregorius episcopus.*
68. I have discussed these phrases and others which the canonists created in reaction to Innocent III's *Quanto personam* in *Pope and Bishops* 16–30.
69. Hostiensis to X 2.22.15 v. *Cum P. tabellio,* S fol. 347r, V fol. 120r, Clm 28152, fol. 242r: "Nec mirum si alii hoc non concedatur nisi principi; sunt enim hec quasi miraculosa et contra naturam."
70. Hostiensis to X 2.1.12 (Cum uenissent) v. *per alios,* S fol. 221v–222r, V fol. 5r, Clm 28152, fol. 152r: "Set et quamuis dicatur dominus quia quamdiu uiuit potest mutare quadrata rotundis et omnia disponere tamquam dominus, salua uiolatione fidei." It is characteristic of Hostiensis's ecclesiology that the gloss continued by limiting the pope's authority: "tamen uere loquendo nec ipse nec alius prelatus dominus est; immo bona ecclesie communia sunt, xvi. q.i. c. finali, infra de prebend. c.iii. Vnde nec pape licet alienare, xii. q.ii. Non liceat pape, nec successio in Dei ecclesia locum habet, supra de fil. presbit. Ex transmissa, in fine. Et hec est ratio naturalis quare prelatus in causa ecclesie potest esse et iudex et testis, sicut et unus de collegio in causa collegii, infra de testibus, Insuper, et supra de offic. ord. Irrefragabilis § Excessus."
71. Brian Tierney, *Foundations of the Conciliar Theory: The Contribution of the Medieval Canonists from Gratian to the Great Schism* (Cambridge: 1955) 151–153; 164–165 and "Hostiensis and Collegiality" 401–409. Pennington, *Pope and Bishops* 128–129, 132–134, 146–149, 176–177, 187–189, 192–193.

We do not know who first fashioned these terms or why they became fashionable, but around 1230 the terminology can be found almost simultaneously in the works of Godfrey of Poitiers, William of Auxerre, Alexander of Hales, Odo Rigaldi, and Hugh of St. Cher. William Courtenay best sums up the meaning of these new definitions in theological thought:

> (No theologian) speaks about two powers in God, but rather of two ways of speaking about divine power. One way was to discuss power in the abstract, without taking into consideration God's will and actions as revealed in the present order. The other way considers divine power according to what God has in fact chosen to do. Some things impossible for God in light of the present order, *de potentia ordinata*, are possible to God if one only considers divine power by itself . . . [*Potestas*] *absoluta* was never intended as a description for some form of divine action. God never acts—and can never act—in an "absolute" way.[72]

The theological works of Alexander of Hales, which Hostiensis made mention of in his *Lectura,* are important for definitions of God's "potestas absoluta." In fact, Hostiensis may have discovered "potestas absoluta" in this Franciscan theologian's works.[73] Whatever the case, Hostiensis borrowed the term "potestas absoluta" from the theologians and applied it to the pope. Unlike God's "potestas absoluta," Hostiensis's pope was empowered to act with this exalted power. He was the first human being to wield this sublime might. To modern sensibilities, it may seem almost blasphemous to equate papal with divine authority. It is deliciously paradoxical that a term with which theologians described God's inaction became a term signifying great authority and power for terrestrial princes. Hostiensis found "potestas absoluta" suit-

---

72. *Capacity and Volition: A History of the Distinction of Absolute and Ordained Power* (Quodlibet, Ricerche e strumenti di filosofia medievale; Bergamo: 1990) 74; for the early history of the term in theological thought, see pp. 65–79. See also his earlier work: "Nominalism and Late Medieval Religion," *The Pursuit of Holiness in late Medieval and Renaissance Religion,* ed. C. Trinkaus and H. Oberman (Leiden: 1974) 39. Two important recent studies bearing upon God's absolute power are Berndt Hamm, *Promissio, Pactum, Ordinatio: Freiheit und Selbstbindung Gottes in der scholastischen Gnadenlehre* (Tübingen: 1977) and Klaus Bannach, *Die Lehre von der doppelten Macht Gottes bei Wilhelm von Ockham: Problemgeschichtliche Voraussetzungen und Bedeutung* (Wiesbaden: 1975). The best examination of "potestas absoluta's" development as a term of political power is Francis Oakley, *Omnipotence, Covenant, and Order: An Excursion in the History of Ideas from Abelard to Leibniz* (Ithaca and London: 1984). Cf. Courtenay's critical remarks in *Speculum* 60 (1985) 1006–1009.

73. Only in the second recension: Hostiensis to X 1.15.1 v. *potestatem,* S fol. 116v–117r, V fol. 112r–112v, Clm 13015, fol. 168r–168v, Clm 28152, fol. 72r–v (Not in Oxford, New College 205): "Vnde et secundum fratrem Alexand. de ordine Minorum: Ecclesia est multitudo fidelium siue uniuersitas Christianorum."

able and attractive—although he may not have understood the theology of the term—and he created comfortable places for it in his rhetoric. He concluded that if the pope's authority, law, and consistory were divine, his power should bear the same name as God's.

Book three of his *Lectura* on the Decretals of Gregory IX contains Hostiensis's most elaborate statements on papal power. In the first recension of the third book (ca. 1255–1265), he used the term "potestas absoluta" to define the pope's authority for the first time. He had not employed it in his *Summa* or in his *Commentary* on the *Novellae* of Innocent IV that he finished just a few years earlier (ca. 1253). When he revised his *Lectura* at the end of his life (1270–1271), he used "potestas absoluta" only two more times but did expand its meaning slightly.

Hostiensis's comments on a decretal of Alexander III *Ex publico* (X 3.32.7) and on three decretals of Innocent III, *Proposuit* (X 3.8.4), *Magnae devotionis* (X 3.34.7), *Cum ad monasterium* (X 3.35.6), offer his most detailed and coherent analysis of papal power. These passages are crucial for understanding his theory of papal monarchy. He referred to *Proposuit* almost invariably when he discussed papal "plenitudo potestatis" in his *Summa* and *Lectura*. Without a doubt, he considered his comments on this decretal a summing up of his doctrine on "potestas absoluta" and on the relationship of the pope to the law and to those subject to him.[74]

Innocent III had sent *Proposuit* to the dean and chapter of Cambrai in the first year of his pontificate. He ordered the chapter to grant a prebend to Thebaldus that had been bestowed upon him by his predecessor, Pope Celestine III. The chapter, however, had disobeyed Celestine's mandate and had given it to another. Consequently, Celestine personally invested Thebaldus with the prebend. Despite papal intervention, Thebaldus did not receive his prebend. From the letter, we can gather that he had petitioned the new pope to intervene again in the case after Innocent had already sent an earlier letter to the chapter ordering the installation of Thebaldus. As a delaying tactic, the chapter had replied that granting a prebend of a living person to another cleric was contrary to canon law.

Innocent enunciated a fundamental principle of monarchical power in *Proposuit*: the pope could, if circumstances demanded, dispense from canon law, *de iure*, with his plenitude of power, even if, in this case,

---

74. One may see Hostiensis's reliance on "Proposuit" in the texts printed by Watt, "Term 'Plentitudo potestatis,'" 178–187.

it was not necessary. At present, the prebend was not occupied since the chapter's grant had been invalidated by Celestine. Therefore, the chapter should remove any current occupant of the prebend and grant Thebaldus his rights immediately.[75]

During the next four centuries, *Proposuit* intrigued the canonists and stimulated them to consider papal power when they commented on it. Innocent insisted that the pope could dispense from the provisions of canon law, but this principle would have been a commonplace for anyone who had studied in Bologna. Nonetheless, the ramifications of these commonplaces—in this case, the maxim "Princeps legibus solutus est" (the prince is not bound by the laws)—had not yet penetrated the nooks and crannies of distant episcopal courts. Indeed, in some places, like England, the prince's authority to dispense from positive law was still only hesitantly accepted in the middle of the thirteenth century. As Brian Tierney has convincingly demonstrated, although the English lawyer known as Bracton granted that the king was "legibus solutus" (that is, he could make new law and was not subject to the law's sanctions), he probably would not have accepted the idea that the king could dispense from the law *de iure*. Bracton seems to believe that, once the law is established, the king is held to observe it.[76]

Innocent's claim that the pope could dispense from canon law was a comparatively new idea in curial circles as well. The last quarter of the twelfth century had seen a rise in the number of educated cardinals, and during the same time, the popes took a much more active interest in the developing universities.[77] By the beginning of the thirteenth century, Innocent III could remark that the Roman curia had no lack of lawyers. Their ubiquitous presence at the papal court and curia helped to sharpen and refine the content of papal letters.

The papal curia had only recently developed juridical sophistication. Thirty years earlier, a wily bishop of Meaux objected to Pope Alexander

75. *Die Register Innocenz' III.: 1. Pontifikatsjahr,* eds. Othmar Hageneder and Anton Haidacher (Graz-Köln: 1964) no. 127, p. 191–193. Po. 126. It was included in 3 Comp. 3.8.1 and later in X 3.8.4. The sentence from which we may deduce the chapter's objection also contains Innocent's formulation of papal prerogatives: "Licet autem intentionis nostre non sit investituras de vacaturis factas contra canonum instituta ratas habere, qui secundum plenitudinem potestatis de iure possumus supra ius dispensare."

76. Brian Tierney, "Bracton on Government," *Speculum* 38 (1963) 295–317. See also Michael Blecker, "The King's Partners in Bracton," *Studi senesi* 96 (1984) 66–118.

77. Peter Classen, "Rom und Paris: Kurie und Universität im 12. Jahrhundert," *Studium und Gesellschaft im Mittelalter* ed. Johannes Fried (MGH Schriften 29; Stuttgart: 1983) 143–169; Miethke, "Kirche und die Universitäten" 296–303; Werner Maleczek, "Das Papsttum und die Anfänge der Universität im Mittelalter," *Römische historische Mitteilungen* 27 (1985) 85–143.

III that since a papal mandate violated the provisions of a decree of the Third Lateran Council (1179), the mandate was not valid. Alexander III replied that his mandate had predated the canon of the Third Lateran, therefore, the canon did not apply. In modern juristic language, the pope contended that the validity of his mandate could not be negated by subsequent legislation.[78] One should not read too much into Alexander's words, but it is worth noting that his reply was, in legal terms, quite different from Innocent's. From the wording of his letter, Alexander seems to have conceded that, if his mandate had been issued after the council, it would not have been valid. He would have been bound by his own decree. By the time of Innocent III, any first-year law student could have pointed out the fallaciousness of Alexander's implied concession. In *Proposuit,* Innocent or a lawyer at his curia wrote a response that demonstrates a much more sophisticated understanding of legislative theory and the relationship of the prince and the law. The pope could dispense from positive law, his own decrees or conciliar canons, because he was "supra ius" (above the law). His power was not limited by time or precedent.

Hostiensis wrote two long glosses to Innocent's words "possumus supra ius dispensare" (we can dispense from the law) in the first recension of his *Lectura.* To the words "supra ius" (from the law), he outlined the prince's power to subvert law:[79]

> As if he would say: "We are bound by no law, but are placed above all laws and councils. . . . Nevertheless, we will rarely deviate from the common law. It is proper that we do this, even though we are not bound to do so, as in the Digest, *Princeps* and the Codex, *Digna vox.* We write [rescripts] that injure the rights of a third party only under certain circumstances. . . . But, when we have expressed our will, we must be obeyed, although it may be difficult."

78. S. Löwenfeld, *Epistolae pontificum Romanorum ineditae* (Leipzig: 1885) 182–183: "Nolumus enim quod constitutio quam in concilio fecimus, impediat, quod a nobis ante concilium fuisse dinoscitur inchoatum." On this case see Pennington, "'Epistolae Alexandrinae': A Collection of Pope Alexander III's Letters," *Miscellanea Rolando Bandinelli: Papa Alessandro III,* ed. Filippo Liotta. (Siena: 1986) 337–353.

79. Hostiensis, *Lectura* to X 3.8.4 (Proposuit) S fol. 38v, V fol. 35r, Oxford, New College 205, fol. 128r, Bamberg, Staatsbibl. Can. 56 III, fol. 56r–56v, v. *supra ius:* "quasi dicat nullo iure constringimur, immo sumus positi supra omnia iura atque concilia, supra de elect. Significasti § penult. set tamen perraro a iure communi uolumus deuiare. Hoc enim decet nos, licet non astringat, ff. de constit. princ. Princeps, C. de legibus, Digna uox. Et ideo nec precise scribimus de facili contra ius alterius, ut supra de rescript. c.ii. Verum ex quo de uoluntate nostra constat, ei obediendum est, etsi postquam durum sit, xix. di. In memoriam et c. Enim uero, ix. q.iii. Cuncta per mundum et c. Per principalem, ff. qui et a quibus manu. li. non fi. Prospexit."

This definition of papal authority conforms entirely to the views of contemporary jurists on the relationship of the prince and the law. *Digna vox* was a key text. In a slightly paradoxical argument, the jurists, when they glossed *Digna vox,* averred that the prince should conform to the provisions of the law, although he himself was not bound by it.[80]

Having freed the pope from positive law, Hostiensis turned to the question that had intrigued three generations of canonists: could the pope be accused of a crime?[81] No man, he wrote, could bring suit against the pope or condemn him, except in the case of heresy; in that case the pope could be subject to the "ecclesia" (the Church). Otherwise, even if the emperor, the clergy, and the Christian people were all convened at the same time, they could not judge him. The pope had his soul in his own hands, warned Hostiensis, and a more terrible punishment than any earthly judgment awaited him if he strayed.[82]

After having established that the pope was immune from judgment, Hostiensis treated a third aspect of papal power: when should a subject obey the pope:[83]

80. See Brian Tierney's analysis of Accursius's glosses touching this issue in "The Prince is not Bound by the Laws: Accursius and the Origins of the Modern State," *Comparative Studies in Society and History* 5 (1963) 378–400.

81. Tierney's account of the pope's liability to be judged in canon law is still the standard treatment: *Foundations of the Conciliar Theory* 56–67 and passim; also "Pope and Council: Some New Decretist Texts," *Mediaeval Studies* 19 (1957) 197–218.

82. Hostiensis, *Lectura* to X 3.8.4 (Proposuit) loc. cit.: "tamen regulam tibi trado quod papa suiipsius tantam potestatem habet, quod et si faciat et dicat quicquid placuerit, accusari non potest, neque damnari ab homine, dummodo non sit hereticus, ut xl. di. Si papa. Potest tamen et debet moneri in secreto et etiam palam, si palam peccet mortaliter, nam uelit (curare), nolit (accusare), ipse subiacet euangelice ueritati quo ad monitionem faciendam, quia cuilibet dictum est, ii. q.i. Si peccauerit (c. 19). Set quo ad hoc quod ibi dicit, dic ecclesie non subiacet nisi in heresi. Dicam ergo hoc, si sit inpenitens ecclesie, idest Deo orando quod ipsum inspiret, et ecclesie triumphanti ut oret pro ipso; alias autem etsi imperator et totus clerus et populus simul conueniant, ipsum non poterunt iudicare, tamen caueat sibi quia etsi anima sua in manibus suis, tamen eidem pre ceteris si sic decesserit iudicium terribilius iminet et intolerabilior cruciatus, ut patet ix. q.iii. Nemo iudicabit et c. Aliorum et sequentibus."

83. Ibid.: "In subditis autem tantam habet plenitudinem potestatis quod ex quo aliquid precipit, obediendum est, etiam si dubium sit utrum mortale sit, dummodo conscientia uinci possit; sic intellige xxiii. q.i. Quid culpatur et not. supra de rescript. Si quando [X 1.3.5] Set certum sit quod illud quod precipit est mortale, recognoscendus est papa Celestis, xi. q.iii. Iulianus et c. Qui resistit et multis aliis capitulis ibi positis, quia ecclesia triumphans numquam fallit, nec fallitur. Ideo si conscientia tua tibi dictet quod non obedias, non recedas ab ea set excommunicationem sustineas patienter, infra de sent. excom. A uobis ii. et c. Inquisitioni, etiam si errorea sit, nisi possis deponere errorem, infra de simon. Per tuas ii. Vbicumque ergo peccatum mortale insurgit ex lege diuina non debes obedire, ubi uero ex lege humana siue canonica semper obediendum est, ut supra de constit. c. finali et si intellige quod hic dicit, 'supra ius,' scilicet positiuum, supra de consuet. c. finali, quod qui potuit instituere, potest destituere, xii. qi. Certe, et successor, supra de elect. Innotuit § Multa, et patet in his que not. supra de prebend. Extirpande § i. De hoc tamen not. plenius supra de tempor. ordin. Ad aures § i."

[The pope] has so great a fullness of power over subjects that when he commands anything, he must be obeyed, even if there is doubt whether what he
has commanded would be a mortal sin, provided that one's conscience can
be convinced of the command's justness. . . . But if one is certain that the
pope's command would result in a mortal sin, then the heavenly Pope should
be obeyed. . . . The Church triumphant never fails, and has not failed. If
your conscience dictates that you should not obey, you should stand by
your conscience, but endure excommunication patiently . . . even if your
conscience is in error, unless you can detect it. . . . In every case in which
you would commit a mortal sin by breaking divine law, you should not obey.
If a mortal sin is committed by breaking human or canonical law, then the
pope should always be obeyed. . . . And thus you should understand that
when Innocent says "above the law," it means positive law.

I have not translated this passage literally, as the text is too tightly written. On the one hand, Hostiensis's thought is quite traditional: the pope
exercises great authority over those subject to him and, when the prince
is described as "legibus solutus" or "supra ius," the prince is not bound
by the sanctions of positive law. His insistence that a subject must resist
a command of the pope if it runs counter to conscience is not traditional. In other glosses he went further. He clearly stated that if a subject's conscience were violated, even in matters of positive law, the
pope's commands should not be obeyed.[84]

To Innocent III's words, "we can legally dispense from the law,"
Hostiensis discussed other papal prerogatives: when the pope may dispense from divine law. The first part of the gloss was a repetition of
earlier canonistic thought. The pope, he stated, may dispense from the
mandates of the Apostle and the rules of the Old Testament. He cannot
dispense from the "universal state of the Church."[85] These were commonplaces that had been part of canonistic doctrine since the last quarter of the twelfth century.[86] At that point, he departed from traditional
thought and put forward claims for papal dispensing powers that no
canonist had ever made:[87]

84. Pennington, *Pope and Bishops* 132–134.
85. Hostiensis to X 3.8.4 (Proposuit) v. *dispensare*, S, fol. 38v, V, fol. 35r, Oxford,
New College 205, fol. 128r, Bamberg, Staatsbibliothek, Can. 56, III, fol. 55v: "Etiam
contra Apostolum sine lesione tamen fidei, xxxiiii. di. Lector, et canonem Apostoli,
lxxviii. di. Presbiter et § sequenti et c. Si triginta, et contra uetus testamentum quo ad
decimas, infra de decim. Ex parte, et in uoto, infra de uoto, c.i. et iuramento, xv. q.vi.
c. ii. supra de rescript. Constitutus. Non potest tamen contra uniuersalem statum ecclesie dispensare, xxiiii. q.i. Memor sum et c. Si ea destruere, quod intelligo in fidei
subuersione."
86. There is an extensive literature treating this subject; see Pennington, *Pope and
Bishops* 70 n. 87.
87. Hostiensis to X 3.8.4 (Proposuit) v. *dispensare*: "alias ei non aufero, etsi uelit
mutare quadrata rotundis. Quid enim si uellet facere statutum quod omnes clerici de

Otherwise I do not deny him anything, even if he wishes to change squares into circles. But what if he wants to issue a statute that all the clergy could marry, since divine law does not prohibit clerical marriages? (But, [a contrary argument to this proposition would be that] he cannot dispense from the monastic rule forbidding a monk to have property). . . . This alone you should believe: he can dispense in all things provided that he does not violate the faith and provided that his dispensation does not lead to a mortal sin, subversion of the faith, or danger for the salvation of souls. In these matters he has no power against God. . . . So, he may dispense from canon law generally and from divine law when he is not prohibited from dispensing and where there is no obvious mortal sin.

The gloss has a rough edge. The question—could the pope abolish clerical celibacy?—is followed by what seems to be a *non sequitur* or a gap in the text: the pope cannot dispense from the monastic rule that the monks may own property. However, the manuscripts all agree on the text; it is not a faulty text but Hostiensis's argument that is elliptical. His statement that the pope cannot grant monks the right to own property is a contrary argument that he does not believe. In other glosses, he argued forcefully that the pope could grant such dispensations.[88] Hostiensis concluded that "this alone you should believe: [the pope] can dispense in all things." Hostiensis gave the pope vast authority, particularly in matters touching the constitution of the Church and the life of the clergy. He also permitted the pope to dispense from the provisions of divine law.

In his analysis of the decretal *Proposuit*, Hostiensis laid aside the rhetoric that canon law was divine. As is clear from these glosses, canon law was human, positive law. The relationship of the pope to canon law was the same as that of any prince to the legal system over which he presided. Hostiensis explored this question in more detail, however, when he commented on *Magnae devotionis*. This decretal of Innocent III was crucial for understanding canonistic doctrine of dispensation. Innocent had commented that when the pope dispensed from a crusade vow, three things must be observed: "what is licit, what is proper,

---

mundo contraherent, cum nec hoc prohibeat lex diuina? Nec potest dispensare ut monachus habeat proprium, quod dic ut not. infra de stat. mon. Cum ad monasterium § finali [X 3.35.6]. Hoc solum tene quod in omnibus potest dispensare dummodo non sit contra fidem, et dummodo per dispensationem suam euidenter non nutriatur mortale peccatum. Nec inducat subuersionem fidei nec periculum animarum, nam in talibus nullam habet contra Deum penitus potestatem, sic intellige xxv. q.i. Sunt quidam, xv. di Sicut. Ergo contra legem canonicam potest dispensare indistincte, et contra diuinum ubi sibi non est prohibitum dispensare, nec peccatum mortale est euidenter."

88. Pennington, *Pope and Bishops* 67–69; see Hostiensis's commentary on *Cum ad monasterium* discussed below.

and what is expedient" (quid liceat ... quid deceat ... quid expe-diat).[89] Hostiensis noted that these three rules regulating papal dispen-sations are important in all matters. The Roman Church and the pope ought to consider these criteria very carefully.[90] He continued:[91]

> I ask, therefore, what can the apostolic see do? Response: What have I asked? Rather what can it not do? It can do all things provided that it does not deviate from the faith.

He then listed the cases and detailed some of the crimes for which the pope could be judged: when he fell into heresy, when he sinned against divine law contained in the Old and New testaments, or when he sinned against the Ten Commandments. Continuing the argument that he had begun in his commentary on *Proposuit,* he noted that if the pope committed a mortal sin against the precepts of canon law, he could not be judged. In those matters regulated by positive law, the pope could do anything he pleased.[92]

At this point, Hostiensis turned to examine what "licit, proper, and expedient" meant. He posed the question: If all things are permitted to the pope, was everything he did to be considered proper? He argued that this depended on "cause" (causa), a norm of medieval law that was deeply ingrained in the thought of the jurists. Although the theory of "cause" developed by the jurists may seem frustratingly abstract, one cannot understand their concept of authority without it. It must be taken seriously as a fundamental principle governing the exercise of princely power.[93] As Brian Tierney has observed, modern legal phi-losophers have sophisticated theories describing the norms on which

89. On the canonists and the crusade vow see James A. Brundage, *Medieval Canon Law and the Crusader* (Madison-Milwaukee: 1969).

90. Hostiensis to X 3.34.7 (Magne devotionis) v. *tria,* S, fol. 134v, V, fol. 127r, Ox-ford, New College 205, fol. 154r, Bamberg, Staatsbibl. Can. 56, III, fol. 196v–197r: "que semper in omnibus de quibus agitur non est uanum considerare, arg. iiii. di. Denique, in fine [D.4 c.6], xi. q.ii. Aliud [C.11 q.1 c.34], specialiter tamen hec debet ecclesia Romana et papa attendere qui super omnes est (Bamberg and S: sunt, V: supersunt), supra de elect. Licet § finali [X 1.6.6]."

91. Ibid.: "Quero igitur quid licet sedi apostolice? Rn. quid quesiui? Immo quid non licet? Omnia enim licent ei dummodo non faciat contra fidem."

92. Ibid.: "Saluo eo quod papa dummodo a fide non deuiet per neminem poterit con-demnari ut patet in eo quod not. supra de concess. preb. Proposuit [X 3.8.4] et est hoc intelligendum quo ad transgressionem Decalogi et omnia alia quorum commissio uel omissio ex lege diuina, que scilicet in nouo et ueteri testamento continetur mortalis iudicatur, ut patet in eo quod leg. et not. infra de usur. Super eo [X 5.19.4] et supra de consuet. c. finali [X 1.4.11]. Secus in hiis que ex lege canonica mortalia sunt, nam in illis omnibus licet quicquidlibet, ut patet de conces. preb. Proposuit."

93. Cortese's masterful study, *La norma,* vol. 1, chapters 3–6, pp. 97–296.

contemporary legal systems are based. Medieval jurists may not have worn their norms on their sleeves; nevertheless they viewed them as a set of obligations that bound the prince and his subjects.[94] These norms were articulated in the writings of the jurists, and they blossomed in the soul of every baron who thought himself wronged.

Having in mind these norms that bound the prince, Hostiensis perceived no contradiction in writing that if the pope did not have sufficient cause, his action was not proper (non decet) immediately after he claimed all things were permitted to the pope.[95] In his references, he cited *Digna vox*, a law from Justinian's Code, which was a touchstone for juristic discussions of the prince's obligation to respect cause and norms. As these examples show, it is very difficult to determine the exact force of what is "proper" in Hostiensis's thought. When he wrote, "If cause is not present, or is not sufficient, it is not proper for him to deviate from the law,"[96] he does not make clear whether the pope is bound to observe the law or whether he is only admonished to do so.

The glosses of the civilians to *Digna vox* raise the same problem of interpretation.[97] Tierney has argued that when Hostiensis used "decet" to describe the pope's obligation to consult the cardinals in important matters, his use of "decet" had obligatory force.[98] Certainly, as Tierney has stated the case in his study of the glosses on *Digna vox*, Accursius and other medieval jurists thought "law . . . created a universal obligation of obedience . . . [the jurists'] arguments fall into place without self-contradiction."[99] This is true for Hostiensis as well. Unarticulated norms permeate medieval juridical thought, and when we interpret his thought or that of other jurists, we must analyze their glosses with these

94. Tierney, "The Prince is not Bound by the Laws" 394–395.

95. Hostiensis to X 3.34.7 (Magne devotionis) v. *tria*, loc. cit.: "Licet autem secundum predicta sic omnia pape liceant, quero utrum ipsum hec omnia deceant? Respondeo aut causa subest sufficiens quare a iure scripto debeat deuiare aut non. Si subest talis causa omnia quecumque licent, decent, et quecumque decent, licent, arg. infra eodem capitulo § finali, infra de accus. Cum dilecti § i. ver. penult. cum suis concordantiis [X 5.1.18]."

96. Ibid.: "Si uero causa non subest, uel subest set non sufficiens, non decet ipsum aliquatenus a iure deuiare, C. de leg. et consit. Digna uox [Cod. 1.14(17).4], xi. q.i. Peruenit [C.11 q.1 c.39], infra de statu mon. In singulis § Porro [X 3.35.7]."

97. Accursius's glosses to "Digna vox" are discussed by Tierney, "The Prince is not Bound by the Laws" 393–399.

98. "Hostiensis and Collegiality," *Proceedings of the Fourth International Congress of Medieval Canon Law*, ed. Stephan Kuttner (MIC, Series C, 5; Città del Vaticano: 1976) 401–409. John Watt disagrees: "Hostiensis on *Per venerabilem*: The Role of the College of Cardinals," *Authority and Power: Studies on Medieval Law and Government Presented to Walter Ullmann*, ed. Brian Tierney and Peter Linehan (Cambridge: 1980) 99–113.

99. Tierney, "The Prince is not Bound by the Laws" 395.

norms and their ubiquitousness in our minds. Their presence and meanings can never be satisfactorily proven, for they lie beneath the surface of their texts.

The pope must act according to what was licit, proper, and, finally, expedient. Hostiensis defined expediency in terms of another ubiquitous concept in medieval legal thought, the primacy of public over private utility.[100] He declared, "The utility of the state and especially the Church of God and the salvation of souls is always to be preferred to private utility," and concluded, "In this place I put down this rule: when it is asked whether something is expedient, always excepting a perversion of justice, a greater is always preferred to a lesser utility provided that it is licit."[101] As we shall see momentarily, this rule is crucial for understanding his more extreme claims of papal power.

Hostiensis's most significant contribution to political thought was his incorporation of "potestas absoluta" (absolute power) into the language of power. He used "potestas absoluta" to describe the pope's authority to dispense from the laws of marriage and from the monastic vow, institutions established by divine law, and to define the pope's jurisdictional superiority over the hierarchy of the Church. Both types of power posed slightly different questions about the nature of papal authority. God established marriage and its law; the ceremony of uniting a husband and wife was a sacrament of the Church. Many canonists thought that the vow was also regulated by divine law, and some jurists thought that the pope did not have the authority to dispense from a vow that had been properly made.

In fact, the pope's jurisdictional authority in the Church rested upon slightly different juristic grounds. When the pope united two bishoprics, or translated or deposed bishops, he acted in matters that, in the language of the canonists, encroached upon the "status ecclesiae" (state of the Church). The canonists often argued that the pope could never destroy the "status ecclesiae" but that he had special authority over bishops.[102] The central question governing both these problems was this: the pope was not bound by positive law, he was "legibus solutus,"

100. Cortese, *La norma* I 105, 128, 185–186, 264–269. For further bibliography and other examples of Hostiensis's use of "utilitas publica," see Pennington, *Pope and Bishops* 108, and "A 'Quaestio' of Henricus de Segusio" 91–96.

101. Hostiensis to X 3.34.7 (Magne devotionis) v. *tria*, loc. cit.: "Vtilitas tamen rei publice atque maxime ecclesie Dei et salutis animarum est utilitati priuate in omnibus preferenda, supra de regul. Licet § Illa uer. i. . . . in hoc membro talem trado regulam quod quando queritur utrum id, de quo agitur, expediat, semper salua peruersione iustitie, dummodo illud liceat, minori utilitati maior est preferenda."

102. See *Pope and Bishops*, chapters 1–3.

but what authority did he wield over higher laws (divine and natural law) and an ecclesiastical constitution that Christ himself had established (the "status ecclesiae")?

For the first part of the question, marriage was the most delicate problem. God had established the rules of marriage in the Old Testament, and Christ gave new force and importance to a monogamous marriage. But human society was imperfect. Sometimes the laws of God had to be accommodated to human conditions.[103]

The pope's absolute power and marriage law met when Hostiensis commented on *Ex publico,* a decretal of Alexander III, in which the pope had declared that a wife whose marriage had not yet been consummated could enter a monastic order if she acted immediately, even if her husband objected. On the other hand, a wife whose marriage had been consummated could not enter a monastery without her husband's permission.[104] According to medieval jurisprudence, then, an unconsummated marriage created obligations between the two parties that *could be* permanently binding and, in this case, both the husband and the wife should normally agree to one of them entering a monastery.

Hostiensis entered this dense thicket of ideas, laden with treacherous traps of interpretation, in a long gloss to the word "consummated" when he commented on *Ex publico.* It was key text for papal power, and he revised his opinion considerably in the second recension of his *Lectura.*[105] Originally he had written that when Alexander allowed the wife to enter a nunnery, even though her husband objected, he exercised his absolute power:[106]

---

103. On the law of marriage in the medieval church, see Rudolf Weigand, *Die bedingte Eheschliessung im kanonischen Recht, 1: Die Entwicklung der bedingten Eheschliessung im kanonischen Recht: Ein Beitrag zur Geschichte der Kanonistik von Gratian bis Gregor IX., 2: Zur weiteren Geschichte* (2 vols. Münchener Theologische Studien, Kanonistische Abteilung 16, 39; München: 1963; St. Ottilien: 1980) and the up-to-date bibliography in the notes of James A. Brundage, "Marriage and Sexuality in the Decretals of Pope Alexander III," *Miscellanea Rolando Bandinelli: Papa Alessandro III,* ed. Filippo Liotta (Siena: 1986) 57–83.

104. X 3.32.7.

105. I have printed both recensions in "An Earlier Recension of Hostiensis's Lectura" 83–84.

106. Hostiensis to X 3.32.7 (Ex publico) v. *consummatum,* Oxford, New College 205, fol. 151r, Florence, Laur. Fesul. 117, fol. 107r: "Hac etiam ratione considerata possent sponsi de presenti ante carnis copulam auctoritate pape se adinuicem absoluere, sicut legitur in sponsalibus de futuro, infra de spons. c.ii. quia contrarius actus congruus interuenire potest, arg. infra de reg. iuris, Omnes res, licet altero inuito hoc non posset, arg. C. de acc. et obl. Sicut. Sed post carnis copulam non posset hoc fieri, quia nec actus contrarius congruus interuenire posset, arg. ff. de pact. Ab emptione. Hoc autem intelligo de potestate absoluta, non de potestate ordinata, nisi alia causa subesset; non enim fit quod hic statuitur sine causa. Potuit ergo papa circa non consummatum matrimonium hanc constitutionem facere etiam de potestate ordinata."

Since the marriage has not been consummated, a couple may part with papal permission . . . because an equal good has been substituted for the marriage . . . but after consummation, this is no longer possible. . . . I understand that when the pope permitted the wife to enter a monastery without her husband's permission, he exercised his absolute, not his ordained power, unless there were another [here not expressed] reason for his action. Alexander did not issue this decretal without cause. Therefore, the pope might have promulgated this constitution even with his ordained power.

The pope could allow a spouse to separate from an unwilling partner by exercising his absolute power. But Hostiensis believed that Alexander acted with reason and doubted that Alexander would have sanctioned the wife's transfer into a religious order without good cause. If circumstances were appropriate, he speculated, the pope might have issued his mandate with his ordained power, that is, the authority that he exercised when he acted according to the norms established by positive canon law. Nonetheless, the decretal gave no reason, explicit or implicit, for Alexander's decision. If Alexander had acted with cause, argued Hostiensis, then his ordained authority might have been sufficient. Hostiensis's subtle analysis of *Ex publico* is a perfect example of the complexities inherent in medieval legal reasoning.

In his second recension, Hostiensis made two major additions to this gloss. The first he added immediately after the sentence "Alexander did not issue this decretal without cause." Unfortunately, the insertion muddled his thought considerably:[107]

But most likely it can be said that since the church has the power of restricting or relaxing impediments to marriage . . . it can legislate that a spouse can enter a religious order, even though the other spouse is opposed, and, at the same time, permit the other to remarry, the impediment of first marriage notwithstanding. Cardinal deacon Matteo Rosso Orsini argued this position in my presence.[108] If you would ask, from where does this great power of the church come, see the decretals of Innocent III, *Cum ex illo, Inter corporalia,* and *Quanto personam* in the title, concerning the translation of bishops.

107. Loc. cit. Vienna, Nationalbibl. 2055, fol. 108r, Florence, Laur. Fesul. 117, fol. 107r, S, vol. 2, fol. 125v, V, vol. 3, fol. 118rb–118va: "Set et probabiliter dici potest quod cum ecclesia circa impedimenta matrimonii restringenda uel laxanda potestatem habeat, ut patet in eo quod legi et not. infra de consang. Non debet, statuere potuit ut hoc, quod coniunx ante carnis copulam etiam inuito consorte posset religionem intrare, et alius in seculo remanens cum alia contrahere, impedimento hoc non obstante. Et hanc rationem reddidit mihi dominus Mattheus sancte Marie in Porticu diaconus cardinalis. Et si queras unde procedit tanta potestas ecclesie, uide quod leg. et not. supra de translat. episc. c.i. respon. i. et c.ii. et iii. [X 1.7.1–3]."

108. Matteo Rosso Orsini, Cardinal deacon 1262–1305; see Peter Herde, *Cölestin V. (Peter vom Morrone): Der Engelpapst* (Päpste und Papsttum 16; Stuttgart: 1981) 34–36.

Hostiensis affirmed the pope's right to dissolve unconsummated marriages and defended the cardinal's claims with references to Innocent III's decretals in which, as we have seen, Innocent claimed that the pope sometimes employed divine, rather than human, ordained, authority, because the pope does not exercise the office of man, but that of the true God on earth.

Cardinal Orsini's "great power" was clearly "absolute power." But, Hostiensis did not stitch this addition skillfully into his *Lectura*. Immediately after the above passage, the first recension of his gloss continued: "Therefore, the pope could have promulgated this constitution, even with his ordained power," which in the second recension of his commentary seems to refer to the opinion of Cardinal Orsini, instead of Pope Alexander's authority. Only by comparing the text of the Oxford manuscript with his second recension can we follow the logic of Hostiensis's thought. If he had acted with cause, Pope Alexander, Hostiensis meant to say, could have promulgated *Ex publico* ("this constitution") with his ordained power. The pope must use his absolute power if he wished to act in the matters catalogued by Cardinal Orsini.

In his second addition, Hostiensis underlined the points he had already made. With a just cause, the pope may interpret and promulgate laws regulating non-consummated marriages. The pope, however, had no authority over consummated marriages. He concluded:[109]

> When, therefore, there has been no joining of bodies, we do not offend God. And in this case, we can make laws, insofar as we please, with our absolute power, that is plenitude of power. This is true. But it is not expedient that we loosen the reins too much; it is not safe.

In his last thoughts on the subject, Hostiensis made a subtle change of emphasis. He accentuated cause a little less—although he still insisted there should be a just cause—and, by including the opinion of Cardinal Orsini, he seems less inclined to limit papal power over non-consummated marriages in any way. Finally, he equates papal "absolute" power and "plenitude" of power, the latter traditional term being commonly used to define the highest papal authority.

Hostiensis refined his conception of "potestas absoluta" when he discussed the rules governing monastic vows. Pope Innocent III's decretal,

109. Hostiensis to X 3.32.7 (Ex publico) Vienna, Nationalbibl. 2055, fol. 108r, S, vol. 2, fol. 125v, V, vol. 2, fol. 118rb–118va: "Vbi ergo deest coniunctio corporum, nichil facimus contra Deum. Et ideo circa tale matrimonium possumus statuere quicquid placet de potestate nostra absoluta, idest de plenitudine potestatis, quod etiam uerum est. Set non expedit quod in hoc casu nimis laxemus habenas nec etiam tutum est." I have discussed the textual tradition of this text in "An earlier Recension" 82–84.

Cum ad monasterium, provided his point of departure. Paradoxically, Innocent had limited, rather than exalted, papal power in *Cum ad monasterium.* He wrote the decretal in 1202 to the abbot and monks at Subiaco in which he gave them basic instructions for monastic life: rules governing clothing, food, and private property. At the conclusion of the decretal, Innocent noted that the abbot may not permit a monk to own property, because the vows of poverty and chastity are annexed to the monastic rule.[110] The Lord Pope, concluded Innocent, cannot dispense in these matters.[111]

Spurred on by Innocent's remark, the canonists discussed papal right of dispensation when they commented on *Cum ad monasterium* after it had been incorporated into the canonical collections. Although some canonists supported Innocent's generalization, Hostiensis noted that Johannes Teutonicus and Vincentius Hispanus agreed that the pope could not dispense from the monastic rule; however, they thought the pope could change a monk into a layman. Then the ex-monk could own property and marry. Hostiensis mused:[112]

> Others say that, although the monastic vow is part of the very substance of the monastic life, nevertheless, the pope can do this with his plenitude of power, as if one would say that he acts not with his ordained, but with his absolute power. With this power he can change the substance of a thing . . . and make something out of nothing.[113] . . . And one may not object that this is contrary to Innocent's statement, because when the pope says that he cannot, this is understood as "it is not appropriate that he do this,"

110. Innocent spent summers in Subiaco, see Karl Hampe, "Eine Schilderung des Sommeraufenthaltes der römischen Kurie unter Innocenz III. in Subiaco 1202," *Historische Vierteljahrschrift* 8 (1905) 509–535.

111. X 3.35.6 (Cum ad monasterium): "Nec estimet abbas quod super habenda proprietate possit cum aliquo monacho dispensare, quia abdicatio proprietatis, sicut et custodia castitatis, adeo est annexa regule monachali, ut contra eam nec summus pontifex possit licentiam indulgere."

112. Hostiensis to X 3.35.6 (Cum ad monasterium), v. *annexa,* Oxford, New College 205, fol. 156v, Bamberg, Staatsbibl. Can. 56, III, fol. 208v, S, fol. 142v, V, fol. 134r: "Alii dicunt quod licet uotum sit de substantia monachatus, tamen hoc potest de plenitudine potestatis, quasi dicat non de potestate ordinata, set de absoluta, secundum quam potest mutare substantiam rei, C. de rei uxor. act. l. unica [Cod. 5.13.1] et eo quod nihil est aliquid facit, iii. q.vi. Hec quippe [C.3 q.6 c.10]. Arg. de con. di. ii. Reuera [De con. D.2 c.69] et not. supra de transact. c.i. [X 1.36.1]. Nec obstat quod hic dicitur, quia quod sequitur 'possit' exponendum est, idest potentie sue non congruit, sicut et exponitur illud Hieronymi: 'Cum Deus omnia possit, hoc solum non potest, suscitare uirginem post ruinam,' xxxii. q.v. Si Paulus [C.32 q.5 c.11], idest non congruit potentie sue. Vel de solito cursu, quia non consueuit hoc facere; posset tamen si uellet, sic expone et hic 'Vel hoc non potest papa sine causa, set ex magna causa et Deo magis placente hoc posset.' Hanc amplector ut patet in eo quod not. supra titulo i. c.i. in fine" [Cum peregrinationis, X 3.34.1?].

113. These last two statements are not exaggerated papal claims, but illustrate mundane aspects of papal judicial power, see Pennington, *Pope and Bishops* 26–29.

just as Jerome said: "God can do all things, but this alone he may not do: restore virginity to a woman after she has fallen" . . . that is "it is not appropriate that he do this." Or he [the pope] is not accustomed to do this in the normal course of events; he could, nevertheless, do this if he wished. And so you may explain this decretal thus: "The pope may not dispense from the monastic vow without cause, but if he has an important reason (causa) that is pleasing to God, he can do it."

Hostiensis had borrowed "potestas absoluta" from the theologians, and here he discussed it in traditional theological terms. Jerome's fallen virgin had been a favorite subject of the theologians when they analyzed God's actual and potential powers.[114] Comparing God's power and the pope's, Hostiensis emphasized that the pope could dispense from the monastic rule, but normally refrained from exercising this authority. However, the pope must have good reasons for his actions (differing at this point from God's absolute power). The pope should employ his absolute power only when he adheres to the principle that the prince must act with cause. According to the theologians, God would not, it should be remembered, ever exercise his absolute power, but here Hostiensis transformed a potential into a real power. In response to this transformation, Innocent III might have been pleased to have his authority compared to God's but surprised that his clear statement could bear a completely contrary meaning.

In the second recension of his *Lectura* on *Cum ad monasterium*, Hostiensis wrote a long, additional gloss to the same words in which he gave several different examples of what he meant by the principle that the pope must act with "cause." Whenever the pope dispensed from the monastic rule, cause must be "just," "genuine," and "great." If not, the pope and the monk to whom he gave the dispensation sinned.[115]

A sense of equity permeated Hostiensis's thought. A dispensation could be valid even when strictly speaking it should have been invalid. He gave a striking example of principles of justness and equity overriding principles of power. If the pope permitted a monk to marry when

114. Oakley, *Omnipotence, Covenant, and Order*, chapter 2, 41–65; Courtenay, *Capacity and Volition* 25–86.
115. X 3.35.6 (Cum ad monasterium) v. *nec summus pontifex* (bis), S, fol. 142v–143r, V, fol. 134r–134v, Bamberg, Staatsbibl. Can. 56, III, fol. 208v–209r, Vienna, Nationalbibl. 2055, fol. 124r–124v: "nisi ex causa; quamuis enim papa dispensare possit; si tamen iusta causa dispensationis non subsit, peccat, et papa dispensans, necnon et ille cum quo dispensatur. Numquam etiam ualet dispensatio pape in proprio concedendo monacho et similibus, licet ex causa posset concedere monacho quod peregrinetur et uiaticum secum portet; quod tamen non possidebit suo nomine set monasterii. Vnde nec de eo testari poterit, et hec uera sint nisi magna et uera causa subesset."

there was no necessity or utility for granting a dispensation, then, if the monk's wife believed that the marriage was good and licit, the marriage was valid, but the monk could not demand the conjugal debt without sinning.[116] However, if the pope granted a monk the right to own property without cause, then the dispensation was not valid. Hostiensis invoked the rights of parties in a bilateral contract to justify his position. A monk's right of owning property did not prejudice a third party, but the dispensation to marry did.[117] The monk's wife would have been injured if the dispensation were declared invalid; therefore, for her the pope's act remained valid, even though it had been without cause.

Throughout the complexities of these arguments, Hostiensis's thought remains elegant and coherent. He based his theory of papal dispensations firmly on the doctrine he developed when he discussed papal authority in his commentary on the decretal that became the Roman and canon lawyers' most important benchmark for the prince's power—*Proposuit*. The pope must always exercise his authority licitly, properly, expediently, and for the common good. If the pope did not observe these rules, his action was neither licit nor valid.

Of course, Hostiensis's thought is not completely without contradictions. He argued that the pope must always have cause when he dispensed from a vow or the state of the Church, but if he dispensed from positive law, the law of a human legislator, the pope did not need a reason, only his will was sufficient.[118] Yet in a gloss that he wrote for

116. Ibid.: "Set quid si dispenset papa cum monacho in casu in quo dispensandum non esset: puta quod uxorem ducat, nec est necessitas uel utilitas dispensandi? Respondeo si mulier quam ducit dispensationem factam credit bonam et licitam, tenet matrimonium, et tenetur monachus reddere debitum, set ipsum sine peccato exigere non potest."

117. Ibid.: "Si uero concederet papa alicui monacho quod haberet proprium et causa non subesset, omnino dispensatio nulla esset, nec ipsum excusaret. Ratio diuersitatis hec est: quia ex dispensatione habendi proprium nemini preiudicatur, nec alicui prodest uel obest nisi illi cum quo dispensatur. Vnde illi nisi subsit utilitas non ualet dispensatio. Secus autem est in matrimonio ubi dispensatio prodest uel preiudicat alii, scilicet coniugi. Et ideo dicendum est tenere matrimonium ne illa cum qua contrahit auctoritate principis decipi uideatur, arg. C. de his qui uen. etat. impet. l.i. [Cod. 2.44(45).1] supra de donat. Per tuas § finali. [X 3.24.5] Monacho tamen non prodest quam semper peccat debitum exigendo."

118. Ibid.: "Dicunt etiam quidam et forte non male, quod sicut in his que sunt contra uotum tacitum uel expressum uel contra euangelium non prodest pape dispensatio, nisi ex causa facta. Idem intelligendum est si dispenset in his que sunt contra statum ecclesie generalem, arg. xxiiii. q.i. Memor sum et c. Si ea distruerem. Hoc tamen non est uerum in his dispensationibus que tantum fiunt contra ius positiuum, sicut apparet in statutis editis de ordinibus infra certa interstitia temporum faciendis, lxxxvii. di. per totum. Vel quod quis non posset habere duas curas, ut not. supra de prebend. Cum iam dudum. In his enim dispensationibus sufficit sola uoluntas dispensatoris etiam sine causa, quod ex hoc probatur, quia si sola uoluntaria constitutio sit causa quare aliquid prohibetur, per consequens et sola uoluntas contraria causa erit quare prohibitio relaxetur, quia eius est

the second recension of his *Lectura* on *Cum ad monasterium*, Hostiensis quoted a gloss of Innocent IV that monastic poverty and chastity were added to the monastic rule by enactments of positive law. The pope could, therefore, completely abolish these provisions.[119] Hostiensis seems to have tacitly rejected Innocent's doctrine. He continued to maintain that the pope must have cause when he dispensed from the rule that a monk could not own property. If he had thought that monastic poverty were merely a provision of positive law, he should not have held steadfastly to his doctrine that the pope must exercise his absolute power in these matters—not at least if he were consistent.[120]

Hostiensis carried his argument even further when he alleged that the pope could allow a monk to own property. He noted that if Christendom or a part of it would be in danger unless a monk were allowed to become king, the pope could give him permission to leave the monastery. His reason was the same as he had given in *Proposuit*: common good is to be preferred to private good.[121] Or, he continued, if nobility of a land threatened to make an infidel or tyrant king if the son of a king who had taken the monastic habit did not become king, the pope

---

destruere ius qui illud condidit et interpretari, ff. de iud. Quod iussit [Dig. 42.1.14] infra de sent. excom. Inter alia [X 5.39.31]." On *Cum ad monasterium* see the discussion of Courtenay, *Capacity and Volition* 93–94.

119. Ibid.: v. *annexa*, Bamberg, Staatsbibl. Can. 56, III, fol. 208v, Vienna, Nationalbibl. 2055, fol. 123r: "Hec sunt annexa ordini de iure positiuo, quod sic probo. Monachus enim nichil aliud est quam solitarius et tristis, xvi. q.i. Placuit. [C.16 q.1 c.8] Quicquid ergo ultra hoc additum est de iure positiuo impositum est, ex quo apparet quod papa potest dispensare cum monacho ut proprium habeat uel uxorem ducat, cum nemini dubium sit quin ipsam religionem siue ordinem et naturam siue substantiam quam dedit ordini, ex toto tollere possit, secundum dominum nostrum." See Innocent IV, *Commentarium* loc. cit.

120. Hostiensis to 3.35.6 v. *nec summus pontifex* (bis), S, fol. 142v–143r, V, fol. 134r–134v, Bamberg, Staatsbibl. Can. 56, III, fol. 208v–209r, Vienna, Nationalbibl. 2055, fol. 124r–124v: "Princeps etiam suis legibus non ligatur quamuis ipsas eum deceat obseruare, C. de legibus, Digna uox, et res de facili reuertitur ad suam naturam, ff. de pactis, Si unus § Pactus ne peteret uer. Quodsi non ut tolleret. Alii tamen quam pape contra iura sine causa dispensare non licet, quodsi presumpserit non ualet dispensatio uel reuocatur et ipse punitur, li. di. Qui in aliqua. Set ex causa potest papa dispensare cum monacho ut proprium habeant."

121. Ibid.: "Quid enim si tota Christianitas uel etiam alia pars ipsius esset in periculo nisi monachus fieret rex, forte quia non est alius qui sciret uel posset regnum regere? Nonne dices quod monachus fiat rex in hoc casu? Nonne quilibet debet se totum offerre Deo in holocaustum, ut ei in eo quod sibi plus placet preeligat seruire? Set pre omnibus placet ei creaturam suam rationabilem et corporalem conseruare pro qua etiam ipse animam suam dedit. Minori etiam bono maius est preponendum et priuate communis utilitas preferenda, supra de renun. Licet, xi. q.iii. Si quis non recte, vii. q.i. Scias. Preterea si propter communem utilitatem potest monachus fieri episcopus, supra de regular. Licet, et etiam clericus siue rector incuratus, lvi. di. Priscis, xvi. q.i. Ne pro cuiuslibet, et patet in eo quod legitur et notatur supra c. proximo. Quare non eodem modo et rex?"

could grant a dispensation.[122] Do you think, fumed Hostiensis, that God is so cruel that he would not want his vicar to provide for Christendom? God himself, he reflected, would prefer the common good.[123]

In his commentary on *Ex publico* and *Cum ad monasterium*, Hostiensis discussed "potestas absoluta" solely in terms of the pope's authority to dispense from the provisions of divine laws governing marriage and a solemn vow.[124] Papal dispensatory rights did not, however, grant him authority to change or abrogate divine law. He was not "legibus solutus" from the provisions of divine or natural law. In fact, dispensations are not, strictly speaking, legislative acts. They are judicial or administrative acts. Consequently, one might have assumed that Hostiensis intended to use the term to describe only this rather narrow papal prerogative. However, he used the term once more in his commentary on a decretal of Pope Celestine III. In this gloss, he applied "potestas absoluta" to the pope's constitutional authority.

In *Sicut unire*, Celestine had written that the pope has the authority to unite and subject one bishopric to another, and bishops have the same authority over churches in their diocese.[125] In other words, the bishops were popes in their own diocese. When they glossed this decretal, the canonists expanded upon Celestine's statement and created long lists of papal prerogatives that bishops did not share. In his first recension, Hostiensis included a poem in which he detailed the prerogatives that only the pope possessed: he could not be judged; only he could judge bishops, issue a general law, call a general council, approve, consecrate, anoint, and depose the emperor, among many others. He then registered a caveat to the general force of Celestine's dictum, noting that the analogy within the dictum was not completely accurate. The pope could unite a bishopric without the consent of the bishops;

---

122. Ibid.: "Quid enim si non potest Christianitas salua esse nisi regnum in suum proprium accipiat et relinquat suis filiis quos forte ante monachatum suscepit? Quid etiam si dicant ei illi, qui possunt dare regnum, cuius est puella heres, 'parati sumus tibi dare puellam et regnum, quodsi renuas dabimus eam tali tyranno uel etiam infideli.'"

123. Ibid.: "Nonne in tali casu tantum approbabis contemplationem unius monachi et continentiam unius hominis, et adeo reputabis Deum credelem quod nolit per dispensationem sui uicarii tante multitudini Christianitatis prouideri? Vtique dicendum est quod papa in tali casu poterit dispensare, cum ei ad maiora potestas sua extendi uideatur . . . Set credendum est quod Deo magis placeat ut quod communiter est utile eligatur."

124. See also Ludwig Buisson, *Potestas und Caritas: Die päpstliche Gewalt im Spätmittelalter* (2nd Ed. Köln-Wien: 1982) 88–89, on Hostiensis's doctrine in "Cum monasterium" and the papal right of dispensation in general, pp. 74–124.

125. X 5.31.8 (Sicut unire): "Sicut unire episcopatus atque potestati subiicere alienae, ad summum pontificem pertinere dignoscitur, ita episcopi est ecclesiarum suae diocesis unio et subiectio earumdem."

a bishop, on the other hand, must have the consent of the clergy and of both churches when he united two churches.[126]

In his second recension, Hostiensis connected "potestas absoluta" to the pope's general authority to exercise jurisdiction over the entire Church:[127]

> But the pope does not customarily act in this case [unification of bishoprics] or in other matters that are reserved to his authority alone without the advice of his brothers, that is, the cardinals. And he cannot do this with his ordinary power, as in *Novit*, although he may with his absolute power, as in *Proposuit*.

As is the case with a number of glosses that he added in his second recension, Hostiensis formulated this gloss poorly. His point seems to have been this: The pope can act alone when he unites a bishopric or in other matters reserved to his authority alone, but normally he consults the cardinals. The pope cannot unite a bishopric with his ordinary power, and his reference to *Novit* supports his conviction that the pope should act with the consent of the cardinals in these matters. In his commentary on *Novit*, Hostiensis wrote that a bishop and chapter formed one body. As such, the bishop should never do anything of importance without the advice of his chapter.[128] Hostiensis seems to believe that the same principles apply to the College of Cardinals. The point of *Novit* was that a bishop must consult his clergy when he exercised his normal jurisdiction in matters of significance, and the decretal had become the *locus classicus* where jurists created their vision of corporate church in the thirteenth century. Hostiensis concluded with an ambiguous final clause: "And he cannot do this with his ordinary power, as in *Novit*, although he may with his absolute power, as in *Proposuit*."

126. Hostiensis to X 5.31.8 (Sicut unire), v. *ita episcopi*, Oxford, New College 205, fol. 219r, Florence, Laur. Fesul. 117, fol. 238v, S, vol. II, fol. 312r, V, vol. V, fol. 72v: "Set non eodem modo, quia papa hoc potest facere sine consilio ecclesiarum, ix. q.iii. Cuncta per mundum et c. Per principalem [C.9 q.3 c.17 and c.21] et arg. infra eodem capitulo in fine. Set episcopus hoc non potest absque laudatione clericorum et consensu ambarum ecclesiarum, supra de his que fiunt a prelat. c.i. [X 3.10.1] supra de rebus eccles. non alien. c.i. [X 3.13.1]."
127. Ibid.: "Et not. supra eodem capitulo, respon. i. ver. 'Neque duas.' Set nec papa hec uel alios casus sibi specialiter reseruatos, ut in premissis versibus, consueuit expedire sine consilio fratrum suorum, idest cardinalium. Nec istud potest facere de potestate ordinaria, arg. supra de his que fiunt a prelat. Nouit [X 1.10.4] licet secus sit de absoluta, supra de concess. preben. Proposuit" [X 3.8.4]. See Tierney, "Hostiensis and Collegiality" 408–409 and Johannes Andreae's misunderstanding of this text in chapter 3. This text is key to understanding Hostiensis's views on the relationship of the pope to the cardinals.
128. See the texts in *Pope and Bishops* 72 n. 92.

The text is subtly equivocal and ambiguous. The key to its understanding, however, resides in the meaning of "this" (istud). Is the antecedent of "istud" an act of the pope without the cardinals, or is it the pope's prerogative to unite churches? If the first, the sentence means that the pope must use absolute power when he acts without the cardinals; if the second, it means that the pope must always exercise absolute power when he wields jurisdiction in matters of extraordinary importance or outside his normal jurisdiction—whether he consults the cardinals or not.[129] In any case, the text is equivocal and Hostiensis's intended meaning, in this instance, cannot be known.

Whatever the exact meaning of his gloss may have been, Hostiensis's use of "potestas absoluta" in *Sicut unire* was quite different from his earlier discussions of *Cum ad monasterium* and *Ex publico*. When he used the term to describe the papal prerogative to dispense from divine law, he was in the tradition of Innocent III's decretal *Quanto personam*. Innocent had claimed that he exercised extraordinary, divine authority when he dissolved a marriage between a bishop and his church; that is, when he acted in matters that were not under the jurisdiction of positive canon law. Hostiensis elaborated Innocent's conception of papal monarchy. In *Cum ad monasterium* and *Ex publico*, Hostiensis concurred that the pope could not promulgate divine law, was in fact subject to it, but he also asserted that at certain times and under certain circumstances the pope could exercise dispensatory power over it. In his brief statement to *Sicut unire*, he emphasized that the pope wielded "potestas absoluta" when he regulated the "status ecclesiae"—the structure of the Church—and employed his administrative prerogatives.

In both cases, Hostiensis conceived of papal absolute power as a transcendental authority. The jurists commonly held that the pope was bound by the "state of the Church" ("status ecclesiae") and could not abolish the fundamental constitution of the Church. If the pope wished to alter the constitution of the Church, he must exercise absolute power. Hostiensis's "potestas absoluta" has a different meaning than any definition that the jurists had given to "legibus solutus." He did not define it as signifying the pope's freedom to abrogate or derogate positive canon law. When the pope engaged his absolute power, he participated in God's jurisdiction. He can dispense from divine law because he is the vicar of Christ and represents divine authority on earth.

---

129. Not everyone has seen the ambiguity; cf. Courtenay, *Capacity and Volition* 94.

Hostiensis launched the prince's "potestas absoluta" into the main-stream of Western political thought, and future jurists incorporated it into their descriptions of the prince's authority. The term seemed perfectly matched to the problem of defining the prince's authority to transgress higher norms. Nonetheless, the pope's "potestas absoluta" did not free him from all restraints, even though Hostiensis's flights of rhetorical brilliance can lead a reader astray. He did not lay the foundations of arbitrary power for the prince. When Dieter Wyduckel concludes that Hostiensis's concept of papal power "explodes the medieval legal system," he has been misled by Hostiensis's rhetorical creativity.[130] His rhetoric was rich and filled with novel metaphors. But, as should be clear from our analysis of these texts, Hostiensis formulated these ideas in the context of thirteenth-century juristic thought. The prince could be "legibus solutus," might possess "potestas absoluta," but he must always act with cause. Hostiensis has left the pope little room, despite his elevated terminology and the divine origins of his authority, for arbitrary action.

Unlike Laurentius Hispanus, Hostiensis did not fundamentally shift the way in which the jurists understood power. His conception of papal authority fitted neatly into the commonly accepted juristic norms about how the prince should exercise his power. To underline a point that I have already made: Ennio Cortese has written the most comprehensive analysis of the juristic norms of the twelfth and thirteenth centuries and has demonstrated, exhaustively, the jurists' profound sense of limited power. Hostiensis's thought conforms in almost every respect to the medieval "norms" that Cortese described.[131]

---

130. *Princeps Legibus Solutus* 100.
131. See Brain Tierney's insightful comments in "The Prince is not Bound by the Laws," 394, where he compares the norms of the medieval jurists to the "Grundnormen" of modern jurists.

The Power of the Prince in the Thirteenth and Fourteenth Centuries

                                    ... for us, we will resign
During the life of this old majesty,
To him our absolute power [to Edgar and Kent]:
   you, to your rights;
With boot and such addition as your honors
Have more than merited.
                              —Shakespeare, *King Lear,* Act 5, Scene 3

In act 5, scene 3 of *King Lear,* Albany gave up his authority to old, mad Lear and restored their rights to Edgar and Kent. Shakespeare, of course, was not a political theorist, and one can wonder how he imagined that "absolute power" could be compatible with rights. Rather than creating a singular paradox here, however, Shakespeare artfully fashioned a speech for loyal Albany that pierced the central conundrum of absolute power. Between the time of Hostiensis and Shakespeare, many jurists, philosophers, and theologians had granted the prince absolute power. Yet they rarely defined absolute power as supreme, arbitrary authority obliterating the rights of subjects. Instead, they hemmed absolute power in with an ingenious variety of restrictions. The jurists besieged the fortress of absolute power by investing it with juridical norms, natural law, reason, custom, privilege, obligations, in effect, the "constitution" of the realm. Paradoxically, absolute power never was absolute.[1]

Hostiensis had cast papal absolute power in two different forms: first, the pope was permitted to dispense from divine law; second, he employed absolute power when he exercised prerogatives over the ecclesiastical hierarchy and positive law that were reserved to him alone. From a legal point of view, Hostiensis's first definition justified his new terminology. A prince did not have the authority to dispense from laws

1. See in particular Wyduckel, *Princeps legibus solutus* 16–30 for a discussion of historical opinion on the role of absolute power in early modern political theory with rich bibliographical references.

that were outside his jurisdiction. By adopting God's "potestas absoluta" and applying it to the papal office, Hostiensis invented a transcendental definition of papal authority for acts normally outside the pope's jurisdictional competence. The pope exercised this dispensatory authority in the private, not the public forum. His absolute power affected the individual but not the public law of the Church.

Hostiensis's second definition of papal absolute power was not as skillfully conceived. He did not break new ground juristically and, in fact, the new term took its place alongside older definitions of the pope's suzerainty over the ecclesiastical hierarchy and canonical positive law: "princeps legibus solutus" and "plenitudo potestatis." "Potestas absoluta" might have had one advantage that would have merited its use: it could have justified those rare occasions when the pope acted without cause or reason. Using the new terminology to define arbitrary papal authority, however, does not seem to have occurred to Hostiensis. The juridical norm that the prince must act with cause was too much a fundamental principle of his conception of monarchy.

In this chapter, we shall explore the authority of the prince in the writings of Italian, French, and to a lesser extent, of the secular jurists, who blended earlier definitions of power with "potestas absoluta." In addition, we shall probe the thought of the theologians.[2] First, however, we shall focus upon the various ways the jurists thought that the prince was "legibus solutus" (loosed from the laws), and how they integrated the Roman law definitions of the prince's power into the medieval *ius commune*. As we explore their thought, we shall ask a series of questions in this and the following chapters: How did the jurists react to the terminology that Hostiensis introduced? Did they accept "potestas absoluta" as a transcendental power of the prince? How did "potestas absoluta" mingle with older definitions of authority? Nevertheless, before we turn to absolute power, we must begin with an examination of the jurists' use of the famous phrase "princeps legibus solutus est" (the prince is not bound by the laws) in the thirteenth and fourteenth centuries. Only then can we place "potestas absoluta" in its juridical context.

PRINCEPS LEGIBUS SOLUTUS

The medieval jurists borrowed the concept "the prince is not bound (or: is loosed from) by the laws" from Roman law. The formulation

2. For the thought of the theologians see Courtenay, *Capacity and Volition* 87–188.

occurs four times in Justinian's codification.[3] The most important formulation comes from a fragment of Ulpian's commentary to the Lex
Julia and Papia:[4]

> The prince is not bound by the laws. The empress, however, is not freed
> from the law, although the princes bestow the same privileges on her as they
> themselves possess.

Of all the texts in Justinian's codification, this is the clearest statement
of the emperor's superiority to the law.[5] In contrast to earlier usages,
Ulpian did not limit himself to the prince's right to dispense from
the law. For the Roman and medieval jurists, "legibus solutus" was a
shorthand definition of the prince's power to abrogate or derogate his
own laws or the laws, court decisions, and administrative edicts of his
predecessors.

The Roman jurists did not work out a clear and unambiguous doctrine of the prince's legislative authority, however. Any study of law in
pre-modern societies reveals that buried deep within the legal sensibilities of the people, learned and unlearned, is the idea that "good
old law" ought to be preserved and protected. Roman law, even in its
sophisticated Justinian dress, is no exception to this generalization. The
most famous statute that seemed to limit the prince was from the
Codex, *Digna vox,* issued by emperors Theodosius II and Valentinianus
III in 429. *Digna vox,* we must remember, was one of the medieval
jurists' most important "constitutional" texts and a fixed reference
point for their discussions of authority, and we have referred to it several times in the first two chapters:[6]

> It is a statement worthy of the majesty of the ruler for the Prince to profess
> himself bound by the laws. Indeed our authority depends upon the authority
> of the law. And truly it is greater for the imperial government to submit to
> the sovereignty of the laws. By this rescript we declare what we do not per-
> mit ourselves.

If Ulpian's text has a strong absolutistic flavor, Theodosius's and Valentinianus's is quite constitutionalist. Ulpian declared that the prince was

---

3. Dig. 1.3.31(30), 32.[1].23, Cod. 6.23.3, Inst. 2.17.8(7).
4. Dig. 1.3.31(30): "Princeps legibus solutus est; Augusta autem licet legibus soluta
non est, principes tamen eadem illi privilegia tribuunt, quae ipsi habent."
5. Wyduckel, *Princeps legibus solutus* 48–51 and the bibliography he cites.
6. Cod. 1.14(17).4: "Digna vox maiestate regnantis legis alligatum se principem
profiteri. Adeo de auctoritate iuris nostra pendet auctoritas. Et re vera maius imperio est
submittere legibus principatum. Et oraculo praesentis edicti quod nobis licere non
patimur iudicamus."

above all law without qualification; the princes themselves, Theodosius and Valentinianus, declared that they were bound by all law. The ancient Roman jurists who placed these two texts in Justinian's codification set a difficult question of law to their medieval successors.

The intellectual origins of the idea that the emperor ought to submit himself to the law seems to have come from the stoic and Christian traditions.[7] In particular, St. Ambrose anticipated the contents of *Digna vox*. In a letter he defined the essence of what became the central problem of understanding the prince's power:[8]

> What you have prescribed for others, you have prescribed for yourself; the emperor issues laws that he ought to be first to preserve.

The jurists could interpret the phrase "princeps legibus solutus" as being a license for the prince to act arbitrarily only by ignoring *Digna vox*. Although historians have too often tended to view Roman law as a primary source of absolutistic principles in the Middle Ages,[9] even late Roman law was not devoid of constitutional elements.

Medieval civilians, for their part, were not interested in the constitutional history of the Roman Empire, but instead, in making sense of and extracting a coherent set of legal principles from Roman law. They were trained in dialectical argumentation and saw as their task the resolution of the apparent contradictions in Justinian's codification. The two texts quoted above presented them with a difficult problem of interpretation. Because the ancient Roman jurists did not elucidate upon the emperor's authority and prerogatives in any detail, the medieval jurists had to shape their conception of imperial authority with very few points of reference. As such, they interpreted these texts in the context of all the other pertinent passages and, quite naturally, their interpretation was partially shaped by their presuppositions about contemporary political institutions. Nonetheless, they read their texts as models of ancient imperial authority and as a paradigm for con-

7. Wyduckel, *Princeps legibus solutus* 54–60 and Nicolini, *Proprietà* 142–145.

8. Migne, PL 16.1047: "quod praescripsisti alii, praescripsisti et tibi; leges enim imperator fert quas primus ipse custodiat"; also the passages in "De apologia prophetae David ad Theodosium Augustum," *Opera*, ed. C. Schenkl (Corpus scriptorum ecclesiasticorum latinorum 32.2; Prague: 1897) 333 and 363 (Migne PL 14.880 [16.77], 890 [3.8] and 871 [10.51]: "Non . . . solvit potestas iustitiam sed iustitia potestatem; nec legibus rex solutus est, sed leges suo solvit exemplo" [3.8]).

9. E.g., Adhémar Esmein, "La maxime 'Princeps legibus solutus est' dans l'ancien droit public français," *Essays in Legal History,* ed. Paul Vinogradoff (London: 1913) 201–214. See discussion of Tierney, "The Prince is not Bound by the Laws" 378–381, especially, 380 n. 5.

temporary imperial power. When Frederick I asked Martinus and Bulgarus for a definition of his authority, he assumed that the legal principles governing his office and that of the ancient Roman emperors were identical.

In the late twelfth and early thirteenth centuries, Azo and Accursius squeezed the texts in Justinian's compilation to extract a sophisticated theory of imperial power.[10] Because Azo's *Summa super Codice* enjoyed great popularity and Accursius's commentary to the entire *Corpus iuris civilis* became the Ordinary Gloss that was read by students of Roman law for the next four centuries,[11] their interpretations remained of fundamental importance for the rest of the Middle Ages.

Specifically, Azo discussed the relationship of the prince and the law in his analysis of the title "De legibus et constitutionibus principum."[12] All men ought to observe the law, he wrote, because, quoting the Apostle Paul, every soul is subject to the prince.[13] The prince is appointed by God, and all men are obligated to obey his mandates. However, the authority of the prince is limited because he cannot bind his successor. Azo concluded that the prince must persuade his successors to observe his laws and explain to them the reasons for his legislation. The prince receives his authority to legislate from a law, the *Lex regia*. Therefore, the prince should repay his debt to the law by preserving and upholding the source of his authority.[14]

In the notes of Azo's lectures to the Code that Alexander de Sancto Egidio jotted down at the end of Azo's teaching career,[15] the ideas in

10. Piero Fiorelli, "Azzone," DBI 4 (1962) 774–781 and his article on "Accorso," DBI 1 (1960) 118–120. Weimar, "Die legistische Literatur" 173–175.

11. Dolezalek, *Verzeichnis* lists 105 manuscripts and fragments of Azo's *Summa*. It was also translated into French: Brussels, Bibl. royale 9251–9252 and Vat. Regin. lat. 1063.

12. Cod. 1.14(17).

13. *Summa super Codice* to Cod. 1.14(17), Würzburg, Universitätsbibl. M.p.j.f.2, fol. 4v: "Quis debeat obseruare leges et quidem obseruande sunt ab omnibus hominibus ut uniuersi prescripto manifestius cognito, uel inhibita declinent, uel permissa sectantur, ut infra eodem l. Leges sacratissime [Cod. 1.14(17).9] Nam et apostolus ait, omnis anima subdita sit principi tanquam precellenti et ducibus ab eo misis, et idem dicit beatus Aug. in illo c. Quo iure defendis uillas, et Vrbanus(!) in illo c. Cum ad uerum uentum est" [D.8 c.1 and D.96 c.6]. Nicolini, *Proprietà* 150, interprets this passage as meaning that Azo included all men, including the prince, with the adjective "uniuersi." But the next sentence, "Nam omnis anima," contradicts this assumption.

14. Ibid.: "Imperator tamen unus successori suo non potest imperare, set suadere ut leges seruet, et suasionis causam ponere; ut quia de lege, scilicet regia, pendet auctoritas principalis, vel quia per eam populus transtulit omne imperium in principem. Merito et ipse hoc retribuat legi ut seruet eam."

15. This text was published in Paris, 1577, from a manuscript now lost. There is still one manuscript of this "reportatio" extant: Worcester, Cathedral Library, F 29; Fiorelli was mistaken when he wrote that no manuscript of the *Lectura* has been preserved ("Azzone" 779).

his *Summa* were expanded and refined. In these later reflections, Azo argued that many laws demonstrate that the emperor is not bound by the laws; nevertheless, imperial authority depends on the authority of the law.[16] The emperor ought to be bound by the laws because he receives his authority from the *Lex Hortensia*, through which the Roman people bestowed all their rights on the emperor. "Truly," Azo proclaimed, "it is a greater thing for someone to observe the laws than to be emperor," a sentiment that has a striking resonance with the attitude of the author of the *Novella* that we discussed in chapter 1. Frederick Barbarossa had given Martinus the "right to issue a law from his breast" as a reward for loving justice. In this regard, the author of the *Novella* might have written that "it would be a greater thing to promulgate a just law than to be emperor."[17]

Azo continued by expanding on the psychological state of an emperor who binds himself to the law. Subservience to the law is a virtue of the soul; when the prince observes the laws, he does nothing that is not licit and honest, and he represses the pull of his desires.[18] As Juvenal wrote in the *Satires* (7.197), "Imperium is established by fate; if fate wished she could make an consul from a rhetor, or a rhetor from an consul."[19] Finally, Azo underlined his point that the emperor could not command successors to observe his laws because an equal cannot bind an equal. Consequently, the emperor wished to persuade future emperors to obey the law. When the emperor assumed the purple, he swore that he would observe the laws.[20] If they are reported accurately, Azo's final ruminations have a strong constitutionalist flavor, laced with traditional Christian values. The ruler must be virtuous, moral, and exercise restraint.

16. Azo, *Lectura super Codice* (Paris: 1577), p. 40 to Cod. 1.14(17).4: "Pone casum quia bene scis quod imperator non est alligatus legibus, sicut dicunt multe leges, sed tamen adeo de auctoritate iuris pendet auctoritas imperialis, ut Digna uox."

17. See above, chapter 1.

18. Ibid.: "Quia haec est causa quare debet legibus alligari, quia imperium habuit a populo lege Hortensia lata, nam ei et in eum omne ius suum transtulit, ut inst. de iure natur. § Sed et quod [Inst. 1.2.6]. Tertio commendat causam; et re uera quia maius est si aliquis leges obseruet quam si esset imperator. Primum enim de uirtute animi est quia cum quis obseruet leges, non facit nisi licit et honesta, et carnem refrenat a suis desideriis."

19. Ibid.: "Imperium autem est a fortuna, unde si fortuna volet fiet de rhetore consul, si volet haec eadem fiet de consule rhetor."

20. Ibid.: "Quarto et ultimo ponit exemplum imperatoris in seipso cum dicit et oraculo presentis edicti quod nobis licere non patimur, idest quod nos facimus, nec patimur quod non simus legibus alligati, indicamus vobis futuris imperatoribus. Imperare enim non posset quia par in parem non habet imperium, ut ff. de arbit. Nam magistratus et ad Treb. Ille a quo § Tempestiuum. Et bene dicit 'oraculo' quia per legem istam orat futurum imperatorem quod ita faciat cum ei imperare non possit, ut supra dixi . . . Vnde et iurat imperator quando assumit imperium se obseruaturum leges."

In his *Apparatus* to the Digest, Azo discussed the relationship of the prince and the law briefly: the prince was not bound by his own laws or by the laws of others.[21] However, he added one significant point to his remarks on the Code: the prince submitted to the law through his will, as in *Digna vox,* since at the time of his election he promised to obey the law.[22] A contemporary of Azo, Placentinus, had also emphasized that the prince's will was the vehicle through which he subjected himself to the law.[23] By the beginning of the thirteenth century, the prince's will had become the focal point for discussions of the prince's relationship to the law. As we have seen, Laurentius Hispanus and the canonists emphasized the priority of the prince's will over reason;[24] in the civilians' discussions of the prince's authority, they created a doctrine that the prince was loosed from all law but voluntarily "willed" himself to observe the law.

The inherent paradox of this construct did not escape the jurists. Azo observed dryly: "If the prince would say that 'I am bound by the laws,' he would lie."[25] Accursius and later jurists pointed out that *Digna vox* was a "Falsa vox."[26] No matter what the prince said, he was not bound to the law. Although their thought may seem paradoxical to us, they believed the impossible: the prince could bind himself to the law. Their solution was not good law because they had not yet developed satisfactory definitions of power into which they could incorporate Roman law descriptions of authority.

Azo's great contemporary, Accursius, wrote a more elliptical, but more coherent, set of glosses to the same texts, although the format of Accursius's gloss makes his thought more difficult to understand than

21. Azo to Dig. 1.3.31 (Princeps legibus solutus), v. *solutus,* Clm 3887, fol. 4v and Clm 14028, fol. 4r: "Ab alio conditis, et est ratio ut C. eodem l.ii. Digna uox, uel a seipso, quod dic ut infra de arbitris l. penult. et l. Nam magistratus. az."
22. Ibid.: "Voluntate tamen sua seipsum subicere, ut C. eodem l.ii. Digna uox, maxime ideo quia semper cum eligitur cauet se obseruaturum legem. az."
23. Placentinus, *Summa super Codice* (Mainz: 1536; repr. Torino: 1962), p. 17: "Inquit imperator leges obseruari debere a subiectis ex necessitate, a principibus ex uoluntate. Hocque imperator dicit suadendo, 'Digna uox,' inquit. Suasionis causa ponendo cum dicit quia de auctoritate legis, pendet auctoritas regis."
24. See chapter 2, above.
25. Azo, *Lectura super Codice* to Cod. 1.14(17).4, p. 40: "Nam si diceret, ego sum legibus obligatus, mentiretur."
26. Accursius to Cod. 1.14(17).4 v. *Digna vox,* Clm 3501, fol. 39v, Clm 3880, fol. 25v, Clm 3884, fol. 20r: "Ponit casum et eius rationem et commendationem et exemplum. Set quomodo est digna uox cum sit falsum, ut ff. eodem, Princeps et ff. de leg. iii. Ex imperfecto, et in authen. de consul. § finali, col.iv. et infra de testa. Ex imperfecto? Respondeo digna est si dicat se uelle, non quod sit, ut inst. quibus mod. test. infir. § finali [et in prealleg. l. Ex imperfecto *add.* Edd. omnes]. Alii dicunt quod hic permittatur mentiri, ut inst. de act. §Alie, quod non placet. Ac."

Azo's more expansive treatment. He wrote tightly and briefly, inter-weaving legal citations that were clear to contemporaries but obscure for us. To *Princeps legibus solutus* (Dig. 1.3.31), he wrote:[27]

> The prince is loosed from the laws. That is from laws promulgated by another as at Dig. 4.8.4, or by himself as at Dig. 4.8.51. Nevertheless he subjects himself [to the law] by his own will as at Cod. 1.14.4 and Inst. 2.17.8 and also relevant are Cod. 6.23.3, Cod. 6.61.7, Dig. 32.[1].23 and Dist. 8 c.2 of the Decretum.

To the word *principatum* (government) in *Digna vox,* he added:[28]

> Understand this rather than subjecting the laws to imperial government, as if one would say "it is more honorable and fitting since imperium is decided by fate."

He then quoted Juvenal's famous maxim. Brian Tierney, who dissected the intricate references and cross-references of Accursius's gloss,[29] came to the following conclusions:

> For Accursius the emperor was "loosed from the laws" only in the sense that there existed no legal machinery for bringing him to justice if he broke them. He did not associate the words "legibus solutus" with any ideas of arbitrary government.[30] . . . He never argued that it could be licit for an emperor to break the law, nor would he have countenanced such a sugges-tion. . . . Fidelity to the law which was required of all men, had to be main-tained in the case of the Prince alone through internal rather than external discipline.[31]

A comparison with Azo's comments reveals that Accursius added noth-ing. Indeed, almost every phrase is taken from Azo.

Tierney concluded that although he began by exploring a "famous 'absolutist' text . . . at the end of the trail we find ourselves led to a sort of rhapsody on the rule of law."[32] Even if we are guided by Tierney's

27. Accursius, v. *Princeps legibus,* Clm 3503, fol. 8r, Clm 3506, fol. 8v, Clm 6201, fol. 10r, Clm 14022, fol. 8r: "Ab alio conditis, ut infra de arbit. Nam magistratus, uel a seipso, ut infra et arbit. l. penult. Voluntate tamen sua seipsum subicit, ut C. eodem l. Digna et in inst. quibus modis test. infir. in fine, et facit C. de testa. § Ex imperfecto et C. de bon. que lib. Cum multa et infra de leg. iii. Ex imperfecto et in decret. di.viii. c. Que contra." Translation in text is taken from Tierney, "The Prince is Not Bound by the Laws" 387.

28. Accursius to Cod. 1.14(17).4, v. *principatum,* Clm 3501, fol. 39v, Clm 3880, fol. 25v, Clm 3884, fol. 20r: "Subaudi quam leges principatui siue imperio, quasi dicit maior est honor et maior conuenientia, cum imperium sit de fortuna, unde dicitur: 'Si fortuna uolet, fiet de rhetore consul, si uolet hec eadem, fiet de consule rhetor.'"

29. "The Prince is Not Bound by the Laws" 387–398.

30. Ibid. 390.

31. Ibid. 392.

32. Ibid. 394.

lucid analysis, Accursius's rhapsody is not easy to understand. Helmut Walther has recently concluded that the jurists attempted to temper the absolutism of "princeps legibus solutus" by binding the power of the prince with natural law and the common good.[33] It is true, almost a platitude, that the prince was bound by higher laws and limited by the larger interests of his subjects and the "state" (status) of the domain over which he ruled. The canonists called this second limiting factor the "status ecclesiae," while the civilians spoke more commonly of the "utilitas publica." As we have just seen, however, the jurists did not apply natural law or the common good to the texts we have been examining.

Walther also argues that Accursius and the other jurists believed that all law was from God, therefore, when Accursius bound the prince to the *Lex regia,* he bound the prince to a law sanctioned by God. Thus, "for Accursius the problem of sovereignty is solved outside of considerations of positive law" (ist für Accursius das Souveränitätsproblem jenseits rechtspositivistischer Überlegungen gelöst.)[34] Walther's interpretation may make good logical sense to the twentieth-century mind— Accursius's arguments are not easily followed—but there is simply no support for his argument in the writings of the medieval lawyers on *Digna vox.* The jurists did believe that all law came from God, but they laid out the boundaries between divine law and positive law with unambiguous precision, a point we have already made in the previous chapter and shall explore further in the following chapter. Azo and Accursius considered the *Lex regia* positive law. If they had classified it as a higher law, the whole problem would not have occupied their time or have exercised their ingenuity. They grappled with a difficult and paradoxical problem: how can the prince be superior to positive law and still be bound to it? They had not yet freed themselves from the language of Roman law, nor had they created a language to replace it or re-

---

33. *Imperiales Königtum* 117. The comment of Cinus to "Dignus vox" that Walther quotes (n. 11), "Imperator est solutus legibus de necessitate, tamen de honestate ipse uult ligari legibus, quia honor reputatur uinculum sacri iuris et utilitas ipsius," does not bind the emperor to a higher law or to the common good. For the interpretation of this text, see the discussion below.

34. Walther argues that in these passages the jurists were concerned with personal "superioritas" (p. 117 n. 11). But his argument is a series of statements about these texts rather than an analysis of them. He does not define what he means by "personenbezogenen Superioritas" and brings forward no texts that might have clarified his meaning. Wyduckel, *Princeps legibus solutus* 53, also asserts that Tierney's argument "zu sehr vom modernen Konstitutionalismus her deutet," but does not explain what he means by this statement.

define it. In this regard, it seems that Tierney's reflections are still appropriate:[35]

> [Accursius was not] a twentieth-century jurist "born out of due time," but [we wish] rather to call attention to certain perennial elements in the Western tradition of government. . . . The concept of sovereignty was not lacking in the thirteenth century; the peculiar difficulties of reconciling the concept with any meaningful definition of the "rule of law" have not disappeared in the twentieth.

The thirteenth-century jurists tried to bind the prince to the law without violating the maxim "princeps legibus solutus" or "par in parem imperium non habet." The result was not elegant law.[36] The tone of Azo's and Accursius's glosses are generally more "constitutionalist" than those of the canonists we examined in the previous chapter. After careful examination, however, the canonists and civilians came to similar conclusions with only insignificant differences between them.

The jurists who wrote immediately after Azo and Accursius accepted their interpretation of these texts and added little of significance. In the middle of the thirteenth century, Odofredus noted that the emperor was not bound by the laws of his predecessors because "an equal could not bind an equal." Further, the prince could not bind himself to his own laws.[37] He must, however, observe the laws. In his commentary to *Digna vox*, Odofredus emphasized that the prince should obey the laws because he derived his authority from the *Lex regia*, repeating Azo's admonition.[38] The emperor's definition of his authority is excellent, Odofredus continued, because, again borrowing from Azo, it is a greater virtue to observe the laws than to be a prince. Odofredus concluded sardonically that, because princes are men, they gain their office

35. Tierney, "The Prince is Not Bound by the Laws" 399–400.
36. See Wyduckel, *Princeps legibus solutus,* 52–54, who emphasizes the importance of the will in the jurists' analysis of "Legibus solutus."
37. Odofredus to Dig. 1.3.31(30) v. *legibus solutus est,* (Princeps legibus solutus) (Lyon: 1550), fol. 14v: "Subaudi et sic non tenetur seruare leges ab aliis imperatoribus conditas, quia pars in parem non habet imperium, ut infra de arbit. l. Nam et magistratus et infra ad Trebell. l. Ille a quo § Intempestiuum. Similiter non est subiectus suis legibus ut eas teneatur seruare, quia nemo potest sibi legem dicere a qua sibi recedere non liceat, ut infra de arbit. l. penult. et infra de legat. iii. l. Si quis in principio et l. Testamenti in principio. Set licet princeps legibus sit solutus tamen equum est ut ipse legem obseruet, ut C. eodem l. Digna et facit ad hoc C. de testamen. l. Ex imperfecto et infra de legat. iii. l. Ex imperfecto."
38. Odofredus to Cod. 1.14(17).4 (Digna uox) (Lyon: 1480), fol. 45v: "Respond. imperator et dicit dignum est quod imperator seruet leges quas fecit, unde dicit 'Digna uox est maiestate regnantis legibus alligatum se principem profiteri.' Et est ratio qua re debet seruare leges quas fecit, quia auctoritas imperii nostri dicit imperator pendet ex legis potestate."

by prayers or power. Often a prince is not worthy of being the common legate or podestà of a city.[39]

As the Italian legal historian, Nicolini, has pointed out, the late medieval jurists made just one addition to the analysis of these texts.[40] At the end of the thirteenth century, Jacques de Révigny scornfully rejected his predecessors' attempts to reconcile "princeps legibus solutus" with *Digna vox*. "*Digna vox*," he commented playfully, "is *Falsa vox* (false voice)."[41] If the emperor submits his will to the laws, he shackles himself because of his honesty, not from necessity.[42] Although most jurists rejected the autocratic favor that Jacques gave to his interpretation of *Digna vox*, a number of them found his formulation elegant— and perhaps less problematic juristically—than Azo's and Accursius's formulations. Nonetheless, Jacques's emphasis on the prince's honesty rather than on his will persuaded only a few jurists. Dante's friend, Cinus of Pistoia, was influenced by Révigny and added that "honor is considered a fetter and the commonweal (utilitas) of the sacred law."[43] Here, the "sacred law" is the civil law itself and the honor of the prince functions in two ways to limit the arbitrariness of the law: first, it is a bond; second, it considers the public weal whenever the prince acts.[44] Cinus explained the contradiction between the emperor's obligation to submit himself to the law and the emperor's duty to augment his authority as being only apparent. When the emperor submits to the law, he does not diminish but augments his dignity. "For what, saving honesty, cannot be done, is considered a bond."[45] Jacques and Cinus, how-

39. Ibid.: "Responsio imperatoris est optima quia maior uirtus est seruare legem quam principem esse, quia seruare leges est ab animi uirtute. Set quod homines sunt principes, est precio uel precibus uel potentia, quia aliquando uocant indignum, quia sepe uocant talem qui non est dignus esse nuntius communis uel esse potestas unius ciuitatis."

40. *Proprietà* 153–155.

41. Jacques de Révigny to Cod. 1.14(17).4 (Digna vox) (Paris: 1519), fol. 33r: "immo falsa vox est." See Nicolini, *Proprietà* 131 n. 1.

42. Ibid.: "Dicit glossa: hic non dicitur quod princeps sit legibus ligatus, set dicit hic quod digna vox est si velit se subijcere sponte . . . vel verius non de necessitate, sed de honestate."

43. Cinus to Cod. 1.14.(17).4 (Digna vox) (Frankfurt: 1578), fol. 25v–26r: "DIGNA VOX: Tamen ipse dicit se ligatum; non tamen est verum. Ita dicit glossa hic. Set non bene intelligit, salua reuerentia sua. Dico ergo quod imperator est solutus legibus de necessitate, tamen de honestate ipse uult ligari legibus, quia honor reputatur uinculum sacri iuris, et utilitas ipsius."

44. A common usage in Roman law; see Cod. 1.14(17).9. Nov. 83 pr., Cod. 4.32.20.

45. Ibid.: "Et inter ceteros ipse suam dignitatem augere debet, ut augusto nomini deseruiat per officium, ut instit. de donat. § i. [Inst. 2.7.1] Ad hoc respondet ipsemet imperator in hac lege quia dignitatem suam ob hoc non minuit, immo auget, 'quia re uera' etc. [maius imperio est submittere legibus principatum]. Vnde honor est essse in tali ligamine et deductus esse extra, ut supra dixi. Nam quod salua honestate fieri non potest, ligamen reputatur, ut ff. ex quibus caus. mai. l. In eadem" [Dig. 4.6.10].

ever, did not convince Bartolus of Sassoferrato, the most important Romanist of the fourteenth century, with their arguments. Bartolus simply repeated the definitions of Azo and Accursius.[46] "Honesty," whatever that meant to Jacques and Cinus, did not have a greater binding force on the prince than honor or justice and did not replace the will as a juristic concept to limit the prince's power.[47] Although some jurists in the fourteenth and fifteenth centuries enhanced the authority of the prince by declaring that whatever the prince did should be considered just and equitable, many other jurists seem not to have embraced this early manifestation of absolutism.[48]

The reluctance of the civilians to speculate more ingeniously about the conundrum of *Digna vox* is puzzling. Dieter Wyduckel has recently observed that the ingenuity of the canonists' definitions of power and authority stems from the mass of new papal legislation promulgated by a living prince with which they had to contend. The interpreters of Roman law were bound to their texts in the *Corpus iuris civilis* of Justinian, and their thought was more static than that of the canonists. The constant stream of new decretals constantly reminded the canonists that law was changeable and that change was not to be despised or feared.[49] As such, one finds no eulogies for the "good old law" in the writings of the canonists.

Early in the fourteenth century (before 1317), however, Johannes Andreae formulated a remarkable definition of princely power that had, as far as I know, no later echoes before Panormitanus formulated a similar description of power in the fifteenth century.[50] Johannes com-

46. Bartolus to Cod. 1.14(17).4 (Digna vox) (Venice: 1476). Nürnberg, Cent. II 84, fol. 26v: "Op. quod in ueritate princeps est solutus legibus, ut ff. eodem l. Princeps. Solutio. Fateor quod ipse est solutus legibus, tamen equum et dignum est quod legibus uiuat. Ita loquitur hic. Vnde ipse submittit se legibus de uoluntate, non de necessitate. Ita debes intelligere hanc legem."
47. Theologians emphasized the duty of the prince to live according to the laws just as insistently as the jurists. Aegidius Romanus wrote that divine grace was essential if the rulers of others would live justly. See the discussion of the fourteenth-century theologians in Stürner, *Peccatum und Potestas* 193–207.
48. Baldus de Ubaldis to Dig. 1.4.1 (Quod principi placuit): "Principi nihil presumitur placere nisi iustum et equum," See Norbert Horn, *Aequitas in den Lehren des Baldus* (Forschungen zur neueren Privatrechtsgeschichte, 11; Cologne-Graz: 1968) 53; or as Baldus worded the same idea in a consilium (Milan 1.333, Venice 3.285): "Item in principe quia disponit tanquam de re propria creditur uerbis eius et motiuum ipsius habetur pro ratione certissima . . . et in mandatis principis non requiritur causa . . . Item princeps iura utilia potest concedere sine causa . . . nam ipse et ratio idem est." The thought of the late medieval jurists will be discussed in more detail below in chapter 6; see also Cortese, *Norma* II 272–282. On the differences between the Milanese and Venetian editions of Baldus's consilia, see Pennington, "The Consilia of Baldus de Ubaldis."
49. Wyduckel, *Ius Publicum*, 94.
50. See chapter 6.

bined the idea of the prince's will as the source of all law with the notion that the prince's will had its source in the common good (communis utilitas) of his subjects:[51]

> But say that positive law resides in the will of the prince, as much by promulgating law as by changing it. . . . The will of the prince, moreover, resides in the common good of his subjects . . . but their common good changes according to changing times; therefore, in the same way, for this reason, positive law changes.

At another place in his *Additiones* to the same chapter, Johannes underlined the mutability of positive law. Borrowing his terminology from a novel of Justinian, he wrote that positive law is enacted, rescinded, and changed daily because "our entire state" is always in flux.[52] Two ideas in these glosses are new: that law and the common good are not constants but mutable and that the prince's will exists in the common good of his subjects. Although early fourteenth-century jurists certainly understood that law could be changed, they usually stressed its stability, not its mutability, and placed much emphasis on the role of necessity for changing positive law. In their eyes law should never be changed by whim; there should always be good and necessary reasons for changes.[53] In reaching these conclusions, Johannes Andreae was also influenced by earlier juristic definitions that the prince's will was the source of all law, but should, nevertheless, conform to the common good. Johannes was ahead of his times and seems to have known it. When he revised his *Additiones* later in life, he eliminated these definitions of the prince's will from the final revision of his commentary.[54]

Whether out of timidity or prudence, the jurists always stopped short

51. Johannes Andreae, Repetitio and "Additiones II" to X 1.4.11 (Cum tanto), Nürnberg, Stadtbibl. Cent. II 60, fol. 71r and Clm 15703, fol. 26v: "Set dic quod ius positiuum consistit in uoluntate principis tam in concedendo quam in mutando, ix. q.iii. Cuncta (c.17 and 18) et inst. de iure natural. § Set quod principi. Voluntas autem principis consistit in communi utilitate subditorum ut in Prohemio vi. libro in principio. Set communis utilitas subditorum mutatur secundum uarietatem temporum, ergo eodem modo mutabitur ius positiuum per talem rationem."
52. Ibid. fol. 25v–26r: "iuri positiuo: nedum naturali. naturali siue diuino cuius transgressio periculum satis inducit, de quo dicitur supra in prima parte. Et dicitur ius positiuum, quia cottidie ponitur, tollitur, et mutatur. Vnde dicit lex quod totus noster status sub motu consistit, in authen. de non alien. per. rebus eccles. § Vt autem, coll. ii. [Authen. 2.1 (Nov. 7).2]."
53. Wolf, "Gesetzgebung" 548–552, who cites Thomas Aquinas, *Summa theologica* 1.2.97.1: "lex recte mutari potest propter mutationem conditionum hominum."
54. Johannes Andreae to X 1.4.11 (Cum tanto) *Novella* (Venice: 1581), I, fol. 61v: "Omnis lex positiua deriuatur et cautatur a lege naturae et a lege diuina, supra in Proemio . . . nec aliter enim uniuersum ecclesiae nostrae consistere posset, nisi regularet per maiores et ipsorum leges."

of saying the prince's will was the common good, even though theological thought anticipated this linkage. Thomas Aquinas and his followers, for example, may have partially inspired Johannes's thought. As Aegidius Romanus remarked in *De regimine principum* (3.2.27), "there is no law which is not promulgated by him whose task it is to rule for the common good." [55] Or as Thomas himself defined law: "Law is nothing else than a reasonable ordination for the common good, by him who has the care of the community." [56] These definitions, however, only anticipate Johannes's and do not enter the potentially dangerous terrain that Johannes fashioned. If, as Johannes thought in his early career, the prince's will really resided or existed in the "common good" of his subjects, his power could be challenged and his authority bound by them. Johannes must have realized the danger in this logic and retreated from the idea in his later writings. As we shall see in the following section, Johannes's early views might have also been shaped by a strand of thought among contemporary jurists that "princes" were bound by the law.

We can draw several conclusions from our discussion of "legibus solutus." Although it has been asserted that the jurists attempted to bind the prince with natural law and the common good as they worked out the meaning of "legibus solutus," they did not use higher laws to shackle the prince. [57] Even though they bypassed higher law, they did not interpret "legibus solutus" absolutistically. As the preceding chapters have shown, they colored the clause with very few hues of arbitrary authority. As we shall see in the following chapters, natural law was not an effective means of limiting princely authority unless the jurists were in agreement about what natural law was and unless the prince violated it directly. Further, as we have seen already in Hostiensis's thought, the "common good" was only one of a number of criteria that could be used to determine the validity of the prince's actions. More important, the jurists did not often connect the common good and

---

55. Gagnér, *Gesetzgebung* 360–361 (There is no modern edition of this work; citation from Rome: 1482 edition): "Nulla est ergo lex quae non sit edita ab eo cuius est dirigere in bonum commune."

56. Thomas Aquinas, *Summa theologica* 1.2.90.3: "quae nihil est aliud quam quaedam rationis ordinatio ad bonum commune, ab eo qui curam communitatis habet." See Gagnér, *Gesetzgebung* 270.

57. Walther, *Imperiales Königtum* 117: "Sie [the jurists] bemühen sich deshalb darum, den im Satz vom 'Princeps legibus solutus' angelegten Absolutismus durch die Bindung des Herrschers an ein höher stehendes Naturrecht und an das Staatswohl unschädlich zu machen." He cites a passsage from Cinus's Commentary to the Code, discussed above at fnn. 43 and 45 to support his generalization.

"legibus solutus" in their commentaries. They never connected "legibus solutus" and natural law and were careful to explain that the prince was not "legibus solutus" from natural law. The jurists understood very well that natural law transcended the prince's positive law and was not subject to his authority.

THE PRINCE IS BOUND BY THE LAW

The jurists often used "prince" when they described the authority of magistrates. In earlier sources "prince" was even used loosely for lower magistrates.[58] By the middle of the thirteenth century, the jurists reserved the title for monarchs who had no superiors. Hostiensis was one of the first jurists, if not the first, to state explicitly what they had tacitly assumed for at least a half century: the "pope," he said, could be substituted for "prince," and "pope" for "emperor."[59] Later jurists assumed that the prince could be the emperor, a king, a podestà, or the pope. As Marinus de Caramanico wrote in the prologue to his commentary on the Liber Augustalis, "the name, 'prince,' is commonly used for a king and as well as for the emperor."[60] Bartolus extended the definition to include the Italian city-states with the phrase "Civitas sibi princeps est" (The city-state is a "prince").[61] Baldus formulated an elegant aphorism that expressed the relationship between the secular and ecclesiastical powers in fourteenth-century juristic thought when he transposed the famous maxim that the king was emperor in his own kingdom by substituting the pope for the king and the king for the emperor: "whatever the king can do in his kingdom, the pope can do in the ecclesiastical monarchy."[62]

58. E.g., bishops in a decretal of unknown origin, included in 1 Comp. 1.25.3 (X 1.33.2): "Si quis venerit contra decretum episcopi, ab ecclesia abiiciatur. In libro Regum legitur: 'Qui non obedierit principi, moritatur.' Et in concilio Agathensi, quod anathematizetur." This quotation is not in Kings or elsewhere; there is similar passage in Deut. 17.12.

59. Hostiensis to X 1.33.2 v. qui non obedierit principi, V, fol. 170r: "idest pape, de con. di.i Corpora, uel idest episcopo, xxxv. di Ecclesie. Sic econuerso ponitur pontifex pro imperatore, x. di. De capitulis."

60. "Quod principis nomen est commune tam regi, ut patet in aut. Vt preponatur nomen imperatoris § Si quis enim [Authen. 5 (= Nov. 47).3 pr] quam imperatori, ut ff. de constit. prin. l.i. [Dig. 1.4.1]." Edition of this entire text in Calasso, Glossatori 188–189. Marinus then lists others who are called "prince" in Roman law.

61. Bartolus of Sassoferrato to Dig. 4.4.3. See Wyduckel, Ius publicum 67. Julius Kirshner, "Civitas sibi faciat civem: Bartolus of Sassoferrato's Doctrine on the Making of a Citizen," Speculum 48 (1973) 694–713.

62. Baldus de Ubaldis, X 2.1.12 v. Cum venissent, Clm 3629, fol. 15r–15v, Ed. 1478, unfol.: "et in summa quicquid potest rex in suo regno potest papa in ecclesiastica monarchia, sicut olim omnia a regibus gubernabantur, ut ff. de orig. iur. l.ii. in prin. ita et

Although most jurists adopted "princeps" as a generic title to define a ruler who had no superior, not all jurists approved of the definition. In the second half of the thirteenth century, a number of jurists attempted to fashion a more restricted definition of the prince. They argued that "prince" could only be used to describe the emperor as defined by Roman law. The prince had prerogatives and authority that kings did not possess. In particular, these jurists insisted that kings could not lay claims to the authority granted to the emperor by Roman law. If a king were not a prince, he could not possess the attributes of princely authority: he was not "legibus solutus" and he did not exercise "potestas absoluta." Although this attempt to bind national monarchs to the laws of their lands failed to persuade future generations of lawyers, their arguments allow us to understand better the lawyers' thought when they discussed the prince and the law. In a parallel development, a few learned lawyers of the *ius commune* even fashioned theories that bound the "prince" himself to the laws.

When the academic jurists considered the constitutional status of the national monarchs, they often equated the authority of a king with that of the emperor. By the late Middle Ages, after the national monarchs had established themselves as not only equal to, but, in real life, more powerful than the emperors, this equation, king equals emperor, became an unexceptional commonplace. However, the academic lawyers rarely allow us to see European kings as the jurists themselves must have seen them: embroiled in disputes with their nobles over rights enshrined in customary law—"the good old law"—or hard pressed by developing institutions, like parliament, that demanded a share in the power to tax, wage war, judge, and legislate.

We can catch fleeting glimpses of the real world in the writings of those few nonacademic lawyers whose works have survived, the two best known being Phillipe de Beaumanoir and Henry Bracton.[63] Beau-

---

hodie quicquid regi placet legis habet uigorem." Cf. Canning, *The Political Thought of Baldus de Ubaldis* (Cambridge Studies in Medieval Life and Thought 4, 6; Cambridge: 1987) 63, 237, where he interprets this passage as being a confirmation of papal temporal authority.

63. The literature on Bracton is bountiful. As he completed his edition and translation of the treatise that has been attributed to the English judge, Henry Bracton, Samuel Thorne was beset by reservations over whether Bracton was, indeed, the author of the tract; *On the Laws and Customs of England* (Cambridge, Mass.: 1968–1977) III, pp. xv-lii. Brian Tierney's analysis of Bracton's thought on the relationship of the king and the law is masterful: "Bracton on Government," *Speculum* 38 (1963) 295–317. See most recently, Michael Blecker, "The King's Partners in Bracton," *Studi senesi* 96 (1984) 66–118. On Beaumanoir's political thought, see S. J. T. Miller, "The Position of the King in Bracton and Beaumanoir," *Speculum* 31 (1956) 263–296.

manoir said little about the relationship of the king and the law in his tract; in comparison, Bracton was garrulous. This difference may reflect the two countries' separate histories. Beaumanoir's France was not as turbulent as Bracton's England, which had been rocked by one constitutional and legal crisis after another. From Magna Carta to the Baron's Revolt of 1258, the issue of whether the king was obligated to observe customary law dominated English politics. Beaumanoir did quote the Roman law tag, what pleases the prince has the force of law,[64] but he had a quite limited conception of royal legislative power. The king could issue new laws during wartime or in preparation for war. When he did issue a new law it must have a reasonable cause, benefit the commonweal, be consented to, and not violate the law of God or morals.[65] He said nothing about whether the king was subject to his own laws or those of his predecessors, but the tone of his remarks conveys a sense that royal power had firmly established boundaries.

When Bracton discussed the relationship of the king and the law, he tried to explain the status of the king in English law and to incorporate into his work the new (for English lawyers) Roman law doctrines that we have been discussing. He cooked a heady broth. Historians have squabbled over whether Bracton understood Roman law (ancient or medieval) and whether his thought was consistent. On the one hand, Bracton could write:[66]

> The king ought not be subject to man, but to God and the law, because the law makes the king. There is no king where the will rules and not law.

Bracton emphasized the king's duty to obey the law and specifically rejected the idea, common among the academic lawyers by the middle of the thirteenth century, that although the prince's will was the source of law, he voluntarily subjected himself to the law through his will. He adamantly rejected the notion that the prince's will could be superior to law. On the other hand, Bracton could quote passages of Roman law

64. *Coutumes de Clermont en Beauvaisis*, ed. A. Salmon (2 vols. Paris: 1899–1900; repr. Paris: 1970) II 63: "ce qu'il li plest a fere doit estre tenu pour loi." On Beaumanoir's conception of law, see the discussion by Armin Wolf, "Gesetzgebung," *Handbuch*, ed. Coing, 644.

65. Ibid. II 261: "ou tans de guerre ou tans que l'en se doute de guerre . . . (II 264) Tout soit il ainsi que li rois puist fere nouveaus etablissemens, il doit mout prendre garde qu'il les face par resnable cause et pour le commun pourfir et par grant conseil, et especiaument qu'il ne soient pas fet contre Dieu ne contre bonnes meurs."

66. *On the Laws and Customs of England*, II 33 (Woodbine II 33, fol. 5b): "Ipse autem rex non debet esse sub homine sed sub Deo et sub lege, quia lex facit regem. Attribuat igitur rex legi quod lex attribuit ei, videlicet dominationem et potestatem. Non est enim rex ubi dominatur voluntas et non lex."

that underlined the superiority of the king to the law of his predecessors and any person or corporation within his kingdom:[67]

> The king does not have an equal in his own kingdom, since an equal cannot have power over an equal. Much less then can he have a superior.

A jurist at Bologna would have extracted a coherent doctrine of legislative sovereignty by the year 1200, but we cannot know, and never will know, what Bracton meant when he borrowed these sentences from the academic jurists. Before we could truly grapple with his thought, we would have to discover and edit the Ur-Bracton, free of interpolations and additions. However, the manuscript tradition of his text precludes our ever having such a text. Bracton probably did wish to bind the English king to English law. To quote Tierney, however, he "was working with intractable materials. His work was essentially an attempt to fit a massive structure of English private law into the rather flimsy framework of Romanesque public law."[68] We might add that Bracton built a structure of thought that tottered dangerously close to collapse because he did not know Roman and canon law well enough to make a better job of it. Neither Beaumanoir nor Bracton adopted the new terminology that the academic lawyers had used to describe the prince's power and authority.

There were Bractons among the academic lawyers as well, but with this difference: they had a keen sense that the prince must be limited and knew Roman and canon law well enough to limit his sovereignty without creating a hopelessly confused system of thought. Guido of Suzzara surfaces here as one of the most interesting Roman lawyers in the second half of the thirteenth century in the arena of public law and political theory. He taught in Reggio Emilia, Padua, Bologna, and served in the curia of Charles of Anjou.

Guido (who died ca. 1291) is not well known. Perhaps this is because he did not write a major commentary, preferring "additiones" to the Digest and Code.[69] "Additiones" were supplementary glosses to the Ordinary Gloss and were, by their nature, more ephemeral than the mas-

67. Ibid. II 33 (Woodbine II 33, fol. 5b): "Parem autem non habet rex in regno suo quia sic amitteret preceptum cum par in parem non habet imperium. Item nec multo fortius superiorem."

68. "Bracton on Government" 316–317.

69. See P. Torelli and E. P. Vicini, "Documenti su Guido da Suzzara," *Rassegna per la storia dell'Università di Modena e della cultura superiore modenese* (Modena: 1929) 63–89; P. Torelli, "Sulle orme di Guido da Suzzara," *Scritti vari dedicati al prof. E. Masè-Dari* (Modena: 1935) 58–78 (reprinted in his *Scritti di storia del diritto italiano* [Milano: 1959] 293–348) and Federico Martino, *Ricerche sull'opera di Guido da Suzzara le "Su-*

sive commentaries of Odofredus or Hostiensis, attracting thereby less attention from later scholars. Although jurists wrote "additiones" to their own works and the works of others at an early date,[70] they became an important literary genre only in the second half of the thirteenth century.[71] Guido wrote several different versions of his "additiones"—or "suppletiones" as they are called in some manuscripts—at several different times. Because they were often copied, at times carelessly, into the margins of the Digest and Code manuscripts, their textual traditions are quite poor. They are archetypical "textes vivantes" (living texts).

Guido had Bracton's conviction that monarchy should be limited, but, unlike Bracton, his knowledge of Roman law permitted him to create a doctrine of constitutional sovereignty within a framework of Roman law. The result was a tour de force. In an "additio" to the Digest in which he commented on the words of "The prince is not bound by the laws," Guido stripped kings of their legal prerogatives:[72]

> Note that the prince is not bound by the laws. Are kings? [That is, Guido asks, "Are kings princes?"] Certainly they are bound because no one is loosed from the laws other than the prince. Although here [in the text of the Digest] the prince is not bound by the laws, he submits himself to them voluntarily.

Guido most likely wrote this gloss in the 1270s.[73] He returned to the older idea that there could be only one prince, the emperor. Only that prince enjoyed the prerogatives granted him by Roman law. He did not argue for the return of an imperial world order but was convinced that kings could not exercise the same prerogatives as the emperor in Roman law, implicitly rejecting the maxim "a king is emperor in his own kingdom." He did not, however, exalt the power of the prince. Echoing a century of commentary on the words "legibus solutus," he subjected the prince to the law.

---

pleciones" (Studi e ricerche dei "Quaderni catanesi," 3; Catania: 1981); Gérard Fransen, "Guy de Suzaria, Dictionnaire d'histoire et de géographie ecclésiastiques 22 (1988) 1291. Savigny, Geschichte V 387–398.

70. See my remarks about the textual tradition of Azo's Summa Codicis in chapter 1.

71. Horn, "Legistische Literatur," Handbuch, ed. Coing, 331–333.

72. Guido of Suzzara, Suppletiones to Dig. 1.3.31(31) (Princeps legibus), Clm 6201, fol. 10v: "l. Princeps, 'solutus legibus': nota principem esse solutum legibus. Quid de regibus? Certe illi astricti sunt quia non inuenitur aliquis solutus nisi princeps, et licet hic solutus sit, tamen seipsum sponte subicit legi, ut C. eodem l. Digna [Cod. 1.14(17).4], inst. quibus modis testa. infr. cum similibus." This gloss is also preserved in Paris, B.N. 4488, fol. 321r, but is corrupt. The section on kings being bound to the law is omitted by Paris, B.N. 4489, fol. 4r.

73. Martino, Ricerche 45–49.

Frederick Barbarossa's question—"Am I the lord of the world?"—does not seem to have interested Guido. He did not trouble himself whether kings are subject to the emperor—there was, after all, most likely no reigning emperor, or only Rudolf of Hapsburg, on the imperial throne at the time he wrote this passage—nor did he wish to argue that kings have the same prerogatives as the emperor. Rather, his point is quite the opposite: kings are not princes; they are not above law but are bound to it.

Guido's viewpoint was radical and disappeared swiftly with the rise of the strong monarchies. I have found only a few later jurists who espoused it. Albericus de Rosate (died 1360), for example, noted that the king of France did not recognize a superior, but he insisted that, independent or not, the French king and others cannot transgress the laws. Only the "prince" (emperor) is not bound by the laws. All kings are "de iure" subjects of the emperor.[74]

Although a short-lived sentiment, "the king is bound by the laws" did intrigue French lawyers in the late thirteenth century. At that time, French ambitions at home and in Italy encouraged jurists to formulate a doctrine of royal independence from the emperor and a theory that the king could exercise the same authority as the "prince" in Roman law.[75] But for every action there is a reaction. Most historians have interpreted a famous text commonly attributed to Jacques de Révigny as only answering the question of whether the French king was subject to the emperor. Additionally, however, Jacques broached the problem as to whether the French king was a "prince" in his kingdom.[76]

Jacques told a story in which a French count raised the flag of rebel-

74. Albericus de Rosate, *Commentaria super Digesto* (2 vols. Venice: 1585; repr. Torino: 1974), fol. 31r to Dig. !.3.30(31): "Et ex hoc patet quod rex Franciae licet non recognoscat superiorem et alii reges non possunt leges transgredi, cum de solo principe inveniatur quod sit solutus legibus et quia omnes reges de iure sunt subditi imperio." See Savigny, *Geschichte* VI 126–136.

75. See Friedrich Bock, "Kaisertum, Kurie und Nationalstaat im Beginn des 14. Jahrhunderts," *Römische Quartalschrift für christliche Altertumskunde und für Kirchengeschichte* 44 (1936) 105–122; 169–220.

76. First published by Pierre de Tourtoulon, *Les oeuvres de Jacques de Révigny (Jacobus de Ravanis) d'après deux manuscrits de la Bibliothque Nationale* (Etudes sur le droit écrit; Paris: 1898) 48–49, also printed by Calasso, *Glossatori*, 44. The question is added to the margin of a manuscript of the Code, Paris, B.N. 14350, fol. 185r. There is no direct attribution to Révigny. The rubric reads: "Hic redit dominus meus ad illa que omiserat de illo § Preiudiciales." Because the manuscript contains Jacques's Commentary on the Institutes (fol. 141r–186r), Tourtoulon thought the question must be Révigny's. For now, the question of authorship must remain open. See Marguerite Boulet-Sautel, "Le concept de souveraineté chez Jacques Révigny," *Actes du congrès sur l'ancienne université d'Orléans (XIIIe-XVIIIe siècles)* (Orleans: 1961) 17–27. See Savigny, *Geschichte* V 605–614.

lion against the king and demanded that his vassals render him aid.[77] He posed two questions: whether the vassals were obligated to help the count and, if they did, whether they would be excused from the accusation of treason on the grounds that they were just obeying the count's command.[78] Jacques responded that the vassals would not be obligated to help the count because they could not be bound by their oath of fealty to defend their lord when he acted illicitly. If vassals joined a rebellion, they committed crimes.[79] In a key passage, Jacques concluded his argument:[80]

> And because, [some jurists say] the rebels break the Lex Julia [treating treason], it is proved that the king is "prince" because he does not recognize a superior. I say that they do rebel against the prince, but not, however, as some say, because the king is a prince; rather because the crime is committed against the magistrate of the prince, as it states in the "Lex Iulia." . . . Because France and Spain were once under imperial authority . . . they always will be.

Jacques considered the king of France to be, legally speaking, a magistrate of the emperor, but not himself a "prince." Révigny's unstated corollary is that the king did not, therefore, possess or exercise the prerogatives of the prince embedded in Roman law.

Jean de Blanot (ca. 1256) may have been one of those jurists who thought that rebels against the king broke the Lex Julia.[81] He addressed the same problem briefly in his tract on actions, mentioning that a re-

---

77. The best and most recent treatment of French feudal law in the twelfth and thirteenth centuries is Gérard Giordanengo, Le droit féodal dans les pays de droit écrit: L'exemple de la Provence et du Dauphiné XIIe-début XIV siècle (Bibliothèques des Écoles Françaises d'Athènes et de Rome 266; Rome: 1988); see especially his chapter on "Le droit féodal savant," 111–152. On academic feudal law, see the pathbreaking work of Peter Weimar, "Die Handschriften des Liber feudorum und seiner Glossen," Rivista internazionale di diritto comune 1 (1990) 31–98.

78. Calasso, Glossatori 44: "Quidam est comes in regno Franciae insurgit contra regem, uult congregare exercitum suum contra superiorem, mandat omnibus fidelibus suis ut iuuent eum. Queritur an debeant eum iuuare contra superiorem. Supposito quod non, si pareant ei de facto numquid excusabuntur propter iussum eius?"

79. Ibid.: "Ad primam respondetur non debent ei parere, in sacramento fidelitatis non ueniunt illicita, quia sacramentum simpliciter factum non se extendit ad illicita. Committit ille qui se eleuat contra superiorem, ut ff. de cond. ind. l. Si procurator § Celsus [Dig. 12.6.6], ff. que in fraud. cred. l. Si pater [Dig. 42.9.12]."

80. Ibid.: Et quod committant in lege Iulia maiestatis, probatur quod rex princeps est quia non cognoscit superiorem. Dico hoc est in principem, non sicut ipsi dicunt quod rex princeps sit, set quia committatur in magistratum principis, et ff. ad leg. Iul. mai. l.i. quia Francia et Yspania semel fuerunt sub imperio, C. de off. pref. pret. Aff. l.ii. circa principium, et ideo semper erant, ut alias probaui per l. C. de prescript. xxx. uel xl. ann. l. Comperit [Cod. 7.39.6]." I have incorporated Feenstra's corrections, "Rex Franciae," 892, n. 50, to Tourtoulon's text.

81. Savigny, Geschichte V 495–501.

bellion of the barons could be considered treason because they were involved in the death of a magistrate of the Roman people, but decided that "more truly [it is treason] because they have directly rebelled against the prince." [82] Roman law justified the charge of treason for acts committed without the permission of the "prince" or for illegal acts against the magistrates of the Roman people. [83] Jacques de Révigny insisted that this law vindicated the charge of treason against those who rebelled against the king and, at the same time, contrary to Jean de Blanot, denied that the king was a "prince." Jacques's comment that "some say the king is a prince" should, I think, be interpreted as meaning that some say—Jean de Blanot, for example—that the French king should be considered to have the same legal status and prerogatives as the emperor in Roman law. Besides granting him the title of prince, they also bestowed the other Roman attributes of sovereignty, especially that of "legibus solutus," upon the king. Jacques, of course, rejected their arguments. [84]

If my interpretation of Révigny's question is correct, other French jurists supported him. In the early fourteenth century, Pierre Jame d'Aurillac taught at Montpellier (he is sometimes cited by contemporary jurists as Petrus de Montepessulano). He composed an important tract on procedure that bears the title *Aurea practica* in the printed edi-

82. Text is printed by Calasso, *Glossatori* 114 and also, with collations of several manuscripts, by Robert Feenstra, "Jean de Blanot et la formule 'Rex Francie in regno suo princeps est,'" *Etudes d'histoire du droit canonique dédiées à Gabriel Le Bras* (Paris: 1965) II 885–895 at 890 (which we print here): "Dicendum est tamen contrarium, quod baro ille qui insurgit contra regem videtur incidere in legem Iuliam maiestatis ex illo capite, quia videtur machinatus in mortem magistratus populi Romani, vel verius quia directo videtur fecisse contra principem, nam rex Franciae in regno suo princeps est, nam in temporalibus superiorem non recognoscit, et facit ad hoc ff. ad leg. Iul. ma. l.i. [Dig. 48.4.1]." Bartholomaeus of Capua even thought that treason could be committed against counts and barons in a gloss to Dig. 7.1.7.1 v. *et iure dominii*: "Nota quod si vasallus comitis vel baronis committit crimen lese magistatis quod bona eius perveniant ad comitem vel baronem, non ad regem." Printed in *Iuris Interpretes saec. XIII*, ed Eduard Meijers (Naples: 1924) 210.
83. Dig. 48.4.1: "quo obsides iniussu principis interciderent . . . quo quis magistratus populi Romani quive imperium potestatemve habet occidatur."
84. A question of Révigny published by Maffei, "Il giudice testimone" 74–75, throws some doubt on Révigny's authorship of Tourtoulon's question. In the question Maffei discovered in a Bolognese manuscript, Révigny describes a judge "who is above the laws like the prince" and states that such a judge could render judgments against the laws or customs. It is not clear from the context whether the judge whom Révigny says is "supra leges ut princeps" can only be the emperor. To describe this "prince" he cites "Digna vox" and "Princeps legibus solutus" [Cod. 1.14(17).4 and Dig. 1.3.31], from which one might conclude he means the emperor, but from the context of the question, he seems to have two groups of judges in mind: one group who are above the law and another who are not. If, indeed, he has a group of judges in mind, then Révigny's doctrine in this question conflicts with that we have been discussing.

tions. He died after 1351.[85] In much of his work, he wrote about the relationship of the emperor and the French king in traditional terms. Although the emperor was lord of the world, the French king was not subject to him by law or in fact.[86] He conceded that the emperor was the universal lord of Christendom, but only in high office, not in deed (saltem aptitudine, non actu).[87] Around 1330, Pierre wrote four "additiones" to his work on procedure. In the first he discussed the question of whether a feudal vassal could alienate a fief to the Church without the permission of his feudal lord. Feudal law dictated that such an alienation of property needed the lord's assent. Pierre commented:[88]

> Some jurists give another reason: whoever alienates property to the Church could commit treason, and consequently the property could be confiscated by the king [according to the Roman law governing treason]. . . . But they are mistaken. The king does not call himself emperor, although he wishes to be. Thus the [Roman] law governing treason does not apply.

Later jurists understood Pierre's argument exactly. An anonymous scribe added a marginal gloss to one of the Paris manuscripts in which he protested: "Rather Pierre Jame is mistaken, the king is emperor in his own kingdom."[89] Even as late as the sixteenth century, Charles De Grassaille quoted Pierre's opinion and noted that Pierre was mistaken. In his list of privileges of the French king he declared with some ceremony that "the king of France is emperor in his own kingdom."[90]

---

85. Savigny, *Geschichte* VI 37–39; Horn, "Die legistische Literatur," *Handbuch*, ed. Coing, 282; Paul Fournier, "Pierre Jame (Petrus Jacobi) d'Aurillac, jurisconsulte," *Histoire littéraire de la France* 36 (1922) 481–521. R. Grand, "Un jurisconsulte du XIVe siècle, Pierre Jacobi," *Bibliothèque de l'École de Chartes* 79 (1918) 68–101. Giordanengo, *Le droit féodal* 138–139, n. 104. Pierre Jame's work is of great practical interest, treating a series of cases touching on many subjects. He entitled the work "Libellus libellorum," which the first printers changed to *Aurea practica*. Editions were printed at Lyons in 1493, 1501, 1511, 1519, 1527, 1535, 1539. A last edition was printed at Cologne in 1575.

86. Fournier, "Pierre Jame" 510.

87. Fournier, "Pierre Jame" 511.

88. Pierre Jame d'Aurillac (de Aureliaco), Additiones, Paris, B.N. lat. 4571, fol. 101v and Paris, B.N. lat. 4446, fol. 90r: "Item reddunt aliam rationem, scilicet quia ille qui alienat in ecclesiam posset committere crimen lese maiestatis, et ita ille res possent cedere lucro regis, set ecclesia non posset illud committere. Set illi deficiunt quia rex non uocat se imperatorem, set ille uelle esse, et ita in eo non habet locum id crimen sub illo nomine."

89. Paris, B.N. 4446, fol. 90r: "immo deficit Pe. Ja. salua sui gratia . . . et rex Francie est imperator in suo regno."

90. Karolus Degrassalius Carcassonsis (De Grassaille), *Regalium Franciae libri duo iura omnia et dignitates Christianissorum Galliae regum* (Paris: 1545) 316: "Ad id quod dicit [Petrus Jacobi] quod in rege non cadit crimen lesae maiestatis, quia non dicit se imperatorem quamvis vellet esse, respondetur quod illud est falsum quia rex Franciae est imperator in suo regno, secundum Bald. in l. Exemplo, C. de probat. et habet omnia iura imperatoris, ut specifice supra i. parte in xi. [where De Grassaille discussed royal power]

Other evidence sheds light on those few academic jurists who bound the prince to the law. Another French jurist, Pierre de Mornay, disputed a question in December, 1278, that a student recorded. It is preserved in a London manuscript. Mornay was a distinguished jurist and an advisor to Phillip the Good and Phillip the Fair of France. Advisor, jurist, and bishop of Orléans and Auxerre, he was a man of many parts.[91] The custom of Brittany was, began Mornay, that if anyone were summoned before the count's court in either a criminal or a civil matter, that person could appeal to the king of France. When such an appeal had been made, the count of Brittany could carry the case no further. The king of France, who wished to abolish the right of appeal and remit it to the count, finally did so without consulting the barons of Brittany.[92] The rule that an appeal brought all proceedings in the court of first instance to a halt had been in place for ecclesiastical cases since the twelfth century. It had become a central principle of the *ius commune*. The French king may have wished—if Mornay's hypothetical case has any basis in fact—to restrict appeals to Paris for the very same reason that the papacy had made an abortive attempt to stem the flow of appeals to Rome in the late twelfth century. Pope Clement III (1187–1191), for instance, had tried in vain to stop the flood of litigation engulfing Rome by limiting appeals to the papal curia.[93]

---

iure probatum extitit. Et ideo dicitur habere supremam iurisdictionem secundum Fran. Cur. in consil. 49, col. xxxiii. et Corse. in adde. ad Panor. in c. Que in ecclesiarum, de col. ii. constit. et est Monarcha in suo regno secundum Soz. in consil. 68 et 165." On De Grassaille, see Francesco Ercole, *Da Bartolo all'Althusio: Saggi sulla storia del pensiero pubblicistico del Rinascimento italiano* (Collana storica, 44; Firenze: 1932) 172 n. 2. Calasso, *Glossatori* 146, Helmut Quaritsch, *Souveränität: Enstehung und Entwicklung des Begriffs in Frankreich und Deutschland vom 13. Jh. bis 1806* (Schriften zur Verfassungsgeschichte, 38; Berlin: 1986) 30–31, and Julian H. Franklin, *Jean Bodin and the Rise of Absolutist Theory* (Cambridge: 1973) 6–9.

91. J. Favier, "Les légistes et le gouvernement de Philippe le Bel," *Journal des savants* (1969) 92–108; Meijers, *Etudes* III 81–83; Sten Gagnér, *Studien zur Ideengeschichte der Gesetzgebung* 333–363.

92. London, British Library, Arundel 459, fol. 70v: "Tertia questio fuit talis. Consuetudo fuit in Britannia quod si aliquis de iurisdictione comitis Britannie conueniebatur coram comite siue in ciuili siue in criminali causa, poterat prouocare uel appellare ad regem Francie, et sic comes amplius manus suas apponere non potuit. Deinde rex Francie uoluit comiti istud ius remittere, immo de facto ponamus remisit, baronibus de Britannia non uocatis." Beaumanoir would have also objected to legislation without consent; see above. Three questions on fol. 70v are attributed to Mornay. The other two begin: 1. "Duo pone Titius et Seius habent iurisdictiones contiguas." 2. "Comes Blesen. auus istius comitis, concessit cuidam abbatie decimam."

93. See Stanley Chodorow, "Dishonest Litigation in the Church Courts, 1140–1198," *Law, Church, and Society: Essays in Honor of Stephan Kuttner*, ed. K. Pennington and R. Somerville (Philadelphia: 1977) 190–192; see also the discussion and detailed bibliography of Ludwig Falkenstein, "Appellationen an den Papst und Delega-

The Breton barons protested. "Lord king," they admonished, "your grant is not valid. It prejudices us and the whole land. Further, you did not summon us when you made this grant."

The king was not swayed. "It is valid, and we are not obligated to summon you in this matter."[94]

As the wording makes clear, this was not a real case. Pierre introduced an imaginary situation and asked whether the king could take away the right of appeal from the barons of Brittany without their consent. His student recorded that first Pierre presented the case for the king. According to the law in Justinian's Code, *Quotiens,* Pierre argued, the king's grant was valid. Since the king of France did not have a superior in his lands, he considered himself a "prince"—although, Pierre felt compelled to add, this is an error. Because the king thinks himself a prince, he could grant a rescript to his subjects on whatever matter he wished, provided that the rights of any third party were not completely destroyed. Since the king did not subvert the rights of the barons or other subjects, he could take away their right of appeal.[95] As we shall see in the following chapter, the jurists commonly discussed the question of when the prince could grant rescripts that injured a third party in their commentaries on *Quotiens.*[96] If the king's grant were valid, its validity rested on this law.

As one may gather from the "pro" allegations, Pierre took the side of the barons. His student reported his succinct conclusion: "what would be tolerated when done to a few is considered a great error when done to many."[97] Mornay refused to entertain the idea that the king of

tionsgerichtsbarkeit am Beispiel Alexanders III. und Heinrichs von Frankreich," *Zeitschrift für Kirchengeschichte* 97 (1986) 36–65.

94. London, B. L. Arundel 459, fol. 70v: "Dicunt barones, 'Domine rex, remissio uestra non ualet quia cedit nobis et toti terre in preiudicium, et nos in hac remissione facienda non uocastis.' Dicit rex, 'immo ualet, nec uos tenebar uocare ad hoc.'"

95. Ibid.: "Queritur numquid remissio ualuit uel non. Et in hac questione doctor breuiter transiuit. Primo arguit quod ualeret per legem, C. de prec. imper. offic. Quotiens [Cod. 1.19(22).2]. Ex quo enim rex Francie non reputat in terris habere superiorem se, et sic quodam errore reputat se principem. Potest concedere rescriptum in sibi subditos quantumque uoluerit, dum tamen ius aduersarii in totum non leditur uel perimatur, ad exemplum principis qui et hoc potest per legem antedictam. Per huiusmodi autem remissionem non tollitur ius baronum in totum nec etiam aliorum subditorum, ergo etc."

96. On this problem see the excellent and generally ignored (by historians of political thought) work of Nicolini, *La proprietà* 107–134.

97. London, B. L. Arundel 459, fol. 70v: "Set doctor contrarium determindando dixit: 'Nam aliquod tolleratur in personis aliorum paucorum, quod reputaretur error magnus et inquietas magna in personis multis uel alicuius prouincie, quod probatur ff. de uulg. et pup. subst. l. Ex facto, circa prin. [Dig. 28.6.43], C. de donat. Sancimus [Cod. 8.53(54).34] et maxime per legem ff. de offic. procon. et leg. l. Solent, in fine [Dig. 1.16.6]. Dominus Petrus de Morneio, anno Domini m.cc.lxxviii. die ueneris ante natalem Domini istas questiones disputauit."

France could legislate in matters that touched the interests of the great barons without their consent, and he would not permit the king to abolish an important procedural right. He conceded that in individual cases the king might take away the rights of a few, but never the rights of the majority. In the late thirteenth century, this was not an unusual opinion.[98]

We can draw several conclusions from these jurists about the meaning of the maxim "the king is emperor in his own kingdom." First, at least in the cases we have discussed, Calasso's argument that the maxim only means that the king exercises the same powers in his kingdom as the emperor but still recognized him "de iure" as his superior cannot be supported. Second, these passages are another piece of evidence for my earlier argument (above and in chapter 1) that the jurists were not particularly interested in the question that has fascinated modern historians: when did the jurists recognize that the national kings were independent of the emperor? They were far more preoccupied with the relationship of the king and his subjects or of the king to the law than they were in his relationship to the emperor. As Mornay made clear to his listeners, he might grant that the king recognizes no superior (at least he does not reject this part of the argument), but he will not concede that the king exercises the authority of the "prince," that is, the emperor, granted to him by the laws of Justinian's codification. Pierre de Mornay believed the customs and laws of France limited the king and not the universal sovereignty of the emperor. Historians who have focused on "a king is emperor in his own kingdom" and its counterpoint "the emperor is lord of the world," as a touchstone of medieval thought on sovereignty, have seen only one dimension of the jurists' concerns.[99]

Besides Mornay's questions, the London manuscript also contains three questions by "Ja. de Bol.," who is, most likely, Jacobus of Bologna. There is a question of Jacobus of Bologna dated 1275 and preserved in another London manuscript.[100] The same man probably wrote

---

98. See Pennington, *Pope and Bishops* 68–69.

99. The literature is very large. Aside from the work of Calasso, Feenstra, Wyduckel, and Boulet-Sautel already cited, see Walther, *Imperiales Königtum* 65–111; Walter Ullmann, "The Development of the Medieval Idea of Sovereignty," EHR 64 (1949) 1–33; Gaines Post, *Studies in Medieval Legal Thought: Public Law and the State 1100–1322* (Princeton: 1964); Francesco Ercole, "L'Origine francese di una nota formola Bartoliana," *Archivio storico italiano* 73 (1915) 241–294 and "Sulla origine francese e le vicende in Italia della formola: 'Rex superiorem non recognoscens est princeps in regno suo,'" *Archivio storico italiano* 7 16 (1931) 197–238.

100. London, British Library Arundel 493, 22r–48r, a collection of 92 questions dating before 1300. On these quaestiones and related quaestiones in Bamberg, Can. 48, Darmstadt, and Vatican manuscripts, see Martin Bertram, "Kanonistische Quaestionensammlungen von Bartholomäus Brixiensis bis Johannes Andreae," *Proceedings of the*

all four questions. The rubric for the former questions states that they were disputed in the same year as Mornay's, that is, 1278. The first deals with a disputed papal provision to the church of Carleton by a certain provost who bestowed benefices sometimes as canon and sometimes as provost. The pope had ordered him to grant the next vacancy to a certain poor cleric but had addressed him only as provost.[101] Jacobus asked whether the provost was obligated to make a provision that fell to his canonical office and concluded that since the pope was a prince and that since the grants of a prince ought to be interpreted broadly, the provost had to make the provision.[102] Jacobus's conclusion is not unusual although his emphasis that the pope is a "prince" is. Be that as it may, the papal and the imperial office had long been united in the theory of the canonists. Glosses from the late twelfth century on referred to the pope as prince. Hostiensis had connected the two offices explicitly,[103] and Jacobus pointedly remarked that the pope *is a prince* to justify the pope's exercising an imperial prerogative. His emphasis is significant and is yet another indication that the jurists of the late thirteenth century were carefully distinguishing between those lords who exercised the office of "prince" and those who did not.

Although the evidence for this development is sparse, we should not underestimate its importance in legal thought simply because we are not inundated with texts. Civilians and canonists here seemingly suffered the same fate: the former had few occasions to address the issue of royal power in their glosses and commentaries; the latter had very few texts that prompted them to treat the problem. In this regard, the question of the rebel barons referred to briefly by Jean de Blanot and disputed by Jacques de Révigny must have been discussed more than once in

---

Seventh International Congress of Medieval Canon Law, ed. Peter Linehan (MIC, Series C, 8; Città del Vaticano: 1988) 265–281 at 270–271.

101. London, British Library Arundel 459, fol. 70v–71r: "Eodem anno die Sabbati ante Dominicam esto mihi disputauit dominus Ja. de Bol. tales questiones. Prima fuit. In ecclesia Carleten. consuetudo est quod quicumque debet esse prepositus de uniuersitate [nitintate] debet esse canonicus illius ecclesie, modo ita est quod ille prepositus quedam beneficia confert ratione qua prepositus et quedam ratione qua canonicus. Ponamus ergo papa mandat preposito Carleten. non expresso nomine proprio set nomine dignitatis quantus prouideat H. pauperi clerico de primo beneficio spectante ad collationem suam. Deinde uacat quoddam beneficium spectans ad collationem suam non quia prepositus est, set quia canonicus ecclesie predicte. Venit H. clericus et uult habere hoc beneficium. Prepositus se opponit."

102. Ibid. fol. 71r: "Papa est pater omnium, C. de sum. trin. et fid. cat. epistola Victor [Cod. 1.1.8.7]. Item ipse est princeps et beneficia principis latissime sunt interpretanda." For the interpretation of this maxim by the canonists, see Pennington *Pope and Bishops*, 170–177.

103. See above note 59.

France, yet the topic has left only these few traces. Since, however, two such geographically distant jurists, Jacques de Révigny and Guido of Suzzara, tried to restrict the authority of kings at approximately the same time, one should not, as a few historians have been inclined to do, view this question as a "French" or "Italian" problem. Rather, it should be considered with greater breadth as a current of juristic thought that provoked widespread interest.

Marinus de Caramanico provides the best evidence that the jurists vigorously debated whether kings were "princes" in the late thirteenth century. In his Prologue to the *Liber Augustalis,* which Frederick II issued as king of Sicily and not as emperor of the Romans, Marinus wrote a long tract in which he defended Frederick's right to promulgate the constitutions and argued, at length, for the authority of kings to exercise all the prerogatives normally attributed to the emperor. He finished his gloss to the *Liber Augustalis* sometime after 1278, and it soon became the Ordinary Gloss.[104] Had Marinus written his prologue fifty years earlier or later, I suspect that he would not have belabored the question of royal legislative authority. But he glossed a collection of royal laws at a time when Guido of Suzzara and others were attacking the "princely" authority of kings. He knew the positions of the French jurists on treason, and he had undoubtedly met Guido of Suzzara during Guido's stay in the Regno and probably knew his opinions on royal power.

Marinus cited the famous text from Justinian's Institutes—"what pleases the prince has the force of law"—at the beginning of his prologue and noted that no one should believe that this text only referred to the emperor, because a "free king, who was subject to no one" could promulgate laws, even against the "ius commune" or Roman law.[105]

---

104. See Wolf, "Gesetzgebung," *Handbuch,* ed. Coing, 698–699; Pennington, "Gregory IX, Emperor Frederick II, and the Constitutions of Melfi," *Popes, Teachers and Canon Law in the Middle Ages: Festschrift for Brian Tierney,* ed. Stanley Chodorow and James Ross Sweeney (Ithaca, N.Y.: 1989) 53–61. Marinus's Prologue is printed in A. Cervonius, *Constitutiones Regni Siciliarum libri III* (Naples: 1773) and by Calasso, *Glossatori* 179–205, from Vatican manuscripts: Vat. lat. 1437 and Vat. Reg. lat. 1948. On the date of Marinus's commentary, see the appendix in G. Vallone, *Iurisdictio Domini: Introduzione a Matteo d'Afflitto ed alla cultura giuridica meridionale tra Quattro e Cinquecento* (Collana di studi storici e giuridici 1; Lecce: 1985) 177–182. Vallone demonstrates convincingly that Marinus's gloss must have been written between 1278 and 1285.

105. Calasso, *Glossatori* 179–180: "Et neminem moveat quod preallegata Romana iura tantum in principe, idest Romanorum imperatore obtineat, cui soli concessum est condere legem . . . Sed in rege libero, qui nullius alterius potestati subiectus est, idem dicimus, scilicet ut rex ipse possit condere legem . . . Ideoque audacter dicimus, ut videlicet inter subditos regni sui possit rex constitutionem facere, et contrariam etiam communi Romano iuri constituere legem."

The laws and decretals also agree that the kings and the emperor reign in temporals and have fullness of power.[106] Marinus thus maintained that royal and imperial laws justify the ownership of earthly possessions; an emperor possesses all things in the empire, a king has the same rights in his kingdom.[107] Kings are consecrated in the same manner as emperors, and the symbols of their authority are the same.[108]

Marinus dissected the meaning of "prince." The reader may note that he emphasized for the skeptical that consuls are called "princes" and that "prince" is common both to kings and emperors. Any "monarch" can be thought of as a "prince," for the etymology of the word is derived from the "first head." All laws that discuss the authority of the "prince," therefore, apply to the emperor, kings, and anyone else who would hold "monarchy" over subjects living according to Roman law.[109] Marinus's qualification that the prince exercises this authority over people who recognize Roman law may be subtle acknowledgment that other peoples, like the French and English, were not ruled by princes.

Marinus turned to the question of whether the king of Sicily could be independent since he was the vassal of the pope.[110] He concluded that the pope granted the king full power over the kingdom and that the king's authority was not limited. As such, Sicilians could also commit treason against the king, although some argue, as Marinus noted, that only the emperor has "sovereignty" (maiestas). In this sense, lesser rulers did not have "maiestas" and could not claim that their "maiestas" had been injured. Sovereignty is nothing less than "superiority" (majoritas); indeed, a people that is superior (and not subjected to any authority) is said to have sovereignty.[111]

106. Ibid. 181: "quod vero regalis sicut imperialis dignitas in temporalibus precellat et plenitudinem habeat potestatis iuria et decreta concordant."
107. Ibid. 182: "Item alibi quod res terrene per iura regum possidentur, idest iure humano quod in potestate est regum et quod est in legibus regum sive imperatorum, quia ipsa iura humana per imperatores et reges seculi Deus distribuit humano generi . . . Ex quo apparet quod sicut dicimus omnia esse imperatoris, ut C. de quad. prescrip. l. Bene a Zenone [Cod. 7.37.3], ita possumus et in rege dicere de rebus omnibus regni sui." See discussion of this text in chapter 1.
108. Ibid. 185.
109. Ibid. 188–189: "Immo si bene lector curiosus advertat, non sine misterio legislator, ubi recitat quomodo evenit novissime ut necesse esset per unum reipublice consuli, istum unum nominat principem . . . Quod principis nomen est commune tam regi . . . quam imperatori . . . nec non cuilibet alteri qui esset monarcha quocumque nomine censeretur. Nam princeps per ethimologiam dicitur, idest primum caput, et sic dat intelligere quod iura omnia que loquuntur in principe intelligantur in rege vel imperatore seu quocumque alio qui haberet in subditis iure Romano viventibus monarchiam."
110. Discussed by Calasso, *Glossatori*, 133–136.
111. Ibid. 199–200: "Iam enim amodo liquet quod crimen lese maiestatis et perduel-

Marinus is almost certainly combating the opinions of Guido and the French jurists in the above passage. Next, Marinus outlined the authority of the king: he may legitimate bastards and no appeal can be made from his decisions.[112] Again, from the forcefulness of his arguments, Marinus knew some jurists who denied that these prerogatives pertained to kings.[113]

Both Ercole and Calasso recognized the importance of Marinus's Prologue and used it energetically to defend their theses. Ercole insisted that Marinus derived his inspiration from French jurists who developed the idea that the king was emperor in his own kingdom; Calasso saw Marinus as the culmination of Italian juridical thought that created the doctrine of independent national monarchies. Both, however, are slightly off the mark. The story is more complicated and interesting than they imagined.[114] Whether the king was independent of the emperor was a secondary concern. Marinus's primary preoccupation was the king's relationship to the law or, to ask the question in the language of the day, was the king a prince? I also think the evidence shows that Marinus was, as Ercole thought, influenced by the French jurists, although their influence on him was entirely different from Ercole's conception of it. Marinus was reacting against those French jurists (and Guido of Suzzara) who denied that the king was above the law because he was not a prince. This web of ideas called into question the very legitimacy of the *Liber Augustalis*. Marinus had to rebut them. Their conceptions of royal sovereignty called into question the authority of the book of laws on which he was commenting.

This episode in the development of medieval political thought about the authority of kings was quickly forgotten. By the end of the fourteenth century, no academic jurist denied that a king had the same authority as the emperor. Charles De Grassaille's long and florid list of privileges that the French king possessed is a final panegyric for the maxim "The king of France is emperor in his own kingdom."[115] We

---

lionis committitur in regem Sicilie, quamvis quidam nimia subtilitate tenti temptaverunt contrarium dicere, allegantes maiestatem tantum esse in imperatore . . . sed ipsi perperam sunt locuti, nam et in rege dicitur esse maiestas . . . Nihil enim sonat aliud maiestas quam maioritas, et ideo etiam populus, qui est superior, dicitur habere maiestatem."

112. Ibid. 201–202.

113. Ibid. 201: "Liquet etiam ammodo per rationes easdem quod a rege Sicilie appellari non potest, nam, cum sit princeps, stultum est, idest supervacuum, dicere fas esse a principe appellari."

114. Brian Tierney, "Some Recent Works," 612–619, provides a lucid analysis of this dispute.

115. De Grassaille, *Regalium Franciae libri duo* 316ff.

might call this brief moment when the academic jurists seem to have tried to transform the prince into a feudal, rather than a Roman ruler, the "flowering of feudal constitutionalism." From the evidence that remains, Guido of Suzzara may have been the chief proponent of "feudal constitutionalism."

In a remarkable gloss, Guido went one step further than any earlier jurist in binding the prince to the law. He not only thought that kings were bound by the law because they were not princes, he proposed that the prince himself was bound. Although the prince submitted himself voluntarily to the laws at the beginning, thereafter his submission was no longer voluntary, rather a necessity. In this context, Guido's arguments were juristically sophisticated and clever. He compared the prince's submission to the law to the act of arbitration. Litigants may enter into arbitration freely, but once they have agreed to arbitration they cannot withdraw their consent. The same is true, he noted, of the Roman law contract of loan (commodatum).[116]

Guido's argument was astute and a convincing explanation for the efficacy of the coronation oath's obligating the prince to observe the law. Again, as with the French jurists, Guido's thought had no influence on later legists. He was, it seems, a devout believer in an extreme doctrine of limited monarchy. As we shall see in the following chapter, jurists accepted Guido's arguments about the prince's obligation to respect certain judicial rights of his subjects, but not his limitations on the "princeps."

POTESTAS ABSOLUTA ET ORDINATA
(CA. 1270–1350)

Having explored the nuances of meaning with which the jurists enriched "legibus solutus," we can now turn to "potestas absoluta." When Hostiensis applied the phrase to the papal authority, one could have anticipated that it might have become standard terminology for

---

116. Guido of Suzzara, Suppletiones to Dig. 1.3.31(30) (Princeps legibus), Clm 6201, fol. 10v: "Item cum ipse se sponte subiaciat legibus ut probatum est in legibus nunc allegatis, quod ergo a principio fuit ei uoluntarium, scilicet se subicere legibus, postquam sic se subiecit necessitatis est. Sicut dicimus in compromisso subeundo quod ab initio est uoluntarium, postea necessitatis est, ut infra de arbit. l.iii. § Tam esti neminem [Dig. 4.8.3.1] sic in commodato, infra commod. l. In commodato § Sicut [Dig. 13.6.17?] et in similibus constat, C. de act. et oblig. l. Sicut [Cod. 4.10.5] Quis autem erit iudex in ea questione? Respon. Procurator Cesaris, ut C. ubi cause fis. agi. l. Ad fiscum [Cod. 3.26.5] et C. si aduersus fis. l.ii. [Cod. 2.36(37).2]. G." Cortese, La norma, I 158–159 n. 22, from the Parsian manuscripts, whose texts are inferior to Clm 6201.

legal discussions of princely authority. The theologians had explored God's absolute power in the thirteenth and fourteenth centuries with enthusiasm, and analogies between heavenly and earthly paradigms were popular. Nevertheless, if one may judge its popularity by the number of times it occurred in canon and Roman law glosses, Hostiensis's novelty was not a smashing success. In the following pages, I shall trace its use by representative theologians and jurists in the period after Hostiensis. I shall eschew a discussion of kindred, but not necessarily identical terms, "legibus solutus" and "plenitudo potestatis" for two reasons. First, because "potestas absoluta" becomes a term that describes the prince's ultimate sovereignty in later thought, I wish to trace its history more clearly than has previously been done. Second, I think that historians make a mistake when they simply collate these three terms together. As we have already seen in the work of Hostiensis, "potestas absoluta" had a life separate from "plenitudo potestatis" or "legibus solutus," and we shall focus on exactly how later jurists defined the term. Although the boundaries they draw are by far not clear or always coherent, they are worth recognizing.[117]

Medieval theologians adopted the distinction between God's ordained and absolute powers, and even Protestants accepted this part of Catholic speculative thinking. Martin Luther used the term, if with reservations, and "potentia absoluta et ordinata" appears as late as the eighteenth century in the writings of New England puritans. In Western thought, absolute power became an expression of one man's authority over another. As democratic ideals have replaced monarchy as a model of government, absolute power became a pejorative term in political discourse. Finally, Lord Acton dealt "potestas absoluta" a cruel blow with his famous aphorism: "power tends to corrupt and absolute power corrupts absolutely."

The bestowal of absolute power on God opened an extended theological discourse in the late Middle Ages. The new terminology prodded theologians to consider the relationship of man and the deity in a new light. Some theologians came to despair of knowing God through His

---

117. The most recent and comprehensive study of "potestas absoluta" is Courtenay, *Capacity and Volition*. For other treatments of "potestas absoluta" during this early period, see Oakley, *Omnipotence*, passim, Wyduckel, *Princeps legibus solutus* 97–101; 120–129; 130–137; Wyduckel, *Ius publicum* 58; 96–102; Cortese, *La norma* I 162–165; Nicolini, *Proprietà* 115–151; William J. Courtenay, "The Dialectic of Omnipotence in the High and Late Middle Ages," *Divine Omniscience and Omnipotence in Medieval Philosophy: Islamic, Jewish and Christian Perspectives*, ed. Tamar Rudavsky (Dordrecht-Boston-Lancaster: 1985) 243–269.

works. If God could at any moment change the world he had fashioned
into something else through his absolute power—a vacuum was an intriguing possibility—the theologians asked themselves how a truth obtained from observation and experimentation could be proven a truth.
God might overturn the results tomorrow. This realization, as Edward
Grant has noted, "encouraged innumerable invocations of God's absolute power in a variety of hypothetical physical situations."[118] According to Grant, Christian thinkers consequently could reject the received
truths of ancient science. Not only was the credibility of the ancients
undermined, but William Ockham put forward the idea of God's ultimate unknowability—an idea that gained widespread acceptance in the
late Middle Ages.[119] Further yet, Ockham and his followers established
the primacy of God's will over reason, "ratio"—a concept dear to the
medieval soul and a reversal of Aquinas's priorities and those of earlier
thinkers.[120]

As we have seen, the theologians were not the first to subordinate
reason to the prince's will.[121] That was the work of the jurists. The primacy of will over reason was a major transformation of juridical and
theological ways of understanding political authority.

Like the jurists, the theologians applied the terminology of absolute
power to the human prince. In his seventh Quodlibet, Ockham observed that God's ordinary power is to be understood as his authority
when he acts in accordance with the laws ordained and enacted by him.
God performed all other acts through his absolute power—if he so decided. Ockham concluded: "Just as the pope cannot do some things according to the laws ordained by him that he may absolutely do."[122] In
other words, the pope is "legibus solutus."

118. Edward Grant, "The Condemnation of 1277, God's Absolute Power, and Physical Thought in the Late Middle Ages," *Viator* 10 (1979) 239. See Courtenay's cautionary
remarks about Grant's article in *Capacity and Volition* 95, 108–109.

119. Jürgen Miethke, *Ockhams Weg zur Sozialphilosophie* (Berlin 1969) 137–156.
Klaus Bannach, *Die Lehre von der doppelten Macht Gottes bei Wilhelm von Ockham:
Problemgeschichtliche Voraussetzungen und Bedeutung* (Wiesbaden: 1975). Mary Anne
Pernoud, "The Theory of the *Potentia Dei* according to Aquinas, Scotus and Ockham,"
Antonianum 47 (1972) 69–95.

120. See Courtenay, *Capacity and Volition* 115–172 and Wyduckel, *Princeps legibus
solutus* 124–129.

121. Laurentius Hispanus was the first to subjugate reason to the will in Western
thought; see chapter 2.

122. *Quodlibeta septem*, ed. Joseph Wey, *Opera theologica* 9 (St. Bonaventure, N.Y.:
1980), pp. 585–586; "Aliter accipitur 'posse' pro posse facere omne illud quod non in-
cludit contradictionem fieri, sive Deus ordinaverit se hoc facturum sive non, quia multa
potest Deus facere quae non vult facere . . . et illa dicitur Deus posse de potentia absoluta.
Sicut papa aliqua non potest secundum iura statuta ab eo, quae tamen absolute potest."
Cf. Courtenay, *Capacity and Volition* 121–122, who states that "Ockham was attempt-

When Ockham discussed the authority of the pope or the prince, he normally used the term "plenitudo potestatis."[123] Whether applied to the pope or the emperor, "plenitudo potestatis" did not allow the prince to violate divine or natural law, although the pope could, with cause, dispense from higher laws.[124] Equating plenitude of power to absolute power in the tract he wrote to reveal the errors of Pope Benedict XII, Ockham observed that some (presumably at the papal court) held that papal plenitude of power was the equivalent of absolute power inside and outside the Church. They claimed that the pope could do all things (in temporal and spiritual matters) excepting only his transgressing natural or divine law.[125] Ockham disputed this expanded definition of absolute power vigorously.

Although jurists certainly used the term "potestas absoluta," the papal curia was a complicated place. Ockham's trusty foe, Pope John XXII, rebuked those who equated God's absolute power with the pope's, and he pointed out that papal power to change those things that have been ordained by others stems from the inability of man to foresee the future. Therefore, necessity and cause dictated change.[126] In-

---

ing to maintain that the pope was bound to uphold and abide by his laws once instituted." Ockham knew law well enough, I think, that he would not have taken such an eccentric position. No other theologian or jurist bound the pope to positive canon law. See also Courtenay's remarks on p. 109 where he equates papal infallibility and the pope's being bound to the laws of his predecessors. However, no statute of strictly positive law could be infallible unless it restated a divine law or unless it expressed a fundamental doctrine of the Christian faith.

123. See William of Ockham, *Dialogus de potestate papae et imperatoris* (Frankfurt: 1614; repr. Monumenta politica rariora, 1; Torino: 1966) 3.3.4 (p. 774–775), 3.3.12 (p. 783), 1.3.26 (p. 922–923).

124. Ibid. 3.3.4, pp. 775: "Nam papa dispensat contra Deum in iuramento et in voto . . . ergo multofortius papa potest omnia, quae non sunt contra legem Dei nec contra ius naturae . . . habet potestatem a Christo super omnia licita, quae naturali aequitati non obviant."

125. Ockham, *Tractatus contra Benedictum* 6.2, *Opera politica*, eds. R. F. Bennett and H. S. Offler (Manchester: 1956) III 273: "Ista autem radix in quadam alia est fundata quod scilicet papa habet a Christo plenitudinem potestatis, tam in spiritualibus quam in temporalibus, ut de potentia absoluta omnia possit quae non sunt contra legem divinam vel legem naturae." For a discussion of this passage, see Eugenio Randi, "La vergine e il papa: *Potentia Dei absoluta* e *Plenitudo potestatis* papale nel XIV secolo," *History of Political Thought* 5 (1984) 425–445 at 431.

126. An unpublished sermon of John XXII in Paris, B.N. 3290 and partially edited by Randi, "La vergine e il papa," 433–434: "Alii dicunt intelligimus ordinatam potentiam illam qua Deus ordinavit ab eterno fienda; absolutam vero illam que potest suspendere illa que ab eterno sint ordinata. Sicut est de papa, ut dicunt, qui de plenitudine potestatis potest immutare illa que ab aliis ordinata sint, maxime si non tangant fidem. Frater nec istud intelligo nec verum credo, unde quod papa possit immutare illa que ab aliis ordinata sunt hoc est propter defectum humanae providentie, que non potest omnia previdere. Et ideo quando veniunt casus et necessitates improvise oportet quod aliter ordinetur in multis." Cf. Courtenay, *Capacity and Volition* 147–162.

deed, John objected to the distinction of God's absolute and ordained power.[127] That John would not apply the theologian's definition of absolute power to God or to the pope does not mean that he would not have used the jurists' definition. He was trained in law and would have probably had little difficulty explaining absolute power as the pope's being "legibus solutus."[128] The pope acted in accordance with the law when he exercised his ordained power; he acted above the law and with absolute power when he legislated, dispensed, or contravened positive law.

Another important publicist of the period, and a high papalist, Aegidius Romanus, attributed absolute power to the pope and made the same distinction as Ockham:[129]

> If, therefore, the pope is without bit and halter when exercising absolute power, he nevertheless ought to impose a halter and bit upon himself by observing the laws and the rights [of his subjects]. For, although he is above the law when he treats positive law, he should give certainty to rights and laws, by governing the Church entrusted to him according to them.

Aegidius is not only "encouraging self-limits on royal or papal 'absolutist' behavior,"[130] but, more important, expressing a legal doctrine that, as we have seen, in the first two sections of this chapter, was already a commonplace by the middle of the thirteenth century. The prince should live according to the law and should bind himself to the law. This commonsensical dictum could be found in Roman law and was pervasive in legal and theological thought.[131] Even English judges,

---

127. Ibid.: "Unde dico secundum hoc quod est impossibile habere potentiam absolutam et ordinatum respectu eiusdem effectus, quia implicaret contradictio manifesta."

128. For an extended discussion of John's thought, see Tierney, *Papal Infallibility* 171–204. Also James Heft, *John XXII and Papal Teaching Authority* (Texts and Studies in Religion, 27; Lewiston-Queenston: 1986). John taught civil law at Cahors and canon law at Toulouse. Also Eugenio Randi, "Ockham, John XXII and the Absolute Power of God," *Franciscan Studies* 46 (1986) 205–216.

129. Aegidius Romanus, *De ecclesiastica potestate,* ed. Richard Scholz (Vienna: 1929, repr. Aalen: 1961) 181: "Si ergo summus pontifex secundum suum posse absolutum est alias sine freno et sine capistro, ipse tamen debet sibi frenum et capistrum imponere, in se ipso observando leges et iura. Nam licet ipse sit supra iura, loquendo de iuribus positivis, ut tamen det suis iuribus et suis legibus firmitatem, decet eum secundum leges et iura commissam sibi ecclesiam gubernare." See *Giles of Rome on Ecclesiastical Power: The "De ecclesiastica potestate" of Aegidius Romanus,* trans. R. W. Dyson (Woodbridge-Dover: 1986) 178; also Wilks, *Problem of Sovereignty* 307–308.

130. Courtenay, *Speculum* 60 (1985) 1008. Also his comments in "Dialectic of Omnipotence," 264–265 n. 33.

131. The best discussion of "limited monarchy" in thirteenth-century thought is Brian Tierney, "Bracton on Government," *Speculum* 38 (1963) 295–317 and "'The Prince is Not Bound by the Law': Accursius and the Origins of the Modern State," *Comparative Studies in Society and History* 5 (1963) 378–400, and, of course, Cortese, *La norma.*

who one might presume knew little of theological niceties, placed "bits and halters" on their king.

Other theologians, however, were not as restrained as Ockham and Aegidius. They took theological discussions of God's absolute power and applied God's power to the pope. Guillaume de Pierre Godin—if he really is the author of the tract a recent editor has attributed to him— claimed that the pope, exercising "potestas absoluta," may take ecclesiastical jurisdiction away from every bishop and rule the Church through legates.[132] The pope could act without cause and without any limitations. Hostiensis would have found Godin's argument that the pope could violate the "status ecclesiae" intolerable, but Godin's position does reflect a logical extension of one side of Hostiensis's discussion of papal power.

Other theologians defined papal absolute power as the exercise of certain prerogatives under special circumstances. Ever since Pope Innocent III had claimed to wield authority in the secular sphere "diversis causis inspectis," the canonists had tried to give some juridical precision to this claim.[133] Conrad of Megenburg (1309–1374) explained this extraordinary papal power as "potestas absoluta":[134]

> The pope may deprive the princes of their power to elect the emperor with his absolute power.... With this power the pope is above positive and human law.

Conrad's definition corresponds to Hostiensis's efforts of giving absolute power a technical meaning; he saw it as justification for the pope's right to act when he did not normally have jurisdiction—a greater claim to authority than being simply "legibus solutus." Opicinus Canistris

132. Guillaume de Pierre Godin, *Tractatus de causa immediata ecclesiastice potestatis*, ed. William D. McCready (Toronto: 1982) 295: "Eodem modo de potentia absoluta posset papa ecclesiam regere per episcopos legatos annuales missos ad tempus ad provincias et dioceses, sicut olim imperatores regebant mundum per presides, per consules et legatos." See D. Van den Auweele's critique of McCready's edition and editorial principles in "A propos de la tradition manuscrite du 'De causa immediata ecclesiastice potestatis' de Guillaume de Pierre Godin (+ 1366)," *Recherches de théologie ancienne et médiévale* 51 (1984) 183–205. Cf. Randi, "La vergine e il papa," 438–439.

133. See Pennington, "Pope Innocent III's Views on Church and State: A Gloss to *Per venerabilem*," *Law, Church and Society: Essays in Honor of Stephan Kuttner*, ed. Kenneth Pennington and Robert Somerville (Philadelphia: 1977) 49–67, with the literature cited there.

134. Conrad of Megenberg, *Oeconomica*, ed. S. Krüger (MGH, Staatsschriften, 6; Stuttgart: 1977) II 53–55: "Papa ex potestate absoluta potest principes electione privare et ipse eligere vacante imperio, posito etiam quod principes eligere velint et possint canonice concordari . . . Ista etenim potestate papa est super iura positiva et humana." Quoted by Randi, "La vergine e il papa," 436–437.

adopted a similar doctrine in a tract dedicated to Pope John XXII in 1329.[135]

The jurists were, it seems, reluctant to incorporate absolute power into their thought. I have found only a few late thirteenth-century lawyers who discussed the prince's "potestas absoluta." Giovanni Anguissola (ca. 1295), who wrote about the prince's authority in a gloss to the Digest,[136] depicted the prince as having two powers: ordinary and absolute. By his ordinary power, the prince should observe the law, but is not bound by it. When he exercises absolute power, he need not observe positive law because he is not bound by it. However, the prince is bound by divine law.[137] If this is an accurate report of Johannes's thought, he simply replaced "legibus solutus" with "potestas absoluta."

Andrea de Isernia's commentary (ca. 1315) to *Super feudis* discussed ecclesiastical and secular "potestas absoluta." The pope possessed absolute and ordained power and exercised absolute power outside the order of the legal system. But he may not act without cause.[138] The prince also may not confiscate the private property of his subjects without cause, because dominium is protected by natural law. If the prince acts without cause, he exercises his absolute, not his ordained, authority. Even though no one may judge him when he resorts to his "potestas absoluta," he still sins against God, just as he sins when he imposes a new tax without cause.[139] By distinguishing between the proper and the

135. Opicinus de Canistris, *De preminentia spiritualis imperii*, ed. Richard Scholz *Unbekannte kirchenpolitische Streitschriften aus der Zeit Ludwigs des Bayern (1327–1354)*, 2: *Analysen und Texte* (Bibliothek des Deutschen Historischen Instituts in Rom, 10; Rome: 1914) 97: "Licet autem summus pontifex utriusque gladii iurisdictionem habeat ac etiam executionem de potentia absoluta, non debet tamen per se gladium temporalem in vindictam exhimere, sed potius alii tradere." Quoted by Randi, "La vergine e il papa," 437.

136. Luigi Prosdocimi, "Anguissola, Giovanni," DBI 3 (1961) 317–318.

137. Franciscus Curtius Papiensis reported Johannes's opinion in consilium 65 (Milan: 1496), unfol.: "Joh. Fran. de Anguisolis . . . in l. Princeps, ff. de leg. et const. prin. [Dig. 1.3.31(30)] quod in sententia principis non requitur ordo iuris quia secundum eum princeps habet duplicem potestatem, videlicet ordinariam et absolutam, et in ordinaria censetur sub lege quantum ad observantiam, non quo ad vinculum. In absoluta vero non est sub lege, nec quo ad observantiam nec quo ad vinculum in iure positivo, quamvis in iure divino omnino subsit, c. Sunt quidam xxv. q.i."

138. *Lectura in usibus feudorum* (Naples: 1477), fol. 105v, to 2.55(56) § Vectigalia: "Et licet in papa sit potestas absoluta et ordinata, absolutam exercet preter iuris ordinem, sed non sine causa, quantumcumque vocatus sit in plenitudinem, alii in partes solicitudinis, iii. q.vi. Multum, alias videtur clavis errare."

139. Ibid.: § Flumina navigabilia, fol. 104v: "Non potest rem privati sine causa tollere, quia dominium erat suum iure naturali gentium quod non potest princeps mutare . . . Sic debent intelligi iura de potestate principis loquentia ut semper cum causa faciat, sicut diximus super verbo 'Vectigalia' . . . Alias si sine cause, potestate absoluta, non ordinata, licet non habeat hominem qui sua facta deiudicet, ut dicit glo. super illud Psal. Tibi soli peccavi. Certum est quod peccat apud Deum, sicut quando sine causa imponit novum vectigal dicit Innoc. extra de censi. Innovamus."

improper use of absolute power, Andrea fitted "potestas absoluta" into the earlier paradigm. The prince's power is not enhanced by absolute power; rather, it is another term for "legibus solutus" or "plenitudo potestatis." The prince may act; his act may be legally binding; but he may fall into sin for it. His absolute power does not justify an unjust act.

Albericus de Rosate (ca. 1340–1360) wrote the most extended and nuanced discussion of absolute power and may have been the first jurist to define "potestas absoluta" as the prince's right to exercise his authority arbitrarily but "de iure."[140] Although Nicolini carefully examined Albericus's analysis of absolute power almost fifty years ago, historians have not given him his due in the history of political theory.[141]

Stimulated by the story of Martinus, Bulgarus, and Frederick Barbarossa, Albericus discussed absolute power in his commentary on Justinian's Digest.[142] Martinus, he said, had alleged that the emperor possessed all imperium, including all property and total dominion; he was not just sovereign over all property in order to protect it, as Bulgarus thought.[143] He declared that all the jurists agreed with Bulgarus that the emperor was not the lord of all things and added that Jacobus Buttrigarius thought that the pope might be lord of all ecclesiastical property but only in the sense that he exercised care and solicitude over the Church.[144]

Influenced by the French jurist, Jacques de Révigny, who had broken decisively from the consensus of most thirteenth-century jurists to limit the prince's power, Albericus put forward a series of counterarguments against received opinion.[145] First, although the jurists had alleged that two people could not own property concurrently, Albericus noted that this did not apply to the emperor, but only to private individuals. The emperor is exempt from the legal order, and he exercises the office of God on earth in temporal matters just as the pope takes His place in

---

140. Luigi Prosdocimi, "Alberico da Rosciate e la giurisprudenza italiana nel secolo XIV," *Rivista di storia del diritto italiano* 29 (1956) 67–74.

141. Nicolini, *Proprietà* 132–142.

142. Albericus de Rosate, *Commentarium super Digesto* (2 vols. Venice: 1585; repr. Torino: 1974).

143. Albericus to Dig. § Omnem (Introductory constitution), fol. 4v: "Dixit quod imperator erat dominus totius imperii quo ad proprietatem et totale dominium, non solum quo ad protectionem et iurisdictionem, ut sensit Bul."

144. Ibid.: "Tenet Iaco. de Are. quod imperator non sit dominus rerum singularium, nisi quo ad iurisdictionem et protectionem, approbans in hoc Bul. opinionem quam etiam glos. approbat, et communiter omnes doctores . . . et hanc etiam sequebatur Iacob. Butri. dicens eum non esse dominum rerum singularium, nisi cura et solicitudine, sic et papa in rebus ecclesiasticis."

145. Cortese, *La norma* II 453–460 has printed the pertinent glosses of Révigny.

spiritual affairs.[146] Albericus's teacher, Ricardus Malumbra (died 1334), he maintained that the emperor was lord of even the property of individuals.[147] To justify this claim, he relied on the arguments of Johannes Teutonicus in the Ordinary Gloss to the Decretum.[148] Everyone owns or possesses property through Roman law. If the laws of the emperor were destroyed, no one could claim that this was mine.[149]

Albericus next considered whether the emperor could confiscate the goods of his subjects. If the emperor is lord of all the property of individuals, the answer is clear: he may.[150] If the emperor is not lord of all such property, the answer is somewhat more complex: a person who is not the lord of property may sometimes alienate it. Again, however, the common opinion of the doctors is that the prince may not confiscate private property. To further support his contention, Albericus cited two familiar arguments: private property had been established by the law of nations and the emperor is bound by laws outside his legislative competence.[151] Although one could argue that the emperor could confiscate property for the public good, ordinarily he could not.[152] One might also argue, Albericus continued, that while the emperor could not confiscate private property, he could deny the right to bring suit since this right was derived from civil law.[153]

---

146. Ibid.: "Sed huic arg. posset responderi quod duo insolidum non possunt esse domini, scilicet privati, sed privatus et imperator sic, quia imperator excluditur a regulis iuris, ut C. de legibus l. Digna vox, nam et Deus est dominus omnium, ut in psalmo, 'Domini est terra et plenitudo eius,' etc. et imperator est in terris loco Dei, quo ad temporalia, et papa, quo ad spiritualia."

147. Ricardus's major commentaries on the Digest do not seem to have survived.

148. See chapter 1.

149. Ibid.: "Dominus meus dominus Ricardus Malumbrae indistincte tenebat imperatorem esse dominum (dominium Ed.) etiam rerum singularium, et ad hoc inducebat quoddam decretum quod videtur valde bene probare, 8 dist. Quo iure villas defendas ecclesiae [c.1], ubi expresse dicitur quod quilibet dicit possessiones et res suas propter iura imperatorum, et amotis legibus imperatorum non est qui dicere possit, haec est res mea, cum igitur imperator non sit ligatus legibus, ut dicta l. Digna vox, et leges possit ad libitum mutare. Sequitur quod ista consideratione sit dominus etiam rerum singularium."

150. Ibid.: "An possit res singulorum eis auferre et alienare, si teneremus opinionem quod sit dominus quaestio cessaret."

151. Ibid.: "Si autem teneamus aliam opinionem tunc procedit quaestio, quia etiam non dominus alienat quandoque, ut inst. qui alien. licet in principio . . . et communiter doctores tenent quod non sequentes opinionem Bul. . . . et quia dominia sunt distincta de iuregentium . . . et tale ius est immutabile per ius civile . . . Item quia non est mos imperatoris alterius iura tollere."

152. Ibid.: "adhuc posset allegari pro opinione Mart. infra de offic. pro. l. Barbarius [Dig. 1.14.3], sed ibi speciale favore publicae utilitatis."

153. Ibid.: "quod si fiscus vendat rem alienam quod dominus eam revocare vel vendicare non potest. Sed dici potest, ut dixi ad l. Barbarius [Dig. 1.14.3], vel dic quod ibi non perdit dominium, quod est de iure gentium sed actionem que est de iure civili."

For the contrary arguments, Albericus turned again to Ricardus Malumbra and Jacques de Révigny,[154] who had both agreed that the emperor could issue a peremptory law in which he stated that his decree was valid even though it conflicted with another law (non obstante aliqua lege). Nevertheless, the emperor could not completely take the rights of another away through such a law.[155]

Jacques de Révigny wrote that the prince's power was not limited and that he could confiscate property without cause from his "plenitudo potestatis," although Jacques tempered his absolutism with the traditional warning that the emperor would be judged by God for his sins.[156] Albericus applied the terminology of "potestas absoluta" to the problem. If the emperor acts without a just cause and contrary to "honesty," he sins gravely if he were exercising his ordained and limited power. Then he may not confiscate property and the opinion of Bulgarus is correct.[157] If the emperor acts with his absolute power and "plenitudo potestatis" that is over all law, then the opinion of Martinus is true. The emperor may act with cause in certain special cases and (may do) the same in other cases (with his absolute power). No one may judge him whether the cause is just or not; only God judges him, just as only God judges the pope.[158] Although he repeated Jacques de Révigny's warning that God would judge the prince if he sinned, Albericus clearly thought that the prince could act justly, "de iure," without cause.[159]

Today, "absolutism," derived from its adjectival use in "absolute power," is defined as the unrestricted exercise of authority by a govern-

154. Jacques de Révigny's gloss to Justinian's constitution *Omnem* has been printed by Cortese, *La norma* II 452–454. Jacques agreed with Martinus that the emperor was the lord of all things in the world, that he could confiscate private property without cause, and that actions are established by civil law and therefore can be taken away by the emperor.

155. Ibid.: "Sed qui tenent opinionem Mart. sicut dominus Ric. Malumbre et etiam Iacob. de Ra. allegant adhuc pro dicta opinione quia certum est quod imperator ex certa scientia potest concedere peremptoriam, dicendo non obstante aliqua lege, vel non obstante dicta lege Quotiens, de prec. imperat. offer. sed non concedendo peremptoriam ex toto tollit ius alterius."

156. Cortese, *La norma* II 453: "Sua enim potentia non est limitata, de plenitudine potestatis sue potest hoc facere. Caveat sibi, minister Dei est, aut. de fide instrum. § i. coll. vi. [Nov. 73 pr. § 1 = Authen. 6.3.76] cum non minus iudicabitur quam ipse iudicat."

157. Albericus to *Omnem* loc. cit.: "Dicit tamen quod si sine iusta causa hoc faciat graviter peccat. Aut ergo querimus de ordinata et limitata potestate et honestate, et tunc non potest, et ita posset intelligi opinio Bul."

158. Ibid.: "Aut de absoluta et plenitudine potestatis quae est supra omnem legem et tunc est vera opinio Mar. nam qua ratione potest in casibus specialibus ex iusta causa hoc facere, eadem in aliis. Nec erit qui dijudicare possit, si iusta causa vel non, quia ipse facta subditorum iudicat, sua iudicat solus Deus, sicut de papa."

159. See Canning's discussion of these issues in "Law, Sovereignty" 456–460.

ment or person. Although other jurists like Révigny anticipated his absolutism, Albericus may have been the first jurist to use "potestas absoluta" as a definition of the prince's authority to act unjustly, without cause, and arbitrarily.

The political thought of Albericus is rich and innovative.[160] Although it is unusual in the work of a civilian, he treated imperial and papal power as being part of one cloth and carefully sorted out the characteristics of each in detail.[161] When he discussed papal and imperial power, he relied on Dante's *Monarchia* and John of Paris's *De regia potestate et papali* for their views on the separation of secular and ecclesiastical authority.[162] Consequently, Albericus defended an unusual position in the Middle Ages, advocating a strict separation of church and state, exalting imperial authority, and granting the pope the same authority within the Church as the emperor exercised in the state.

Among the canonists, Johannes Andreae was one of the few who adopted the terminology of absolute power. When he glossed *Sicut unire* in the second recension of his *Additiones* to the Gregoriana, he fashioned a definition of absolute power that seems to have been a misreading of Hostiensis. In cases that were reserved to the pope, the pope should obtain the consent of the cardinals. If he ignored the cardinals, he exercised his absolute power.[163] Since Johannes altered his definition to conform to that of Hostiensis in his *Novella*, we cannot know whether he changed his mind or whether he realized that he had misread Hostiensis's text.[164] But whatever the case, like Hostiensis, Jo-

160. On Albericus's thought see Canning, *Baldus de Ubaldus* passim and Nicolini, *Proprietà* passim.

161. In his gloss to "Princeps legibus solutus," Dig. 1.3.31(30), he noted at the beginning: "Quod hic dicitur de principe idem intelligas in papa."

162. *Commentaria super Codice* (2 vols. Venice: 1585; repr. Torino: 1979), II fol. 108r, to Cod. 7.37.3.

163. Johannes Andreae to X 5.31.8, Clm 15703, fol. 297v and Clm 14026, fol. 158v, [ita] episcopi: "non per omnia quia episcopus non potest hoc facere sine consensu capituli, quod non requiritur in papa. Item papa cum causa et sine causa, licet male faciat si sine causa faciat; episcopus autem nonnisi cum causa, et tunc cum consensu capituli, nec facit hoc episcopus sine consensu ecclesiarum uniuntur. Refert tamen Host. quod papa quando facit aliquid de reseruatis requirit consensum fratrum suorum, et dicit quod illud est de ordinata (ordinaria Clm 15703) potestate, non de absoluta, scilicet quod papa eos requirere teneatur." For a description of Johannes's *Additiones* see Pennington, "Johannes Andreae's *Additiones*," esp. pp. 334–335.

164. *Novella* (Venice 1581) V, fol. 92v.: "*ita*: istud uerbum et 'sicut,' quod precedit non sunt omnino similitudinaria, quia episcopus facit hoc de consensu capituli ad quod papa non tenetur. Item episcopus hoc non facit sine collaudatione ambarum ecclesiarum, de his que fiunt a prelat. c. primo (X 3.10.1), de rebus eccles. non alien. c. primo (X 3.13.1), quod falsum est, ut in clem. de rebus eccles. non alien. Si una (Clem. 3.4.2), ad quod papa non tenetur. ix. q.iii. Cuncta per mundum et c. Principalem (C.9 q.3 c.18 and 21), secundum Host., qui dicit hic hunc casum uel alios specialiter reseruatos papa

hannes viewed absolute power as the pope's authority to alter the un-written constitution of the Church, the "status ecclesiae" in his early work. As we have seen, this concept is quite different from the prince's being "legibus solutus."

Johannes also used "absolute power" when he glossed *Cum mona-sterium*. His remark was short and cryptic. Bernardus Parmensis had written in his Ordinary Gloss to the Decretals that "some say that the pope may permit a monk to own property from his fullness of power" ("propter plenitudinem potestatis").[165] Johannes noted that Bernardus almost seems to be speaking of absolute rather than ordinary power.[166] Here too he follows Hostiensis's argument. One of Hostiensis's defini-tions of absolute power was the pope's power to derogate divine law.[167] Like Hostiensis, Johannes conceived of absolute power as the pope's authority to transcend his normal jurisdiction and executive authority, not as an equivalent of "princeps legibus solutus." There is no hint, however, in Johannes's thought that "potestas absoluta" sanctioned arbitrary power.

We shall further explore the prince's absolute power and the jurists' interpretation of it in chapter 6. Two points can be made at this time. First, most jurists did not view absolute power as absolute. They did not concede that it granted the prince the authority to act arbitrarily. Unlike God's absolute power, it was not a theoretical authority, but one that the prince could employ in the exercise of his office.[168] Second, most jurists did not conclude that the prince's absolute power tran-scended natural or divine law, or the normal, established, "constitu-tional" order. Hostiensis had defined the pope's absolute power as his authority to transcend natural and divine law and to subvert the state of the Church (status ecclesiae) in certain limited cases. A few theolo-gians enhanced the prince's power with the term. Nevertheless, one may

non consueuit expedire sine consilio cardinalium. Dicit etiam eum non posse de potestate ordinata, de his que fiunt a prelat. Nouit (X 3.10.4), licet secus de absoluta, de conces, prebend. Proposuit (X 3.8.4)."

165. Bernardus Parmensis to X 3.35.6 v. *abdicatio proprietatis*: "Alii dicunt quod potest dispensare propter plenitudinem potestatis quod monachus habeat proprium."

166. Johannes Andreae, Additiones II to X 3.35.6, Clm 14026, fol. 120v, Clm 15703, fol. 229r: "Eadem glossa ibi 'propter plenitudinem potestatis' dicit quasi dicat de absoluta non ordinaria potestate." Johannes repeated the gloss in his Novella, III, fol. 179v. It is not in Additiones I (Clm 6351, fol. 72v).

167. See chapter 2.

168. Cf. Wilks, *Problem of Sovereignty* 441: "the distinction between the *potestas absoluta* and the *potestas ordinaria* is one between the theory and practice of the ruler's power."

generalize that a more powerful prince wielding real "potestas absoluta" was not attractive to the canonists, theologians, or civilians before that time (ca. 1360).

This last point raises an intriguing, but unanswerable question: why were the jurists reluctant to adopt absolute power and apply it to the prince? As we have seen, they had no difficulty calling the prince "legibus solutus." They readily granted him "plenitudo potestatis." When Laurentius Hispanus introduced a similar term, "pro ratione voluntas," into political discourse during the first decades of the thirteenth century, by the century's end it had become a standard maxim with which the jurists defined the source of the prince's legislative authority. "Pro ratione voluntas" has an absolutistic ring, and non-jurists sometimes used it to describe arbitrary or tyrannical authority.[169] Nonetheless, in spite of its absolutistic flavor, the jurists incorporated it into their thought. In a recent article on Calvin's attitude towards God's absolute power, David Steinmetz writes that Calvin "finds it impossible to make those points (about the freedom and transcendence of God's power) by appealing to the theological distinction between the absolute and ordained power of God. Absolute power is for him disordered power, omnipotence divorced from justice."[170] Could the jurists have had a similar distaste for the prince's absolute power? On the basis of what evidence we have—the "constitutionalism" of the jurists and their tenacious adherence to the norms of the *ius commune*—one is tempted to think "perhaps."

---

169. See Pennington, *Pope and Bishops* 34–38.
170. David C. Steinmetz, "Calvin and the Absolute Power of God," *The Journal of Medieval and Renaissance Studies* 18 (1988) 65–79 at 79.

Natural Law and Positive Law

Due Process and the Prince

Actiones omnes sunt a iure civili.
—Accursius to Dig. 1.1.5

By the middle of the fourteenth century, a new doctrine of authority had emerged in the writings of the jurists that penetrated every crack and crevice of the *ius commune*. The jurists struggled to reconcile the old and the new terminology describing the prince's power. In the end, they made a simple barter. For the old norms of custom, feudal obligations, honor, loyalty, reason, and tradition they exchanged cause, necessity, and the public good.

As the jurists defined the authority of the prince with greater precision and subtlety, they discovered that the older norms, even with new names, could not be easily incorporated into the new jurisprudence of power. A prince who was "legibus solutus," whose will was the source of all positive law, whose decrees abrogated any custom, who exercised "plenitudo potestatis" and, occasionally, "potestas absoluta," became a being who was no longer constrained by vague notions of cause, necessity, the public good, natural law, and reason. Nevertheless, the jurists never abandoned their atavistic beliefs in limited princely power: they had no place in their souls for a Leviathan. The new jurisprudence of lordship was haunted by the specter of past traditions, bonds, and customary laws.

Ennio Cortese has brilliantly and exhaustively demonstrated how well the twelfth- and thirteenth-century jurists first defined these norms and how tenaciously they clung to them.[1] For the most part, however,

---

1. *La norma giuridica*. Historians of political thought have ignored Cortese's book and conclusions. They still write about concepts like "legibus solutus" as if the jurists used it to define the absolute and arbitrary authority of the prince.

119

the norms were exhortations, not precise legal concepts, and their enforcement was difficult, if not impossible. A law might be rendered nugatory if promulgated without cause, but how could one define cause? The jurists were not blind to the difficulties. Those who tended to grant great authority to the prince simply concluded that the prince's will and cause were synonymous. In a recent essay, Joseph Canning rightly noted that cause and reason did not offer robust protection from the prince's arbitrary authority.[2]

> Juristic thought could only offer a limited enforceability for higher norms; but the jurists nevertheless considered such norms to have real value even if in practice they were usually unenforceable—a view far removed from any positivist theory rejecting the existence of norms which cannot be enforced.

To be sure, only an extraordinarily doughty lawyer would have pointed out to his prince that his laws were invalid because they were bereft of cause and reason.

The jurists acknowledged other norms that transcended positive law: divine law, natural law, and the law of nations, "ius gentium." Human positive law could not transgress the provisions of these higher laws, although the jurists conceded that higher laws might occasionally be derogated, even if the prince could not abrogate them. For example, the prince could derogate the divine command of "Thou shalt not kill" by mandating a judicial murder. Some historians of political thought have concluded, just as Jean Bodin recognized in the sixteenth century, that "given these limitations, no ruler could be considered truly absolute."[3] A legal positivist of the nineteenth century, for example, would refuse to recognize that any law transcended human positive law. We have seen that the medieval jurists did not measure the prince's "potestas absoluta" by that standard. Rather, they defined "potestas absoluta" as transcending positive law but not as liberating the prince from the shackles of natural and divine law.

The horrors of the twentieth century have sparked a revival of interest in transcendental systems of law. Many modern jurists have argued for the superiority of norms over the positive law of the nation state. Today few jurists would hold, as no jurist of medieval and early modern Europe held, that positive law should reign supreme and un-

---

2. "Law, Sovereignty and Corporation Theory, 1300–1450," *The Cambridge History of Medieval Political Thought, c. 350–c. 1450*, ed. J. H. Burns (Cambridge: 1988); see also *Pope and Bishops* 71–73.

3. Canning, "Law, Sovereignty" 455.

trammeled over all other norms. Modern philosophers of law have concluded that using transitory nineteenth-century concepts of sovereignty as a benchmark of what political authority should be is either teleological at best or wrong at worst. From the point of view of someone writing in the late twentieth century, the inexorable progress of jurisprudence toward an epiphany of the human legislator's will is not a necessary, desirable, inevitable, or historically accurate account of the history of legislative sovereignty in the West.[4]

At this juncture, two points become apparent. A jurist might reject all transcendental norms and still create a prince whose will was shackled by norms of other sorts. A twelfth-century vassal's steadfast belief in the inviolability of individual rights and privileges is a good example of the importance of non-transcendental norms in medieval society. Conversely, a few medieval jurists, like Albericus de Rosate, recognized the transcendental norms of natural and divine law and still offered a theory of government that was impressively absolutistic.

Earlier theorizing about natural law suffered from the same problem as juristic definitions of "cause" and "reason." Jurists of the twelfth and early thirteenth centuries readily granted that natural law transcended positive law, but were, until the middle of the thirteenth century, reluctant to list specific mandates of natural law that infringed upon the authority of the prince. In the following pages, I shall explore the prince's power in the writings of the jurists of the thirteenth and early fourteenth centuries and its relationship to norms of judicial procedure. We shall see that a doctrine of due process evolved in the late thirteenth century establishing absolute norms protecting a litigant's right to a trial. This right even transcended the "potestas absoluta" of the prince. Ironically, while the jurists created and adopted the prince's "potestas absoluta," they simultaneously bound his power absolutely.

4. The revival of interest in natural law after World War II is a confirmation of this statement. The bibliography is enormous. See the work of two Germans who approach the problem from diametrically opposed viewpoints, Josef Funk, *Primat des Naturrechtes: Die Transzendenz des Naturrechtes gegenüber dem positiven Recht* (Mödling bei Wien: 1952), Ernst Bloch, *Natural Law and Human Dignity*, trans. Dennis J. Schmidt (Cambridge and London: 1986). A detailed bibliography contained in *Naturrecht oder Rechtspositivismus?*, ed. Werner Maihofer (Wege der Forschung 116, Darmstadt: 1962) 580–622. For a recent discussion of sovereignty in the modern world, see Hurst Hannum, *Autonomy, Sovereignty, and Self-Determination: The Accommodation of Conflicting Rights* (Philadelphia: 1990), 14–26, who notes that a customary international law (*ius cogens*) has developed in a small number of cases that can be said to limit the sovereignty of states. The *ius cogens* is, of course, like natural law, a theoretical ideal, not a concrete reality. Hannum accepts, however, the principle that *iura cogentes* exist and transcend positive law.

NATURAL LAW AND THE
RIGHTS OF SUBJECTS

The varieties of juristic thought touching the source(s), content, provisions, and sanctions of natural law are complex. As Rudolf Weigand remarked in his magisterial study of natural law in the works of the twelfth- and early thirteenth-century canon and Roman lawyers, "the discussion of natural law has never ceased since ancient times, particularly since Plato and Aristotle."[5] The jurists of the Middle Ages inherited definitions of natural law from Roman law, the Stoics, and the Church fathers. The Roman jurist Ulpian defined natural law as being something akin to animal instinct. "Natural law is what Nature teaches all animals."[6] Justinian's compilers placed this text at the very beginning of the Digest and, consequently, every jurist knew this definition and its implication that rational and nonrational creatures obey the same laws. In his *Republic,* Cicero connected reason and natural law:[7]

> There is in fact a true law, namely right reason, which is in accordance with nature, applies to all men, and is unchangeable and eternal.

Cicero's definition became a commonplace in the ancient world and, in one form or another, found its way into law, theology, and philosophy.

Of course, the medieval lawyers forged the definitions that they found in their sources into a coherent doctrine. Azo gave typical definitions:

> Natural law can be understood in several ways. . . . Natural law is what nature, i.e., God, teaches all animals.[8] . . . Natural law is sometimes called the law established by the common diligence of men, and so the law of nations can be called natural law. . . . Natural law is called that which is contained in the Mosaic law and the New Testament.[9]

5. *Die Naturrechtslehre der Legisten und Dekretisten von Irnerius bis Accursius und von Gratian bis Johannes Teutonicus* (Münchener Theologische Studien, Kanonistische Abteilung 26, München: 1967) 1.

6. Dig. 1.1.1.3: "Ius naturale est quod natura omnia animalia docuit; nam ius istud non humani generis proprium, sed omnium animalium quae in terra quae in mari nascuntur, avium quoque commune est."

7. Book 3, chapter 22. The passage is preserved in Lactantius's Institutes 6.8.

8. Azo, *Summa Institutionum* 1.2 (Lyon: 1557) fol. 269r, Aschaffenburg, Stiftsbibl. Perg. 15, fol. 134v–135r, Bamberg, Staatsbibl. jur. 24, fol. 190r: "Ius autem naturale pluribus modis dicitur. Primus est ut dicatur a natura animati motus, quiddam instinctu nature proueniens quo singula animalia ad aliquid faciendum inducuntur. Vnde dicitur ius naturale est quod natura, idest ipse Deus, docuit omnia animalia." Weigand, *Naturrechtslehre* 52 § 76.

9. Azo, loc. cit.: "Dicitur etiam quandoque ius naturale ius communi (commune Ed.) hominum industria statutum, et ita ius gentium potest dici ius naturale, ut infra de rerum diu. § Singulorum. Item dicitur naturale quod in lege mosiaca uel in euangelio continetur, ut legitur in decretis." Weigand, *Naturrechtslehre* 52–53 § 76.

Some jurists distinguished more clearly than Azo between natural law and the law of nations (ius gentium).[10] Others defined natural law as being closely connected with equity and reason.[11] Azo's assertion that God *is* nature, however, was not as radical as it may seem at first sight. By the early thirteenth century the idea was a commonplace. An alternative formulation that explains the idea in juristic terms was this: "nature is the divine will." In this sense, natural law and nature reflected the will of God.[12] Consequently, natural law, like divine law, emanated from God's will. Although their descriptions of natural law varied, the jurists emphatically agreed on one thing: in the hierarchy of laws natural law is immutable, always takes precedence over positive law, and nullifies positive law when the two come into conflict.[13]

The Latin "ius" has two definitions: law or right. "Ius naturale" can mean natural law, but it can also mean a natural right. In a recent series of articles, Brian Tierney has explored medieval juridical and theological conceptions of natural law and natural rights. As he has persuasively argued, the medieval jurists were the first to develop a theory of individual rights that corresponds to modern ideas of immutable "human rights."[14] Tierney has shown that while the jurists most often used "ius naturale" to mean natural law, they were not oblivious to its other possible meaning, a natural right.[15] The twelfth- and thirteenth-century jurists had a well-developed general conception of rights, but these

10. Weigand, *Naturrechtslehre* 28–30, 33–39, 61–62, 82–83.

11. Ibid. 39, in which he quotes Rogerius's *Quaestiones super Institutis*: "Dicitur quoque ius naturale, id est ius equissimum." Also pp. 23–24, 102, 127, 193–196.

12. Weigand, *Naturrechtslehre* 59–60; Brian Tierney, "'Natura id est Deus': A Case of Juristic Panthesim?" *Journal of the History of Ideas* 24 (1963) 307–322; Ugo Gualazzini, "Natura id est Deus," SG 3 (1955) 413–424; Cortese, *La norma* II 45, 57–58.12.

13. Weigand, *Naturrechtslehre* 114–119; 361–368; 386–394. The Carlyle's account of natural law in ancient and medieval thought can still be read with profit, *History of Medieval Political Theory in the West* (Edinburgh and London: 1962) vol. 1, chapters 1–7 and vol. 2, chapter 3. See also Gaines Post, *Studies in Medieval Legal Thought* 521–551; Charles Lefebvre's chapter on natural law in *Histoire de droit et des institutions de l'Eglise en Occident: L'Age classique 1140–1378, Sources et théorie du droit* (Paris: 1965) 367–384; Janet Coleman, "Property and Poverty," *The Cambridge History of Medieval Political Thought* 607–615.

14. "Tuck on Rights: Some Medieval Problems," *History of Political Thought* 4 (1983) 429–441; "Natural Law and Canon Law in Ockham's *Dialogus*," *Aspects of Late Medieval Government and Society: Essays Presented to J. R. Lander*, ed. J. G. Rowe (Toronto: 1986); "Villey, Ockham and the Origin of Individual Rights," *The Weightier Matters of the Law: Essays on Law and Religion*, ed. John White, Jr. and F. S. Alexander (American Academy of Religion Studies in Religion, 51; Atlanta: 1988) 1–31; "Origins of Natural Rights Language: Texts and Contexts, 1150–1250," *History of Political Thought* 10 (1989) 615–646; "Aristotle and the American Indians—Again: Two Critical Discussions," *Cristianesimo nella storia* 12 (1991) 295–322.

15. Tierney, "Villey, Ockham," 3–10; "Origins of Natural Rights Language" 629–646; and most recently, "*Ius dictum est a iure possidendo*: Law and Rights in *Decretales*, 5.40.12," *Church and Sovereignty: Essays in Honour of Michael Wilks*, ed. D. Wood

rights or norms were not, for the most part, sacrosanct.[16] They could be violated.

From the early twelfth century on, the jurists began to establish a limited number of immutable rights that they averred were established and protected by natural law—a defining moment in the history of juristic discourse on rights. As Tierney has put it:[17]

> If we tried to trace out all the threads that led from the web of medieval rights language to the fully formed natural rights theories of the seventeenth century, we would have to explore many areas of discourse [and] . . . they would include rights of property, rights of consent to government, rights of self-defense, rights of infidels, marriage rights.

Although the jurists did not call these rights natural, they developed doctrines that supported a theory of subjective, immutable, individual rights.

Once the jurists had created immutable rights, their next step led to an inevitable clash between power and rights. For example, could the prince abrogate rights of his subjects emanating from a law over which he had no power or jurisdiction? Ultimately, the jurists concluded that these rights protected subjects from the authority of the prince. By the end of the thirteenth century, they had fashioned a theory of rights for the *ius commune* that was sophisticated and elegant.

The first right that jurists grappled with was the distinction between "meus" and "tuus:" an individual's right to own and protect private property. Roman law stated that a person obtained ownership of jewels found on the seashore and wild animals by natural law.[18] Property was acquired by possessing a *res nullius* (property of no one). The Church fathers, on the other hand, almost universally believed that property was a consequence of sin and greed.[19] If ownership were a consequence of sin, then no one could have an uncontestable right to any property. For the most part, the jurists rejected a doctrine stipulating that property rights evolved from sinful avariciousness but vacillated between accepting property as a right granted by natural law or conceding that at

---

(Studies in Church History, Subsidia 9. Oxford: 1991) 457–466, where he discusses the meaning of "ius" in the writings of the canonists.

16. Ennio Cortese's masterly study, *La norma*, passim, is the most thorough analysis of these ideas in this period.

17. Tierney, "Origins of Natural Rights" 639.

18. Dig. 1.8.3 and Inst. 2.1.12.

19. Wolfgang Stürner, *Peccatum und Potestas: Der Sündenfall und die Entstehung der herrscherlichen Gewalt im mittelalterlichen Staatsdenken* (Sigmaringen: 1987) 61 and passim, whose notes contain an exhaustive bibliography.

one time all goods were held in common. If all goods were once held in common, property rights may have arisen from illegitimate usurpation if not from sin.

By the early thirteenth century, the jurists took another tack. Azo and Accursius both agreed that even if property rights could not be found in natural law, they could be traced to the Ten Commandments. When God forbade stealing, He protected private property. Since divine law took precedence over natural law and since natural law could be thought of as having been promulgated by God, property rights could be logically considered a part of natural law.[20] As we have seen in chapter 1, from very early on the jurists argued that the prince could not take the property rights of his subjects away without cause.

After they had established property's status in natural and divine law, the jurists recognized contracts and pacts as rights.[21] By the early thirteenth century, they understood the issues well enough to discuss the paradox that under certain circumstances civil law abrogated contracts. Normally, a contract was inviolate under rule that "faith ought to be preserved" (fidem servare debet). Azo wrote that "It [to restore property to defrauded minors] is against natural law that protects pacts, as in Dig. 2.14.1.1 [where Ulpian described a pact as natural equity] and in this sense civil law can be called natural."[22] At first, they did not ask if the prince was bound by his contracts with his subjects, even though one might have expected them to ask the question since the inviolability of the feudal contract might have led them to consider the problem.

Guido of Suzzara was one of the first jurists, if not the first, to grap-

20. Weigand, Naturrechtslehre 92–99. Weigand makes the point, that has not always been heeded (p. 99), that we should not confuse legal texts that discuss "natural possession" as meaning that these objects are possessed by natural law.

21. Weigand, Naturrechtslehre 100–106.

22. Azo, Institutes 1.2, (Lyon: 1557), fol. 269v. Aschaffenburg, Stiftsbibl. Perg. 15, fol. 135r, Bamberg, Staatsbibl. jur. 24, fol. 190r: "Est tamen contra [etiam Ed.] ius naturale quod tuetur pacta, ut ff. de pactis l.i., in principio, et in hac significatione ius naturale potest dici ciuile." Cf. Weigand, Naturrechtslehre 54–55, 57, 102–103. Manfred Laufs, Politik und Recht bei Innozenz III.: Kaiserprivilegien, Thronstreitregister und Egerer Goldbulle in der Reichs- und Rekuperationspolitik Papst Innozenz III. (Köln-Wien: 1980) 263–273, attempts to place the dispute between Innocent III and Philip of Hohenstaufen in the context of the jurists' ideas about contracts. See also Elisabeth Vodola, Excommunication in the Middle Ages (Berkeley-Los Angeles-London: 1986) 128–135, who discusses whether excommunicants' contracts were protected or maintained by natural law; Wyduckel, Princeps legibus solutus 82–87. C. Karsten, Die Lehre vom Vertrage bei den italienischen Juristen des Mittelalters: Ein Beitrag zur inneren Geschichte der Reception des römischen Rechts in Deutschland (Rostock: 1882; repr. Amsterdam: 1967) 136–140; 172–173.

ple with the binding power of the feudal contract on the prince. We
have noted the originality of his thought in the last chapter, and here
too he sparked with new ideas. His *Suppletiones* have been preserved
in several different recensions as separate works or as marginal additions to manuscripts of the Code and Digest.[23] Although relatively
unknown to modern historians, Guido was not ignored by his contemporaries and jurists of the next generation.

Guido's views on contracts have been known for some time. In his
commentary on the Code, Cinus of Pistoia mentioned that Guido
had written a question whether the emperor was bound by pacts that
he made with a city or a baron when Guido glossed *Digna vox*.[24]
Most historians have cited Guido's opinion from Cinus's commentary, but Cinus's summary of Guido's thought was quite misleading.
Guido's gloss, written in the 1260s and 1270s,[25] is worth quoting in its
entirety:[26]

> Note that if the emperor makes peace with any city or with any count or
> baron, and enters into any agreements, he is bound to observe them; he can-
> not contravene nor break them. . . . He also cannot break agreements that
> his predecessors made. . . . The maxim, an equal cannot have authority does
> not apply in this case . . . because the emperor does not have an equal as
> long as he lives, and a successor, his own heir, has to preserve the arrange-
> ments of his predecessors.

Guido did not write a formal *quaestio,* and contrary to Cinus his treatment of contract was much broader than just the feudal contract. He
applied his theory to any contract or agreement that the prince might
make.[27] He based his conclusions on a text of the Roman law of inheri-

23. A manuscript of the Digestum vetus in Munich, Clm 6201, contains a much better text of his Suppletiones to that section of the Digest than the Paris manuscripts do.
24. Cinus to Cod. 1.14(17).4 (Digna vox) (Frankfurt: 1578), fol. 25v–26r, Florence,
Bibl. naz. Magliabec. Cl. XXIX.169, fol. 29r, Paris, B.N. lat. 4547, fol. 18v: "Vltimo
sciendum est quod Guido de Suza. formauit hic [at this law] questionem utrum si imperator ineat aliqua pacta cum aliqua ciuitate uel barone, teneatur ea obseruare, tam ipse
quam eius successor."
25. Martino, *Ricerche* 45–49.
26. Guido of Suzzara, Suppletiones to Cod. 1.14(17).4 (Digna vox), Paris, B.N. lat.
4489, fol. 33v: "Infra eodem, Digna, 'alligatum': Nota quod si imperator facit pacem
cum aliqua ciuitate seu cum aliquo comite uel barone, et ineat aliqua pacta, teneretur ea
obseruare, nec potest uenire contra uel ea infringere, ut hic et qui testa. fac. pos. l. Si
quis [Cod. 6.22.6] et de testa. l. Ex imperfecto [Cod. 6.23.3] Item nec pacta facta per
suos antecessores potest infringere, ut infra de rest. milit. l. Que a patre [Cod. 2.51.7] et
de rebus alien. uel non alien. l. Venditrici [Cod. 4.51.3] Nec obstat quod dicitur quod
par in parem non habet imperium, ut ff. de iniur. Nec magistratibus [Dig. 47.10.32] et
ad Trebell. Ille a quo § Tempestiuum [Dig. 36.1.13.4] quod imperator dum uiuit parem
non habet, et successor suus heres habet seruare facta predecessorum ut dictum est. G."
27. Canning, "Law, Sovereignty" 461–462 interprets these ideas as being primarily
feudal; that they were partly feudal cannot be doubted, but the jurists applied this principle to all contracts.

tance in which Ulpian observed that even a consul or praetor who had been instituted as a testamentary heir should submit himself to the law.[28]

Guido took up the issue again when he wrote on the famous text in the Digest *Princeps legibus solutus* (the prince was not bound by the laws).[29] In versions of his *Suppletiones* preserved in Munich and Paris, Guido began by asking a more general question than the one he asked when commenting on *Digna vox*: is the prince bound by the contracts he makes with anyone? Since the prince is not bound by the laws and cannot be summoned to court, how can a subject make a binding contract with him? Further, Guido noted that a text in the *Digest* proclaimed the emperor to be the "Lord of the world." We have seen that the emperor's universal lordship and the property rights of his subjects had been a lively topic of discussion in the law schools. Into this debate Guido introduced the subject of contracts.[30]

The above questions, however, were fodder for Guido's cannons, and he dismantled each systematically. The law of nations sanctioned contracts and was, therefore, immutable. Again turning to the law of inheritance, he noted that the prince could not confiscate a legacy even if the testament were faulty.[31] His closing and most weighty argument, which we discussed in the previous chapter, concerned the prince's submission to the law. The prince may, at first, submit himself to the law voluntarily, but after he has bound himself to the law—in this case, by entering into an agreement—he must by necessity conform to the law.

28. Dig. 36.1.13.4.
29. Dig. 1.3.31(30).
30. Guido of Suzzara, Suppletiones to Dig. 1.3.31(30) (Princeps legibus), Clm 6201, fol. 10v: "Quid si princeps pactum faciat cum aliquo, teneturne seruare ut possit conueniri ex contractu quam iniuit cum aliquo? Et uidetur quod non teneatur seruare, nec possit conueniri, arg. huius legis, quia hic dicitur ipsum esse solutum legibus. Item alibi dicitur ipsum esse dominum mundi, infra ad leg. Ro. de iac. l. Deprecatio [Dig. 14.2.8] Item sicut pactum inter dominum et seruum non ualet, ut C. de transact. l. Interpositas [Cod. 2.4.13] ita hic dicitur in questione premissa." Cortese, *La norma* 1.158–159, printed this text from Paris, B.N. lat. 4489, fol. 4r. The text in both Paris manuscripts is inferior to the Munich (also Paris, B.N. lat. 4488, fol. 321r).
31. Ibid.: "Econtra uidetur quod princeps debeat seruare contractus quos facit cum aliquo, quia contractus iuris gentium sunt, ut supra de iust. et iur. l. Ex his [Dig. 1.1.5] Cui iuri non potuerit derogare princeps, cum tale ius sit immutabile, ut inst. de iure natural. § Set naturalia [Inst. 1.2.11] Item ex imperfecto testamento princeps legatum uel fideicommissum non sumit [MS summit], ut infra de legat. iii. Ex imperfecto [Dig. 32.1.23] Item 'cum ipse princeps uel augusta heredes instituuntur, ius commune cum ceteris habent,' ut C. de hered. inst. l. Cum heredes [Cod. 6.22.7] Item ipse pacta et contractus precepit aliis seruare, ergo quod ei uidetur iustum, in personam aliorum, seruare debet in sua, ut infra de cond. indeb. l. Frater a fratre [Dig. 12.6.38] et infra de pact. l. Cum in eo [Dig. 2.14.44(45)] Item 'non debet nasci iniuriarum occasio, unde ius nascitur,' ut C. unde ui l. Meminerint [Cod. 8.4.6] et hoc esse uerum, scilicet istum arg. ult. allegatum in questione ista."

Guido then compared the prince's submission to the law to an act of arbitration. Litigants may enter into arbitration freely, but once they agree to arbitrate, they cannot withdraw their consent.[32]

Cortese printed two other versions of Guido's gloss to *Digna vox* from two Vatican manuscripts. In the first (Vat. lat. 1428), Guido repeated the above argument rather closely, but put more emphasis on the immutability of natural law. A contract was sanctioned by natural law, and the prince was freed only from positive, not natural, law.[33] Guido's argument has a fatal flaw: as Azo recognized, there were always circumstances under which even natural law could be broken.[34] In his *Suppletiones* (Vat. Ross. lat. 582), Guido used the argument borrowed from the Roman law of inheritance, but did not develop it as fully as he did in the Munich and Paris texts. Perhaps, most important, in neither version did he put forward the argument that the prince was bound to the law after he had voluntarily submitted to it.

One would like to know the chronology of these different versions. Unfortunately, that is impossible to establish. On the basis of these passages, one would be tempted to conclude that Guido wrote the version in Vat. lat. 1428 first and then the text in Vat. Ross. lat. 582. Guido's final thoughts were contained in the texts of the Munich and Paris manuscripts. If Guido's thought did develop in a logically consistent way (by no means a certainty), these texts demonstrate that he returned to this problem with greater understanding each time he treated it.

Cinus of Pistoia incorporated Guido's commentary into his *Lectura*

32. Ibid.: "Item cum ipse se sponte subiaciat legibus ut probatum est in legibus nunc allegatis, quod ergo a principio fuit ei uoluntarium, scilicet se subicere legibus, postquam sic se subiecit necessitatis est. Sicut dicimus in compromisso subeundo quod ab initio est uoluntarium, postea necessitatis est, ut infra de arbit. l.iii. § Tam etsi neminem [Dig. 4.8.3.1] sic in commodato, infra commod. l. In commodato § Sicut [Dig. 13.6.17.3] et in similibus constat, C. de act. et oblig. l. Sicut [Cod. 4.10.5] Quis autem erit iudex in ea questione? Respon. Procurator Cesaris, ut C. ubi cause fis. agi. l. Ad fiscum [Cod. 3.26.5] et C. si aduersus fis. l.ii. [Cod. 2.36(37).2]. G."

33. Cortese, *La norma* 1.156–157: "Item et alia ratione, quia quamquam sit legibus solutus, tamen naturalibus iuribus et etiam gentium et que quasi naturalia dicuntur nunquam solutus est, ut ff. de iustitia et iure, l. Omnes uero homines, etc. [Dig. 1.1.9] ut eadem lege dicitur. Et huiusmodi concessiones siue obligaciones sunt de iure gentium, ut ff. de iustitia et iure, l. Ex hoc iure [Dig. 1.1.5], ergo illis iuribus alligatus est, ut dictum est."

34. Or divine law; see Weigand, *Naturrechtslehre* 168–173. Canning, *Baldus de Ubaldis* 76–79. The locus classicus for a discussion of legislating against divine law was Cod. 1.19(22).7 (Rescripta). Cortese discusses the derogation, never the abrogation, of divine law in the thought of the jurists, *La norma* vol. 1, chapter 3.

on the Codex. He seems to have known only Guido's commentary on *Digna vox* and not those on *Princeps*. Although he concurred with Guido's conclusions, Cinus relied almost exclusively on a contract's origins in natural law to bind the prince to it.[35] Cinus abhorred breaking faith; natural laws dictate that pacts should be honored, even those that princes conclude with enemies. Nothing greater is owed to a man than the honoring of pacts. Therefore, the contract of the prince is law.[36] Although French jurists developed a slightly different theory of contract at the same time, later jurists almost unanimously accepted Guido's paradigm.[37]

The jurists understood that contracts were only a small part of natural law. Natural and divine law established general rules that princes broke with regularity. The complexity of their thought can be illustrated through their discussion of a text in the Code, *Rescripta,* in which the emperors Theodosius and Valentinianus had decreed that all rescripts contravening law were invalid.[38] The early jurists simply stated that no rescript could abrogate divine or natural law. Cortese quoted a text of Johannes Bassianus:[39]

35. Cinus to Cod. 1.14(17).4 (Digna vox), Florence, Bibl. naz. Magliabec. Cl. XXIX.169, fol. 29r, Paris, B.N. lat. 4547, fol. 18v, Frankfurt: 1578, fol. 25v–26r: "Vltimo sciendum est quod Guido de Suza. formauit hic questionem utrum si imperator ineat aliqua pacta cum aliqua ciuitate uel barone, teneatur ea obseruare, tam ipse quam eius successor?"

36. Ibid.: "Videtur quod non, ut l. Princeps, ff. eodem et ff. de leg. iii. l. Si quis in principio, et quia par in parem non habet imperium, ut l. Nam magistratus, ff. de arbit. [Dig. 4.8.4] et l. Ille a quo § Tempestiuum, ff. ad Trebel. [Dig. 36.1.13.4] Pro hac parte facit infra de lib. causa Cum affirmes [Cod. 7.16.8] et infra de transact. l. Interpositas [Cod. 2.4.13] et infra de decur. l. Euacuatis, lib. x. [Cod. 10.32(31).19]. Econtra uidetur quod sic, nam graue est fidem fallere, ut ff. de const. pecu. l.i. [Dig. 13.5.1] et naturalia iura suadent pacta seruari, et fides etiam hostibus est seruanda, ut ff. de leg. i. l.ult. [Dig. 30.1.128] de censi. l.i. [Dig. 50.15.1] Preterea ad hoc facit hec lex, quia honestas ligat etiam principem, ut hic patet per ea que supra dixi et nichil magis debetur homini quam pacta seruare, ut l.i. ff. de pact. [Dig. 2.14.1] Ad hoc facit infra de testa. [Ed. et MSS qui testa. fac. pos.] l. Ex imperfecto [Cod. 6.23.3] et ff. de leg. ii. Ex imperfecto [Dig. 32.1.23] et infra de restit. milit. l. Que a patre [Cod. 2.51.7] Preterea contractus principis est lex, ut infra de donat. inter uir. et uxor. l.ult. [Cod. 5.16.27] Ergo etc. et hanc legem et hanc partem tenet ipse Guido, ad quod optime facit extra probat. c.i. [X 2.19.1]."

37. See Cortese, *La norma* 135 (Jacques de Révigny) and 136 (Pierre de Belleperche); also Karsten, *Lehre vom Vertrage* 136–140. Canning, *Baldus de Ubaldis* 82–86, where Baldus's opinion, which simply follows Cinus's, is discussed.

38. Cod. 1.19(22).7 (Rescripta).

39. Cortese, *La norma* I 110 n. 26, from Vat. Chigi E.VII.218, fol. 82v: "Ita sententio et observo nullum rescriptum que est iuri evangelio contrarium, quod dicimus naturale et divinum, ut si tibi concedat quemvis occidere, nullius erit momenti." Cortese discusses this issue on pp. 97–142. Annalisa Belloni, "Baziano, cioè Giovanni Bassiano, legista e canonista del secolo XII," TRG 57 (1985) 69–85, argues that Bazianus the canonist and Johannes Bassianus were the same person.

> I think and believe that no rescript is of any moment that is contrary to the law of the Gospels, what we call natural and divine law, as if for example it would be granted to you [the right] to kill someone.

The jurists soon realized that this question was complex and not susceptible to simple answers, and upon reflection they discovered that general rules were impossible. One solution was to distinguish among different types of natural law. The prince could abrogate some provisions of natural law with impunity, others, particularly those that contained moral precepts, were less vulnerable to his authority.

In certain cases, the prince could or should derogate natural law. For example, the law of God forbade killing, but society must sometimes sanction killing. Order demanded that the prince preserve the peace. In the late thirteenth century, Johannes Bassianus's naive definition had been stood on its head. Pierre de Belleperche stated what had become a commonplace: the prince could, with sufficient cause, issue a rescript derogating natural law.[40]

The question continued to interest the jurists. Cinus devoted a long commentary on *Rescripta*. He quoted Jacques de Révigny and Pierre de Belleperche that the emperor issued a rescript against natural law either with or without sufficient cause. In the first case, for example, the emperor might decree that all captives taken in war be made slaves because he wished to save them from death. Although the law of nature granted men freedom, the prince could rescind that law for compelling reasons. However, if the prince issued a rescript contrary to natural law without sufficient cause, it would not be valid.[41] Indeed, under certain carefully circumscribed conditions, the emperor can derogate divine law, but he may never abrogate it. Nonetheless, he can interpret divine law. For example, he may specify how many witnesses are necessary for a valid testament even though divine law dictates that two or three witnesses are sufficient. He may not, Cinus noted dryly, issue a rescript permitting me to marry my mother.[42] Moral precepts were impervious to the prince's power.

40. Cortese, *La norma* I 136: "aut illud rescriptum est contra ius naturale vel gentium, et tunc dico quod cum causa sufficienti valet." Commentary to Institutes, 1.2.

41. Cinus to Cod. 1.19(22).7 (Rescripta), Florence, Bibl. naz. XXIX.169, fol. 40v–41v, Frankfurt: 1578, fol. 36r–36v: "In hac questione respon. secundum Iacobum de Rauen. et Petrum quod aut uult imperator contra ius naturale rescribere causa subsistente, aut sine causa. Primo casu, uidelicet uidet imperator quod in bello capti statim occidebantur, ne liberi remanerent, et ideo ut seruarentur statuit, quod capti fierent serui hostium, bene ualet. Et sic causa subsistente rescriptum contra ius naturale bene ualeret. Secundo casu quando causa non subest non posset, sic posset dici in sententia quod causa subsistente lata tollit iura naturalia, ut l. Quod ad statum."

42. Ibid.: "Tertio quero numquid imperator potest rescribere contra iura diuina?

Judicial murder provided another argument for Cinus. The emperor may decree that a man be hanged or killed. Even if the criminal had not committed a crime for which he ought to be killed, one may presume cause and justice in the prince's sentence. In such cases, the prince is above the law and considered to be incorruptible.[43] If the prince acts without cause, he sins. A judge, however, who judges according to a law that was issued without cause does not sin, for the emperor is "Lex animata."[44] Cinus precluded an inferior magistrate's having the sins of the prince visited upon him.

As this brief survey of juristic opinion on the prince's relationship to natural and divine law illustrates, their thought was subtle and complex. They granted the prince some power to contravene natural and divine law but were fully aware that any rule that they might create was susceptible to exceptions. We should also be careful not to give the language of the jurists too much precision. In particular, we should not fall into the fallacy of defining a "natural right" as a "human right," which has become an important element of late-twentieth-century rights discourse. The lawyers approached rights, natural law, and its precepts from a number of different angles and instinctively recoiled from simple solutions to hard problems. They did, however, evolve a precocious theory of rights for defendants whom the prince judged in

---

Videtur quod non, quia imperator est seruus Dei, ut infra de offic. prefect. affr. l.i. [Cod. 1.27(30).1] ergo non potest tollere legem domini sui, arg. ff. de arbit. l. Nam et magistratus [Dig. 4.8.4] et ad Trebell. l. Ille a quo § Tempestiuum [Dig. 36.1.13.4] Sed uidetur contra, saltem cum distinctione, ecce sicut imperator est subiectus Deo, sic et quilibet iudex est subiectus sibi. Sed sententia lata per iudicem, si quidem feratur non expresso errore in sententia ualet, ergo idem in rescripto principis, arg. infra quando prouoc. non est l.i. [Cod. 7.64.1] In ista questione distinguendum est aut imperator scribit ad interpretationem legis diuine, et sic ei derogando, et tunc potest, sicut pater in testamentis ubi requiritur maior numerus testium, licet lex diuina dicat quod in ore duorum uel trium stat omne uerbum. Ibi distinguit lex principis inter testamentum et alia negocia. Aut uult scribere contra legem diuinam abrogando eam, et tunc refert aut rescribit super his que non possunt procedere causa subsistente, aut rescribit quod ego contraham cum matre mea. Istud non ualet, ut infra de nupt. Celebrandis [Cod. 5.4.19]."

43. Ibid.: "aut rescribit contra legem diuinam, in eo quod potest causa subsistente procedere, ut rescribit talem suspendendum, occidendum, uel similia, tunc quantum ad obseruandum tenet, quia siue sit uerum siue falsum, quod commiserit illud per quod debeat occidi, tamen presumendum est quod causa subsit et sententia sua presumitur semper iusta. Vnde ab eo non appellatur, et princeps est supra legem, adeo secundum conscientiam suam iudicare potest, quia semper presumitur incorruptibilis."

44. Ibid.: "Et est presumptio pro eo quod facit quod iuste facit, ita quod non admittitur probatio in contrarium, secundum Jaco. de Rauen. Verumtamen, si uerum est, non subesse causam, negari non potest quod princeps peccat. Tamen iudex qui iudicat secundum eius mandatum non peccat, cum ipse sit lex animata in terris, ut in authen. de consulibus [Authen. 4.3(Nov. 105)] Et iudex secundum legem iudicare habet, a simili, si iudex iudicat secundum legem iniquam et consuetudinem iniquam non peccat, quia iudex subest legi, cui necesse habet obedire."

his court. In the middle of the thirteenth century, the jurists began to argue that the prince must grant certain procedural rights to all defendants whether he acted with cause or not. We shall now turn to that development.

NATURAL LAW AND THE JUDICIAL PROCESS

The evolution of judicial procedure in the eleventh and twelfth centuries can be described as the replacement of irrational methods of proof by rational procedures. As with every sweeping generalization, one may object to each term. The ordeal was not as irrational as it appears at first glance, and the judicial process that replaced it was not completely rational. Further, the ordeal never dominated judicial procedure completely throughout Europe in the early Middle Ages. Written and oral evidence never disappeared entirely from the courts as a means of deciding disputes, and we must not characterize the procedure of the entire period as primitive and backward.[45]

The older, unilateral ordeals (primarily oaths, hot and cold water, and hot iron) were means of rendering judicial decisions in the early Middle Ages. Whether they were rational or not, they extricated justice from the more dangerous private forum of feuds and transferred justice to a public forum in which litigants received a definitive judgment. The decision became a part of folk memory, and victors could defend their rights against future claims. Ordeals have been called "irrational" because they did not depend on oral or written evidence or on a body of theoretical rules and principles, but on God's intervention into human affairs. Judges did not pass sentence; they simple read God's will as revealed through the ritual of the ordeal. In Italy these judgments were called "Paribiles," that is, "open and manifest judgments." Historians have called the belief that God's hand could intervene regularly in human affairs as immanent justice.

We have become more sensitive to the rationality of the ordeal. It followed generally understood rules, involved the community in each decision, and provided an opportunity to the litigants, under the surveillance of their neighbors, to reach a compromise.[46]

45. The concluding essay in *The Settlement of Disputes in Early Medieval Europe*, ed. Wendy Davies and Paul Fouracre (Cambridge: 1986) 207–240, is a powerful argument against simplistic views of early medieval procedure.

46. Stephen D. White, *"Pactum . . . legem vincit amor judicium*: The Settlement of Disputes by Compromise in Eleventh-Century Western France," *The American Journal of Legal History* 22 (1978) 281–295.

During the twelfth and thirteenth centuries, the ordeal disappeared in many parts of Western Europe and was replaced with a system of judicial procedure that rested primarily on oral and written evidence. This change marks an important point in the transformation of Western European society. Reason, not the supernatural, now was the primary determinate in the resolution of conflicts. Although it is a mistake to view this development as purely a triumph of reason over superstition—the new contained its share of the irrational, the most striking being torture and the retention of oath-taking, (compurgation)—this change established norms that still rule modern judicial procedure.[47]

Within the past fifteen years, Peter Brown, Rebecca Coleman, Paul Hyams, Charles Radding, and Robert Bartlett have tried to understand why the ordeal gave way to a quite different form of judicial proof in the twelfth and thirteenth centuries.[48] The question is of fundamental importance for evaluating the rise of the law schools and the legal profession in Italy and elsewhere. The older explanatory model viewed the ordeal as irrational, assumed that society in the eleventh and twelfth centuries became more sophisticated (merchants, craftsmen, bankers, and their ilk were unlikely to appreciate a dunking in a cold pond or the sweet smell of burnt flesh), and noted that the study of Roman and canon law created a new class in society, lawyers. Finally, during the twelfth century the clergy, in particular, began to realize that the ordeal

47. The best synthesis of these developments is still R. C. van Caenegem, "La preuve dans le droit du moyen âge occidental: Rapport de synthèse." *La preuve: Moyen Age et temps modernes* (Recueils de la Société Jean Bodin 17.2; Brussels: 1965) 691–753. His essay has been translated and provided with additional bibliography by J. R. Sweeney and D. A. Flanary in *Mededelingen van de Koninklijke Academie voor Wetenschappen, Letteren en Schone Kunsten van België* 45 (Brussels: 1983) 85–127, under the title "Methods of Proof in Western Medieval Law." See also my short summary, "Law, Procedure of, 1000–1500," DMA 7 (New York: 1986) 502–506.
48. Peter Brown, "Society and the Supernatural: A Medieval Change," *Daedalus* 104 (1975) 133–151; Rebecca Coleman, "Reason and Unreason in Early Medieval Law," *Journal of Interdisciplinary History* 4 (1974) 571–591; Paul Hyams, "Trial by Ordeal: The Key to Proof in the Early Common Law," *On the Laws and Customs of England: Essays in Honor of Samuel E. Thorne*, ed. M. S. Arnold et al. (Chapel Hill: 1981) 90–126 and "Henry II and Ganelon," *The Syracuse Scholar* 4 (1983) 23–35; Charles Radding, "Superstition to Science: Nature, Fortune and the Passing of the Medieval Ordeal," *The American Historical Review* 84 (1979) 945–969; Robert Bartlett, *Trial by Fire and Water: The Medieval Judicial Ordeal* (Oxford: 1986). See also H. Nottarp, *Gottesurteilstudien* (Munich: 1956); Dominique Barthélemy, "Présence de l'aveu dans le déroulement des ordalies (IXème-XIVème) siècles," *L'Aveu: Antiquité et moyen âge: Actes de la table ronde organisée par l'Ecole française de Rome* (Rome: 1986) 315–340 and "Diversité des ordalies médiévales," *Revue historique* 280 (1988) 3–25. N. Grippari, "Le jugement de Dieu ou la mise en jeu du pouvoir," *Revue historique* 278 (1987) 281–291; William Ian Miller, "Ordeal in Iceland," *Scandinavian Studies* 60 (1988) 189–218; Colin Morris, "*Judicium Dei*: The Social and Political Significance of the Ordeal in the Eleventh Century," *Studies in Church History* 12 (1975) 95–112.

was fundamentally flawed. Consequently, in 1215 Pope Innocent III promulgated a canon at the Fourth Lateran Council prohibiting them from participating in the procedure. The ordeal, already dying, quickly passed away (with only the odd lingering recrudescence here or there).

The paradoxes underlying newer explanatory models have demanded resolution, and historians have attempted to supply answers to difficult questions. If, as many historians have argued, the ordeal was rational, why then was one rational system substituted for another? Using a model of a child's mental development borrowed from Jean Piaget, Radding has maintained that the collective mentality of Europeans matured during the eleventh century. Their perception of what was rational changed. They no longer believed in immanent justice meted out fairly from above by God; therefore, they abandoned the ordeal.[49]

Bartlett does not accept Radding's argument that ideas about the efficacy of immanent justice changed.[50] He does believe that the ordeal was so rational that it sailed smartly forward under full sail until floundering on the rocks of Fourth Lateran. Since it was used rationally, Bartlett conjectures that it would not have been imposed indiscriminately on litigants. Therefore, he argues that the ordeal was mandated in only a few, limited cases, particularly those for which other, written or oral, proofs were lacking. However, the clergy was unhappy with the ordeal, canon and Roman law did not accept it, and, in a triumph of ideas over customary usage, the Church decided to abolish it in the early thirteenth century. His lapidary conclusion:[51] "[the clergy] did not abandon it because it was irrational, it became irrational because they abandoned it."

A weakness of both Radding and Bartlett's work is that they ignore procedural developments in the ecclesiastical and secular courts of the eleventh and twelfth centuries, the substantial literature treating judicial procedure (written between ca. 1075 and 1215),[52] and the rise of

49. Radding has expanded the scope of his argument in A World Made by Men: Cognition and Society, 400–1200 (Chapel Hill and London: 1985). Very few, if any, historians accept Radding's thesis; see John Contreni's review in Speculum 63 (1988) 709–714. Almost all the essays in Settlement of Disputes offer evidence that refutes Radding's thesis (see especially remarks in conclusion, pp. 222–223).

50. Trial by Fire and Water, pp. 161–163 is a particularly convincing refutation of Radding's thesis that the group psychology of medieval men was altered in the twelfth century. See my review of Bartlett's book in The Journal of Ecclesiastical History 39 (1988) 263–266. Much of what I argue in that review applies equally well to Radding's article.

51. Trial by Fire and Water 86.

52. The work of Knut Wolfgang Nörr is particularly important. His chapter in Handbuch, ed. Coing, "Die Literatur zum gemeinen Zivilprozeß," with its rich bibliography, is a survey of the problem.

trained jurists in Italian cities during the late eleventh and twelfth centuries.[53] A rich literature developed in the late eleventh and twelfth centuries that described a procedure not based on fire and water, but on evidence and arguments.[54] These tracts were not written as academic exercises, but for practical purposes. Although the first examples are from Italy and Southern France, by the second half of the twelfth century they appeared all over Europe.

As Fowler-Magerl has noted, the jurists of the Middle Ages approached the judicial process differently than the Roman jurists.[55] This difference is not because they understood the world differently, but because they valued different elements of procedure and placed much weight on the rights of the litigants during a trial. Consequently, she contends that any understanding of procedure during this period must begin with an analysis of the twelfth-century *ordines iudiciarii*.

Brown and Hyams see the ordeal as a rational procedure in small communities, but as these communities became more populous in the twelfth century, however, the ordeal was no longer suitable for its new environment. Hyams believes, rightly I think, that laymen (most of his evidence comes from England) were largely unhappy with the ordeal as a procedure long before the Lateran Council. He would argue that laymen voted against the ordeal with their feet.

The history of how the Romano-canonical process—the technical term for this procedure was *ordo iudiciarius*—became the model for the courts of continental legal systems remains to be written. That its roots predate the Fourth Lateran Council is certain. From at least 1150 on, when the evidence becomes plentiful, Church courts all over Europe no longer used the ordeal to decide ecclesiastical cases. This fact is attested by the vast number of papal decretals that describe implicitly and sometimes explicitly the procedures of the *ordo iudiciarius*.

The centralization of papal legislative and judicial power in the eleventh century had introduced far-reaching changes in how ecclesiastical justice functioned. Not only were the rules of procedure transformed, but litigants began to appeal their cases to Rome. The *Dictatus papae* of Pope Gregory VII reflects this development. *Dictatus* 20 stipulated that "no one shall dare to condemn one who appeals to the apos-

53. See above all Johannes Fried, *Die Entstehung des Juristenstandes im 12. Jahrhundert: Zur sozialen Stellung und politischen Bedeutung gelehrter Juristen in Bologna und Modena* (Forschungen zur neueren Privatrechtsgeschichte 21; Köln-Wien: 1974).
54. The work of Linda Fowler-Magerl is of fundamental importance; *Repertorien zur Frühzeit der gelehrten Rechte: Ordo iudiciorum vel ordo iudiciarius* (Ius commune, Sonderhefte 19; Frankfurt am Main: 1984).
55. Fowler-Magerl, *Ordo iudiciarius* 2.

tolic chair." Appeal from the decision of an ordeal—the judgment of God—was impossible. The inexorable logic of the pope's dictum demanded that the old systems of proof not be used. As the papal court became the court of last resort, ecclesiastical procedure had to adapt to a system of proof that was based on written and oral evidence. Papal letters of the twelfth century pullulate with references to witnesses and their testimony.

Sometime before 1141, Bulgarus, the famous doctor of Roman law, wrote a short procedural tract for Haimeric, the papal chancellor.[56] This is certain evidence that the papal court had abandoned or was abandoning the ordeal completely. Contemporaries concluded that the revival of Roman law made the ordeal unpalatable to the Church. In the 1180s, Ralph Niger, the English theologian, applauded the Roman church's adoption of the procedural rules of Roman law and condemned the effluvium of Lombard, French, German and English law.[57]

The tension between the procedure of the *ordo iudiciarius* and the justice of the secular courts has left its mark in twelfth-century papal letters. Although the term *ordo iudiciarius* dates back to the early Middle Ages,[58] from about the middle of the twelfth century it was used to describe the procedure of the Romano-canonical process in ecclesiastical letters.[59] Litigants and institutions obtained letters from the papacy guaranteeing that their cases would be heard according to the rules of the *ordo iudiciarius*, a clear indication that they wished to protect themselves from other forms of proof, mostly likely the ordeal or other forms

56. Fowler-Magerl, *Ordo iudiciarius* 35–40.
57. Ludwig Schmugge, "*Codicis Iustiniani et Institutionum baiulus*: Eine neue Quelle zu Magister Pepo von Bologna," *Ius commune* 6 (1977) 4: "monomachia et iudicium aque et iudicium ferri et similia non approbat curia Romana." A little later, Ralph notes (p. 5): "De fece igitur legis Lombarde et similium pravarum constitutionum Alemanie et Anglie et Francie et aliorum regnorum, que non reguntur romano iure . . . " He particularly objected to the monetary fines levied by Germanic legal systems for criminal and civil offenses. See also Paolo Colliva, "Pepo legis doctor," *Atti e memorie della Deputazione di storia patria per le provincie di Romagna* 29–30 (1978–1979) 153–162, for a discussion of this point and Carlo Dolcini, *Velut aurora surgente: Pepo, il vescovo Pietro e l'origine dello studium bolognese* (Istituto Storico Italiano per il Medio Evo, Studi storici, 180; Roma: 1987) 35–37.
58. Fowler-Magerl, *Ordo iudiciarius* 10–11.
59. E.g., *Papsturkunden in Frankreich, 7: Nördliche Ile-de-France und Vermandois,* ed. Dietrich Lohrmann (Abhandlungen der Akademie der Wissenschaften in Göttingen, Phil.-Historische Klasse, 95; Göttingen: 1976) no. 162 (1173–1174), no. 237 (1165–1181), no. 322a (1192); Pope Innocent II ordered the abbot of St. Augustine's in Canterbury to expel disobedient monks by using the "ordo iudiciarius," *Papsturkunden in England, 1: Bibliotheken und Archive in London,* ed. Walter Holtzmann (Abhandlungen der Akademie der Wissenschaften in Göttingen, phil.-historische Klasse 25; Berlin: 1931), no. 23 (1141), p. 248.

of secular, customary justice.[60] No letter states explicitly what the other, alternative procedures might have been, but hints abound. All the letters in which litigants ask for or the papacy instructs that the *ordo* be used are from Northern Europe. I have not yet found any letters from Southern Europe in which a petitioner asks that the *ordo* be used. This indirect evidence may indicate that secular procedure in Italy, Southern France, and Spain was already patterned after the *ordo* by the mid-twelfth century.

The impetus to establish the *ordo* as normative probably protected the interests of the judges as well as the litigants. Using language that resonated with Justinian's metaphors, Alexander III wrote to the papal legate Henry, cardinal-deacon of Sts. Nereus and Achilleus, that a dispute settled with the *ordo* should not be called into doubt. "Rather a judgment rendered through the *ordo* should receive the authority of our confirmation."[61]

Papal letters are cryptic, difficult to interpret, and do not yield their secrets easily. When Alexander wrote to Master Vacarius, the distinguished Italian jurist,[62] and the Abbot of Vaudey in 1179 that they should investigate the circumstances under which a certain S. despoiled a cleric of a church "without the *ordo iudiciarius*," we may suspect that S. did not forcibly take possession of the church but dispossessed O. by some other means. Papal letters often make a clear distinction between armed, unlawful occupation of disputed property and what seems to be a disagreement about what procedure should be followed. If the cleric had been violently dispossessed, Alexander would have explicitly noted that crucial fact.[63] This suspicion is reinforced later in the dispository section of the letter when the pope orders the judges-

60. See the examples published by Charles Duggan and Stanley Chodorow in *Decretales ineditae saeculi XII, from the Papers of Walther Holtzmann* (MIC, Series B, 4; Città del Vaticano: 1982) 137: "nec eum super eadem molestari sine ordine iudiciario permittatis." Other examples in letters 17 (p. 31), 35 (p. 58), 46 (p. 81), 65 (p. 112). See also the texts in *Papsturkunden in England*, ed. Holtzmann, I, no. 132 (1174–1176), pp. 401–402, no. 146 (1177), pp. 417–419.

61. *Papsturkunden in Frankreich*, 2: *Normandie*, ed. Johannes Ramackers (Abhandlungen der Gesellschaft der Wissenschaften zu Göttingen, philologish-historische Klasse³ 21; Göttingen: 1937), no. 107, pp. 196–197: "Nulla igitur ratione permittimus que sub examine . . . legitime terminata noscuntur, iterum in uestram iniuriam contra iuris rationem reuocari in dubium. Quin potius ordine iudiciario promulgata sententia confirmationis robur meretur accipere."

62. Leonard E. Boyle, "Vacarius," DMA 12 (1989) 343–344.

63. See Chodorow and Duggan, *Decretales ineditae* 40, 51, 54, 59, 165 for a few examples. When a cleric has been dispossessed violently, that fact is normally clearly stated with the words (or similar formulations): "manus uiolentas inicere" or "uiolentia eis illata de eadem fuerunt ecclesia spoliati."

delegate to restore O. to his church and to prevent him from being vexed "against the form of the law." [64]

If one judges from extant letters, the pontificate of Alexander III seems to have been critical for this development. For example, Alexander wrote to the bishops of Glasgow and Whithorn that they should hear all cases that laymen under their jurisdiction or others might bring against the property and possessions of the abbey of Holcultram. They should judge these matters according to [the rules of] the *ordo iudiciarius* and should not permit any disputes to be heard in secular forums or in secular courts.[65] Alexander instructed Bishop Henry of Bayeux in a letter to stop laymen from summoning clerics to lay courts. Laymen must bring their suits to the episcopal court and submit, if they wish, to the *ordo iudiciarius*.[66] Alexander also ordered that the archbishops, bishops, and archdeacons who exercised jurisdiction over the houses of Sempringham should not permit laymen to trouble the monks "outside the 'ordo iuris.'"[67]

This evidence is not conclusive. The pope is enforcing two principles in these cases. The first principle traced its origins to the reform movement of the eleventh century: all matters touching ecclesiastical matters should be heard in Church courts; the second was new and evolved

64. *Papsturkunden in England*, ed. Holtzmann, I, no. 169, pp. 440–441: "idem S. contra prestitum iuramentum ueniens predictum O. predicta ecclesia absque ordine iudiciario spoliauit . . . nostra freti auctoritate nullius contradictione uel appellatione obstante restituatis nec ipsum contra formam iuris a quoquam grauari exinde permittatis." The exact meaning of "contra formam iuris" or "contra ordinem iuris" depends on the context of the case. The situation is never explained. For other examples in letters of this period see *Papsturkunden in England: II: Die kirchlichen Archive und Bibliotheken* (Abhandlungen der Akademie der Wissenschaften in Göttingen, philologisch-historische Klasse³ 14; Berlin: 1935), no. 176 (1166–1179), pp. 367–368, no. 236 and 237 (1186), pp. 429–431.

65. *Scotia pontificia: Papal Letters to Scotland before the Pontificate of Innocent III* (Oxford: 1982) no. 98, p. 94–95: "Verum si qui adversus illos super hiis agere forte voluerint, sub examine vestro secum exinde iudiciario ordine experiantur, nec eos super aliquibus possessionibus suis sibi aut monasterio suo pia dèvotione collatis extra curiam ecclesiasticam ad seculare forum aliqua ratione trahi permittatis aut eius iudicium quoquo modo subire." The date of this letter is 1175–1181 and also printed in *Papsturkunden in England: III: Oxford, Cambridge, kleinere Bibliotheken und Archive und Nachträge aus London*, ed. Walther Holtzmann (Abhandlungen der Akademie der Wissenschaften in Göttingen, philologisch-historische Klasse³ 33; Berlin: 1952), no. 316 (1175–1181), p. 432.

66. *Papsturkunden in Frankreich, 2: Normandie*, ed. Johannes Ramackers, no. 143, pp. 240–241: "ne uiros ecclesiasticos ad secularia iudicia trahant neque causas ecclesiasticas tractare uel episcopalia iura exinde percipere presumant. Sed si quid habent aduersus uiros ecclesiasticos, cum eis in curia tua uel illius ecclesiastice persone, ad quam causa ipsa spectauerit, si uoluerint, ordine iudiciario experiantur."

67. *Papsturkunden in England*, ed. Holtzmann, I, no. 185 (1159–1181), p. 455: "ne canonicos aut moniales . . . a quolibet contra iuris ordinem fatigari."

out of the revival of jurisprudence during the twelfth century: the *ordo iudiciarius* should be the procedural process used to settle ecclesiastical disputes.

One cannot always discover what facts are concealed beneath the formulas of a papal mandate, but when Alexander prohibited the abbot and monks of Clairmarais from disturbing the rights of another monastery "against the 'ordo iuris'" because their actions would injure their religious vocation, we may, perhaps, presume that the abbot was using customary secular law to claim his rights.[68] This interpretation of the letter is reinforced by Alexander's conclusion that if the monks wished to litigate, they should do so before an elected judge and according to the *ordo iudiciarius*.[69] For a short time in the late twelfth century, monasteries sometimes included a clause in their papal privileges stipulating that their court cases must be judged according to the *ordo*.[70]

A papal letter is occasionally explicit enough to allow a brief glimpse of the struggle between the rules of the new *ordo* and the customary law of proof and contract. Two letters of Alexander III illuminate the situation in England sometime in the late 1160s. In the first, Alexander mandated that Roger, the archbishop of York, and Hugo, the bishop of Durham, should not permit laymen in their dioceses to obtain possession of the lands of the abbey of Rievaulx (Helmsley, Yorkshire) through the secular courts. Their parishioners were accustomed to occupy the abbey's lands "by whatever means" and then to vindicating their right to the property by means of "a certain customary contract that they call gage" in a secular court. Consequently, the abbot and the monks frequently were unjustly despoiled of their property without the benefit of the *ordo iudiciarius*.[71] In a second letter to the same

68. *Papsturkunden in Frankreich*, 3: *Artois*, ed. Johannes Ramackers (Abhandlungen der Gesellschaft der Wissenschaften zu Göttingen, 23; Göttingen: 1940), no. 63 (1173), p. 123: "quatinus iura et possessiones . . . eis in pace et quiete dimittatis nec . . . per uos aut per alios indebite molestare aut quolibet modo uexare contra iuris ordinem presumatis. Si enim eos exinde minus rationabiliter grauare presumpseritis, religionem uestram plurimum dedeceret."

69. Ibid.: "Ceterum si aduersus iamdictos abbatem et fratres de iustitia uestra confidentes agere uolueritis, coram iudice ab utraque parte communiter electo ordine iudiciario experiamini."

70. *Papsturkunden in England*, ed. Holtzmann, I, no. 135 (1174–1176), pp. 404–405 (Papal privilege for the abbey of Stone).

71. *Papsturkunden in England*, ed. Holtzmann, I, no. 105, p. 370 (1167–1169): "Ad aures nostras peruenisse noscatis, quod cum aliqui parrochiani uestri sibi quamlibet possessionem abbatis et fratrum de Rieualle uendicare uoluerint, eam quoquo modo occupare consueuerunt et deinde, postquam ipsam qualitercumque intrauerint, se ius suum sicut mos est seculari curia euicturos sub cuiusdam consuetudinis obligatione quam guagium uocant soliti sunt offerre, unde frequenter contingit, quod iamdicti abbas et fratres suis possessionibus iniuste et absque ordine iudiciario spoliantur."

recipients Alexander issued a general mandate that all cases involving the abbey's possessions should be heard in their courts according to the *ordo iudiciarius*.[72] The formula of prohibition in the dispository section of the letter is exactly the same as that of the abbey of Holcultram, but in this case we are informed, if only sketchily, about the background of the complaint. If we knew more about English procedure and law of gage at this time, we could better understand the situation at Rievaulx.[73] We would like to know how the monks were despoiled of their right and what procedural devices were used. But whatever the case, clerics found their own system of justice a more equitable system than that offered by secular law.

This evidence would seem to indicate that the increasingly frequent use of the technical term *ordo iudiciarius* in papal letters undoubtedly forbids not only violent dispossession but also dispossession by procedures other than the Romano-canonical process.[74] In the mid-twelfth century, ecclesiastical litigants sought justice in secular courts, but royal justice could be capricious and serendipitous. Van Caenegem has drawn attention to a property case between the Abbey of Abingdon and a certain Turstin whose course and conclusion illustrates secular justice of the time to be "arbitrary, even irresponsible."[75]

Two English cases from the 1170s illustrate the clash between the rough and ready tactics of secular litigants and the reliance, indeed dependence, of ecclesiastical corporations on the' *ordo iudiciarius*. The canons of Frideswide and Oseney took a dispute to the papal curia over the church of St. Mary Magdalen in Oxford. Pope Eugenius III gave judgment for the canons of Oseney "according to the *ordo iudiciarius*."[76] A certain Hugh violently dispossessed the canons, and the case

---

72. Ibid. no. 107, p. 371.

73. On gage see Frederick Pollock and Frederic Maitland, *The History of English Law before the Time of Edward I,* ed. S. F. C. Milsom (2 vols. Cambridge: 1968) II 117–124.

74. The language used in papal letters to forbid non-judicial or violent dispossession is quite different. A typical formula is: "Nulli ergo hominum liceat predictum locum temere perturbare aut eius possessiones auferre vel ablatas retinere, minuere seu quibuscumque vexationibus fatigare." Printed by O. Hageneder and A. Haidacher, *Die Register Innocenz' III., 1: 1. Pontifikatsjahr: Texte* (Graz-Köln: 1964) xlix. This formula had been used in papal privileges much earlier: e.g., *Papsturkunden in England,* ed. Holtzmann, no. 10 (1120), p. 232; *Papsturkunden in Frankreich,* ed. Lohrmann, no. 62 (1147), pp. 320–321. Very often the entire clause is abbreviated to "'Decernimus ergo,'" etc.," e.g., Ibid. nos. 61, 63, 64, 67.

75. Raoul C. Van Caenegem, *The Birth of English Common Law* (Cambridge: 1973) 35–36.

76. *Papsturkunden in England,* ed. Holtzmann, III, no. 213 (1174), pp. 346–348: "... tandem fuit ordine iudiciario terminata et sentencia scripti apostolici munimine

was reopened under Bishop Bartholomaeus of Exeter and the dean of Chichester, John. One of the canons from the Frideswide appealed the case to Rome. Bartholomaeus and John decided on the basis of the evidence that the appeal was frivolous. They ordered the archdeacon of Oxford to put the canons of Oseney back in possession of the church. Not daunted, the canons of Frideswide arrived at the church with armed men and seized it. Alexander delegated the case to bishops Gilbert of London and Roger of Worcester with the remark that he wished to rectify "all things that are against the order of the law." [77] The entire proceedings had taken place according to the rules of the *ordo,* but the admonitions of the decretal to adhere to the "order of the law" are clearly directed at the canons of Frideswide's violent dispossession of the canons of Oseney.

The circumstances surrounding another dispute between the monks from the monastery of Fountains and the archbishop of York are not as clear. After having received a papal mandate containing instructions from Alexander, Archbishop Roger of York heard testimony from the monks of the abbey of Fountains that their abbot had given the archbishop a grange at Wartsale without their consent. [78] In spite of their pleas, the archbishop refused to return the grange to them. In a second mandate, Alexander delegated the case to the bishop of Chester, the abbot of Ford, and the dean of Chichester. [79] They were to hear the evidence, and if the facts were as Alexander understood them they should restore the grange to the monks and abbot. Afterward, if the archbishop wished to contest his right to the grange, the judges-delegate should decide the case according to the rules of the *ordo iudiciarius.*

The explanation that Alexander gave to explain the abbot's reasons for "committing" the grange to the archbishop was rather odd in his first mandate. The monks had possession of the grange before the archbishop had received his episcopal office and held it in peace. The abbot granted the grange to the archbishop hoping that he would be inclined to mercy if the abbot quickly satisfied him. [80] The archbishop, however,

---

roborata." See Christopher Cheney, *From Becket to Langton: English Church Government 1170–1213* (Manchester: 1956) 114.

77. Ibid.: "Sepedictis uero fratribus uolentes omnia que contra iuris ordinem sunt ad religionis statum reuocare et suam iustitiam conseruare . . ."

78. Ibid. no. 194 (1173), p. 330–331.

79. Ibid. no. 208 (1173), p. 341–342.

80. Ibid. no. 194, p. 331: "quod de quadam grangia, quam temporibus antecessorum T. H. et W. ex concessione ipsorum ut dicitur in pace tenuerant, calumpniam eis infligens, abbas bonis uerbis tuis et promissionibus delinitus eandem grangiam sine consilio et

did not temper his justice with mercy and closed his ears to the monks' importuning. The monks hoped for an egg; the archbishop gave them a scorpion.[81]

If we see this dispute as a confrontation between an imperious bishop and a weak-kneed abbot, the facts do not quite make sense. The relationships between the three parties—archbishop, abbot, and monks—cannot be reconstructed, but the archbishop must have given the abbot alternatives in the first hearing that forced the abbot to hope for mercy rather than justice. The alternatives might have been to undergo a wager according to the rules of English land law or lose the grange.[82] Alexander's mandates become understandable from this perspective. He instructed the archbishop and the judges-delegate that the grange must be returned to the monks and abbot if they had had possession of it and if the abbot had committed it to the archbishop without the monks' consent. If the archbishop wished to contest his right to the grange, the case would be heard according to the rules of the *ordo iudiciarius* and before judges-delegate.

In contrast to the obscurity surrounding the events at Archbishop Roger's court, the implications of Alexander's mandates are straightforward. The *ordo iudiciarius* was the instrument and the norm by which disputes within the ecclesiastical hierarchy must be settled. As Alexander thundered in another letter, "we decree that no one shall dare to excommunicate, place under interdict, or suspend churches or clerics without the *ordo iudiciarius,* unless the crime is notorious."[83]

Realizing the importance of the procedure and undoubtedly understanding lay and some clerical objections to it, twelfth-century jurists built imposing theoretical foundations for the *ordo iudiciarius* and justified it as a norm of judicial procedure by ingeniously tracing its origins to Adam and Eve in paradise, or to the Old Testament. The first topic that Paucapalea (ca. 1150) treated in the Prologue of his *Summa* on the Decretum was the origins of the ecclesiastical procedure. He noted that

---

uoluntate fratrum suorum misericordie tue commisit tanto te facilius sperans ad misericordiam inclinandum, quanto uoluntati tue citius satisfecit."

81. Luke 11.12.

82. Stephen D. White, "Proposing the Ordeal and Avoiding It: Strategy and Power in Western French Litigation, 1050 to 1110," unpublished paper forthcoming in *Power and Society in the Twelfth Century,* has written an intriguing study on the use of the ordeal as a weapon to impose settlements on litigants. The archbishop may have offered the ordeal or some other wager to the monks who decided that it was an unpleasant and unwanted alternative. Consequently, they put their hope in the archbishop's mercy.

83. Ibid., no. 261 (1179), p. 392.

the *ordo iudiciarius* originated in paradise when Adam pleaded innocent to the Lord's accusation. He complained to God that: "My wife, whom You gave to me, gave [the apple] to me, and I ate it." Paucapalea's point is subtle but would not be lost on later jurists: even though God is omniscient, he too must summon defendants and hear their pleas. Paucapalea added another piece of evidence that the *ordo* had a biblical justification. When Moses decreed that the truth could be found in the testimony of two or three witnesses, he articulated a basic rule of evidence in the *ordo* and confirmed the procedure's antiquity.[84]

Stephen of Tournai (ca. 1165) analyzed the story of Adam and Eve and dissected it. He pointed out that Adam raised, as it were, a formal objection (exceptio), to the Lord God's complaint (actio) and shifted the blame on his wife or the serpent.[85] "Exceptio" and "actio" were technical terms that were essential parts of the *ordo iudiciarius*.[86] Stephen was the first canonist to define the *ordo*.[87]

> The defendant shall be summoned before his own judge and be legitimately called by three edicts or one peremptory edict. He must be permitted to have legitimate delays. The accusation must be formally presented in writing. Legitimate witnesses must be produced. A decision may be rendered only after someone has been convicted or confessed. The decision must be in writing.

84. Paucapalea, Prologue to Summa, ed. Johann F. von Schulte (Giessen: 1890, repr. Aalen: 1965) 1: "Quoniam in omnibus rebus animadvertitur, id esse perfectum, quod his omnibus ex partibus constat, exordium vero cuiusque rei potentissima pars est, ideoque mihi videtur, agendarum causarum formam ecclesiastici iuris originem eiusque processum non esse inutile ignorantibus reserare . . . Placitandi forma in paradiso primum videtur inventa, dum prothoplastus de inobedientiae crimine ibidem a domino interrogatus criminis relatione sive remotione usus culpam in coniugem removisse autumat dicens, 'mulier, quam dedisti, dedit mihi et comedi' (Genesis 3.12). Deinde in veteri lege nobis tradita, dum Moyses in lege sua ait: 'In ore duorum vel trium testium stabit omne verbum.'"

85. Stephen of Tournai, Prologue to Summa, printed by Herbert Kalb, *Studien zur Summa Stephans von Tournai: Ein Beitrag zur kanonistischen Wissenshaftsgeschichte des späten 12. Jahrhunderts* (Forschungen zur Rechts- und Kulturgeschichte, 12; Innsbruck: 1983) 114 and Fowler-Magerl, *Ordo iudiciarius* 1 n. 1: "Cum enim Adam de inobedientia argueretur a Domino, quasi actioni exceptionem obiciens relationem criminis in coniugem."

86. See Fowler-Magerl, *Ordo iudiciarius* 7–8 on the twelfth-century jurists' understanding of the terms "prescriptio" and "exceptio."

87. Stephen of Tournai to C.2 q.1 v. *an in manifestis*, printed by Fowler-Magerl, *Ordo iudiciarius* 27–28 n. 76: "Videndum quod ordo iudiciarius dicitur, ut apud suum iudicem quis conveniatur, ut legitime vocetur ad causam tribus edictis vel uno peremptorio pro omnibus, ut vocato legitime prestentur inducie, ut accusatio sollempniter et in scriptis fiat, ut testes legitimi producantur, ut nonnisi in convictum vel confessum feratur [sententia]; que sententia nonnisi in scriptis fieri debet, nisi sint breves lites et maxime vilium."

This litany of admonitions indicates that by the second half of the twelfth century, the jurists were conscious of a defendant's right to a trial and of the defendant's right to have the trial conducted according to the rules of the *ordo iudiciarius*.[88] In this regard, "actio" could mean the particular formulary of Roman procedure by which the plaintiff brought suit, the whole judicial proceedings, or, as a passage in Justinian's *Institutes* put it, "the right of an individual to sue in a trial for what is due to him."[89] In this last sense "actio" meant "ius" or right.[90] This right did not inhere in each human being. As we shall see from the following discussion, the jurists wavered between justifying this right on the basis of the objective right of a subject to receive justice and a subjective right of a subject to have a case fully heard in court.[91] Only after the jurists concluded that parts of the judicial process were protected by natural law did they clearly articulate a subjective, almost inalienable, right of defendants to have their day in court.

Fowler-Magerl has described what she sees as a significant shift of emphasis in the judicial procedure of the twelfth century. In classical Roman law, the litigants had very few rights to intervene in or to alter the pace of the proceedings. The Roman jurists considered the *ordo iudiciarius* an indispensable extension of public authority. Medieval jurists, she argues, saw it as a right of the litigants. In Roman law, the litigants could not object to a judge whom they considered partial nor could they delay proceedings easily.[92] The medieval "ordines," on the other hand, granted litigants a range of devices with which they could control the tempo of a case. They could raise objections to the plaintiff, the judge, and the witnesses and thereby delay or halt the course of a case.[93]

Even though we do not have a proper history of twelfth-century judicial procedure, Fowler-Magerl may well be right to see a sharp contrast between ancient and medieval practices. Most legal systems of any

88. The author of *Summa 'Elegantius in iure diuino seu Coloniensis,* ed. Gérard Fransen (MIC, Series A, 1.2; Città del Vaticano: 1978) 52, repeats Stephen's gloss.

89. Inst. 4.6 pr.: "Actio autem nihil aliud est quam ius persequendi iudicio quod sibi debetur."

90. See the discussion of Brian Tierney, "Villey, Ockham," 7.

91. See Tierney, "Villey, Ockham," 1–10 for an excellent discussion of this distinction. In "Origins of Natural Rights" 620–638, Tierney continued the discussion of the meaning of "ius" and carefully examined the jurists' definitions of it.

92. The best account of procedure at the time of Justinian (the procedure the medieval jurists took as their model) is Dieter Simon, *Untersuchungen zum Justinianischen Zivilprozeß* (München: 1969).

93. Fowler-Magerl, *Ordo iudiciarius* 28; see also her remarks on pp. 9, 13.

sophistication have some conception of "due process" in their procedure as well as the germ of the notion that a defendant has the right to be heard. The Old Testament and Roman law required that a defendant be given an opportunity for self-defense in court.[94] The medieval jurists probably would have translated "due process"—a key concept of American and English law—as "servare ordinem iuris."[95]

The idea was not foreign to the world of the ordeal. There too a man or woman had the right to prove his or her innocence. In the *Romance of Tristan*, King Mark condemned Tristan and Isolt to death without a trial when they were caught in *flagrante delicto*. The people of the Kingdom were dismayed because they had not been tried and cried out: "King, you would do them too great a wrong if they were not first brought to trial. Afterwards put them to death."[96] Although their plea to the king might seem to be a simple call for fair play, notorious crimes presented a particularly difficult case for jurists who wished to defend a litigant's right to his day in court. They did not find it easy to justify a trial for a defendant whose crime was known to all or who had committed it, as Tristan had, in the presence of the prince himself.

We know almost nothing about the norms governing judicial procedure in the early Middle Ages. From the ninth century on, however, there is substantial evidence that a defendant's right to a trial was an accepted norm.[97] The jurists formulated a maxim that a defendant must be canonically summoned and publicly convicted. A few texts in Roman law supported a defendant's right to be heard in court.[98] In his famous decretal *Venerabilem,* Innocent III stated that if a defendant had not been cited, witnesses could not present testimony against the defen-

94. See the remarks of Richard M. Fraher, "'Ut nullus describatur reus prius quam convincatur': Presumption of Innocence in Medieval Canon Law," *Proceedings of the Sixth International Congress of Medieval Canon Law,* ed. S. Kuttner and K. Pennington (MIC, Series C, 7; Città del Vaticano: 1985) 494.

95. The term "due process" dates back to the Middle Ages. The first instance of its use was in a Statute of King Edward III, 28 Edward III, c.3 (1354), *The Statutes of the Realm* (London: 1810) I 345: "saunz estre mesne en respons par due proces de lei." My thanks to Professor William Wiecek who brought this passage to my attention.

96. Beroul, *The Romance of Tristan,* trans. A. S. Fedrick (Hammondsworth: 1970) 67. On the trials in Tristan, see E. C. York, "Isolt's Ordeal: English Legal Customs in the Medieval Tristan Legend," *Studies in Philology* 68 (1971) 1–9. See also Nancy Ostreicher, *Trial Scenes in Medieval Romance: The Evolution of their Structure and Function* (PhD dissertation, Columbia University, 1980); John A. Alford and Dennis P. Sennif, *Literature and Law in the Middle Ages* (New York: 1984).

97. See the discussion in Fowler-Magerl, *Ordo iudiciarius* 14–19. Gratian gathered some of these texts together in C.3 q.9, where he treated the question whether someone may be accused *in absentia.*

98. Cod. 9.2.6 and 9.40.1; Dig. 48.17.1. My thanks to Professor Richard Fraher for these references.

dant.[99] Although this general principle was well established in canon law,[100] it was not, however, an absolute right. The jurists attempted to draw distinctions between those crimes that required a trial and those that did not. For the canonists the locus classicus of this question was Gratian's *Decretum* (C.2 q.1). Gratian included texts that permitted a judge to condemn someone without a trial if the crime committed was "manifest" or "notorious." Later canonists refined and altered these concepts. In the end, however, the jurists commonly agreed that under certain circumstances, usually when a crime was heinous and notorious, a judge could render a decision against a defendant without a trial.[101]

Even before the revival of jurisprudence in the twelfth century, the question was not just theoretical. During the struggle between Pope Gregory VII and the Emperor Henry IV, Gregory excommunicated the German bishops who had taken part in the Synod at Worms. Gregory's summary action at a Lenten Synod in Rome in 1076 led to an exchange of letters by Bernoldus and Adelbertus of Constance to Bernoldus's former teacher, Bernhardus of Hildesheim.[102] Bernhardus inveighed that Gregory did not have the right to excommunicate the bishops without a trial. He conceded that if the bishops had been summoned but refused to appear, their condemnation would have been justified.[103] Bernoldus insisted, however, that the pope could excommunicate criminals without a trial if their crimes were public and they were contumacious.[104] Petrus Crassus raised the same issue when he defended Henry IV in 1084. Citing texts from Roman and canon law, Petrus declared that

99. X 1.6.34: "Si cognitoris absente altera partium videtur perperam processisse, cum citata non fuerit."

100. E.g. X 2.20.2 and C.3 q.9. Azo discussed the question whether witnesses could be heard and a sentence rendered if one of the parties had been legitimately summoned but did not appear. See Belloni, *Questioni civilistiche* 159–161.

101. Fowler-Magerl, *Ordo iudiciarius* 13–28 treats this problem in juristic thought from the early Middle Ages to the twelfth century. See also Richard M. Fraher, "Ut nullus describatur reus" 493–506 and "Preventing Crime in the High Middle Ages: The Medieval Lawyers' Search for Deterrence," *Popes, Teachers, and the Canon Law in the Middle Ages: Festschrift for Brian Tierney*, ed. Stanley Chodorow and James R. Sweeney (Ithaca: 1989) 224–227. Gratian treated the question whether a defendant could be condemned *in absentia* in C.3 q.9.

102. Fowler-Magerl, *Ordo iudiciarius* 20–21.

103. *Libelli de lite imperatorum et pontificum saeculis XI. et XII. conscripti* (MGH 2; Hannover: 1892) 30: "Fecit quidem papa quod est apostolicum, dum damnavit quos dixeras publicos et contumaces aut confessos veraciter, aut convictos regulariter, aut si vocati canonice ad reddendae rationis iudicium venire noluerunt."

104. Ibid.: "Iuxta hunc modum domnus apostolicus publicos et contumaces apostolicae sedis proscriptores satis canonice damnavit etiam absentes."

since Gregory had refused to hear the king's advocates and had condemned him *in absentia,* his sentence was not just.[105]

In spite of objections, the pope's right to render a sentence without granting due process became well established. Hostiensis defended Pope Innocent IV's deposition of Frederick II at the First Council of Lyons in 1245 effortlessly. Notorious crimes, he concluded, particularly those committed against the Church, need no formal juridical examination.[106] The papacy granted exceptions to the normal rules of due process for lesser crimes as well. By the beginning of the fourteenth century, ecclesiastical courts employed the shortened, summary procedure in cases that ranged from marriage to benefices.[107]

A primary reason why the jurists accepted the right of the prince to subvert the judicial process was that they considered legal procedure ("actiones") to be a part of the civil law, that is, positive law and, therefore, completely under his legislative and administrative competence. Two Roman law texts that outlined a mythological history of early Roman law provided authoritative proof that "actiones" were a part of positive law. The Roman jurisconsult Papinianus had declared that the Praetorian law, the Roman law governing procedure, was a part of the civil law.[108] Another jurisconsult, Pomponius, described the origins of the "actiones" at the time of the Twelve Tables: "the three laws were born, the laws of the Twelve Tables, and from these tables arose the civil law, and from them actions of law were composed."[109] Con-

105. *Libelli de lite imperatorum et pontificum saeculis XI. et XII. conscripti* (MGH 1; Hannover: 1891) 446–447. See Dolcini, *Velut aurora surgente* 43–52 for a discussion of Crassus and this dispute. See also Wolfgang Stürner, *Peccatum und Potestas: Der Sündenfall und die Entstehung der herrscherlichen Gewalt im mittelalterlichen Staatsdenken* (Beiträge zur Geschichte und Quellenkunde des Mittelalters 11; Sigmaringen: 1987) 125–126 with bibliography in n. 5.

106. Hostiensis to X 1.6.34 v. *progenitores* and his Summa, de electione, X 1.6 § 106. Nedum in prelatis. The text is edited by John Watt, "Medieval Deposition Theory: A Neglected Canonist *Consultatio,*" *Studies in Church History,* ed. G. J. Cumming (London: 1965) II 207–210 at 210: "Set hec quomodo cum tantus princeps sic nec accusetur nec denuncietur nec citatus sit nec convictus; quod citatus fuerit, hoc certum est. Set esto quod non fuerit—quero quare si apostolus Corinthium absentem et irrequisitum contempnauit, ii. q.i. De manifesta, infra de appell. Cum sit Romana, in fine? Certe quia 'excessus notorius examinatione non indiget' . . . pater sanctissime considera quod idem est in eodem, scilicet excommunicatio publica, periurium manifestum ac persecutio diuulgata quam progenitores eius et ipse presumpserunt in apostolicam sedem et in alias ecclesias exercere." At another place, Hostiensis suggested that the "voluntas" of the pope in matters that touched procedure was almost absolute, X 5.2.31 v. *voluimus,* (Ed. 1581), fol. 21va.

107. Clem. 2.1.2 (Dispendiosam).

108. Dig. 1.1.7 (Ius autem civile est).

109. Dig. 1.2.2.6: "Deinde ex his legibus eodem tempore fere actiones compositae

sequently, by the early thirteenth century, the jurists had no doubts that
the "actiones" were a part of the civil law, even if, as we have seen,
some canonists traced some elements of the *ordo iudiciarius* back to
paradise. Accursius summed up a commonplace of juristic thought
when he wrote in his Ordinary Gloss to the Digest that "actiones," in
contrast to contracts, are derived from the civil law, as Pomponius had
noted in his history incorporated into the Digest.[110]

In the middle of the thirteenth century, at a time when some historians have seen medieval conceptions of due process rapidly being
eroded by the introduction of torture and by a fierce determination of
ecclesiastical and secular magistrates to eradicate crime,[111] the jurists
began to reshape their thinking about the origins of the judicial process
and about the rights of defendants. The jurists had been preoccupied
with theories of rights and the creation of norms since the twelfth century, and their tentative gropings for rights exploded into a passionate
embrace during the second half of the thirteenth century.[112] Theories of
inviolable individual rights to property, to contracts, to bear arms, and
to due process were spawned in the deep pools of juristic thought.[113]

Paradoxically, the jurists created new doctrines of rights at the same
time that they fitted the prince with resplendent rhetorical garments that
they fashioned to exalt his authority. We may suffer with the illusion
that only democratic societies can create and defend human rights, but
history can still provoke surprise. Perhaps the jurists' conceptions of
power may have been a factor that prodded them to place a harness
on the prince's authority. As they became aware of the implications of
the doctrine that all positive law resided in the will of the prince, the
jurists may have responded to a deeply felt conviction that the right to
a trial should not be left solely to his arbitrary will. Whatever their
reasons were, the jurists changed their minds about the origins of the
ordo iudiciarius and the rights of litigants in the judicial process. They
began to argue that the *ordo* was not derived from civil law, but from

---

sunt, quibus inter se homines disceptarent . . . et ita in eodem paene tempore tria haec
iura nata sunt: lege duodecim tabularum ex his fluere coepit ius civile, ex isdem legis actiones compositae sunt."
    110. Accursius to Dig. 1.1.5 (Ex hoc iure gentium) v. *obligationes*, Clm 6201, fol.
4v: "set actiones omnes sunt a iure civili, ut infra titulo i. l.ii. § Deinde [Dig. 1.2.2.6]."
I do not know which jurist first asked whether "actiones" are derived from civil law.
Although the earlier "ordines" define what "actiones" were, they say nothing about from
whence they came.
    111. Bartlett, *Trial by Fire and Water* 139–143; Fraher, "Preventing Crime" 227–
233.
    112. See the work of Tierney cited in note 14 above, and Cortese, *La norma giuridica*.
    113. Cf. Fraher, "Preventing Crime" 230–231.

natural law or the law of nations. They begot an inviolable right to due process.

The jurists who first discussed this problem often referred to a gloss of Pope Innocent IV when they redefined the origins of "actiones." Indeed, although he does not quite meet the issue, Innocent IV was the first jurist to broach the question of whether the prince has an absolute right to take an action away from a subject.[114] Between 1246 and 1254, Innocent IV wrote his commentary on a decretal that Pope Innocent III had sent to Matthew, the bishop of Ceneda.[115] Innocent III had informed Matthew that he was striking down the laws of Treviso and Conegliano permitting a layman who held a fief from an ecclesiastical institution to alienate it if he were needy.[116]

Innocent IV began his commentary with the observation that even if these laws did not touch ecclesiastical persons and institutions, they would still be invalid because they injured the rights of a third party. Since the matter concerned dominion and obligations, a third party held these rights from natural law. Unlike actions, dominion and obligations are not derived from civil law or from the emperor.[117] No law or rescript was valid if it violated natural law, unless there was a just cause.[118] Up to this point, Innocent repeated platitudes with which no jurist would have disagreed.

Innocent then asked a much more interesting question. What if the prince issued a rescript or statute that forbade a litigant from bringing a suit in court? First, he argued that if such a rescript or statute completely destroyed the right to bring suit it was not valid unless it had a "non obstante" clause, that is, a clause that recognized the legal objections to a provision of the law, but overrode them.[119] The concept of

114. At least I have not found earlier discussions that would anticipate his gloss.

115. On Innocent IV, see Melloni, *Innocenzo IV* 26–30, 59–98 and Schulte, *Quellen* II 91–94.

116. X 1.2.7, Po. 641, March 23, 1199. *Die Register Innocenz' III.*, 2: 2. *Pontifikatsjahr: Texte*, ed. O. Hageneder, W. Maleczek, and A. Strnad (Rom-Wien: 1979) no. 7, p. 14.

117. Innocent IV to X 1.2.7 v. *constituerunt* (Venice: 1495) unfol., Clm 6350, fol. 1vb, Clm 15704, fol. 1vb: "Super rebus etiam laicorum hoc statuere non possent cum tale statutum esset in lesionem iuris alterius et eius iuris quod ad aliquem spectat uel acquiritur de iure naturali, ut sunt dominia, obligationes et huiusmodi. Et non datur a iure civili uel ab imperatore uel actiones, ut ff. de iust. et iure Ex hoc [Dig. 1.1.5], instit. de rerum diui. § Fere et § Preterea per illum [Instit. 2.1.12 and 20]."

118. Ibid.: "Et dico non ualere legem uel rescriptum in preiudicium naturalis iuris nisi iusta causa interueniat."

119. Ibid.: "Si ex eo perimatur ius omnino uel ex toto deneget agendi potestatem non ualet nisi adiiciatur non obstante lege aliqua, ff. de lega. iii. Si quis, in principio. C. de testa. authen. Hoc inter liberos."

"non obstante" was a commonplace in medieval legislative theory.[120] Innocent meant that such a general prohibition could not be licit unless the prince signified that he understood the implications of his actions. He concluded his argument with a statement of great originality:[121]

> But then some say that although it may be sustained that [the prince] takes an action away, nevertheless he cannot take away [the duty] that he render justice. This would be against natural law. If, indeed, the right is not taken away, but only postponed, [the law] is valid.

I do not know of other jurists who maintained that a prince could not abolish the judicial process or ignore an action because he was bound by natural law to render justice. Perhaps these ideas were circulating in the schools. Whatever the case, from this time on the issue became an important one in juristic thought, and Innocent's brief comments provided a "pièce justicative" to establish a right of due process for the next four centuries.

Hostiensis copied Innocent's commentary (to X 1.2.7) into his own, but left out the crucial passage that the prince was bound by natural law to render justice. As a result, he shortened Innocent's comments almost to the point of incomprehensibility.[122] Hostiensis's omission was not intentional. He incorporated the essence of Innocent's gloss in another part of his *Lectura*. Although he concurred with Innocent that the pope should never pervert the *ordo iudiciarius* and was always obligated to render justice, still there were exceptions. Sometimes a case might be delayed because of scandal, or public utility might dictate that the common good might take precedence over private utility.[123] At

---

120. For an example of its use, see Leonard E. Boyle, "Robert Grosseteste and the Pastoral Care," *Medieval and Renaissance Studies: Proceedings of the Southeastern Institute of Medieval and Renaissance Studies, Summer, 1976,* ed. Dale B. J. Randall (Medieval and Renaissance Series, 8; Durham: 1979) 3–51 at 30–33. Its use in the twelfth century has been explored by Brigitte Meduna, *Studien zum Formular der päpstlichen Justizbriefe von Alexander III. bis Innocenz III. (1159–1216): Die "non obstantibus"-Formel* (Österreichische Akademie der Wissenschaften, Phil.-Hist. Klasse, 536; Vienna: 1989).

121. Innocent IV to 1.2.7: "Sed et tunc ut quidam dicunt licet sustineatur quod auferat actionem tamen quin reddat iustitiam auferre non potest, cum esset contra ius naturale. Si vero non auferatur ius, sed differatur, tenet, C. de precibus imper. Quotiens [Cod. 1.19(22).2]."

122. Hostiensis to X 1.2.7 (Quae in ecclesiarum) Oxford, New College 205, fol. 5r, (Venice: 1581), I fol. 9r: "ubi uero rescriptum uel statutum lederet alterius ius de iure ciuili proueniens, sicut sunt actiones, ff. de orig. iur. l.ii. Set ex toto perimitur non ualet, nisi dicat 'non obstante tali lege,' arg. ff. de leg. iii. Si quis, in prin. . . . Si autem non aufert, set differt ualet, C. de prec. imper. of. Quotiens."

123. Hostiensis to X 3.34.7 (Magne devotionis), v. *tria*, Ed. 1581, fol. 127r, Ed. 1512, fol. 134v, Oxford, New College 205, fol. 154r, Bamberg, Can. 56, fol. 196v–197r:

another place in his commentary, he noted that even the devil should have his day in court, an idea that later jurists found intriguing.[124] Nonetheless, he did not link the pope's duty to render justice with natural law. Rather, Hostiensis emphasized the occasions when the pope could subvert due process.[125]

A little later, the Roman lawyer Odofredus de Denariis discussed the prince's authority to deny his subject's right to an action in his commentary on Justinian's *Code* (1255–1264).[126] He was inspired by a constitution of the Emperor Anastasius in which the emperor decreed that no rescript or pragmatic sanction should be observed if it seemed to prejudice any litigant.[127] Odofredus posed the question by contrasting the right that someone has to property with the right he has to an action:[128]

> I do not have dominion from the prince that I have acquired from my lord through "traditio" [a method of transferring property in Roman law], but from natural reason. The emperor cannot abolish natural reason. But I have [my right] to an action from the emperor . . . the emperor is "Lex animata" . . . and because he may grant an action, he can deny it. But some

---

"Cum igitur secundum predictum modum omnia sic liceant pape et sic deceant, numquid et omnia expediunt? Respondeo: si ordine iudiciario agatur semper expedit iustitiam facere, et numquam ipsam peruertere, super quo uide not. supra de re iud. In causis [X 2.27.19], licet quandoque propter scandalum differatur, quod dic ut not. supra de iud. Nouit § i. uer. Ceterum [X 2.1.13] et de renun. Nisi cum pridem § Pro graui quoque scandalo [X 1.9.10]. Vtilitas tamen rei publice atque maxime ecclesie Dei et salutis animarum est utilitati priuate in omnibus preferenda, supra de regul. Licet § Illa uer. i. et de postul. prelat. Bone i. § i. uer. i. et per hoc euidenter comprobatur quod not. supra eodem, c.i. ad finem. Expedit etiam quandoque rigorem temperare saluis substantialibus ueritatis, dilationes amputare, et lites abbreuiare potissime in electionibus et similibus, supra de appell. Oblate § penult. quod etsi in omni iudice uerum sit, ut supra de dolo et contum. Finem, cum suis concordantiis [X 2.14.5]."

124. Hostiensis to X 2.25.5 v. *sed equitas.*

125. On Hostiensis's concepts of due process, see Gallagher, *Canon Law and the Christian Community: The Role of Law in the Church According to the Summa Aurea of Cardinal Hostiensis* (Analecta Gregoriana, 208; Rome: 1978) 154–162.

126. Cortese, *La norma* I 131–141, seems to have been the first modern historian to have noticed this strand of juristic thought. On Odofredus, see Savigny, *Geschichte* V 356–380.

127. Cod. 1.22 (25).6 (Omnes).

128. Odofredus to Cod. 1.22(25).6 (Omnes) Ed. Lyon: 1480, unfol. Vienna, Nationalbibl. Ink. 26.A.5, sine loco et anno (Hain—), fol. 52r–52v: "Audite: dominium mihi quesitum per traditionem mihi factam a domino, non habeo a principe, immo naturali ratione, et imperator non potest tollere naturalem rationem; set actionem habeo ab imperatore, i. a. l. ut ff. de origin. iur. l.ii. § Deinde [Dig. 1.2.2.6], et imperator est lex animata in terris, ut in authen. de consul. et ideo quia dat actionem, potest tollere. Set dicet aliquis male dicis. Nonne rei uendicatio est ciuilis? Et sic aut imperator potest mihi tollere eam, et sic tollis mihi dominium rei mee, quia per eam uendicamus dominium, ut infra de rei uend. l. Doce [Cod. 3.32.9], aut non potest tollere; et tu dixisti quia imperator potuit tollere actiones ciuiles si dicat 'non obstante tali lege.'"

would say that you are arguing falsely [that is, the argument is wrong no matter which position is adopted]. Is not the vindication of a thing ["vindicatio rei" is a technical term of Roman law that means asserting one's right to something] a matter of civil law? Consequently, either the emperor may deny my action, and you can take my dominion away from me, because we defend our rights through an action . . . or he may not. You have argued that the emperor may take a civil action away if he states "non obstante tali lege."

After having posed the question whether the emperor can take away dominion by denying an action, Odofredus dealt with it in three different ways. First he pointed out that sometimes one could claim ownership of a thing without an action.[129] But with this observation, he begged the question. Then he went to the heart of the matter. The emperor can, he argued, deny an action for the recovery of a right that is derived from the civil or praetorian law, in other words, positive law. When, however, the right is based on the law of nations, the emperor cannot.[130] And thirdly, he continued, one might argue that since the emperor cannot take my dominion of a thing away, therefore, he cannot take the consequences of that dominion away, that is, the right to bring an action to recover it. He conceded that the prince could take "any other personal action away if he had a just cause."[131]

Guido of Suzzara picked up some of the threads of Odofredus's argument.[132] Like Odofredus, he focused on the connection between a right protected by natural law and a person's right to seek a remedy in court. In his *Suppletiones* to Justinian's *Code,* Guido noted that the emperor cannot take away an action that might deprive a person of ownership. If the emperor, he went on, could take away a legitimate action

129. Ibid.: "Ad quod respondeo duobus modis: Et uno modo sic. Dominium rei mee non potest mihi auferre imperator, set rei uendicationem sic. Si dicis non possum rem meam petere ab alio nisi per rei uendicationem, respondeo non. Si tu es dominus, aliter potes habere rem tuam, quia si cadat a possessione alter, et tu nanciscaris possessionem, retinebis eam per retentionem quia multa retinemus per retentionem que, etc. ut ff. de cond. indeb. l. Si in area."

130. Ibid.: "Vel possum dicere secundo modo quod imperator non potest tollere mihi rei uendicationem, quia per hoc tolleret mihi dominium rei mee. Et hoc uerum est cum res mea est apud alium constituta, quia cum quid prohibetur et id per quod peruenitur ad illud etc. ut ff. de sponsa. l. Oratione; quod enim supra dictum est: intelligo cum actio ciuilis competit mihi pro his que non sunt iurisgentium, set pro his que sunt quesita iure ciuili uel pretorio."

131. Ibid.: "Vel dicatis tertio modo, sicut imperator non potest auferre dominium rei mee, nec sequelam dominii, scilicet rei uindicationis, set aliam personalem actionem bene potest mihi auferre uel ex causa iusta uel dic si diceret 'non obstante tali lege.'" See the remarks of Cortese, *La norma* I 133–134.

132. For bibliography and Guido's importance in late-thirteenth-century legal thought, see chapter 3, n. 69, above.

with a rescript, then he would remove the impediment of civil law that someone cannot go to law without an action.[133] The implicit point of Guido's gloss is that the emperor cannot confiscate private property by preventing a subject from bringing suit because the subject's right would still exist and could be presumably vindicated, whether the prince granted the subject an action or not.

Guido broached the question again in his glosses on the *Digest*. He asked if the podestà of a city were asked to enforce a municipal law depriving someone of their castle or some other right without any cause, would the podestà be bound to uphold this statute since the podestà had sworn to uphold all the statutes of the city? His first point was succinct:[134]

> It is plain that the statute is not valid, for even the prince should not take my property away, unless there is just cause, and should not [deny] my right, such as an action . . . rather the officials of the prince can be resisted by the people if they attempt to confiscate my property.

Although Guido did not explicitly argue that an action was protected by natural law, that is the almost inevitable implication of his argument. An annotator of his text in the Parisian manuscript with the initial "e" (Egidius?) understood the thrust of his argument. "Guido's opinion is true if actions are derived from the law of nations," he commented.[135] Guido had slightly changed the tenor of the argument. He no longer

133. Guido of Suzzara, Suppletiones to Cod. 1.19(22).2 (Quotiens), Paris, B.N. lat. 4489, fol. 34r: "Infra eodem, in glossa ad finem: Vel dic quod actionem mihi competentem imperator non potest tollere per rescriptum, nam sic per consequens posset mihi auferre dominium rei mee, quod tamen falsum est. Et cum aliquid prohibetur, et omne id, etc. ut ff. de spon. l. Oratio [Dig. 23.1.15] et leg. sum. rei fu. et alien. ne prosti. l. finali [?] Item quod non refert quid equipollentibus fiat, ut ff. si certum pet. l. Certum est [Dig. 12.1.6] uel si dicatur quod imperator possit mihi tollere per rescriptum actionem mihi competentem, que est de iure ciuili, remouebitur impedimentum quod ius ciuile posuit, scilicet quod aliquis sine actione non potest experiri, ut ff. de negot. gest. Si pupilli [Dig. 3.5.5(6)] et de admin. tu. l. Quotiens § Si temporali [Dig. 26.7.9(10).2] ut et alias aliquis sine actione experitur, ut infra de contrahend. et commit. stip. l. Nuda [Cod. 8.37(38).5] et ff. de uerb. oblig. l. Si citius. [Dig. 45.1.?] G."

134. Guido of Suzzara, Suppletiones to Dig. 1.1.9 (Omnes populi), Clm 6201, fol. 5v: "Item quero si statutum sit in ciuitate de castro alicuius uel de alia re sine causa occupando, [et] potestas iurauit generaliter seruare omnia statuta, teneturne istud statutum seruare? Planum est quod statutum non ualet, nam etiam princeps, nisi iusta causa subesset, non debet mihi rem meam auferre, immo nec ius meum, puta actionem, ut C. de prec. imperat. offic. l. Quotiens [Cod. 1.19(22).2] et l. Rescripta [Cod. 1.19(22).7] de diuer. rescript. l. finali [Cod. 1.23(26).7] infra de constit. prin. l.i. in fine [Dig. 1.4.1] immo officialibus principis a priuatis potest resisti si contra ius rem meam uellent auferre, ut C. de iure fisc. l. Prohibitum et l. Facultas, lib. x. [Cod. 10.1.5 and 7]."

135. Paris, B.N. lat. 4489, fol. 34r: "et hec oppinio maxime uera est si dicas actiones esse de iure gentium, quod dic ut dixi, ff. de orig. iur. l.ii. Deinde ex hiis [Dig. 1.2.2.6] e." Paris 4489 abounds with additiones to Guido's text, most signed "e."

reminded his readers that actions were established by civil law. He equated the right of ownership and the right of due process. If the right to own property were based on natural law, then the right to defend that property must also be grounded in natural law. Therefore, the prince may not take either right away.

The jurists after Guido quickly made the connection that Odofredus and Guido anticipated. An anonymous glossator of the *Digest* may have been the first to write that actions are derived from the law of nations. While commenting on a law stating that if Seius's property were confiscated he could direct Titius to buy the property, the jurist observed that if Titius did not buy it for Seius or if Titius would not relinquish it to him, Seius could still bring an action on mandate (a gratuitous contract in Roman law).[136] His argument is ingenious:[137]

> Note that one may argue from this paragraph that actions are derived from the law of nations. This may be proven thus: a person who is sent into exile loses everything according to civil law, and yet he does not lose his right to an action. Therefore we may say that actions are derived from the law of nations.

He stretched the meaning of the text in the *Digest* considerably when he assumed that the person being dispossessed will be exiled, but his argument is, nonetheless, clever. Significantly, he did not specify whether all actions are derived from the law of nations or only those actions based on the law of contract. Although he most likely believed the latter, from his gloss one could assume that he would have grounded all actions in the law of nations.

Jacobus de Arena (died ca. 1296), a student of Guido of Suzzara, taught at Bologna, Padua, and Toulouse.[138] Guido directly influenced his thought on the origins of actions. By the end of the thirteenth century, the jurists were writing long commentaries on the fourth book of Justinian's *Institutes* in which actions were treated. Jacobus drew out all the implications of Guido's comments on contracts and actions. His

---

136. Dig. 17.1.22.5 (Si tibi mandavero).

137. Dig. 17.1.22.5 v. *His cuius bona*, Clm 6201, fol. 261r: "Not. arg. ex isto § quod actiones sunt de iure gentium, quod sit probatum, nam deportatio facit omnia amittere que sunt de iure ciuili, et cum hic iste fuit deportatus, et a[d]mittat actiones, igitur dicamus quod sint de iure gentium." The gloss went on to present a counterargument: "Hoc reprobant doctores et intelligunt istum § quod non fuit hic facta deportatio, set intelligunt quando fuit facta publice tantum mouentur ex lege ex hoc iure gentium, supra de iust. et iure, licet hic glo. eum indistincte intelligat in deportato." Paleographically the text of this gloss is contemporary to the layer of Guido of Suzzara's glosses in the same manuscript.

138. Savigny, *Geschichte* V 399–407.

gloss is the first extended argument that certain actions are based on the law of nations, and it is worth quoting in its entirety.[139]

> I ask by what law are actions established? The doctors say that they come from civil law, for the law states that actions are constructed from these laws . . . and these laws are derived from civil law. . . . My teacher [Guido of Suzzara] argued that contracts are established by all legal systems, and Accursius stated that there are certain obligations that are praetorian or civil, hence actions are also either civil or praetorian. Of course, those actions that the law of nations does not recognize, it could not establish. Certainly these [actions] are civil or praetorian. But those actions that arise from contracts of the law of nations are established by the law of nations. And because of this, obligations are a part of the law of nations. It would be absurd if men were bound [by contracts] according to the law of nations and could not bring suit, for then contracts would be useless. Consequently, in order to avoid this difficulty, there were actions then [when men were ruled by the law of nations].

Like Guido, Jacobus maintained that contracts were found in all legal systems; therefore, actions vindicating contracts must precede the civil law. The idea was becoming a platitude.

At the end of the thirteenth century, the jurists moved slowly toward the realization that in cases involving contracts a defendant had a fundamental right for a hearing and a defense.[140] Since this right was founded on a higher law, the prince could not unilaterally deprive a subject of it. Although these ideas did not immediately sweep the field—one can find examples of jurists steadfastly maintaining that actions were a part of civil law—they did become firmly entrenched in the literature.

The modern concept of due process includes much more than just simply the right to a trial. A defendant must be properly cited, must have the opportunity to present evidence on his or her behalf, must have the right of counsel, could have the right to remain silent, and must only

---

139. Jacobus de Arena to Institutes 4.6, "Lectura super titulo De actionibus" in *Super iure civili* (Lyon: 1541) fol. 262r: "Quero quo iure inducte sunt actiones? Doctores dicunt quod de iure civili, nam lex dicit ex his legibus composite sunt actiones, ff. de orig. iur. l.ii. § Deinde ex hiis, et leges sunt de iure civili, ut dicto §. Dominus meus dicit quod exemplo quocumque iuris obligatio inducitur, et Accursius dicit quod quedam sunt obligationes pretorie seu civiles, unde et actiones sunt civiles vel pretorie, quoniam illas actiones quas iurisgentium ignoravit non potuit inducere iusgentium, immo sunt de iure civili et pretorio. Set ille actiones que descendunt ex contractibus iure gentium, ille actiones sunt de iure gentium, et propter hoc obligationes sunt de iuregentium, ut ff. de iust. et iure l. Ex hoc iure. Set absurdum fuerit in iuregentium si homines erunt obligati et non poterunt exigi. Ergo pro nihilo erant obligationes. Vnde ut evitetur istud inconveniens, et actiones erant tunc temporis." See Cortese, *La norma* I 132 n. 86.

140. To paraphrase the wording of the United States Supreme Court, *Ballard v. Hunter*, 204 U.S. 241, 27 Sup. Ct. 261, 51 L. Ed. 461.

be convicted if the evidence is clear and unambiguous. And, finally, the plaintiff or prosecutor, not the defendant, must bear the burden of proof. A corollary of this last concept is the idea that the defendant is innocent until proven guilty. Some of these ideas were already well established in Roman law and were adopted by the jurists. The maxims "the burden of proof lies with the accuser, not the defendant," [141] and "in doubtful matters the defendant is favored, not the plaintiff " [142] were commonplaces of medieval law. [143]

The evolution of the jurists' thought concerning a defendant's right to have his or her suit heard must be placed in the larger context of their concern with other elements of what we call due process. Richard Fraher has argued, correctly I think, that as early as the twelfth century, many of those concepts we think of as being essential to due process were already present in medieval law. [144] Consequently, we must glance briefly at other elements of late-thirteenth-century thought about a just trial.

Of all these concepts the presumption of innocence was, perhaps, the most sophisticated. [145] By the end of the thirteenth century, the jurists had begun to realize that the presumed innocence of the defendant was an important element of a just trial and due process. The first explicit

141. Paul, Dig. 22.3.2: "Ei incumbit probatio qui dicit, non qui negat." Also Marcus, Dig. 22.3.21: "Semper necessitas probandi incumbit illi, qui agit."
142. De regulis iuris of Boniface VIII, no. 11: "Cum sunt partium iura obscura, reo favendum est potius quam actori."
143. See Fraher, "Ut nullus describatur reus," 494–495 and D. Clementi, "The Anglo-Saxon Origins of the Principle 'Innocent until Proved Guilty,'" Herrschaftsverträge, Wahlkapitulationen, Fundamentalgesetze, ed. Rudolf Vierhaus (Studies Presented to the International Commission for the History of Representative and Parliamentary Institutions, 59; Veröffentlichungen des Max-Plank-Instituts für Geschichte 56; Göttingen: 1977) 68–76. Clementi comments that the maxim, innocent until proved guilty, was present in Anglo-Saxon law and foreign to continental legal systems. His conclusions are quite questionable for the past and the present. Since the Convention for the Protection of Human Rights, signed by thirteen European countries on November 4, 1950, the maxim "innocent until proved guilty" has been formally adopted in most civil law jurisdictions (article 6, paragraph 2). Richard Hemholz has explored the defendant's privilege to remain silent in "Origins of the Privilege against Self-incrimination: The Role of the European 'ius commune,'" New York University Law Review 65 (1990) 962–990.
144. "Ut nullus describatur reus," 494–503. I am not sure that we may equate the maxim "Ut nullus describatur reus prius quam convincatur" with "a man is innocent until proved guilty." The difference between "described" and "presumed" is significant. In the first case, there might not be any impediments to the court treating the man as guilty, while the statement that a man is presumed innocent implies that the legal definitions and safeguards surrounding the concept "presumptio" in legal thought would protect his status. But this is a quibble. The maxim is, as Fraher argues, a part of the jurists' concern with due process.
145. On the origins of medieval ideas of presumption, see André Gouron, "Aux racines de la théorie des présomptions," Rivista internazionale di diritto comune 1 (1990) 99–109, with full bibliographical references.

formulation of the presumption of innocence known to me is in an anonymous question of a French jurist (ca. 1270). He wrote that in criminal cases the legislators of laws have decreed, in order to maintain the equity of a judgment and avoid the precipice of iniquity, that a man who has not been proven with absolute clarity to have committed a crime is presumed innocent. Further, he continued, it is better to leave a criminal unpunished than to condemn an innocent man.[146] A key text in his argument was a decretal of Pope Innocent III, *Dudum,* sent to the archdeacon and provost of Milan in 1207.[147] Innocent had admonished the archdeacon and provost that when a cleric carried a papal mandate providing him with a benefice, he did not have to prove himself worthy. "He may be presumed worthy unless the contrary may be shown." Innocent might have been surprised by the importance that future jurists attached to his words. They became a justification for the presumption of innocence from the thirteenth to the nineteenth centuries. Supreme Court Justice Edward Douglass White cited the same decretal in 1894 when he traced the history of a presumption of innocence in the Western legal tradition.[148] Of course, Innocent III had no intention of establishing, nor any concept of, a general presumption of innocence, but later jurists interpreted his text as justifying it.[149]

One last problem concerning due process in the late thirteenth century must be addressed, albeit tentatively and incompletely. Torture fundamentally undermines any idea of due process. Historians have generally assumed that torture became a regular part of the judicial process by this time.[150] They have reached this conclusion primarily on the

---

146. *Responsa doctorum Tholosanorum* (Rechtshistorisch Instituut, Leiden 2.8; Haarlem: 1938), quaestio 50, pp. 116–120: "In sententiis namque condempnatoriis super criminibus proferendis iurium conditores, ut equitatis iudicium servaretur et iniquitatis precipicium vitaretur, vivaciter pensarunt ac veraciter statuerunt, ut super crimine quilibet innocens presumatur qui comisisse facinus clarissime non probatur, ut C. qui milit. non pos. l. Super servis, lib. xii. [Cod. 12.33.6], extra de presumpt. c. Dudum [X 2.23.16], 'satius fore inpunitum facinus relinqui quam innocentem dampnari,' ut ff. de penis l. Absentem, in principio [Dig. 48.19.5]"; the quote is from the text in the Digest, 48.19.5.
147. X 2.23.16, Po. 3093.
148. *Coffin v. U.S.,* 156 U.S. 432, 455. Cf. Fraher, "Ut nullus describatur reus," p. 493 n. 2. The source of White's (or his clerk's) knowledge would be interesting to explore; on White in general, see Robert B. Highsaw, *Edward Douglass White: Defender of the Conservative Faith* (Southern Biography Series; Baton Rouge-London: 1981), who does not, unfortunately, treat *Coffin v. U.S.*
149. Another decretal in which Innocent made a very similar statement was also important, X 1.12.1, Po. 2717: "quem indignum esse non novit, dignum debeat estimare."
150. See John Langbein, *Torture and the Law of Proof: Europe and England in the Ancien Régime* (Chicago-London: 1977) 3–17, 45–49; Mirjan Damaska, "The Death of Legal Torture," *Yale Law Journal* 87 (1978) 860–884; Fraher, "Ut nullus describatur

basis of the theoretical literature concerning torture that discussed the use of torture in ecclesiastical and secular courts and, in particular, the growing use of torture to expose heretics.

There are two reasons for wondering whether this picture is correct. First, we have little evidence of how often and when torture was used in thirteenth- and fourteenth-century courts. Until the surviving records of those courts are studied, especially in the archives of Italy, we cannot say much about how theory corresponded to practice. Theory severely limited the use of torture in most cases. Only a thorough examination of actual courtroom procedure will give us some idea of whether these limitations were respected in practice.[151] Second, historians have not adequately explored two other sources that throw light on the use of torture: the commentaries of the jurists and the statutes of the city-states. Although Guilielmus Durantis wrote almost nothing about torture and its use in his comprehensive *Speculum* on procedure,[152] Johannes Andreae touched upon the subject several times in his *Additiones* to it.[153] Many Italian city-states promulgated laws that prohibited their citizens from being tortured unless they were of notorious reputation (mala fama). As early as 1241, Vercelli promulgated a statute that "no man [citizen of Vercelli] is to be tortured."[154] A marginal gloss in the manuscript of the statutes added:[155]

> The podestà or rector is held to observe this law without exception or dispensation [the meaning of "precise" in juristic Latin] and to enforce its observance. He cannot seek to have its provisions changed or altered. The correctors of the statutes are not permitted to change, delete, or omit the

---

reus," 505 and "Preventing Crime" 230–231; Bartlett, *Trial by Fire and Water* 139–146; 158–159. Edward Peter's remarks, in *Torture* (New Perspectives of the Past, Oxford-New York: 1985) 44–62, are a very sophisticated and balanced reading of the available evidence.

151. A first step has been taken by Laura Ikins Stern's book on Florentine Criminal Law that will be published by Johns Hopkins University Press.

152. *Speculum iudiciale* II de praesumptionibus § Species (p. 740).

153. *Additiones ad Speculum iudiciale* (Basel: 1574) v. *l. unica*, II de praesumptionibus § Species (p. 738); v. *in predict. c. Veniens*, III de notoriis criminibus § Scias (p. 45) and § Fama (p. 47).

154. "Statuta communis Vercellarum." Ed. Giovambattista Adriani. *Leges Municipales*, Vol. 2. (Historiae Patriae Monumenta 16; Augusta Taurinorum (Torino: 1876) col. 1224.

155. Ibid.: "et potestas seu rector communis Vercellarum precise teneatur hoc capitulum attendere et observare et attendi et observari facere. Nec inde possit vel debeat petere recipere vel habere licentiam vel absolutionem vel remissionem conscilio credencie vel arengi vel alio modo vel ingenio. Nec istud capitulum possit mutari vel deleri vel omitti per emendatores statuti vel per aliquam aliam personam. Sed semper precise in statuto communis Vercellarum remaneat. Super quod quilibet potestas seu rector communis Vercell. iurare debeat."

statute. The podestà or rector ought to swear an oath to uphold these provisions.

The statutes of Chieri in 1311 contained an identical provision.[156] Fiorelli has explored the statutes of the Italian city-states and discovered that almost all of them established provisions limiting the use of torture on citizens of good reputation.[157] Johannes Andreae reported that Hostiensis referred to "the statutes of cities that prohibited torture unless there was a grave presumption of guilt."[158]

Johannes's remarks are supported by the statutes of Bologna of 1288.[159] As one might have expected, they protect the people of Bologna who belonged to a guild or who are considered members of the "populus Bononie" because of privilege, ordinance, decree or statute from being tortured without "legitimate proofs" that have been examined by the lord captain.[160] The lord captain must approve the use of torture in the presence of the defendant or one of the defendant's family, six "anziani" or consuls, four officials of the commune, and a notary.[161] If these provisions were violated, the podestà would be condemned to a fine of 1,000 Bolognese pounds and exclusion from municipal government.[162]

---

156. Luigi Cibrario, *Delle storie di Chieri libri quattro* (2 vols. Torino: 1827) II 186.

157. Piero Fiorelli, *La tortura giudiziaria nel diritto comune* (Ius nostrum 1–2; 2 vols. Milan: 1953–54) I 91–94, nn. 22–32. See Fraher's comments on a Florentine statute in "Preventing Crime" 230.

158. Cited by Johannes Andreae in his Additiones to the *Speculum iudiciale* (Basel: 1574) III de notoriis criminibus § Scias (p. 45): "Dicebat autem Host. quod in statutis civitatum, quae prohibent poni aliquos ad tormenta, nisi adsint violentae praesumptiones." I have not found this passage in Hostiensis's works.

159. Printed by Hermann Kantorowicz, "Studien zum altitalienischen Strafprozess," *Zeitschrift für gesamte Strafrechtswissenschaft* 44 (1924) 97–130, reprinted in his *Rechtshistorische Schriften* (Karlsruhe: 1970) 311–340. See his comments on the use of statutes as a source for judicial procedure, pp. 313–314 n. 17.

160. Ibid., 327–328: "Salvo et reservato, quod nullus, qui sit de societatibus artium vel armorum, cambii vel merchadandie populi Bononie, vel intelligatur esse de populo Bononie ex forma alicuius privilegii, ordinamenti, statuti vel provisionis aut reformationis communis vel populi Bononie, possit vel debeat modo aliquo vel ingenio tormentari vel subici aliquibus tormentis tondoli vel tirelli vel cuiuscunque generis tormentorum . . . nisi prius contra eum essent legittime probationes inducte vel saltim probate violente presumptiones et indicia manifesta."

161. Ibid., 328: "Et nisi dominus capitaneus populi Bononie omnia acta viderit et ea examinaverit et approbaverit acta recepta. In ipso casu et tunc possit fieri tormentatio cum expressa licentia domini capitanei vel eius vicarii et in eius presentia vel unius de sua familia et in presentia sex ancianorum vel consulum et quatuor officialium communis Bononie, audientium et intelligentium confessionem ipsius et videntium tormenta predicta, et in presentia notarii, qui prepositus est ad scribendum confessiones mallefactorum—et aliter non."

162. Ibid.: "Et si contra predicta vel aliquod predictorum fiat per dominum potestatem vel aliquem de sua familia, ipso iure sit exclusus a regimine civitatis et condempnetur per dominum capitaneum in mille libras bononenorum."

If the captain of the people, the anziani, and the consuls did not enforce this statute, they were subject to the same penalty. The statute was to be observed without exception and dispensation.[163]

Scholars have long recognized that the jurists who wrote theoretical tracts defining the use of torture in the courts limited the employment of torture.[164] One may wonder, cynically perhaps, whether these limitations of the statutes and of the jurists were observed in practice. Even without the necessary careful exploration of court cases in the Italian cities, we might conclude that the jurists' and the communes' careful protection of an individual's right to due process, even from torture, was perfectly congruent with the jurists' preoccupation with procedural doctrine during this period. These statutes may not have saved noncitizens from being "put to the question," but they might have spared a citizen or two.

The rules of the Bolognese statutes are particularly striking. The decision to torture was not left to a judge or judges, but to a large number of magistrates. All of this would seem to indicate that torture was considered an evil that infringed on the rights of a free individual—a "citizen" of the city-state[165]—of honorable reputation.[166] If so—we can only reach tentative conclusions until we have some idea of how torture was actually used in the late thirteenth and early fourteenth centuries—the general limitations placed on torture in these statutes would be in harmony with contemporary ideas about a defendant's right to due process.

The most sophisticated and complete summing up of juristic thinking

163. Ibid.: "Et nihilominus dominus capitaneus possit et debeat talem captum auferre et de fortia domini potestatis et communis Bononie libere relaxare ad ipsius voluntatem. Et si predicta non servaverit dominus capitaneus, penam similem patiatur, et loco ipsius domini capitanei anciani et consules, qui tunc fuerint, tenantur exequi omnia et singula supradicta. Quod statutum in omnibus suis partibus sit precisum et precise debeat observari."

164. Fiorelli, *Tortura* I 131–179 (tracts on torture); I 243–326 (doctrine).

165. On conceptions of citizenship in Italy, see Julius Kirshner, "'Civitas sibi faciat civem': Bartolus of Sassoferrato's Doctrine of the Making of a Citizen," *Speculum* 48 (1973) 694–713 and the bibliography listed in n. 1, p. 694.

166. Johannes Fried has examined the use of torture in the prosecution of the Templars and has emphasized that even in the case of heresy where torture was unquestionably permitted, the judges were careful to observe the rules governing its use. "Wille, Freiwilligkeit und Geständnis um 1300: Zur Beurteilung des letzten Templergroßmeisters Jacques de Molay," *Historisches Jahrbuch* 105 (1985) 388–425. Fried has printed an excellent bibliography on torture pp. 389–390 nn. 5–6. The first mention of torture in German sources has been assumed to have been in the statutes of Vienna in the 1220s. Othmar Hageneder, "Zum ersten Zeugnis für Anwendung der Folter in Deutschland," *Geschichte und ihre Quellen: Festschrift für Friedrich Hausmann zum 70. Geburstag* (Graz: 1991) 143–148, has shown that this text must date to the late thirteenth century (ca. 1275).

about due process in the late thirteenth and early fourteenth centuries is found in the work of a canonist, Johannes Monachus. He was French, studied in Paris, became bishop of Meaux and an advisor to Philip the Fair, and died in 1313.[167] While glossing a "decretalis extravagans" of Boniface VIII (*Rem non novam*) he commented extensively on the rights of a defendant.[168] Johannes had been undoubtedly goaded by Boniface's rash decree that seemed to ignore the developing jurisprudence of due process that we have just examined. The pope had promulgated *Rem non novam* in 1303, in which he stipulated that papal summons were valid whether defendants knew of them or not.[169] Johannes asked a key question that went to the heart of procedural protection for defendants: could the pope, on the basis of this decretal, proceed against a person without a summons? Johannes concluded that the pope was only above positive law, not natural law. Since a summons had been established by natural law, no pope could omit it.[170] He insisted that no judge, even the pope, could come to a just decision unless the defendant was present in court.[171] When a crime is notorious, the judge may proceed in a sum-

167. Hans-Peter Glöckner, "Johannes Monachus," DMA 7 (1986) 120–121. Schulte, *Quellen* II 191–193.

168. *Extravagantes communes* 2.3.1; on the collection of extravagantes that Johannes glossed and other similar collections, see Jacqueline Tarrant, *Extrauagantes Iohannis XXII* (MIC, Series B, 6; Città del Vaticano: 1983) 1–21. On Johannes's glosses to the extravagantes, see R. M. Johannessen, "Cardinal Jean Lemoine and the Authorship of the Glosses to Unam sanctam," BMCL 18 (1988) 33–41. On his gloss to *Rem non novam*, see Johannessen, "Cardinal Jean Lemoine's Gloss to *Rem non novam* and the Reinstatement of the Colonna Cardinals," *Proceedings of the Eighth International Congress of Medieval Canon Law, San Diego*, ed. Stanley Chodorow. (MIC, Series C, 9; Città del Vaticano: 1992) 309–320.

169. Pope Clement V viscerated *Rem non novam* with *Dudum*, Clem. 2.1.1.

170. Johannes Monachus to Extravag. com. 2.3.1 (Rem non novam) v. *Non obstantibus aliquibus privilegiis*, London, BL Royal 10.E.i., fol. 214r, London, Lambeth Palace 13, fol. 363v–364r: "Ad euidentiam premissorum quero an papa procedere contra aliquem ualeat citatione non premissa? Et uidetur quod sic quia est supra ius, extra. de conces. preb. Proposuit [X 3.8.4]. Item quia princeps solutus est legibus, ff. de legibus et senatuscon. Princeps [Dig. 1.3.31(30)]. Item papa habet plenitudinem potestatis, ii. q.vi. Decreto [C.2 q.6 c.11], extra. de pen. et rem. Cum ex eo, in fine [X 5.38.14], extra. de usu pal. Ad honorem [X 1.8.4]. Sed contra. Citatio est principium processus iudiciarii ut supra not. et habetur extra. de probat. Quoniam contra [X. 2.19.11], et ad finem iudiciorum que est sententia, ff. de re iud. l.i. [Dig. 42.1.1] attingi sine principio non potest . . . Nullus potest supra ius quod non condidit, sed conditum presupponit. Sed papa uel purus homo nullum dictorum iurium condidit, sed alias conditum presupponit, xxv. q.i. Sunt quidam [C.25 q.1 c.6], igitur supra nullum illorum potest. Maior patet, minor etiam manifesta est quantum ad legem eternam, uel ius eternum, diuinum, naturale, et quantum ad ius humanum quod deriuatur a naturali . . . sequitur ergo conclusio, scilicet, quod papa non potest nisi supra ius quinto modo dictum, scilicet supra ius pure positiuum."

171. Ibid.: "Restat igitur uidere si citatio sit de iure naturali uel de humano deriuato a naturali ut conclusio ex principio: quia si papa circa talia iura nihil possit ut ex precedentibus patet, consequens est quod contra nullum possit procedere citatione non pre-

mary fashion in some parts of the process, but the summons and judgment must be observed.[172]

Johannes held that a summons to court (citatio) and a judgment (sententia) were integral parts of the judicial procedure because Genesis 3.12 proved that both were indispensable.[173] He referred to the story of Adam and Eve that Paucapalea and Stephen of Tournai had introduced into the canonical tradition and that Guilielmus Durantis had given its final form in the Prologue of his *Speculum iudiciale*: Even God had been bound to summon Adam to render a defense.[174] Perhaps drawing upon the question of the anonymous French jurist cited above or impelled by the inner logic of God's judgment of Adam, Johannes took medieval conceptions of due process one step further: Everyone is presumed innocent unless they are proven culpable. The law, he insisted, is more inclined to absolve than to condemn.[175] An argument could be made that the pope or some other judge might know the truth about a case from secret sources, but Johannes did not think that this was a valid objection. A judge is not a private person and does not judge as one. He is a public person, and he should learn the truth publicly.[176] Although the prince's will has the force of law if it is regulated by reason, his will is not, according to Aristotle, "a secure rule." When

---

missa . . . Cum igitur non potest ad plenum factum et iustum uel iniustum sine presentia eius qui iudicari debet cognosci et sciri, xxx. q.v. § His ita, in fine [C.30 q.5 p.c.9], extra. de re iud. Cum Bertholdus [X 2.27.18], xi. q.iii. Eorum [C.11 q.3 c.76]. Tunc necesse est ipsum citari et uocari; nec papa hoc potest omittere, et minus alius iudex, quia sic omitteretur cognitio que ad iudicium de necessitate requiritur . . . Et sic patet secundum et tertium simul, scilicet quod citatio est de iure naturali et per consequens quod papa contra aliquem procedere non potest nisi citatione premissa."

172. Ibid.: "Et hoc probat hec constitutio euidenter. Hoc liquet etiam in notoriis in quibus licet iuris ordo non sit seruandus usquequaque, seruandus in citando et in sententiando, extra. de iureiur. Ad nostram [X 2.24.21], ii. q.i. Imprimis [C.2 q.1 c.7], extra. de diuort. Porro [X 4.19.3], ii. q.i. Manifesta [C.2 q.1 c.15], not. extra. de accus. Qualiter, ibi, 'Descendam' [X 5.1.17]."

173. Ibid.: "Et Gen. xviii. ubi factum erat notorium attamen Deus uoluit probare quam iudicare . . . Nec obstat extra. de accus. c. Euidentia [X 5.1.9], nec ibi tollitur citatio nec sententia quia Gen. iii. probatur utrumque necessarium."

174. Proemium, *Speculum iuris* (Basel: 1574) 5: "Hinc est quod iudiciorum ordo et placitandi usus in paradiso videtur exordium habuisse. Nam Adam de inobedientia a Domino redargutus, quasi actori exceptionem obiiciens, relationem criminis in coniugem, immo in coniugis actorem convertit, dicens: Mulier quam mihi sociam dedisti me decepit."

175. Johannes Monachus to Extrav. Com. 2.3.1: "Item quilibet presumitur innocens nisi probetur nocens, extra. de presum. c. Dudum [X 2.23.16], extra. de scrut. in ord. fac. c. unico [X 1.12.1], ff. de manumis. test. l. Seruos [Dig. 40.4.20] et ius est promptius ad absoluendum quam ad condemnandum."

176. Ibid.: "Sed forte dices quod papa uel alius iudex nouit causam et ueritatem neogotii secreto, ut est priuata persona. Dicendum est quod hoc non sufficit quia iudex non iudicat ut priuata persona, sed ut publica et ideo publice debet sibi innotescere ueritas, scilicet per leges publicas, diuinas, uel humanas in communi."

the prince judges without a discussion and examination of a case, his will is not informed by reason.[177] Finally, Johannes cited Aristotle again. There are two types of principalities: despotic and politic. The first is similar to a slave and his master. The slave has no right to resist. The second is a polity of free people, who have the right of resistance. A free polity governs the Church; it is not a despotism.[178]

Johannes's gloss is a remarkable defense and justification of due process in law. As we have seen, nothing in his gloss was without antecedents, but no jurist before him had written such a thorough analysis of a defendant's right to a public, proper, and orderly trial. Contrasting Johannes's treatment with that of Guilielmus Durantis's composed a few decades earlier reveals important differences that reflect the metamorphosis of juristic thought about due process at the end of the thirteenth century. Scholars have relied on Durantis for much of what they know about medieval procedure. He wrote a first version of his *Speculum iudiciale* between 1271 and 1276, later revising it between 1289 and 1291.[179] Guilielmus noted several times that a defendant had a right to a defense;[180] he observed that an excommunicate, even the devil, deserved to have his case heard.[181] He also thought that those accused of notorious crimes should have a proper trial.[182] But having

177. Ibid.: "Ad tertium dicendum est quod uoluntas principis legis habet uigorem, si sit ratione regulata, et fiat animo condendi legem cuius forma traditur C. de leg. Humanum [Cod. 1.14(17).8], quia uoluntas de se non est securus canon, ut Philosophus dicit ii. Polit. Cum autem princeps iudicat uel sententiat sine cause discussione et examinatione non habet uoluntatem regulatam secundum rectum iudicium rationis."

178. Ibid.: "Ad quartum dicendum est quod secundum Philosophum in i. Polit. duplex est principatus, despoticus et politicus. Primus est domini ad seruum qui non habet ius resistendi, eo quod seruus est domini totaliter secundum quod huiusmodi. Secundus est principatus liberorum, qui habent ius in aliquo resistendi, et talis est principatus ecclesie circa subditos. Non enim est uerisimile quod principatus ecclesie sit despoticus. Non enim sumus ancille filii, sed libere, qua libertate Christus non liberauit, ad Galat. iv. Joh. Monac. Cardinalis."

179. Ronald J. Zawilla, "Durand, Guillaume," DMA 4 (1984) 314–315. Schulte, *Quellen* II 144–156.

180. *Speculum iuris* II de exceptionibus § Nunc (p. 532): "Propter naturam defensionis nulli tracto ad iudicium auferendae: alias saepe innocens condemnaretur. Et quia ex quo defensio mihi conceditur, et per consequens omnis, sine quibus defendi non possem, conceduntur." Also III de notoriis criminibus § Scias, in fine (p. 45): "nulli est de iure legitima defensio deneganda." The exception to this rule was that if the case was notorious and the defendant contumacious, a judge might sentence him in his absence.

181. *Speculum iuris* III de inquisitione § Vltimo (p. 42): "Et si proprium non habeat, abbas non privabit eum defensione, quae excommunicato, et etiam diabolo, si in iudicio adesset, non negaretur, ut extra de except. Cum inter et xi. q.iii. Eorum." He borrowed this idea and the wording from Hostiensis's *Summa*, see Gallagher, *Canon Law* 160.

182. *Speculum iuris* III de notoriis criminibus § Iam (p. 52): "Item dicit Innoc. iiii. quod in notorio facti, quod est notum aliis, et non iudici, et in notorio iuris, et in notorio praesumptionis est ordo iudiciarius observandus, ut not. plene extra de cohab. cler. et mulier. Tua."

written his great work just as the jurists developed radically new ideas about the juridical process, his work reflects the presuppositions of the earlier period. He wrote nothing about the judicial procedure being based on a higher law, and he did not systematically describe the rights of defendants at court. His *Speculum* became the standard textbook on procedure in the later Middle Ages and early modern period. If he had composed his *Speculum* thirty years later, he probably would have written sympathetically about these issues. As it was, future readers found little of the significant changes in the doctrine of due process that we have just discussed in the pages of his book. The *ius commune* of early modern Europe may have been the poorer for it.

CHAPTER 5

Henry VII and Robert of Naples

Where are the evidence that do accuse me? What
lawful quest have given their verdict up unto the
frowning judge? Or who pronounced the bitter
sentence of poor Clarence's death? Before I be
convict by course of law, To threaten me with
death is most unlawful.

—Shakespeare, *King Richard III*, Act I, scene 4

In his privilege for the scholars of Bologna, Frederick Barbarossa observed that "their knowledge [of Roman law] illuminates the world, leading men to obey God and us, his ministers."[1] A fractious dispute of the early fourteenth century between the German Emperor Henry VII and King Robert of Naples put Frederick's trust in Roman law to the test. Walter Ullmann wrote that the core of this controversy was whether "the emperor was in reality the 'dominus mundi' as the law books clamorously maintained."[2] Ullmann may not, as I shall argue, have gotten the importance of the dispute exactly right.[3] But, as is so often the case in Ullmann's work, even when he is wrong in detail, he

1. Koeppler, "Frederick Barbarossa," 607: "quorum sicentia mundus illuminatur, ad obediendum deo et nobis, ministris eius."
2. Walter Ullmann, "The Development of the Medieval Idea of Sovereignty," EHR 64 (1949) 1–33, at p. 1. Ullmann returned to this topic in his essay "Zur Entwicklung des Souveränitätsbegriffs im Spätmittelalter," *Festschrift Nikolaus Grass zum 60. Geburtstag* (2 vols. Innsbruck: 1974–1975) I 9–27, reprinted in *Scholarship and Politics in the Middle Ages* (Collected Studies; London: 1978). On the idea of "Weltherrschaft" in the later Middle Ages see Friedrich Heer, "Zur Kontinuität des Reichgedankens im Spätmittelalter," MIÖG 58 (1950) 336–350, Friedrich Baethgen, "Zur Geschichte der Weltherrschaftsidee im späteren Mittelalter," *Festschrift Percy Ernst Schramm zu seinem 70. Geburtstag* (2 vols. Wiesbaden: 1964) I 189–203, Kurt-Ulrich Jäschke, "Zu universalen und regionalen Reichskonzeptionen beim Tode Kaiser Heinrichs VII." *Festschrift für Berent Schwineköper* (Sigmaringen: 1982) 415–435 and Hageneder, "Weltherrschaft" 271–278.
3. Helmut G. Walther, "Die Gegner Ockhams: Zur Korporationslehre der mittelalterlichen Legisten," *Politische Institutionen im gesellschaftlichen Umbruch: Ideengeschichtliche Beiträge zur Theorie politischer Institutionen*, ed. G. Göhler, K. Lenk, H. Münkler, and M. Walther (Opladen: 1990) 129 n. 18.

is right about the essence of the matter. The controversy did focus more precisely on the authority of the emperor over other Christian kings than any earlier confrontation between emperor or king, and pope. The contentious issues forced the jurists to define large questions: Could the emperor bring a treasonous vassal to trial who was an independent king? Was the emperor truly lord of the world? Could he exercise jurisdiction over kings? Could he condemn a vassal without a trial? Did the emperor have to observe the rules of judicial procedure before he rendered sentence on a contumacious vassal? The clash of imperial and royal prerogatives stimulated jurists to clarify questions that went to the heart of procedural norms.

After his selection by six of the electoral princes on November 27, 1308, Henry, count of Luxemburg, was crowned King of the Romans at Aachen, January 6, 1309. He became emperor-elect. No German king had been crowned in Italy since Frederick II. By the end of the summer he had contacted Pope Clement V and arranged for an imperial coronation in Rome.[4] The king of the Angevin kingdom of Sicily, Robert of Naples (or, as he was otherwise known, Robert of Anjou) was a major obstacle to Henry's plans. Although Clement immediately proposed a marriage joining the houses of Luxemburg and Anjou by uniting Henry's daughter, Beatrice, with Robert's son, Charles, the pope's initiative was doomed from the start.[5] Robert was a recognized leader of the Guelf party in Florence and in the other northern city-states. Henry had much to gain from an alliance with Robert; what Robert thought he might gain is harder to discern. Henry could use Robert's support to reassert imperial prerogatives in Italy. In return Robert could receive military aid against his Aragonese rival and enemy, King Frederick II of Trinacria, who held the island of Sicily, but Henry's ability to furnish real aid to Robert was slight. More impor-

4. William M. Bowsky, *Henry VII in Italy: The Conflict of Empire and City-State, 1310–1313* (Lincoln, Nebraska: 1960) 17–23. Friedrich Schneider, *Kaiser Heinrich VII* (3 vols. Greiz-Leipzig: 1924–1928). G. Sommerfeldt, "König Heinrich VII. und die lombardischen Städte in den Jahren 1310–1312," *Deutsche Zeitschrift für Geschichtswissenschaft* 2 (1889) 97–155. W. Israel, *König Robert von Neapel und Kaiser Heinrich VII.: Die Ereignisse bis zur Krönung in Rom* (Berlin: 1903); G. Irmer, *Die Romfahrt Kaiser Heinrichs VII. im Bildercyclus des Codex Balduini Trevirensis* (Berlin: 1881); Franz-Josef Heyen, *Kaiser Heinrichs Romfahrt: Die Bilderchronik von Kaiser Heinrich VII. und Kurfürst Balduin von Luxemburg (1308–1313)* (Boppard am Rhein: 1965); C. R. Wenck, *Clemens V. und Heinrich VII.: Die Anfänge des französischen Papsttums: Ein Beitrag zur Geschichte des 14. Jahrhunderts* (Halle: 1882). K. Hitzfeld, "Die letzte Gesandtschaft Heinrichs VII. nach Avignon und ihre Folgen," *Historisches Jahrbuch* 83 (1964) 43–53.
5. Agostino Paravicini Bagliani, "Clemente V," DBI 26 (Roma: 1982) 3–16, with an excellent bibliography.

tantly, Robert might lose his allies among the Guelfs if he allied himself too closely with Henry.

Clement V probably viewed the alliance with enthusiasm. The Aragonese control of Sicily had been a festering thorn in the side of the papacy since the Sicilian Vespers. Further, an alliance between the houses of Anjou and Luxemburg would have appealed to a pope residing in Avignon.[6]

After crossing the Alps, Henry arrived in the Piedmontese town of Susa, the birthplace of Hostiensis, on October 23, 1310. From the moment Henry touched Italian soil, Robert feigned loyalty that was belied by his actions. Although Henry restored Ghibelline exiles and appointed imperial vicars, he strove to placate the sensitivities of the Guelfs. He restored peace between dissident parties in Chieri and Asti, if only temporarily. In Milan, where he was crowned king of Italy with the traditional iron crown, he could not bring concord. Cremona and Brescia revolted; Henry's treatment of the rebels was harsh. The Guelfs rekindled their fears of the emperor. Florence, Lucca, Siena, and Bologna joined together to prevent Henry from reaching Rome. Nevertheless, with the aid of Genoa and Pisa, old imperial cities, Henry reached Rome in the spring of 1312.

His reception did not befit his station or his aspirations. Robert had sent his brother, John of Gravina, to Rome with a sizable army. After bloody street fighting, Henry realized that he would not be crowned in St. Peter's. John's troops held Castel Sant'Angelo and the area between it and the Capitoline. Reluctantly, because their mandate specified St. Peter's, the cardinals sent by Clement V crowned Henry in the Basilica of St. John in Lateran on June 29, 1312.[7]

Henry sent an encyclical letter announcing his election to the princes of Europe.[8] In a long arenga he declared that although the rule (principatus) had been divided in earlier centuries among various nations, God's established order dictated that all men should be subject to one

---

6. Bowsky, *Henry VII* 23–53, argues that Robert may have been more interested in an alliance with Henry than I have indicated. R. Caggese, *Roberto d'Angiò e i suoi tempi* (2 vols. Firenze: 1921–1930). Walter Goetz, *König Robert von Neapel (1309–1343), seine Persönlichkeit und sein Verhältnis zum Humanismus* (Tübingen: 1910). A. Cutolo, "Arrigo VII e Roberto d'Angiò," *Archivio storico per le provincie napoletane* 18 (1932) 5–30; G. M. Monti, "Da Carlo I a Roberto de Angiò," *Archivio storico per le provincie napoletane* 18 (1932) 101–117. Paravicini Bagliani, "Clemente V," 10.

7. Bowsky, *Henry VII* 54–167.

8. *Constitutiones et acta publica imperatorum et regum,* 4.2: *Inde ab A. MCCXCVIII usque ad A. MCCCXIII,* ed. J. Schwalm (MGH, Legum sectio, 4; Hannover-Leipzig: 1911) no. 801, pp. 801–804.

prince, in imitation of the celestial hierarchy.[9] With the translation of imperium to the Romans, God established the city of Rome as the future seat of ecclesiastical and imperial power.[10] Subsequently, Christ instituted the eternal priesthood in Rome.[11] As the "King of kings and the Lord of lords," Christ drew all things under his exalted office and placed all things under the imperium of his sovereignty [at Rome].[12]

Royal responses to Henry's letter offer interesting contrasts. King Edward II's chancery congratulated the new emperor politely.[13] Philip the Fair's lawyers read the arenga tendentiously. Henry had carefully avoided making the claim that the kingdoms of Europe were subject to the empire but did imply that God's plan would be more closely followed if they were. Philip rejected Henry's implication and stated baldly that France had never, since the time of Christ, recognized a temporal superior.[14] Philip had a pressing political point to make as well. Henry had sent one of his letters to the city of Lyon and called its citizens subjects. Philip made it clear that Lyon was part of the kingdom of France and did not belong to the empire.[15]

Clement V sent a letter to Henry that reached him shortly after his coronation. He demanded that Henry promise not to invade the Regno and asked Henry to submit his dispute with Robert to papal arbitration. He asked them both to submit to a year's truce.[16]

9. Ibid. 802: "super cuncta que fecit tribueret principatum et ut creatura tam nobilis a celestium ierarchia non differret similitudine ordinis . . . sic universi homines distincti regnis et provinciis separati uni principi monarche subessent, quatinus eo consurgeret machina mundi preclarior."

10. Ibid.: "dictum imperium transiit ad Romanos provide Dei disponente clemencia, quod illuc preiret imperialis excellencie thronus, ubi futura erat sacerdotalis et apostolica sedes."

11. Ibid.: "ac in eodem loco pontificis et imperatoris auctoritas refulgeret illius vicariam representans imaginem, qui pro nobis ex intemerato virginis utero natus."

12. Ibid.: "ipse sacerdocium eternum instituit ac tamquam rex regum et dominus dominorum ad culminis sui fastigium omnia trahens sub sue ditionis imperio universa subgessit."

13. Ibid. no. 812, p. 814.

14. Ibid. no. 811, pp. 812–814: "Notorie namque et generaliter predicatur ab omnibus et ubique, quod a tempore Christi citra regnum Francorum solum regem suum sub ipso Ihesu Christo rege regum et domino dominorum ac omnimode creature dominatore habuit, nullum temporalem superiorem cognoscens aut habens, quocumque imperatore regnante."

15. Ibid.: "in litteris vestris . . . ipsos (cives Lugdunenses) fideles vestros et subditos appellastis, cum in nullo predecessoribus vestris fuerint nec vobis sint subditi aut vobis ad aliquam fidelitatem teneantur astricti, sed semper fuerunt notorie in et de regno Francie et prestante Domino sunt et erunt."

16. Bowsky, *Henry VII* 168–169; Martin Thilo, *Das Recht der Entscheidung über Krieg und Frieden im Streite Kaiser Heinrichs VII. mit der römischen Kurie: Ein Beitrag zur Geschichte des Verhältnisses von sacerdotium und imperium und des Wandels vom Weltimperium zum nationalen Königtum* (Historische Studien 343; Berlin: 1938) 68–115, esp. 90–103.

Christendom had only recently recovered from the dispute over national sovereignty between Pope Boniface VIII and King Philip the Fair of France. One can draw intriguing parallels between Boniface and Henry VII. Both laid claims to universal lordship and hoped to breathe new life into an institution that claimed universal jurisdiction over all Christians. Both were faced with opponents and situations they did not understand. Henry's personal and political position was, like Boniface's, tenuous. He had lost his wife, his brother, and most of his army by the time of his coronation. He also lost patience with Robert of Naples. Henry, like Boniface, did not hold patience as a conspicuous virtue. Instead of retreating from what had become a quagmire, he took the only step left. He sent legates to King Frederick II of Trinacria, and they concluded pacts of mutual assistance. Henry broke with Robert definitively.[17] If Henry misjudged the Italian political situation badly, he committed an even graver error by binding himself with the Aragonese king, Frederick II, who would prove a completely ineffective ally.

Henry moved north. At Arezzo, on September 12, 1312, he issued a solemn proclamation directed against Robert of Naples and had it posted on the door of the cathedral. He fulfilled his prediction to Frederick of Trinacria that he would accuse Robert of treason.[18] He summoned Robert to appear before him within three months to answer charges that he supported rebels in Lombardy and Tuscany, that his legates promoted treaties inimical to imperial interests, and that his brother and allies waged war on him in the streets of Rome.

At this early stage of the dispute Henry already knew that he was on shaky legal ground. He claimed that he could not have the proclamation delivered because the roads were too dangerous. His messengers would have been seized and killed. Henry announced that he intended to proceed even if Robert did not appear at his court in person.[19]

After leaving Arezzo, Frederick besieged Florence. Without sufficient troops or supplies, the siege was a predictable failure, and his fortunes turned from bad to worse. Robert of Naples supported rebellious

17. Bowsky, *Henry VII* 169–170.
18. *Constitutiones*, ed. Schwalm no. 821, pp. 823–824. On the canon law of treason see Vito Piergiovanni, "La lesa maestà nella canonistica fino ad Uguccione," *Materiali per una storia della cultura giuridica* 2 (1972) 53–88. Also F. Ghisalberti, "Sulla teoria dei delitti di lesa maestà nel diritto comune," *Archivio giuridico Filippo Serafini* 166 (1955) 160ff.
19. Ibid. no. 848, pp. 854–856: "hec citatio ad eius possit pervenire notitiam, et quia litteras et nuntios ad eum transmittere non valemus propter viarum discrimina . . . quod nulli nostri nuntii ad eum possint accedere . . . ipso per contumaciam absente nichilominus procedere tam ad sententiam quam ad alia, prout de iure facere debebimus et poterimus, eius absentia non obstante."

Tuscan and Lombard communes and became the leader of the Guelf league. At Poggibonsi, which he renamed the "Imperial Mount," Henry issued empty, meaningless edicts condemning Robert and the rebels of Tuscany.[20] Then, in the middle of March, he returned to Pisa and promulgated two laws which provided the legal justifications for his decrees of condemnation. The first, *Ad reprimendum*, was a general constitution in which the emperor decreed that whoever committed the crime of treason against the emperor or king of the Romans could be condemned *in absentia* in summary judicial proceedings.[21] Echoing Boniface VIII's decretal, *Unam sanctam*, he declared that every soul was subject to the Roman prince.[22] The second, *Quoniam nuper est*, answered the question, "Who was a rebel?"[23] The law schools quickly incorporated both edicts into the *Corpus iuris civilis*. Finally, on April 26, 1313, Henry issued his definitive condemnation of Robert of Naples.[24] Robert's crimes were public and notorious, declared Henry, and we, who are not subject to the laws, could have proceeded against him even if he had not been cited.[25] We did not condemn him summarily due to our imperial clemency but have held a hearing and cited him legitimately. Robert did not appear for the hearing, and having heard and recorded the testimony of witnesses, we condemned him in an interlocutory judgment. We now make this judgment definitive.[26] Robert was condemned to be beheaded and his lands confiscated.[27]

The war of paper turned into a war of deeds. Henry was bolstered by his Ghibelline allies and set out from Pisa, after much delay and, again, with inadequate forces, on August 8, 1313. He marched on Siena, where, in spite of his hope for treachery from imperial supporters

20. *Constitutiones*, ed. Schwalm, no. 913, pp. 925–926 (Feb. 12, 1313). Interlocutory judgment against Robert of Naples. Ibid. no. 915, pp. 929–933 (Feb. 23, 1313). Condemnation of rebels.

21. Ibid. no. 929, pp. 965–966: "in quocunque lese maiestatis crimine et maxime ubi contra Romanorum imperatores vel reges aliquid quod dictum crimen tangat asseratur commissum, possit procedi per accusationem vel inquisitionem seu denuntiationem summarie et de plano sine strepitu et figura iudicii." The incipit of the original decree was *Ad reprimenda*, but was changed after having been incorporated into the *Corpus iuris civilis*.

22. Ibid. no. 929, p. 965: "verum etiam divina precepta, quibus iubetur quod omnis anima Romano principi sit subiecta."

23. Ibid. no. 931, pp. 966–967.

24. Ibid. no. 946, pp. 985–990.

25. Ibid. p. 987: "Hec siquidem ad nos deferente clamore notorio et in pluribus etiam rerum experientia edocente, licet ipsa tam publica et notoria essent, quod nulla possent tergiversatione celari, et nos qui legibus subiecti non sumus contra dictum Robertum propter premissa ipso inrequisito potuissemus procedere."

26. Ibid. pp. 987–988 lines 35–47 and 1–4.

27. Bowsky, *Henry VII* 183–184.

within the city's walls, his entrance was barred. Perhaps despondent, certainly thwarted, Henry fell ill and died on August 24, 1313.[28]

THE PAPAL AND IMPERIAL POLEMICS

The struggle between Henry and Robert is an event of the first rank in legal history. It generated a significant amount of polemical literature, most of it in the form of consilia, and also produced papal and imperial legislation that dealt with the issues of imperial jurisdiction, the relationship between the church and the state, and the rules governing the judicial process. The dispute is a splendid example of politics and legal theory swirling about and creating unpredictable turbulence; it is also an illustration of how rapidly the issues of a political dispute could become common coin in the law schools and influence the doctrine of the *ius commune*.

Henry's chancery produced *Ad reprimendum* and *Quoniam nuper est*. Pope Clement V issued three constitutions: (1) *Pastoralis cura*[29] in which he reacted directly to *Ad reprimendum*; (2) *Romani principes* in which Clement reminded Henry of his duty to observe the oaths that he had sworn to the pope;[30] and, somewhat later; (3) *Saepe* in which he clarified the rules of judicial procedure that had arisen over the meaning of "simpliciter et de plano, ac sine strepitu et figura iudicii" (simply and plainly, without clamor and the normal forms of procedure), a phrase used in Henry's letters condemning Robert and a common fixture of papal letters to judges-delegate in certain cases.[31]

This flurry of legislation had a long-lasting influence. Stephan Kuttner has called *Saepe* "the most important single piece of medieval legislation in the history of summary judicial procedure."[32] *Pastoralis cura* became a locus classicus in medieval law for the discussion of due pro-

---

28. Ibid. 192–205.
29. Clem. 2.11.2, issued at Carpentras, March, 1314 on the same day as *Romani principes*. See the text printed by W. Dönniges, *Acta Henrici VII. imperatoris Romanorum et monumenta quaedam alia Medii Aevi* (2 vols. Berlin: 1839) II 241–243.
30. Clem. 2.9.1.
31. Clem. 5.11.2. Kuttner dates the text between May 6, 1312 and March 21, 1314, "probably closer to the later date;" "The Date of the Constitution 'Saepe': The Vatican Manuscripts and the Roman Edition of the Clementines," *Mélanges Eugène Tisserant* (Studi e Testi 234; Città del Vaticano: 1964) 427–452 at p. 432; reprinted in *Medieval Councils, Decretals, and Collections of Canon Law* (Collected Studies Series; London: 1980).
32. "The Date of the Constitution 'Saepe,'" p. 427. On the doctrine of summary judicial procedure, see Charles Lefebvre, "Les origines romaines de la procédure sommaire aux XII et XIII s.," *Ephemerides iuris canonici* 12 (1956) 149–197.

cess. Both decrees were milestones for the development of a doctrine of due process in the *ius commune*.

From the beginning, there must have been questions circulating in the courts and schools about Henry's right to condemn Robert without a trial. Robert had little to fear from the emperor as the fiasco of Henry's coronation in Rome had demonstrated. Since Henry could not confront Robert on the battlefield, he decided to proceed against him legally.

Jurists who supported the emperor wrote the earliest tracts. An anonymous jurist wrote the first consilium that defended Henry from papal interference in his Italian affairs.[33] Quite likely he composed it in Sicily, sometime in late 1312 or early 1313, before Henry promulgated *Ad reprimendum*. Johannes de Calvoruso, a civilian, has been proposed as the author of the consilium, but the evidence for his authorship is very weak.[34] The author dealt with three major questions: (1) Could the pope impose a truce on the emperor? (2) Did the emperor have jurisdiction over all kings, including the king of Sicily (was he "dominus mundi")? (3) Could the emperor condemn his enemies without due process?

If the jurist was a civilian like Calvoruso, he did not turn to Roman law while shaping a defense for Henry. Rather, he based most of conclusions on canon law.[35] Although he referred to the *Lex Rhodia* and *Bene a Zenone*[36] to justify his claim that the emperor was the "lord of the world," the glosses of Johannes Teutonicus and Bernardus Parmensis to Gratian's Decretum and Innocent III's decretal, *Venerabilem*, were his centerpieces for justifying the emperor's universal authority.[37] The Emperor Justinian, the grandfather of medieval Roman law, would have thought it ironic that in the middle of the fourteenth century, a jurist had to turn to the jurisprudence of canon law to defend the emperor from the pope. Roman law contained no texts that put the emperor's case as forcefully—or as bluntly. The anonymous jurist concluded that the pope could not impose a truce on the emperor nor could he interfere in temporal affairs, because he would then be putting his

---

33. *Constitutiones*, ed. Schwalm no. 1248, pp. 1308–1317.

34. Thilo, *Das Recht der Entscheidung* 8–15, who based his conclusions on a suggestion first made by Karl Leopold Hitzfeld, *Studien zu den religiösen und politischen Anschauungen Friedrichs III. von Sizilien* (Historische Studien, 193; Berlin: 1930) 76–125, at 124. Hitzfeld dated the consilium in August, 1312 (pp. 94–95).

35. He cited canon law 35 times; Roman law 30. But a count of citations does not fully demonstrate the extent to which he depended on canon law.

36. Dig. 14.2.9 and Cod. 7.37.3; see above chapter 1.

37. Johannes Teutonicus to D.63 c.22 and 3 Comp. 1.6.19 and Bernardus Parmensis to X 1.6.34; on these glosses see chapter 1.

"scythe into another's field." Quoting a proverb that Innocent III had already used a century earlier, the author underlined a traditional position on the separation of ecclesiastical and temporal power that dated back to the time of Pope Gelasius I in the fifth century.[38]

When considered from a purely legal point of view, two questions were most important. Could the emperor condemn his enemies without a trial? And could the emperor bring someone to trial who was de facto outside his jurisdiction? Although he devoted most of his text to proving that the pope cannot exercise any jurisdiction over the emperor in temporal matters, the anonymous jurist addressed both in two short sections.

First, he asked whether the emperor could punish the crimes of his enemies without an examination and the "ordo [iudiciarius]."[39] He thought there was no doubt that he could when the crimes were notorious. As proof he cited canon law—a passage of Augustine discussing the death of Abel in which he observed that notorious crimes did not "need the clamor of an accuser" and Gratian's discussion (at C.1 q.2.)[40]

The Bible continued to be a gold mine of examples with which to defend or dismiss due process. Although we have seen that by the middle of the twelfth century, the jurists had cited God's condemnation of Adam and Eve as a justification for due process, this jurist read other parts of the Bible. He pointed out that neither Cain's guilt and condemnation nor the fornicator who had married his stepmother needed the formalities of a trial. St. Paul condemned the fornicator without a trial and without even being in Corinth.[41] Consequently the enemies of the prince may be punished without examination or witnesses. Using the same maxim with which Hostiensis defended Innocent IV's deposition of Frederick II, he concluded that "notorious crimes do not need proof."[42]

38. *Constitutiones*, ed. Schwalm no. 1248, pp. 1310, lines 28–29, and 1313, lines 32–35; Innocent III in *Venerabilem*, X 1.6.34.
39. Ibid., p. 1314: "an possit imperator sine hiis que sunt ordinis et absque alia penitus examinactione hostium crimina ferire."
40. Ibid.: "quia vere potest absque accusatore et ordine, ut extra. de accusat. Evidentia [X 5.1.2] et ii. q.i. De manifesta et c. Deus omnipotens § Quando autem" [C.2 q.1 c.17 and 20].
41. Ibid.: "iuxta illud quod scribatur per apostolum ad Corinthios v [1 Corinth. 5.1–6], scilicet quod fornicator ille, in quem sine examinactione sententia apostolica processerat, publice coram omnibus novercam suam pro uxore habebat, et ideo apostolus absens facie, presens autem auctoritate Spiritus sancti eum, qui hoc admisit, tradidit Sathane in interitum carnis."
42. Unfortunately the text is fragmentary at this point. Ibid.: "Set hostes principis nec poterant moneri nec debebant ... citra examinactionem feriri possint per eundem principem, nec sit opus testibus vel alia [lacuna of 12–13 letters in text] extra. de cohabit.

To the question of whether the emperor could condemn someone
outside his jurisdiction, he responded that the imperial condemnation
of Robert was just because the emperor held sovereignty over the entire
world. Sicily is a part of the empire. Even though some ecclesiastical
canons might support the claim that the island is part of the Patrimony
of St. Peter, the canonists, as he had noted earlier, acknowledge that
the emperor is lord of the world.[43]

The boundaries within which the emperor could exercise his jurisdiction was a key issue with practical ramifications. As Henry struggled
with the cities that rallied to Robert, he sought to levy sentences against
them. Milanzo, who was one of Henry's imperial judges, wrote an opinion justifying Henry's expropriation of Robert's lands.[44] He concluded
that Henry's punishment of Robert was just and that he could also
render judgments against Bologna and the cities of Romagna for their
treasonous crimes against Padua and Treviso.[45] Milanzo's main argument was insupportable. Since Robert had been condemned, the imperial treasury confiscated his lands (La Romagna). Therefore, Henry
could exercise jurisdiction over the cities of La Romagna.[46] Milanzo's
sycophantic reasoning violated every norm of the *ius commune*.

Henry needed good legal counsel, not unenforceable claims. A jurist
from Pavia, Johannes Branchazolus, sent Henry a treatise on the "Powers of the Pope and of the Emperor," in which he justified imperial authority.[47] Just as the bees have one king, nature fashioned one ruler for
the human race. If no one would uphold it, law could not exist in a
city.[48] Relying on the glosses of the canonists, Johannes trumpeted that

---

mul. et cler. c. Tua [X 3.2.8] . . . notoria probactione non indigent, ff. qui sat. cog. Si
vero § Qui pro rei [Dig. 2.8.5.1]."

43. Ibid., p. 1315: "Totus enim mundus imperatoris est . . . Et specialter dico de
Sicilia quod est de imperio . . . licet quidam canones dicant quod Sicilia est de patrimonio
beati Petri ut infra. Set et canoniste fatentur ut supradictum est quod imperator est
dominus mundi."

44. Ibid., pp. 1015–1017; first printed by Wilhelm Dönniges, *Acta Henrici VII.* no.
32, II 79–87. See also Dönniges, *Kritik der Quellen für die Geschichte Heinrichs des VII.
des Luxemburgers* (Berlin: 1841), who critically examined the historical sources.

45. Ibid., p. 1015: "Si ergo lata est sententia contra Robertum et feratur, sicut de
iure ferri potest, contra commune et homines de Bononia, contra communitates et
homines de Romaniola propter delicta et crimina lese maiestatis commissa super ter-
ritorio imperii et contra commune et homines civitatis Padue et contra commune et
homines civitatis Trivisii."

46. Ibid., p. 1016: "quia civitas Bononie et civitates Romaniole et communitates ipsarum terrarum per sententiam latam contra Robertum olim regem Sicilie sunt incor-
porati in fiscum imperii pro eo tempore." See Bowsky, *Henry VII* 183.

47. E. E. Stengel, *Nova Alamanniae* (Berlin: 1921) I.1 no. 90, pp. 44–52. Also
Bowsky, *Henry VII* 185.

48. *Nova Alamanniae* 45–46: "in apibus naturaliter unus rex est."

the emperor was the lord of the world and all nations were under him. He expanded on his metaphor of the bees. Just as a beekeeper keeps them in a hive and releases them at his will, so too the emperor arranges human society.[49] The emperor rules in temporal and spiritual matters because he is the king of all things and the head of the Church.[50] Petrarch would use the metaphor of the bees' making honey to describe creative genius, but metaphors that work in the realm of literature do not always work in law.[51] No fourteenth-century judge would have taken Johannes's argument seriously.

Still, it was Dante Alighieri who produced the most famous defense of imperial authority during this time, his *Monarchia* (written ca. 1312–1314).[52] However, *Monarchia* was not a work of jurisprudence. Although Dante made most of the same general points as Johannes Branchazolus, he justified Henry's position with literary and theological arguments for imperial authority[53] that also would not stand the careful scrutiny of a judge.

Of the surviving materials, the tracts defending Robert and the papacy far outnumber those supporting Henry VII.[54] Two treatises that predate Henry's death answer ten questions arising from the dispute.[55] The first is a juridical analysis, the second theological. Although the second is incomplete, it probably dealt with all the questions disputed in the first. The authors of these tracts are unknown, but they both reflect "official" papal thinking. Since the manuscripts containing them were originally in the papal library, the tracts were probably written at the

49. Ibid., p. 49: "Preparat enim homo apibus vasa suis, in que reducte ibidem facit quelibet, in quam se recolligit, domum suam ibique recondit sagaciter fructum suum. Inde tamen exire non possunt preter domini voluntatem . . . sic hominibus imperator preparat loca diversa et varias civitates . . . inde preter ipsius voluntatem exire nequeunt si velit eisdem exitum denegare, cum sit viarum dominus et omnium publicorum, ut in constit. feudorum Que sint regalie, c. uno [Const. feud. 2.57] sicque per se ipsum se quilibet voluntarie carceravit et sic dominatur omnibus merito imperator."

50. Ibid.: "Dominatur in spiritualibus et divinis quoniam rex est omnium rerum, etiam divinarum, ut ff. de legibus l.ii. cum capud sit ecclesie."

51. Petrarch, *Rerum familiarum libri I–VIII*, trans. Aldo S. Bernardo (Albany, New York: 1975) 1.7.

52. The date of his treatise has been disputed although some date it as late as 1317. For a short summary of opinion see Robert Hollander, "Dante Alighieri," DMA 4 (1984) 94–105 at 102–103.

53. Bowsky, *Henry VII* 187–189; Charles T. Davis, *Dante and the Idea of Rome* (Oxford: 1957) 263ff; Michele Maccarrone, "Il terzo libro della 'Monarchia,'" *Studi Danteschi* 33 (1955) 5–142; and Kantorowicz, *The King's Two Bodies* 451–495.

54. See Bowsky, *Henry VII* 189–192; Davis, *Dante and the Idea of Rome* 180–185.

55. *Constitutiones*, ed. Schwalm, [1.] no. 1249–1250, pp. 1317–1341; [2.] no. 1251, pp. 1342–1362, lacking the beginning and end of the tract, answers questions 2–6 (beginning).

papal court in Avignon.[56] The focus of the questions is entirely on issues of feudal law and of "church and state": (1) Could Henry's oath to Clement be considered an oath of fealty? (2) Could the pope impose a truce on Robert and Henry without having summoned them? (3) Could the pope demand an oath from Henry not to damage the Regno? (4) Could Henry deprive Robert of his royal office that the king held immediately from the pope? The answers to the first three questions were affirmative, the last was negative.

The problems posed by these two anonymous treatises were not new. Only a few years earlier, during his dispute with Philip IV of France, Pope Boniface VIII had endorsed the universality of the empire and the *de iure* subordination of all princes to the emperor, but changing political circumstances created a radical metamorphosis of papal ideology.[57] Papal polemicists returned to the doctrine first articulated by Pope Innocent III in *Per venerabilem*: "the king of France recognizes no superior in temporal affairs."[58] The authors of both papal treatises subjected the emperor to the pope and the state to the Church. "All men are subject to the pope by reason of sin . . . who is the father and teacher and pastor of all men," proclaimed the jurist.[59] Henry cannot judge Robert because "those laws [that proclaim the emperor's universality] were valid during the time of the Roman empire, but the law of nations introduced separate dominions and separate kingdoms. The Roman empire now has boundaries and limits."[60] Because the Romans obtained their empire through violence, he continued, the empire may be dissolved through violence.[61]

56. Ibid., pp. 1317 and 1342. The legal consilium is contained in Archives départ. de la Lozère, Série G nr. 1036; the theological in Paris, B.N. lat. 4113, fol. 7r–17r. See P. Gachon, "Etude sur le manuscrit G. 1036 des Archives départmentales de la Lozère: Pièces relatives au débat de pape Clément V avec l'empereur Henri VII," *Mémoires de la Société archéologique de Montpellier* (Montpellier: 1894).

57. Calasso, *Glossatori* 80–81. Boniface wrote of French claims: "regem Romanorum qui est promovendus in imperatorem et monarcham omnium regum et principum terrenorum. Nec insurgat his superbia gallicano: quae dicit quod non recognoscit superiorem. Mentiuntur, quia de iure sunt et esse debent sub rege romano et imperatore." *Constitutiones*, ed. Schwalm, nr. 173, p. 139. See Walther, *Imperiales Königtum* 148–149, 213.

58. See above, chapter 1.

59. Ibid. no. 1250, p. 1324.

60. Ibid. p. 1338: "et habent iura illa pro tempore et pro rebus que subiacebant Romano imperio, sed sicut iure gentium sunt rerum dominia distincta et regna condita et bella introducta, sic eodem iure et ratione fuerunt regna translata et mutata et dominia mutata et iterum distincta. Unde Romanum imperium habet fines et limites."

61. Ibid. p. 1339: "Preterea scimus quod per violentiam et occupationem Romanum crevit imperium, unde si homines se subtrahant, cum vident opportunitatem et regna per se constituant, inconveniens non videtur, cum omnis res, per quas causas introducitur, per easdem dissolvi possit."

The issue of due process was broached by the second question—could the pope impose a truce on Henry and Robert without having cited them—and the answer was simple. The facts of the case were notorious. The pope acted on the principle that when there was danger in delay he could cut short normal judicial procedures, such as a summons and the solemnity of admonitions.[62] In the end, Clement did not act through the normal judicial process but by command as Henry's superior.[63]

The arguments of the anonymous theologian were crudely hierocratic. In his answer to the second question—could the pope impose a truce without having cited Henry and Robert—he argued that the pope had both swords, the temporal and the spiritual. The pope delegated the exercise of the temporal sword to the emperor, but retained "plenitudo potestatis" over him in temporal affairs.[64] Exercising jurisdiction over temporal and spiritual affairs from divine and natural law, the pope is the prince of Christendom.[65] Since his power is instituted for the public welfare, the prince has the authority to suppress war. He noted that the pope was like a "most perfect doctor of medicine." Consequently, he had all the means to prevent wars and impose truces or penalties on the body of the faithful.[66] The niceties of due process were completely lost on this writer, and he had nothing to say about the justness of the pope's acting without having cited the defendants.

In a fragmentary consilium, another anonymous jurist argued that the universality of the Roman empire had long since disappeared.[67] He noted that the city of Rome, which had preeminence over the whole world, is no longer that commonwealth (Res publica) of which the law books spoke. The time of Roman hegemony has passed. Roman sovereignty has been divided. Hence, since Rome no longer exists, one cannot commit treason against it. Today that republic resides in the Roman pontiff who has great power and both swords.[68] "At present it is clear

---

62. Ibid., p. 1327: "potuit dominus papa treugas indicere, partibus non vocatis et etiam invitis, quia cum non posset non esse notorium, quod ex eorum guerra et discordia . . . multa pericula animarum et corporum et scandala orirentur . . . et etiam ubi proceditur in notoriis, si est in mora periculum, potest omitti citatio et monitionum solemnitas, ut not. Innoc. extra. de cohab. cler. et mul. c. Tua [X 3.2.8]." The papal author relies on the decretal "Tua," as did his imperial counterpart, see n. 42 above.

63. Ibid.: "Preterea istud non est actus iudicialis, sed preceptum quoddam, quod fit ex officio superioris, ut periculis occurratur, et est dilatorium, non peremptorium."

64. Ibid. no. 1251, p. 1346.

65. Ibid., p. 1347.

66. Ibid., pp. 1348–1349.

67. Walther, *Imperiales Königtum* 102–103, for reasons that he does not give, attributes this consilium to Robert's Protonotary and Logothete, Bartholomeus of Capua.

68. *Acta imperii Angliae et Franciae ab a. 1267 ad a. 1313: Dokumente vornehmlich*

for all to see that many kings, princes, marquises, counts, barons, and city-states have dominion."[69] The kings of France, Sicily, Spain, Aragon, England, Portugal, Armenia, Hungary, and Cyprus are subject only to themselves.[70] He concluded by citing two legal maxims: when examining Roman law the reason of the law should be considered rather than its literal meaning. And if the reason of the law no longer holds, then neither does the law.[71] This anonymous jurist put forward a remarkably commonsensical defense of national monarchies.[72]

Even after Henry's death had removed any immediate threat to papal and Angevin rule in Italy, Clement V still felt compelled to answer the legal challenge posed by Henry's legislation and his condemnation of Robert. His first step was to ask Oldradus de Ponte, one of the most distinguished jurists at Avignon, for two consilia on the legal issues involved in the affair.[73] Gachon discovered a manuscript containing a

---

zur Geschichte der auswärtigen Beziehungen Deutschlands, ed. Fritz Kern (Tübingen: 1911), nr. 295, pp. 244–247, at 244: "et ubicumque notorium est per mundum, nec (om. ?) ipsa Romana civitas que olim communiter quasi preerat toti mundo, aliquarum provinciarum aut terrarum habet sub se gubernationem, regimen vel administrationem . . . reges et diversos principes orbis terre in (MS: ñ) sui tantum districtus satistenuerit coartari, constat hodie non esse rem publicam illam de qua leges predicte locuntur, sed fore penitus addissolutam, unde nec contra ipsam committi potest crimen predictum, quod vocatur perduellionis." Kern noted in his edition that this passage is corrupt; I have telescoped it to make its meaning clearer. A subject of Robert wrote it (p. 245: "noster dominus rex,") and a corrupt text is preserved in Paris, B.N. lat. 4046, fol. 218v–219v. See C. Müller, Der Kampf Ludwigs des Baiern mit der römischen Curie (Tübingen: 1879) I 393ff. Davis, Dante and the Idea of Rome 184–185.

69. Ibid., p. 246: "Sed hodie satis est apertum videre quod dominium habet in mundo tot regibus, principibus, tot marchionibus, tot comitibus, et aliis baronibus et communitatibus."

70. Ibid.

71. Ibid., p. 247: "Cum enim plus attendenda sit ratio legis quam ipsa lex, ut ff. de fonte l.i. Hoc interdictum [Dig. 43.22.7] cessante ratione legis cessare et deffiniri debet ipsa lex, ut ff. de repud. l.ult. [Dig. 24.2.11.2]."

72. Ptolomey of Lucca, "Tractatus de iurisdictione ecclesie super regnum Sicilie et Apulie," ed. S. Baluze and J. D. Mansi, Miscellanea (Lucca: 1761) I 468–473, wrote a tract defending Robert; see Bowsky, Henry VII 190. See also the three consilia for Robert discussed by G. M. Monti, "La dottrina antiimperiale degli Angioini di Napoli: I loro vicariati imperiali e Bartolomeo di Capua," Studi di storia e diritto in onore di Arrigo Solmi (Milano: 1941) II 11–54, A. Nitschke, "Die Reden des Logotheten Bartholomäus von Capua," QF 35 (1955) 266–274, Walther, Imperiales Königtum 102.

73. Schulte, Quellen II 232–233; Savigny, Geschichte V 471. If the consilia added to fifteenth-century editions are authentic, Oldradus died after 1343, not ca. 1335 as most reference works state; see Consilium 333 (Rome: 1478) unfol. (Venice: 1571) fol. 166v: "et quod confessus est tortus et non questioni positus, non uidetur ei obesse, quia de uulgaribus tantum confessus est, et quia nullis indiciis precedentibus confessus fuit et contra priuilegium concessum Hebreis per reginam." There is, however, no manuscript evidence that this consilium is Oldradus's, and the evidence taken from it must be treated cautiously. The queen to whom he referred is Giovanna I (1343–1381). See Attilio Milano, Storia degli ebrei in Italia (Torino: 1963) 186. The privilege is printed by Nunzio Federigo Faraglia, Codice diplomatico sulmonese (Lanciano: 1888) 263. Also N. F. Faraglia, Storia della regina Giovanna II d'Angio (Lanciano: 1904) 334.

consilium of Oldradus and two others that had formerly been in the papal library at Avignon.[74] The manuscript must have been a dossier put together at the papal court to provide a juristic basis for the legislation that Clement planned. One of the consilia was written after Henry's death, but before Clement promulgated *Pastoralis cura.*[75]

Oldradus probably wrote his opinions during the same period. He composed the first (number 43 of the printed edition) at the request of the cardinals at Avignon.[76] Gachon's manuscript may contain a draft of this consilium.[77] After it had served its purpose in the Curia, he included it in his collection of consilia.[78] The second (number 69) cannot be dated, but is undoubtedly connected with the controversy between Henry and Robert.[79] Many of Oldradus's consilia were written for specific cases, and his work marks the beginning of a juristic literary genre that would rapidly become the most important vehicle for the dissemination of doctrine and for legal change in the *ius commune* during the late Middle Ages. Jurists had composed consilia that gave practical advice to judges since the twelfth century. In the twelfth and thirteenth centuries, they had commonly collected abstract "quaestiones," but Oldradus and later jurists put together collections of consilia that rendered opinions on actual court cases.[80]

74. Oldradus de Ponte (not identified by Schwalm), *Constitutiones,* ed. Schwalm, nr. 1254, pp. 1373–1378; nr. 1255, pp. 1378–1398; and the consilium already discussed above, nr. 1249–1250, pp. 1317–1341. See the still valuable study of Eduard Will, *Die Gutachten des Oldradus de Ponte zum Prozeß Heinrichs VII. gegen Robert von Neapel: Nebst der Biographie des Oldradus* (Abhandlungen zur mittleren und neueren Geschichte, 65; Berlin-Leipzig: 1917), 20–21.

75. Ibid. nr. 1255, p. 1378: "ab imperatore nunc mortuo."

76. Oldradus de Ponte, *Consilia* (Rome: 1472) (unfoliated) (nr. 43), Clm 3638, fol. 26r–27r (43), Clm 5463, fol. 43r–44r (nr. 81, olim 87): "predicta conscripsi cupiens super his scire a maioribus dominis meis cardinalibus ueritatem." Will, *Die Gutachten* 20–62, was the first to point out the relationship of the decretal and Oldradus's consilia, and he compared the consilia and the decretal in detail.

77. See note 56, above.

78. The textual tradition of Oldradus's consilia needs to be explored. There are at least three different manuscript collections of his consilia in the manuscripts: one contains 220 consilia (Clm 5463), the other 264 (Clm 3638). The first incunabular edition printed the text containing 264 consilia (Rome: 1472), but a second Roman edition (1478) expanded this number to 333. This Roman edition added consilia 265–274 that were not Oldradus's, but were often added to manuscripts of his consilia (e.g., Clm 3638), and then printed consilia 275–333 from an unknown source. I have not found a manuscript containing these consilia, and they must, therefore, be treated with caution. Gero Dolezalek has examined a manuscript owned by Antiquariat Keip, Frankfurt am Main, that contains 264 consilia, but in a different order from the vulgate. A thorough examination of the textual tradition may help to date the different stages of their composition and, consequently, the individual consilia.

79. (Rome: 1472) (unfoliated) (nr. 69), Clm 3638, fol. 36r–37v (nr. 69), Clm 5463, fol. 114v–117r (nr. 186); Will, *Die Gutachten* 51–62.

80. See Peter Weimar and Norbert Horn, *Handbuch,* ed. Coing, pp. 241–250 and 336–341. On Oldradus's consilia, see Baldwin Aistermann, *Beiträge zum Konflikt Jo-*

In the first, Oldradus dealt almost exclusively with the question of due process. He posed a series of questions about the legitimacy of Henry's summons of Robert to his court. Is a summons issued to a place where a defendant has notorious enemies invalid? If so, is a subsequent trial and judgment also invalid?[81] Oldradus argued that two considerations must be taken into account when examining a summons: the "execution of intent" and the manner through which the summons is brought.[82] The execution of intent is the defendant's knowledge of the summons and the defendant's ability for self-defense. This cannot be omitted.[83] Oldradus observed that the right of self-defense is granted to everyone in extrajudicial matters by natural law and, consequently, people have the right to defend themselves by natural law.[84] There can

---

hanns XXII. mit dem deutschen Königtum (Dissertation Freiburg im Breisgau; Bonn: 1909), consilia 180, 191; Joshusa Starr, "Jewish Life in Crete under the Rule of Venice," *Proceedings of the American Academy for Jewish Research* 12 (1942) 59–114 at 64–65 (reprinted in *Medieval Jewish Life: Studies from the Proceedings of the American Academy for Jewish Research*) (New York: 1976), consilium 36; Guido Kisch, *The Jews in Medieval Germany: A Study of Their Legal and Social Status* (2d Ed. New York: 1970), 559, consilium 87 and 466–467, nn. 105, 108, consilium 33; K. Pennington, "Bartolomé de Las Casas and the Tradition of Medieval Law," *Church History* 39 (1970) 149–161 and James Muldoon, *Popes, Lawyers, and Infidels: The Church and the Non-Christian World 1250–1550* (Philadelphia: 1979) 20–21, consilium 264; Karl Mommsen, "Oldradus de Ponte als Gutachter für das Kloster Allerheiligen in Schaffhausen," ZRG Kan. Abt. 62 (1976) 173–193. Norman Zacour, *Jews and Saracens in the Consilia of Oldradus de Ponte* (Studies and Texts; Toronto: 1990), has edited the Latin texts and translated several consilia without collating manuscripts. Since consilium 333 has not yet been found in any manuscript bearing an attribution to Oldradus (or, indeed, in any manuscript at all), his authorship of it must be treated with great caution.

81. (Rome: 1472) (unfoliated) (nr. 43), Clm 3638, fol. 25v–27r (43), Clm 5463, fol. 43r–44r (nr. 81, olim 87): "Queritur utrum citatio facta in loco ubi communiter habitant inimici notorii citati absente longe ipso citato ex hoc reddatur nulla, et per consequens processus et sententia subsecuta." Another consilium, nr. 88, treats due process as well, but was written after *Pastoralis* had been issued. Its text is truncated in the printed editions.

82. Ibid.: "Pro examinatione eorum de quibus queritur primo illud puto uidendum utrum citatio, si sit de esse iudicii ita quod pretermissa per principem sententiam nullam reddat et potissime criminalem? Circa quod dicendum uidetur quod in citatione consideratur duo, scilicet effectus intentus et ad ipsum peruehiendi modus."

83. Ibid.: "Effectus intentus est scientia citati et facultas defendendi. Et hoc non uidetur posse obmitti quin ueniat uere uel interpretatiue, ut in c. Nos in quemquam [C. q.1. c.1]."

84. Ibid.: "Sicut enim iure nature permissa est unicuique defensio contra extraiudicialem uiolentiam, ut ff. de iust. et iur. l. Vt uim [Dig. 1.1.3] et ad leg. Aquil. l. Scientiam § Qui cum aliter [Dig. 9.2.45(46).4] Adeoque in brutis uiget huius permissio, ut ff. si quad. paup. fec. dicatur l.i. § Cum arietes [Dig. 9.1.1.11], sic et aduersus uiolentiam iudicialem, ut ff. de iniuriis l. Nec magistratibus [Dig. 47.10.32] extra de rest. spol. Conquerente [X 2.13.7] et ff. ad leg. Aquil. l. Quemadmodum § Magistratus [Dig. 9.2.29.7] et C. de iure fisci l. Facultas et l. Prohibitum [Cod. 10.1.7 et 5] Verum quia omnis licitus defendendi modus debet commensurari modo offendendi qui intenditur, ut C. unde ui l. Si quis in tantam [Cod. 8.4.7] et C. de iureiur. l.i. [Cod. 2.58(59).1] et ibi not. Idcirco

be no defense, however, without knowledge. If the prince would render a judgment without all necessary knowledge, he would take a defense away from a person that is granted by natural law. This, concluded Oldradus, the prince may not do.[85] A summons is the means by which knowledge is brought to the court.[86] The means by which a summons is delivered is not established by natural law. A summons can be delivered by a nuncio, letter, or edict. The means are regulated by positive law and the prince can, therefore, summon anyone as he wishes.[87]

Oldradus did not cite his sources. His general argument is closest to that of Johannes Monachus and parallels the Frenchman's in many respects.[88] It is somewhat surprising that Oldradus did not know of Johannes's gloss to Rem non novam since Monachus wrote it sometime between 1305 and his death in 1313. Still, the same network of ideas obviously influenced both jurists. They each concentrated on the argument that natural law granted a defense to each defendant. Both jurists adopted the argument of the Roman lawyers that parts of all actions were derived from natural law.[89]

In consilium 69, Oldradus grappled with the other issue raised by the dispute: did the emperor exercise jurisdiction over other kings and over the king of Sicily? He drew his arguments from many sources and decisively rejected the emperor's claim that he was "dominus mundi." The Roman people could not have bestowed more power on the emperor than they themselves held. They did not exercise authority over other nations, therefore, they could not make him lord of the world. God did not establish imperial rule since there were no scriptural justifi-

---

in iudicialibus licet iure nature cuilibet se defendere iudicialiter, non iniuriis et obprobriis, ut C. de postul. l. Quisquis [Cod. 2.6.6]."

85. Ibid.: "sed quia defensio sine scientia esse non potest, necessaria est omnino scientia uera uel interpretiua, et cum princeps hac non precedente iudicat, subtrahit homini defensionem iure nature concessam. Set hoc non potest princeps, ut inst. de iure nat. gen. et ciu. § Set naturalia [Inst. 1.2.11] et not. Compos. in c.p. Sicut extra de elect. [et not.— elect. om. Clm 3638] ergo etc."

86. Ibid.: "Modus autem inducendi hanc scientiam uere uel interpretiue est citatio, et ideo cum inchoatur modus offendendi, statim datur possibilitas defendendi per citationem, et hoc est quod textus dicit 'omnium autem actionum instituendarum principium ab ea parte edicti proficiscitur quam pretor edicit de in ius uocandi.'"

87. Ibid.: "Set citationes habent suos modos quia aliquando per nuncium et aliquando per epistolas et aliquando per edicta . . . et est quidam modus citationum in ipsarum iteratione consistens . . . et ad hunc modum non uidetur princeps artari, arg. expressum ff. de manu. l. Apud eum [Dig. 40.1.14] quia isti non sunt modi de iure nature, set de iure simpliciter positiuo cui princeps non est necessario alligatus, ut ff. de leg. et sent. consul. l. Princeps [Dig. 1.3.31(30)] et C. eodem titulo l. Digna [Cod. 1.14(17).4]."

88. See chapter 4.

89. See chapter 4.

cations for it. He repeated the metaphor of the bees of Johannes Branch-azolus, but rejected Johannes's conclusion: "One bee who is king," he wrote, "is not king of all bees."

One feature of Oldradus's consilium is particularly striking: unlike the theological tract discussed above and other contemporary polemical tracts, he did not deny the universality of the emperor by subjecting him to the pope. Oldradus was no hierocrat. His comment at the end of the consilium is telling. After reviewing the arguments of the canonists for the emperor's sovereignty, he concluded that their thought was a result of their nationalities: Johannes Teutonicus was a German, the others were Italians, therefore, as subjects of the emperor, they supported his claims of sovereignty. Only the Spanish opposed German claims.[90] Oldradus's consilium became a focal point for considering the universal authority of the emperor in the later Middle Ages. Jurists and publicists incorporated it into their works, and supporters of the late medieval empire combatted its thesis.[91]

In these consilia, Oldradus put forward two arguments to justify Robert of Naples's position. The first, as we have seen, was new and had slowly evolved in the thought of the jurists during the previous fifty years. The prince could not deny a subject the right of due process be-cause this right was grounded in natural law. The second argument was not as new and had been debated for two centuries. Oldradus main-tained that the emperor was not "dominus mundi" and did not exercise jurisdiction outside the borders of the German empire.

In his otherwise excellent study of Oldradus's consilia, Eduard Will seriously underestimated the force of Oldradus's arguments in con-silium 43. He observed that since Robert could not justify his actions in a court of law, Oldradus was reduced to "sophistry" when he de-fended him.[92] Will concluded that the arguments of consilium 43 were not valid unless one presupposed Oldradus's rejection of universal em-

90. Oldradus de Ponte, *Consilia* (Rome: 1472), unfol. (nr. 69), Clm 3638, fol. 37v (nr. 69), Clm 5463, fol. 117r (nr. 186): "maxime quia subditi imperatoris, ut apparet in Ioanne, qui erat Theutonicus (Almanus 5463) et alii Italici. Sed Hispani nouerant (notauerant Ed.) contra." A modern historian, E. J. Meijers, in a book review of Mochi Onory's *Fonti canonistiche* and Calasso's *Glossatori*, TRG 20 (1952) 113–125 at 122, makes the same point: "Le sentiment national était ici le facteur décisif." Meijers referred to Oldradus's last lines as support for his opinion (p. 124).

91. Albericus de Rosate included the consilium in his commentary on Cod. 1.1(4).1, Philippe de Maziére in his "Somnium viridarii." Hieronymus Balbus wrote a tract attack-ing Oldradus and defending imperial prerogatives, printed in M. Goldast, *Politica im-perialia* (Frankfurt: 1614). See Will, *Die Gutachten* 53–55, for other examples.

92. *Die Gutachten* 37.

pire in consilum 69.[93] Other historians have missed the weightiness of Oldradus's defense of Robert on procedural grounds because they were not aware of the juristic background.[94]

The dispute between Robert of Naples and Henry VII was important because it introduced ideas of due process and the relationship of natural law to due process into a wider political arena and into the *ius commune*. As we have seen, the issue of the emperor's universal power was not nearly as important, weighty, or as difficult for the jurists. The Roman lawyers had never seriously considered the emperor to be "dominus mundi" in the sense that he exercised universal jurisdiction over all people and their property. Somewhat ironically, Henry VII's jurists could only call upon canonists of the early thirteenth century to bolster their claims against Robert and Pope Clement. Significantly, we must remember that if we accept these canonistic glosses literally, we probably misinterpret them.[95] Henry's jurists needed a defense and took from what they thought might lend weight to their arguments.

Later jurists did continue to attribute universal lordship to the emperor. Bartolus of Sassoferrato and Baldus de Ubaldis claimed that the emperor was *de iure* "dominus mundi," but their claims are hedged with *de facto* exceptions of every sort. It is difficult to determine what either jurist might have seen as the practical implications of the emperor's *de iure* universal sovereignty. In the end, the historian must conclude that they argued only for a theoretical overlordship with few if any concrete consequences.[96]

The anonymous jurist who wrote the consilium contained in the Avignonese dossier discovered by Gachon provided a more detailed defense of due process than Oldradus.[97] He combined his answers to the first four questions of Oldradus's consilium into a disquisition on the duty of a judge to give a defendant an opportunity for self-defense. The issue had also been raised in Robert's protest that Bartholomeus of Capua may have written.[98] A judge who would summon a person to a

---

93. *Die Gutachten* 51.
94. E.g., Walther, *Imperiales Königtum* 215, writes that Oldradus did not deal with the substance of the case in consilium 43, but onlyl with "formale Einwände."
95. See chapter 1.
96. C. N. S. Woolf, *Bartolus of Sassoferrato: His Position in the History of Medieval Political Thought* (Cambridge: 1913) 21–28, 37–53; Canning, *Baldus de Ubaldis* 64–70, 113–127, 211–213; Walther, *Imperiales Königtum* 85–111; Wilks, *Problem of Sovereignty* 433–451.
97. Archives départ. de la Lozère, Série G nr. 1036, fol. 18r–29v, *Constitutiones*, ed. Schwalm, nr. 1255, pp. 1378–1398.
98. *Constitutiones*, ed. Schwalm, nr. 1252, pp. 1362–1369, at 1365: "Constat enim quod defensionem personarum et rerum eciam tam iuris quam facti omnes leges om-

place infested with enemies would violate natural reason and equity.[99] A summons had as its purpose the notification of a defendant so that a defense would not be denied to the defendant. If a summons is not properly carried out and, as a consequence, a person has a defense taken away, such a summons is contrary to natural reason and to divine and human law.[100] One may not object that the emperor is "legibus solutus" and can, therefore, particularly for the crime of treason, omit a summons and proceed to a judgment. "We say that a defense, and consequently a summons, is established by natural law, not only by civil law."[101] If these rules were not followed, he emphasized, "there would be no difference between guilty and innocent persons. The prince could willfully condemn whom he wished. The power of life and death over his subjects would be entirely in his hands. There would not be civil or royal power, but only tyrannical authority. Natural reason concedes a defense not only to people, but also to animals."[102]

Johannes Monachus had insisted that if a judge rendered a sentence without examining the defendant personally, his will was not informed by reason.[103] In Robert's defense, the anonymous jurist noted that a summons permits a judge to examine the truth and render a just sentence. Reason required that the judge hear the defense of the defendant in court. A judge could not have "full knowledge" of a case if a defen-

---

niaque iura permittunt, sive quis loquatur de iure divino sive naturali eciam brutis indito." Gennaro Maria Monti, "La dottrina antiimperiale degli Angioini di Napoli: I loro vicariati imperiali e Bartolomeo di Capua," *Studi di storia e diritto in onore di Arrigo Solmi* (Milan: 1941) II 11–54, attributes this text to Bartholomeus (p. 23), and August Nitschke, "Die Reden des Logotheten Bartholomäus von Capua," QF 35 (1955) 226–274, at 254, inclines, carefully, to agree. Walther, *Imperiales Königtum* 102, simply assigns authorship to him. Calasso, *Glossatori* 136–138, has his doubts.

99. Ibid., p. 1387.

100. Ibid., p. 1389: "Habet enim citatio modum suum ad effectum et finem certum ordinatum, effectum quidem et finem habet, ut in citati noticiam perveniat, ut sibi sua defensio non negetur, sed concedetur . . . Unde si citatio fiat taliter quod citatus nesciat vel verisimiliter scire non possit cum per consequens sibi defensio subtrahatur, citatio talis contra rationem naturalem et divinam et humana iura non valet, nec lata sententia virtute ipsius."

101. Ibid., p. 1390: "Nec obstat si dicatur quod imperator legibus est solutus et ideo obmissa citatione legitima ad diffinitivam, maxime in crimine lese maiestatis, potuit secundum legem suam quam super hoc edidit procedere. Dicimus enim quod defensio et per consequens citatio est de iure naturali, non solum de iure civili, ff. de iust. et iure l. Vt vim [Dig. 1.13]."

102. Ibid., p. 1390: "Alias non esset differentia inter nocentes et innocentes, sed posset princeps pro voluntate condempnare quem vellet, et esset penes eum potestas in subditis vite et necis nec esset regia nec civilis, sed tirannica potestas in eo contra rationem naturalem, que nedum hominibus, sed etiam brutis defensionem adversus periculum concedit."

103. See chapter 4.

dant did not appear before him. Natural and divine law dictated due process.[104] Even God, who knows all things, called Adam, Cain, and the Sodomites to him before he rendered a sentence on them. Consequently, a summons must be made according to natural reason in notorious crimes. Many things might be alleged for the defendant that would be hidden from the judge who had not examined the defendant personally.[105]

Although the emperor is "living civil law on earth," he cannot dispense with or change these laws. He is not loosed from natural law.[106] One may not justify the emperor's proceeding against an absent defendant according to his own legislation *Ad reprimendum,* because that law does not extend to non-subjects and because even that law requires a legitimate summons.[107] Therefore, Henry's condemnation of Robert was not valid.[108]

PAPAL LEGISLATION AND THE REACTION OF THE LAWYERS

The consilia of Oldradus provide the historical, intellectual, and judicial background for the promulgation of the most significant set of papal decretals touching upon procedure in the Middle Ages. The dispute between Henry VII and Robert of Naples was a key moment. The heat of that conflict gave life and meaning to the ruminations of the jurists. Speculative glosses gave way to normative legislation for the *ius commune.* Robert's quarrel with Henry did not spawn defendants' rights—that honor belongs to the jurists of the late thirteenth century.

104. Ibid.: "Ad hoc enim fit citatio ut iudex veritatem examinet et recte iudicare possit deffensionibus rei auditis et ab eo presente queratur ratio, aliter non posset examinari negocium vel recte sententia ferri . . . Hoc autem, scilicet cognitio plena iudicis et deffensio reo naturali et divino iure promissa, non fieret si citatio obmitteretur, et posset omitti."

105. Ibid.: "Hoc etiam divino probatur exemplo, ut patet in Genesi de Adam, Caym, et Sodomitis, quos requisivit et vocavit Dominus, antequam sententiam ferret in eos, ut sciret eis presentibus, si res sic se habebat, et excusationes si quas haberent audiret, licet omnia essent sibi notoria sicut Deo . . . In notoriis etiam est citatio facienda ratione naturali, cum multe possint esse deffensiones pro reo, que iudici latent."

106. Ibid., p. 1391: "Imperator igitur qui est lex animata civilis in terris . . . iura talia tollere vel mutare non potest . . . Unde ipse imperator a tali lege non est solutus, instit. de iure nat. gen. et civ. § Sed naturalia."

107. Ibid.: "Non obstat etiam lex quam imperator predictus edidit, que incipit 'Ad reprimenda,' quod in talibus procedi possit etiam contra absentem . . . ad non subditos extendi non potest . . . Item lex illa requirit citationem legitimam, que hic non processit, ut ex premissis apparet, nec ipse illam tollere potuit."

108. Ibid.: "Ex hiis igitur patet nullam fuisse sententiam quod citatio legitima non processit, nec ille contra quem fuit lata sententia potuit contumax reputari."

Nonetheless the dispute did provide the vehicle to bring those rights out of the realm of theory and into cantankerous school rooms and courts of medieval Europe.

Henry VII responded to the challenge of Clement and Robert by issuing *Ad reprimendum* and *Quoniam nuper est*. Clement V countered with *Pastoralis cura* and *Romani principes*.[109] In *Romani principes*, Clement defined the oath that Henry made to the pope as one of fealty. Consequently, Henry was obliged to respect the rights and possessions of the Roman church.[110] At roughly the same time, he issued *Saepe contingit* to resolve further procedural questions raised by the dispute.[111] Even after the strife had ended, jurists continued to link the issue of due process with the controversy.

Nicolaus de Orsone wrote a consilium in which he disputed the right of the king of Sicily to allow royal judges to proceed against notorious suspects of violent crimes without a hearing, in the interest of public order.[112] Nicolaus observed that the judges put defendants immediately to the rack, even though they wished to provide the court with witnesses on their behalf.[113] Nicolaus rehearsed all the arguments for the defendants that had been used during the dispute between Henry and Robert. "Defenses are introduced and pertain to a person through natural law. Therefore they cannot be taken away."[114] Ironically, perhaps, he further noted that during the controversy with Henry VII, Robert

109. *Pastoralis* and *Romani principes* were issued at Carpentras in March, 1314. Dönniges, *Acta imperi* II 237–243, printed them from originals. They were later inserted into Clement's legislation issued by John XXII in 1317, at the beginning of his pontificate, the *Clementines*, under Clem. 2.9.1 and 2.11.2.

110. Clem. 2.9.1: "Sub eodem etiam iuramento promisit, quod tam ipsam Romanam ecclesiam, quam alias ecclesias, libertatem ecclesiasticam, bona, iura, prelatos et ministros ecclesiarum ipsarum manuteneret, conservaret atque defenderet suo posse."

111. See above, n. 31.

112. Ennio Cortese, "Nicolaus de Ursone de Salerno: Un'opera ignota sulle lettere arbitrarie angioine nella tradizione dei trattati sulla tortura," *Per Francesco Calasso: Studi degli allievi* (Roma: 1978) 191–284 at 251: Bartholomeus de Capua issued the decree: "cum consilio iudicis tibi dati per curiam, sine strepitu eciam, procedere ualeas, eciam ordine iudiciario pretermisso." On the importance of Bartholomeus see Monti, "La dottrina anti-imperiale" 11–54, Nitschke, "Die Reden des Logotheten Bartholomäus von Capua," 231, for a list of Bartholomeus's legal works.

113. Ibid., p. 252: "Et quia officiales, autoritate predictarum litterarum, 'De iuris censura,' contra aliquos multociens procedunt testes examinando et uolendo illos, contra quos procedunt, ponere questionibus et tormentis; et pro parte ipsorum allegatur et petitur, quia uolunt se defendere, quod audiantur in suis iustis defensionibus et quod detur eis copia nominum et dictorum testium contra eos productorum et examinatorum, quia uolunt contra ipsos excipere et opponere."

114. Ibid., p. 256: "defensiones sunt inducte et competunt alicui de iure naturali, scilicet divino, gentium, et primeuo, quo homines et animalia ad aliquid faciendum docentur seu inducuntur . . . et sic, si sint de iure naturali debent esse firme et immutabiles . . . et per consequens per regem, seu ius ciuile, tolli ipse defensiones non possent."

himself commissioned a consilium that contained these same arguments in his defense.[115] Subsequently, Clement V and his entire college had determined that a defense was established by natural law and could not be obviated by the emperor or king. To confirm this doctrine, Clement issued *Pastoralis cura*.[116]

Modern historians have not seen the importance of procedural elements in *Pastoralis cura*. In fact, they have seen only one issue here: the sovereignty of the emperor, pope, and kings. Walter Ullmann argued that Clement "clearly brought the material side of the idea of sovereignty precisely forward and thereby took a large step in defining sovereignty."[117] Helmut Walther thinks that Clement annulled the judgment of Henry against Robert on the basis of the pope's superiority over imperial authority.[118] Eduard Will, the first historian to deal with the problem at length, refused to recognize the significance of the procedural issues in the decretal.[119] Other specialized studies also shunt these issues to the side.[120]

After one has examined the thought of the jurists on procedure in the late thirteenth and early fourteenth centuries, *Pastoralis cura* appears in a different light. Clement made four major points: (1) a defendant could not be summoned to a dangerous place; (2) Robert could not be summoned from outside the borders of the empire; (3) Robert did hold fiefs from the emperor, but he was domiciled in the Regno, his own kingdom; and (4) Robert was a vassal of the pope. Finally, in the depositive clauses of the decretal, Clement declared that all of these points nullified Henry's actions. Additionally, because Robert had been

115. Ibid., p. 257: "Quid plura? Per consilium totum domini nostri regis, in casu ubi per dominum Herricum, qui se imperatorem nominabat, procedebatur contra dominum nostrum regem et per eum defensiones eidem domino nostro regi tollebantur, fuit allegatum quod hoc non poterat fieri per ipsum dominum Herricum, quia ipsa defensio erat de iure naturali." The consilium referred to could be that printed in *Constitutiones*, ed. Schwalm, nr. 1252 or 1255. Or the fragmentary text edited by Kern, *Acta imperii* nr. 295 (see above, n. 68). In any case, Bartholomeus of Capua's authorship of any of these consilia is thrown into doubt because Nicolaus would have certainly pointed out that Bartholomeus had defended these very principles during the dispute.

116. Ibid.: "Et postea per bone memorie dominum Clementem papam v. et totum eius collegium determinatum fuit quod defensiones, cum sint de iure naturali, non possunt tolli per imperatorem uel regem, et de hoc fecit unam constitutionem decretalem, ut in constitutionibus Clementinis de re iudicata c. Pastoralis, lib. vii."

117. Ullmann, "Sourveränitätsbegriff" 16.

118. *Imperiales Königtum* 218.

119. *Die Gutachten* 37.

120. Georges Lizerand, "Les constitutions 'Romani principes' et 'Pastoralis cura' et leurs sources," *Nouvelle revue historique de droit français et étranger* 37 (1913) 725–757; Mario delle Piane, "Intorno ad una bolla papale: La 'Pastoralis cura' di Clemente V," *Rivista di storia del diritto italiano* 31 (1958) 21–56. Piane concludes that *Pastoralis* is "dunque un'affermazione di teocrazia" (p. 56).

stripped of his right to defend himself, Henry's condemnation was invalid. A defense is a fundamental principle of natural law and cannot be taken away by the emperor.[121]

At the end of the decretal, in a passage that historians have focused on, Clement concluded that he took his action because papal authority was superior to imperial authority, because the throne of the empire was vacant, and because he exercised plenitude of power granted by Christ himself. The pope's (or any bishop's) right to exercise secular jurisdiction when there was no emperor had been established by Innocent III in his famous decretal, Licet.[122]

In these last lines of Pastoralis, Clement justified his right to review Henry's condemnation of Robert and, in light of the evidence, to annul it. He declared that Henry's condemnation was invalid because the emperor had violated the precepts of natural law. By issuing Pastoralis, Clement publicized Henry's errors and instituted new norms for the courts of Christendom. He certainly did not espouse a doctrine that the pope was the secular superior of the emperor or exercised hegemony over him.

Clement's statement, however, that Robert lived "outside imperial jurisdiction" is hardly new. Long before, Pope Innocent III had acknowledged in the decretal Per venerabilem that the king of France recognized no superior.[123] Fundamentally, the importance of Pastoralis lies outside the framework of public law. Clement's decretal established that a key element of the judicial process was inviolable because natural law demanded that people be given an opportunity to defend themselves in court. Pastoralis established an essential element of due process and protected it from the will of the prince.

The pope had to deal with one last issue. In Ad reprimendum, Henry maintained that he could dispense with many of the normal rules of procedure in the case of summary trials for serious crimes like treason.

---

121. Clem. 2.11.2: "Ceterum defectus suppletio, circa processus adhibita supra dictos, non tantum ualet ad iustificationem ipsorum et sententiae supra dictae, quantum ad eorum suggillationem et notam: cum nullam super premissis potestatem haberet imperator in regem, sibi alias, quam ut praefertur, non subditum, non citatum legitime aut remissum, et extra districtum ipsius continue ac notorie consistentem. Nec predicta suppletio circa subditum etiam ad ea potuisset de ratione referri, per quae de crimine praesertim sic gravi delato defensionis, quae a iure provenit naturali, facultas adimi valuisset, cum illa imperatori tollere non licuerit, quae iuris naturalis exsistunt."

122. X 2.2.10. For the doctrine of Licet, see John A. Watt, The Theory of Papal Monarchy in the Thirteenth Century: The Contribution of the Canonists (London: 1965) 41–43.

123. X 4.17.13; again see Watt, Papal Monarchy 37–38; 40–41; 53–56.

Henry or his jurists borrowed this doctrine from canon law. Canonical procedure had long recognized that certain serious matters should be handled swiftly and without delay. The canonists created summary judicial procedure that proceeded "simpliciter et de plano, ac sine strepitu et figura iudicii" (simply and plainly, without clamor and the normal forms of procedure). As we have seen, this is exactly the procedure that Henry incorporated into *Ad reprimendum* and explicitly adopted when he condemned Robert.[124]

The result of these events must have led to confusion in the papal curia. Summary procedure had been recently defined by the canon *Dispendiosam* at the Council of Vienne.[125] This canon had simply listed which cases could be treated summarily—benefices, tithes, marriage, and usury—but not how they were to be handled. The lawyers must have disagreed over exactly what could be omitted. Some jurists may have thought that Henry could take procedural short cuts during Robert's trial because the clause "simpliciter et de plano, ac sine strepitu et figura iudicii" had never been carefully defined. The jurists noticed the problem, and Johannes Andreae wrote that he was responsible for pressing the lords and lawyers of the curia to define the words "de plano sine strepitu et figura iudicii."[126]

The result was *Saepe contingit*, which Clement issued "proprio motu" as a constitution—that is, the pope had no reason or motive other than that he wished to change the law. Its provisions conformed to the doctrine governing the judicial process developed by the jurists and established by *Pastoralis*. In the Clementines, it was placed under the title "The significance of words" because, by defining the words "de plano sine strepitu et figura iudicii," it drew the boundaries of how abbreviated summary judicial procedure could be. Clement first specified the areas that a judge could trim from the judicial process: the "libellum" was not required; holidays must not be observed; objections, appeals, and witnesses could be limited. However, Clement insisted that a judge may not omit necessary proofs or legitimate defenses from the proceedings. A summons and an oath denying calumny cannot be excluded.[127]

124. *Constitutiones,* ed. Schwalm, nr. 946, p. 989: "alioquin tantundem camere nostre persolvant et ad id sine strepitu et figura iudicii conpellantur."

125. Later incorporated into Clem. 2.1.2.

126. Quoted by Kuttner, "Constitution 'Saepe,'" 430.

127. Clem. 5.11.2: "Non sic tamen iudex litem abbreviet quin probationes necessariae et defensiones legitimae admittantur. Citationem vero ac praestationem iuramenti de calumnia vel malitia, sive de veritate dicenda, ne veritas occultetur, per commissionem

The relationship between the dispute of Henry and Robert and the promulgation of *Pastoralis* and *Saepe* is obvious. Clement issued *Saepe* in the immediate aftermath of the controversy—it is a rare example of a great dispute in the public forum having a substantial and immediate impact on a legal system.

Lawyers needed to be informed of the provisions of *Saepe*. Johannes Andreae, who wrote (ca. 1322) the Ordinary Gloss to the *Clementines*, the official collection of canon law that contained both *Pastoralis* and *Saepe*, underlined the significance of *Saepe* by glossing and lecturing on the new decretal soon after its promulgation, even before Pope John XXII issued the *Clementines* on November 1, 1317.[128] A rare copy of Johannes's first lectures on *Saepe* may be contained in an Erlangen manuscript.[129]

The canonists were quick to gloss the *Clementines* and incorporate its provisions into the *ius commune*. Johannes Andreae, Guillielmus de Monte Lauduno, Jesselin de Cassagnes, and Paulus de Liazariis all glossed the *Clementines* shortly after their promulgation, posing new questions about the rules of procedure and exploring new areas of law that might be regulated by principles of natural law.[130]

Johannes Andreae grappled with a question that the jurists had long debated: do the rules governing arbitration differ from those regulating the *ordo iudiciarius*? Some Roman lawyers had argued that by virtue of his special office an arbiter could ignore the normal legal norms and rights of the parties.[131] Johannes, however, decided that an arbiter could take many procedural short cuts but must still observe the rules established by *Pastoralis* for proofs and defenses.[132]

---

huiusmodi intelligimus non excludi." Oldradus de Ponte may have had a hand in the intellectual preparation of *Saepe* too. See his consilium treating the words "sine strepitu iudicii et figura:" nr. 115 in vulgate edition; nr. 34 in Clm 5463, fol. 22r–22v.

128. Kuttner, "Constitution 'Saepe,'" 430–432.

129. Johannes Andreae, repetitio to *Saepe contingit*, Clem. 5.11.2, Erlangen, Universitätsbibl. 358, fol. 47r–49r. See "Johannes Andreae's Additiones to the Decretals of Gregory IX," ZRG Kan. Abt. 74 (1988) 345. The text of the Erlangen manuscript is exactly the same as that of Johannes's Ordinary Gloss.

130. See Guido Rossi, "Contributi alla biografia del canonista Giovanni d'Andrea: L'insegnamento di Novella e Bettina, sue figlie, ed i presunti 'responsa' di Milancia, sua moglie," *Rivista trimestale di diritto e procedura civile* 11 (1957) 1451–1502, Stephan Kuttner, "The Apostillae of Johannes Andreae on the Clementines," *Etudes d'histoire du droit canonique dédiées à Gabriel Le Bras* (2 vols. Paris: 1965) I: 195–201, Jacqueline Tarrant, "The Life and Works of Jesselin de Cassagnes," BMCL 9 (1979) 37–64, Thomas M. Izbicki, "New Notes on Late Medieval Jurists: III. Commentators on the Clementines according to Johannes Calderinus," BMCL 10 (1980) 62–65.

131. Johannes Andreae to Clem. 2.11.2 v. *imperatori tollere non licuerit*.

132. Johannes Andreae to Clem. 5.11.2 v. *defensiones legitimae*: "Et facit haec lit-

When he commented on a letter of Pope Gregory the Great in which Gregory had declared that he had no power to render a judgment against a defendant who had not been in court, Johannes asserted that Gregory's statement applied only to his "juridical," not his absolute power.[133] Although his gloss may be too brief to bear much interpretation, he seemed to equate "potestas ordinata" and "potentia iuridica." Thus, the pope may violate due process only with his absolute power, which permitted him to transcend the normal limits of his power. Absolute power enabled the pope to derogate a provision of a legal system that was beyond his legislative and jurisdictional authority. This is one of the few examples that I have found before 1350 in which a jurist has adopted the definition of absolute power formulated, if only tentatively, by Hostiensis a half century earlier. Johannes may have been the first jurist to declare that the pope was not bound by the provisions of *Pastoralis*. He would not, of course, have maintained that the pope could abolish due process without cause, but his conception of "potestas absoluta," if we may extrapolate from this brief comment and those who have already discussed in chapter 3,[134] bordered on granting the prince absolute sovereignty.

Guilielmus de Monte Lauduno, for his part, observed that the emperor could remedy any defect of positive law. In such matters he can make something out of nothing.[135] This paradoxical statement was an old idea first formulated by the canonists of the early thirteenth century.[136] The emperor may not, however, take away those things that someone possesses from natural law, except with a just judgment and cause. A judgment, however, could not be just unless a defendant were

---

tera . . . et iura predicta ad quaestionem Legistarum de Potestate qui habet arbitrium, an teneatur iustitiam partis seruare vel possit illam contra iura et iustitiam condemnare et voluntate uti. Et teneat quod iustitia et legitima partis defensio non tollitur per dationem arbitrii . . . et optime probat constitutio Clem. supra de re iud. Pastoralis." Johannes had some interest in the office of the potestà; see Pennington, "Johannes Andreae's Additiones" 336–337.

133. Johannes Andreae to X 2.12.1 (Susceptis) v. *possumus*, (Venice: 1581, repr. Torino: 1963), II, fol. 63v: "de iuridica potentia loquitur, non de absoluta, sic infra de fide instrum. c.i."

134. See chapter 3.

135. Guilielmus de Monte Lauduno to Clem 2.11.2 (Pastoralis), Bamberg Can. 76, fol. 44r–47r, Bamberg Can. 77, fol. 35r–37v, v. *nec predicta suppletio*: "Nota quod licet imperialis potestas possit de iure omnes defectus iuris positiui supplere, et remotis prioribus formis seu solempnitatibus nouas apponere. Et sic in talibus de nihilo aliquid facere, C. comm. de leg. l.ii. C. de rei [uxor] act. l.una." Guillaume Mollat, "Guillaume de Montelauzun," DDC 5 (1953) 1078–1079.

136. See Pennington, *Pope and Bishops* 17–29.

allowed the right of self-defense. Even if the devil asked for a hearing, he must be granted a legitimate defense.[137]

In the middle of the fourteenth century, the jurists discovered the rights of children, perhaps having been spurred by *Pastoralis* to think about what other rights might be protected by natural law. In his gloss on *Pastoralis*, Guilielmus turned from due process to the rights of children to inherit their patrimony. From this it follows, he observed, that the hereditary portion due to children by natural law cannot be taken away by a crime of the father. If the children would hear of their father's condemnation and abscond with their inheritance, they would not be obligated to make restitution to the prince, at least according to the internal forum.[138] Johannes Andreae agreed that children must receive their due. If a statute permitted a father to cease supporting his children when they reached the age of eighteen, it was invalid. The nurturing of children is a part of natural law.[139]

Jesselin de Cassagnes, a judge at the Roman Rota (court) at Avignon and an eminent jurist, concurred with the provisions of *Pastoralis*. The emperor could take away those things governed by positive law, but he could not deny anyone the right of self-defense. Self-defense and the repulsion of force with force are established by natural law.[140] Jesselin,

137. Guilielmus de Monte Lauduno to Clem. 2.11.2 (Pastoralis), Bamberg Can. 76, fol. 44r–47r, Bamberg Can. 77, fol. 35r–37v, v. *nec predicta suppletio:* "Non tamen illa que alicui de iure naturali competunt illi aufferre licet, nisi per sententiam iuste et rite latam uel alias ex iusta causa, ne sit contra C. de bon. damp. per totum. De quo per Innoc. supra de constit. Que in ecclesiarum, et sic cum omnis defensio cuique competat, realis uel uerbalis, sic quod uim ui repellant, omnia iura clament, saltim causa moderamine inculpate tutele, supra de restit. spol. c.i. de except. Cum inter, de homicid. Significasti. Hec nemini auferri potest, maxime in iudiciis in quibus debet esse tanta equitas. Quod etiam dyabolo si mendicandus esset, non est legitima defensio auferenda, ut in dicto capitulo Cum inter."

138. Ibid.: "Ex quo sequitur quod portio iure naturali debita filiis, si alias penitus egeant, non potest propter delictum patris quam ius grauissimum de iure auferri, ex quo iure naturali debetur, supra de testi. Raynuncius. Vnde est arg. quod si filii audita condempnatione patris furtim per uim uel dolose suam partem abscondant et asportant, non tenentur in foro saltim anime restitutionem principi faciendam ex quo iure sibi retinere possunt, ergo iuste, supra de uerb. sign. Ius dictum."

139. Johannes Andreae *Additiones* to the *Speculum iuris* 4.3 "Qui filii sint legitimi," (Basel: 1574), II, 462: "statutum continens quod pater non teneatur alere filium maiorem xviii. annis non tenet, cum educatio illorum sit de iure naturali."

140. Jesselin de Cassagnes to Clem. 2.11.2 v. *naturalis existant,* Paris, B.N. lat. 4105, fol. 19v–20v, Paris, B.N. lat. 14331, fol. 128r, Paris, B.N. 16902, fol. 90r: "Nota per imperatorem id quod de iure naturali est tolli non posse, ff. de petit. l. Quidam [Dig. 28.5.47(46)?], notatur C. de prec. imp. off. l. Quotiens [Cod. 1.19(22).2], et de hoc dicas ut not. per Innoc. de constit. Que in ecclesiarum [X 1.2.7], de immun. eccles. c. Quia plerique [X 3.49.8]. Secus est in illis que sunt de iure positiuo ciuili, ut dictis iuribus et C. comm. de leg. l.ii. [Cod. 6.43.2] de rei uxor. act. l.i. [Cod. 5.13.1]. Hec autem de iure naturali reputantur: defensio et per uim uis repulsio, ut dicta l. Vt uim [Dig. 1.1.3]." Tarrant, "Jesselin" 37–64.

however, could not accept Guilielmus's and Johannes's stance on the rights of children. Although some jurists had argued that the legitimate portion of an inheritance due to a son cannot be taken away even for the most heinous crime of the father, Jesselin asserted that a son can be deprived of his portion by contract. This is a matter of civil law, informed by "natural instinct." Therefore, municipal statutes for their part may take these rights away from children.[141]

Paulus de Liazariis dealt with due process and arbitration in his commentary. Like Johannes Andreae, the authority of the podestà intrigued him.[142] A "judicial" defense was a defendant's right,[143] even when a party had agreed to arbitration. We have seen that the Italian jurists were preoccupied with the authority of the podestà, and Paulus wondered whether a podestà who had agreed to arbitrate a dispute was exempt from the rules in *Pastoralis*. He concluded that a podestà may not condemn a person unjustly because a legitimate defense is not precluded by arbitration; the podestà may omit those things which pertain to the facts of a case, but not matters that touch on the rights of the defendant.[144]

Except for Johannes Andreae, most canonists who glossed *Pastoralis* did not ask the crucial question regarding the pope: was he bound by the provisions of the decretal? The point became relevant during the dispute between Pope John XXII and Emperor Louis IV of Bavaria not long after the promulgation of *Pastoralis*.

Clearly, the issues involved in the above controversy are enormously

141. Ibid.: "Et ex hoc sequitur quod ob delictum patris licet grauisssimum legitima iure nature debita, de testa. Raynuncius [X 3.26.16], filio tolli non potest secundum aliquos. Tu dic in hoc contra, cum et per contractum [MSS *add.* es] alienum paternum illa tollatur, ff. de inoffic. test. l. Papinianus § Quoniam autem quarta [Dig. 5.2.8.8]. Et de iure ciuili debetur licet instinctu naturali, et ideo etiam per statutum municipale tolli potest, ut de hoc plene not. per Dinum de reg. iur. c. Indultum, lib. vi. [VI (5.13).17]."

142. See chapter 2.

143. Paulus de Liazariis to Clem. 2.11.2 (Pastoralis), Bamberg Can. 79, fol. 39v, Nürnberg Stadtbibl. II 60, fol. 115r–116r, Vienna, N.B. 2078, fol. 33v, v. *defensionis*: "iudicialis, et uerum de sent. excomm. Si uera § ii. et xxiii. q.iii. Non inferenda." *licuerit*: "facit hec littera ad id quod not. Innoc. et Compo. de const. Que in ecclesiarum, [X 1.2.7] ff. de const. prin. l.i. in fine [Dig. 1.4.1] C. si contra ius uel util. pub. l. finali [Cod. 1.22(25).6] Host. in Summa de rescript. § Quas uires, uer. Potest autem, et Cyn. post Jac. de Ra. et Pe. de Bellap. C. de precibus imperat. offer. Rescripta [Cod. 1.19(22).7]." R. Chabanne, "Paulus de Liazariis," DDC 6 (1957) 1276–1277.

144. Ibid.: "Facit etiam ad questionem an potestas habens arbitrium teneatur facere iustitiam, et dicendum est quod sic, nec per hoc condemnare potest iniuste, quia legitima defensio non tollitur per dationem arbitrii, arg. C. de inoffic. testa. Si quando [Cod. 3.28.35] ff. de condit. indeb. Si procurator, in prin. [Dig. 12.6.6] . . . Operabit autem predictum arbitrium ut non teneatur ad sollempnitates que figuram iudicii respiciunt ut sunt repente, citationes, satisfactiones et similia, non quo ad ea que sunt acta rei uel litis, ut sint illa que respiciunt factum, sicut sunt confessiones, attestationes, et similia; de quibus per Innoc. et Host. de testi. Causam."

complicated—more complicated than those between Henry VII and Robert of Naples. The split between the conventual and spiritual Franciscans had driven a wider than usual wedge between papal and imperial claims.[145] John XXII excommunicated Louis and deposed him without having heard the emperor's defense. In his third appeal to the pope of May, 1324, in which he relied on Italian jurists and on the consilium for Henry VII of 1312,[146] Louis objected that he had not been present at the trial. Positive law, scripture, papal custom, and divine law demanded that a defendant be present to face all accusers.[147] John had anticipated Louis's objection. The pope had given him three months to obey his commands. If Louis disobeyed, the pope would proceed notwithstanding Louis's absence.[148] From this evidence, one might assume that the wily old jurist thought that crimes against the papal office—crimes of heresy by definition—were exempt from the strictures of *Pastoralis*.[149] Although the conflict was the last major "trial by invective" between the empire and the papacy during the Middle Ages, it

145. On the intellectual ramifications of this dispute see Richard Scholz, *Unbekannte kirchenpolitische Streitschriften aus der Zeit Ludwigs des Bayern (1327–1354)* (Bibliothek des Deutschen Historischen Instituts in Rome, 9–10; Rome: 1911–1914); Brian Tierney, *Origins of Papal Infallibility 1150–1350: A Study on the Concepts of Infallibility, Sovereignty and Tradition in the Middle Ages* (Studies in the History of Christian Thought, 6; Leiden: 1972) 171–272; James Heft, *John XXII and Papal Teaching Authority* (Texts and Studies in Religion, 27; Lewiston-Queenston: 1986); still useful is C. Müller, *Der Kampf Ludwigs des Baiern mit der römischen Curie* (Tübingen: 1879); F. Hofmann, *Der Anteil der Minoriten am Kampf Ludwigs des Bayern* (Münster: 1959).

146. *Constitutiones*, ed. J. Schwalm, 4.2, nr. 1248.

147. *Constitutiones et acta publica imperatorum et regum, 5: Inde ab a. MCCCXII ad a. MCCCXXIV*, ed. Jacobus Schwalm (MGH, Legum sectio 4; Hannover-Leipzig: 1911–1913) nr. 909, p. 725: "omnino defuit pars citata, quia nec fuimus presens nec per contumaciam absens nec aliqua de nobis facta fuit citatio, prout expostulat ordo iuris, cum scriptura sacra testetur, non esse consuetudinem Romanis pontificibus, dampnare aliquem hominem, priusquam is qui accusatur presentes habeat accusatores locumque ad defendendum se accipiat ad abluenda crimina, et divina lex non iudicat hominem, nisi audierit ab ipso prius et cognoverit, quid fecerit." The various appeals of Louis are discussed by Jacob Schwalm, *Die Appellationen König Ludwigs des Bayern von 1324* (Weimar: 1906) and Friedrich Bock, "Die Appellationsschriften König Ludwigs IV. in den Jahren 1323/24," DA 4 (1941) 179–205.

148. Ibid. nr. 792 (Oct. 8, 1323), p. 618, repeated in the later condemnations of March, 1324 (nr. 881) and July, 1324 (nr. 944): "Per presentium seriem intimantes eidem, quod si in premissis per eum infra prefatum terminum exequendis negligens fuerit vel remissus, nos contra ipsum ad publicationem penarum, in quas propter premissos excessus notorios incidisse noscitur vel incidet in futurum, et alias quantum suadebit iustitia eius non obstante absentia procedemus."

149. In a consilium written for Castruccio Castracani, Ugolino da Celle conceded that if the emperor were guilty of heresy, he could be deposed by the pope, see *Nova Alamanniae*, ed. E. E. Stengel, nr. 123, pp. 71–79 at 77. Heft, *John XXII and Papal Teaching Authority* 106–120, discusses the various shades of meaning the word "heresy" had in the fourteenth century.

did not have the same importance as earlier disputes for the history of the *ius commune*. No legislation arose from the controversy to memorialize it for future generations of jurists.

Long after John XXII and Louis of Bavaria, Simone da Borsano raised the issue of the pope's being bound by the tenets of *Pastoralis* (ca. 1361–1370). Simone was a man of many parts: jurist, archdeacon of Bologna, archbishop of Milan, cardinal priest of Sts. Giovanni and Paolo. He played an important role in the events leading to the Great Schism and declared for Pope Clement VII at the end of his life (August, 1381).[150]

Simone discussed both major issues in *Pastoralis*: was Robert subject to Henry and could the emperor deprive him of his defense in court? He thought that someone who was not subject to Henry's authority could not commit treason against him. Since treason, by definition, meant that a greater power, or "majesty" (maiestas) must be injured, Robert could not have been accused of treason because he was not subject to him by feudal law (ex debito).[151] Simone agreed that the emperor could not take away Robert's defense because he held this right from natural law, but not all actions had been instituted by natural law. The emperor could take away actions of civil positive law. However, he must not deprive someone of justice.[152] Innocent IV's doctrine of justice was still alive and well in the fourteenth century.

Although the pope and the emperor were "legibus solutus" (not bound by the law), could they condemn someone without a hearing? Referring to the decretals on which Hostiensis had developed his views of the pope's absolute power, Simone drew a distinction between papal

---

150. Domenico Maffei, "La biblioteca di Gimignano Inghirami e la 'Lectura Clementinarum' di Simone da Borsano," *Proceedings of the Third International Congress of Medieval Canon Law, Strasbourg,* ed. Stephan Kuttner (MIC, Series C, 4; Città del Vaticano: 1971) 217–236 and "Dottori e studenti nel pensiero di Simone da Borsano," *Posta Scripta: Essays on Medieval Law and the Emergence of the European State in Honor of Gaines Post,* ed. J. R. Strayer and D. E. Queller (SG 15; Rome: 1972) 229–249; I. Walter and H. J. Becker, "Brossano (Borsano), Simone da," DBI 14 (1972) 470–474.

151. Simone da Borsano, Reportationes to Clem. 2.11.2 v. *uel ab eis,* Florence, Laur. Edili 55, fol. 194r: "Primo notandum est crimen lese maiestatis non per subditum non posse committi quia ex quo non est in eum potestas atque superioris, non posse esse lesio maioris potestatis, unde dicitur maiestas, et ex qua cui subditus non est ex debito." On the legal usage of "ex debito" see Pennington, *Canadian Journal of History* 11 (1976) 367–370.

152. Ibid.: "Tertio not. per imperatorem defensionem non posse tolli quia defensio est de iure naturali . . . et eodem modo licet princeps posset auferre actionem que est de iure ciuili positiuo, ff. de orig. iur. l.ii. § Deinde [Dig. 1.2.2.8], non tamen posset tollere iustitiam que est naturalem et diuinam, ut not. Innoc. de constit. Que in ecclesiarum."

and imperial authority. The pope dispensed with many things that others could not, but his dispensation must always be "with cause." The emperor, however, is only above positive law.[153] If Simone had lived in the eighteenth century, he might have written, two princes, one law, but not equal under the *ius commune*.

By and large, the canonists did not quibble about the provisions of *Pastoralis*. They accepted the argument that the emperor did not have jurisdiction outside the empire and that a defense was a right protected by natural law. The canonists did not cite Henry VII's constitution *Ad reprimendum* in their commentaries and, curiously, the civilians did not write commentaries on Henry VII's *Ad reprimendum*, with the notable exception of Bartolus of Sassoferrato. Sometime after 1355, Bartolus composed a long tract on Henry VII's decree that became the Ordinary Gloss.[154] Paradoxically, Bartolus's extensive commentary on Henry VII's imperial decree, whose central provisions had been rejected by the pope and the canonists, became a principal vehicle for establishing the new doctrines of due process in those lands governed by the *ius commune*. For the next three centuries, his commentary and the decree were included in most manuscripts and printed editions of the *Corpus iuris civilis*. The tract also circulated separately.

Bartolus knew the canonistic literature and interpreted *Ad reprimendum* through the procedural norms of the canonists. His "pro-papal" commentary on *Ad reprimendum* is surprising only if one would view a fourteenth-century civilian anachronistically: a jurist who put the interests of universal empire before national kingdoms, Italian city-states,

---

153. Ibid., fol. 196v: "Opponitur contra quartum not. quod possit contra non citatum procedi per papam quia supra ius est, de conces. prebend. Proposuit [X 3.8.4] et plenitudinem habet potestatis, de auct. et usu pal. Ad honorem [X 1.8.4]. Et idem de principe quia legibus solutus est, ff. de legibus l. Princeps [Dig. 1.3.31(30)]. Solutio. Dic quod papa est supra ius quia in multis dispensat ubi alii non possunt, que tamen dispensatio debet esse cum causa, de prebend. De multa [X 3.5.28], Ad l. Princeps respondetur quod solutus est in positiuis; nec obstat quod not. Goff. et Ost. sequitur ibi de iud. re. Tenor [X 2.27.10] quia sententia [non] ualet in absentem non contumacem nisi per appellatione, C. quomodo et quando iudex l. Ab eo [Cod. 7.43.3] quia istud debet intelligi si sit citatus." See chapter 2 for Hostiensis's glosses to *Proposuit* and *Ad honorem*.

154. The literature on Bartolus is enormous. See Francesco Calasso, "Bartolo da Sassoferrato," DBI 6 (1964) 640–669 at 659–660; Emilio Betti, "La dottrina costruita da Bartolo sulla constitutio 'Ad reprimendum,'" *Bartolo da Sassoferrato: Studi e documenti per il VI centenario* (2 vols. Milan: 1962) II 37–47; Cecil N. Sidney Woolf, *Bartolus of Sassoferrato: His Position in the History of Medieval Political Thought* (Cambridge: 1913); Diego Quaglioni, *Politica e diritto nel trecento italiano: Il "De tyranno" di Bartolo da Sassoferrato (1314–1357), con l'edizione critica dei trattati "De Guelphis et Gebellinis," "De regimine civitatis," e "De tyranno"* (Il pensiero politico, biblioteca 11; Florence: 1983); Walther, *Imperiales Königtum* 176–186. Still useful is Savigny, *Geschichte* VI 137–184. Most recently, Elena Brizio, "Una indicizzazione 'automatica' dei consilia di Bartolo da Sassoferrato," *Studi senesi* 102 (1991) 101–349.

or the Church. In his commentary on *Ad reprimendum,* Bartolus dealt not only with procedural norms but confronted the entire range of problems that jurists had raised about imperial and princely power for centuries.

Bartolus's famous statement about the emperor helps us to understand his thought: "Whoever would say that the emperor is not lord and monarch of the entire world would be a heretic." [155] Despite this grandiose, pro-imperial rhetoric, Bartolus affirmed the old doctrines of the twelfth-century jurists: the emperor did not own all things, the emperor did not have jurisdiction over all kings, and the Donation of Constantine had been validly granted by Constantine. Exasperated historians who have looked for unity in his thought have expected a defense of Roman power from a civilian. We should not impose our paradoxes on him. Anyone who has read the previous pages of this book should understand that Bartolus simply adhered to traditional doctrines of the *ius commune* that he could not ignore. [156]

Ad reprimendum had established two points: the emperor could summon Robert to his court and he could dispense with the normal rules of judicial procedure. [157] Bartolus granted that before the birth of Christ the emperor had been the true "dominus mundi," but since then imperium resided in Christ and his vicar on earth, the pope. The pope transfers this imperium to the secular prince. [158] Bartolus referred to a question that Cinus of Pistoia had disputed in Siena, which seemed to offer support for at least one of Henry VII's claims in *Ad reprimendum.* According to Bartolus, Cinus declared that the provision of *Pastoralis* denying that the prince had the right to summon a subject outside his jurisdiction was "an error of the canonists." [159]

155. Bartolus to Dig. 49.15.24, Clm 5475, fol. 305rb–305va and Clm 17763, fol. 313rb: "Et forte si quis diceret dominum imperatorem non esse dominum et monarcham totius orbis, esset hereticus, quia diceret contra determinationem ecclesiae, contra textum sancti evangelii, dum dicit 'Exiuit edictum a Cesare Augusto ut describeretur totus orbis uniuersus,' ut habes Luce ii. uel iii. c." On this passage see Woolf, *Bartolus* 23–31.
156. See discussion of Walther, *Imperiales Königtum* 176–186. Woolf, *Bartolus* 34, finds Bartolus "a very shy thinker wherever the papacy is concerned."
157. See above, n. 21.
158. Bartolus of Sassoferrato to *Ad reprimendum* (Ed. 1472), fol. 1r–23r, Clm 6643, fol. 133r–150v at Ed. fol. 3r, Clm 6643, fol. 133v, v. *totius orbis:* "Vltimo adueniente Christo istud Romanum imperium incipit esse Christi imperium, et ideo apud Christi uicarium est uterque gladius, scilicet spiritualis et temporalis . . . Dic ergo quod ante Christum imperium Romamum dependebat ab eo solo et imperator recte dicebatur quod dominus mundi est, et omnia sua sunt. Post Christum uerum enim imperium est apud Christum et eius uicarium, et per papam transfertur in principem secularem, ut extra de elect. Venerabilem [X 1.6.34]."
159. Bartolus to loc. cit., Ed. fol. 14v, Clm 6643, fol. 143r, v. *per edictum:* "Set an predictis modis possit quis citari ubicumque sit, etiam extra territorium ciuitatis, quod

The consilium has survived, and we can follow Cinus's argument.[160] Cinus envisioned two kinds of summons: one was an exercise of jurisdiction, the second only of notification. The first, declared Cinus, could not be issued outside a judge's jurisdiction, the second could be.[161] Cinus conceded that the Rector of Siena could punish a citizen for committing a murder in Paris on the familiar grounds that serious crimes should be punished for the public good,[162] but not because the Rector could exercise jurisdiction in Paris. Contrary to Bartolus, Cinus did not, at least in this consilium, reject the doctrine of *Pastoralis* and his views expressed in it cannot be called pro-imperial.[163]

Bartolus himself did not, even in part, deny the lawfulness of *Pastoralis*. He noted, wrongly, that Clement's constitution had been pro-

---

uidetur, ut C. de epis. et cler. l. Omnes § Si uero apparitor [Cod. 1.3(6).32.5 in med.] et de offic. prefec. urb. l.ii [Cod. 1.28(31).2] ubi subditum suum citat quis etiam extra territorium. In contrarium est casus extra de re iud. Pastoralis, ubi declaratur quod imperator non potest citare per se eum qui est in terris ecclesie, set debet superiori nunciare ut ei nuncietur. Cynus in quadam disputatione dicit quod illud fuit positum ex errore canonistarum." Cinus had been Bartolus's teacher, and he acknowledged that Cinus had a powerful impact on his juristic formation.

160. Cino da Pistoia, Le "*Quaestiones*" e i "*Consilia,*" ed. Gennaro Maria Monti (Milan: 1942) printed the consilium, "Rector civitatis," for the first time pp. 59–74. P. S. Leicht, "Cino da Pistoia e la citazione di Re Roberto da parte d'Arrigo VII," *Archivio storico italiano* 112 (1954) 313–320. See also Monti, *Cino da Pistoia giurista con bibliografia e tre appendici di documenti inediti* (Città del Castello: 1924) 101–105. Savigny, *Geschichte* VI 71–97.

161. Cino da Pistoia, *Quaestiones* 66: "Michi videtur quod etiam per nunptium et epistulam possit actus mere citationis fieri, nam sicut quidam moderniores notaverunt et bene, omnis citatio habet in se duo extrema. Unum extremum est actus pronunptiationis quo iudex interloquitur citationem fiendam, et iste actus non potest fieri extra territorium, quia est actus jurisdictionis et extra territorium ius dicit, etc. Secundum extremum est ipse actus mere citationis qui non est actus jurisdictionis, sed notificationis, et iste potest ubique exercere." Cinus wrote a few lines further that some jurists interpreted a key passage of *Pastoralis* in a certain way, and they were not correct, loc. cit. p. 67: "Illud 'tanquam' est similitudinarium et debet subaudiri 'apud' secundum quosdam quorum opinio non est vera." Bartolus assumed that the "secundum quosdam" were the canonists; Cinus himself wrote nothing about the "errors of the canonists."

162. Ibid., p. 70: "et sicut res publica Romani imperii consistit in sacerdotibus et magistratibus localibus ita et in hac vindicta interesse suum consistit quam vindictam magistratus Senensis exercere debet quia ne talia malleficia remaneant inpunita, dicitur publice utile considerationi argumenta." On the idea that the punishment of crime is in the interest of the public good, see Fraher, "Preventing Crime in the High Middle Ages," see chapter 4, n. 101.

163. Contrary to what several historians have concluded, cf. Monti's introduction to *Quaestiones* 58: "[La] celebre *Quaestio* 'Rector civitatis' conferma delle dottrine politiche di Cino in senso imperiale e anticurialista." In fact, Cinus's conclusions would support the pope's, the emperor's, or any magistrate's right to exercise jurisdiction outside the territorial limits of their sovereignty. The doctrine of "crimina impunita remaneant" could be any judge's justification for exercising extra-territorial jurisdiction. On the roots of the doctrine see Richard M. Fraher, "The Theoretical Justification for the New Criminal Law of the High Middle Ages: 'Rei publice interest, ne crimina remaneant impunita,'" *University of Illinois Law Review* (1984) 577–595.

mulgated in a general council; therefore, it would not have contained an error since a council consists of a great number of learned men.[164] This concept has a striking resonance with the maxim in which Bartolus signified a primitive concept of popular sovereignty: "concilium representat mentem populi" (a council represents the mind of the people), except that here he alleged that the authority of learning, not its source, gives legislation greater validity.[165]

Following Paulus de Liazariis, Bartolus made a distinction between Cinus's case, the city of Siena's summoning one of its citizens outside its territory, and a judge's summoning a person over whom the judge did not have jurisdiction. In the first case, a summons might have validity, in the second not.[166] In the case of Henry and Robert, Bartolus concluded that the emperor did not have the right to summon him, particularly since he resided within the lands of the Church. The pope, on the other hand, could lawfully summon anyone from anywhere. "He is the vicar of Christ, whose earth it is and whose plenitude."[167]

To the second point of Ad reprimendum, Bartolus acknowledged that the constitution had to be interpreted through Pastoralis and Saepe. A judge is obligated to observe all the judicial norms that have been established by the law of nations and natural reason.[168] Bartolus discussed all those parts of the judicial process that he thought were

164. Bartolus to loc. cit., Ed. fol. 14v, Clm 6643, fol. 143r, v. per edictum: "Set cum illa decretalis fuerit facta in concilio generali ubi fuit magna copia intelligentium, non est uerisimile, quod ibi fuerit erratum, unde temeraria est dicta solutio contra."

165. Walter Ullmann, "De Bartoli sententia: Concilium repraesentat mentem populi," Bartolo da Sassoferrato: Studi e documenti per il VI centenario (Milan: 1962) II 705–733. See also Tierney, "Only the Truth has Authority."

166. Ibid.: "Dominus Paulus de Liazariis dicit quod in dicto capitulo quod ille qui est iudex alicuius ratione domicilii potest citare illum extra territorium quacumque citatione uerbali, cum talis absens alium superiorem isto non habet, per quem citari posset." The "citatio verbalis" is probably the equivalent to Cinus's "citatio notificationis." Paulus de Liazariis to Clem. 2.11.2 (Pastoralis), Bamberg Can. 79, fol. 39v, Nürnberg Stadtbibl. II 60, fol. 115r–116r, Vienna, N.B. 2078, fol. 33v, has a long section on whether someone may be summoned when he commits a delict outside his own territory.

167. Ibid.: "Secundo, quia est directo contra casum huius constitutionis et, quod sic intellexit etiam imperator, patet, quia citationem factam de rege Roberto existente extra territorium asseruit legitime factam. Et loquitur hic de citatione facta a quocumque qui iurisdictione preest. Item in causa capitali. Et si dicis hic imperator non potuit, concedo in terris ecclesie. Dic ergo quod papa potest iure quemlibet ubique existentem citare, quia ipse est uicarius Christi cuius est terra, et plenitudo (orbis add. Ed.) eius, ut extra. de iud. in Clem. c.i. [Clem. 2.1.1]."

168. Ibid., Ed. fol. 11r, Clm 6643, fol. 139v, v. et figura iudicii: "Tu dic quod iudex per hec uerba releuatur ab omni forma et figura iudicii inducta a iure ciuili, et tenetur seruare omnem figuram formam iudicii inductam de iure gentium uel naturali ratione . . . Quid ergo de sermone huius uerbi dicam: intellige idem si omnia coniungerentur. Quid hoc important per singulas partes iudicii prosequamur latius quam in dicto capitulo 'Sepe' [Clem. 5.11.2]."

essential. Although he held the view that actions themselves were part
of the civil law,[169] a summons was necessary; after all, God had called
Adam to judgment.[170] Petitions, exceptions, delays, and proofs must
also always be allowed because natural law had instituted them. Even
the legal maxim that someone may not be judged twice for the same
crime is a precept of natural law.[171] Therefore, although the significance
of the words "sine strepitu et figura iudicii" is that a judge's will is freed
of the rules of the civil law, a judge must nevertheless preserve the
equity of the law of nations and natural equity. The old question of
the podestà is thus solved: the podestà may dispense with the solem-
nities of law, but the podestà may not perpetrate an injustice.[172] Bartolus's reinterpretation of the key clauses of *Ad reprimendum* might be
cited as another example of his willingness to subject imperial to papal
prerogatives, in this case imperial to papal law. However, one must
recognize that Bartolus's interpretation of *Ad reprimendum* reflected
the jurisprudence of the *ius commune*. I have not yet found any late
fourteenth-century lawyers who argued that essential parts of the judicial process were not established by natural law.[173]

169. Bartolus to Cod. 1.19.2, (Venice: 1476) unfol., Nürnberg, Cent. II 84, fol. 27r:
"[potest tolli] quedam de iure ciuili, ut actiones; quedam de iure gentium, ut dominium
[imperator non tolli potest]." See Woolf, *Bartolus* 47.
170. Ibid.: "Quero ergo an sit necesse ut pars citetur? Respondeo sic, ut infra in hac
lege innuitur. Idem quia hoc est de iure naturali, nam primum hominem citauit Deus dicens 'Adam, Adam, ubi es?' Hoc est probatur extra de re iud. Clem. Pastoralis [Clem.
2.11.2] ubi sententia domini imperatoris Henrici qui fecit hanc legem et postea condem-
nauit Robertum regem Iherusalem et Sicilie cassatur, ob hoc quod citatio non fuit facta
legitime et probatur in dicto capitulo 'Sepe.'"
171. Ibid., Ed. fol. 11v; Clm 6643, fol. 140r: "Item an poterit opponi exceptio rei
iudicate uel finite ad impediendum processum. Respondeo sic, quia de iure naturali est
ne iudicetur bis in idipsum."
172. Ibid., Ed. fol. 12v, Clm 6643, fol. 141v, v. *iurisdictioni preest uidetur expedire*:
"Si uero per uerba significantia liberam uoluntatem tunc est liber a regulis iuris ciuilis,
debet tamen seruare equitatem iuris gentium seu naturalem equitatem que idem est per
dicta iura et est casus de re iud. in Clem. Pastoralis, nam imperator solutus est legibus
et ex uigore sue potestatis tulit ibi sententiam, tamen quia in quibusdam fecit ibi contra
naturalem equitatem ideo sententia cassatur. Et ideo patet quod in casu nostre legis ubi
procedit absque figura iudicii, si committur iudici per uerba significantia, arbitrium boni
uiri debet seruare regulas iurisgentium, quia hec uerba predicta 'sine figura iudicii' important siue committantur per uerba significantia uoluntatem liberam. Et per hoc patet soluta
questio quando potestati datur liberum arbitrium an propter hoc poterit facere parti
iniustitiam? Certe non, quia hoc est contra naturalem equitatem; set potest omittere
solemnitates iuris ciuilis. De hoc per glossam in dicta Clem. Sepe, super uerbo 'defensiones'; dixi de dona. l. Si [cum] filiusfamilias [Dig. 39.5.2]."
173. There seems to have been unanimity among the jurists on this point; see, for
example, Ranieri Arsendi's comments (ca. 1342–1344) printed by F. Martino, *Dottrine
di giuristi e realtà cittadine nell'Italia del trecento: Ranieri Arsendi a Pisa e a Padova*
(Studi e ricerche die 'Quaderni catanesi', 5; Catania: 1984) 145: "Set nunquid actio sit
de iure civili vel gentium? Et videtur quod gentium . . . et hoc tenet Iacobus de Bellovisu,

Bartolus's student, Baldus de Ubaldis, accepted the provisions of *Pastoralis* completely. Although he concurred with Bartolus that an action was a part of civil law and could be taken away, he conceded that the prince was obligated by other parts of the judicial process. He could not deprive a defendant of self-defense in court. The prince had an obligation to summon a defendant because a summons is established by the law of nations. The prince must examine the truth in a courtroom because the search for truth is a mandate of the law of nations.[174] Although the pope was the vicar of Christ, Baldus was not certain that he could condemn a feudal vassal of the Church without summoning that vassal. He presented only "pro et contra" arguments.[175] The end of the fourteenth century saw the provisions of *Pastoralis* established as the regulatory norms of judicial procedure in Roman and canon law; nevertheless the papal "prince" was not yet bound by his own legislation.

---

set Dynus tenet quod sint de iure civili . . . set ego dico quod materia ex qua actiones producuntur in esse bene est de iure gentium . . . Forma autem sive inventio actionum sive modi agendi bene sunt de iure civili."

174. Baldus to Cod. 1.14(17).11, Ed. sine anno et loco (Hain *2279): "Est et aliud speciale quia princeps non tenetur seruare ordinem iudiciorum in procedendo, ut not. Innoc. extra de re iud. c. In causis [X 2.27.19]. Debet tamen pars citari; alias non ualet sententia principis, et potest opponi de nullitate, et textus est hic notabile cum sua glossa. Ideo enim pars est citanda ut possit se defendere, que defensio est de iure gentium seu naturali, et ideo non potest auferri, ut ff. de re milit. l.iii. § Si ad diem [Dig. 49.16.3.7] et in c. Pastoralis, de re iud. in Clem. [Clem. 2.11.2] ff. de adopt. Adoptio per iura facta et l. Nam ita diuus, cum si. [Dig. 1.7.38 and 39] Item coram principe requiritur examinatio et uentilatio ueritatis, quia inquisitio ueritatis est de iure gentium. Vnde licet solemnitates legales non teneatur princeps obseruare, obseruantiam tamen iure gentium non debet deesse, quia pertinet ad naturalem equitatem, et hoc est quod uult littera dum dicit 'cognitionaliter.'"

175. Baldus de Ubaldis, *Prologus* to *Lectura super usibus feudorum* (Rome: sine anno [Hain *2316]) unfol., Clm 6632, fol. 96v, Clm 26912, fol. 140r: "Potest etiam papa contra omnes tenentes terram ecclesie sententiam ferre eis non citatis, ut not. in c. Cum olim, extra. de re iud. in Clem. Vel dic quod et si papa non posset hoc ex ordine, potest tamen et debet [et debet *om.* Clm 26912] fauore uniuersalis ecclesie, idest Romane, ex plenitudine potestatis; arg. contra de re iud. c. Pastoralis, in Clem."

The Authority of the Prince in the Late Middle Ages

Decius: Most mighty Caesar,
  Let me know some cause

  . . .

Caesar: The cause is my will.
  —Shakespeare, *Julius*
    Caesar, Act 2, scene 2

Ever since the jurists of the early thirteenth century focused on the will of the prince as being the source of his authority and power, they fretted whether the prince could act without reason or without cause. They had created a potential Leviathan and worried about loosing the bonds that kept him tame. Some jurists solved the problem by conceding that inferior princes could not act arbitrarily, all the while admitting that the emperor and the pope could. Other jurists maintained that the emperor must act with cause, but not the pope, whose authority transcended all others.

Shakespeare lived in an age when theories of absolutism were fashionable and may have written *Julius Caesar* with an eye on his own prince, James I. In *Macbeth* (Act 3, scene 1), which may have been written specifically for James, Macbeth orders Banquo's death with the words: "I could with barefaced power sweep him from my sight and bid my will avouch it." No jurist ever formulated a more dramatic description of power. However, while Macbeth may have recognized no fetters on brutal action, Shakespeare was undoubtedly not endorsing ruthlessness here. A prince with a keen ear might have learned something about the illusion of absolute power from Macbeth's tragedy.

An important part of our story is the synthesis that the late medieval jurists fashioned from earlier theories of princely authority. Of course, they do not create new terminology or doctrine, but do refine and expand earlier thought. In this chapter, I shall discuss the thought of

Baldus de Ubaldis and Panormitanus, two jurists who were particularly important for synthesizing doctrines of sovereignty for the *ius commune* and whose opinions were cited frequently by later jurists.

Baldus de Ubaldis was one of the great lawyers of the late fourteenth century. His teacher, Bartolus of Sassoferrato, surpassed him in reputation, but at his death in 1400 Baldus's fame had approached if not exceeded his master's. Bartolus had written at a pace to make the most dedicated printer dizzy. His eminence rested on a shelf of volumes of extraordinary bulk. For his part, Baldus was only slightly less prolific.

Baldus was central Italian by birth and culture. He was a native of Perugia, attended the law school there, and afterward taught at his Alma Mater. Like so many of his contemporaries, he relished public forums and immersed himself in practical affairs. He practiced law, held public offices, performed important diplomatic missions, and at the end of his life was called to the University of Pavia by Giangaleazzo Visconti.[1]

As Joseph Canning has pointed out, Baldus did not write any political tracts. While his teacher, Bartolus, wrote on politics and political institutions, Baldus contented himself with the materials of Roman and canon law.[2] Helmut Walther has pointed out, rightly I think, that "Baldus undoubtedly went further than any other medieval civilian in shaping political theory."[3] However, because we do not have any specific tract by Baldus on "political authority," his scattered glosses do not always present his ideas coherently. Canning has discovered a striking example of this in his careful study of Baldus's thought. Unlike almost all his contemporaries, Baldus believed that property rights were not sacrosanct. The prince could, Baldus seems to maintain, deprive his subjects of their property without cause. Did Baldus break with the tra-

---

1. Joseph Canning, *The Political Thought of Baldus de Ubaldis* (Cambridge Studies in Medieval Life and Thought⁴ 6; Cambridge: 1987) 1–6. K. Pennington, "The Consilia of Baldus de Ubaldis," *Tijdschrift voor Rechtsgeschiedenis* 56 (1988) 85–92 and "The Authority of the Prince in a Consilium of Baldus de Ubaldis," *Studia in honorem Em.mi Card. Alfons M. Stickler* (Rome: 1992) 483–515. See also Norbert Horn, *Aequitas in den Lehren des Baldus* (Forschungen zur neueren Privatrechtsgeschichte, 11; Köln-Graz: 1968) and G. Chevrier, "Baldi de Ubaldi," DDC 2 (1937) 39–52. Savigny, *Geschichte* VI 208–248. Most recently, see Vincenzo Colli, "Il cod. 351 della Biblioteca Capitolare 'Feliniana' di Lucca: Editori quattrocenteschi e 'Libri consiliorum' di Baldo degli Ubaldi (1327–1400)," *Scritti di storia del diritto offerti dagli allievi a Domenico Maffei*, ed. Mario Ascheri (Medioevo e Umanesimo, 78; Padova: 1992) 255–282.
2. Diego Quaglioni, *Politica e diritto nel trecento italiano: Il "De Tyranno" di Bartolo da Sassoferrato (1314–1357), con l'edizione critica dei trattati "De Guelphis et Gebellinis," "De regimine civitatis" e "De tyranno"* (Il pensiero politico 11; Florence: 1983) has edited three of Bartolus's works.
3. Walther, "Die Gegner Ockhams" 131.

dition of "natural law jurisprudence" that we have seen develop from the twelfth century?

For two centuries, jurists had paused at a constitution of the Emperors Theodosius and Valentinian on the validity of rescripts to discuss whether the prince could issue a rescript that contravened natural or divine law. The jurists unanimously concluded that the prince could dispense from the provisions of natural law *with cause*. Baldus wrote:[4]

> Thirdly, the doctors ask whether the emperor can issue rescripts contrary to the law of nations. Accursius says that he may not. The prince's rescript may not take dominium away from anyone without cause. Although with some kind of cause he may. . . . A cause is considered to be a "ratio motiva" of the prince. In the statute of the people "causa motiva" is not required, only a probable or worthy cause.

The key phrase in this passage is "A cause is considered to be a 'ratio motiva' of the prince." Canning has translated this as "whatever reason motivates the emperor himself is considered cause enough."[5] The translation is not an unreasonable one, and Canning was puzzled that Baldus "should adopt this view on property and leave the emperor limited in other important respects."[6] As we have seen, property rights were grounded in natural law, just as other limitations on the prince's authority were. Canning concludes that Baldus's conception of absolute power was "more in tune with absolutist theories of the seventeenth century."[7] If Canning is correct in his interpretation of Baldus's conception of sovereignty, Baldus could be considered a key figure who might have influenced later advocates of arbitrary absolutism. Consequently, for our understanding of the historical continuity of medieval and early modern political thought, Baldus's conception of princely authority is of singular importance. He was a thinker of renown until well into the seventeenth century.[8]

Yet reading Baldus can be exasperating. He could be opaque, even purposefully obscure. In order to understand Baldus's views on the re-

---

4. Baldus to Cod. 1.19(22).7 (Rescripta) (Sine anno, Hain *2279): "Tertio querunt doctores numquid imperator potest rescribere contra ius gentium. Glossa uidetur dicere quod non, unde per rescriptum principis non potest alicui sine causa auferri dominium; sed cum aliquali bene potest, ff. de natural. rest. l. Queris [Dig. 40.11.3], de euic. l. Lucius [Dig. 21.2.11], de leg. ii. Qui solidum § i. [Dig. 31.1.78(80).1], de rei uen. l. Item si uerberatum [Dig. 6.1.15]. Et habetur pro causa quelibet ratio motiua ipsius principis; secus est in statuto populi, quia non debet inesse causa motiua, sed debet inesse causa probabilis et condigna."

5. Canning, *Baldus de Ubaldis* 81.

6. Canning, *Baldus de Ubaldis* 82.

7. Ibid.

8. See the remarks of Canning, *Baldus de Ubaldis* 228–229.

lationship of the prince and natural law, we shall review other passages in which he dealt with the prince's power to transcend the traditional limits on his authority. Finally, we shall better be able to place the troublesome passage with which we began in its proper context.

In a consilium that he wrote for Giangaleazzo Visconti in which he defended the Duke of Milan's right to assume by right of privilege lordships formerly held by the Roman emperor, Baldus struggled with the irreconcilable conflict of his obligations and loyalty to Giangaleazzo and his adherence to a conviction that the prince could not subvert a legal instrument that was based on natural law. He revised the consilium extensively and at several different times.[9] We know of these revisions from a Vatican manuscript, and they show that he purposely obfuscated his line of argument and his thought. In the end, however, he clearly avowed that the prince could not break a contract with his subject. The prince is bound to observe a contract by natural law. With cause, of course, the prince could annul a contract,[10] but cause would have to be proved. It is odd, to say the least, that Baldus could not bring himself to break with the "medieval natural law tradition" of the jurists when he handled Giangaleazzo's problem that was encumbered with considerable political delicacy. It is odder still that he could write in at least one place in his commentaries that the prince could dispossess subjects' private property without cause, "ratio motiva." With this vexing problem of interpretation in mind, we shall review Baldus's conception of princely sovereignty.

Canning has distinguished the various meanings of "princeps" or prince in Baldus's thought. He demonstrated that Baldus used the term to refer to the emperor, to the pope, and sometimes to rulers in general. Consequently, one must be careful not to confuse any jurist's meaning by misunderstanding to which prince he referred. Although the prince could designate a particular ruler, by the late fourteenth century the jurists had adopted a generalized definition of prince: it included all monarchs who exercised sovereign power.

9. Salvatore Fodale, "Baldo degli Ubaldi difensore di Urbano VI e signore di Biscina," *Quaderni medievali* 17 (1984) 73–85, gives another example of Baldus's having revised his opinion about the legitimacy of Pope Urban VI's election.

10. Baldus de Ubaldis, *Consilia*, 3.326–3.327 (Milan edition) 3.279 (Venice); I have edited this consilium from the manuscripts in "The Authority of the Prince": "dico quod ex contractu imperatoris obligatur fiscus . . . quam obligationem imperator non potest rescindere quia est de naturali, et hoc casu in principe non presumitur causa." Canning, *Baldus de Ubaldis* 82–86, discusses Baldus's theory of contract, both private and feudal. He does not stress the crucial point that Baldus believed that the prince could not break a contract without cause and that when he broke a contract, he was not presumed to have acted with cause.

Baldus expressed his conception of princely power in his commentary on one of the most famous texts in Justinian's *Digest*, *Princeps*, which was a formulation of princely authority by the Roman jurist, Ulpian: "What pleases the prince has the force of law." [11] This passage had provided two centuries of jurists with the inspiration to reflect on the prince's authority over positive law and his relationship to higher norms. The question of whether the prince could abrogate or derogate positive law was straightforward and simple. Ever since in the early thirteenth century Laurentius Hispanus had perceived that the prince's will could be defined as the source of all positive law, the jurists conceded that the prince could alter or change positive law as he wished. [12] He could enact laws that were unjust, unreasonable, and arbitrary if he fancied, for "his will was reason." Baldus adopted the paradigm of his predecessors without a demur. [13]

Higher norms presented greater difficulties. As we have seen, the jurists granted the prince authority to dispense from the norms of natural or divine law, but they were careful to circumscribe his authority. Baldus discussed the relationship of the prince and higher norms when he commented on *Princeps* and the words "What pleases the prince has the force of law:" [14]

> "What pleases the prince" ought to be considered law. And law is not only what has the form of a constitution, but that which has the form of a contract. . . . Rather [a contract] is even greater because, although the prince is not bound by the law of law, he is bound by the law of contract, as Cinus has shown in the law, *Digna vox*.

Following his predecessors, Baldus considered the law governing the creation and maintenance of a contract to be grounded in natural law. Guido of Suzzara and Cinus of Pistoia had championed this view, and

11. Dig. 1.4.1. On this passage and others in Roman law that touched upon the authority of the emperor, see Peter Stein, "Roman Law," *The Cambridge History of Medieval Political Thought c. 350–c.1450*, ed. J. H. Burns (Cambridge: 1988) 37–47 at 46.

12. See above, chapter 2 and Pennington, *Pope and Bishops* 17–23 and "Law, Legislative Authority, and Theories of Government, 1150–1300," *Cambridge History of Medieval Political Thought* 427–430.

13. Canning, *Baldus de Ubaldis* 74–76.

14. Baldus to Dig. 1.4.1 (Quod principi placet) Munich, Staatsbibl. Clm 6640, fol. 43v–44r; (Venice: 1493), fol. 24v–25r. There are two commentaries to this law in the printed edition; Clm 6640 has only the first: "Pro lege haberi debet quod principi placet. Et non solum est lex quod habet formam constitutionis, sed id quod habet formam contractus, l. penult. de donat. inter uir. et uxor. [Dig. 24.1.66(67)]. Immo plus quod licet princeps non ligetur lege legis, ligatur lege conuentionis, C. de leg. l. Digna uox [Cod. 1.14(17).4] per Cy. et infra de iur. om. iud. l. Est receptum [Dig. 2.1.14]." The textual tradition of Baldus's commentary on the *Digest* must still be explored.

their arguments had prevailed in the *ius commune*.[15] In his commentary to *Digna vox*, Baldus had quoted Cinus's opinion that he now cited with approval:[16] "Master Cinus says that if a pact contains natural justice and equity that such a pact should be preserved."

Baldus then made it clear that he thought that the prince was bound by public contracts—such as feudal contracts and peace treaties—and private contracts. Although Guido of Suzzara seemed to believe that all the prince's contracts could bind his heirs, Baldus distinguished between public contracts that could bind the prince's successors and those that could not. In doing so he drew a neat distinction between acts of the prince as head of state and his acts as a private person. Although the jurists had not yet worked out boundaries between the prince's public and private person, Baldus took a major step in that direction in his commentaries on *Princeps* and *Digna vox*:[17]

> I say that the prince is bound [by contracts] and not his successor. The prince's contract cannot bind his successor, because his successor does not have a "cause" from him . . . a right (ius) does not pass to a successor, but is created again at the time of election. . . . This is true except in the case of a contract that he makes [while executing a function that is inherent] in the nature of customary usage of his office, such as the granting of fiefs.

Baldus had given a clearer and more general explanation of this distinction in his commentary on *Digna vox*:[18]

> If the emperor concludes a peace or agreement with his subjects for the general and public good, those pacts ought not be infringed by his successor,

15. For a discussion of their thought see chapter 4.

16. Baldus to Cod. 1.14(17).4 (Digna vox), (Sine loco et anno, Hain *2279), unfol. (Venice: 1474) unfol.: "Dominus Cynus dicit quod si istud pactum habet in se iustitiam naturalem et equitatem quod istud pactum est seruandum."

17. Baldus to Dig. 1.4.1, Edd. cit.: "Ipse dico, non successor, quia contractus principis non transit in successorem, quia successor non habet ab eo causam; ad hoc infra de pignor. l. Lex uectigali, [Dig. 20.1.31] infra loca. l. Si quis domum, [Dig. 19.2.9] quia ius non transit ad successorem, sed de nouo creatur per electionem, extra de prebend. c. Dilecto [X 3.5.25]. Facit quod not. in simili in l. Quesitum § finali de procurat. [Dig. 1.19.? or Cod. 2.12(13).?] Et hoc uerum nisi faciat ea que sunt de natura uel consuetudine sui officii, sicut est infeudare, arg. in auth. constit. que de dignit. § Illud. [Auth. 6.9 (Nov. 81).2]."

18. Baldus to Cod. 1.14(17).4, Ed. cit.: "Si imperator facit pacem uel capitulum cum subditis propter generale et publicum bonum, quod ista non debent infringi per successorem, nisi ex parte subditorum interuenisset dolus uel fraus. Allegat extra. de probat. c.i. [X 2.19.1] de cond. inde. l. In summa [Dig. 12.6.65] Tu allega glossam ordinariam que directe loquitur de capitulis pacis Constantie in authen. de defen. ciu. § Nulla, col. iii. [Authen. 3.2(Nov. 15).2] et ideo pacta que fierent hodie cum regibus Francorum et Anglie porrigerentur ad successores, intelligo si fierent nomine sue gentis que sunt approbata de iure gentium, ut ff. de pact. l. Conuentionem. [Dig. 2.14.5] Personale enim pactum non transiret ad successorem, sed reale pactum bene transit."

unless the subjects commit fraud or wrong-doing. . . . I understand that the pacts made today between the kings of France and England extend to their successors if they are concluded in the name of their people and if they are approved by "ius gentium."

In both of these examples, Baldus supported the idea that the territory and people over which the prince rules have an independent juridical existence. Matters touching the public good or done in the name of the people add another dimension to any act of the prince.[19] The prince cannot break these pacts without cause, and his successors must also maintain them. Baldus conceived of the territory and people over which the prince ruled as an unitary entity that had rights that should be preserved and that should remain inviolable. We call this entity a "state." For Baldus it had no name.[20]

Baldus had no doubts that the prince was bound by his contracts because the law of contracts was based on natural law. He also thought that certain contracts of public law bound the prince's successors.[21] The question remains, however, of whether Baldus believed that the prince could expropriate private property without cause. In *Princeps,* for example, he discussed other limitations of princely authority that restricted the prince's power to disregard higher norms. In a section of his commentary in which he presented pro and contra arguments for the prince's right to subvert natural law, Baldus gave a general and rather abstract definition of these limitations. First, he observed that the prince must always do what is possible and honest. He may not do the impossible. The impossible, he noted, is the opposite of what is necessary. What is necessary, he concluded, is divine and natural law. Second, he presented an objection to this generalization. Although a natural obligation is not greater than a natural release (e.g., from a debt), the prince can annul such a release; for instance, an agreement between a creditor and debtor in which the creditor will not bring suit against the debtor for the fulfillment of the obligation (pactum de non petendo).[22] Consequently, the prince can derogate the right of a subject

19. For further discussion of "bonum publicum" in the thought of the jurists, see nn. 99–115.

20. This idea was not unique to Baldus, see Canning, *Baldus de Ubaldis* 206–208 and his discussion of corporate theory and the "populus" on pp. 185–206.

21. Another example of Baldus's conviction that contracts are inviolable can be found in Pennington, "Authority of the Prince" (see n. 1).

22. Baldus, Dig. 1.4.1 Ed. cit.: "Not. tamen quod hec auctoritas 'quicquid principi placet' debet intelligi, scilicet possibile et honestum, nam impossibilia princeps non potest. Illud autem est impossibile cuius contrarium est necessarium. Est autem necessarium ius diuinum. Item ius naturale. Sed contra hoc opponitur quia non plus potest naturalis ob-

to be free from suit in a matter in which the subject's right is protected by natural law.

Baldus answered this objection and added a series of concrete examples illustrating limitations of the prince's authority. First, he explained that a clause in a contract that stipulated that a suit could not be brought by the creditor is an "exception"—that is, a defense by a defendant to a plaintiff's claim—and all exceptions are part of positive, not natural law. Therefore, the objection is not an example of the prince's right to derogate the law of nations. No prince can promulgate a law that violates God's mandates.[23] Second, the prince could not order his subjects to commit adultery with rebels; he could not order fathers to stop feeding their sons.[24] As another illustration of the prince's limitations, Baldus referred to Henry VII's decree, *Ad reprimendum*, which we discussed in the last chapter. The prince may not, he observed, promulgate a law stating that natural law had no place in his legislation. Clement V, we should recall, had rejected Henry's claim that he could ignore natural law in his decretal *Pastoralis*.[25]

In addition, Baldus insisted on other limitations to princely authority. The prince could not permit men to steal but could allow his men to plunder the possessions of the enemy. Nor could the prince issue decrees that would permit heresy or usury.[26] Then there was the subject of property. The prince, Baldus declared, could not take away ownership (dominium) from a subject without cause, nor could he deprive that subject of jurisdiction, that is, the ownership of private property.[27]

---

ligatio quam naturalis liberatio, sed princeps potest tollere liberationem; puta pacti de non petendo, ut l.iii. § [Si] is pro quo, infra quod quisque iuris [Dig. 2.2.3.3] Ergo etc."

23. Ibid.: "Solutio. Ibi non tollit naturalem liberationem, ut eadem lege § finali, sed exceptiones pacti, nam omnes exceptiones sunt de iure ciuili, sicut actiones, unde tollitur exceptio, idest eius propositio et forma. Sed non causa et materia. Sic non potest tolli ius gentium, supra titulo i. l. penult. [Dig. 1.3.40(39)] et instit. de iure naturali § Ius autem gentium [Inst. 1.2.2 in medio] et ideo si principi placet quod Deo non placet, non habet legis uigorem."

24. Ibid.: "Item si principi placet quod unusquisque possit adulterari in rebelles, non habet uigorem (uim Clm 6640) legis quia scriptum est non mecaberis . . . Item si principi placet quod nullus pater teneatur alimentare filium, non ualet."

25. Ibid.: "Item si principi placet quod lex nature non habeat locum in suis actis, tale beneplacitum non est lex, extra de re iud. Pastoralis, in Clem. [Clem. 2.11.2]."

26. Ibid.: "Item si principi placet quod homines possint licite furari, tale beneplacitum non est lex nisi in rebus hostium, C. de commer. et mer. l.i. [Cod. 4.63.2] et infra de alea. l.i. § Quod autem. [Dig. 11.5.1.3] Item si principi placet heresis uel usura, certe hoc non habet legis uigorem, ut not. C. de usur. auth. Ad hec [Cod. 4.32.16 (ex Nov. 34.1)]."

27. Ibid.: "Item not. quod sicut princeps non debet alicui auferre dominium sine causa, ita nec propriam iurisdictionem, ut l. Qui fuere, de statu hom. [Dig. 1.5.20] sed iurisdictionem commissam uel precariam auferre potest libere, ut infra de iud. l. Iudicium soluitur."

To further his point, Baldus cited a text from the *Digest* in which Ulpian had stated that if a man was seized by madness he still retained his status, dignity, magistracy, and power, just as he retained his ownership of his own things.[28] Another text in Baldus's commentary on the Decretals of Gregory IX bears upon this question. He asked the old question first posed by the jurists in connection with the stories surrounding Martinus and Bulgarus: could the prince give my property as a gift? From his answer he meant to solve the question of whether the prince could give a subject's property to someone who had not been mentioned in the will. Baldus responded, as had almost all previous jurists, by citing the opinion of Guido de Baysio with approval. A testament could not be broken by the privilege of the prince, even if the privilege preceded the will.[29]

These passages return us to the problem of the text of Baldus that I cited at the beginning of this chapter:

> The prince may not take dominium away from anyone without cause. Although with some kind of cause he may. . . . A cause is considered to be a "ratio motiva" of the prince.

But what exactly did Baldus mean by "ratio motiva"? This passage is not a model of clarity. A. J. Carlyle, for one, read the same text and came to the opposite conclusion as Canning.[30] Ennio Cortese noted that the sixteenth-century jurist, Philippus Decius, cited this text from Baldus's *Commentary* to justify his assertion that the prince could confiscate property without cause, but he is not sure Decius interpreted the passage correctly.[31] As we have seen, Canning translated this sentence as "whatever reason motivates the emperor himself is considered cause enough." As such, one may not object to this interpretation of the passage, for it could be exactly what Baldus meant.

Several other explanations of this anomaly in Baldus's thought are possible, however. First, Baldus may have written this passage early in

28. Dig. 1.5.20: "Qui furere coepit, et statum et dignitatem in qua fuit et magistratum et potestatem videtur retinere, sicut rei suae dominum retinet."

29. Baldus de Ubaldis to X 2.1.12 (Cum venissent) Munich, Staatsbibl. Clm 3629, fol. 15r–15v (Milan: 1478) unfol.: "Quero an imperator possit rem meam donare. Not. Archidia. ix. q.ult. Per principalem [C.9 q.3 c.21] ubi omnino uide an principis priuilegium rumpat testamentum. Dicit Archidia. quod non, licet priuilegium procedat, quia fauorabilius est testamentum quam priuilegium. Dicit Archidia. lxxxviii. di. Episcopus [D.88 c.5]."

30. *History of Mediaeval Political Theory* VI 85.

31. Cortese, *La norma* I p. 138 n.96. and II p. 274. Nicolini, *Proprietà* 147–151 and passim, did not discuss the passage, but thought Baldus's position was that the emperor must have cause to expropriate property.

his career, and it does not reflect his later opinion. "Ratio motiva" may not have meant that any reason justified the prince's action, but only a reason informed by cause. If this last interpretation of the text is correct, it would bring other texts where Baldus discusses property into congruence and would eliminate what seems to be a startling discordant note in Baldus's strict adherence to the doctrine that the prince cannot violate or subvert the provisions of natural law without cause.

Yet the passage remains puzzling. Earlier jurists had debated the question long and thoroughly, and the issues were clear by the late fourteenth century. Did Baldus deviate from the clear doctrine of the *ius commune*?

The passage is worth quoting again, in full:[32]

> Thirdly, the doctors ask whether the emperor can issue rescripts contrary to the law of nations. Accursius says that he may not. The prince's rescript may not take dominium away without cause. Although with some kind of cause he may. . . . A cause is considered to be a "ratio motiva." In a statute of the people "causa motiva" is not required, only a probable or worthy cause. . . . From what has been said, it appears that if the emperor made someone count of the Palatinate and gave him the power of legitimizing bastards, even after the death of the parents, that if relatives inherited a bastard's parents' property and thereby were made lords before the count legitimized him, the count's action would not prejudice the relatives because lordship is established by the law of nations and cannot be taken away by a rescript of the prince without cause. Here there was no cause unless, perhaps, the father had preordained the legitimizing of his bastard son.

The key phrase for proper interpretation here is "a cause can be any reason that motivates the prince." Canning has interpreted "quelibet ratio motiva" as the equivalent of "sine cause" (without cause). This would undoubtedly be correct if Baldus had written "quelibet causa

---

32. Baldus to Cod. 1.19(22).7 (Rescripta) (Sine loco et anno [Hain *2279]): "Tertio querunt doctores numquid imperator potest rescribere contra ius gentium. Glossa uidetur dicere quod non, unde per rescriptum principis non potest alicui sine causa auferri dominium; sed cum aliquali bene potest, ff. de natural. rest. l. Queris [Dig. 40.11.3], de euic. l. Lucius [Dig. 21.2.11], de leg. ii. Qui solidum § i. [Dig. 31.1.78(80).1], de rei uen. l. Item si uerberatum [Dig. 6.1.15]. Et habetur pro causa quelibet ratio motiua ipsius principis; secus est in statuto populi, quia non debet inesse causa motiua, sed debet inesse causa probabilis et condigna; alias non uidetur, ut ff. qui et a quibus l. Si priuatus [Dig. 40.9.17]. Ex predictis apparet quod si imperator aliquem facit comitem Palatinum et dat sibi potestatem legitimandi spurios, etiam post mortem parentum, quod si ante legitimationem alii consanguinei adiuerunt hereditatem et per consequens erant effecti domini, quod ista legitimatio non preiudicat eis quia cum dominium sit de iuregentium, per rescriptum principis non potest auferri sine causa, et hic nulla subest causa nisi forte pater hoc preordinasset, ut not. Bar. in l. Gallus § Et quid si tantum, de libe. et posthu. et ibi dixi [Dig. 28.2.29]." See Canning, *Baldus de Ubaldis* 81, 156–157, 238, 259.

motiva." But "ratio" had a very special meaning for the medieval jurists. It informed cause, it assumed justice, and it precluded arbitrary actions.[33] Further, as Cortese remarked, the example with which Baldus followed his statement seems to preclude any absolutistic interpretation of his statement. Baldus's story of the bastard and his relatives seems to confirm that if a right had been granted on the authority of the prince, he could not abrogate the right if the law of nations protected it. Consequently, if Baldus considered the case of the bastard as being governed by the prince's "ratio motiva," then "ratio motiva" had limits and was not arbitrary. In this instance, the prince could not restore the bastard's property to him without cause.

Baldus's final thought seems to clinch the argument. He ended his gloss with the observation that the prince had no cause—and therefore could not deprive the bastard's relatives of their property—"unless the father had preordained the legitimizing of his bastard son." Thus, if the father had requested that his son be legitimized before his death, the prince could restore his patrimony to his son. In that case the prince is not acting without cause but is restoring what the father intended his son to have. "Ratio motiva" is not the prince's arbitrary will; rather, it is a defense of filial rights to property that transcended all other claims.

Canning cites another text from Baldus's commentary to *Bene a Zenone* to support his interpretation of "ratio motiva," but, again, I think the text is ambiguous.[34]

> The property of private individuals does not belong to the prince . . . nevertheless the emperor may confiscate it with his absolute power and treat it as his own property, as I have said in the preceding law, especially if there is an existing cause (maxime causa subsistente).

One may read "maxime causa subsistente," which I have translated as "especially if there is an existing cause," as "a just cause is not essential," as Canning has understood the passage. Baldus's meaning would then be, "with absolute power the prince may expropriate property, especially (maxime) if there were a cause." His implication would be

---

33. Once again, Cortese, *La norma* passim, is the most thorough argument for my generalization.

34. Baldus to Cod. 7.37.7 (Sine anno et loco [Hain *2279]) unfol.: "Bona vero singularium personarum non sunt principis . . . de his tamen imperator disponere potest ex͞ potestate absoluta ut de propriis, ut supra dixi super lege proxima, et maxime causa subsistente." Cf. Canning, *Baldus de Ubaldis* 81 n. 40. The second text, to Cod. 7.37.2, that Canning cites is an allegation ("hec est causa contra illos") and is not necessarily Baldus's own opinion.

that if there were no cause, the prince could still confiscate a subject's possessions. A few later jurists did, in fact, interpret Baldus as having justified a prince's abrogation of the natural law and of the law of nations without cause.[35] However, given the weight of the evidence, particularly the fact that Baldus unequivocally insisted that the prince could not break contracts and that he could not deprive his subjects of due process, one might safely assume that Baldus did not conceive of the prince's absolute power as transcending natural law. Medieval jurists were not always logically consistent, but in this case the inconsistency of his opinions would be so great that one should assume that Baldus was not being self-contradictory. It is difficult to believe that Baldus would have permitted the prince to derogate natural law without cause in one case and not in another. Of course, an alternative explanation might be that Baldus changed his mind later in life. He may have been a young absolutist and an old constitutionalist. Unfortunately, we have no firm chronology of his writings nor do we have studies of the manuscript traditions of his work. Nonetheless, an exploration of the textual histories of his various works might shed more light on the question.

Baldus, however, did adopt the terminology of absolute power. His prince had the look of absolutism if not, as I have argued, the substance. Absolute power, we must remember, was not a given. Even in the late Middle Ages, many jurists seem to have avoided "potestas absoluta." In contrast to his teacher, Bartolus, who never seems to have employed the phrase, Baldus, as we shall see, used "potestas absoluta" frequently.

In a gloss to *Imperium* of Justinian's Digest, Baldus described the different types of authority exercised by princes and magistrates and posited two types of imperium. High magistrates held "merum imperium," and this power was limited by law.[36] The prince, on the other hand, exercised absolute "merum imperium" with his plenitude of power, and he alone held this power.[37] "Merum imperium" is absolute in the prince and limited in inferiors. The prince's imperium may be defined as the absolute power of the emperor granted to him by the *Lex regia* (the

35. Cortese, *La norma* II 274, citing Decius' consilia, nr. 146 and 198.
36. Baldus to Dig. 2.1.3 (Imperium) Clm 6640, fol. 100r–102r; (Venice 1493), fol. 70v–72r (1st Repetitio in Ed.): "Tu dic quod duplex est merum imperium. Quoddam est merum imperium a iure limitatum, et istud residet in presidibus et etiam in maioribus magistratibus ut glossa dicit."
37. Ibid.: "Quoddam est merum imperium absolutum cum plenitudine potestatis, et istud non est nisi in principe. Vnde princeps ita non potest delegare causas meri imperii sicut alias, ut C. qui pro sua iuris l.i. in fine [Cod. 3.3.1]."

law by which the Roman people had bestowed authority on the emperor). In the pope, this authority may be defined as the absolute power conceded to him by God in spiritual affairs.[38]

Although Baldus placed absolute power squarely in the person of the prince, he did not define its relationship to law, nor did he indicate whether the prince could subvert justice or derogate higher norms with this power. In his *Commentary* on the Decretals, Baldus wrote that "the power of the prince ought not be disputed, because his supreme power (suprema potestas)—a favorite term of Baldus and an equivalent for "potestas absoluta"—is subject to no rule, except immutable divine and natural law."[39] Then Baldus tempered the force of this "rule" considerably by observing that every rule needs solemn and rational interpretation.[40] When Baldus commented on *Digna vox* in the Code, however, his definition of absolute power was less nuanced:[41]

> The prince should live according to the laws because his authority depends on the law. Take note that this phrase ought to be understood as the obligation of honesty that should be greatest in the prince. But this phrase may not be understood absolutely, because the supreme and absolute power of the prince is not subject to the law.

Consequently, *Digna vox* applies to the prince's ordinary, not his absolute, power.

Baldus applied the same principles of authority to the pope in his Prologue to the *Decretals of Gregory IX*. The bishop of Rome possesses the fullness of the keys, the highest and unfettered power, that is called

38. Ibid., Clm 6640, fol. 100v, (Venice: 1493) fol. 71v: "Dico quod prima distinctio est illa quod est duplex, scilicet absolutum in principe et limitatum in inferiore. Prout est in principe diffinitur sic: [fol. 101r] merum imperium est absoluta potestas imperatori concessa per legem regiam. In papa diffiniretur sic: merum imperium est absoluta potestas apostolico in spiritualibus a Deo concessa." On this gloss is Wyduckel, *Ius publicum* 58–59.

39. Baldus to X 2.1.12 (Venice: 1595; repr. Torino: 1971), fol. 158v, Clm 3629, fol. 15r–15v: "Illud tamen scias quod de potentia principis non est disputandum quia suprema potestas eius nulli subiacet regule, nisi soli legi diuine uel naturali immutabili, ut plene not. et leg. C. si contra ius uel util. publ. l. finali [Cod. 1.22(25).6]."

40. Ibid.: "Et scias quod omne uerbum abbreuiatum ut puta regula iuris, quia omnis regula potest dici uerbum abbreuiatum, indiget solempni et sana interpretatione." Cf. Wyduckel, *Princeps legibus solutus* 81.

41. Baldus to Cod. 1.14(17).4 (Digna vox) Ed. sine loco et anno (Hain *2279) unfol. Venice: 1474, unfol.: "Princeps debet uiuere secundum leges quia ex lege eiusdem pendet auctoritas. Hoc dicto intellige quod istud uerbum debet intelligi de debito honestatis que summa debet in principe. Sed non intelligitur precise quia suprema et absoluta potestas principis non est sub lege. Vnde lex ista habet respectum ad potestatem ordinariam, non ad potestatem absolutam." Canning, *Baldus de Ubaldis* 75, 238.

power loosed (potestas absoluta) from all the bonds of the canons and from any limiting rules, except the apostolic and evangelical precepts.[42]

In another gloss to the *Decretals,* Baldus noted that all the rights of the imperial fisc (the public treasury) reside in the prince, and he may concede them to any person. The rights of each person, however, do not reside in the prince, and they may not come into his possession, unless he exercises his absolute power with reasonable cause—such as for the public good.[43] Unlike the ambiguous passages that we cited above, this text limits princely power and has the solid ring of thirteenth-century juristic thought.

Baldus further discussed the authority of the prince and his absolute power in two consilia.[44] In a discussion of the emperor's right to create new dignities and to subject previously established authorities to them, he defined the emperor's position in the world: the emperor is the lord of the world, he is God on earth, and he is the servant of God.[45] Drawing upon papal sources, Baldus noted that the emperor had sometimes been given less flattering names. But whenever he acted contrary to law, he employed his absolute power:[46]

> As in another Psalm, "Justly judge the sons of men," the same words that appear on the emperor's seal. If the emperor writes one thing in the text, namely what is unjust and wicked, and another on his seal, he contradicts

42. Baldus to Prologue of Decretals (Venice: 1585, repr. Aalen: 1970) fol. 2v: "cui data est clavium plenitudo, et summa libera potestas, que appellatur potestas absoluta ab omnibus uinculis canonum et ab omni regula arctatiua, preterquam ab euangelica et apostolica." Canning, *Baldus de Ubaldis* 31, 231.

43. Baldus to X 2.26.13 (Venice: 1585) fol. 244v: "Nota quod omnia iura fiscalia sunt principis et ea concedere potest cuilibet persone, sed iura singularium personarum non sunt principis, nec ueniunt in eius possessionem (confessionesm Ed.), ut hic patet de iuribus castellani, nisi princeps ex potestate absoluta et rationabili causa aliter et specialiter prouideret . . . nam propter publicam utilitatem ecclesie uel populi posset uni concedi et alii auferri, item propter libertatem ecclesie." See Canning, *Baldus de Ubaldis* 80–81, 240.

44. On the textual problems connected with Baldus's consilia see Pennington, "The Consilia of Baldus de Ubaldis" and "Authority of the Prince."

45. Baldus, *Consilia* (Venice: 1491) 3.280, (Milan: 1491–1493) 1.328: "Imperator est dominus mundi . . . Item est Deus in terris . . . Item imperator est servus Dei."

46. Ibid.: "Et iterum in alio psalmo: 'Iuste iudicate filii hominum,' que verba sigillo imperatoris sunt impressa et si imperator unum scribit in textu, videlicet quod est iniustum et iniquum et aliud in sigillo, est contrarius sibiipsi. Et aliquando vocatur coluber tortuosus, quando est scismaticus, de elect. Venerabilem, aliquando aspis periculosus quando non vult audire nec facere quod equum est pro mundi pace, ut in c. Ad apostolice, de re iud. lib. vi. Quicquid tamen agitur supra legem absoluta potestas est, nec est subditorum corripere, quia ut ait Aristoteles, nullum inferius participat id quod superius est, sed obedire oportet. Nam hic maxime bonum obedientie sentitur ubi discolis dominis flexis genibus obeditur."

himself. He is sometimes called a treacherous snake when he is a schismatic . . . and sometimes a dangerous viper, when he does not do what is just for the peace of the world. . . . Whatever, nevertheless, he does contrary to law [he does with] his absolute power, and subjects may not reproach him. As Aristotle says, an inferior shares in nothing of a superior but must obey. The good of obedience is most greatly experienced when a rebel obeys his lords on bended knee.[47]

Baldus qualified the emperor's willful authority that permeates this text. In decisions of arbitration, the prince may act without expressing the "cause" of his decision.[48] If, nevertheless, he decided and determined matters governed by natural law or the law of nations, he must express a specific cause.[49] Here again Baldus respected the transcendental authority of higher norms.

In another consilium treating imperial authority to create new or abrogate old dignities, Baldus delved more thoroughly into the same problem:[50]

The doctors say that the emperor cannot bind himself to the law. Thus a prince who granted a privilege can revoke it by a contrary mandate, if not by ordained law, then by his absolute power, as in the *Authentica*, since the revocation, bestowal, and nature of a privilege spring from the same source, the will of the prince. The prince cannot take his own free will away nor that of another.

Baldus then retreated quickly from this absolutistic description of the prince's power:[51]

47. Baldus's reference to Aristotle has not been found; see Canning, *Baldus de Ubaldis* 73, n. 12.
48. This was a question frequently disputed by the jurists; see chapter 5.
49. Ibid.: "Porro in principe si loquitur in arbitrariis non requiritur causa. Si vero loquitur in rebus decisis et determinatis naturali lege vel moribus gentium aut exprimit causam specifice et statur verbis suis proprio motu prolatis."
50. Edited in Pennington, "Authority of the Prince" 497: "Dicunt doctores quod imperator non potest sibi legem imponere. Vnde privilegium suum princeps qui illud concessit potest contrario imperio revocare, etsi non de lege ordinata, tamen de potentia absoluta, ut in authen. de defen. civ. § Interim [Authen. 3.2 (Nov. 15).1], ut inde procedat privatio, unde processit habitus et collatio, maxime cum privilegia ex solius principis voluntate dependeant et liberum arbitrium alii vel sibiipsi non possit auferre."
51. Ibid., 498: "Set ego non credo quod ita fragilia sint que princeps facit auctoritate Dei, nisi facta exorbitarent, quia immunitatis prohibite a iure facta concessio nullum commodum affert . . . Preterea princeps potest se subicere rationi . . . Finaliter concludo opinionem meam quod hiis que fecit ipse uel sui antecessores legitime non potest sine causa derogare, quia totum est unum imperium, unde non debet contradicere sibiipsi." Baldus and the Donation of Constantine are discussed by Domenico Maffei, *La donazione di Costantino nei giuristi medievali* (Milano: 1969) 193–207 and Canning, *Baldus de Ubaldis* 47–48.

But I do not believe that the mandates of the prince enacted by the authority of God are so fragile, unless the prince's acts would deviate [from higher norms] because a concession of an immunity prohibited by law does not convey any privilege. . . . The prince can subject himself to reason. . . . Finally, I conclude that in these matters, whatever the prince or his predecessors legitimately do, cannot be derogated without cause, because imperium is one and complete, whence the prince cannot contradict himself.

Baldus thus limited the prince's supreme authority to positive law and to the limits of his territory. Nothing resists the prince's plenitude of power except divine law and immutable natural law. The prince can remedy all defects of positive law, except when the matter touches his limited power. All jurisdiction is terminated by boundaries, even the emperor's.[52] In this sense, Baldus agreed with those jurists who defined "potestas absoluta" as freeing the prince from positive law. He did not, as did Albericus de Rosate, permit the prince to act arbitrarily and without cause.[53]

Although later jurists only rarely cited Baldus as an advocate of unbridled princely authority, they did refer frequently to his brother, Angelus de Ubaldis, as an extreme proponent of arbitrary absolute power. Although his brother's reputation lent him added luster, Angelus was also a respected jurist in his own right. Like his brother, he studied in Perugia. Although not nearly as prolific as Baldus, his opinions on princely power percolate in the commentaries of the late medieval jurists. In the sixteenth century, jurists cited Angelus's commentary on the famous text in Justinian's Digest, Princeps legibus solutus est (The prince is not bound by the laws), when they wanted to summon a jurist who believed in the prince's absolute power.

In Princeps, for example, Angelus discussed the issue whether the prince could obviate the ordo iudiciarius and defined "potestas absoluta." He noted that the prince could ignore those sections of the ordo that were governed by civil law. However, the right of defense and the right to be summoned to court were almost an "order of natural law" (quasi ordo iuris naturalis).[54]

52. Baldus, Consilia (Venice: 1491) 3.239 (Milan: 1493) 1.257: "Plenitudo potestatis nihil resistit nisi duo tantum, scilicet ius divinum et immutabile ius naturale et necessarium, ut inst. de iure nat. § Sed naturalia . . . Ex his apparent soluta omnia quesita quia plenitudo potestatis omnia supplet nisi constaret de non plenitudine sed de potestate limitata quia limitibus omnis iurisdictio terminatur, ut ff. de iuris. om. iud. l. finali." Cf. discussion of emperor's jurisdiction in Canning, Baldus de Ubaldis 46–47.
53. On Albericus, see chapter 3, above.
54. Angelus de Ubaldis to Dig. 1.3.31 (Princeps) (Milan: 1477) unfol. (Lyon: 1534)

Angelus's discussion of due process led him to consider the prince's power. The prince had two powers, ordained and absolute. Ordained power, while subject to the observance of the law, was not bound by it. Absolute power, on the other hand, was not subject either to the observance or the authority of the law. Yet the prince was bound by natural and divine law.[55] In another place, Angelus raised the question of private property. He noted that the prince could take a subject's right away and concede it to another with his absolute power. During the war that Perugia waged against the Church, Popes Gregory XI and Urban V had confiscated the goods of individuals in the city.[56] He referred to the same events in another passage. The Apostolic See had made valid grants in Perugia to certain noblemen which the pope had expropriated from the patrimonies of commoners who were citizens. "This is a case," noted Angelus, "in which the emperor, exercising his fullness of power, can deprive us of our dominium without any cause. Whoever denies it is a liar."[57] Later jurists were intrigued by his opinion and amused by his language.

Despite these unequivocal statements supporting the prince's absolute power, Angelus was either not consistent or changed his mind. Again, as with his brother's writings, studies of the manuscripts of his

I, fol. 9v: "Quero an sententia principis requiratur ordo iuris? Innoc. dicit quod non, de re iud. c. In causis, tu habes tex. et infra de constit. prin. l.i. in uerbo destruit et in uerbo de plano dato; tamen quod non requiritur ordo iuris ciuilis, tamen bene requiritur ordo qui est quasi ordo iuris naturalis, uidelicet quod ille contra quem admittatur ad defensionem ideo citetur, ut not. C. de leg. l. finali, in prin. et est casus de sententia et re iud. c. Pastoralis, in fine." Savigny, *Geschichte* VI 249–255.

55. Ibid.: "Et dic quod princeps habet duplicem potestatem ordinatam et absolutam. Ordinata est sub lege quantum ad obseruantiam, licet non quo ad uinculum. Absoluta non est sub lege nec quo ad obseruantiam nec quo ad uinculum. Et loquor de iure ciuili quia iuri naturali et diuino omnino est suppositus, ut not. Innoc. de statu monach. c. Quemadmodum, ubi omnino uide."

56. Angelus de Ubaldis to Dig. 2.2.3.3 (Milan: 1477) unfol. (Lyon: 1534) I fol. 29v: "In eadem glossa in fine patet ergo quod ex absoluta potestate imperator potest tollere mihi ius meum et alteri concedere. Et hoc tenet Cy. in l. Bene a Zenone, C. de quadrien. prescript. et hoc not. multum pro certis concessionibus factis quibusdam nobilibus et Perusinis de bonis singularium personarum per Greg. vi. (sic) et Urban. v. [1362–1370] quando illa ciuitas habebat guerram cum ecclesia. Inferior autem a principe hoc non potest, not. gl. in l.ii. post medium, C. qui sit lon. consue."

57. Angelus de Ubaldis to Dig. 6.1.15 (Item si uerberatum) (Milan: 1477) unfol. (Lyon: 1534) I fol. 116r: "Sequitur in glo. et militibus assignatus, hic est casus quod imperator de plenitudine potestatis auferre potest nobis dominium etiam nulla causa suadente et qui contrarium dicunt mentiuntur, casus est in l.ii. de in l. Bene a Zenone, C. de quadrien. prescript. Vnde concessiones apostolice dudum in Perusio facte de patrimonio quorundam plebeorum ciuium quibusdam nobilibus ualent, cum fuerint facte ex certa scientia et de plenitudine potestatis facit, infra eadem de usufruct. l. Si pendentes § Si quid colacarii [Dig. 7.1.27(33).3]."

works and their textual traditions might throw light on how his thought developed. Lacking these we can only point to puzzling contradictions in his thought. In a later section of his commentary on the *Digest,* he upheld the traditional view that the prince could not take private property away from a subject without cause.[58] In one of his consilia he held the same view. The city-state and the prince cannot deprive a subject of property without that subject's having committed a wrong. Angelus granted that a city-state could take the private property of a citizen away, but there must be compensation. "Therefore," he concluded, "to take away private property without cause is to deny me justice. A law or a rescript that denies me justice is invalid because it violates the law of nature."[59]

Again, are these fundamental contradictions in the writings of Baldus and Angelus merely the result of inconsistent or contradictory thought? There are good reasons for thinking otherwise. A more immediate and compelling explanation may account for Baldus's and Angelus's unusual comments on the power of the prince to confiscate property. They may have written about the prince and property with more than a little personal animus. According to Paulus de Castro, Pope Urban VI granted Baldus a castle near Gubbio that the pope afterward granted

58. Angelus de Ubaldis to Dig. 21.2.11 (Lyon: 1534) II fol. 71r: "Not. quod hic uidetur tex. quod princeps dominum rei mee mihi auferre non potest et alteri donare concor. supra de rei uend. Item si uerberatum, post prin. Item tenet Martinus, C. de quadrien. prescript. Bene a Zenone. Contrarium tenet gl. C. de prec. imper. off. Quotiens, C. de in ius uoc. l.ii. in gl. "Parua," quia princeps potest tollere ea que sunt de iure ciuili ut actiones. Sed dominia rerum cum sint de iure gentium quod immutari non potest, etiam ex certa scientia [non potest] nam princeps rerum priuatarum non est dominus quod patet, quia directa rei uendicatio soli domino datur, ut supra de rei uend. In rem, in prin. Si ergo tibi datur rei uendicatio, ergo tu es dominus, non princeps. Quando ergo loquitur de dominio quod de iure ciuili, queretur quod est in multis modis: puta usucap. C. de pac. not. in l. In rem. Forte princeps posset disponere uelle suum, arg. illius gl. not. C. de prec. imper. off. Quotiens. Intelligamus ergo hic quod ex causa legitima talia predia fuerunt publicata, secus sine causa. Sed quomodo cotidie uidemus in ciuitatibus fieri legem et auferri iura alteri quesita ne hoc fieri? Certe consilium ciuitatis potest faciendo seu condendo legem generalem, ut l. Venditor § Si constat supra commun. pred."
59. Angelus de Ubaldis, *Consilia* (Treviso: 1477) unfol. (Lyon: 1532) fol. 55r–55v: "Non enim potest ciuitas aut princeps non interueniente delicto uel quasi delicto priuare subditum suum dominio rei sue expedite et simpliciter. Hinc est quod gl. dicit principem non esse dominum mei libri, C. de quadrien. prescript. l. Bene a Zenone. Not. in l. Deprecatio, ff. ad l. Rhod. de iactu. Nec obstat § Si constat et § Si quid cloacarii, quia concedo quod cum reipublice expedi per statutum populi auferre potest res priuato et applicari rei publice dummodo in recompensationem eius quod aufertur aliquid tribuatur et ita loquantur illa iura et hoc fuit de mente Innoc. de consue. c.i. in ii. col. Facit C. de prec. imper. off. l. Quotiens. Preterea auferre mihi meum pro nulla causa est mihi iustitiam denegare. Lex autem uel rescriptum continens ut mihi iustitia denegetur, etsi habet clausulam derogatoriam non obstat lex aliqua, non tenet tanquam contra ius naturale, ut not. Innoc. de constit. Que ecclesiarum."

to another. Although Baldus brought suit in the Roman curia to recover the property, he never gained possession of it.[60] Consequently,
Angelus's explicit and Baldus's equivocal comments on the prince's relationship to property may reflect both disappointment, rancor, and
irony. When Angelus concluded that anyone was a liar who said that
the prince could not confiscate property without cause, he might have
been emphasizing harsh reality rather than the theory of property in
the *ius commune* that every jurist learned. Rather than endorsing a
theory of power, he may only have been describing its effect on him
and on others.

This explanation of Angelus's eccentric position may be much more
satisfying to the historian than simply attributing incoherence to him.
It was, after all, rare for a jurist to claim that the prince could subvert
rights protected by higher norms. By the end of the fourteenth century,
the *ius commune* had protected property rights for over two centuries.
Nonetheless, we must not try to fit the thought of the jurists into patterns neat and tidy. As our reading of the evidence has demonstrated,
we cannot know with certainty whether Baldus and Angelus deviated
from the established doctrines governing the expropriation of private
property. Equivocation of doctrine always plays an important role in
any development of law that stretches over several centuries. And,
as we have seen, the ambiguities in the commentaries of Baldus and
Angelus provided some jurists of the sixteenth century with opinions
of great authority with which they could construct a new theory of absolutism that was not shackled by the limitations of the *ius commune*.

The other jurist of the late Middle Ages whose thought had extraordinary influence on the jurists of the sixteenth century was the canonist,
Nicholas de Tudeschis, also known as Panormitanus or Abbas Siculus
(1386–1445). Born in Catania, he studied law at Bologna, where he sat
at the feet of Antonius de Butrio, whom he referred to often as "magister meus." Cardinal Zabarella may have taught him at Padua as well.
After receiving his doctorate, he taught at Bologna, Parma, and Siena
from 1411–1432. In 1425, he was named abbot of the Sicilian monastery of St. Maria of Maniaco and, in 1434, archbishop of Palermo. Pope
Eugenius IV selected him to participate in a papal delegation to the

---

60. Paulus de Castro to Cod. 1.14.2, *Commentaria super Codice* (Lyon: 1531), fol.
25v: "Baldus in multis locis allegat quia tangebat eum, nam papa Urbanus VI. primo sibi
contulerat unum castrum quod vocatur Festina in comitatu Augubii, et postea illud idem
contulit alteri, et numquam Baldus potuit habere possessionem, licet multum litigaverit
cum illo in Romana curia." Savigny, *Geschichte* VI 232–233, n. f.

Council of Basel in 1431. He defended papal interests until 1433 when Eugenius's dissolution of the council converted him into a conciliarist.[61] Although Nicholas became a committed foe of papal monarchy during the continuation of the Council of Basel from 1436–1439, he had already written most of his legal works by that time. Consequently, his most radical thoughts about papal monarchy are not reflected in his juridical works.[62]

Panormitanus was the great decretalist of the fifteenth century. Other jurists may have written more or been more learned and subtle, but his commentary on the *Decretals of Gregory IX* achieved remarkable and unparalleled popularity by the end of the century. Readers' demand induced early printers to produce over twenty incunable editions.[63]

Knut Wolfgang Nörr has written an excellent study of Panormitanus's theory of papal monarchy and ecclesiology. For the purposes of this study, I shall concentrate narrowly on the themes that we have been following: Panormitanus's definitions and limitations of princely authority and his conception of due process.

In his juridical works, Panormitanus described the power of the pope in very traditional terms. In his later conciliar tracts, his views changed considerably. The pope was the vicar of Christ, exercised the office of the true God on earth, and employed divine authority when he deposed bishops. Although the pope possessed absolute power, Panormitanus limited it to papal authority to change written law.[64] Papal fullness of power and absolute power were the same. Panormitanus informed his readers that sometimes we call the pope's power absolute, at other times we call it fullness of power.[65] That his doctrine of power was platitudi-

61. Antony Black, *Council and Commune: The Conciliar Movement and the Fifteenth-Century Heritage* (London: 1979) 92–105 and "The Conciliar Movement," *The Cambridge History of Medieval Political Thought c.350–c. 1450*, ed. J. H. Burns (Cambridge: 1988) 575–578.

62. On Panormitanus see Knut Wolfgang Nörr, *Kirche und Konzil bei Nicolaus de Tudeschis (Panormitanus)* (Graz-Cologne: 1964) and Charles Lefebvre, "Panormitain," DDC 6 (1957) 1195–1215. Schulte, *Quellen* II 312–327. For the textual tradition of his commentary on the Decretals see K. Pennington, "Panormitanus's Lectura on the Decretals of Gregory IX," *Fälschungen im Mittelalter: Internationaler Kongreß der Monumenta Germaniae Historica München, 16–19 September 1986: Gefälschte Rechtstexte: Der bestrafte Fälscher* (Schriften der Monumenta Germaniae Historica 33.1–6; Hannover: 1988) II 363–373. On his recently discovered commentary on the *Decretum*, see Antony Black, "Panormitanus on the Decretum," *Traditio* 26 (1970) 440–444. This work was composed at the Council of Basel and is preserved in a single manuscript, Lucca, Bibloteca Capitolare Feliniana 160, fol. 250v–263v. He wrote only on D.1.

63. Pennington, "Panormitanus's Lectura" 368.
64. Nörr, *Kirche und Konzil* 46–47.
65. Nörr, *Kirche und Konzil* 48, commentary to X 1.3.10.

nous reminds us that few jurists were treating power creatively in the first half of the fifteenth century.

If the terminology of papal power did not pique Panormitanus's interest, other issues touching upon the authority of the prince did. The second title of the *Decretals of Gregory IX,* "De constitutionibus," offered Panormitanus an opportunity to discuss the relationship of the prince and the law. First, he noted that a corporation cannot issue a statute that injures the rights of an individual, especially if the person's right is protected by the law of nations. Innocent IV equated the law of nations, he observed, with natural law.[66] He then moved on to a more general consideration of the relationship of natural law to civil law. Civil law (by which he meant positive law) could not abrogate those things that have been established by natural law. According to Innocent IV, the prince cannot take my property away unless he has cause.[67] Panormitanus discussed the prince's relationship to divine, natural, and civil law using the same categories that Cinus of Pistoia had used. He distinguished between divine laws that were limited, such as the command "thou shalt not kill," and those that were not limited in any way, such as the prohibition that a son could not marry his mother. In the first case, the prince could regulate divine law, in the second case not.[68]

Panormitanus repeated the platitudes that had become a part of the *ius commune*'s litany of princely authority. The prince could legislate against the provisions of natural law only with cause. For example, the prince may deprive a subject of property with cause. The emperor, for

66. Panormitanus to X 1.2.7 (Que in ecclesiarum) (Venice: 1497) I, fol. 18v–19v, Munich, Staatsbibl. Clm 5473, fol. 17r–17v and Clm 6551, unfol.: "Set quo ad terminos huius decretalis est dubium numquid valet tantum respectu laicorum? Innoc., Hosti. et Compost. tenent non, quia non potest universitas statuere in preiudicium eorum que competunt singulis de iure gentium ut sunt dominia, i. di. Ius gentium, [D.1 c.9] et hoc ius gentium potest appellari ius naturale secundum Innoc. quasi naturali ratione inductum."

67. Ibid.: "Ius autem civile non potest tollere ea que sunt iuris naturalis, instit. de iure nat. § Sed naturalia [Instit. 1.2.11] et v. di. per totum. Vnde secundum Innoc. etiam princeps non potest sine causa tollere michi dominium rei mee, licet cum causa possit, ut in l. Item si verberatum, ff. de rei ven. [Dig. 6.1.15]."

68. Ibid.: "Primo numquid princeps possit statuere contra legem divinam, secundo utrum contra ius gentium, tertio numquid contra ius civile. Circa primum sit brevis conclusio quodsi vult statuere in eo articulo qui reperitur limitatus et potest, scilicet distinguendo interpretando et adiuvando ius divinum; Exemplum. In lege divina inter cetera continetur illud preceptum 'Non occides,' tamen reperitur postmodum limitatum, scilicet qui occiderit occidatur. Vnde patet quod primum preceptum non est indistincte observandum. Ideo potest princeps statuere distinguendo et interpretando qui possint occidi pro hoc, C. si quis sine iudice se vindic. per totum [Cod. 3.27] et ad legem Cornel. de sicar. per totum [Cod. 9.16] et in multis aliis locis. Si vero preceptum divinum non reperitur limitatum et tunc aut nulla potest subesse causa legitima limitandi et non potest princeps statuere, ut puta si vellet statuere quod quis potest contrahere matrimonium cum matre."

his part, has universal jurisdiction, but he does not have dominion over private property.[69] Neither the pope nor the emperor can deprive the infidels of their property without cause, although they may transgress natural law if there is only slight injury to a subject's rights. An example of this would be if the prince granted a debtor a delay from being summoned to court. He could not, however, prevent the creditors from summoning the debtor forever.[70]

By the fifteenth century, the counterpoint between the prince's absolute power and his subjects' rights to due process had become a sensitive touchstone through which we can determine the jurists' attitudes toward authority. Remarkably, we can trace a significant change in Panormitanus's thought about the relationship of the prince's power and the judicial process in the various recensions of his works. In his commentary to *Quae in ecclesiarum,* which was probably written before 1431, he wrote that an action is a part of civil law, although some jurists think otherwise. Therefore, the emperor may dispense with it.[71] Panormitanus expanded this point when he commented on the decretal *Susceptis* in book two of the *Decretals.* He raised the question whether the pope could render a judgment without having summoned the defen-

69. Ibid.: "Circa secundum numquid princeps possit statuere contra ea que sunt iuris gentium et iuris naturalis. Et brevis conclusio doctorum, ubi supra, est quod ex causa rationabili potest. Videmus enim quod per prescriptionem inductam a iure positivo privatur quis re sua. Item propter delictum confiscantur bona alicuius, ad hoc c. Vergentis, infra de heret. [X 5.7.10] et C. de bon. dampnato, per totum. [Cod. 4.49] Ad idem c. Ita quorumdam, de iudeis [X 5.6.6] ubi papa certo casu inducit servitutem contra libertatem que est de iure naturali. Si autem non subest causa et est certum, non potest princeps statuere vel rescribere [prescribere Clm 5473, Ed.] in preiudicium privati secundum communem opinionem legistarum et canonistarum, pro hoc Clem. Pastoralis, de re iud. [Clem 2.11.2] ubi expresse dicitur imperatorem non posse tollere eas que sunt de iure naturali et sic non potest imperator alicui auferre rem suam sine causa quia imperator, licet habeat iurisdictionem in universo, non tamen dominium rerum privatarum que ab olim fuerunt concesse occupantibus, ut instit. de rer. div. quasi per totum. [Instit. 2.1]."

70. Ibid.: "Sed causa existente potest ut supra dixi et est causa legitima favor publicus, ut l. Item si verberatum, ff. de rei vend. [Dig. 6.1.15] et not. in l. Anciocensium, ff. de privil. cred. [Dig. 42.5(6).37(21)] et hec procedunt etiam respectu bonorum infidelium nam sine causa nec papa nec imperator potest auferre bona eis, de quo plene dic ut not. Innoc. in c. Quod super his, de voto. [X 3.34.8] Potest tamen princeps modicam lesionem auferre, ut puta dare debitori dilationem ut non possit interim conveniri a suis creditoribus, ut in l. Quotiens, C. de prec. imper. offic. [Cod. 1.19(22).2] secus si in totum vellet concedere ut non possit conveniri aliquando, quia sine causa hoc non potest, ut not. ibi glo. et Innoc. hic."

71. Ibid.: "Licet enim secundum Innoc. possit imperator mihi tollere actionem que est de iure civili, per l.ii. ff. de orig. iuris, [Dig. 1.2.2] et est communis opinio, licet quidam contra ut not. in l. Ex hoc iure, ff. de iust. et iur. [Dig. 1.1.5] Non tamen potest facere quin iustitia mihi reddatur, unde reditur ad primevum ius in quo non erant actiones sed manu regia administrabatur iustitia, dicta l.ii. et sic habes casum in quo sine actione formali quis potest agere ex sola obligatione iuris gentium."

dant to court.[72] Panormitanus maintained that the pope had the power to dispense with a trial since he was above the law. He noted that Johannes Andreae distinguished between the pope's ordained and absolute power and concluded that he could not violate the judicial process with his ordained power, only with his absolute. Cardinal Zabarella, however, who had been his teacher, understood the question "simply and absolutely." The pope, Zabarella insisted, could not render a judgment against someone who had not been summoned.[73]

Zabarella had, indeed, staunchly defended the provisions of *Pastoralis*.[74] A canonist, conciliarist, and cardinal, he had an intense commitment to the corporate structure of the Church. He lived through the Great Schism and died at the Council of Constance. With the reestablishment of papal monarchy by Popes Martin V and Eugenius IV, the world must have looked very different to Panormitanus than it had to Zabarella.[75] As we have seen, Johannes Andreae had been one of the first canonists to pose the question of whether the pope was bound by the rules of the *ordo iudiciarius* established by *Pastoralis*. His answer

72. Panormitanus to X 2.12.1 (Susceptis) (Venice: 1497), vol. 3, fol. 127r, Munich, Staatsbibl. Clm 5474, fol. 221v–222r, Clm 6536, unfol., Clm 23685, fol. 256r: "Not. ultimo et tene menti quod etiam princeps uel papa non potest parte absente et non uocata causam diffinire. Vnde pondera tex. qui proponit negationem uerbo potest ex quo infertur hoc esse de necessitate iuxta theoricam glo. in regula Beneficium, de reg. iur. lib. vi. [VI 5.13.1]."

73. Ibid.: "Sed hoc non uidetur posse procedere quia papa est supra ius, ut in c. Proposuit, de concess. prebend. [X 3.8.4] et l. Princeps, ff. de leg. [Dig. 1.3.31(30)]. Ergo potest procedere non seruata hac solempnitate citationis. Jo. And. metu contrarii intellexit tex. de iuridica seu ordinata [ordinaria Clm 6536] potentia non de absoluta, simile infra de fide instrum. c.i. [X 2.22.1]. Dominus meus dominus F. Cardinalis intellexit textum simpliciter et absolute quia diffinire contra inauditam partem esset tollere defensionem que est de iure naturali quod princeps non potest, de re iud. Clem. Pastoralis [Clem 2.11.2]. Pro suo dicto adduco Bar. in l. Filiusfamilias, ff. de donat. [Dig. 39.5.7] ubi dicit citationem esse de iure gentium."

74. Francesco Zabarella to Clem. 2.11.2 (Pastoralis) (Rome: 1477), fol. 147v–148r, Clm 3631, fol. 126r, Clm 6539, fol. 135r: "Nota quod licet imperator possit supplere defectus iuris positiui et in hoc de nichilo aliquid facere, C. de rei uxor. act. l. una, commun. de leg. l.ii., non potest alicui auferre que sibi competunt de iure naturali; pro hoc quod dicitur in glo.ii. et inst. de iure naturali § Sed naturalia, v. di § Naturale [D.5 a.c.1], et sic non tollit defensionem que est de iure naturali, ut hic, et in hoc singulariter cotidie allegatur . . . nota ex hoc quod clausula illa que ponitur in priuilegiis seu processibus 'supplentes ex plenitudine potestatis omnes defectus si quis fuerit defectus,' etc. intelligitur quo ad defectus iuris positiui, pro hoc de elect. Illa [X 1.6.39], de transact. c.i. [X 1.36.1]."

75. On Zabarella, see Tierney, *Conciliar Theory* 220–237, Thomas Morrissey, "Cardinal Zabarella on Papal and Episcopal Authority," *Proceedings of the Patristic, Medieval and Renaissance Conference* 1 (Villanova: 1976) 39–52, T. Sartore, "Un discorso inedito di Francesco Zabarella a Bonifacio IX sull'autorità del papa," *Rivista di storia della chiesa in Italia* 20 (1966) 375–388.

had been a firm negative, and he put forward the thesis that the pope's absolute power was not limited by the rules of natural law.[76]

In the 1430s, Panormitanus adopted the views of Johannes Andreae. He rejected Zabarella's position and noted that the prince may eliminate the right to present a defense in court if "it is certain" that a defense is not the defendant's due. In such a case, not only the prince, but an inferior judge can ignore due process.[77] The prince should normally summon litigants to court, but if he were to omit a summons, he is always presumed to have acted with cause. In this regard, Pope Clement V could object to Henry VII's having condemned Robert of Naples without trial because Robert was not directly subject to Henry. If Henry had been his "natural lord," he could have judged him. It is always presumed that a natural lord acts with cause.[78]

Panormitanus's early commentaries on *Susceptis* and *Quae in ecclesiarum* were completely out of step with the jurisprudence of the *ius commune*. Although we cannot survey the writings of all the lawyers, Johannes of Imola and Petrus of Ancharano are representative.[79] Like Zabarella, whose position at Padua he held from 1406 to 1407, Johannes (Giovanni Nicoletti da Imola) rejected any infringement on the right of due process. He taught at Pavia, Bologna, and Siena and glossed *Pas-*

76. See above, chapter 5, for a discussion of Johannes's thought.

77. Panormitanus to X 2.12.1 (Susceptis) ed. cit.: "Ex quo infert quod si princeps dat alicui potestatem ut possit procedere sine iuris sollempnitate nihilominus tenetur citare; sed in contrarium allego glossam in l. Meminerint, C. unde ui [Cod. 8.4.6], que innuit imperatorem posse dare facultatem occupandi possessionem sine citatione, licet aliud sit in iudice inferiori, ut l. finali, C. si per uim uel alio modo [Cod. 8.5.2] et not. glossa in l. Iuste, ff. de acqui. pos. [Dig. 41.2.11] Concludo sic quod aut certum est absenti defensionem non competere, et non requiritur citatio etiam per inferiorem, quia citatio fit ut ueniat citatus ad se defendendum, in Clem. Pastoralis preallegata, ergo frustra fieret citatio, pro hoc textus optimus in c. Cum olim, de re iud. [X 2.27.12] et l.ii. et quod ibi not. Bart. de admin. re. ad ciu. pertin. [Dig. 50.8.2] aut potest competere defensio et tunc inferior non procedit sine citatione ad actum preiudicialem, ut dicta lege finali et iii. q.ix. Caueant et c. Omnia [C.3 q.9 c.2 and 4] et supra de constit. Ecclesia [X 1.2.10]."

78. Ibid.: "Princeps uero regulariter citare debet, sed si non citat et procedat ex certa scientia uel dat facultatem procedendi sine citatione ualet quod agitur quia in eo presumitur causa etiam si tollat ipsum dominium, licet enim non possit tollere ea que sunt de iure gentium sine causa. Tamen si facit, presumitur in eo causa, ut not. doctores in l. finali, C. si contra ius uel util. publ. [Cod. 1.22(25).6] et in c. Que in ecclesiarum, de constit. [X 1.2.7] Facit Clem. una, de probat. [Clem. 2.7.1] et quod not. Innoc. in c. Inquisitioni, de sent. excom. [X 5.39.44] Non obstat Clem. Pastoralis, ubi presumitur causa quia ibi imperator non erat iudex illius regis, sed papa, sed pretendebat iurisdictionem ratione delicti. Vnde licet presumatur causa in principe domino naturali, secus in alio non domino, nisi ratione accidentie, pro hoc quod not. idem Innoc. in dicto cap. Inquisitioni."

79. R. Naz, "Jean d'Imola," DDC 6 (1957) 107–110. Charles Lefebvre and R. Chabanne, "Pierre d'Ancarano ou d'Ancharano," DDC 6 (1957) 1464–1471.

toralis about 1421 when Panormitanus had just begun to write his commentaries on the Decretals.[80] Johannes declared that the right of a defendant to appear in court was protected by natural law. Quoting Guiliellmus Durantis, he cinched his argument by insisting that even the devil must have a hearing. Ownership is a right of natural law, and the prince cannot confiscate it without cause.[81] A summons to court is an element of procedure that natural and divine law have established. Although Henry VII promulgated *Ad reprimendum* to establish the right of the emperor to subvert due process, a constitution of the prince cannot abrogate natural law. A defense and the testimony of witnesses in court are rights that must be extended to every litigant.[82]

Petrus of Ancharano was involved in the disputes of the Great Schism and wrote several consilia between 1405 and 1409 on papal power.[83] He maintained that a statute of a city-state could not forbid a defendant to challenge a court decision because the decision was void for some reason. The *ius commune*, he noted, left no room for doubt. The statute would be too general, as it would forbid appeals even when essential elements of procedure had been overlooked or bypassed. This would violate the rules of the *ordo iudiciarius*; *Pastoralis* rendered null any decision without due process. The prince cannot abrogate natural law by eliminating those parts of the procedural process that have their origins in it.[84]

80. Belloni, *Professori giuristi* 236–242.

81. Johannes of Imola, to Clem. 2.11.2 (Pastoralis), Clm 6523, fol. 111vb–118ra at fol. 114rb (Venice: 1480, unfol.): "In § Ceterum primo per hanc Cle. que hic dicit principem non posse tollere iura naturalia et consequenter nec defensionem que illo iure est inducta, et que secundum Guil. etiam diabolo concedenda est . . . Gl. 'licuerit' colligere uoluit ex littera quod ea que sunt iuris naturalis non possunt tolli per superiorem, etiam papam uel imperatorem, quod inducit ad not. per Innoc. de const. Que in ecclesiarum [X 1.2.7] . . . uidelicet quod dominium rei sue non posset alicui aufferri sine causa quia est de iure naturali siue gentium. Inducit etiam ad questionem de qua in Cle. Sepe in uerbo 'defensionis' infra de uerb. sig. [Clem. 5.11.2] ut uidelicet dato quod alicui iudici concedatur liberum arbitrium."

82. Johannes de Imola to Clem. 5.11.2 [Saepe], Clm 6523, fol. 271r–276v (Venice: 1480) Unfol.: "Primo querit [Joh. de Leg.] de citatione que est initium iudicii, ut inst. de pena tem. liti. § finali [Inst. 4.16.3] numquid illa intelligatur remissa an uero requiratur, et dicit quod requiritur citatio, nec uidetur remissa. Mouetur quia illa est de iure naturali et diuina ut patet ex eo quod Deus citauit Adam cum dixit 'Adam, Adam ubi es?' Hoc etiam probatur in Clem. Pastoralis, de re iud. [Clem. 2.11.2] ergo per consequens non intelligitur remissa, quia defensio que est de iure naturali nemini est deneganda, ut probatur in dicta Clem. Pastoralis, ff. de iust. et iur. l. Vt uim [Dig. 1.1.3] et l.i. C. unde ui [Cod. 8.4.1] de rest. spol. Olim el. i. [X 2.13.12]. Ad hoc etiam extrauagans Henrici imperatoris que incipit Ad reprimendam, quam Bartholus glosauit; ex dictis Bar. hic sumpsit Joh. de Lig. que hic scribit . . . Ius autem naturale tollere non potest principis constitutio, not. Innoc. de const. Que in ecclesiarum [X 1.2.7] et not. in l. finali C. si contra ius uel util. pub. [Cod. 1.22(25).6]."

83. Lefebvre and Chabanne, "Pierre" 1466–1469.

84. Petrus de Ancharano, Consilium 212 (Rome: 1474; Venice: 1490): "Statutum

In another consilium, Petrus specifically denied that the pope could violate the essential rules of due process.[85] The pope could interpret or modify divine law with his legislation, but contracts were sacrosanct and outside his power since they rested on natural law.[86] The pope can interpret natural or divine law and can "impede" contracts—that is, he could make it impossible to make a contract—but that is the limit of his power.[87]

Whatever reasons dulled Panormitanus's sensitivity to issues of due process, he changed his mind completely in a later addition to his commentary on *Susceptis,* which he probably wrote after 1430.[88] As if he had read *Pastoralis* for the first time, he cited its text to prove that the prince may not deprive a subject of a summons or a defense in court. He noted that a summons and defense are derived from natural law and referred to Baldus's commentary on the question with approval.[89]

---

quo cauetur quod non possit contra sententiam opponi de nullitate, utrum possit nullitas quod non fuerit pars citata? . . . De iure communi questio nullam continet dubitationem quod talis sententia quam et citatio peremptoria non precessit est ipso iure nulla . . . Subsequenter ex aliis deductis in allegationibus pro hac parte factis dictum statutum non impedit hanc speciem nullitatis, licet generaliter loquatur; constat namque omne iudicium incipere a citatione, ut instit. de pena. te. li. in fine, et not. in c. Ecclesia sancte Marie, de constit. et in quolibet actu in quo potest petendi lesio est quis citandus, l. De unoquoque, de re iud. Item eius obmissio reddit sententiam nullam, ut l. Ea que C. quomodo et quando iud. Item textus iuris nouissimi dicit citationem esse speciem defensionis defendent (sic Edd.) et a iure naturali que non potest per principem (principum Edd.) auferri, ut Clem. Pastoralis, de re iud."

85. Ibid. Consilium 166: "et maxime ut dixi faciendo siue statuendo hoc sine cause cognitione que est substantia cuiuscumque iudicii et sine qua etiam sententia pape non ualet, ut not. Bart. C. de sent. l. Prolatam [Cod. 7.45.4] . . . et dixi in c.i. de offic. deleg. lib.vi." In consilium 272, Petrus argued that an inquisitorial trial of a Jew is void if proper judicial procedure is not followed.

86. Petrus de Ancharano to VI 1.3.10 (Si propter) (Venice: 1501), fol. 18r: (Repetitio dated 1394 at Bologna) "nunc expediam per modum lecture: Octauo not. in uer. 'nisi' quod papa potest expresse tollere ius alicui competens et priuilegia reuocare et statuta que conferunt ius certe persone quod intellige super beneficiis quorum dispositio et omnis ordinatio ab eo dependet, ut in c.ii. infra de prebend. Vnde in ipsis potest preiudicare patrono laico super iure presentandi, ut in c. Dilectus de iure patron. Diuina dominia uero et obligationes que descendunt a iure gentium non uidetur quod possit alicui sine causa conferre, quod dic ut not. Jo. And. post Innoc. in c. Que in ecclesiarum, de constit."

87. Petrus de Ancharano, Repetitio to Canonum statuta (X 1.2.1) (Rome: 1475) Unfol. Clm 3625 Unfol.: "Patet etiam ex his quod papa [potest] ius diuinum interpretari et modificari et per suas constitutiones, contractus et dispositiones que fundatur in iure naturali et gentium impedire, ut sit ex his nullum uinculum uel obligatio contrahatur; hoc idem facit ius ciuile ut l. Cum lex, ff. de fideius."

88. On Panormitanus's "additiones" to his commentary on the Decretals and the problems dating them, see Pennington, "Panormitanus's Lectura," 371–373.

89. Panormitanus's additio to X 2.12.1 (Susceptis); Munich, Staatsbibl. Clm 6536 and Clm 23685 omit it, Clm 5474, fol. 222r and the ed. cit. have it: "Sed in contrarium facit textus in dicta Clem. Pastoralis, ut uer. 'Nunc predicta suppletio,' ubi expresse dicitur quod etiam contra subditum non potest princeps supplere defectum citationis uel defensionis, quia cum illa sit de iure naturali non potest per principem tolli, ut ibi et uide

Baldus had written that a decision of the prince could be nullified if he
had not summoned a defendant to his court or if he had prevented the
defendant from pursuing a defense. God, continued Panormitanus, had
instituted the summons and recognition of a defendant. Echoing the
Decretists of the twelfth century, he pointed out that God had summoned the Sodomites and Adam before condemning them.[90] He
touched upon due process again in his commentary on *Inter quatuor.*
The prince ought not proceed against a defendant who was absent because the prince exercised his "ordained" justice and power when he
sat as judge. Even with his absolute power the prince could only ignore
those parts of the judicial process that were not a part of natural law.
Again, the prince must summon a defendant and grant the defendant
an opportunity to present a defense.[91]

In a later gloss to the decretal *Cum olim,* Panormitanus cited the arguments of Bartolus and Baldus that the prince could ignore due process
if he acted through his fullness of power and specified that he acted with
"certain knowledge." In doubt one may presume that the prince has
acted justly.[92] Panormitanus did not mean to infer that the prince could

---

textum iuncta glossa in l. finali, C. de leg. [Cod. 1.14(17).12(11)] qui aperte tenuit non
ualere sententiam principis sine citatione lata etiam in causa ciuili quod apertius ibi deter-
minat Baldus."

90. Ibid.: "Nam citatio fit ut ueniat ad se defendendum. Debet ergo princeps citare
partes hac de causa ut ibi innuitur quibus interuenientibus presumendum est pro sententia
principis et non aliter. Vnde tenet Baldus quod istis non interuenientibus potest allegari
et opponi de nullitate etiam contra principis sententiam. Et hoc mihi plus placet, et sic
puto limitandum et restringendum Cynum in l. Rescripta, C. de prec. imper. [Cod.
1.19(22).7] et Joh. And. hoc facit c.i. de feudo sine culpa non amit., col. x. [L.F.
1.20(21).1] ubi dicitur quod non debet quis priuare feudum etiam per principem antequam de culpa sit conuictus. Item citationem et cause cognitionem Deus instituisse
uidetur et aperte colligitur ii. q.i. Deus omnipotens [C.2 q.1 c.20], ubi dicitur quod Deus
noluit punire peccata Sodomorum nisi descenderet et uideret etc. nec Adam de suo peccato, nisi prius eum uocasset et defensionem suam audiuisset, ut habetur Gen. iii. et uide
quod dico in c. Cum olim, de re iud. [X 2.27.12]."

91. Panormitanus to X 1.33.8 (Inter quatuor) (Venice: 1497) II fol. 114v, Munich,
Staatsbibl. Clm 5473, fol. 258v–259r, Clm 6551, unfol.: "Secundo nota quod etiam princeps non debet procedere contra absentem non citatum quod indubie procedit in ordinata
iustitia et potentia, ut in c.i. de causa pos. et prop. [X 2.12.1] et ii. q.i. c. Nos in quemquam, [C.2 q.1 c.1] et in l. Meminerint, C. unde vi [Cod. 8.4.6] An autem de absoluta
potestate possit procedere sine citatione contra absentem? Puto quod in his que sunt in
potestate ipsius principis hoc potest; secus autem in his in quibus princeps non habet
plenam dispositionem, quia tollere citationem est tollere defensionem que est de iure
naturali, contra quam princeps venire non potest. Hoc probari videtur in Clem. Pastoralis, de re iud. [Clem. 2.11.2] Facit quod not. Bar. in l. Cum mulier, ff. solut. matrim
[Dig. 24.3.47(49)]."

92. Panormitanus to X 2.27.12 (Cum olim) (Venice: 1497) vol. 5, fol. 54r–54v, Clm
6537, unfol.: "An autem princeps possit ex plenitudine potestatis talem gratiam nullo
uocato concedere, uide quod not. Bart. et Bald. in locis preallegatis et in dubio pre-

derogate natural law in this passage, only that he could remedy a defect of procedure that was governed by positive law. He made this clear in his commentary on *Ea quae*:[93]

> I say that it is necessary that a judgment is rendered justly and reasonably and that it is confirmed by the pope, namely by ordained justice. But the pope may confirm an unjust judgment or one that has omitted the judicial process. . . . But if the judgment lacks natural justice the prince may not confirm it or remedy its defects.

In his discussion of *Cum olim*, Panormitanus injected another element into the discussion. Panormitanus's teacher, Antonius de Butrio, had written that if the facts were notorious, the pope can dispense with the *ordo iudiciarius*. The pope could render a judgment without a summons when he, the cardinals, and others were present during the crime for which someone is judged.[94] De Burtio seems to have been one of the last major figures who held steadfastly to this doctrine.[95] Later jurists frequently cited his opinion.

Panormitanus resolved the problem in two ways. Following the older opinion of Cinus of Pistoia, he conceded that, when there is doubt, the prince's judgment of a subject is valid. Still, the prince could not condemn a non-subject without a trial.[96] If the crime were sufficiently

---

sumeretur causa si dicit ex certa scientia fecit. Ad hoc quod not. idem Bartol. in l. finali C. si contra ius et util. publ. [Cod. 1.22(25).6] et Cyn. in l. Prescriptione, C. eodem titulo [Cod. 1.22(25).2] et ita late in facto consului."

93. Panormitanus to X 2.27.4 (Ea que) (Venice: 1497) V fol. 47r, Munich, Staatsbibl. Clm 6537, unfol.: " . . . dico enim quod exigitur quod iuste et rationabiliter fuit lata sententia ad hoc ut per papam confirmetur, scilicet ex iustitia ordinata. Sed ex plenitudine potestatis potest sententiam confirmare quantumcumque iniustam et sine iudiciario ordine prolatam, ut leg. et not. in c. Hec quippe iii. q.vi. [C.3 q.6 c.10] Not. gl. in c. Nullus, ix. q.ii. [C.9 q.2 c.1, 3 or 5] Facit tex. in c. Ad petitionem, de accus. [X 5.1.22] quod intelligo in dependentibus a libera potestate principis ut in beneficialibus uel in supplendo defectum ordinis positiui, et ita loquuntur iura superius allegata. Sed si sententia deficit in iustitia naturali non potest per principem confirmari seu defectus suppleri, ut est textus not. in Clem. Pastoralis, de re iud. [Clem. 2.11.2]."

94. Antonius de Butrio, to X 2.27.12 (Cum olim), *Commentarium* (Venice 1578) II fol. 119v: "Notorium autem esse poterat [papa]. Nam hic interfuerat Innocentius papa tunc cardinalis cum aliis. Nota ergo casus in quasi notoriis proceditur ad sententiam absque citatione, licet alias secundum communem opinionem exigatur citatio, ut in materia. Puto quod processus pape in notoriis valeat absque citatione quia non subiicitur forme et maxime quando notorium surgit ex his quae acta sunt coram eo. Ab aliis potest dici quod licet debeant citari, omissio citationis non vitiet processum."

95. Antonius de Butrio to X 1.2.7 (Quae in ecclesiarum) (Venice: 1578) I fol. 14v–15r discusses whether actions are based in civil or natural law and whether the prince can ignore the formalities of the judicial process without cause.

96. Ibid.: "Fateor tamen quod in dubio presumeretur pro processu principis contra subiectum, ut not. Cyn. in Rescripta, C. de prec. imper. [1.19(22).7], ubi dicit quod si

notorious, however, Panormitanus, adopting Butrio's opinion, seemed
to concede that the prince could act without a summons for both subjects and non-subjects[97]:

> I prefer the opinion [i.e., that the prince's judgment is invalid without a sum-
> mons and defense] more and without distinction when the deed is not notori-
> ous. The prince's judgment is null without a summons and a hearing even
> when rendered on his subject.

Although he referred to his opinion in his addition to Susceptis, he
seems to have contradicted himself. When God preserved due process
for Adam and the Sodomites, He certainly knew that they were guilty.
His omniscience guaranteed that their sins were notorious. If Panormitanus had reflected on the point, he might have seen that notoriety
could not be an exception to the normal rules governing due process.
Not, at least, if he wished to use God as an example that the prince
should emulate.

Discussing the relationship between heavenly and terrestrial judgment in his commentary on Pope Innocent III's famous decretal De
multa, Panormitanus emphasized that the pope's judgment should conform to the judgment of God.[98] He stressed that the law rested on the
foundation of the "public good" and natural reason. The pope should
not dispense from the public good for a private interest. This, he said,
would be dissipation, not dispensation.[99] He concluded that Innocent
IV was wrong when he wrote that the pope could dispense from positive

---

princeps sine alia cause cognitione mandat alicui ut aliquem suspendat, potest ille sine
peccato exequi, quia pro principe presumitur quod iuste procedat, quod est notandum
facit l. Si uindicari, de pen. [Cod. 9.47.20] et xi. q.iii. Cum apud [C.11 q.3 c.69], sed
respectu non subditi quem dicit aliqua ratione suum forum sortiri non presumeretur pro
sententia principis."

97. Ibid.: "et uide ad predicta c.i. de causa pos. et prop. [X 2.12.1] et quod ibi dixi
in additione. Nam mihi plus placet ut indistincte ex quo factum non est notorium; sententia principis etiam in subiectum sit nulla absque citatione et cause cognitione."

98. X 3.5.28. On the importance of De multa in the canonical tradition see Pennington, Pope and bishops 135–148.

99. Panormitanus to X 3.5.28 (De multa) (Venice: 1497) VI fol. 34r, Clm 6534,
fol. 58r, Clm 23696, fol. 114r: "Vnde obstat quia cum apud Deum non sit acceptio
personarum, ita nec apud papam esse debet ut in c. Nouit, supra de iud. [X 2.1.13]
nam iudicium papa debet esse conforme iudicio Dei, in c. Vt nostrum, ut eccles. ben.
[X 3.12.1] . . . Item ius commune est fundata super bono publico, iiii. di. Erit autem lex
[D.4 c.2] et super naturali ratione, i. di. Consuetudo [D.1 c.5] sed bonum publicum non
est relaxandum propter considerationem priuatam, ut in c. Bone, infra de postul. prelat.
[X 1.5.3 or 4] . . . Concludendo ergo breuiter dic quod dispensatio non debet fieri ob
causam priuatam, sed publicam, alias non dicitur dispensatio, sed dissipatio."

law "with only his will." The pope ought not derogate a law that is based on the public good.[100]

In the early thirteenth century, Laurentius Hispanus had conceived of positive law as having its origins in the will of the prince. Juvenal's aphorism, "Pro ratione voluntas"—his will is held to be reason—became the maxim through which the jurists expressed the prince's sovereignty over positive law.[101] A consequence of Laurentius's genius was that jurists realized that they could not limit the authority of the prince over positive law. As we have seen, as the language of princely authority became more sophisticated and exalted, the jurists sought to circumscribe the prince's power with natural law. They did not create other norms through which his authority could be limited.

Before Laurentius, the jurists used reason to encumber the will of the prince. If a law were not based on reason, it was invalid. St. Thomas Aquinas drew upon this older and, by this time, antiquated system of thought when he wrote about law in his *Summa theologica*. Aquinas objected to the concept of law without reason:[102]

> Law is a certain rule and measure. . . . First, as in that which measures and rules, and since this is a characteristic of reason, in this way law is in reason alone. . . . Reason has its power of moving from the will . . . but in order that the will has the reason of law in those things that it commands, it is necessary that it be informed by some reason. And in this way it is understood that the will of the prince has the force of law. Otherwise the will of the prince would be a sin rather than law.

Panormitanus drew inspiration from the above passage or one similar to it. In a later gloss to *Quae in ecclesiarum,* an important decretal for his conception of princely power, he acknowledged his debt to

100. Ibid.: "Ex predictis infero contra theoricam Innoc. in c. Cum ad monasterium, de statu reg. [X 3.35.6] ubi dicit papam posse supra ius positiuum dispensare ex sola uoluntate, nam puto quod licet illud procedat quo ad ecclesiam militantem, quia nulli licet de suo iudicio iudicare, secus tamen puto quo ad Deum, nam non debet sine causa relaxare ius fundatum super bono publico cum teneatur ex officio pascere oues suas et facere sicut bonus dispensator, Luce x.c."

101. Pennington, *Pope and bishops* 17–37.

102. *Summa theologiae* 1.2 q.90.1: "Lex quaedam regula est et mensura . . . Uno modo, sicut in mensurante et regulante. Et quia hoc est proprium rationis, ideo per hunc modum lex est in ratione sola . . . ratio habet vim movendi a voluntate . . . Sed voluntas de his quae imperantur, ad hoc quod legis rationem habeat, oportet quod sit aliqua ratione regulata. Et hoc modo intelligitur quod voluntas principis habet vigorem legis; alioquin voluntas principis magis esset iniquitas quam lex." On this passage and its importance, see Pennington, "Law, Legislation, and Government" 429–430. Aquinas also used the phrase "bonum commune" in his *Summa*; see 1.2 q.90.4: "(lex) . . . quaedam rationis ordinatio ad bonum commune."

St. Thomas. He also reiterated his belief that the prince could sin if he violated positive law without cause, even if his belief was, as he noted, contrary to the entire juristic tradition of the *ius commune*.[103] While commenting on *De multa*, he argued that the validity of positive law rested on the public good, not on the will of the prince. He proposed a change in legal thinking just as radical as Laurentius's had been: law was established (fundatum) on the public good. The public good lay outside and transcended the prince's will and could serve as a bridle through which arbitrary authority could be reined in. Panormitanus seems to have equated the "public good" with the collective interests of society. As we have seen, the jurists had limited the prince's authority by divine and natural law, but they had not yet created a theory that would limit the prince's authority over positive law without calling upon higher norms. Panormitanus fashioned a secular concept that stressed the importance of society's interests that the prince could not usurp or ignore. The notion that society had a collective "good" that should be preserved became an important part of later political thought.[104]

Like "potestas absoluta et ordinata" in the thirteenth century, "bonum publicum" began to pullulate in the writings of the jurists and the theologians, and we may never be able to sort out who coined it.[105] In the sixteenth century, jurists developed the term. Johannes Corasius, for instance, called the public good "immutable, constant, and eternal . . . the final goal of law."[106]

The public good was different from, but related to, the much older

103. Panormitanus to X 1.2.7 (Que in ecclesiarum) (Venice: 1497) I fol. 18v–19v, Munich, Staatsbibl. Clm 5473, fol. 17r–17v, Clm 6551, unfol.: "Circa tertium, an possit princeps scribere seu statuere contra ius positivum, et communiter tenetur quod sic, quia est supra ius positivum, ut in c. Proposuit, de conces. preb. [X 3.8.4] et vide quod latius not. in d. l. Rescripta et d. l. finali, C. de prec. imper. offic. Ego tamen dicerem quod ubi non subest legitima causa veniendi contra ius positivum, princeps peccat illud violando quia debet facere ut bonus paterfamilias, quia data est ei potestas pascendi oves, non autem turbandi seu molestandi et debet procedere ex rectitudine iustitie et equitatis, non autem ex affectione speciali. Vide quod dixi post beatum Tho. in c. De multa, de prebend. [X 3.5.28]." See Canning, "Law, Sovereignty and Corporation Theory" 459–460.

104. Panormitanus may not be the first to use this term in this sense; I know of no earlier jurist or theologian.

105. Johannes of Segovia used the term "bonum publicum" in the same sense as Panormitanus in his treatise, *Decem Advisamenta* in 1439. Text is printed by Antony Black, *Monarchy and Community: Political Ideas in the Later Conciliar Controversy 1430–1450* (Cambridge Studies in Medieval Life and Thought 2; Cambridge: 1970) 148. Baldus had used the term in his thought too, see n. 18, above.

106. A. London Fell, *Origins of Legislative Sovereignty and the Legislative State, Vol. 1: Corasius and the Renaissance Systematization of Roman Law* (Königstein-Cambridge, Mass. 1983) 198–205, discusses Corasius's use of the term.

public utility (utilitas publica), which has also been commonly translated as the common or the public good.[107] The jurists used public utility
as an example of "cause," that is, a reason for which the prince could
subvert the legal order, derogate natural law, or abrogate positive
law.[108] Johannes Andreae had formulated a similar conception of law
in an early work that did not influence later juristic thought. He had
written that the will of the prince resided in the common good (communis utilitas) of his subjects.[109] Baldus had come very close to expressing the same idea in one of his consilia:[110]

> One should note that the original purpose of creating the imperial office was
> the good and utility of the people (res publica), not private interests of an
> individual emperor, say the Emperor Charles. Therefore if the emperor
> waged war on the republics, it would not be against natural reason to throw
> off the yoke of such great servitude.

Baldus employed the traditional terminology of the jurists and combined the "good" and the "utility" of society. The example that Baldus
chose to illustrate his thought was a platitude of medieval juristic
thought. Most jurists would have agreed that the principle of self-
defense, a fundamental element of natural law, justified the prince's
subjects' throwing off his savage yoke if he waged war against them.[111]

Baldus had conceived of the public good (bonum publicum) as a

107. The idea of the public utility or the common good had a long history in juristic
thought. See Thomas Honsell, "Gemeinwohl und öffentliches Interesse im klassischen
römischen Recht," ZRG Rom. Abt. 95 (1978) 93–137, Michael Hoeflich, "The Concept
of Utilitas Populi in Early Ecclesiastical Law and Government," ZRG Kan. Abt. 67
(1981) 37–74, Jean Gaudemet, "Utilitas publica," Revue historique de droit francais et
étranger 29 (1951) 465–499. Nicolini, Proprietà 243–263 discusses the expropriation of
property in the commentaries of the late medieval jurists. The jurists commonly permitted
the prince to confiscate property for "utilitas publica."

108. Walter Ullmann has argued in several different places that "utilitas publica" was
conceded by the prince to the people in the thought of the jurists of the high Middle Ages,
e.g. "Historical Jurisprudence, Historial Politiology and the History of the Middle Ages,"
La storia del diritto nel quadro delle scienze storiche: Atti del primo Congresso internazionale delle Società italiana di storia del diritto (Florence: 1965) 206–207, reprinted
in Jurisprudence in the Middle Ages (Collected Studies; London: 1980). There seems to
be little evidence for his assumption.

109. See chapter 3.

110. Baldus de Ubaldis, Consilia Venice 3.283, Milan 1.333: "Notandum est ergo
quod originalis intentio creationis imperii fuit bonum et utilitas rei publice non private,
puta Caroli imperatoris. Ergo si imperator in respublicas seviret, excutere ab eo iugum
tante servitutis non esset contrarium rationi naturali." Text discussed by Canning, Baldus
de Ubaldis 91.

111. For the natural law of self-defense in juristic and theological thought, see Frederick H. Russell, The Just War in the Middle Ages (Cambridge Studies in Medieval Life
and Thought 8; Cambridge: 1975) 95–98, 106–108, 145–146, 164–165, 175–176, 184,
191 and passim.

norm that could also make contracts or treaties inviolable. If the emperor made a treaty for the public good, his successor could not break it unless his subjects committed a wrong.[112] Panormitanus took the same term and transformed it into a theory of political authority in which the power of the prince could be harnessed by a norm that did not rely on a higher law. Baldus had rested contracts, which jurists had already argued the prince could not break because they were agreements established by natural law, on the public good. Such contracts also bound the prince's successors. Panormitanus, however, argued that all law derived its force and inviolability from the public good.

Panormitanus gave his clearest and most precise explanation of the public good when he discussed the ecclesiastical polity. In his commentary on *Sua nobis*, Panormitanus took up the question that had been first raised in the early thirteenth century: could the pope depose a bishop without cause?[113] First, he rehearsed the traditional arguments for the pope's right to depose one bishop without cause. He noted that the pope could not do away with all bishops, a principle that had been long accepted by the canonists.[114] He compared the bishop's office to a marriage. A marriage could not be dissolved without cause and neither could a bishop's bond to his church. In the case of the bishop, another justification for a papal deposition could be public utility.[115] Up to this

112. Baldus to Cod. 1.14(17).4, Ed. cit.: "Si imperator facit pacem uel capitulum cum subditis propter generale et publicum bonum, quod ista non debent infringi per successorem, nisi ex parte subditorum interuenisset dolus uel fraus."

113. See Pennington, *Pope and Bishops* 75–114.

114. Panormitanus to X 2.30.9 (Sua nobis) (Venice: 1497) V fol. 131r–131v, Munich, Staatsbibl. Clm 6537, unfol.: "In ea glossa ibi 'nec honorem meum,' reputo; hec glossa seu ratio decidendi facit ad questionem de qua solet esse contentio inter scholasticos: utrum papa possit deponere unum episcopum sine causa. Et uidetur primo quod sic per glossam in c. Per principalem, ix. q.iii. [C.9 q.3 c.21], que dicit quod quemadmodum princeps potest priuare subditum re sua, ut in l. Bene a Zenone, C. de quadri. prescript. [Cod. 7.37.3], sic et papa unum episcopum, sed omnes episcopos non potest quia esset contra uniuersalem statum ecclesie. Debet ergo intelligi ut possit sine causa propter exceptionem quam facit. Item papa habet plenam potestatem in ecclesia militante, et omnes recipiunt dignitatem ab eo, xxii. di. c.i. et ii. et maxime hoc uidetur uerum quia episcopatus uidetur de iure positiuo. Nam olim tempore Christi non erant proprie episcopi, sed propter scisma apostoli congregato concilio presbiterorum statuerunt ut ordinarentur episcopi qui essent super alias . . . ergo uidetur quod papa possit episcopum remouere, arg. in c. Significasti, de elect. [X 1.6.4] et in c. Ad honorem, de auct. et usu pallii [X 1.8.4]."

115. Ibid.: "Sed his non obstantibus conclude sic quod aut nulla prorsus causa subest in remouendo ita quod nec utilitas publica suadet, et tunc non potest quia quemadmodum in contrahendo coniugio spirituali requiritur consensus promouendi, ut in c. Cum inter canonicos, de elect. [X 1.6.21] et in c. finali de translat. prelat. [X 1.7.4] Ita et fortius in dissoluendo, quia nichil tam naturale quam quod unumquodque dissoluatur eodem uinculo quo ligatum est, ut in c.i. de regul. iur. [X 5.41.1] et in c. Nichil tam naturale, ff. eodem [Dig. 50.17.35(36)] Optime facit l.i. et ii. C. quando ab empt. lic. dis. [Cod.

point, his conclusion was well within the boundaries of traditional canonistic thought.

Panormitanus's next step was more radical. He applied the same logic to episcopal translations and refused to permit the pope to transfer a bishop to another diocese or to another office without the bishop's consent or without cause. The pope could act, however, if the transfer were a matter of public utility. He justified this exception with an example of a bishop who was being unjustly persecuted by his people. In such a case, the pope could transfer him, even unwillingly, for the good of the Church.[116] He concluded by drawing a comparison to the prince:[117]

> He says that the prince may dispossess his subject of his property for the benefit of society, but he cannot without cause . . . anyone ought to sacrifice himself for the preservation of the public good.

Panormitanus used "utilitas publica" and "bonum publicum" in very different ways. Public utility justified the prince's actions. If there were a reason for the prince's actions that rested upon public utility, the jurists had conceded that he could violate the rights of his subjects. Today we concede the same right to the state. The public good, on the other hand, was the right and just order of a polity. The term is amor-

---

4.45.1 and 2] Item coniugium spirituale facilius contrahitur quam dissoluitur, in c. Inter corporalia, de translat. prelat. [X 1.7.2] sed non potest contrahi sine consensu pro-mouendi, ut supra dixi, ergo nec dissolui. Item sicut Deus reseruauit sibi dissolutionem coniugii carnalis, ita presumendum est quod reseruauerit sibi dissolutionem coniugii spiritualis com illud sit dignius; ita dicit textus in d.c. Inter corporalia, et quando papa illud dissoluit deponendo uel transferendo episcopum, hoc facit potius diuina potestate quam humana, quia quos Deus coniunxit, homo non separat, ita dicit textus in d.c. Inter corporalia, sed papa non potest obligationem iure diuina contractam sine causa dis-soluere, xxv. q.i. Sunt quidam [C.25 q.1 c.6], ergo non potest hoc coniugium sine causa dissoluere."

116. Ibid.: "Numquid papa possit transferre episcopum inuitum de uno episcopatu ad alium seu ad aliam dignitatem? Conclusio est quod omni causa cessante non potest quia in dissolutione coniugii requiritur consensus sponsi, sed [potest] si subesset causa publicam utilitatem concernens, licet episcopus non esset in culpa. Exemplum. Populus prosequitur episcopum sine causa iusta, et magis indurescit cor hominum contra ecclesias, tunc potest papa ut uicarius Dei, ut totum corpus ecclesie sit sanum, illud membrum prescidere. Sed debet sibi dare bonum cambium ex quo sine culpa sit remotio, ut notanter dicit Innoc. in c. Nisi, de renun. [X 1.9.10]." Richard Kay has argued that Dante thought that translations were an abuse, *Dante's Swift and Strong: Essays on Inferno XV* (Lawrence, Kansas: 1978) 115. Panormitanus is the only canonist I know who might have thought that they were. See Pennington, *Pope and Bishops* 100.

117. Ibid.: "Dicit [i.e., Glossa ordinaria] enim principem priuare posse subditum re sua, debet enim intelligi quando subest aliqua causa, puta propter fauorem rei publice, nam sine causa non potest, notat Innoc. in c. Que in ecclesiarum, de constit. [X 1.2.7] et doctores iuris ciuilis C. si contra ius uel util. publ. l. finali [Cod. 1.22(25).6], nam propter bonum publicum conseruandum quisque debet seipsum exponere, maxime in fauorem animarum."

phous, but later thinkers would embellish its attributes. If pressed, Panormitanus might have defined the public good as the state of the church ("status ecclesiae") or the "status regni" (state of the realm), older terms that the jurists had long employed to describe the right order of a society.[118]

Renaissance historians have noted a similar term in treatises describing the Italian communes during the fifteenth century, the "common good" (bonum commune) or the "good of the commune" (bonum communis). The common good was juxtaposed to discord, party factionalism, and strife, but was also defined as the collective good of society.[119] As Antony Black has written, "Common good also meant maintenance of procedures of facilities, such as common law and sound coinage, which make normal relationships and orderly exchange possible."[120] In these senses, the common good is close, perhaps identical, to Panormitanus's public good.

Baldus and, even more, Panormitanus adhered to the older ideals of "medieval constitutionalism." Their prince was sovereign and exercised authority over positive law, but was hardly absolute. They did not create a system of political thought, although they could have debated any question of political theory that a sixteenth-century jurist might have posed.[121] Historians have debated whether medieval thinkers have anticipated concepts developed by thinkers of the sixteenth century and have spilled much ink defending the modernity of Bodin and his colleagues against the accusation that they merely adopted the terminology of their medieval predecessors.[122] This debate misses the point. The evolution of political thought in the West is complex and varied. Baldus

---

118. These ideas date back to the twelfth century; see Tierney, *Conciliar Theory* 50–59, 194–195 and passim; Post, *Medieval Legal Thought* chapters 6–8; on the general definition of "status," see Calasso, *Glossatori* 18–22 and Ennio Cortese, *Il problema della sovranità nel pensiero giuridico medioevale* (Rome: 1966) 1–28. The literature on this question is very large and is discussed by those who have studied medieval constitutional thought.

119. Nicholai Rubinstein, "Political Ideas in Sienese Art: The Frescos by Ambrogio Lorenzetti and Taddeo de Bartolo," *Journal of the Warburg and Courtauld Institutes* 21 (1958) 179–207 and Antony Black, *Guilds and Civil Society in European Political Thought from the Twelfth Century to the Present* (London: 1984) 70.

120. Antony Black, "The Individual and Society," *The Cambridge History of Medieval Political Thought c.350–c.1450*, ed. J. H. Burns (Cambridge: 1988) 596.

121. See the remarks of Canning, *Baldus de Ubaldis* 1–2 and 228–229.

122. A recent example of this tendency of modern historiography is Helmut Quaritsch, *Souveränität: Entsteung und Entwicklung des Begriffs in Frankreich und Deutschland vom 13. Jh. bis 1806* (Schriften zur Verfassungsgeschichte, 38; Berlin: 1986) and the sprawling three volumes of A. London Fell, *Origins of Legislative Sovereignty*.

and Panormitanus cannot be fitted into neat categories or described by pithy phrases. They influenced a broad range of later thinkers, and therein lies their importance for the history of political ideas. Our understanding of the authority of the prince in the late Middle Ages owes much to them.

The Pazzi Conspiracy and the Jurists

If the assassination
Could trammel up the
consequence, and catch
With his surcease success.
—Shakespeare, *Macbeth,*
  Act 1, Scene 7

Machiavelli was nine years old in 1478 when the Pazzi, a rich Florentine banking family, and the Archbishop of Pisa, with at least the support of Pope Sixtus IV, formed a conspiracy to rid Florence of the Medici.[1] On Sunday, April 26, the assassins who had been hired by the conspirators wounded Lorenzo de' Medici and killed his brother during Mass in the cathedral. The people of Florence supported the Medici, and in the blood bath that followed, the archbishop and many of the Pazzi were summarily executed. In his *History of Florence,* written in his later years, Machiavelli concluded that the people rallied to the Medici because of their "prudence and liberality."[2]

People had become hardened to political assassinations during the fifteenth century, but the death of Giuliano de' Medici shocked them. The attack on Lorenzo and his brother had established a new benchmark for amoral political behavior. The images of Giuliano lying in a pool of his own blood on the floor of the cathedral in Florence and of Lorenzo scrambling into the sacristy for safety were powerful symbols

---

1. See Sebastian De Grazia, *Machiavelli in Hell* (Princeton: 1989) 9–16 for an evocative description of these events.

2. Niccolò Machiavelli, *Istorie fiorentine* (Milano: 1968) book 8, chapter 9, p. 454: "tanta era la fortuna e la grazia che quella casa, per sua prudenza e liberalità, si aveva acquistata." For an analysis of "prudenza" in Machiavelli and other political thinkers, see J. G. A. Pocock's *Machiavellian Moment: Florentine Political Thought and the Atlantic Republican Tradition* (Princeton: 1975) under "prudence" in the index.

of perfidiousness and betrayal. History may teach us that absolutism and tyranny can be tempered by assassination, but the lesson is bitter medicine for which only a few acquire a taste.

Giuliano's death brought neither quick surcease nor immediate success for either side. Violence ruled the streets of Florence. Lorenzo remained in power and, when assassination failed, Pope Sixtus IV brought other weapons to bear on Medici power: excommunication and interdict. The protagonists of this story were worthy foes. On the one side stood Sixtus, the spiritual leader of Christendom and temporal prince of Central Italy; on the other, Lorenzo, first citizen of Florence, poet, patron, and the embodiment of the Renaissance.

In the early nineteenth century, Lorenzo Pignotti mentioned a number of jurists who wrote consilia defending Lorenzo from the papal excommunication levied on him after the Pazzi Conspiracy. Although historians have explored the intense acrimony between Lorenzo and the pope as a political problem, few have explored the legal aspects of the controversy.[3]

Lorenzo himself had no doubts about the unjustness of Pope Sixtus IV's actions after he had escaped the assassins' knives. On June 19, 1478, he wrote to René of Anjou:[4]

> I know that the only crime I have committed against the pope is, and God is my witness, that I live and that I did not suffer death. . . . On our side we have canon law, on our side we have natural and political law, on our side we have truth and innocence, on our side God and mankind.

3. *Storia della Toscana* (Firenze: 1826) VIII 132–133, note 18. There is surprisingly little literature on the conspiracy in modern times. The most detailed accounts, discussed in part below, are dated. See the bibliography in the edition of Angelo Poliziano, *Della congiura dei Pazzi (Coniurationis commentarium)*, ed. A. Perosa (Padua: 1958) and F. Morandini, "Il conflitto tra Lorenzo il Magnifico e Sisto IV dopo la congiura dei Pazzi: Dal carteggio di Lorenzo con Girolamo Morelli, ambasciatore fiorentio a Milano," *Archivio storico italiano* 107 (1949) 113–154.

4. Historians had thought that this letter was sent to King Louis XI of France. This misattribution has occurred even after Nicolai Rubinstein published his edition of the letter (cf. Harold Acton, *The Pazzi Conspiracy: The Plot Against the Medici* [London: 1979] 99). Lorenzo de' Medici, *Lettere*, 3: 1478–1479, ed. Nicolai Rubinstein (Firenze: 1977) 72–74: "Ego enim mihi sum conscius, Deus autem testis adest, nihil me commisisse contra pontificem nisi quod vivam, quod me interfici non sim passus, quod omnipotentis Dei gratia me protexit; hoc meum est peccatum, hoc scelus, ob hoc unum exterminari excommunicarique sum meritus. Deum tamen optimum cordium scrutatorem iustissimum iudicem, meae innocentiae testem minime permissurum credo, ut quem illemet inter suas aras et sacra, ante sui corporis sacramentum a sacrilegis illis nos ab hac etiam iniustissima calumnia defensum velit. Nobiscum faciunt canonicae leges, nobiscum ius naturale et politicum, nobiscum veritas et innocentia, nobiscum Deus atque homines sunt."

Sixtus's bull of June 1, 1478 had condemned Lorenzo as a son of iniquity and a rebel against the Church. Sixtus used the new printing press
to give wide circulation to his condemnation.[5]

Machiavelli wrote that the pope had proved himself a wolf rather
than a shepherd and that the Florentines filled Italy with accounts of
papal treachery against their government, exposing the impiety and injustice of Sixtus to all.[6] The Florentine consilia were a part of this propaganda effort. In an apologia probably written by Bartolomeo Scala,
the Signoria of Florence responded to Sixtus's letter on July 21.[7] He rejected Sixtus's allegation that Lorenzo was a tyrant. The pope had the
authority, he observed, to wage war against the Turks, but not to wage
war against a Christian ruler.[8] Both Sixtus's original bull and the Signoria's response to it were pieces of propaganda aimed at a larger public.[9] Erich Frantz argued that the letter of the Signoria avoided answering Sixtus's clearly formulated accusations.[10] But, if the Signoria had
not replied to the papal accusation with precise rejoinders, it enlisted
a number of jurists who quickly responded to Sixtus's bull with detailed rebuttals. Lorenzo and his advisors must have been aware that
they needed more than propaganda to discredit Sixtus's excommunication and interdict.[11] By the end of July, 1478, he had already received

5. The bulls excommunicating Lorenzo and placing Florence under interdict were
printed, presumably in Rome, by G. Bonattus. Listed by Hain as *14816. Angelo Fabroni,
Adnotationes et monumenta ad Laurentii Medicis magnifici vitam pertinentia (2 vols.
Pisa: 1784) 2.121–129, printed *Iniquitatis filius.* Contemporaries noted the pope's use
of the new technology; see Alison Brown, *Bartolomeo Scala, 1430–1497, Chancellor of
Florence: The Humanist as Bureaucrat* (Princeton, N.J.: 1979) 159, n. 68, citing a letter
of L. Botta: "perchè non sequendo pace, me pare essere certo ch'el pontefice con le con-
suete justificationi sue le faria mettere in stampa et le mandaria ad sua justificatione ad
tutti li potentati christiani." Rubinstein, *Lettere* 48–49, notes that original copies of the
bull and its printing are very rare. He draws attention to a copy in the Bibliothèque
nationale, Paris and a copy of Hain *14816 in Munich, Staatsbibliothek (correct signature is 4° Inc. s.a. 1672a). A. Sorbelli, "La scomunica di Lorenzo de' Medici in un raro
incunabulo romano," *L'Archiginnasio* 31 (1937) 331–335.
6. Machiavelli, *Istorie fiorentine* book 8, chapter 11, p. 459: "E poiché il papa si era
dimostro lupo e non pastore . . . con tutti quelli modi potevono la causa loro giustifica-
vono, e tutta la Italia del tradimento fatto contro allo stato loro riempierono, mostrando
la impietà del pontifice e la ingiustizia sua."
7. Brown, *Bartolomeo Scala* 85–87, discusses this letter and Scala's authorship of it.
8. Pignotti, *Storia* VIII 220–225. Sixtus's bull is also printed by Mansi, Rainaldi, and
Baluze, *Miscell.* vol. 1.
9. Erich Frantz, *Sixtus IV. und die Republik Florenz* (Regensburg: 1880) 225–229,
partially prints the letter of the Signoria and discusses it.
10. Ibid. 228: "Vermeidet jede sachgemässe Widerlegung der vom Papste erhobenen,
klar formulirten Anklagen und enthält im Grunde nichts als eine schwache Apotheose
der Mediceer." Frantz's book is a tendentious defense of Sixtus.
11. The most famous defense of Lorenzo was by the Humanist, Angelo Poliziano,
first printed in the fifteenth century: Also edited by A. Perosa (Padua: 1958) see note 3.

tightly argued and lengthy consilia that were impressive defenses of his position.

The eighteenth-century Italian historians, Fabroni and Pignotti, noted that seven jurists "and others" wrote in defense of Lorenzo.[12] I have tracked down four long consilia comprising twenty-one folios in the printed editions, containing extensive discussions of the political and the legal ramifications of the Pazzi Conspiracy. The consilia are of great importance for issues that we have been following. They discuss the authority of the prince, the necessity of due process, and the prince's relationship to the law. If we may say that the dispute between Henry VII and Robert of Naples enshrined due process in the doctrine of the *ius commune,* the polemical consilia generated by the Pazzi conspiracy demonstrate how deeply the doctrine was embedded in juristic thought by the end of the fifteenth century.

Of the four consilia that I have found, two appear in a collection printed under the name of Franciscus Curtius Papiensis.[13] The first was written by Bartolomeo Sozzini (Socinus) (1436–1507).[14] Poliziano mentioned this consilium in a letter written to Lorenzo on August 24, 1478; consequently, Sozzini must have finished it before this date.[15] The second was signed by the doctors of Florence representing the entire college of doctors (undoubtedly the doctors of law).[16]

While he was teaching at Siena, Francesco Accolti wrote a defense of Lorenzo that is published among his consilia.[17] In November 1478, he complained to Lorenzo that the legate of the Duke of Calabria had

12. Fabroni, *Adnotationes* I 81 and Pignotti, *Storia della Toscana* VIII 133 n. 18 also lists Lancilloto, Bolgarino, Andrea Panormita, and Pier Antonio Cornio as having written consilia. Perhaps they participated in writing the consilium of the College of the Doctors of law.

13. Printed as Consilia 20 and 21 (Milan: 1496).

14. Savigny, *Geschichte* VI 345–355. John Tedeschi, "Notes Toward a Genealogy of the Sozzini Family," *Italian Reformation Studies in Honor of Laelius Socinus,* ed. John A. Tedeschi (Università di Siena, Facoltà di Giurisprudenza Collana di Studi "Pietro Rossi," Nuova Serie, 4; Firenze: 1965) 275–313 at 287–291.

15. Fabroni, *Adnotationes et monumenta* 2.183: "Per costui vi mando e consigli di Messer Bartolommeo Sozzini. Holli sollecitati a ogni hora et trovato li scriptori; et elli ancora vi ha usata diligentia somma. Ma non si è potuto far più presto." Cf. Brown, *Bartolomeo Scala* 158, n. 65.

16. Franciscus Curtius Papiensis, *Consilia* (Milan: 1496) [Hain *5871], no. 21 (unfoliated): "Et ita salva semper determinatione sancte matris ecclesie iuris esse putamus, nos doctores Floren. prius inter nos communicato consilio representantes totum collegium doctorum Floren., et in fidem premissorum solito sigilo collegii nostri sigillari fecimus." Adriana Campitelli and Filippo Liotta have found another consilium subscribed by the "Collegium Florentinum" in Vat. lat. 8069. See their article "Notizia del ms. Vat. lat. 8069." *Annali di storia del diritto* 5/6 (1961–1962) 395.

17. Savigny, *Geschichte* VI 328–341; Savigny mentions the consilium on the Pazzi Conspiracy, p. 332.

petitioned that the magistrates of Siena should take him captive. Francesco believed it was because he had written the consilium for Lorenzo. He was undoubtedly right. Some of his language in the consilium was intemperate. Fortunately, he informed Lorenzo; the legate's request was not granted.[18] Shortly afterward, in the spring of 1479 he began teaching at Pisa.[19]

The Florentines went rather far afield in their search for legal counsel. They asked a noted jurist of the time who has since sunk into obscurity, Girolamo Torti (Hieronimus de Tortis), to write a consilium. He had been educated at Pavia, Ferrara, and Bologna, taught at Pavia for thirty-two years, and died in 1484. His consilium was published separately in a slim folio volume.[20]

If Sixtus commissioned jurists to write pro-papal consilia, they have not survived. I have found one brief allusion to the controversy in the writings of the Neapolitan jurist, Giovanni Antonio Carafa, who wrote approvingly of Sixtus's sanctions against the Florentines in his commentary on the rule of law, Peccatum, in the Liber Sextus.[21] Unlike the dispute between Henry VII and Robert of Naples, the papal position is barely represented in the sources.

When Lorenzo wrote to René of Anjou in the middle of June 1478, he must have known about the main arguments that could be made in his defense. The rhetorical flourish of his elegantly cadenced litany—that canon law, natural law, and God supported him—should not obscure the essential truth of his statement.[22] All the consilia make the same argument: two centuries of Romano-canonical procedural law

18. Fabroni, Adnotationes 2.135–136.
19. "Accolti, Francesco," DBI 1 (Rome: 1960) 104–105.
20. One of the incunabula does not have a place or a date, Hain *15579; the other was published at Pavia in 1485, Hain *15580. It was also printed in the sixteenth century by Vincentius de Portonariis after the consilia of Antonio de Butrio (Lyon: 1534) and (Lyon: 1554). Gero Dolezalek, Verzeichnis der Handschriften zum römischen Recht (4 vols. Frankfurt am Main: 1972) lists several manuscripts: Escorial D.II.6, Bologna, CS 193, 262, and Ravenna, Bibl. Class. 485. The beginning rubric of Hain *15579 calls him "de Tortis." Diplovatatius, Liber de claris iuris consultis, ed. F. Schulz, H. Kantorwicz, and G. Rabotti (SG 10; Bologna: 1968) 396–397, spells his name "Hiernonymus Tortus." Jason de Mayno wrote a funeral oration for him, see Annalisa Belloni, Professori giuristi a Padova nel secolo XV: Profili bio-bibliografici e cattedre (Frankfurt am Main: 1986) 227. See also Girolamo Tiraboschi, Storia della letteratura italiana (Naples: 1780) vol. 6.1, pp. 403–405.
21. Quoted by Ennio Cortese from Vat. lat. 5922 in "Sulla scienza giuridica a Napoli tra quattro e cinquecento," Scuole diritto a società nel mezzogiorno medievale d'Italia (Catania: 1985) I 83 n. 139.
22. Rubinstein, Lettere 72–74 writes little about the contents of the letter and nothing about the author. Poliziano was working in the chancery and may have been responsible for it.

supported Lorenzo, and these procedural rules were not just a part of positive canon law but were based on a higher, natural law that the pope must also maintain.

Each of the consilia discussed questions of law and questions of fact. The jurists established that when Sixtus condemned Lorenzo, he had violated due process. As we have seen, most jurists no longer had any doubt that the supreme prince of Christendom was bound by the procedural rules of *Pastoralis*. The pope was hoist to his own petard.

The jurists played at being historians. They analyzed the concatenation of events that immediately followed the assassination of Giuliano de' Medici and used "facts" to support their legal arguments. Machiavelli dealt with the events after the Medici regained control of the city with a single sentence: "Since a change of government had not been brought about in Florence as the pope and king desired, they decided to wage war to achieve what they had not accomplished through the conspiracy."[23] The jurists presented detailed information about the period before war broke out in order to prove that Lorenzo had acted lawfully and prudently. There is no internal evidence with which we can date the consilia, and none of the jurists used one of the other consilia. We cannot, therefore, reconstruct the chronology of their composition. Most likely, they were all written simultaneously within months of Sixtus's bull of excommunication.

The anonymous doctors of law who wrote the consilium for the Florentine College began by stating their conclusion: Pope Sixtus had inflicted an injustice on the people and magistrates of Florence and, especially, on Lorenzo de' Medici.[24] Jurists did not normally state their conclusions at the beginning of a consilium, and their political purpose is underlined by their departure from the standard structure of consilia. However, the consilium's political purpose should not obscure its legal importance. In the late Middle Ages, consilia served as tools with which litigants argued their cases and as advisory opinions, often written at the request of a judge and presented to a court.[25] The juristic lines be-

23. *Istorie fiorentine*, book 8, chapter 10, p. 456: "Ma non essendo sequìta in Firenze la mutazione dello stato, come il papa e il re desideravono, deliberorono quello che non avevono potuto fare per congiure farlo per guerra."

24. Franciscus Curtius Papiensis, *Consilia* (Milan: 1496) [Hain *5871], unfoliated, no. 21: "Tum propter plurima quibus iustissimis rationibus doceri potest nullitas proposite sententie et non vera insinuatione sed improba ut credimus a Sixto pontifice maximo assistentium importunitate suggesta a qua ortam putamus evidentem iniusticiam contra Florentinum populum et eius supremos magistratus civesque primarios et presertim contra Laur. de Medicis."

25. Mario Ascheri, "Rechtsprechungssammlungen," *Handbuch der Quellen und*

tween the opinions of a private jurist and the decisions of a judge were sometimes not clear. The question was often posed and debated of whether a judge who requested a "consilium sapientis" for a particular case was bound to follow its conclusions in his decision.[26] When Lorenzo de' Medici chose jurists to write consilia, he selected an instrument for his defense that was the primary weapon of the fifteenth-century jurists.

The doctors of laws first treated the pope's right to condemn Lorenzo. They concentrated on the central question of whether the absolute power of the prince allowed him to render a decision or issue a condemnation of a defendant without having summoned that defendant to court. Noting that some jurists argued for the prince's right to violate the normal rules of procedure when he exercised his "absolute fullness of power,"[27] they presented three other cases in which the prince could transgress the established procedural rules: if the prince was motivated by a just cause, when the prince judged a notorious crime, when the prince censured a subject.[28]

Although the format of the consilia demanded that the jurists outline the best case for the pope, they gave the papal theoretical defense little space. They concentrated on questions of fact and compared Sixtus's

---

Literatur der neueren europäischen Privatrechtsgeschichte, 2.2: Neuere Zeit (1500–1800): Das Zeitalter des gemeinen Rechts: Gesetzgebung und Rechtsprechung, ed. Helmut Coing (München: 1976) 1113–1221.

26. See Mario Ascheri, "'Consilium sapientis', perizia medica e 'res iudicata': Diritto dei 'dottori' e istituzioni communali," *Proceedings of the Fifth International Congress of Medieval Canon Law,* ed. Stephan Kuttner and Kenneth Pennington (Città del Vaticano: 1980) 533–579.

27. Franciscus Curtius Papiensis, *Consilia:* "Aut consistit in citatione et tunc licet defectus citationis in actu in quo quis potest ledi reddat regulariter actum nullum etiam in principe maxime in actibus iusticie, c.i. de causa pos. et prop. Cle. Pastoralis, v. 'Ceterum,' de re iud. Tamen predicta regula plures recipit limitationes. Prima est quando princeps intendit uti plenitudine potestatis. Ita format Host. et Jo. An. in c. In nostra, de procur. et ita contingit in casu isto. Minor probatur quia paria sunt principem uti velle plenitudine potestatis absoluta se exprimere vel gerere actum supra potestatem ordinariam et apponere clausulam non obstante, ut firmat Baldus et scribentes post eum in l. Si testamentum, C. de testa. Sed princeps hic procedendo sine citatione fecit actum potestatis absolute et in fine adiecit clausulam 'non obstante.'"

28. Ibid.: "Secunda limitatio datur ubicumque princeps ad procedendum sine citatione movetur aliqua iusta causa, ita firmant glo. in l. antepen. ff. ex qui. ca. ma. (Dig. 4.6.45) et Bal. in l.ii. C. quomodo et quando iud. (Cod. 7.43.2) Sed iusta causa in dubio presumitur in principe secundum Jaco. Butri. et alios in l. finali C. si contra ius vel util. pub. (Cod. 1.22.6); canoniste in c. Que in ecclesiarum, de constit. (X 1.2.7) Tertia limitatio est ubicumque fieret processus super notorio, tex. in c. Quanto, de translat. prelat. (X 1.7.3) in c. Cum sit in fine, de app. (X 2.28.5) sed in casu nostro processum fuit tanquam super notorio et constare videtur fuisse notorium . . . Quarta allegatur limitatio ut speciale sit in sententiis censure, c. Sacro de sent. excom. (X 5.39.48) c. De illicita, xxiiii. q.iii. (c.6)."

bull of excommunication with what they believed happened immediately after the assassination. Sixtus claimed that Lorenzo had violently seized the archbishop of Pisa, Francesco Salviati, after the assassination and hanged him. Salviati had been, without question, a member of the conspiracy, but Sixtus could have quite properly condemned Lorenzo if he had taken part in his execution.

Lorenzo could not have participated in the murder of Salviati, claimed the jurists, because he was carried wounded to his home after the assassination and did not leave again for ten days.[29] The archbishop and his conspirators had confessed their roles and were hanged by the people who had rushed to help the priors. The priors and the eight men of the balìa (Otto di Balìa) were blameless for the death of Salviati.[30] In contrast to the allegations of Sixtus's bull, they did not detain the archbishop, and they did not hang him or order his hanging.[31] Their main point was that Sixtus could not have condemned Lorenzo, the priors, and the eight men of the balìa because their crimes were not notorious. Further, they had not ordered the capture of Cardinal deacon Raffaele Riario-Sansoni of San Giorgio. The young cardinal was frightened, and the citizens of Florence had brought him to the Palazzo Vecchio for his safety, not forcibly, and at his own request.[32] The jurists

29. Ibid.: "Iulianum interfectum et Laurentium vulneratum dixisse putamus hec enim ex confessione propria archiepiscopi et coniuratorum, nedum in manifestum sed in notorium iuris transivit; notoriumque est Laurentium ante assertam capturam archiepiscopi fuisse vulneratum et in domum deductum quam introeunte vidente et assistente maiore parte populi x. dies non exivit, ex quo notorium sit nullo modo ipsum in archiepiscopum manus iniecisse."

30. Ibid.: "Probatur autem ut diximus ex dicta notorietate. Addit priores et octo viros bailie. Fidelius veritatem scriptor expressisset si archiepiscopum armatum et cum sateletibus priores et inermes insultasse et ferro petivisse recitasset . . . Subiungit archiepiscopum captum per plures horas fuisse detentum in palatio dicto. Et similiter in fine dicit esse notorium. Fatemur enim fuisse captum, sed negamus Laurentium aut priores cepisse. Fuit enim captus a quibusdam qui prioribus invasis succurrerunt qui statim intellecto ab eo negotio et forma factionis et coniurationis sue timentes seditionem invalescere et audientes milites quam plurimos ex Tipherno et foro Cornelii in favorem archiepiscopi appropinquare ut subueniret patrie periclitanti eum ut in processu dicitur suspenderunt."

31. Ibid.: "Qui ergo dixit pontifici notorium esse archiepiscopum in dicto palatio fuisse detentum non bene legit quia detentio clerici maxime tam brevis numquam potest transire in notorium, nisi carceres vel alius locus detentionis essent patentes populo transeunti . . . Subsequenter dicit [Sixtus] archiepiscopum communicato consilio predictorum fuisse suspensum etc. Negatur ipsos nominatos suspendisse aut fecisse suspendi. Negatur etiam communicatio consilii et eorum asserta notorietas."

32. Ibid.: "Non enim captus fuit dominus cardinalis, sed ab octo viris volens et rogans ad palatium deductus est ne a populo propter vehemens iudicium quod contra eum de conscientia cedis in Julianium et de seditione laborabat offenderetur. Et ita cum fuisse honorificentissime tractatum in dicto palatio littere dicti cardinalis ad pontificem et actio gratiarum nomine pontificis ab apostolico nuncio exposita manifestissime testantur. . . . Ait pretrea petenti sibi per legatum liberationem cardinalis fuisse contumaciter dene-

admitted that members of the cardinal's entourage were killed. However, they and the rebels attacked the priors in the Palazzo Vecchio, and the priors had only defended themselves, not knowing from their secular garb that their attackers were clerics.[33] Machiavelli did not report most of these details but noted that Salviati found the priors at dinner. They discovered very quickly that the archbishop and his entourage had attacked the Palazzo Vecchio and acted in self-defense. If Machiavelli knew, he did not reveal who ordered the archbishop hanged.[34]

Next the jurists turned to the interdict that Sixtus had imposed on the city of Florence. It was invalid for several reasons. First, Sixtus did not hear representatives of the city in court.[35] Second, a city cannot be punished for the act of a single citizen. Even if the city's bell were sounded and its citizens roused, Florence should not bear the responsibility for a murder committed during this time. Only if the act had been planned could the city be held culpable.[36] One may not object, they continued, that the priors held jurisdiction, represented the corporate city, were responsible for the death of the archbishop, and, therefore, that the city could be punished for their actions. The priors did not have supreme, perpetual, and complete jurisdiction over the city. For that reason they did not act as representatives of the whole city. Echoing Roman law and the medieval juristic doctrine of representation, the jurists declared that supreme, perpetual, and complete jurisdiction resides in the people of Florence and their councils.[37] Finally, the Archbishop Salviati had attacked the priors, and whatever they or the people

---

gatam inspiciantur scripture responsionis nostre quam ne falsa fieret relatio in scriptis dedimus."

33. Ibid.: "Quod autem dicitur clericos etiam familiares cardinalis fuisse occisos fatemur, sed debet adiungi eos ingressos fuisse palatium et armis insultasse dominos priores et in tumultum defensionis non apparuisse eos fuisse clericos."

34. *Istorie fiorentine,* book 8, chapter 7, p. 452.

35. Franciscus Curtius Papiensis, loc. cit.: "Primus modus non est casus noster, quia non intentatur in processu et quando intentaretur obstaret intentioni pontificis quia nihil actum fuit communicato consilio et precedente deliberatione eorum qui representant totam civitatem, et sic non dicitur civitas deliquisse."

36. Ibid.: "Si totus populus ad pulsationem campane et cum vexilo iverit ad aliquem occidendum non dicitur civitas occidisse sed singulares, si non precessit tractatus et deliberatio predicta, que non precessit in casu nostro."

37. Ibid.: "Nec obstat quod priores et alii nominati sunt magistratus habentes iurisdictionem et per consequens eo respectu videtur civitas esse ipsorum . . . nam respondetur quod ratio iurisdictionis tunc operatur dictum effectum, quando esset suprema, perpetua, et in solidum, et competeretur iure proprio et non representativo pro alio . . . Assignant rationem quia non debet alter propter delictum alterius gravari, sed priores et alii nominati non habent iurisdictionem supremam aut perpetuam et in solidum, quia illa est apud populum et consilia per que populus representatur."

of Florence did to fend off the assault was justified self-defense.[38] The most important juristic argument of the consilium was left to near the end:[39]

> We come to this conclusion about the order and the process of the pope's condemnation: it was invalid by law. Every judicial act in which a party can be injured cannot be carried out if the party is not heard or summoned to court. The act is invalid especially if it is an act of justice and not of grace. This is proven by the decretal of Pope Clement, *Pastoralis*.

The Florentine lawyers did not have to search far and wide to establish Lorenzo's right to defend himself from Sixtus's condemnation. By the end of the fifteenth century, the arguments were common coin of the *ius commune*.

At the beginning of the final section of the consilium, the jurists responded to the arguments that supported Sixtus's condemnation. The kernel of the case was whether the prince may dispense with normal judicial process if he is "moved by a just cause."[40] When the prince acts, the jurists stressed, he must use his fullness of power and have a just cause. However, the pope and the emperor are not above the law of nations or natural law. The prince may only dispense from natural law if he has fullness of power and cause.[41] Although the prince is presumed to have cause when he acts, if he alleges a cause that is invalid, then any other cause that he may express is not presumed valid. In this case, Sixtus justified his actions by declaring that he was rendering judgment on notorious crimes and did not, therefore, need to attend to the niceties

---

38. Ibid.: "Sed archiepiscopus prius insultavit dominos priores et occupavit palatium, et sic prius offendit populum Floren. ergo quicumque Florentinus eum percusserit vel interfecerit presumitur fecisse ad defensionem." This argument and their defense of the cardinal's detention occupy more than a folio of text.

39. Ibid.: "Idest circa ordinem et processum istius declaratorie ponimus istam conclusionem: videtur quod dicta declaratio sit ipso iure nulla. Probatur sic: omnis actus iudicialis in quo pars possit ledi non fiat parte inaudita et non citata. Est ipso iure nullus maxime si est actus iusticie et non gratie. Casus est in Clem. Pastoralis § Ceterum, de re iud."

40. See above, note 28.

41. Franciscus Curtius Papiensis, *Consilia*, no. 21: "Ad secundam limitationem que est de substantia cause respondemus quod ad hoc ut ista limitatio procedat oportet duo concurrere copulative: primum quod utatur plenitudine potestatis, secundum quod moveatur ex iusta causa subsistente. Probatur: papa et imperator non sunt supra ius gentium et naturale § fin. inst. de iure nat. et si quandoque per eos dispensari concedatur dicitur concedi de plenitudine potestatis, c. Proposuit, de conces. preb. Sed numquam conceditur talis dispensatio nisi subsistente legitima causa ut firmant omnes in l. finali C. si contra ius et in c. Que in ecclesiarum de constit. Ergo ad dispensandum quod non requiritur citatio que est de iure gentium vel naturali dicto § 'Ceterum' requiritur copulative plenitudo potestatis."

of the judicial process. But, as the jurists had already proven, Sixtus was mistaken. Lorenzo's crimes were not, and could not have been, notorious.[42] They admitted that if Lorenzo's crimes had been notorious, the pope could have condemned him without a trial, although many doctors had come to different conclusions.[43] Finally, they concluded that the interdict that Sixtus had placed on the city of Florence was also invalid. If the archbishop of Pisa were under the jurisdiction of Florence or if he were the Florentine archbishop, then the interdict would have been just. Sixtus committed an intolerable error of law.[44]

In their defense of Lorenzo, the doctors of law had singled out Francesco Accolti as the greatest living jurist, and Lorenzo enlisted Accolti in his stable of juristic champions.[45] At the beginning of his consilium, Accolti noted that Sixtus had done two things in his letters of excommunication and interdict: first, he deduced a number of offenses that Lorenzo had committed against the pope and the state of the Holy Roman Church that aggravated the situation leading to Giuliano's death; second, he levied the appropriate penalties for these crimes.[46]

42. Ibid.: "Item potest addi quod quando concedamus in principe presumi causam illud procederet quando nullam expressit. Sed si unam expressit licet invalidam non presumeretur alia valida. Probatur ista conclusio in terminis recte intuenti in l. Cum de in rem verso, de usur. iuncta. l. Si certis annis, C. de pac. Sed in isto processu exprimitur una causa que esset sufficiens ad procedendum sine citatione, si esset vera, videlicet totalis notorietas. Ergo alia causa non debet presumi. Non enim tractandum est de coniectura et presumptione ubi est voluntas expressa . . . Sed in hoc processu est expressa causa notorietatis que est falsa et insufficiens, ergo etc."

43. Ibid.: "Et licet in hac materia an in notoriis requiritur citatio doctores multum variaverunt ut plene recitant Anto. de Bu. et moderni in dicto capitulo Vestra (X 3.2.7). Tamen ista est communis et vera opinio et de intentione omnium modernorum quod ubi notorium sit defensionem non competere, tunc procedi possit sine citatione quia tunc non tollitur defensio si non subest, et tunc procedat opinio illorum qui dicunt citationem non requiri ubi vero appareret defensionem competere vel esset dubium utrum competeret procedat opinio contraria quam tenuit glo. in c. Ad nostram el terzo de iureiur. et in c. Cum sit § finali."

44. Ibid.: "Secundo ostenditur nulla dicta declaratio in ea parte in qua declarat interdictam civitatem Floren. cum duabus vicinioribus, nam de iure id non potest fieri nisi offendens fuerit dominus dictarum civitatum secundum quod supra plene declaravimus. Vel si civitas offenderit episcopum proprium, sed ex processu apparet et notorie constat quod isti declarati et presertim Laurentius non erant domini dictarum civitatum eo modo quo requiritur ad hunc effectum et iste archiepiscopus erat Pisane civitatis et non Floren."

45. Ibid.: "Ibi subtiliter declarat maximus iurisconsultus etate nostra Franciscus Arety." This is not a reference to Accolti's defense of Lorenzo, but to his commentary on the Decretals of Gregory IX.

46. Franciscus de Accoltis Aretinus, Consilia (Pisa: 1482) [Hain *36] no. 165, unfoliated: "Et quia summus pontifex in hac sua declaratoria duo principaliter facit. Primo enim ad aggravationem cedis facte in urbe Florentina cumulat et deducit plurima crimina et offensas quas dicit in se in statumque sancte Romane ecclesie fuisse commissas. Secundo narrat que nuperrime in urbe Florentina gesta sunt et pro delictis in ea turbatione commissis penas statutas a iure predictos incurrisse."

Following the organization of Sixtus's bull, Accolti discussed those crimes that the pope believed led to Giuliano's murder. Lorenzo's first offense was his support of Niccolò Vitelli when he defended Città di Castello from papal troops. Machiavelli believed that although Lorenzo's support had been inadequate, this event was the beginning of Sixtus's animosity towards the Medici.[47] Accolti observed that Sixtus had already absolved Lorenzo of any wrongdoing and that "no crime from which one had been absolved could be used to prove another."[48] Further, since Florentines had defended Niccolò because of a treaty between them that had been approved by the Apostolic See, Accolti cannot imagine how their action could be considered culpable. It could be argued that defending a feudal lord, even in an unjust action, was just.[49]

Lorenzo and the Florentines denied all the other crimes of which they were accused. Even if the pope had been informed of their crimes, they were not proven and could not be proven. A thousand witnesses do not constitute proof if their testimony is taken when the accused is not present.[50] As Bartolus of Sassoferrato had pointed out, such testimony is not even sufficient proof for a judge to torture a defendant.[51]

In general, Accolti's argument—in order for a judge to hear a case, he must summon both parties—follows that of the doctors of law. Another aspect of procedural rules of proof had to be dealt with: could Sixtus's witnesses have produced a "half proof?"—that is, a proof which could not provide a basis for a judge to condemn a defendant but did have a certain weight in court. In the past some jurists, like Bartolus, had argued that they might, but Accolti had never been pleased

---

47. Machiavelli, *Istorie fiorentine*, book 7, chapter 331, p. 430: "il primi semi della nimicizia intra Sisto e i Medici."

48. Accoltis, *loc. cit.*: "Sed in nullum de quo fuit soluta pena potest adduci ad qualificandum aliud maleficium."

49. Ibid.: "Et tenet Bal. in c. Domino guerram hic finitur l. Conradi, ubi post longam disputationem concludit speciale esse in vasallo ex consuetudine feudorum quo teneatur defendere dominum etiam iniuste, ut ibi dicitur. . . . Sed si domini Florentini defenderunt dominum Nicolaum ex federe approbato per sedem apostolicam ne expelleretur iniuste de domo sua et de sua civitate hic non video in quas censuras aut penas inciderunt."

50. Ibid.: "Ad reliqua vero crimina que magnis et excellentissimis Florentinis obiciuntur et nominatim prestantissimo et magnifico viro Laurentio Medici est una responsio generalis: quia ipsi negant se talia commisisse . . . ergo frusta obiciuntur eis crimina que non sunt probata, licet fortasse ab aliquibus instructus fuerit illa esse commissa. Manifestum tamen non est etiam si essent mille testes quia per eos nullum fit indicium sufficiens, ex quo recepti sunt parte non citata neque intentato crimine contra eos."

51. Ibid.: "Vnde dicit Bartolus in l. finali, in fine, ff. de quest. quod per testes examinatos in generali inquisitione non sit indicium sufficiens ad torturam, ex quo sunt recepti parte non citata neque intentato iudicio contra eam."

with their position.[52] Since Sixtus had not summoned Lorenzo, if witnesses had constituted a "half-proof," the pope would not have been justified condemning him on the basis of this testimony. Even if we were to concede, sniffed Accolti, that the pope should be believed, if the deeds were not done in his presence, we have an equivocation in which one person is exempted from normal rules in two ways in the same matter. Either one person should be believed, or one person should be believed about something heard from a witness, violating the rule *Licet ex quadam* that evidence from a witness who is not present cannot be accepted in court. Both positions violate procedural rules and, moreover, the same person cannot break both rules in the same case.[53] In the end, Accolti concurred with the Florentine doctors of law, stipulating that not even the pope could dispense with a legal defense.[54]

Accolti continued his commentary on Sixtus's bull by taking up the section in which the pope had accused Lorenzo of supporting the condottiere Carlo Fortebraccio's campaign against Perugia. "I am embarrassed to hear the voice of the pope in this section," he lamented. One may easily gather from papal letters written to Lorenzo during the prior September that Sixtus had declared Lorenzo innocent in this affair.[55]

> Then, a few months later, O most holy Father, you heap enormous crimes upon him. I am not the truth handed down from heaven. I can only say that there is not enough honesty in him who sits on the throne of God and of Christ when he indulges in such inconstancy.

52. Ibid.: "Utrum autem iste probationes recepte inter alios facerent semiplenam probationem posset forte dubitari per ea que tradit Bar. in l. Admonendi, ff. de iureiur. ubi videtur sentire quod sic cum quadam modificatione ut ibi per eum quem sequitur Anton. de Butrio in c. finali, de iureiur. Hec tamen opinio numquam mihi placuit quia videtur contra textus in c. Inter dilectos, circa medium, de fide instrum. ubi dicitur quod attestationes recepte inter alios nichil nocent aliis."

53. Ibid.: "Sed dixi secundum mentem Bal. in l. secunda, C. de eden. quod probationes recepte inter alios faciunt semiplenam probationem contra illum qui fuit pars primi iudicii . . . si concedimus quod soli summo pontifici credatur etiam de gestis non coram se hic concurrit ex una causa duplex specialitas circa idem: videlicet quod uni soli crederetur; item quod crederetur ei de eo quod audivit ab alio contra regulam positam in c. Licet ex quadam, de testi. [X 2.20.47] . . . Sed duplex specialitas non debet concurrere circa idem ex eadem causa."

54. Ibid.: "Non enim potest summus pontifex defensionem citationis auferre." He promises to return to this point later.

55. Ibid.: "Quinimo crimen quod infertur magnifico Laurentio de rebellione civitatis Perusine. Adeo manifeste refellitur ut erubescam vocem summi pontificis in hac parte. Nam ex litteris suis scriptis ad eundem magnificum virum de mense septembris proxime preteriti declaratur quod de crimine illo habet eum pro innocente et innoxio . . . unde ergo beatissime pater post paucos menses etiam multa et enormia crimina in eum congeris tu videris: 'Meum non est ponere os in celum.' Hoc tantum dixerim in eo qui sedet in throno Dei et Christi eius non est satis honestum tanta varietate uti."

The pope does not have, concluded Accolti, sufficient memory of the past.[56]

The main body of Sixtus's letter had treated the Pazzi Conspiracy, and Accolti confronted those sections by posing four questions. First, was Sixtus correct to proceed against Lorenzo as if he had committed a notorious and inexcusable crime? Second, if the crime were notorious, was it inexcusable? Third, was the prince required to summon a defendant who had committed a notorious crime? Fourth, were there any reasons that would have excused the crimes?

Accolti's answer to the first question was the same as the Florentine lawyers: Lorenzo had been wounded in the attack and had been immediately placed under the care of doctors who feared that he had been struck with a poisoned weapon. He was not present when the archbishop had been hanged and was completely ignorant of the event.[57] Those who captured the cardinal and hanged the archbishop did not act because of Lorenzo's injuries, but because a state of crisis existed: rebels had occupied the Palazzo Vecchio and had harmed the republic by killing Giuliano and wounding Lorenzo.[58] If Lorenzo had ratified the actions of the Florentines, he could not have been punished with the severe penalties that the pope had levied. These penalties were justified only for those who had ordered such crimes.[59]

To the second question, Accolti cited Antonio de Butrio. No crime could be so notorious that the defendant might not have secret reasons or circumstances that might excuse him.[60] Although Butrio thought that the pope was not bound by the rules of the *ordo iudiciarius*, particularly in notorious crimes, he seems to have applied the provisions of *Pastoralis* to less exalted judges.

---

56. Ibid.: "apparet summum pontificem non satis fuisse memorem preteritorum."

57. Ibid.: "Ipse vulneratus et consternatus pavore ac dolore acerbissimo aut in sacrario maioris ecclesie inclusus aut certe domi intendens erat ad curationem proprii vulneris de quo ob veneni suspitionem vehementissime erat sollicitus . . . Credo facile probari posse non fuit presens Laurentius quando archiepiscopus fuit suspensus, quinimo hoc tunc penitus ignoravit."

58. Ibid.: "In casu autem nostro hii qui ceperunt cardinalem et suspenderunt archiepiscopum potuerunt hoc facere non propter iniuriam illatam Laurentio sed propter turbationem status que erat incepta in occupatione palatii et etiam propter iniuriam illatam rei publice in cede Iuliani et insultu et vulnere Laurentii."

59. Ibid.: "Licet ergo notorium esset Laurentium ista habere rata per hoc tamen non posset puniri ut malum committens et quantum ad delicta commissa in personam aliorum et hoc est de iure expeditum."

60. Ibid.: "Anton. de But. in c. Vestra (X 3.2.7) preallegato dicit quod nullum maleficium potest esse ita notorium ut non possit habere excusationes sive circumstantias occultas excusantes."

As a point of law, the third question was the most important: Could the pope conduct a trial of a notorious crime without having summoned one of the parties? Although a number of jurists—Johannes Andreae, Antonio de Butrio, and Baldus—seemed to permit the prince to judge a person without having summoned him to court, Accolti pointed out that their opinions directly contradicted the text of *Pastoralis*.[61] Divine law established the summons to court. God's calling Adam and Eve to judgment in the Book of Genesis is certain proof of the summon's divine origins. Neither the pope nor the emperor can dispense with this part of the judicial process because no one can ignore a precept of divine law.[62]

Accolti returned to the facts of the case. The pope, he alleged, not only misrepresented the facts in his letter, but overlooked them. When the archbishop was captured in the Palazzo Vecchio, he was not clothed in clerical garb and was armed. He had been taken trying to seize the Palazzo and the "Vexillifer iustitiae." He had fomented sedition and could be hanged, therefore, without incurring excommunication.[63] The canon law is clear, declared Accolti. If a cleric is bearing arms and not wearing clerical garb, his killer does not fall into excommunication.[64]

Accolti emphasized that Lorenzo did not know about the death of the archbishop and the capture of the cardinal, and he did not ratify either deed at the time or in such a manner that he could be punished for the ratification. No one knows, he added, who hanged the archbishop. Although Florentines in the piazza saw his body hanging from the Palazzo, they could not have known whether the priors, the eight, or others had carried out the execution.[65]

61. Ibid.: "Sed cum reverentia ista dicta sunt expresse contra tex. in Clem. Pastoralis § Ceterum, in secundo responso de re iud. ubi pontifex expresse declarat quod etiam contra subditum in causa criminali princeps non potest ex certa scientia supplere defectum citationis quia esset tollere defensionem que est de iure naturali."

62. Ibid.: "Citatio sit de iure divino, ii. q.i. c. Deus omnipotens, et patet ex libro Genesis quia citavit Deus Adam contra illud preceptum negativum quod non posset procedi non citata parte in causa in qua non potest verti cognitio. Papa vel imperator non dispensavit quia numquam in tali precepto reperitur in lege divina dispensatum."

63. Ibid.: "Ego que ad ius pertinent deinceps prosequar: dicimus ergo primo quod archiepiscopus dum fuit captus et suspensus inventus est sine vestibus clericalibus et cum armis in palatio magnificorum dominorum, idest sine habitu clericali. . . . Fuit inventus in palatio magnificorum dominorum cum vellet palatium capere cum manus in vexilliferum iusticie voluisse inicere et sic inventus est sine habitu cum armis inmiscens se enormibus sceleribus, idest turbationi status excitans seditionem. Ergo potuit occidi et suspendi sine pena excommunicationis."

64. Ibid.: "Casus est in c. Cum non ab homine § finali, et in c. Perpendimus, de sent. excom. que decretalis videtur esse facta propter casum nostrum et utrobique tenent omnes doctores."

65. Ibid.: "Laurentius neque scivit mortem archiepiscopi neque capturam cardinalis

Accolti made two final arguments. First, the Florentines accused the archbishop of having paid assassins to kill Lorenzo, violating canon law. The decretal *Pro humani* permitted any Christian to kill someone who paid an assassin with impunity. Some earlier jurists, like Johannes Andreae, had held that this decretal was limited to non-Christians who perpetrated assassinations, but Johannes de Imola and Dominicus de Sancto Geminiano thought that any paid assassination was covered under the provisions of this decretal.[66] Second, he returned to an earlier contention that a cleric could be slain if his killer acted in self-defense. He admitted that the archbishop had been killed without a trial. However, his death was justified since he had fomented a "bloody sedition." Indeed, if a citizen did not defend the fatherland, that citizen would lose the right of "civility."[67]

The third jurist enlisted to defend Lorenzo was an old friend of Florence. Messer Bartolomeo Sozzini was born in Siena, the son of the jurist Mariano Sozzini, under whom he studied. He continued his studies at Bologna where he heard lectures of Francesco Accolti. He taught canon law and Roman law at Siena, Ferrara, Florence, Padua, and Pavia. When the Pazzi Conspiracy occurred he was teaching at Pisa. He was also a frequent advocate at the papal curia. He left a considerable corpus of written work, mainly Roman law, but one canonical work, a set of *additiones* to his father's commentary on the titles of the Decretals.[68]

---

nec etiam ratificavit saltim taliter quod ex illa ratificatione potuerit puniri, ut supra est probatum. Et licet esset notorium archiepiscopum fuisse suspensum, non tamen notorium est qui fecerit suspendi. Licet enim populus videret ex platea archiepiscopum suspensum, non tamen poterat videre utrum domini vel octo, utrum omnes vel maior pars hoc fieri facerent et qui essent illi."

66. Ibid.: "Tertio allegant domini Florentini quod dominus archiepiscopus mandaverat cuidam ut occideret Laurentium et pro premio promiserunt sibi direptionem domus Laurentii, quodsi est verum ex solo mandato, licet effectus non sit secutus, videtur incidere in penas que ponuntur in c. Pro humani, de homicid. lib.vi. . . . Arch. ibi et Joh. And. cum quo sentio tenent quod illa constitutio solum habeat locum in certo genere personarum et non generaliter in aliis, sed Joh. de Ymo. ibi et dominus Dominicus tenent oppositum et hanc eorum opinionem multi sequuntur."

67. Ibid.: "Illud etiam in occisione archiepiscopi et aliorum clericorum advertendum quod quando est excitata seditio cruenta ut utar verbis iurisconsulti sicut erat ista occisio que fuit contra iuris ordinem de aliquo videtur fieri causa preveniendi periculum, idest ut obvietur periculo quod imminet et sic causa defensionis ita dicit tex. in l. Si quis filio exheredato § Hi autem, ff. de iniusto testamento [Dig. 28.3.6.8] . . . Debet autem civis defendere statum patrie, alias perdit ius civilitatis secundum Bar. in l.ii. C. de infanti. expo." [Cod. 8.51(52).2]. On the concept of "civility" see Antony Black, *Guilds and Civil Society* 98–108 and passim. Also Roger Chartier, *The Cultural Use of Print in Early Modern France,* trans. Lydia Cochrane (Princeton, N.J.: 1987).

68. The most complete biography with bibliography of editions and manuscripts is Belloni, *Professori giuridici* 168–172. Belloni does not list Florence as a law school where Bartolomeo taught, but he mentions having taught there in this consilium: Bartolomeo

Sozzini knew Angelo Poliziano, and he wrote the introductory paragraphs to his consilium with a rhetorical flourish that might have pleased his friend:[69]

> Who is so cruel or hard that he may not be moved when he sees Lorenzo, a religious, pious, and just man, decorated and polished with every virtue, touched by ignominy and lacerated by harsh words?

Despite his sympathy, Sozzini expressed some doubts about writing a consilium that probed the limits of papal authority. He reminded his readers of the old juristic rule that one should not dispute papal power.[70] However, the first question he posed—were Sixtus's censure and interdict justly promulgated?—was the most important, and the one that he treated most extensively.

His response was a long and complex analysis of the authority of the prince to violate the rules of judicial procedure. Sixtus could be accused of the same error with which Pope Clement had reproved Henry VII in the decretal *Pastoralis*: a condemnation without due process is not a mature judgment.[71] There were, Sozzini noted, several arguments that could justify the pope's having rendered a judgment without a summons. One may presume, as Cinus of Pistoia had, that the prince was motivated by a just cause or that when there is doubt about the justness

---

Sozzini (Socinus), *Consilium* No. 20 in Franciscus Curtius Papiensis, *Consilia* (Milan: 1496), unfol.: "In contrariam partem ancipitem animum diu fluctuantem Florentinorum auctor [auctoritas Ed.] reuocat apud quos cum magno salario et honore ius ciuile tot annos interpretor." Diplovatatius wrote a short biography of him in the sixteenth century, *Liber de claris iuris consultis* 412–414. Savigny, *Geschichte* VI 345–353, has important details about his life and works. Tedeschi, "Notes Toward a Genealogy" 287–291 contains valuable manuscript information and important corrections to the standard accounts of his life. Dolezalek, *Verzeichnis* lists works and manuscripts. On the basis of this consilium, one might revise Lauro Martines's summary of Sozzini's importance in Florence; see *Lawyers and Statecraft in Renaissance Florence* (Princeton: 1968) 481.

69. Bartolomeo Sozzini (Socinus), *Consilium* No. 20 in Franciscus Curtius Papiensis, *Consilia* (Milan: 1496), unfol.: "Quis est tam ferreus tam durus ut non comoveatur cum videat dictum Laurentium virum pium religiosum iustum et omnibus virtutibus ornatum atque excultum, ignomina affectum et verbis iniuriosis lacesitum."

70. Ibid.: "Sepenumero animo reuolui si hanc prouinciam assumerem et modo in istam modo in illam partem me conuertebam nonnulla a scribendo me deterrebant nec pauca ad scribendum hortabantur. Videbatur quodammodo alienum ab homine Christiano et quasi hereticum de summi pontificis potestate diserere." On the juristic tradition behind the last phrase, see Pennington, *Pope and Bishops* 22–28.

71. Ibid.: "Unde potest illud dici de quo pontifex reprehendit Henricum imperator qui tulerat sententiam contra regem Robertum contra ipsum pontificem retorqueri, scilicet quod in absentem nec citatum legitime ac inaudita parte et per consequens non maturo fuit iudicio, sed precipitatione et presertim de tanto crimine promulgata ut dicit textus in dicta Clem. Pastoralis."

of his actions, the prince exercised his absolute power.[72] Sozzini conceded that the pope might have used the "non obstantibus legibus in contrarium facientibus"—that any contrary laws should be ignored when obeying the papal mandate.[73] The "non obstantibus" clause, however, only abrogates papal decrees that prohibit the laying of excommunication on persons or interdiction on places and renders null any privileges or exemptions that Lorenzo and others may possess. The "non obstantibus" clause may not derogate a defense in court since natural law supported that right.[74] Although the pope sometimes uses his fullness of power to rectify defects in the judicial process, in doubtful cases he only corrects those matters touching positive law.[75]

Once having dealt with these general issues, Sozzini turned to more concrete problems and asked whether one could distinguish between a subject and non-subject. Encouraged by the distinction made by Pope Clement in *Pastoralis*, jurists had concluded that the prince could take the right of defense away from a subject. Clement had objected that Henry VII could not judge Robert of Naples because he was not subject to the emperor. The implication was that if Robert had been his subject, Henry's action would have been justified.

Sozzini found this argument specious. He cited the opinions of Panormitanus, Angelus de Ubaldis, and Alexander Tartagni.[76] One may

72. Ibid.: "In dubio autem presumitur quod princeps motus fuerit ex iusta causa, ut declarat Cynus in l. finali C. de prec. impe. offe. . . . Sed ad hanc obiectionem respondeo quod quando princeps procedit ex potestate ordinaria, ista opinio non potest procedere quia tunc licet princeps sit supra leges, ut in c. Proposuit de conces. preb. l. Princeps ff. de leg., tamen non potest sine citatione procedere . . . Secundo quod quamquam princeps de ordinaria potestate non possit parte non citata procedere, tamen de absoluta cum causa potest que causa in dubio presumitur, ut dixi et sic bene procedere potuit parte non citata. Ita concludit Jo. An. in addit. Spec. tit. de sen. § Iuxta."

73. The "non obstantibus" clause had long been used in the papal chancellery; on its usage see Brigitte Meduna, *Studien zum Formular der päpstlichen Justizbriefe*.

74. Sozzini, *Consilium*: "Sed contra hoc posset quispiam replicare quod immo pontifex in casu nostro uti voluit plenitudine potestatis quoniam in sententia censure apposita est clausula 'non obstantibus legibus in contrarium facientibus' . . . Sed ad hoc possumus respondere quod si recte ponderetur dicta clausula 'non obstantibus,' solum duo respicit. Primo enim tollit constitutionem et ordinationem apostolicam quibus talis sententia interdicti, excommunicationis vel privationis in personas et loca prohibetur ferri. Secundo tollit priuilegia, exemptiones vel indulgentias quas habent Laurentius et alii in quos lata est sententia per que effectus promulgate sententie impediretur."

75. Ibid.: "nam videmus quod si papa de plenitudine potestatis supplet omnes defectus non intelligitur velle supplere in dubio circa defectus citationis, sed tantum circa solemnitates iuris positivi, ut est textus ubi hoc concludit Zen. et sequitur Imol. in dicta Clem. Pastoralis."

76. On Alexander, see Aurelius Sabattani, *De vita et operibus Alexandri Tartagni de Imola* (Quaderni di Studi senesi 27; Milan: 1972).

not presume that when the prince proceeds against a subject that he is always motivated by a just cause.[77]

Notoriety was the last and most difficult issue that Sozzini confronted in the first section of the consilium. Notorious crimes had always occupied a special place in the jurisprudence of medieval procedure. Indeed, jurists often made exceptions to the normal rules of procedure in notorious crimes. Sixtus's most powerful argument, which he used in his bull of condemnation, was that Lorenzo's crimes were notorious; for this reason, the pope could ignore procedural niceties. Antonio de Butrio had also argued that the pope could violate due process in notorious crimes, claiming support of a number of pre-fourteenth-century jurists.[78]

Sozzini responded that the pope could only render a judgment in a case in which there was absolutely no doubt that the defendant could muster no defense. Lorenzo, however, had a defense—which he would discuss later.[79] He made a distinction between those crimes committed in the presence of the pope and those crimes that were not. He conceded that when the pope was an eyewitness, he could judge the defendant summarily, without a summons and in his absence.[80] Juristically the

77. Sozzini, *Consilium*: "Quinimmo dominus Abbas in locis preallegatis et dominus Alex. post Angelum in l. Si sic in principio in fi. iii. col. de le. i. tenent quod etiam princeps contra subditum non potest supplere defectum citationis et defensionis quia cum illa sit de iure naturali non potest per principem tolli, per textum ubi est casus in dicta Clem. Pastoralis . . . Secundo potest responderi quod non presumitur quod iusta causa interveniat ubi princeps procedit parte non citata et non auditis defensionibus, ut voluit singulariter Baldus per tex. ibi in dicta lege finali C. de leg. quia tollere citationem est tollere defensionem prout etiam dicit Bar. in extravagan. Ad reprimendam in verso 'sine figura,' et sic non potest per principem tolli, ut est casus in dicta Clem. Pastoralis . . . Alias frustra requireretur iusta causa ad hoc ut princeps procedendo de plenitudine potestatis tollere posset citationem si semper causa iusta presumeretur."

78. Ibid.: "Ceterum et tertio videtur quod summus pontifex possit se defendere quia ut supra dictum est ipse se fundat quod erat delictum notorium quo casu non videbatur quod requireretur citatio per tex. cum glo. in dicto c. Cum olim, per quem dicit ibi dominus Antonius quod processus pape notoriis valet sine citatione. Vnde dicunt ibi Hosti. et Jo. An. quod papa potest ferre sententiam contra tenentes terras et rationes ecclesie etiam illis non citatis."

79. Ibid.: "Sed ad hoc respondeo quod illud procedit quando res esset ita notoria quod certum esset nullam absenti defensionem competere, et ita procedunt iura et auctoritates allegate, secus ubi esset dubium an abensti posset competere aliqua defensio vel non, quia tunc etiam in notoriis requiritur citatio . . . [ut] dicit Hosti. quod nullus absens quantumcunque notorius criminosus est excommunicandum nisi primo sit citatus, cum multi dicantur notorii qui tamen non sunt, ut c. Consuluit, de appell. et quia forte notorius habuit legitimas defensiones que sunt admittende. . . . In casu autem nostro nedum erat dubium quod defensio competeret, sed quod fortius est, ut in quarta dubitatione ostendetur, quasi certum erat defensionem competere."

80. Ibid.: "Sed ad hanc obiectionem respondeo quod aliquando sumus in his que sunt gesta a pontifice vel coram se, et tunc indubitanter procedit tex. cum ibi not. in dicta Clem. Litteris, et hic non est casus noster."

matter was straightforward. Although the pope held supreme power, he did not exercise supreme authority over natural law. Therefore, he must respect and preserve its precepts.[81]

In his final conclusion, Sozzini seemed to deny any possibility that the pope could ignore due process, despite what he had written about the pope's right to judge crimes that had been committed in his presence. God, he wrote, who knows all things and who knows whether a defendant can put forward a defense, summoned Adam and heard his testimony before he condemned him. The Lord granted the same privilege to the Sodomites. Sozzini's implicit point, of course, was that the pope should not practice a lesser standard of justice than God.[82]

Yet a major question remained to be answered. The canonists had always held that an excommunication could be unjust, but still have legal force. Excommunication was a punishment that cleansed the soul, an ointment that healed a troubled spirit. Therefore, the canonists had argued that even unjust excommunications were valid.[83] Sozzini acknowledged the force of this argument but insisted that in this case, since the pope had not summoned Lorenzo, he had rendered his decision without having heard the evidence. Worse, the pope believed false information. Lorenzo's excommunication could not be valid.[84]

Sozzini turned to the muse of history and analyzed the events that Sixtus IV had used as evidence of Lorenzo's perfidy in his bull of condemnation. He listed five objections to Sixtus's narrative of the events surrounding the attack on Lorenzo and Giuliano and discussed them in a section that covered five large folio pages. Sozzini demonstrated an intimate knowledge of the events. One wonders from where he got his information. The first accusation in Sixtus's bull had been a condemnation of Lorenzo's support of Niccolò Vitelli when he had attempted

---

81. Ibid.: "Hac suprema potestate hoc casu uti non potest super his super quibus non habet plenam potestatem. Ita dicit prefatus dominus Fran. in dicto c. Cum a nobis, allegando textum in dicta Clem. Pastoralis. Et ita potest procedere quod ibi dicit dominus Abbas dum vult assertioni pape non stari in his in quibus non habet supremam potestatem super dispositiones [dispositio ed.] a iuregentium vel divino, prout est citatio."

82. Ibid.: "Nam Deus cui omnia sunt in aperto an competat vel non competat defensio antequam puniret Adam de peccato inobedientie vocavit eum et audivit defensiones suas ut habetur in Genesi primo et noluit punire peccata Sodomorum nisi descenderet et videret."

83. Elisabeth Vodola, *Excommunication in the Middle Ages* (Berkeley, Los Angeles, London: 1986) 101.

84. Sozzini, *Consilium,* loc. cit.: "Potest etiam nullitas sentientie demonstrari etiam alia via valet quia multa fuerunt per falsitatem suggestam et multa tacita propter que fuit talis sententia promulgata prout demonstrabitur in quarta dubitatione, unde papa motus fuit ex falsis causis ad talem sententiam proferendam, et sic dicta sententia nulla censeri debet."

to regain Città di Castello in 1475 from which papal troops had driven him in 1474. Sozzini offered a more detailed defense of Lorenzo's dealings with Niccolò than Francesco Accolti. He began by reminding his readers that the treaty between Lorenzo and the citizens of Città di Castello had been approved by Pope Paul II. The treaty had specified that the citizens were subject to the Apostolic See in some matters, but free in others. Consequently, they had every right to appeal to Florence for aid in their defense since the two cities were bound together by a papally approved contract. The pope could not break this treaty arbitrarily. Rather, he is held to observe it, just as the emperor had to observe the Treaty of Constance.[85]

Sozzini maintained that Sixtus gained possession of Città di Castello because of the letters that Lorenzo had written to Niccolò.[86] Florence had removed Niccolò and sent him to Pisa. Consequently, the pope regained his lordship of the city more promptly than he would have without Lorenzo's intervention.[87]

What was the truth? The events surrounding the sudden revolt of the citizens of Città di Castello on October 17, 1475, are still difficult to reconstruct, and the role that Lorenzo played is not altogether clear. The supporters of Niccolò did call upon him to assist their throwing off the yoke of papal government. Sixtus may have had good reason, but little evidence, to suspect Lorenzo's complicity.[88] As we have seen, Machiavelli thought that Lorenzo proffered aid to Niccolò.

In his bull of condemnation, *Iniquitatis filius,* Sixtus IV had accused Lorenzo of helping the condottiere, Carlo Fortebraccio, when he attacked Perugia in 1477. Sozzini also examined this complex affair in

85. Ibid.: "Contractum enim fuerat fedus inter Floren. et Tiferantes sciente et approbante pontifice Paulo quod eis licitum fuit per ea que not. Bart. . . . Item Tiferantes qui tamen in his que in eorum capitulis continentur dicebantur subditi in aliis censebantur liberi . . . Petierunt auxilium a Floren. confederatis quibus cum esset licitum se defendere et propter hoc bellum facere . . . si auxilium prestiterunt iuste, videntur hoc fecisse cum ad hoc ex federe contracto tenerentur . . . Nec videtur quod capitula Civitatis Castelli que dicebatur secundum quid non simpliciter subdita et dictas confederationes potuerit pontifex ita ex abrupto tollere et irritare, immo tenebatur eas servare, not. per Bald. in c.i. per illum textum de probat. ubi dicit quod imperator servare tenetur capitula contracta inter eum et civitates Longobardie in pace Constan."

86. Ibid.: "Quinimmo ut fertur nisi pontifex verum inficiari vellet, per mensem citius propter litteras Laur. ad Nicolaum Vitellum dictam civitatem obtinuit et pro certo non ita de facili lis extincta fuisset si Florentini manum apposuissent."

87. Ibid.: "Remotus enim fuit postremo dictus Nicolaus ex agro vicino et in agrum Pisanum translatus quo paratius pontifex urbe Castelli potiretur. Vnde potest adduci illud Ovidii, exitus acta probat, de quo in l. Rem non novam § finali de iud."

88. See the discussion of Riccardo Fubini in Lorenzo de' Medici, *Lettere,* 2: 1474– 1478 (Florence 1977) 139–142.

much more detail than Francesco Accolti had. Fortebraccio had been dismissed by Venice at the end of 1476 and returned to his homeland. The political situation in Perugia remained unsettled, and Fortebraccio was invited to enter the city. Sixtus wrote to the priors of Perugia that they should not make a pact with Fortebraccio. At the same time, Carlo entered negotiations to regain Montone, his birthplace and his father's possession. With Sixtus's permission, Fortebraccio returned to Montone.

Negotiations turned to military action. Papal and Neapolitan troops thwarted Fortebraccio's hopes in Perugia, and a small papal-Neapolitan army under Federico da Montefeltro besieged Montone, which Fortebraccio's wife, Margherita Malatesta, defended valiantly.[89]

Sozzini had no difficulty unraveling the correct thread of this story. Sixtus's accusations against Lorenzo were off the mark. After all, Lorenzo concluded a treaty with Perugia immediately after Fortebraccio's defeat.[90] Like Accolti, Sozzini cited the letters that Sixtus had sent to Lorenzo exonerating him from blame.[91] Only the confessions of some soldiers captured during the siege of Montone implicated Lorenzo's complicity with Fortebraccio. Sozzini pointed out that confessions extracted from the accomplices in crimes, even in cases of treason, bring only a small presumption of guilt. In any case, since Lorenzo had not been summoned to court, the soldier's confessions were without any value.[92]

Sixtus had accused Lorenzo of assisting another enemy of the papacy, Deifobo di Anguillara, and of having enlisted pirates in his ser-

---

89. Fubini tells this story in his commentary to Lorenzo's letters cited above, *Lettere*, 2: *1474–1478*, 376–380, 386–387, 389–391, 398–401, 416–420; also Rubinstein, *Lettere*, 3: *1478–1479*, 287–288.

90. Sozzini, *Consilium*, loc. cit.: "Minus pro certo verisimile secundo loco videtur quod Laur. et complices per comitem Carolum civitatem Perusinam ab ecclesia Romana abducere conati fuerunt, cum postmodum immediate Florentini cum his Perusinis fedus contraxerint qui comiti Carolo adversabantur signa sunt ista amicitie, ut habetur in pace Constan. in verbo 'societatem.' Ex quibus constat illos qui comiti Carolo adversabantur non factos inimicos Floren. quod quidem factum fuisset si Florentini contra eos comitem Carolum iuuassent."

91. Ibid.: "Sed quid plura? Nonne pontifex per plures litteras magnifico Laurentio destinatas fatetur Laurentium a premissis insontem et innoxium, nunc autem contraria et repugnantia in promulgatione sententie reperiuntur."

92. Ibid.: "Verumque et tertio loco negatur obsessum a militibus ecclesie Montonum adiutum fuisse a Laurentio et complicibus, etsi aliqui intercepti pedites contrarium asserant, quanta fides sit eis adhibenda nullus ignorat. Sunt enim hi participes criminis, qui etiam si essemus in crimine lese maiestatis vel etiam in aliis criminibus exceptis (exceptuatis Ed.) facerent tantum presumptionem quamdam . . . Nullam autem contra Laurentium et complices probationem examinati insciis ipsis et non citatis."

vice. Sozzini would have none of it. He argued, quite properly, that in self-defense Lorenzo could have used Christian or non-Christian pirates.[93] He finished this section of the consilium treating the events that preceded the Pazzi Conspiracy with the legal maxim: the defendant is absolved if the plaintiff has not proven the case (actore non probante reum absolvi).[94]

The final section of Sozzini's consilium was devoted to the events of the Pazzi Conspiracy. The most eloquent passages of Sixtus's bull were those in which he recounted the death of Archbishop Francesco Salviati and condemned Lorenzo, the Otto di Balìa, and the Florentine magistrate, the Gonfaloniere di Giustizia. Sozzini repeated in large part what the other jurists had claimed. Salviati and his followers had forcibly occupied the Palazzo Vecchio in secular garb. A number of clerics were killed in the attack. The Florentines captured, interrogated, and hanged Salviati. The situation had been dangerous. Troops supporting the Pazzi were said to be coming from Florenzole and Città di Castello. Jacopo Pazzi was still in the field. The Otto di Balìa and the other Florentines had no choice but to kill the archbishop.

Sozzini stressed that none of the men who supported Lorenzo fell under the strictures of Si quis suadente which stipulated automatic excommunication for all those who "laid violent hands on clerics." This canon was an important text in the canonical tradition, and Sixtus had implicitly referred to it in his bull.[95] Individuals could not fall under the provisions of Si quis suadente, nor could the city. Therefore, Sixtus's interdict on the Florentine state was also unjust. Florence should not have been subjected to a papal interdict because Salviati was neither detained nor hanged with the "consilio et tractu" of the magistrates. His death was the result of individual actions, not an act sanctioned by the "body" of citizens.[96] Sozzini cleverly used corporate theory to fend

93. Sozzini, Consilium, loc. cit.: "Non enim tantum a pyrratis Christianis sed etiam a penitus infidelibus auxilio uti debemus ad defensionem." This was a standard tenet of legal thought since the thirteenth century, see Russell, Just War 198–199.

94. Ibid.: "Vnde concludo dici posse illud vulgare, actore non probante reum absolvi, unde ad ista (istis Ed.) que nec vera nec verisimilia probantur, digni non erant Lauren. et alii condemnari, sed absolvi per regulam."

95. Richard Helmholz, "'Si quis suadente' (C.17 q.4 c.29): Theory and Practice," Proceedings of the Seventh International Congress of Medieval Canon Law, Cambridge, ed. Peter Linehan (Città del Vaticano: 1988) 425–438.

96. Sozzini, Consilium, loc. cit.: "Secunda ratio quia tunc civitas dicitur delinquere in terminis illius tex. [Clem. Si quis suadente] secundum Paulum de Eliaza. quando homines communicato consilio et tractatu hoc fecerunt, et sic delinquerunt ut corpus, non ut singulares."

off papal sanctions.[97] Finally, he observed that if Giovan Battista da Montesecco's statement about the archbishop's involvement in the conspiracy were to be believed, the problem of guilt was easily resolved. Canon law clearly stated that anyone who ordered an assassination is deprived of "dignity, honor, orders, and benefice, and defied by all Christians."[98] Salviati would not have been a cleric when he was murdered and would not, consequently, have been protected by *Si quis suadente*. He had lost his clerical status before his execution.

From the archbishop he turned to the cardinal. The pope could condemn neither Florence nor Lorenzo for the capture of Cardinal Raffaele Riario-Sansoni because the Florentines had not taken him by force and had not mistreated the cardinal. The aroused people of Florence threatened the cardinal, and the Otto di Balìa led him to the Palazzo with honor. He was received in the room of the Gonfaloniere.[99] Sixtus could accuse the Florentines of unjustly imprisoning the cardinal only if they had acted with "dolus." Some of Otto di Balìa and others detained the cardinal. They did not act on behalf of the entire city (communicato consilio collegialiter).[100]

Sozzini put forward one last reason for the cardinal's detention that was not mentioned by any other jurist. The Florentines who lived in Rome were in great danger after the events in Florence became known. They gathered together in the Florentine section of the city on Monte

97. On the corporation in medieval legal thought, see Pierre Michaud-Quantin, *Universitas: Expressions du mouvement communautaire dans le moyen âge* (Paris: 1970); Tierney, *Religion, Law* 87–92; Alberto Melloni, *Innocenzo IV: La concezione e l'esperienza della cristianità come "regimen unius personae"* (Istituto per le Scienze religiose di Bologna, Testi e ricerche di scienze religiose 4; Genova: 1990) 106–130.

98. Sozzini, loc. cit.: "Omitto postremo quod fertur archiepiscopum aliqua promississe Jo. Baptiste de Monte Sicco ut magnificum Laurentium interficeret, quod si verum est omnis tollitur difficultas, quoniam dicitur commississe delictum asassinamenti propter quod ipso facto dicitur privatus dignitate, honore, ordine, et beneficio, et a populo Christiano diffidatus, casus in c.i. de homicid. in vi."

99. Ibid.: "Primo quia existente maximo rumore in populo et iminente maximo periculo cardinali in cuius oculis cedes illa nefantissima commissa est, domini Octo de Bailia multis militibus stipati accesserunt ad cardinalem et honorifice duxerunt ad palatium . . . Confirmatur hoc . . . cum honorifice fuerit ductus et defensus a populo, et non sic erga alios fuerit factum honorifice etiam in palatio receptus in camera vexilliferi, et nil contra eum attentatum est per quas coniecturas tollitur presumptio mali animi si que induceretur a iure."

100. Ibid.: "Tertio ista conclusio probatur quia ut dixi ad hoc ut quis incidat in dictas penas requiritur dolus . . . Ex quo hoc communicato consilio non fuit factum quod caperetur, dato quod homines civitatis fuissent, non dicitur civitas delinquere, tunc dicitur quando id fit communicato consilio collegialiter secundum Jo. And. . . . Sed in casu nostro aliqui ex Octo de Balia cum multis hoc fecerunt. . . . Preterea Octo non fecerunt communicato consilio, hoc est collegialiter, ergo non dicuntur deliquisse."

Jordano where supporters of the cardinal threatened them. The magistrates held the cardinal to protect the Florentines and their goods in Rome.[101]

At the end of the consilium, Sozzini ignited another incandescent display of rhetoric:[102]

> Since the pope holds the highest power, he ought to maintain the highest honesty and equity.... I do not doubt that when the pope learns of these most just defenses that Lorenzo can muster, he will revoke his condemnation. Three things are presumed to mingle in the minds of men and the pope: good will, harmony of reason, and ordained power.... The pope, who is the living font of justice, who disperses darkness like the wind... shall impel all Christians to peace.

This passage may be filled with the rhetoric of propaganda, but its passion should not obscure a significant fact. The rhetoric surrounding and describing the prince had evolved over the last three centuries. A jurist was no longer content to ask him, "Why do you do this?" Rather than stressing the authority and power of the prince, to use thirteenth-century terminology, "pro ratione voluntas," Sozzini preferred to emphasize that the virtues of the prince should be those found in the minds of all men. Finally, he placed his seal and signature on the consilium, acknowledging, at the same time, the overriding authority of the Roman Church.[103]

Of the jurists chosen to defend the Medici and Florence, Girolamo Torti was an outsider who had, it seems, no connection to Florence or to any Florentine. He wrote the consilium while teaching at Pavia and

101. Ibid.: "Ista conclusio primo probatur reali fundamento et vero, nam ex Roma receperunt litteras in triduum, durante quasi eo tumultu, et adhuc armis non depositis, qualiter Floren. ibi morantes auditis que gesta erant Floren. stabant in magno discrimine et personarum et bonorum et quod receperant se in montem Jordanum, et quod certi potentes attinentes domino cardinali multa adversa minabantur, unde ob tutelam suorum et bonorum, ut res citius et placabilius pacaretur, per aliquos dies cardinalem detinuerunt, quod eis licuisse arbitror, cum non solum ob tutelam sui sit licitum iniicere manus in clericum sine metu excommunicationis, sed etiam ob defensionem aliorum et rerum." Cf. Rubinstein, *Lettere* 3.275 n. 9.

102. Ibid.: "Cum enim ipse summam potestatem teneat, summam honestatem et equitatem servare debet ut inquit Bald. consilio incipit 'Premittendum' . . . Sed non dubito auditis verbis et iustissimis causis et defensionibus magnifici Laurentii primatum et totius populi Floren. hanc sententiam revocabit, cum in papa sint illa tria que in mentibus hominum concurrere presumuntur: bona voluntas, modi congruitas, et concessa potestas. Quia papa cum vivus fons iusticie fugans tenebras sicut ventus, ut inquit Bal. in quodam alio consilio suo, quo facto Christianos omnes ad pacem urgebit. Et in hoc opus est potestatem suam exercere et omni dissimulatione semota debet."

103. Ibid.: "Et ita ut supra per me conclusum est arbitror iuris esse. Ego Bartholomeus Sozinus Senen. j.u.doc. et in fidem premissorum me subscripsi et sigillavi salvo semper saniori iudicio et sacrosancte Romane ecclesie."

produced very little else during a long career. The only other notice
we have of him is Jason de Mayno's funeral oration.[104] In contrast to
Sozzini and Accolti, Torti knew much less about the events of the conspiracy although he added details that the other jurists overlooked. He
concentrated his attention on two legal points: whether Sixtus's bull of
condemnation was unjust and whether it was void.

Torti's first point was rather tendentious. He noted that the decretal
which Sixtus had cited as a justification for placing an interdict on Florence specified that it only covered crimes against bishops. Since Riario-
Sansoni was only a cardinal deacon, argued Torti, the provisions of the
decretal do not apply.[105] His second point, however, was more important. The pope cannot place Florence under interdict for the death of
the archbishop because the city did not order his death. Repeating the
formulation of Sozzini, Torti stated that those who represented the entire city did not act "communicato consilio" and with "precedente deliberatione." This fact is proven, he went on, by an inspection of the
record books of the city. There is no trace in them that the city had
considered the case in formal deliberations.[106] Although the priors were
responsible for the death of the archbishop, the city may not be
punished for their acts. They do not have supreme and perpetual jurisdiction over the city; that resides in the people.[107]

Torti repeated the same defense that all the jurists put forward for
Lorenzo. After he had been wounded, he was carried back to the Medici
palace and had remained there until after the archbishop's death. He
could not have participated in the decision to kill Salviati.

Torti then returned to his earlier argument that only a corporate decision of the city, taken by the appropriate magistrates, could justify
Sixtus's penalties. The city, which was a fictional body, could not be

104. Belloni, *Professori giuristi a Padova nel secolo XV* 227. See also Tiraboschi,
Storia della letteratura italiana VI.1, pp. 403–405.
105. Girolamo Torti [Hieronimus de Tortis], *Consilium* [Sine loco et dato, Hain
*15579]: "Nam primo ponderandum est verbum pontificem positum in dicta Cle. prima
propter quod dicunt ibi doctores dictam constitutionem [Clem. de penis c.i.] et eius
penam non verificari, nisi offendatur ille qui habet ordinem episcopalem. Hinc infero
quod pro nulla offensa que diceretur aut esset facta clericis inferioribus haberet locum
dicta constitutio. Nec etiam pro offensione que diceretur facta cardinali predicto, cum
ipse non sit episcopus, sed diaconus, cum ergo nullus sit ordo maior episcopo."
106. Ibid.: "Nichil actum fuerit communicato consilio et precedente deliberatione
eorum qui representant totam civitatem, ex quo ex inspectione librorum in quibus consueuerunt describi reformationes et deliberationes que fiunt per ipsos qui representant
totum populum apparebit in ipso nullam deliberationem scriptam fore super hoc."
107. Ibid.: "Sed priores et alii nominati in processu non habent iurisdictionem supremam nec perpetuam et insolidam, quia illa est penes populum sicut erat in populo
Romano antequam esse translata in principe."

penalized for an act that had not been properly ratified by its governing body.[108] Torti repeated the claim of all the other jurists that the cardinal was held for his safety and that the priors did not have hostile intentions against him when they brought him to the Palazzo Vecchio. Like Sozzini, he emphasized that the cardinal was held hostage to protect Florentines in Rome.[109] All of these points led Torti to the conclusion that Sixtus's bull was unjust.

In the second part of his consilium, Torti dealt with the validity of Sixtus's bull. The key element was whether Sixtus had the power to ignore the strictures of *Pastoralis* when he excommunicated Lorenzo without a summons. Bartolus and everyone else thought that the summons was part of natural law. God himself had cited Adam.[110] Citing Johannes of Imola, Torti added that the prince must have an examination and inquisition of the truth in his court because this is required by the law of nations. Although the prince may receive his jurisdiction from God, the Lord did not give him the power to enact anything without just cause or wrongfully.[111]

Torti treated the power of the prince at the end of his consilium, and he outlined the premises that might justify Sixtus's actions. Some jurists maintained that the prince could take away a subject's right to a defense if he exercised his fullness of power in a civil case, but not in criminal cases or in a case of status.[112] Sixtus had clearly intended to use his ab-

108. Ibid.: "Non inferatur ad civitatem vel simile corpus fictum in his que stricte debent intelligi prout in penalibus ut dixi . . . Et ex hoc dico quod priores et alii representantes civitatem licet denegaverint liberationem ipsius d. cardinalis, tamen ex quo ipsa denegatio fuit excusabilis ut infra dicam, non possumus dicere quod veniant puniendi, et consequenter ex quo non veniunt puniendi non est quid imputetur ipsi civitati si ipsos non punierit."

109. Ibid.: "Et sic iure merito predicta ratione licuit ipsis Florentinis denegare dictam liberationem ex quo suberat iustus timor, ne mercatores et cives Florentini ut dixi Rome offenderentur, prout ex dictis confessionibus verisimiliter et probabiliter poterant dubitare."

110. Ibid.: "pars ipsa ideo venit citanda ut possit se defendere adeo quod citatio dicitur de iure naturali ut concludunt omnes, Bar. primo in extravaganti Ad reprimendam in glossa in verbo 'Et figuram iudicii' ubi dixit quod Deus omnipotens citavit primum hominem delinquentem dicens, 'Adam ubi es.'"

111. Ibid.: "et idem firmant canoniste maxime Joh. de Imola in d. Clem. Pastoralis . . . Not. quod papa non potest, ergo per principem auferri neque tolli cum sit de iure naturali . . . et maxime cum coram principe requiratur ventilatio et examinatio veritatis, quia inquisitio veritatis est de iuregentium et licet solemnitates legum princeps non teneatur observare, observantia tamen iurisgentium non debet deesse, quia pertinet ad naturalem equitatem . . . licet princeps habeat iurisdictionem a Deo ut in auth. quomodo oport. episcop. circa principium, tamen Deus non dedit eis iurisdictionem statuendi aliquid indebite et iniuste."

112. Ibid.: "Not. quod princeps potest de plenitudine potestatis alicui auferre defensionem, et hoc in causa civili et pecuniaria, secus in causa criminali vel in causa status, ut extra de re iud. Clem. Pastoralis."

solute power in his bull.[113] Consequently, observed Torti, one might argue that the prince is always presumed to have acted with cause, particularly in doubtful cases.[114]

Torti thought that even if these premises were correct, which he greatly doubted, the prince needed two things: his fullness of power and a just cause. The pope and the emperor are bound by the provisions of natural law and the law of nations.[115] Baldus, said Torti, had insisted that the prince was bound by his own contract. God placed the prince over positive law, but not over the law of nations or natural law. The prince may dispense from natural law, but only with legitimate cause.[116]

Lorenzo and the priors were not subject to the pope. Therefore, the pope could not exercise fullness of power over them and his act cannot have been presumed to have been carried out with cause:[117]

> This is proven by a simple point of reason. Otherwise *Pastoralis* would throw us upon the whims of the wind if we would say that when the prince moves against someone not subject to him that he would be presumed to have cause. *Pastoralis* would stipulate in vain that the judgment of the prince is not valid when rendered without a summons of a defendant who was not his subject, because the judgment would always be legitimate, since the prince would always be presumed to have cause. That is false and absurd.

113. Ibid.: "Sed in casu nostro princeps intendit uti plenitudine potestatis, ergo valuit sine citatione; et quod voluerit uti plenitudine potestatis deducitur, nam paria sunt principem exprimere se uti velle potestate absoluta vel gerere actum supra potestatem ordinariam, et apponere clausulas 'non obstante,' ita Bald."

114. Ibid.: "Nec obstat etiam predictis si diceretur quod valet processus principis sine citatione, dummodo subsit iusta causa . . . que iusta causa in dubio presumitur in principe secundum communiter doctores."

115. Ibid.: "Quia respondeo si per predictum fundamentum est verum in se de quo summe dubito, ex supradictis tamen dico quod ad hoc ut procedat quod requiruntur duo: primum quod utatur plenitudine potestatis, secundum quod moveatur ex iusta causa que subsistat quod deducitur, quia papa vel imperator non sunt supra iusgentium vel naturale."

116. Ibid.: "Et ideo dixit [Baldus] quod princeps obligatur ex suo contractu, licet enim Deus subfecerit principi leges, non tamen subicit iusgentium vel naturale, et sic quando per eos dispensari conceditur, dicitur concedi de plenitudine potestatis, c. Proposuit, de conces. preb. et ideo dixit Innoc. in c. Innotuit, de elect. quod princeps non valet uti plenitudine potestatis nisi ex causa, et ideo numquam conceditur talis dispensatio nisi subsistente legittima causa, ut firmant communiter doctores in l. finali, C. si contra ius vel uti. pub. et in c. Que in ecclesiarum, de constit."

117. Ibid.: "Hinc infero quod cum contra nominatos in processu tanquam non subditos non habeat plenitudinem potestatis merito non potest tollere citationem, etiam ex causa, propterea quando agitur contra non subditos, non est verum quod causa in dubio presumatur, ut firmat d. Abbas in d.c. Que in ecclesiarum. Et probatur per punctam rationis, nam alias Clem. Pastoralis, nobis serviret de vento si diceremus quod quando agitur contra non subditum quod in dubio presumatur causa in principe, quia frustra diceretur ibi non valere sententiam principis contra non subditum sine citatione, quia immo semper valeret cum semper presumeretur causa, quod est falsum et absurdum, d. Clem. Pastoralis."

If the case were notorious, a summons would not have been required, but the evidence that Sixtus gathered against Lorenzo hardly supported the label of notorious.[118]

Torti rehearsed, in general terms, the evidence that exonerated Lorenzo. He had been wounded, he was not present, and he did not order the archbishop's execution. Antonio de Butrio had argued that the pope could render a judgment without a summons in notorious crimes, but his opinion had been rejected by Johannes de Imola and Panormitanus.[119] Finally, after some rather tortuous argumentation, Torti concluded that the prince could dispense with a summons when it was notorious that a defense must not be granted, but this crime did not fall into that category.[120] Sixtus had been required to summon Lorenzo. Therefore, his bull is not valid.[121]

These consilia, although *ex parte* defenses of the Medici, provide valuable historical information about Florentine perceptions of the aftermath of the murder in the cathedral. The jurists interpreted the facts of the Pazzi Conspiracy to support the interests of the Medici, but their testimony should, nonetheless, be taken seriously as an antidote to papal propaganda. Their "historical arguments" are not contradicted by other sources. Without a doubt, these consilia contain a "Florentine voice" that could have been heard in the streets of the city.

To make that voice heard, both sides enlisted the new technology of printing. Sixtus used the printing press to give wide dissemination of his accusations. Lorenzo sought legal advice from law professors in and outside Florence and hurried one consilium, de Tortis's, into print.

118. Ibid.: "Respondeo quod hec qualitas notorietatis non est vera, quia multa sunt in hoc processu que non sunt notoria nec de sui natura esse potuerunt."

119. Ibid.: "Et similiter per illum textum reprobatur alia decisio Anto. de But. quam posuit in c. Cum olim, de re iud. ibi dixit quod speciale est in processu pape quod citatio non requiratur in huiusmodi notoriis et tamen in d. c. Sepe, est processus pape. Ad idem est tex. in d. Clem. Pastoralis, ubi imperator asserit esse notorium, et tamen sine citatione procedi non potuit. Ideo Joh. de Imol. et d. Abb. reprobant dictam oppinionem domini Anton. ponentes quod regula quod iura requirentia citationem in actu vel anulantia actum factum sine citatione, ita habent locum in principe sicut inferiore per d. Clem. Pastoralis."

120. Ibid.: "Et concludendo in hoc articulo illa videtur communis opinio et vera ex hiis que supra deduxi et ex mente doctorum in locis de quibus supra, quod ubi notorium sit defensionem non competere, tunc procedi possit sine citatione, quia tunc non tollitur defensio si non subest, et ita salvetur opinio eorum qui dicunt citationem non requiri. Vbi vero apparet defensionem competere, ut in casu nostro, vel esset dubium, procedat opinio tenentium quod requiritur citatio, et sic opiniones doctorum de quibus supra et quam ultra doctores supra deductos."

121. Ibid.: "Citatio enim in casu nostro requiritur ad finem, ut possumus nos defendere et allegare causas quare in dictas penas non inciderimus, et maxime in casu nostro ubi clare et vere poterant allegari et de ipsis constari facere ut supra deduxi, que si omittatur reddit actum nullum."

The jurists' defense was not timid. Francesco Salviati had attacked the Palazzo Vecchio with a group of men who were not wearing clerical clothing, and Lorenzo did not participate in the decision to hang him and the others. He did, however, sanction their deaths after the fact. Lorenzo, the priors, and the people of Florence had good reasons for responding to the revolt in the way that they did. Whether the "facts" of the jurists correspond to the truth may be argued. They do reflect the best propaganda effort that the Medici regime could muster; the consilia were not as elegant as Poliziano's defense but were undoubtedly more effective.

Machiavelli saw little that was positive in the sordid story of the Pazzi Conspiracy; he wrote that it produced "stinking fruit." [122] Unlike the conflict between Henry VII and Robert of Naples, it was not a harbinger of new principles of jurisprudence. Nevertheless, the jurists' defense of Lorenzo de' Medici provides a fitting end to the story we have been telling. By the end of the fifteenth century, Lorenzo's dramatic letter to René of Anjou contained more than just rhetoric. Law stood staunchly on his side. In their consilia, the lawyers summarized two centuries of juristic thought about the relationship of the prince and the law. Their task was not daunting. The commentaries of the jurists on the decretal *Pastoralis cura* had created a sophisticated doctrine of "due process" that Pope Sixtus violated when he condemned Lorenzo without a hearing. Defendants' rights to present their cases in court had become so embedded in the *ius commune* that even the prince's absolute power could not dislodge them.

The arguments of the Florentines' jurists were spread far and wide in the sixteenth century. All four consilia that we have discussed were reprinted frequently, and printers signaled their importance. The rubric of Francesco Accolti's consilium that Jacobus Giunta printed at Lyon in 1546 read:[123]

> This famous and notable consilium in which many articles are wisely and extensively examined was written to show the justice of the Florentines, when they were placed under interdict by Pope Sixtus IV, because of their most just defense of their state and because of the most cruel death of Giuliano de' Medici and its vindication.

122. *Istorie fiorentine,* book 7, chapter 31, p. 430: "malissimi frutti."

123. Franciscus de Accoltis Aretinus, *Consilia* (Lyon: Jacobus Giunta: 1546), Consilium 163: "Famosum hoc et notabile consilium in quo quam plures articuli mature et copiose examinantur factum est ad ostendendam Florentinorum iustitiam quando a Sixto pontifice maximo interdicti sunt ob status eorum iustissimam defensionem et ob magnifici Juliani Medicis acerbissimam mortem et vindicatam."

Although the following information about subsequent printings is not complete, it demonstrates the defusion of the consilia. Accolti's consilia were printed in Pisa (1482), Pavia (1494 and 1503), Venice (1572), and in Lyon, the great center of book production (1529, 1536, and 1546). The consilia of the Florentine college and Sozzini were printed in Milan (1496), Zürich (1518), Venice (1580), and Speyer (1603). Girolamo Torti's solitary consilium gained renown and wide circulation when it was reprinted with the consilia of Antonio de Butrio. Leonard Pachel, a distinguished printer, included it in an edition of Butrio's consilia published at Milan (1508).[124] This edition with Torti's consilium was reprinted in Lyon (1534 and 1541), and Venice (1575 and 1582). Like *Pastoralis cura* and the commentaries on it, these consilia became an important part of the *ius commune*'s literature treating sovereignty, power, rights, and due process of law.

124. In the Munich, Staatsbibliothek copy of Pachel's edition, signature 2 Decis. 268m, is the following handwritten note about Torti's death and burial: "Iste celeberrimus consulens sepultus est Ticini in ecclesia diuini Iacobi (apud) portam diue uirginis dell'pertica, eiusque epitaphium est tale quod ego Franciscus Rasso Burgkardus iurisutriusque doctor dum 1543 ibidem eram rescripsi: 'Hieronimi Torti iurecon. etc. reliquum quod superest hoc lapide conditur. Hic Ticini tribus et triginta annis legendi munere perfunctus graui correptus morbo in fata concessit. Anno natiuitatis Dominicae 1484, v. idus Aug.'" My thanks to Wolfgang P. Müller for this transcription and for information about the editions of Butrio's consilia.

Epilogue

The Sixteenth Century and Beyond

[Quidem] allegantes maiestatem
tantum esse in imperatore . . . sed
ipsi perperam sunt locuti, nam et in rege
dicitur esse maiestas . . . . Nihil
enim sonat aliud maiestas quam
maioritas, et ideo etiam
populus, qui est superior,
dicitur habere maiestatem.
— Marinus de Caramanico

Niccolò Machiavelli's prince has cast a long, somber shadow over European political thought for five centuries. If every thick book contains a good, slim volume struggling to free itself, Machiavelli's thin volume has spawned a remarkable number of thick books that toil to explain how a man of genius, talent, imagination, and learning could have written such a cynical view of the prince's purpose.[1] Although scholars have quarreled about Machiavelli's novelty and whether he radically changed the presuppositions of earlier political thought, they have reached some agreement about Machiavelli's intentions when he wrote *The Prince* and about the little book's importance in the history of political thought. They concur that Machiavelli wrote it to ingratiate himself with the Medicis, to instruct his readers in the exercise of political power, and to subvert the principle that power should be limited by the restraints of reason and morality. Modern scholars agree about little else, and a few scholars have found reason to dissent from even these rather self-evident points.

Machiavelli can be refracted through many lenses. He was a human-

---

1. Scholarship on Machiavelli has become a heavy, rather than a cottage, industry. Excellent studies abound. Of those in English, Quentin Skinner's *Machiavelli* (New York: 1981) is another excellent, thin book with a good critical bibliography. J. G. A. Pocock's *Machiavellian Moment* and Felix Gilbert's *Machiavelli and Guicciardini: Politics and History in Sixteenth-Century Florence* (Princeton: 1965) are the two most influential books written in the last twenty-five years on Machiavelli's thought. De Grazia's *Machiavelli in Hell* combines flashes of insight with eccentric assertions.

ist and steeped in the *Studia humanitatis.* He was a republican who
drew his inspiration from the republican traditions of the Italian city-
states and from ancient republican Rome. He was a diplomat, adviser
to princes, and historian who took an active part in the political affairs
of Florence until his fall from power in late 1512 and early 1513, when
he was dismissed, arrested, condemned, imprisoned, and finally exiled.

It has been often said and remains true that the Machiavellian Rev-
olution's, to use Quentin Skinner's term, most radical act was to over-
throw the Christian model of a prince. Medieval and Renaissance hand-
books for princes outlined the duties, obligations, and virtues to which
a ruler should adhere. As Skinner has put it:[2]

> If we examine the moral treatises of Machiavelli's contemporaries we find
> these arguments tirelessly reiterated. But when we turn to *The Prince* we
> find this aspect of humanist morality suddenly and violently overturned.

Scholars have tempered this vision of Machiavelli by placing *The Discourses* and *The Prince* cheek to jowl or by separating them completely.
The republicanism of *The Discourses* permits us to forgive—at least
partially—the author of *The Prince* his transgressions. Or *The Prince*
can be seen as an aberration produced by a desperate office-seeker.[3]

That Machiavelli sundered the traditional bonds of Christian morality governing the behavior of rulers in *The Prince* is a platitude. The
prince's "virtù" was secular and not shackled by a tender moral conscience. When he created an amoral prince, Machiavelli conformed to
the spirit of his times. Many Renaissance writers and artists had long
since liberated artistic expression from traditional moral values. In his
Defense of Poetry, for example, Giovanni Boccaccio had pleaded that
morality and literature should be separated, and as H. W. Janson has
eloquently written, the bronze David of Donatello "would seem to be
the first major work of Renaissance art to pose Boccaccio's question in
visual form."[4]

Christian morality was not the only stick with which a prince could
be measured. We have seen that the jurists created a jurisprudence gov-

---

2. Skinner, *Machiavelli* 37.
3. For a summing up of interpretative scholarship on Machiavelli, the last chapter
of Mark Hulliung, *Citizen Machiavelli* (Princeton: 1983) 219–257, is a useful discussion
of the issues raised in this paragraph. See also Joseph M. Levine, "Method in the History
of Ideas: More, Machiavelli and Quentin Skinner," *Annals of Scholarship: Metastudies
of the Humanities and Social Sciences* 3 (1986) 37–60, for a analysis of some approaches
to Machiavelli.
4. H. W. Janson, *The Sculpture of Donatello* (Princeton: 1963) 86.

erning the prince that also imposed standards of behavior on him. Machiavelli was not a jurist, and *The Prince* was not a legal work. Nevertheless, we may ask how Bartolomeo Scala, for example, a friend of Machiavelli's father, might have responded to the precocious pamphlet of his friend's son. Scala was a key figure in the Florentine government at the time of the Pazzi conspiracy and trained in the jurisprudence of the *ius commune*. He very likely would have recognized that Cesare Borgia's summary execution of Rimirro de Orco without a trial violated the same juristic principles that Pope Sixtus IV had broken when he excommunicated Lorenzo de' Medici. Machiavelli undoubtedly wrote that Borgia's deed was "worthy of imitation by others" without fully understanding the long legal tradition that Borgia ignored.[5]

Scala would have noticed that Machiavelli's prince wielded power that broke the established norms of the *ius commune*. We have traced three centuries of thought about the prince's relationship to law and have seen that the jurists insisted that the prince must always act for the common good, with honesty, for reasons of necessity, and with cause. When Machiavelli wrote that "it is necessary for a prince who wishes to maintain his position to learn how not to be good, and to use this knowledge or not to use it according to necessity," he rejected four centuries of juristic reflections on the limitations of power.[6] The "necessitas" of the lawyers was not bereft of reason, cause, and the public good; rather, reason, cause, and the public good defined necessity.[7]

Had he been a trained jurist, Machiavelli would have rejected the jurisprudence of the *ius commune* as easily has he spurned the moral principles of Christianity. His genius did not wear traditions easily. With his usual perspicacity, Pocock has noted that unlike the absolute monarch whose position was still defined "by his relation to a body of law which was part of the complex scheme of his own legitimation, [Machiavelli's] 'new prince' lacked legitimacy altogether."[8] This was

5. Niccolò Machiavelli, *The Prince*, trans. P. Bondanella and Mark Musa (New York-Oxford: 1984) 26. De Grazia's discussion of this scene, *Machiavelli in Hell*, 327–330, in which he argues that Machiavelli, "our jurist," wished to make "law alive" with a staged punishment is a particularly unusual interpretation of this passage. That Machiavelli should have "had in mind the humane purpose stated in Justinian's *Institutes*," when Borgia, the prince, the *lex animata*, staged the murder of Remirro offers a series of extraordinary assertions that are difficult to reconcile with the norms of the *ius commune* or with classical Roman law.

6. Ibid., p. 52.

7. Not all scholars would agree that Machiavelli's "necessità" is different from the jurists, see J. H. Whitfield, *Machiavelli* (New York: 1975) and Hulliung, *Machiavelli* 224–226.

8. Pocock, *Machiavellian Moment* 159.

so, as Pocock certainly implies, because Machiavelli's prince had no relationship to the law.

Machiavelli was an exception in the sixteenth century. His iconoclasm was unique. Lesser minds were shaped and formed by the principles of law established by four centuries of juristic thought. Due process and absolute power continued to be defined by the doctrines of the *ius commune*. In this concluding epilogue, I will illustrate the vigor and durability of these norms in the dawn of the "Age of Absolutism."

In one of his last writings, *De thesauris in Peru*, Bartolomé de Las Casas launched a trenchant attack on the Spanish conquest of the New World and the subjugation of the Indians to Spanish rule. He had devoted his life to the defense of the Indians and had marshalled a corps of medieval jurists to march for his cause. Although we cannot be sure that Las Casas studied law at the University of Salamanca, he did attend a law school at some time during his life. Only a lawyer could have written the sophisticated legal brief that *De thesauris in Peru* was.[9]

Las Casas built his first line of defense on the premise that legitimate secular power existed outside the Church. The Indians' dominium was just, and Spaniards did not have the right to usurp the Indians' title. Las Casas exploited a tradition supporting his contention in the writings of the medieval jurists that stretched back to the thirteenth century.[10]

Upon first reading *De thesauris* twenty years ago, I thought that one of Las Casas's arguments seemed tendentious and strained. In the last pages of the work, he raised the question of whether the Spaniards could have deprived Indians of their possessions if they had never been called or summoned or received due process of law.[11]

I did not know then that these ideas of due process had become fundamental principles of late medieval jurisprudence. It is not longer

---

9. The literature on Las Casas is enormous. On his legal thought see K. Pennington, "Bartolomé de Las Casas and the Tradition of Medieval Law," *Church History* 39 (1970) 149–161; for a discussion of whether Las Casas adopted a doctrine of natural rights from the medieval lawyers, see Brian Tierney, "Aristotle and the American Indians—Again: Two Critical Discussions," *Cristianesimo nella storia* 12 (1991) 295–322.

10. Ibid., p. 159–160. See also James Muldoon, "*Extra ecclesiam non est imperium*: The Canonists and the Legitimacy of Secular Power," SG 9 (1966) 551–580. More recently, Muldoon's *Popes, Lawyers and Infidels: The Church and the Non-Christian World 1250–1550* (Middle Ages; Philadelphia: 1979) discusses the legal background (p. 3–71) and Las Casas (pp. 140–143, 150–153).

11. *De thesauris in Peru*, Latin text with Spanish translation by Angel Losada García (Madrid: 1958) 394: "Contra predeterminata possunt nonnulla opponi et refricari praesertim quoad possessionem capiendam illius orbis sine vocatione vel citatione incolis facta, vel ordine iuris servato."

surprising that Las Casas resolved this problem by writing a long medi-
tation on the issues raised by Pope Clement V's decretal, *Pastoralis*. He
conceded that the pope could omit a summons if he were rendering
judgment in matters touching ecclesiastical matters or prebends. He
could also judge immediate subjects without summoning them.[12] The
pope can supply any defect in positive law, but he may not violate principles of natural law. Las Casas noted pointedly that the pope or the
prince cannot rely on his fullness of power to correct all defects of law—
plenitudo potestatis corrects only defects of civil law.[13] Rather than
being an interesting flight of juristic fancy, Las Casas had put forward
a respectable argument: because elements of due process had been
omitted, the Indians had been unjustly plundered of their property. He
needed good weapons, and *Pastoralis* augmented his arsenal.

The preservation of medieval doctrines of due process was not re-
Las Casas based his theory of dominium on Pope Innocent IV's
formulation that non-Christians had legitimate dominium. However,
Innocent had allowed two exceptions to the general rule that Christians
could not attack infidels without military cause: if non-believers violated natural law or if they would not allow Christian missionaries into
their territories.[14] Las Casas's opponents alleged that the Indians were
guilty of both wrongs, but he parried these objections to his argument
with the support of *Pastoralis*. He conceded that the pope could institute Christian kings to rule over infidels, but he must act only with due
process of law (servato ordine iuris) and with the free consent of the
people.[15]

The preservation of medieval doctrines of due process was not restricted to polemical writers like Las Casas. The tradition flourished in

---

12. Ibid.: "Papa potest ommittere citationem in sententia definitiva etc. Verum est in
beneficialibus et ecclesiasticis cum legitima et inter subditos intra ecclesiam. Sed extra eam
nihil ad eum coercitiva iurisdictione uti aut per eam judicare ut per multa iam probata
claret."

13. Ibid. 403–404: "Potest etiam supplere iuris defectus et solemnitatum quae non
sunt fundatae in iure naturali; nec valet si dicat princeps vel papa in sua dispositione
supplentes omnem defectum ex plenitudine potestatis, quia intelliguntur defectus iuris
civilis sed non autem naturalis, ut in Clemen. Pastoralis, de re iud. et ibi per Cardinalem
§ penult." For the origins of the concept of *defectus iuris*, see Pennington, *Pope and
Bishops* 64–65.

14. Muldoon, *Popes, Lawyers* 10–11.

15. Las Casas, *De thesauris* 404: "Licet causa fidei praedicandae et gentium illarum
convertendarum summus pontifex potuerit reges nostros instituere quantum in eo fuit in
principes universales illius orbis, intelligitur sine praejudicio notabili regum, dominorum
et iurium suorum et populorum incolarumque ipsum orbem inhabitantium et servato iuris
ordine et consensu habito libero eorumdem dictam institutionem habente ratam caeteris-
que aliis conditionibus et debitis circunstantiis in lege naturali fundatis." Cf. the observa-
tions of Muldoon, *Popes, Lawyers* 151–152.

the sixteenth century and beyond. Due process of law became part of the intellectual baggage of every jurist. They continued to believe that key elements of judicial procedure rested upon the sturdy foundation of natural law.[16] In his treatise on natural law, Samuel Pufendorf wrote that a judge must never render a judgment without having heard the testimony of the parties.[17] Johannes Althusius acknowledged that the petition, summons, proof, and judgment were all elements of natural law. Other parts of judicial procedure could be changed or eliminated, but not these.[18]

When Benedict Carpzov wrote his treatise on procedural law of Saxony, he retold the story of the judgment of Adam and Eve. The twelfth-century canonist, Paucapalea, had first cited the trial in Paradise as an exemplum illustrating proper judicial procedure.[19] Later jurists connected the judgment of Adam with the establishment of the *ordo iudiciarius*. The argument still had persuasive force in the seventeenth century. God, declared Carpzov, instituted judicial procedure when he summoned Adam to defend himself. God heard Adam's defense and then rendered his condemnation of Adam and Eve.[20] Carpzov noted that the elements of the judicial process that must be observed because they were a part of natural law were the summons of litigants, the presentation of evidence, and the defense of the parties.[21]

Knut Wolfgang Nörr has sketched the history of these ideas in later German juristic thought. In the eighteenth century, Justus Henning

16. The best discussion of the later period is Knut Wolfgang Nörr, *Naturrecht und Zivilprozeß: Studien zur Geschichte des deutschen Zivilprozeßrechts während der Naturrechtsperiode bis zum beginnenden 19. Jahrhundert* (Tübinger rechtswissenschaftliche Abhandlungen 41; Tübingen: 1976). The following paragraphs are based on Nörr's book.

17. Samuel Pufendorf, *Elementa iurisprudentiae universalis* (Hagae Comitis: 1660) 1.12.25: "causa utrinque nondum liquido perspecta atque cognita partiumque rationibus et excusationibus non auditis." Nörr, *Naturrecht* 4.

18. Johannes Althusius, *Dicaeologicae libri tres, totum et universum ius in quo utimur methodice complectentes* 3.54 (Frankfurt: 1618): "Naturalia requisita ad causam cognoscendum iure gentium vel naturali inducta, quae factum causae et defensionem partium concernunt, hic etiam necessaria, uti est petitio, citatio, probatio, sententia et personarum litigantium legitimatio . . . Caetera abesse vel pro arbitrio mutari possunt." Nörr, *Naturrecht* 6.

19. See chapter 4.

20. Benedict Carpzov, *Processus iuris in foro Saconico* 1.1.3 (Jena: 1657) p. 8: "Quod ut rectius percipiatur, originem primaevam refert acceptam processus iuri divino ac naturali sive gentium, veluti probat actus iudiciarius, quam ipsemet instituit Deus post lapsum protoplastorum in paradiso, cum Adamum ad se tanquam in ius vocavit et ob transgressionem mandati accusavit, eius exceptionem audivit ac postea sententiam tulit condemnatoriam." Nörr *Naturrecht* 6–7.

21. Nörr, *Naturrecht* 7.

Boehmer discussed the *ordo iudiciarius* as an expression of an "ordo naturalis." Subsequently, the principles of natural law that should regulate judicial procedure were incorporated into the Prussian Codes, although their sources were no longer clearly visible.[22]

If we may draw a long and continuous line from the twelfth to eighteenth centuries when we discuss the development of juristic ideas governing due process in judicial proceedings, the lines delineating the evolution of *potestas absoluta* and juristic definitions of sovereignty are neither neat nor agreed upon.

During the sixteenth century, jurists described the authority of the prince with the same terminology that their predecessors had used since the thirteenth. The prince had "plenitudo potestatis," "potestas absoluta," "ordinata," and was "legibus solutus." Historians cannot agree, however, on whether these terms shifted their meanings in the sixteenth century. The key issue is whether medieval jurists attributed "true" sovereignty to the prince and whether sixteenth-century jurists interpreted these terms as granting the prince absolute power, untrammeled by any limitations.

It is beyond the scope of this book to undo this Gordian knot. We have seen that medieval jurists interpreted these terms in a variety of ways—from what might be described as "constitutional" to "absolutistic." A limited comparison of medieval and early modern definitions of absolute power, however, might be useful without charting the range of meanings that absolute power had in the writings of the late medieval and early modern jurists and publicists in grim detail.

The great Italian-Protestant jurist turned Englishman, Albericus Gentilis, wrote a tract in 1605 in which he discussed the nature of monarchy. He observed that royal power is absolute and without limits. The prince is "legibus solutus," and what pleases the prince has the force of law, for his will is held to be reason.[23] To this point, Hostiensis might have been the author of these words. But then Albericus Gentilis continued: "And they define absolute power as that through which he can take away a right of another, even a great right, without cause."[24] At this, his thirteenth century predecessors would have parted company with him, but not, perhaps, Albericus de Rosate and Guillaume Pierre de Godin.[25]

22. Nörr, *Naturrecht* 8–30.
23. Albericus Gentilis, *Regales disputationes tres* (London: 1605) 8, 11, 24.
24. Ibid., p. 10.
25. See chapter 3.

Another example from the British isles is William Barclay, a Scotsman, educated on the continent in law and subsequently a professor of Roman law at Pont-à-Mousson and Angers. His most significant work of political theory was *De regno et regali potestate*.[26] A. J. Carlyle and Quentin Skinner have called him an absolutist and staunch proponent of divine right monarchy. If one reads Barclay carefully, however, his language and thought is simply a statement of the Roman law principle "princeps legibus solutus est,"—the prince may transcend positive law through his absolute power—and he borrows extensively, often with direct quotes, from the glosses of the canonists.[27] He did not depart, as Albericus de Rosate seems to have done, from Roman and canonical thought governing and limiting the authority of the prince.

To bridge the chasm between medieval and early modern thought on sovereignty, I shall examine the best-known commentary on a ruler's absolute power in the sixteenth century, Jean Bodin's *De republica*.[28] Quentin Skinner has summarized sovereignty in Bodin's *De republica* as "high, absolute, and perpetual power over citizens." The prince "gives laws to all his subjects" without seeking anyone's or any group's consent. Bodin's prince was absolute "and even if his commands are never 'just or honest,' it is still 'not lawful for the subject to break the laws of his prince.' " According to Skinner, Bodin seems to have broken sharply with traditional definitions of absolute power; his prince was absolute as few others before him were.[29]

Bodin created an exalted and rarified vision of political power. Skinner is not the only one dazzled by it. A. London Fell has written that "Roman law provides a framework for his [Bodin's] ideas [about absolute power, but] . . . [his work] does not reveal a shaping influence of medieval jurisprudence."[30] Other historians have given Bodin less

26. (Paris: 1600).
27. R. W. Carlyle and A. J. Carlyle, *A History of Mediaeval Political Theory in the West* (Edinburgh and London: 1962) vol. 6, p. 448, n. 1.
28. The literature on Bodin is extensive. In what follows, I shall cite only the most important items in English. See Julian H. Franklin, *Jean Bodin and the Rise of Absolutist Theory* (Cambridge: 1973). A. London Fell's eccentric and idiosyncratic book, *Origins of Legislative Sovereignty and the Legislative State*, vol. 3: *Bodin's Humanistic Legal System and Rejection of "Medieval Political Theology"* (Königstein-Boston, Mass.: 1987). There is neither a critical edition of his Latin nor his French *Republic* nor a complete translation into any modern Language.
29. This paragraph is based, and the quotations taken from, Quentin Skinner, *The Foundations of Modern Political Thought*, vol. 2: *The Age of Reformation* (Cambridge: 1978) 285–288.
30. Fell, *Bodin's Humanistic Legal System* 103. Kenneth Douglas McRae in his Introduction to Richard Knolles's English translation of the *Republic* in 1606 (Harvard Political Classics; Cambridge: 1962) p. A13: "Bodin's . . . analysis of political authority . . . went far beyond the work of his predecessors." See also M. J. Tooley's introduction to

dramatic readings and have recognized his debt to the past. Julian Franklin and Ralph Giesey have emphasized Bodin's debt to the medieval juristic tradition and moderated the more extravagant claims of other historians.[31]

Bodin himself denied that his *De republica* broke decisively with the past in his prefatory letter to the book.[32] The controversy surrounding the nature of Bodin's contribution to political thought has continued unabated, and I shall examine Bodin's handling of the themes that we have been treating in this book in order to assess how much he adhered to or departed from the thought of the earlier jurists.

Bodin discussed absolute power in Book 1, chapter 8, of the *De republica* and adopted the terminology of power that the jurists had incorporated into the language of jurisprudence. "Maiestas," he wrote, cannot be limited by time, by a greater power, or by any law.[33] "Maiestas" meant that the prince was not bound by the law.[34] In other words, Bodin equated "maiestas" with the prince's absolute power to change, abrogate, or derogate positive law. He explained that the kings of France were loosed from the law and possessed absolute power.[35] To justify his contention, he cited Oldradus de Ponte's consilium that we discussed in chapter 5,[36] in which Oldradus had equated kings with the emperor and insisted that they are not subject to imperial jurisdiction. Bodin defined absolute power with language that is redolent with echoes of the past:[37]

---

his partial translation of the *Republic* (Blackwell's Political Texts; New York: 1955) xiv–xxxix.

31. Franklin, *Jean Bodin and the Rise of Absolutist Theory* 102–113 and Ralph E. Giesey, "Medieval Jurisprudence in Bodin's Concept of Sovereignty," *Jean Bodin: Verhandlungen der Internationalen Bodin-Tagung in München*, ed. Horst Denzer (München: Studien zur Politik, 16; München: 1973) 167–186. See also Giorgio Rebuffa, "Jean Bodin e il 'Princeps legibus solutus.'" *Materiali per una storia della cultura giuridica* 2 (1972) 89–123.

32. Quoted by Franklin, *Jean Bodin* 102.

33. Jean Bodin, *De republica libri sex* (Frankfurt: 1594 and 1609) book 1, chapter 8, 123: "Principio definiendi fuit maiestas quam nec philosophorum nec iurisconsultorum quisquam definiit, quum tamen nihil ad Reipublicae naturam intelligendum maius, aut magis necessarium esse videatur." Ibid., p. 125: "Maiestas vero nec maiore potestate nec legibus ullis, nec tempore definitur."

34. Ibid., p. 129: "Diximus, potestatem legibus solutam congruere maiestati."

35. Ibid., p. 132 " . . . nihilominus tamen rex ipse comitiorum popularium ubique arbiter est ac censor, ut vel populi rogationes probare, vel repudiare possit, quod ipsum Castulonum, deque Francorum regibus confirmant; quos etiam potestatem absolutam, sic enim loquuntur, habere tradunt."

36. Ibid.: "Petrus Belluga cap. Extremo, titulo 10, n. 10 et Oldradus consil. 69."

37. Ibid.: "Quid autem sit absoluta, vel potius soluta lege potestas, nemo definiit. Nam si legibus omnibus solutam definiamus, nullus omnino princeps iura maiestatis habere comperiatur, cum omnes teneat lex divina, lex item naturae, tum etiam lex omnium gentium communis, quae a naturae legibus ac divinis divisas habet rationes."

What is absolute power, or rather power that has been freed from the law? No one has yet defined it. If we define absolute power as that which is above all laws, then no prince possesses the rights of sovereignty. All princes are bound by divine, natural, and the common law of all nations.

Bodin's definition could have been written by any fourteenth-century jurist. As we have seen in chapters 3 and 4, the jurists had always limited the prince's authority by the principles of natural law.

Medieval and Renaissance jurists limited the prince's authority through natural law and by an amorphous concept that they called "status regni" or, in the Church, "status ecclesiae." [38] They defined the state of the realm or the state of the Church as an inviolable body of law, custom, and tradition that was not subject to the authority of the prince. Bodin declared that all laws from which the prince derives his "imperium" cannot be abrogated or derogated. An example, he noted, was the Salic law from which French kings derived their authority and which was the very foundation of the kingdom.[39] This sovereignty, he argued, could not be diminished by assemblies of the people.[40]

Natural law was the kernel of medieval jurisprudence that sprouted into a coherent intellectual system harnessing the will of the prince. Bodin adopted all the limitations of the prince's sovereignty that the jurists had developed during the prior three centuries:[41]

> Those who state that princes are loosed from laws and contracts give great injury to immortal God and nature, unless they except the laws of God and of nature, as well as property and rights protected by just contracts with private persons.

To support his allegation, he cited Accursius's famous gloss to *Princeps* in a marginal footnote, reaching back three centuries for an authority to define princely power. As Brian Tierney brilliantly demonstrated when he dissected Accursius's gloss thirty years ago, although modern historians misread him, Bodin would have understood Accursius's ref-

38. Pennington, *Pope and Bishops* 68–69, n. 82 and Tierney, *Foundations* 50–53, 58–59, 194–195 (status ecclesiae): Gaines Post, *Studies in Medieval Legal Thought: Public Law and the State, 1100–1322* (Princeton: 1964) 241–309 (status regni).
39. Ibid., p. 139: "Quantum vero ad imperii leges attinet, cum sint cum ipsa maiestate coniunctae, principes nec eas abrogare nec iis derogare possunt, cuiusmodi est lex Salica, regni huius firmissimum fundamentum."
40. Ibid., p. 143: "Hoc igitur teneamus, principis maiestatem nec comitiorum convocatione nec senatus populique presentia minui."
41. Ibid., p. 153: "Qui autem principes, legibus et pactis conventis solutos esse statuunt, nisi Dei praepotentis ac naturae leges, tum etiam res ac rationes cum privatis iusta conventione contractas excipiant, maximam immortali Deo ac naturae iniuriam inferunt."

erences and allusions as no modern reader can.[42] Accursius held contracts to be inviolable and secure from the arbitrary power of the
prince.[43] His commentary on *Princeps* is an extended discourse on the
prince's obligation to submit himself to positive law.

Medieval and Renaissance jurists distinguished between contracts
that the prince made with private citizens and those he concluded with
other princes or cities. They also noted that contracts between citizens
and non-citizens had a different legal status. Bodin did not use these
distinctions to augment princely authority by arguing that the prince
could render some contracts invalid but not others. The prince could
not break any contract he entered into; he was bound to uphold the
law.[44] Bodin then cited a recent event in French history to support his
contention. The French parlement had vigorously maintained that
Charles IX could not sunder his agreements with the clergy without
their consent.[45] Bodin rejected the views of those canonists like Panormitanus, Antonio de Butrio, Francesco Zabarella, and Felinus who had
argued that the prince's contracts were "natural obligations" and only
validated by civil law.[46] Although Bodin may not have understood his
predecessors' thought on contracts accurately, he vigorously rejected
any attempt to enhance the authority of the prince to break contracts
arbitrarily. Who can doubt, he asked rhetorically, that obligations and
contracts have the same nature?[47]

In the preceding pages we have followed the intricate development
of juristic ideas about due process of the law. We have noted that when
earlier jurists discussed due process, they invariably raised the issue
whether the prince could subvert judicial procedure through his absolute power or "plenitudo potestatis." We have also seen that early mod-

42. Ibid.: "Accurs. in l. Princeps, de leg." Tierney, "Origins of the Modern State"
387–397. See also Rebuffa, "Jean Bodin" 107–111.

43. See chapters 1 and 2.

44. Ibid., p. 156: "His ita constitutis, sequitur principem summum pactis conventis
aeque ac privatos obligari sive cum exteris sive cum civibus contraxerit. Cum enim princeps mutuae fidei inter privatos ac legum omnium vindex sit, quanto magis datam a se
fidem ac promissa servare tenetur?"

45. Ibid.: "Quod certe curia Parisiorum gravi oratione ad Carol. ix. regem (marginal
footnote: anno 1563 mense martio) non ita pridem satis indicavit, cum negaret a pactis conventis cum collegio pontificum sine ipsorum consensu regi discedere licere, hac
subiecta ratione, quo ius unicuique tribuere teneretur."

46. Ibid.: "Ex quibus intelligitur labi et errare pontificii iuris interpretes (marginal
note refers to: Panor. Butrio Felin. in c.i de probat. Cardin. consil. 147 Donans) qui
negant principem suis conventionibus non alia quam naturali obligatione teneri, propterea quod obligatio iuris civilis propria sit, qui error eripiendus est."

47. Ibid., p. 156–157: "Cui enim dubium esse possit quin obligatio eiusdem sit
naturae atque conventio?"

ern jurists embraced medieval conceptions of due process. When we
turn to Bodin's *De republica,* we find no discussion of due process or
the prince's role in the judicial process. The explanation for this lacuna
is simple. Bodin limited his prince much more than any medieval jurist
would have thought possible: he barred him from the courtroom. Medieval jurists had seen that when the prince presided over a court, he
violated basic legal principles that forbade a judge to participate in a
case that touched his own interests.[48] In Book 4, chapter 6, of *De republica,* Bodin proves that the prince should not serve as a judge in his kingdom. In contrast to his discussion of the prince's absolute power in
Book 1, chapter 8, he cited very few legal citations and gave only a few
references to earlier jurists.[49] His reticence is not inexplicable. No earlier
jurists argued that the prince could not preside over his own court. The
key question is whether Bodin would have adopted the principles of due
process that we have discussed, even if he banned the prince from the
courtroom. He referred to judicial procedure in one brief, but telling
passage:[50]

> Therefore, if a contract is natural and common to all nations, then obliga-
> tions and actions have the same nature. No contract and obligation can be
> conceived that is not common to nature and all nations.

When Bodin linked actions—judicial procedure—and obligations to
natural law, he accepted the limitations that the *ius commune* placed
on the prince: he could not subvert the judicial process. Bodin cited
three texts of Roman law to justify his statement. One of them, *Ex hoc
iure,* was the key passage in the Digest that discussed the origins of judicial procedure.[51]

Bodin's theory of contracts is a key to understanding his relationship
to past jurisprudence. Although some contracts might arise from the

48. The medieval canonists treated this issue in the early thirteenth century; see
Johannes Teutonicus's gloss to 3 Comp. 2.1.2 v. *alios iudicari,* ed. Pennington (Città del
Vaticano: 1981) p. 169–170. The legal principle was expressed as "potest esse papa iudex
in sua causa, cum alius debeat esse iudex quam actor?" Ernst H. Kantorowicz has written
about this strand of medieval legal thought in "Kingship under the Impact of Scientific
Jurisprudence," *Twelfth-Century Europe and the Foundations of Modern Society,* ed.
M. Clagett, G. Post, and R. Reynolds (Madison: 1961) 89–111 at 94–95.
49. Ibid., pp. 703–731.
50. Ibid., p. 157: "Igitur si conventio naturalis est ac gentium omnium communis,
obligationes quoque et actiones, eiusdem esse naturae, consequens est. At nulla fere
conventio, nulla obligatio cogitari potest, quae non sit et naturae et gentium omnium
communis."
51. Ibid.: "l. Indebiti, de condic. indeb. [Dig. 12.6.15] l. 2, rerum amot. [Dig. 25.2.2]
l. Ex hoc iure, de iustitia [Dig. 1.1.5] Bart. Bald. Ang. ibi." See discussion of this text in
chapter 4, above.

positive laws of a city, the prince would still be obligated to observe those agreements even more than a private person. Furthermore, he cannot abrogate these pacts even with his most exalted power. All the most important jurists, noted Bodin, agree on this point.[52] In two footnotes he cited Baldus's commentaries on contracts and the obligations of the prince.[53] Neither the emperor nor the pope are excluded from these strictures.

Like many other late medieval jurists, Bodin considered Angelus de Ubaldis the chief representative of those jurists who granted the pope and emperor inordinate power. We have seen that Angelus's opinion is not as straightforward as his interpreters imagined, but Bodin dubbed him one of those "pernicious adulators" of the prince's power.[54] Nonetheless, Bodin noted that most jurists—citing Cinus, Panormitanus, Baldus, Bartolus, and others—believed that the prince could not arbitrarily expropriate the goods of private citizens.[55] Bodin concurred.

At this point in *De republica,* Bodin delivered a ringing condemnation of absolute power as an arbitrary and tyrannical authority:[56]

Since the jurists abhor that plague and dispute many things of that sort brilliantly, nevertheless they make an absurd exception. They say that if the

52. Ibid.: "Demus tamen aliquot esse pacta conventa quae a legibus civitatis cuiusque manant; quis negare audeat principem civilibus pactis ac stipulationibus arctius obligari quam privatos? Atque ita obligari ut ne summa quidem potestate quam habet, iis derogare possit? Haec enim gravissimorum iurisconsultorum sententiis recepta et probata videmus."

53. Ibid.: "Bal. in § ult., colum. i. tit. que feudum dare. Mart. Laud. in tract. de principe vers. 305. Bald. in l. Princeps de legibus et in cap. i. § Ad haec col. 5 Castrensis in l. Digna vox de legibus, C. Decius consil. 10 nu. 22. Bal. in l. Ex imperfecto de test. C. Decius consil. 404 nu. 8."

54. Ibid., p. 159: "Neque vero nobis est Romanus imperator aut pontifex excipiendus, ut pernitiosis quibusdam adulatoribus video placuisse, qui Caesarem ac summum pontificem, bona privatorum suo iure diripere posse scripserunt." Bodin cited Angelus in a marginal note to this passage: Ibid.: "Angel. in l.3 § Si is, quod quisque iuris [Dig. 2.2.3]."

55. Ibid.: "Quam opinionem ne pontificii quidem iuris interpretes ferre potuerunt. (marginal footnote added: Panor. in cap. 2 de rebus eccles. non alie. Felin. in cap. Quae in ecclesiarum. Raphael. Fulgo in l.ult. si contra ius C. Faber. in § Sed naturalia nu. 2 instit. Bart. et Bald. in l. Item si verberatum § Si quis, de rei vindic. . . . Bald. et Angel. in l.2 de quadrien. C. Bald. in l. Bene a Zenone col. 2 . . . Cinus in l. Rescripta q.3 de precibus C.)." Their opinions are discussed in the preceding chapters.

56. Ibid.: "Sed cum pestem illam abhorreant, ac multa in eo genere praeclare disputent; illud tamen absurde, quod hanc exceptionem subiiciunt, nisi summa, et ut ipsi loquuntur, absoluta potestate uti velit, quod perinde est, acsi dicerent, vi et armis oppressos cives diripere fas esse. Potentiores enim hoc iure adversus inopiam tenuiorem uti consueverunt, quod praedatorium ius rectissime appellant Germani. At Innocentius iiii. pontifex Romanus, iuris utriusque peritissimus, summam illam, sine legibus, solutam potestatem definiit, ordinario iuri derogare posse. Illi vero summam potestatem ad legum divinarum ac naturalium abrogationem pertinere voluerunt."

prince wishes to use his highest, absolute power, that [he may expropriate private property] as if they would say that it is in accordance with divine law to dispossess citizens with force and arms. The Germans call the right of the powerful to despoil the weak the law of pillage. Pope Innocent IV, who was an extraordinarily learned jurist, defined this power as the authority to derogate ordinary law. They claim that this great power of the prince can abrogate divine and natural law.

Bodin did not embrace—what he thought was—Innocent IV's absolutism. He accepted the commonly held limitations on the prince's absolute power and rejected Angelus de Ubaldis and others who granted the prince great power to subvert the established order. Bodin concluded, just as so many of his predecessors had also concluded, that the prince could not expropriate property without a just cause.[57]

Bodin raised the question of whether the prince was bound by the contracts of his predecessors. The jurists had discussed this issue in connection with the Donation of Constantine and had generally agreed that the prince was bound to observe the contractual and testamentary provisions of his predecessors.[58] Bodin also pointed out that the prince's hereditary obligations must be upheld.[59] Why must we discuss this distinction, he asked, since wills and contracts are a part of the law of nations? The answer is simple. The law of nations is not inviolable, unless it is also supported by divine and natural law.[60] The prince may revoke iniquitous laws even if they are part of the law of nations—such as the law of slavery.[61]

A. London Fell has recently argued that Bodin's thought "does not

57. Ibid., p. 162: "Hoc igitur fixum sit, principi alienis opibus ac bonis manus afferre aut ea largiri cuiquam, sine iusta causa, non licere."

58. See Maffei, *Donazione di Costantino* and Pennington, "Authority of the Prince."

59. Ibid., p. 164: "Quibus ergo legibus et quatenus pactis conventis princeps teneatur, nobis exposuisse videmur. Restat explicandum illud, an scilicet rex imperii successor, regum antecedentium promissis, salva maiestate, obligari possit . . . Sic statuo principem maiorum pactis conventis aeque ac privatos obligari, si regnum haereditario iuris obvenerit, vel etiam testamento delatum est."

60. Ibid., p. 167: "At cur, dicet aliquis, ea distinctione opus est, cum omnes principes iure gentium teneantur? Nam eo iure conventiones ac testamenta continentur. (Citing: Bald. in proemio Decretal.) Id. quidem falsum videri possit, si de universo genere statuamus. Demus tamen id verum esse, non propterea consequens est, principem gentium legibus potius quam suis obligari, nisi quatenus cum divinis ac naturae legibus conspirant."

61. Ibid.: "Quas quidem ad leges omnia quae de principum obligatione diximus, revocanda nobis sunt, atsi gentium iura quedam iniqua sint, ea princeps abrogare potest et subditos eo iure ne utantur prohibere. (Marginal note: l. Ex hoc iure, de iustitia. Ioan. Andr. in c. ult. de immunitate eccles.) ut antea docuimus de servitiis, quae iure omnium fere gentium in respublicas pernitioso exemplo invecta, multorum principum salutaribus, ac naturae congruentibus interdictis, sublata fuerunt."

reveal a shaping influence of medieval jurisprudence."[62] He maintains that his citations of medieval jurists were "not clear, accurate, or pertinent."[63] They were, he suggests, "afterthoughts, added in the margins to give greater authority to his ideas."[64]

On the contrary, Bodin's conception of sovereignty was unthinkable without the work of his predecessors. His definition of absolute power was taken from earlier jurists, and the limitations that he placed upon it were adopted from their thought. His argument that contracts, private property, and actions were based on natural and divine law were items that he easily took from the shelves of medieval jurisprudence. He did not cite the opinions of medieval and Renaissance jurists arbitrarily or willfully, but he knew their thought and their idiosyncracies well. We may conclude that Bodin's conception of sovereignty that he expounded in Book 1, chapter 8, of the *De republica* would not have offended the most constitutionally minded jurist of the Middle Ages.[65]

Bodin's contribution to the history of political thought was conceptual rather than substantive. The medieval and Renaissance jurists rarely wrote systematically about sovereignty. When they referred to the *loci classici* of the prince's authority, the glosses and commentaries on these texts did expound a coherent doctrine. But not a coherent work which could be entitled "On Sovereignty." They were content to paste their glosses together in their minds rather than writing an extended commentary on the Prince's *maiestas*. In this sense, Bodin was right when he wrote that no one had ever defined the prince's power—no one had written a systematic tract describing sovereignty. That was Bodin's main contribution to political thought.

The subtle dialectic between the rights of subjects and the power of the prince has an extended and complicated history. As we look back on the development of these ideas we may differ whether continuity or discontinuity of thought reigns supreme between the thirteenth and the

---

62. Fell, *Bodin's Humanistic Legal System* 103.

63. Ibid., p. 102. If A. London Fell had read Rebuffa's article, "Jean Bodin" 107–111, he might have come to a different conclusion.

64. Ibid., p. 101.

65. Although this is not the place to examine all of Bodin's thought, one further point should be stressed. Modern historians have laid great stress on Bodin's theory that the prince could legislate without the consent of his subjects (cf. Fell, *Bodin's Humanistic Legal System* 103). This concept, however, was a platitude of medieval learned jurisprudence and was not a sign of arbitrary or tyrannical authority. Brian Tierney's article, "Only the Truth Has Authority," is an excellent introduction to medieval ideas of consent and legislative authority. See also his comments on the pope's legislative authority in the twelfth century in *Foundations* 28–29. A papal decretal, for example, needed the consent of no one and had the same authority as canons of a General Council.

sixteenth centuries. Or whether medieval and early-modern theories of sovereignty and constitutional thought have any relationship to their modern counterparts.[66] Simple answers cannot describe the complex evolution of Western theories of sovereignty. Nonetheless, to borrow a musical metaphor, the counterpoint between Bodin in the sixteenth century and Baldus in the fourteenth century creates more harmony than dissonance. If they had discussed the absolute power of the prince, Baldus and Bodin would have quarreled little and agreed upon much.

The doctrines of sovereignty and rights that we have explored in the *ius commune* have some relevance for the late twentieth century. Modern jurists and political theorists write and talk about sovereignty without the same understanding of its juridical subtleties and complexities that Baldus and Bodin had, and they encounter particular difficulty when they try to explain how individual rights can be protected or preserved by the modern sovereign state or to understand how sovereignty might be less than absolute.

Today as in the Middle Ages, sovereignty remains a difficult concept. A basic question that bedevils Europeans at present is whether a state may share its sovereignty. Baldus had no difficulty conceding that a state could permit its citizens to fall under the jurisdiction of outside institutions or norms. We have seen that every jurist of the *ius commune* recognized that positive law must surrender to higher norms. Shared sovereignty was a commonplace. The Roman Church exercised jurisdictional rights over the subjects of kings throughout Europe in matters touching marriage and other areas governed by canon law. The European Community has proposed to its members that they relinquish parts of their sovereignty to a new Federation of European States, a supranational state that would give birth to a new *ius commune*. I would not presume to decide on whether a united Europe should or should not be established. I would point out, however, that some

---

66. Cary J. Nederman, "Conciliarism and Constitutionalism: Jean Gerson and Medieval Political Thought," *History of European Ideas* 12 (1990) 189–209 and A. London Fell, *Origins of Legislative Sovereignty and the Legislative State, 4: Medieval or Renaissance Origins? Historiographical Debates and Deconstructions* (New York, Westport, London: 1991) share the same reluctance to see that one may discuss medieval concepts of state, sovereignty, constitutionalism, and legislation without becoming hopelessly anachronistic. A purist might insist that one cannot describe the state, the church, the economy, or any other past institution with modern terminology. Such purity would create great explanatory problems—and ugly jargon. We would have to create terms to define every historical institution. There are, I believe, common elements of sovereignty, legislation, rights, and constitutionalism that can be analyzed and compared without being insensitive to differences between then and now.

English intellectuals have embraced a traditional doctrine of British sovereignty that they firmly believe cannot be, like virginity, compromised. Conor Cruise O'Brien has vividly expressed this sentiment:[67]

> Most citizens of the twelve states which make up the European Community would probably be disagreeably surprised if they knew that the sovereignty of their own state is already scheduled for liquidation. . . . [S]ome of them do [want this]; bureaucrats, for example, and Belgians. But I don't think the principal politicians who have been making the running, rhetorically, in the direction of the federalist goal, really mean that they want to get there. To travel hopefully is just fine, but to *arrive*? Ugh!

Of course, shared sovereignty is a particularly difficult concept for an Englishman who is attached to the British system of government where the power of the state is not limited by a written constitution or by defined "fundamental rights" of citizens. O'Brien imagines shared sovereignty as "liquidation" of national rights—individual as well as corporate rights.

In the early modern period England seemed the very model of a limited constitutional state, but from the eighteenth century onward common lawyers began to insist on the "absolute" sovereignty of Parliament.[68] We are all familiar with modern states that have practiced a rigorous absolutism behind the facade of a liberal constitution. The British seem to practice a flexible constitutionalism behind the facade of an absolute theory of government. As Giovanni Sartori once pointed out, this is puzzling for continental observers.[69] More recently, Jonathan Clark has tried, from the British perspective, to explain the differences between English and continental conceptions of sovereignty. He wrote:[70]

> The problem arises because England's dynastic and religious record endows her with a conception of sovereignty which still contrasts with that of many

67. *Times Literary Supplement*, March 13, 1992, p. 3.

68. During the past half century, however, the theory of parliamentary absolutism derived from Blackstone, Bentham, and Austin has come under mounting criticism. The first problems that evoked a substantial critical literature concerned the relationship between Parliament and the self-governing dominions of the Commonwealth. See e.g., R. T. E. Latham, *The Law and the Commonwealth* (Oxford: 1949). More recently, problems concerning the integration of Britain into Europe and the demand for a British Bill of Rights have given rise to extensive further discussion.

69. And for American observers too, one might add. See Giovanni Sartori, "Constitutionalism: A Preliminary Discussion," *American Political Science Review* 56 (1962) 853–864. For another reaction see A. L. Goodhart, *English Law and Moral Law* (London: 1953).

70. *Times Literary Supplement*, November 29, 1991, p. 15.

of her Continental neighbours, so that the integration, merging, or sharing of sovereignty is an easier intellectual exercise within their traditions of thought. Until the eighteenth century, Continental composite states, most notably France and Spain, similarly stressed their monarchies as unifying principles; but their Roman law traditions, the entrenched local privileges which Roman Law countenanced, and the ultramontane claims of the Roman Catholic Church for long inhibited any development of an idea of a unified sovereignty that could not be shared.

When Clark uses the phrase "unified sovereignty" in this passage, he encompasses more than simply supreme authority and power of the state, what Baldus or Bodin would have called "potestas absoluta," "plenitudo potestatis," or "maiestas." What he primarily seems to mean by "unified sovereignty" is what a jurist of the *ius commune* might have called—if such a legal state had existed—"unified jurisdiction."

Clark is right to observe that the jurisdictional claims of the Roman Catholic Church prevented a concept of unified jurisdiction from emerging in the *ius commune*. He is off the mark when he attributes a key role to the "entrenched local privileges which Roman Law countenanced." Neither the doctrine of Roman law nor its constitutional structure prevented a state with unified jurisdiction from arising during the Middle Ages. If he had substituted *ius commune* for Roman Law in the passage quoted, he would have been exactly right. The jurists of the *ius commune* did recognize a territorial state in which overlapping and sometimes conflicting jurisdictions could coexist. But their recognition of these complex jurisdictional rights did not depend on a doctrine or on principles inherited from Roman, canon, or feudal law. Rather, they realized that such overlapping jurisdictions had evolved in the territorial states of medieval and early modern Europe. The jurists merely described reality. And reality changed over the centuries. When Henry VII claimed jurisdiction over Robert of Naples or Sixtus IV over Lorenzo de' Medici, both universal rulers insisted that their rights to judge their "subjects" be recognized. Henry's claim was rejected, and the dispute became an important turning point in the history of the *ius commune*. On the other hand, Lorenzo recognized the pope's right to judge him but not his right to condemn him without a trial.

On the eve of European integration, Clark wishes to stress that sovereignty in England, unlike that in other European countries and the United States, resides in parliament, whose power is not limited by a constitution or other law-making institutions within the state. Clark and others call this "unitary sovereignty" or "parliamentary absolutism." In tracing the historical reasons why England developed parliamentary absolutism, Clark bestows upon Blackstone and John Austin the mantle of having understood and defined English sovereignty:[71]

> Locke's claim that the people retained "a supreme power to remove or alter the legislative" . . . could not be accepted, insisted Blackstone (because) . . . "so long therefore as the English constitution lasts, we may venture to affirm, that the power of parliament is absolute and without control" . . . Bentham and his chief disciple John Austin . . . strip(ped) Blackstone's unreformed common-law sovereign of its Anglican and natural-law limitations. That done . . . law was merely whatever the sovereign commanded.

This is indeed what Englishmen think that they have created. John Austin's definition of sovereignty has been accepted by both political scientists and historians as a touchstone of what sovereignty *ought* to be in an ideal world and what it has to be in the realm of theory. As Clark argues in his essay, sovereignty did not exist in the Roman world or in the Middle Ages because it did not conform to this definition.[72] But if we ask the same question that we posed through Bodin at the beginning of this book—"what is sovereignty?"—the question might not be simply a restatement of Austin.

A way of testing Austin's conception of sovereignty might be to adopt the same methodology the jurists used when they explored "potestas absoluta." Cinus of Pistoia and Panormitanus argued that the prince's sovereignty could not derogate the principle that a son could not marry his mother.[73] They used the argument borrowed from logic that if one exception can be found that proves a general principle false, the principle must not be true. If the English parliament passed an act that commanded the eldest son of every English family to marry his mother, what position would English constitutional lawyers take? Since most would be ambivalent about the prospect of marrying their mothers, more than likely the majority would appeal to the some higher norm, just as their medieval predecessors appealed to divine law. If my

71. Ibid., p. 16.
72. Ibid., p. 15. Clark's thumbnail sketch of Roman and medieval conceptions of sovereignty is a trifle odd, e.g., "subjects commonly held that a king was absolute only in executing the law, not in any ability to make new law by statute." A. London Fell, *Medieval or Renaissance Origins* 54–68 also insists that medieval rulers did not legislate. He asserts that medieval sovereignty is different from modern sovereignty (which of course no one would deny) and therefore cannot be compared (which I would deny). His argument ignores the work of Armin Wolf, Sten Gagnér, and many others. He does not grapple with the legislative doctrine of the *ius commune* but simply gives thumbnail sketches of secondary works, whose contents he often does not even correctly summarize.
73. See chapter 4 and chapter 6.

suppositions are correct, Bodin's conclusion is just as true of parliamentary absolutism as it was of "potestas absoluta:"

> For if we define freed from all laws [as parliamentary absolutism] no parliament anywhere possesses sovereignty (iura maiestatis), since divine law, the law of nature, and the common law of all people, which is established separately from divine and natural law, bind all parliaments.

However, there are presently no commonly accepted terms of discourse which jurists might use to describe the norm that they would substitute for Bodin's "divine law, the law of nature, and the common law of all people" in English constitutional thought.

If "parliamentary absolutism" does not exist today in fact or in theory, as untrammeled "potestas absoluta" did not exist in the past, and if the modern state is not absolutely sovereign, the implications have significance. Shared, a better word might be limited, sovereignty is not a perversion of states' rights, but a concept that is crucial for protecting a citizen from the state—any state. If we believe that individuals have inalienable rights, we must believe that the sovereignty of the state can be compromised. If accepted, this conclusion creates a problem for modern jurisprudence. Since there is no agreement about what higher norms might be, or what they might be called, or how they might be discovered, by what means might jurists limit the sovereignty of the state?[74] Natural law is generally thought to be too heavily laden with ideas of Christian morality to be used as a secular norm. Jurists have not yet proposed alternatives. Modern constitutional lawyers have two tasks: to recognize that modern sovereignty is not and should not be absolute and to construct a coherent juristic theory of norms.

As this study has demonstrated, a doctrine of individual and inalienable rights first surfaced in Western legal thought in the twelfth and thirteenth centuries. Political systems were not democratic, politics were not liberal, but jurists had a common set of norms to which they gave their consent. These norms were the building blocks upon which they constructed rights of property, obligations, marriage, defense, and due process. Today these rights are often protected against arbitrary magistrates of the sovereign state by constitutions. However, although

---

74. Modern jurists have proposed "ius cogens" as the norm, rule, principle—the meaning of the phrase has not been agreed upon—that could be the foundation of a modern doctrine of rights. However, the concept is still far from being accepted as a norm that transcends the positive law of all states. For a discussion of "ius cogens" in contemporary law, see Karen Parker and Lyn Beth Neylon, "Jus cogens: Compelling the Law of Human Rights," *Hastings International and Comparative Law Review* 12 (1989) 411–463.

constitutions may function as higher norms, their provisions can be changed, or, as we have seen in the late twentieth century, the political societies that create them may disappear. In any case, the rights they protect cannot be considered eternal.

In the introduction of this book, I wrote that rights and sovereignty have waged almost constant war against each other. Today they continue to do battle. Since the Convention for the Protection of Human Rights and Freedoms was adopted by sixteen European countries on November 4, 1950, human rights have been endorsed by heads of government, ratified by treaties, and violated by almost everyone. The culprit is the modern sovereign state, which recognizes the right of its citizens to act contrary to its will only with excruciating difficulty.

If there are higher norms that stand outside the jurisdiction of the state, we have discovered that these norms impose obligations on subjects as well as protect rights. Since the Nürnberg Trials, the principle has been established that a subject of the state cannot appeal to the laws and mandates of the state as a defense for having committed crimes sanctioned by the state. The principles of Nürnberg were reaffirmed and expanded by a German court in January 1992. Two East German border guards were convicted of having killed a man trying to cross the border into West Germany. Theodor Seidel, the judge, was reported to have said:[75]

> Not everything that is legal is right . . . (the defendants) were at the end of a long chain of responsibility . . . (but they had violated) a basic human right. . . . At the end of the 20th century no one has the right to "turn off" his conscience when the issue is killing people on the orders of the authorities.

The *ius commune* recognized norms that protected the rights of the prince's subjects. In a limited way, it also acknowledged that there were some cases in which subjects had an obligation to reject the commands of the prince. However, there were only a few who advocated active rather than passive resistance.[76] Although Judge Seidel's decision has its

75. *The New York Times,* January 21, 1992, Section A, pp. 1–2. The irascible news magazine, *Der Spiegel* (January 27, 1992), published a scathing article that pilloried the presiding judge of Heinrich's trial. *The New York Times,* January 26, 1992, Section E, p. 6, presented a one-sided reaction of American jurists to the German decision.

76. The question was often posed whether a subject was permitted to resist a heretical pope, a tyrannical king, or a command that violated Christian belief, but almost never did the jurists of the *ius commune* propose that a subject was obligated to resist the prince. For a discussion of the evolution of a doctrine that subjects had an obligation to resist tyranny, see Julian H. Franklin, *Constitutionalism and Resistance in the Sixteenth Century: Three Treatises by Hotman, Beza, and Mornay* (New York: 1969) and *Jean*

intellectual roots in the history of rights, a judge of the *ius commune*
would have had difficulty rendering his judgment.

In his discussion of the evolution of a theory of rights in the Western
tradition, Brian Tierney has written that:[77]

> Too often liberal Western values are inflated into general principles of
> human conduct and then proclaimed as universal rights applicable to any
> society regardless of its culture, economy, or religion. But it is a good
> Thomist principle that "abusus non tollit usum." There may still be a core
> of real human rights and good reason to insist on them in our modern world.

The problem remains of deciding what these rights might be and how
they might be recognized by the positive law of the state. There is no
question that the edifice of absolute sovereignty is crumbling. From
quite different directions, human rights and the politics of integration
have worked to undermine its foundations. John Austin's sovereignty
has had a brief period of dominance in the history of political thought,
but its days are clearly numbered. We may, with some satisfaction, reflect that when we return to a conception of sovereignty that recognizes
norms outside the state's positive law, we shall be returning to a system
of thought that has deep roots in Western law.

Bodin and the Rise of Absolutist Theory. Cary J. Nederman, "A Duty to Kill: John of
Salisbury's Theory of Tyrannicide," *The Review of Politics* 50 (1988) 365–389, has argued that John of Salisbury imposed a duty of resistance.
    77. "Aristotle and the American Indians," 304.

Bibliography
of Works Cited

MANUSCRIPTS

Admont, Stiftsbibliothek
   55
     Laurentius Hispanus, *Apparatus* to 3 Comp.
Aschaffenburg, Stiftsbibliothek
    Perg. 15
     Azo, *Summa super Codice* (1st recension)
Bamberg, Staatsbibliothek
    Can. 56, III
     Hostiensis, *Lectura,* Books I–V
    Can. 76
     Guilielmus de Monte Lauduno, *Apparatus ad Clementinas*
    Can. 77
     Guilielmus de Monte Lauduno, *Apparatus ad Clementinas*
    Can. 79
     Paulus de Liazariis, *Apparatus ad Clementinas*
    Jur. 24
     Azo, *Summa super Codice* (1st recension)
    Jur. 25
     Azo, *Summa super Codice* (1st recension)
    Jur. 26
     Azo, *Summa super Codice* (2nd recension)
Erlangen, Universitätsbibliothek
   358
     Johannes Andreae, *Additiones* (to X)
   801
     Azo, *Summa super Codice* (1st recension)

Florence, Archivio di Stato
    Dipl. Pistoia (Città), 12 . . . , nr. 8
    Document without dating clause
Florence, Biblioteca Laurenziana
    Edili 47
    Azo, *Summa super Codice* (1st recension)
    Fesul. 117
    Hostiensis, *Commentarium ad X,* Book 3
    Gaddiano Reliqui 193
    Collection of 32 novelle
    Redi 179
    Bulgarus, Glosses to *Codex*
Florence, Biblioteca Nazionale
    Edili 55
    Simone da Borsano, *Reportationes ad Clementinas*
    Grandi formati 39: Magliabecchiano, Cl.xxix.27
    Odofredus, *Lectura super Digesto veteri*
    Magliabecchiano, Cl. XXIX.169
    Cinus de Pistoia. *Lectura super Codice*
Herford, Cathedral Library
    P.5.xiv
    Azo, *Summa super Codice* (1st recension)
Karlsruhe, Badische Landesbibliothek
    Aug. XL
    Laurentius Hispanus, *Apparatus* to 3 Comp.
Klosterneuburg, Stiftsbibliothek
    119
    Azo, *Summa super Codice* (1st recension)
London, British Library
    Arundel 459, fol. 70v
Pierre de Mornay, *Quaestiones*
    Arundel 493
    Jacobus de Bologna, *Quaestiones*
    Royal 10.E.i.
    Johannes Monachus, to *Extravagantes*
London, Lambeth Palace
    13
    Johannes Monachus, to *Extravagantes*
Munich, Staatsbibliothek
    Clm 22
    Glosses to the Code
    Clm 3501
    Accursius, *Glossa ordinaria ad Codicem*
    Clm 3503
    Accursius, *Glossa ordinaria ad Codicem*
    Clm 3506

Accursius, *Glossa ordinaria ad Codicem*
    Clm 3629
Baldus de Ubaldis, *Lectura super Decretalibus*
    Clm 3631
Francesco Zabarella, *Lectura super Decretalibus*
    Clm 3638
Oldradus de Ponte, *Consilia* (264 consilia)
    Clm 3880
Accursius, *Glossa ordinaria ad Codicem*
    Clm 3884
Accursius, *Glossa ordinaria ad Codicem*
    Clm 3887
Azo, Glosses to *Digestum vetus*
    Clm 5463
Oldradus de Ponte, *Consilia* (220 consilia)
    Clm 5473
Nicolaus de Tudeschis, *Lectura super Decretalibus*
    Clm 5474
Nicolaus de Tudeschis, *Lectura super Decretalibus*
    Clm 5475
Bartolus of Sassoferrato, *Lectura super Digesto novo*
    Clm 6201
Accursius, *Glossa ordinaria ad Codicem*
Guido de Suzaria, *Suppletiones ad Codicem*
    Clm 6350
Innocent IV, *Apparatus ad Decretales Gregorii IX*
    Clm 6351
Johannes Andreae, *Additiones* (to X)
    Clm 6523
Johannes de Imola, *Commentarium ad Clementinas*
    Clm 6534
Nicolaus de Tudeschis, *Lectura super Decretalibus*
    Clm 6536
Nicolaus de Tudeschis, *Lectura super Decretalibus*
    Clm 6537
Nicolaus de Tudeschis, *Lectura super Decretalibus*
    Clm 6539
Francesco Zabarella, *Lectura super Decretalibus*
    Clm 6551
Nicolaus de Tudeschis, *Lectura super Decretalibus*
    Clm 6632
Baldus de Ubaldis, *Lectura super usibus feudorum*
    Clm 6640
Baldus de Ubaldis, *Lectura super Digesto*
    Clm 6643
Bartolus of Sassoferrato, *Commentarium ad Ad reprimendum*
    Clm 13015

Hostiensis, *Lectura,* Books I–V (2nd recension)
    Clm 14022
Accursius, *Glossa ordinaria ad Codicem*
    Clm 14024
Johannes Teutonicus, *Glossa Ordinaria ad Decretum*
    Clm 14026
Johannes Andreae, *Additiones* (to X)
    Clm 14028
Azo, Glosses to *Digestum vetus*
    Clm 15703
Johannes Andreae, *Additiones* (to X)
    Clm 15704
Innocent IV, *Apparatus ad Decretales Gregorii IX*
    Clm 17763
Bartolus of Sassoferrato, *Lectura super Digesto novo*
    Clm 23685
Nicolaus de Tudeschis, *Lectura super Decretalibus*
    Clm 23696
Nicolaus de Tudeschis, *Lectura super Decretalibus*
    Clm 26912
Baldus de Ubaldis, *Lectura super usibus feudorum*
    Clm 28152
Hostiensis, *Lectura,* Books I–V (2nd recension)
Nürnberg, Stadtbibliothek
    Cent. II 60
Johannes Andreae, *Repetitio* and *Additiones II* (to X)
Paulus de Liazariis, *Apparatus ad Clementinas*
    Cent. II 84
Bartolus, *Lectura super prima parte Codicis* (to 5.75)
Olomouc, Statní Archiv
    C.O. 398
Azo, *Summa super Codice* (1st recension)
Oxford, New College
    205
Hostiensis, *Lectura,* Books I–V (1st recension)
Paris, Bibliothèque nationale
    lat. 2376
Azo, *Summa super Codice* (1st recension)
    lat. 4105
Jesselin de Cassagnes, *Apparatus ad Clementinas*
    lat. 4446
Pierre Jame d'Aurillac (de Aureliaco), *Additiones*
    lat. 4542
Azo, *Summa super Codice* (1st recension)
    lat. 4547
Cinus de Pistoia, *Lectura super Codice*
    lat. 4560A

Azo, *Summa super Codice* (1st recension)
  lat. 4571
Pierre Jame d'Aurillac (de Aureliaco), *Additiones*
  lat. 4488
Guido de Suzaria, *Suppletiones ad Digestum vetus et Codicem*
  lat. 4489
Guido de Suzaria, *Suppletiones ad Digestum vetus et Codicem*
  lat. 14331
Jesselin de Cassagnes, *Apparatus de Clementinas*
  lat. 16902
Jesselin de Cassagnes, *Apparatus ad Clementinas*
Pisa Archivio capitolare,
  728
  Document dated 14 August, 1196
Pistoia, Archivio di Stato
  Dipl. S. Michele di Forcale
  Document dated July 21, 1215
Seo de Urgel, Bibl. de la Catedral
  2040
  Azo, *Summa super Codice* (1st recension)
Vatican City, Biblioteca Apostolica
  lat. 1367
  Johannes Teutonicus, *Glossa Ordinaria ad Decretum*
  lat. 2312
  Azo, *Summa super Codice* (1st recension)
Vienna, Nationalbibliothek
  2055
  Hostiensis, *Commentarium ad X*, Book 3
  2078
  Paulus de Liazariis, *Apparatus ad Clementinas*
  2267
  Glosses on the Code
Worcester, Cathedral Library
  F 29
  Azo, *Lectura super Codice*, as reported by Alexander de Sancto Egidio
Würzburg, Universitätsbibliothek
  M.p.j.f.2
  Azo, *Summa super Codice* (1st recension)

PRINTED LEGAL SOURCES

Albericus de Rosate. *Commentaria in Codice*. 2 vols. Venice: 1585. Reprinted
  Bologna: 1979.
———. *Commentaria in Digesto veteri*. 2 vols. Venice: 1585. Reprinted
  Bologna: 1977.
———. *Commentaria super Digesto*. 2 vols. Venice: 1585. Reprinted Torino:
  1974.

Althusius, Johannes. *Dicaeologicae libri tres, totum et universum ius in quo utimur methodice complectentes.* Frankfurt am Main: 1618.

Andrea de Isernia. *Constitutiones Regni Siciliarum libri III.* Ed. A. Cervonius. Naples: 1773.

———. *Lectura in usibus feudorum.* Naples: 1477.

———. *Peregrina Anagnosis Lectura in Constitutionibus Neapolitani Regni.* Lyon: 1533.

Angelus de Ubaldis. *Lectura super Digesto.* Milan: 1477. Lyon: 1534.

———. *Consilia.* Treviso: 1477. Lyon: 1532.

Antonius de Butrio. *Commentarium ad Decretales.* Venice: 1578. Reprinted Torino: 1967.

———. *Consilia.* Milan: 1508. Lyon: 1534 and 1541. Venice: 1575 and 1582.

Azo. *Lectura super Codice,* as reported by Alexander de Sancto Egidio. Paris: 1577. Reprinted Torino: 1966.

———. *Die Quaestiones des Azo.* Ed. Ernst Landsberg. Freiburg i. B.: 1888.

———. *Summa super Codice.* Speyer: 1482. Venice: 1489. Pavia: 1506. Reprinted Torino: 1966. Lyon: 1557. Reprinted Frankfurt a.M.: 1968.

Baldus de Ubaldis. *Consilia.* Venice: 1491. Milan: 1493. Venice: 1575. Reprinted Torino: 1970.

———. *Lectura super Decretalibus.* Milan: 1478. Venice: 1585. Reprinted Torino: 1970.

———. *Lectura super Digesto.* Venice: 1493.

———. *Lectura super Codice.* Sine loco et anno (Hain *2279). Venice: 1474.

———. *Lectura super usibus feudorum.* Rome: sine anno (Hain *2316).

Barclay, William. *De regno et regali potestate.* Paris: 1600.

Bartholomaeus de Capua. *Iuris Interpretes saec. XIII.* Ed. Eduard Meijers et al. Naples: 1924.

Bartolus of Sassoferrato. *Commentarium ad Ad reprimendum.* Sine loco: 1472.

———. *Lectura super Codice.* Venice: 1476.

———. *Lectura super Digesto novo.* Turin: 1577.

———. *Politica e diritto nel trecento italiano: Il "De tyranno" di Bartolo da Sassoferrato (1314–1357), con l'edizione critica dei trattati "De Guelphis et Gebellinis," "De regimine civitatis," e "De tyranno."* Ed. Diego Quaglioni. Il pensiero politico, biblioteca 11. Florence: 1983.

Bernardus Parmensis, *Glossa ordinaria ad Decretales Gregorii noni. Corpus iuris canonici.* Vol. 2. Rome: 1582.

Bodin, Jean. *De republica libri sex.* 3d ed. Frankfurt: 1594 and 1609.

———. *Les six livres de la republique.* Paris: 1577.

Carpzov, Benedict. *Processus iuris in foro Saconico.* Jena: 1657.

Chieri, Statutes. *Statuti civili del comune di Chieri, 1313.* Biblioteca della Società Storica Subalpina, 76.2. Pinerolo: 1913.

Cinus de Pistoia. *Lectura super Codice.* 2 vols. Frankfurt: 1578. Reprinted Torino: 1964.

———. *Le "Quaestiones" e i "Consilia."* Ed. Gennaro Maria Monti. Milan: 1942.

———. *Mostra di documenti e libri.* Ed. Ezelinda Altieri and Giancarlo Savino. Florence: 1971.

Constitutions of Melfi. *Constitutiones Regni Siciliarum libri III*. Ed. A. Cervonius. Naples: 1773.

De Grassalius (De Grassaille), Carolus. *Regalium Franciae libri duo iura omnia et dignitates Christianissorum Galliae Regum*. Paris: 1545.

Dissensiones dominorum sive controversiae veterum iuris Romani interpretum. Ed. Gustav Haenel. Leipzig: 1834. Reprinted Aalen: 1964.

Edward III. Statutes of King Edward III. *The Statutes of the Realm*. Vol. I. London: 1810.

Franciscus Curtius Papiensis. *Consilia*. Milan: 1496. Zürich: 1518. Venice: 1580. Speyer: 1603.

Franciscus de Accoltis Aretinus. *Consilia*. Pisa: 1482. Pavia: 1494 and 1503. Lyon: 1529, 1536, and 1546. Venice: 1572.

Franciscus Zabarella. *Lectura super Decretalibus*. Rome: 1477.

Gentilis, Albericus. *Regales disputationes tres*. London: 1605.

Girolamo Torti (Hieronimus de Tortis). *Consilium*. Sine loco et anno (Hain *15579). Pavia: 1485 (Hain *15580).

Gregor VII. *Register*. Ed. Erich Caspar. MGH, Epistolae selectae. Berlin: 1920.

Guilielmus Durantis. *Speculum iuris*. 2 vols. Basel: 1574. Reprinted Aalen: 1975.

Henry VII, emperor. *Acta Henrici VII. imperatoris Romanorum et monumenta quaedam alia Medii Aevi*. Ed. W. Dönniges. 2 vols. Berlin: 1839.

———. *Constitutiones et acta publica imperatorum et regum*. 4.2: Inde ab A. MCCXCVII usque ad A. MCCCXIII. Ed. J. Schwalm. MGH, Legum sectio, 4. Hannover-Leipzig: 1911.

Henry Bracton. *De legibus de consuetudinibus Angliae*. Ed. George Woodbine. 4 vols. New Haven: 1915–1942. Translated with revisions by Samuel E. Thorne. 4 vols. Cambridge, Mass.: 1968–1977.

Hostiensis. *Lectura super Decretalibus*. Strasbourg: 1512. Venice: 1581. Reprinted Torino: 1963.

Hubaldus Pisanus. *Das Imbreviaturbuch des erzbischöflichen Gerichtsnotars Hubaldus aus Pisa, Mai bis August 1230*. Ed. Gero Dolezalek. Forschungen zur neueren Privatrechtsgeschichte, 13. Köln-Wien: 1969.

Innocent III. *Die Register Innocenz' III.: 1. Pontifikatsjahr*. Ed. Othmar Hageneder and Anton Haidacher. Graz-Köln: 1964.

———. *2. Pontifikatsjahr: Texte*. Ed. O. Hageneder, W. Maleczek, and A. Strnad. Rom-Wien: 1979.

Innocent IV. *Apparatus super quinque libris decretalium*. Frankfurt: 1570. Reprinted Frankfurt: 1968.

Jacobus de Arena. "Lectura super titulo De actionibus." *Super iure civili*. Lyon: 1541.

Johannes XXII. *Extrauagantes Iohannis XXII*. Ed. Jacqueline Tarrant. MIC, Series B, 6. Città del Vaticano: 1983.

Johannes Andreae. *Additiones ad Speculum iudiciale*. Basel: 1574.

———. *Novella on X*. Venice: 1581. Reprinted Torino: 1963.

Johannes de Imola. *Commentarium ad Constitutiones Clementinas*. Venice: 1480.

Johannes Teutonicus. *Apparatus glossarum in Compilationem tertiam.* Ed. K. Pennington. MIC, Series A, 3.1. Città del Vaticano: 1981.

Lateran, Fourth Council of. *Constitutiones Concilii quarti Lateransis.* Ed. Antonio García y García. MIC, Series A, 2. Città del Vaticano: 1981.

Laurentius Hispanus. *The Ecclesiology of Laurentius Hispanus (c. 1180–1248) and His Contribution to the Romanization of Canon Law Jurisprudence with an Edition of the "Apparatus glossarum Laurentii Hispani in Compilationem tertiam."* Ed. Brendan J. McManus. PhD dissertation, Syracuse University, 1991.

Louis IV, emperor. *Constitutiones et acta publica imperatorum et regum.* Vol. 5: *Inde ab a. MCCCXII ad a. MCCCXXIV.* Ed. Jacobus Schwalm. MGH, Legum sectio 4. Hannover-Leipzig: 1911–1913.

Marinus de Caramanico. *Constitutiones Regni Siciliarum libri III.* Ed. A. Cervonius. Naples: 1773.

Nicolaus de Tudeschis (Panormitanus). *Lectura super Decretalibus.* Venice: 1497.

Nicolaus Spinelli. *Lectura institutionum.* Pavia: 1506. Reprinted Opera iuridica rariora, 20. Bologna: 1978.

Odofredus. *Lectura super Codice.* Ed. s.a., s.l. (Hain—. Vienna, Nationalbibl.: Ink. 26.A.5). Lyon: 1480. Lyon: 1552. Reprinted Bologna: 1968–1969.

———. *Lectura super Digesto veteri.* 2 vols. Lyon: 1550. Reprinted Opera iuridica rariora, 2. Bologna: 1967.

Oldradus de Ponte. *Consilia.* Rome: 1472 (264 consilia) Rome: 1478 (333 consilia).

———. *Jews and Saracens in the Consilia of Oldradus de Ponte.* Ed. and trans. Norman Zacour. Studies and Texts. Toronto: 1990.

Papal letters. *Decretales ineditae saeculi XII, from the Papers of Walther Holtzmann.* Ed. Charles Duggan and Stanley Chodorow. MIC, Series B, 4. Città del Vaticano: 1982.

Papal letters. *Papsturkunden in England.* Vol. I: *Bibliotheken und Archive in London.* Ed. Walther Holtzmann. Abhandlungen der Akademie der Wissenschaften in Göttingen, philologish-historische Klasse, NF 25. Berlin: 1931.

———. *Papsturkunden in England.* Vol. II: *Die kirchlichen Archive und Bibliotheken.* Ed. Walther Holtzmann. Abhandlungen der Akademie der Wissenschaften in Göttingen, philologisch-historische Klasse (3d series), 14–15. Berlin: 1935.

———. *Papsturkunden in England.* Vol. III: *Oxford, Cambridge, kleinere Bibliotheken und Archive und Nachträge aus London.* Ed Walther Holtzmann. Abhandlungen der Akademie der Wissenschaften in Göttingen, philologisch-historische Klasse (3d series), 33. Berlin: 1952.

———. *Papsturkunden in Frankreich.* Vol. 2: *Normandie.* Ed. Johannes Ramackers. Abhandlungen der Gesellschaft der Wissenschaften zu Göttingen, philologish-historische Klasse (3d series), 21. Göttingen: 1937.

———. *Papsturkunden in Frankreich.* Vol. 3: *Artois.* Ed. Johannes Ramackers. Abhandlungen der Gesellschaft der Wissenschaften zu Göttingen, philologish-historische Klasse (3d series), 23. Göttingen: 1940.

———. *Papsturkunden in Frankreich.* Vol. 7: *Nördliche Ile-de-France und Vermandois.* Ed. Dietrich Lohrmann. Abhandlungen der Akademie der Wissenschaften in Göttingen (3d series), phil.- historische Klasse, 95. Göttingen: 1976.

———. *Scotia pontificia: Papal Letters to Scotland before the Pontificate of Innocent III.* Ed. Robert Somerville. Oxford: 1982.

Paucapalea. *Prologue to Summa.* Ed. Johann F. von Schulte. Giessen: 1890. Reprinted Aalen: 1965.

Paulus de Castro. *Commentaria super Codice.* Lyon: 1531.

Philippe de Beaumanoir. *Coutumes de Beauvaisis.* Ed. A. Salmon. Collection de textes pour servir l'enseignement de l'histoire. 2 vols. Paris: 1899–1900. Reprinted Paris: 1970.

Pierre Jame d'Aurillac. *Libellus libellorum (Aurea practica).* Lyon: 1493, 1501, 1511, 1519, 1527, 1535, 1539. Cologne: 1575.

Placentinus. *Summa super Codice.* Mainz: 1536. Reprinted Torino: 1962.

Pufendorf, Samuel. *Elementa iurisprudentiae universalis.* Hagae Comitis: 1660.

Responsa doctorum Tholosanorum. Rechtshistorisch Instituut, Leiden 2.8. Haarlem: 1938.

Révigny, Jacques de. *Lectura ad Codicem* (attributed to Pierre de Bellapertica). Paris: 1519.

Sixtus IV, pope. Letters excommunicating Lorenzo de' Medici and placing Florence under interdict. Rome: Sine anno (Hain *14816).

Stephen of Tournai. Prologue to *Summa.* Printed by Herbert Kalb. *Studien zur Summa Stephans von Tournai: Ein Beitrag zur kanonistischen Wissenshaftsgeschichte des späten 12. Jahrhunderts.* Forschungen zur Rechts-und Kulturgeschichte, 12. Innsbruck: 1983.

Sulmone, Statutes. *Codice diplomatico sulmunese.* Ed. Nunzio Federigo Faraglia. Lanciano: 1888.

Summa "Elegantius in iure diuino seu Coloniensis." Ed. Gérard Fransen. MIC, Series A, 1.2 Città del Vaticano: 1978.

Vercelli, statutes. *Statuta communis Vercellarum.* Ed. Giovambattista Adriani. *Historiae Patriae Monumenta.* Leges Municipales. Vol. 2. Augustae Taurinorum: 1876.

HISTORICAL AND THEOLOGICAL SOURCES

Acta imperii Angliae et Franciae ab a. 1267 ad a. 1313: Dokumente vornehmlich zur Geschichte der auswärtigen Beziehungen Deutschlands. Ed. Fritz Kern. Tübingen: 1911.

Aegidius Romanus. *De ecclesiastica potestate.* Ed. Richard Scholz. Vienna: 1929. Reprinted Aalen: 1961.

———. *Giles of Rome on Ecclesiastical Power: The "De ecclesiastica potestate" of Aegidius Romanus.* Trans. R. W. Dyson. Woodbridge-Dover: 1986.

Ambrose, St. "De apologia prophetae David ad Theodosium Augustum." *Opera.* Ed. C. Schenkl. Corpus scriptorum ecclesiasticorum latinorum, 32.2. Prague: 1897.

————. *Epistolae*. Migne PL 16.914–1342.

Aquinas, Thomas. *Summa theologiae*. 4 vols. Torino: 1952–1962.

Bernardus of Hildesheim. *Libelli de lite imperatorum et pontificum saeculis XI. et XII. conscripti*. MGH, 2. Hannover: 1892.

Beroul. *Romance of Tristan*. Trans. A. S. Fedrick. Hammondsworth: 1970.

Boutaric, Edgard. *Actes du Parlement de Paris (1254–1328)*. 2 vols. Paris: 1863–1867.

Carmen de gestis Friderici. MGH, Scriptores 22.

Le carte arcivescovili pisane del secolo XIII. Vol. I: *1201–1238*. Ed. Natale Caturegli. Regesta Chartarum Italiae, 37. Rome: 1974.

Chartularium Studii Bononensis: Documenti per la storia dell'università di Bologna dalle origini fino al secolo XV. Vol. 1. Bologna: 1909.

Le ciento novelle antike. Bologna: 1525.

Conrad of Megenberg. *Oeconomica*. Ed. S. Krüger. MGH, Staatsschriften, 6. Stuttgart: 1977.

Diplovatatius, Thomas. *Liber de claris iuris consultis*. Ed. F. Schulz, H. Kantorowicz, and G. Rabotti. SG, 10. Bologna: 1968.

Goldast, M. *Politica imperialia*. Frankfurt: 1614.

Guillaume de Pierre Godin. *Tractatus de causa immediata ecclesiastice potestatis*. Ed. William D. McCready. Toronto: 1982.

Henry VII, emperor. *Constitutiones et acta publica imperatorum et regum*. Vol. 4.2: *Inde ab a. MCCXCVII. usque ad a. MCCCXIII*. Ed. Jacob Schwalm. MGH, Legum sectio 4. Hannover-Leipzig: 1911.

Henry VII and Louis IV, emperors. *Nova Alamanniae: Urkunden, Briefe und andere Quellen besonders zur deutschen Geschichte des 14. Jahrhunderts*. Ed. Edmund E. Stengel. 2 vols. Berlin: 1921–1930.

Karolus Degrassalius Carcassonsis (De Grassaille). *Regalium Franciae libri duo iura omnia et dignitates Christianissorum Galliae regum*. Paris: 1545.

Las Casas, Bartolomé. *De thesauris in Peru*. Latin text with Spanish translation by Angel Losada García. Madrid: 1958.

Louis IV, emperor. *Constitutiones et acta publica imperatorum et regum*. Vol. 5: *Inde ab a. MCCCXIII. usque ad a. MCCCXXIV*. Ed. Jacob Schwalm. MGH, Legum sectio 4. Hannover-Leipzig: 1909–1913.

Machiavelli, Niccolò. *Istorie fiorentine*. Milano: 1968.

————. *The Prince*. Trans. Peter Bondanella and Mark Musa. Oxford-New York: 1984.

Medici, Lorenzo de'. *Lettere*. Vol. 2: *1474–1478*. Ed. Riccardo Fubini. Florence: 1977.

————. *Lettere*. Vol. 3: *1478–1479*. Ed. Nicolai Rubinstein. Florence: 1977.

Novellino e conti del Duecento. Ed. Sebastiano Lo Nigro. Classici italiani, 4. Torino: 1963.

Oculus pastoralis sive Libellus erudiens futurum rectorem populorum. Antiquitates Italicae medii aevii sive Dissertationes. Ed. L. Muratori. Milan: 1741. IV, 95–128.

————. "Oculus pastoralis pascens officia et continens radium dulcibus pomis suis." *Memorie della Accademia delle scienze di Torino*. Ed. Dora Franceschi. Classe di scienze morali, storiche e filologiche, series 4, vol. 11 (1966) 1–74.

———. *Oculus pastoralis*. Ed. Terence O. Tunberg. PhD dissertation, University of Toronto, 1986.

———. *Speeches from the Oculus pastoralis edited from Cleveland, Public Library, MS. Wq 7890921M-C37*. Ed. Terence O. Tunberg. Toronto Medieval Latin Texts 19. Toronto: 1990.

Opicinus de Canistris. *De preminentia spiritualis imperii*. Ed Richard Scholz. *Unbekannte kirchenpolitische Streitschriften aus der Zeit Ludwigs des Bayern (1327–1354)*. Vol. 2: *Analysen und Texte*. Bibliothek des Deutschen Historischen Instituts in Rom, 10. Rome: 1914.

Otto Morena. *De rebus Laudensibus*. Ed. Philipp Jaffé. MGH, Scriptores, 18. Hannover: 1863 and Ed. F. Güterbock. MGH Scriptores rerum Germanicarum, Nova Series, 7. Berlin: 1930.

———. *Historia Frederici I*. Ed. Ferdinand Güterbock. MGH, Scriptores rerum Germanicarum, Nova series, 7. Berlin: 1930.

Otto of Freising. *Ottonis et Rahewini Gesta Friderici I. imperatoris*. Ed. Georg Waitz and B. von Simson. MGH, Scriptores rerum Germanicarum in usum scholarum. 3d ed. Hannover-Leipzig: 1912.

Petrus Crassus. *Libelli de lite imperatorum et pontificum saeculis XI. et XII. conscripti*. MGH, 1. Hannover: 1891.

Poliziano, Angelo. *Angeli Politiani coniurationis Commentarium*. Sine loco et anno (Hain *13240).

———. *Della congiura dei Pazzi (Coniurationis commentarium)*. Ed. A. Perosa. Padua: 1958.

Ptolomey of Lucca. "Tractatus de iurisdictione ecclesie super regnum Sicilie et Apulie." Ed. S. Baluze and J. D. Mansi. *Miscellanea*. Lucca: 1761: I, 468–473.

William Ockham. *Dialogus de potestate papae et imperatoris*. Frankfurt: 1614. Reprinted Monumenta politica rariora, 1. Torino: 1966.

———. *Quodlibeta septem*. Ed. Joseph Wey. *Opera theologica*, 9. St. Bonaventure, N.Y.: 1980.

———. *Tractatus contra Benedictum*. Vol. 6.2: *Opera politica*. Ed. R. F. Bennett and H. S. Offler. Manchester: 1956.

LITERATURE CITED

Acton, Harold. *The Pazzi Conspiracy: The Plot Against the Medici*. London: 1979.

Aimone-Braida, P. V. "Titoli attribuiti al papa e all'imperatore nella decretistica." *Apollinaris* 59 (1986) 213–249.

Aistermann, Balduin. *Beiträge zum Konflikt Johanns XXII. mit dem deutschen Königtum*. PhD dissertation at Freiburg im Breisgau. Bonn: 1909.

Alford, John A., and Dennis P. Sennif. *Literature and Law in the Middle Ages*. New York: 1984.

Anonymous. "Accolti, Francesco." DBI 1 (Rome: 1960) 104–105.

Appelt, H. "Die Kaiseridee Friedrich Barbarossas." *Sitzungsberichte der Akademie der Wissenschaften in Wien*, phil.-hist. Klasse 252.4. Vienna: 1967.

Ascheri, Mario. "'Consilium sapientis,' perizia medica e 'res iudicata': Diritto dei 'dottori' e istituzioni communali." *Proceedings of the Fifth International Congress of Medieval Canon Law*. Ed. Stephan Kuttner and Kenneth Pennington. Città del Vaticano: 1980: 533–579.

————. "Rechtsprechungssammlungen." *Handbuch der Quellen und Literatur der neueren europäischen Privatrechtsgeschichte*. Vol. 2.2: *Neuere Zeit (1500–1800): Das Zeitalter des gemeinen Rechts: Gesetzgebung und Rechtsprechung*. Ed. Helmut Coing. München: 1976: 1113–1221.

Baethgen, Friedrich. "Zur Geschichte der Weltherrschaftsidee im späteren Mittelalter." *Festschrift Percy Ernst Schramm zu seinem 70. Geburtstag*. 2 vols. Wiesbaden: 1964: I, 189–203.

Bannach, Klaus. *Die Lehre von der doppelten Macht Gottes bei Wilhelm von Ockham: Problemgeschichtliche Voraussetzungen und Bedeutung*. Wiesbaden: 1975.

Barthélemy, Dominique. "Diversité des ordalies médiévales." *Revue historique* 280 (1988) 3–25.

————. "Présence de l'aveu dans le déroulement des ordalies (IXème-XIVème siècles." *L'Aveu: Antiquité et moyen âge: Actes de la table ronde organisée par l'Ecole française de Rome*. Rome: 1986: 315–340.

Bartlett, Robert. *Trial by Fire and Water: The Medieval Judicial Ordeal*. Oxford: 1986.

Baumgärtner, Ingrid. "'De privilegiis doctorum': Über Gelehrtenstand und Doktorwürde im späten Mittelalter." *Historisches Jahrbuch* 106 (1986) 298–332.

Becker, H. J., and I. Walter. "Brossano (Borsano), Simone da." DBI 14 (1972) 470–474.

Bellomo, Manlio. *L'Europa del diritto comune*. Roma: 1989.

Belloni, Annalisa. "Baziano, cioè Giovanni Bassiano, legista e canonista del secolo XII." TRG 57 (1985) 69–85.

————. *Professori giuristi a Padova nel secolo XV: Profili bio-bibliografici e cattedre*. Frankfurt am Main: 1986.

Benson, Robert L. "Plenitudo potestatis: Evolution of a Formula from Gregory IV to Gratian." *Collectanea Stephan Kuttner*. SG, 14. Bologna: 1967: 195–217.

————. "Political 'renovatio': Two Models from Roman Antiquity." *Renaissance and Renewal in the Twelfth Century*. Ed. R. L. Benson and G. Constable. Cambridge, Mass.: 1982: 339–386.

Berges, Wilhelm. *Die Früstenspiegel des hohen und späten Mittelalters*. MGH, Schriften 2. Stuttgart-Leipzig: 1938.

Bertram, Martin. "Kanonistische Quaestionensammlungen von Bartholomäus Brixiensis bis Johannes Andreae." *Proceedings of the Seventh International Congress of Medieval Canon Law*. Ed. Peter Linehan. MIC, Series C, 8. Città del Vaticano: 1988: 265–281.

Betti, Emilio. "La dottrina costruita da Bartolo sulla constitutio 'Ad reprimendum.'" *Bartolo da Sassoferrato: Studi e documenti per il VI centenario.* 2 vols. Milan: 1962: II, 37–47.

Beumann, H. "Zur Entwicklung transpersonaler Staatsvorstellungen." *Das Königtum: Seine geistigen und rechtlichen Grundlagen.* Ed. T. Mayer. Vorträge und Forschungen, 3. Sigmaringen: 1956: 185–224.

Black, Antony. *Council and Commune: The Conciliar Movement and the Fifteenth-Century Heritage.* London: 1979.

———. "The Conciliar Movement." *The Cambridge History of Medieval Political Thought c.350-c.1450.* Ed. J. H. Burns. Cambridge: 1988: 575–587.

———. *Guilds and Civil Society in European Political Thought from the Twelfth Century to the Present.* London: 1984.

———. "The Individual and Society." *The Cambridge History of Medieval Political Thought c.350-c.1450.* Ed. J. H. Burns. Cambridge: 1988: 588–606.

———. *Monarchy and Community: Political Ideas in the Later Conciliar Controversy 1430–1450.* Cambridge Studies in Medieval Life and Thought (3d series), 2. Cambridge: 1970.

———. "Panormitanus on the Decretum." *Traditio* 26 (1970) 440–444.

Black, Robert. *Benedetto Accolti and the Florentine Renaissance.* Cambridge: 1985.

Blecker, Michael. "The King's Partners in Bracton." *Studi senesi* 96 (1984) 66–118.

Bloch, Ernst. *Natural Law and Human Dignity.* Trans. Dennis J. Schmidt. Cambridge, Mass. and London: 1986.

Bock, Friedrich. "Die Appellationsschriften König Ludwigs IV. in den Jahren 1323/24." *DA* 4 (1941) 179–205.

———. "Kaisertum, Kurie und Nationalstaat im Beginn des 14. Jahrhunderts." *Römische Quartalschrift für christliche Altertumskunde und für Kirchengeschichte* 44 (1936) 105–122, 169–220.

———. *Reichsidee und Nationalstaaten vom Untergang des alten Reiches bis zur Kündigung des deutsch-Englischen Bündnisses im Jahre 1341.* München: 1943.

Boulet-Sautel, Marguerite. "Le concept de souveraineté chez Jacques Révigny." *Actes du congrès sur l'ancienne université d'Orléans (XIIIe–XVIIIe siècles).* Orléans: 1961: 17–27.

———. "Le 'princeps' de Guillaume Durand." *Études d'histoire du droit canonique dédiées à Gabriel Le Bras.* Paris: 1965: II, 803–813.

Bowsky, William M. *Henry VII in Italy: The Conflict of Empire and City-State, 1310–1313.* Lincoln, Neb.: 1960.

Boyle, Leonard E. "Robert Grosseteste and the Pastoral Care." *Medieval and Renaissance Studies: Proceedings of the Southeastern Institute of Medieval and Renaissance Studies, Summer, 1976.* Ed. Dale B. J. Randall. Medieval and Renaissance Series, 8. Durham: 1979: 3–51.

———. "Vacarius." *DMA* 12 (1989) 343–344.

Brizio, Elena. "Una indicizzazione 'automatica' dei consilia di Bartolo da Sassoferrato." *Studi senesi* 102 (1991) 101–349.

Brown, Alison. *Bartolomeo Scala, 1430–1497, Chancellor of Florence: The Humanist as Bureaucrat.* Princeton, N.J.: 1979.

Brown, Peter. "Society and the Supernatural: A Medieval Change." *Daedalus* 104 (1975) 133–151.

Brundage, James A. *Medieval Canon Law and the Crusader.* Madison-Milwaukee: 1969.

———. "Marriage and Sexuality in the Decretals of Pope Alexander III." *Miscellanea Rolando Bandinelli: Papa Alessandro III.* Ed. Filippo Liotta. Siena: 1986: 57–83.

Brynteson, William. "Roman Law and Legislation in the Middle Ages." *Speculum* 41 (1966) 420–437.

Buisson, Ludwig. *Potestas und Caritas: Die päpstliche Gewalt im Spätmittelalter.* 2d ed. Forschungen zur kirchlichen Rechtsgeschichte und zum Kirchenrecht, 2. Köln-Wien: 1982.

Burns, J. H. See *The Cambridge History.*

Caggese, R. *Roberto d'Angiò e i suoi tempi.* 2 vols. Firenze: 1921–1930.

Calasso, Francesco. "Bartolo da Sassoferrato." DBI 6 (1964) 640–669.

———. *I glossatori e la teoria della sovranità: Storia di diritto comune pubblico.* 3d ed. Milan: 1957.

The Cambridge History of Medieval Political Thought c.350–c.1450. Ed. J. H. Burns. Cambridge: 1988.

Campitelli, Adriana, and Filippo Liotta. "Notizia del ms. Vat. lat. 8069." *Annali di storia del diritto* 5/6 (1961–1962) 387–406.

Canning, Joseph. "Law, Sovereignty and Corporation Theory, 1300–1450." *The Cambridge History of Medieval Political Thought c.350–c.1450.* Ed. J. H. Burns. Cambridge: 1988: 454–476.

———. *The Political Thought of Baldus de Ubaldis.* Cambridge Studies in Medieval Life and Thought, Fourth Series, 6. Cambridge: 1987.

Carlyle, R. W., and A. J. Carlyle. *A History of Mediaeval Political Theory in the West.* 6. vols. Edinburgh and London: 1962.

Chabanne, R. "Paulus de Liazariis." DDC 6 (1957) 1276–1277.

———. See also Lefebvre, Charles.

Chartier, Roger. *The Cultural Use of Print in Early Modern France.* Trans. Lydia Cochrane. Princeton, N.J.: 1987.

Cheney, Christopher. *From Becket to Langton: English Church Government 1170–1213.* Manchester: 1956.

Chevrier, G. "Baldi de Ubaldi." DDC 2 (1937) 39–52.

Chiapelli, Luigi. "Maestri e scuole in Pistoia fino al secolo XIV." *Archivio storico Italiano* 78 (1920) 160–214.

———. *Nuove ricerche su Cino da Pistoia con testi inediti.* Vol. 1. Pistoia: 1911.

Chodorow, Stanley. "Dishonest Litigation in the Church Courts, 1140–98." *Law, Church, and Society: Essays in Honor of Stephan Kuttner.* Ed. K. Pennington and R. Somerville. Philadelphia: 1977: 187–206.

Cibrario, Luigi. *Delle storie di Chieri libri quattro.* 2 vols. Torino: 1827.

Classen, Peter. "Rom und Paris: Kurie und Universität im 12. Jahrhundert."

Studium und Gesellschaft im Mittelalter. Ed. Johannes Fried. MGH, Schriften 29. Stuttgart: 1983: 143–169.

Clementi, D. "The Anglo-Saxon Origins of the Principle 'Innocent until Proved Guilty.'" *Herrschaftsverträge, Wahlkapitulationen, Fundamentalgesetze.* Ed. Rudolf Vierhaus. Studies Presented to the International Commission for the History of Representative and Parliamentary Institutions, 59. Veröffentlichungen des Max-Plank-Instituts für Geschichte, 56. Göttingen: 1977: 68–76.

Coleman, Janet. "Property and Poverty." *The Cambridge History of Medieval Political Thought c. 350–c. 1450.* Ed. J. H. Burns. Cambridge: 1988: 607–652.

Coleman, Rebecca. "Reason and Unreason in Early Medieval Law." *Journal of Interdisciplinary History* 4 (1974) 571–591.

Colli, Vincenzo. "Il cod. 351 della Biblioteca Capitolare 'Feliniana' di Lucca: Editori quattrocenteschi e 'Libri consiliorum' di Baldo degli Ubaldi (1327–1400)." *Scritti di storia del diritto offerti dagli allievi a Domenico Maffei.* Ed. Mario Ascheri. Medioevo e Umanesimo, 78. Padova: 1992: 255–282.

Colliva, Paolo. "Pepo legis doctor." *Atti e memorie della Deputazione di storia patria per le provincie di Romagna* 29–30 (1978–1979) 153–162.

Colorni, Vittore. "Le tre leggi perdute di Roncaglia (1158) ritrovate in un manuscritto parigino (Bibl. Nat. Cod. Lat. 4677)." *Scritti in memoria di Antonino Giuffrè.* Vol. 1. Milan: 1967: 111–170. Translated into German by Gero Dolezalek. *Die drei verschollenen Gesetze des Reichstages bei Roncaglia, wieder aufgefunden in einer Pariser Handscrift (Bibl. nat. cod. lat. 4677).* Untersuchungen zur deutschen Staats-und Rechtsgeschichte, 12. Aalen: Scientia Verlag, 1969.

Constable, Giles. "The Structure of Medieval Society According to the 'Dictatores' of the Twelfth Century." *Law, Church and Society: Essays in Honor of Stephan Kuttner.* Ed. K. Pennington and R. Somerville. Philadelphia: 1977: 253–267.

Contreni, John. Review of Radding, *A World Made by Men: Cognition and Society, 400–1200.* In *Speculum* 63 (1988) 709–714.

Cortese, Ennio. *La norma giuridica: Spunti teorici nel diritto comune classico.* 2 vols. Ius nostrum, 6. Milan: 1962–1964.

———. "Nicolaus de Ursone de Salerno: Un'opera ignota sulle lettere arbitrarie angioine nella tradizione dei trattati sulla tortura." *Per Francesco Calasso: Studi degli allievi.* Roma: 1978: 191–284.

———. *Il problema della sovranità nel pensiero giuridico medioevale.* Rome: 1966.

———. "Sulla scienza giuridica a Napoli tra quattro e cinquecento." *Scuole diritto e società nel mezzogiorno medievale d'Italia.* Catania: 1985: 33–134.

Courtenay, William. *Capacity and Volition: A History of the Distinction of Absolute and Ordained Power.* Quodlibet, Ricerche e strumenti di filosofia medievale. Bergamo: 1990.

———. "The Dialectic of Omnipotence in the High and Late Middle Ages." *Divine Omniscience and Omnipotence in Medieval Philosophy: Islamic,*

Jewish and Christian Perspectives. Ed. Tamar Rudavsky. Dordrecht-Boston-Lancaster: 1985: 243–269.

———. "Nominalism and Late Medieval Religion." *The Pursuit of Holiness in Late Medieval and Renaissance Religion.* Ed. C. Trinkaus and H. Oberman. Leiden: 1974.

———. Review of Oakley, *Omnipotence, Covenant, and Order: An Excursion in the History of Ideas from Abelard to Leibniz.* In *Speculum* 60 (1985) 1006–1009.

Cutolo, A. "Arrigo VII e Roberto d'Angiò." *Archivio storico per le provincie napoletane* 18 (1932) 5–30.

Damaška, Mirjan. "The Death of Legal Torture." *Yale Law Journal* 87 (1978) 860–884.

Damiata, Marino. *Plenitudo potestatis e Universitas civium in Marsilio da Padova.* Firenze: 1983.

Danusso, Cristina. *Ricerche sulla "Lectura feudorum" di Baldo degli Ubaldi.* Università degli Studi di Milano, Pubblicazioni dell'Istituto di Storia del Diritto Italiano, 16. Milano: 1991.

Davies, Wendy, and Fouracre, Paul. Ed. *The Settlement of Disputes in Early Medieval Europe.* Cambridge: 1986.

Davis, Charles T. *Dante and the Idea of Rome.* Oxford: 1957.

———. *Dante's Italy and Other Essays.* Philadelphia: 1984.

De Grazia, Sebastian. *Machiavelli in Hell.* Princeton: 1989.

delle Piane, Mario. "Intorno ad una bolla papale: La 'Pastoralis cura' di Clemente V." *Rivista di storia del diritto italiano* 31 (1958) 21–56.

Didier, Noël. "Henri de Suse: Evêque de Sisteron (1244–1250)." *Revue historique de droit français et étranger* 31 (1953) 244–270.

———. "Henri de Suse en Angleterre (1236?–1244)." *Studi in onore di Vincenzo Arangio-Ruiz nel XLV anno del suo insegnamento.* Napoli: [1953]: II, 333–351.

———. "Henri de Suse, prieur d'Antibes, prévôt de Grasse (1235?–1245)." SG 2 (Bologna: 1954) 595–617.

Doe, Norman. *Fundamental Authority in late Medieval English Law.* Cambridge Studies in English Legal History. Cambridge: 1990.

Dolcini, Carlo. *Velut aurora surgente: Pepo, il vescovo Pietro e l'origine dello studium bolognese.* Istituto Storico Italiano per il Medio Evo, Studi storici, 180. Roma: 1987.

Dolezalek, Gero. "The *Lectura Codicis* of Odofredus, recensio I and Jacobus Balduini." *The Two Laws: Studies in Medieval Roman and Canon Law Dedicated to Stephan Kuttner.* Studies in Medieval and Early Modern Canon Law, 1. Washington D.C.: 1990: 97–120,

———. *Repertorium manuscriptorum veterum Codicis Iustiniani.* With the Collaboration of Laurent Mayali. Repertorien zur Frühzeit der gelehrten Rechte, Ius commune, Sonderhefte, Texte und Monographien, 23. Frankfurt am Main: 1985.

———. *Verzeichnis der Handschriften zum römischen Recht bis 1600.* 4 vols. Frankfurt: 1972.

Dönniges, Wilhelm. *Kritik der Quellen für die Geschichte Heinrichs des VII. des Luxemburgers.* Berlin: 1841.

Duynstee, Marguerite. "Jean Noaillé et sa Lectura sur le titre de actionibus des Institutes." *Études néelandaises de droit et d'historie présentées à l'Université d'Orléans pour le 750e anniversaire des enseignements juridiques.* Ed. Robert Feenstra and C. M. Ridderikhoff. Bulletin de la Société archéologique et historique de l'Orléanais, N.S. 9. Orléans: 1985: 119–132.

Ercole, Francesco. *Da Bartolo all'Althusio: Saggi sulla storia del pensiero pubblicistico del Rinascimento italiano.* Collana storica, 44. Firenze: 1932.

———. "L'Origine francese di una nota formola Bartoliana." *Archivio storico italiano* (6th series) 73 (1915) 241–294.

———. "Sulla origine francese e le vicende in Italia della formola: 'Rex superiorem non recognoscens est princeps in regno suo.'" *Archivio storico italiano* (7th series) 16 (1931) 197–238.

Esmein, Adhémar. "La maxime 'Princeps legibus solutus est' dans l'ancien droit public français." *Essays in Legal History.* Ed. Paul Vinogradoff. London: 1913: 201–214.

Eubel, Conrad. *Hierarchia catholica medii aevi.* 2 vols. Monasterii: 1913–1923.

Fabroni, Angelo. *Adnotationes et monumenta ad Laurentii Medicis magnifici vitam pertinentia.* 2 vols. Pisa: 1784.

Falkenstein, Ludwig. "Appellationen an den Papst und Delegationsgerichtsbarkeit am Beispiel Alexanders III. und Heinrichs von Frankreich." *Zeitschrift für Kirchengeschichte* 97 (1986) 36–65.

Faraglia, N. F. *Storia della regina Giovanna II d'Angio.* Lanciano: 1904.

Favier, J. "Les légistes et le gouvernment de Philippe le Bel." *Journal des savants* (1969) 92–108.

Fedalto, Giorgio. *La chiesa Latina in oriente.* Vol. 2: *Hierarchia latina orientis.* Studi Religiosi, 3. Verona: 1976.

Fedele, P. "Primato pontificio ed Episcopato con particolare riferimento alla dottrina dell'Ostiense." *Collectanea Stephan Kuttner.* SG, 14.4. Bologna: 1967: 349–367.

Feenstra, Robert. "Jean de Blanot et la formule 'Rex Francie in regno suo princeps est.'" *Études d'histoire du droit canonique dédiées à Gabriel Le Bras.* Paris: 1965: II, 885–895.

Fell, A London. *Origins of Legislative Sovereignty and the Legislative State.* Vol. 1: *Corasius and the Renaissance Systematization of Roman Law.* Königstein-Cambridge, Mass.: 1983.

———. *Origins of Legislative Sovereignty and the Legislative State.* Vol. 3: Bodin's *Humanistic Legal System and Rejection of "Medieval Political Theology."* Königstein-Boston, Mass.: 1987.

———. *Origins of Legislative Sovereignty and the Legislative State.* Vol. 4: *Medieval or Renaissance Origins? Historiographical Debates and Deconstructions.* New York-Westport-London: 1991.

Fichtenau, Heinrich. *Arenga: Spätantike und Mittelalter im Spiegel von Urkundenformeln.* Köln-Wien: 1957.

Finke, Heinrich. *Weltimperialismus und nationale Regungen im späteren Mittelalter.* Freiburg i. Br.: 1916.

Fiorelli, Piero. "Accorso." DBI 1 (1960) 118–120.

————. "Azzone." DBI 4 (1962) 774–781.

————. *La tortura giudiziaria nel diritto comune.* Ius nostrum, 1–2. 2 vols. Milan: 1953–1954.

Fodale, Salvatore. "Baldo degli Ubaldi difensore di Urbano VI e signore di Biscina." *Quaderni medievali* 17 (1984) 73–85.

Fouracre, Paul. See Davies, Wendy.

Fournier, Paul. "Pierre Jame (Petrus Jacobi) d'Aurillac, jurisconsulte." *Histoire littéraire de la France* 36 (1922) 481–521.

Fowler-Magerl, Linda. *Repertorien zur Frühzeit der gelehrten Rechte: Ordo iudiciorum vel ordo iudiciarius.* Ius commune, Sonderhefte 19. Frankfurt am Main: 1984.

Fraher, Richard M. "Preventing Crime in the High Middle Ages: The Medieval Lawyers' Search for Deterrence." *Popes, Teachers, and the Canon Law in the Middle Ages: Festschrift for Brian Tierney.* Ed. Stanley Chodorow and James R. Sweeney. Ithaca: 1989: 212–233.

————. "The Theoretical Justification for the New Criminal Law of the High Middle Ages: 'Rei publice interest, ne crimina remaneant impunita.'" *University of Illinois Law Review* (1984) 577–595.

————. "'Ut nullus describatur reus prius quam convincatur': Presumption of Innocence in Medieval Canon Law." *Proceedings of the Sixth International Congress of Medieval Canon Law.* Ed. S. Kuttner and K. Pennington. MIC, Series C, 7. Città del Vaticano: 1985: 493–506.

Franklin, Julian H. *Constitutionalism and Resistance in the Sixteenth Century: Three Treatises by Hotman, Beza, and Mornay.* New York: 1969.

————. *Jean Bodin and the Rise of Absolutist Theory.* Cambridge: 1973.

Fransen, Gérard. "Guy de Suzaria." *Dictionnaire d'histoire et de géographie ecclésiastiques* 22 (1988) 1291.

Frantz, Erich. *Sixtus IV. und die Republik Florenz.* Regensburg: 1880.

Fried, Johannes. *Die Entstehung des Juristenstandes im 12. Jahrhundert: Zur sozialen Stellung und politischen Bedeutung gelehrter Juristen in Bologna und Modena.* Forschungen zur neueren Privatrechtsgeschichte, 21. Köln-Wien: 1974.

————. "Wille, Freiwilligkeit und Geständnis um 1300: Zur Beurteilung des letzten Templergrossmeisters Jacques de Molay." *Historisches Jahrbuch* 105 (1985) 388–425.

Fuhrmann, Horst. *Germany in the High Middle Ages c. 1050–1200.* Trans. Timothy Reuter. Cambridge: 1986.

Funk, Josef. *Primat des Naturrechtes: Die Tranzendenz des Naturrechtes gegenüber dem positiven Recht.* St.-Gabrieler Studien, 13. Mödling bei Wien: 1952.

Gachon, P. "Etude sur le manuscrit G. 1036 des Archives départmentales de la Lozère: Pièces relatives au débat de pape Clément V avec l'empereur Henri VII." *Mémoires de la Société archéologique de Montpellier.* Montpellier: 1894.

Gagnér, Sten. *Studien zur Ideengeschichte der Gesetzgebung.* Acta Universitatis Upsaliensis, Studi Iuridica Upsaliensia, 1. Stockholm-Uppsala-Göteborg: 1960.

Gallagher, Clarence. *Canon Law and the Christian Community: The Role of Law According to the "Summa aurea" of Cardinal Hostiensis.* Analecta Gregoriana, 208. Rome: 1978.

García y García, Antonio. *Laurentius Hispanus: Datos biográficos y estudio crítico de sus obras.* Madrid-Rome: 1956.

Gaudemet, Jean. "Utilitas publica." *Revue historique de droit francais et étranger* 29 (1951) 465–499.

Georgi, Wolfgang. *Friedrich Barbarossa und die auswärtigen Mächte: Studien zur Aussenpolitik 1159–1180.* Europäische Hochschulschriften, Reihe 3, Geschichte und Hilfswissenschaften, 442. Frankfurt am Main-Bern-New York-Paris: 1990.

Gibbon, Edward. *History of the Decline and Fall of the Roman Empire.* Ed. O. Smeaton. New York: n.d.

Gierke, Otto von. *Johannes Althusius und die Entwicklung der naturrechtlichen Staatstheorien: Zugleich ein Beitrag zur Geschichte der Rechtssystematik.* Untersuchungen zur deutschen Staats- und Rechtsgeschichte, Alte Folge 7. Breslau: 1902. Reprinted 6th ed. Aalen: 1968.

———. *Natural Law and the Theory of Society 1500 to 1800.* Trans. Ernest Barker. Boston: 1957.

Giesey, Ralph E. "Medieval Jurisprudence in Bodin's Concept of Sovereignty." *Jean Bodin: Verhandlungen der Internationalen Bodin-Tagung in München.* Ed. Horst Denzer. Münchener Studien zur Politik, 16. München: 1973: 167–186.

Gilbert, Felix. *Machiavelli and Guicciardini: Politics and History in Sixteenth-Century Florence.* Princeton: 1965.

Gillingham, J. B. "Why did Rahewin stop writing the *Gesta Friderici?*" EHR 83 (1968) 294–303.

Gilmore, Myron Piper. *Argument from Roman Law in Political Thought 1200–1600.* Cambridge, Mass.: 1941.

Giordanengo, Gérard. *Le droit féodal dans les pays de droit écrit: L'exemple de la Provence et du Dauphiné XIIe–début XIV siècle.* Bibliothèques des Écoles Françaises d'Athènes et de Rome, 266. Rome: 1988.

Glöckner, Hans-Peter. "Johannes Monachus." DMA 7 (1986) 120–121.

Goetz, Walter. *König Robert von Neapel (1309–1345), seine Persönlichkeit und sein Verhältnis zum Humanismus.* Tübingen: 1910.

Goodhart, Arthur L. *English Law and the Moral Law.* London: 1953.

Gouron, André. "Aux racines de la théorie des présomptions." *Rivista internazionale di diritto comune* 1 (1990) 99–109.

———. "Coutume contre loi chez les premiers glossateurs." *Renaissance du pouvoir législatif et genèse de l'état.* Ed. A. Gouron and A. Rigaudière. Publications de la Société d'Histoire du Droit et des Institutions des anciens pays de Droit écrit, 3. Montpellier: 1988: 117–130.

Grand, R. "Un jurisconsulte du XIVe siècle, Pierre Jacobi." *Bibliothèque de l'École de Chartes* 79 (1918) 68–101.

Grant, Edward. "The Condemnation of 1277, God's Absolute Power, and Physical Thought in the late Middle Ages." *Viator* 10 (1979) 211–244.

Grippari, N. "Le jugement de Dieu ou la mise en jeu du pouvoir." *Revue historique* 278 (1987) 281–291.

Grundlach, W. "Zu Rahewin." NA 11 (1886) 569–570.

Gualazzini, Ugo. "Natura id est Deus." SG 3 (1955) 413–424.

Gudian, Gunter. "Die grundlegenden Institutionen der Länder." *Handbuch*. Ed. Coing: 401–466.

Güterbock, Ferdinand. "Zur Edition des Geschichtswerks Otto Morenas und seiner Fortsetzer." *Neues Archiv der Gesellschaft für ältere deutsche Geschichtskunde* 48 (1930) 116–147.

Hageneder, Othmar. "Weltherrschaft im Mittelalter." MIÖG 93 (1985) 257–278.

———. "Zum ersten Zeugnis für Anwendung der Folter in Deutschland." *Geschichte und ihre Quellen: Festschrift für Friedrich Hausmann zum 70. Geburtstag*. Graz: 1991: 143–148.

Hamm, Berndt. *Promissio, Pactum, Ordinatio: Freiheit und Selbstbindung Gottes in der scholastischen Gnadenlehre*. Tübingen: 1977.

Hampe, Karl. "Eine Schilderung des Sommeraufenthaltes der römischen Kurie unter Innocenz III. in Subiaco 1202." *Historische Vierteljahrschrift* 8 (1905) 509–535.

Hanauer, G. "Das Berufspodestat im dreizehnten Jahrhundert." MIÖG 23 (1902) 377–426.

Hannum, Hurst. *Autonomy, Sovereignty, and Self-Determination: The Accommodation of Conflicting Rights*. Philadelphia: 1990.

Heer, Friedrich. "Zur Kontinuität des Reichgedankens im Spätmittelalter." MIÖG 58 (1950) 336–350.

Heft, James. *John XXII and Papal Teaching Authority*. Texts and Studies in Religion, 27. Lewiston-Queenston: 1986.

Hellmann, Manfred. "Kaiser Heinrich VII. und Venedig." *Historisches Jahrbuch* 76 (1957) 15–33.

Helmholz, Richard. "Origins of the Privilege against Self-incrimination: The Role of the European 'Ius commune.'" *New York University Law Review* 65 (1990) 962–990.

———. "'Si quis suadente' (C.17 q.4 c.29): Theory and Practice." *Proceedings of the Seventh International Congress of Medieval Canon Law, Cambridge*. Ed. Peter Linehan. Città del Vaticano: 1988: 425–438.

Herde, Peter. *Cölestin V. (Peter vom Morrone): Der Engelpapst*. Päpste und Papsttum, 16. Stuttgart: 1981.

Hertter, Fritz. *Die Podestàliteratur Italiens im 12. und 13. Jahrhundert*. Beiträge zur Kulturgeschichte des Mittelalters und der Renaissance, 7. Leipzig-Berlin: 1910.

Heyen, Franz-Josef. *Kaiser Heinrichs Romfahrt: Die Bilderchronik von Kaiser Heinrich VII. und Kurfürst Balduin von Luxemburg (1308–1313)*. Boppard am Rhein: 1965.

Highsaw, Robert B. *Edward Douglass White: Defender of the Conservative Faith*. Southern Biography Series. Baton Rouge-London: 1981.

Hitzfeld, Karl Leopold. "Die letzte Gesandschaft Heinrichs VII. nach Avignon und ihre Folgen." *Historisches Jahrbuch* 83 (1964) 43–53.

———. *Studien zu den religiösen und politischen Anschauungen Friedrichs III. von Sizilien.* Historische Studien, 193. Berlin: 1930.

Hoeflich, Michael. "The Concept of Utilitas Populi in Early Ecclesiastical Law and Government." ZRG Kan. Abt. 67 (1981) 37–74.

Hofmann, F. *Der Anteil der Minoriten am Kampf Ludwigs des Bayern.* Münster: 1959.

Hollander, Robert. "Dante Alighieri." DMA 4 (1984) 94–105.

Holtzmann, Robert. "Dominium mundi und Imperium merum: Ein Beitrag zur Geschichte des staufischen Reichsgedankens." *Zeitschrift für Kirchengeschichte* 61 (1942) 191–200.

———. "Der Weltherrschaftsgedanke des mittelalterlichen Kaisertums und die Souveränität der europäischen Staaten." HZ 159 (1939) 251–264.

Honsell, Thomas. "Gemeinwohl und öffentliches Interesse im klassischen römischen Recht." ZRG Rom. Abt. 95 (1978) 93–137.

Horn, Norbert. *Aequitas in den Lehren des Baldus.* Forschungen zur neueren Privatrechtsgeschichte, 11. Cologne-Graz: 1968.

———. "Die legistische Literatur der Kommentoren." *Handbuch.* Ed. Coing: 261–364.

Hulliung, Mark. *Citizen Machiavelli.* Princeton: 1983.

Hyams, Paul. "Henry II and Ganelon." *The Syracuse Scholar* 4 (1983) 23–35.

———. "Trial by Ordeal: The Key to Proof in the Early Common Law." *On the Laws and Customs of England: Essays in Honor of Samuel E. Thorne.* Ed. M. S. Arnold et al. Chapel Hill: 1981: 90–126.

Irmer, G. *Die Romfahrt Kaiser Heinrichs VII. im Bildercyclus des Codex Balduini Trevirensis.* Berlin: 1881.

Israel, W. *König Robert von Neapel und Kaiser Heinrich VII.: Die Ereignisse bis zur Krönung in Rom.* Berlin: 1903.

Izbicki, Thomas M. "New Notes on Late Medieval Jurists: III. Commentators on the Clementines According to Johannes Calderinus." BMCL 10 (1980) 62–65.

Janson, H. W. *The Sculpture of Donatello.* Princeton: 1963.

Jäschke, Kurt Ulrich. "Zu universalen und regionalen Reichskonzeptionen beim Tode Kaiser Heinrichs VII." *Festschrift für Berent Schwineköper.* Sigmaringen: 1982: 415–435.

Johannessen, R. M. "Cardinal Jean Lemoine and the Authorship of the Glosses to Unam sanctam." BMCL 18 (1988) 33–41.

———. "Cardinal Jean Lemoine's Gloss to *Rem non novam* and the Reinstatement of the Colonna Cardinals." *Proceedings of the Eighth International Congress of Medieval Canon Law, San Diego,* Ed. Stanley Chodorow. MIC, Series C, 9. Città del Vaticano: 1992: 309–320.

Jurow, K. "Untimely Thoughts: A Re-Consideration of the Origins of Due Process of Law." *American Journal of Legal History* 19 (1975) 265–279.

Kalb, Herbert. *Studien zur Summa Stephans von Tournai: Ein Beitrag zur kanonistischen Wissenschaftsgeschichte des späten 12. Jahrhunderts.* Forschungen zur Rechts- und Kulturgeschichte, 12. Innsbruck: 1983.

Kantorowicz, Ernst H. *The King's Two Bodies: A Study in Mediaeval Political Theology.* Princeton: 1957.

———. "Kingship under the Impact of Scientific Jurisprudence." *Twelfth-Century Europe and the Foundations of Modern Society.* Ed. M. Clagett, G. Post, and R. Reynolds. Madison: 1961: 89–111.

———. "The Sovereignty of the Artist: A Note on Legal Maxims and Renaissance Theories of Art." *Essays in Honor of Erwin Panofsky.* Ed. Millard Meiss. New York: 1961: 267–279.

Kantorowicz, Hermann. "Studien zum altitalienischen Strafprozess." *Zeitschrift für gesamte Strafrechtswissenschaft* 44 (1924) 97–130. Reprinted in *Rechtshistorische Schriften.* Karlsruhe: 1970: 311–340.

Karsten, C. *Die Lehre vom Vertrage bei den italienischen Juristen des Mittelalters: Ein Beitrag zur inneren Geschichte der Reception des römischen Rechts in Deutschland.* Rostock: 1882. Reprinted Amsterdam: 1967.

Kessler, Peter-Josef. "Untersuchungen über die Novellengesetzgebung Papst Innocenz IV." ZRG Kan. Abt. 33 (1944) 65–83.

Kirshner, Julius. "Civitas sibi faciat civem: Bartolus of Sassoferrato's Doctrine on the Making of a Citizen." *Speculum* 48 (1973) 694–713.

Kisch, Guido. *The Jews in Medieval Germany: A Study of Their Legal and Social Status.* 2d ed. New York: 1970.

Koeppler, H. "Frederick Barbarossa and the Schools of Bologna: Some Remarks on the 'Authentica Habita.'" EHR 54 (1939) 577–607.

Kuttner, Stephan. "The Apostillae of Johannes Andreae on the Clementines." *Etudes d'histoire du droit canonique dédiées à Gabriel Le Bras.* 2 vols. Paris: 1965: I, 195–201. Reprinted in *Studies in the History of Medieval Canon Law.* Collected Studies Series. London: 1990.

———. "The Date of the Constitution 'Saepe': The Vatican Manuscripts and the Roman Edition of the Clementines." *Mélanges Eugène Tisserant.* Studi e Testi, 234. Città del Vaticano: 1964: 427–452.

———. "Francesco Zabarella's Commentary on the Decretals: A Note on the Editions and the Vatican Manuscripts." BMCL 16 (1986) 97–101. Reprinted in *Studies in the History of Medieval Canon Law.* Collected Studies Series. London: 1990.

———. *Medieval Councils, Decretals, and Collections of Canon Law.* Collected Studies Series. London: 1980.

Langbein, John. *Torture and the Law of Proof: Europe and England in the Ancien Régime.* Chicago-London: 1977.

Latham, Richard T. E. *The Law and the Commonwealth.* Oxford: 1949.

Laufs, Manfred. *Politik und Recht bei Innozenz III.: Kaiserprivilegien, Thronstreitregister und Egerer Goldbulle in der Reichs– und Rekuperationspolitik Papst Innozenz' III.* Kölner historische Abhandlungen, 26. Köln-Wien: 1980.

Le Bras, Gabriel, Charles Lefebvre, and Jacqueline Rambaud. *Histoire du droit et des institutions de l'église en Occident.* Vol. 7: *L'Age classique, 1140–1378: Sources et théorie du droit.* Paris: 1965.

Lefebvre, Charles. "L'Enseignement de Nicolas de Tudeschis et l'autorité pontificale." *Ephemerides iuris canonici* 14 (1958) 312–339.

————. "Hostiensis." DDC 5 (1953) 1211–1227.

————. "Les origines romaines de la procédure sommaire aux XII et XIII s." *Ephemerides iuris canonici* 12 (1956) 149–197.

————. "Panormitain." DDC 6 (1957) 1195–1215.

Lefebvre, Charles, and R. Chabanne. "Pierre d'Ancarano ou d'Ancharano." DDC 6 (1957) 1464–1471.

Leicht, P. S. "Cino da Pistoia e la citazione di Re Roberto da parte d'Arrigo VII." *Archivio storico italiano* 112 (1954) 313–320.

Leupen, P. *Philip of Leyden, A Fourteenth-Century Jurist: A Study of his Life and Treatise "De cura reipublicae et sorte principantis."* The Hague: 1981.

Levine, Joseph M. "Method in the History of Ideas: More, Machiavelli and Quentin Skinner." *Annals of Scholarship: Metastudies of the Humanities and Social Sciences* 3 (1986) 37–60.

Leyser, Karl. "Frederick Barbarossa, Henry II, and the Hand of St. James." *Medieval Germany and Its Neighbors.* London: 1982: 215–240. Originally published in EHR 90 (1975) 481–506.

————. "Some Reflections on Twelfth-Century Kings and Kingship." *Medieval Germany and its Neighbors 900–1250.* London: 1982: 241–267.

Lieberwirth, R. *Christian Thomasius, über die Folter: Untersuchung zur Geschichte der Folter.* Weimar: 1960.

Lizerand, Georges. "Les constitutions 'Romani principes' et 'Pastoralis cura' et leurs sources." *Nouvelle revue historique de droit français et étranger* 37 (1913) 725–757.

Lohrmann, Dietrich. "Zur Vorgeschichte der Dekretale X 3.17.3: Der Prozess zwischen Beauvais und Chaalis." BMCL 4 (1974) 1–7.

Löwenfeld, S. *Epistolae pontificum Romanorum ineditae.* Leipzig: 1885.

Luca, Luigi de. "L'accettazione popolare della legge canonica nel pensiero di Graziano e dei suoi interpreti." SG 3 (1955) 193–276.

Maccarrone, Michele. "Il terzo libro della 'Monarchia.'" *Studi Danteschi* 33 (1955) 5–142.

McManus, Brendan. *The Ecclesiology of Laurentius Hispanus (c. 1180–1248) and his Contribution or the Romanization of Canon Law Jurisprudence with an Edition of the "Apparatus glossarum Laurentii Hispani in Compilationem tertiam."* PhD dissertation, Syracuse University, 1991.

Maffei, Domenico. "La biblioteca di Gimignano Inghirami e la 'Lectura Clementinarum' di Simone da Borsano." *Proceedings of the Third International Congress of Medieval Canon Law, Strasbourg.* Ed. Stephan Kuttner. MIC, series C, 4. Città del Vaticano: 1971: 217–236.

————. *La donazione di Costantino nei giuristi medievali.* Milan: 1969.

————. "Dottori e studenti nel pensiero di Simone da Borsano." *Posta Scripta: Essays on Medieval Law and the Emergence of the European State in Honor of Gaines Post.* Ed. J. R. Strayer and D. E. Queller. SG, 15. Rome: 1972: 229–249.

————. "Il giudice testimone e una 'quaestio' di Jacques de Révigny (MS Bon. Coll. Hisp. 82)." TRG 35 (1967) 54–76.

Maleczek, Werner. *Papst und Kardinalskolleg von 1191 bis 1216.* Publikationen des Historischen Instituts beim Österreichischen Kulturinstitut in Rom, Abhandlungen, 6. Vienna: 1984.

————. "Das Papsttum und die Anfänge der Universität im Mittelalter."
Römische historische Mitteilungen 27 (1985) 85–143.

Manitius, Max. "Zu Rahewin, Ruotger und Lambert." NA 12 (1887) 361–
385.

Martens, Carl. *Ein Beitrag zur Kritik Ragewins.* Griefswald: 1877.

Martines, Lauro. *Lawyers and Statecraft in Renaissance Florence.* Princeton:
1968.

Martino, Federico. "Aspetti inediti del pensiero di Ranieri Arsendi in alcune
'Additiones' a Bartolo." *Quaderni catanesi di studi classici e medievali* 5
(1983) 177–199.

————. *Dottrine di giuristi e realtà cittadine nell'Italia del trecento: Ranieri Arsendi a Pisa e a Padova.* Studi e ricerche die "Quaderni catanesi," 5. Catania:
1984.

————. "In tema di 'potestas condendi statuta': Indagini sul pensiero di Ranieri
Arsendi a Padova." *Quaderni catanesi di studi classici e medievali* 5 (1983)
461–482.

————. *Ricerche sull'opera di Guido da Suzzara: Le "Supleciones".* Studi e
ricerche dei "Quaderni catanesi," 3. Catania: 1981.

Mattei, Antonio Felice. *Ecclesiae Pisanae historia.* Lucca: 1768–1772.

Mayali, Laurent. "Lex animata: Rationalisation du pouvoir politique et science
juridique (XIIème–XIVème siècles)." *Renaissance du pouvoir législatif et
genèse de l'état.* Ed. André Gouron and Albert Rigaudière. Montpellier:
1988: 155–164.

Meduna, Brigitte. *Studien zum Formular der päpstlichen Justizbriefe von
Alexander III. bis Innocenz III. (1159–1216): Die "non obstantibus"
–Formel.* Österreichische Akademie der Wissenschaften, Phil.-Hist. Klasse,
536. Vienna: 1989.

Meijers, Eduard M. Review of Calasso and Mochi Onory, TRG 20 (1952).

————. *Études d'histoire du droit.* Ed. R. Feenstra and H. F. W. D. Fischer.
4 vols. Leiden: 1956–1966.

Melloni, Alberto. *Innocenzo IV: La concezione e l'esperienza della cristianità
come "regimen unius personae."* Istituto per le Scienze religiose di Bologna,
Testi e ricerche di scienze religiose, 4. Genova: 1990.

Mesini, C. "De codice iuridico N. 3, Pl II l.s. Bibliothecae Malatestianae
(Cesenae)." *Antonianum* 26 (1951) 271–294, 367–385.

Meyer, Georg. *Das Recht der Expropriation.* Leipzig: 1868.

Michaud-Quantin, Pierre. *Universitas: Expressions du mouvement communautaire dans le moyen âge.* Paris: 1970.

Miethke, Jürgen. "Autorität, I." *Theologische Realenzyklopädie* 5 (1979) 17–
32.

————. "Die Kirche und die Universitäten im 13. Jahrhundert." *Schulen und
Studium im sozialen Wandel des hohen und späten Mittelalters.* Ed. Johannes Fried. Vorträge und Forschungen, 30. Sigmaringen: 1986: 285–320.

————. *Ockhams Weg zur Sozialphilosophie.* Berlin: 1969.

Migliorino, Francesco. *Fama e infamia: Problemi della società medievale nel
pensiero giuridico nei secoli XII e XIII.* Catania: 1985.

Milano, Attilio. *Storia degli ebrei in Italia.* Torino: 1963.

Miller, S. J. T. "The Position of the King in Bracton and Beaumanoir." *Speculum* 31 (1956) 263–296.

Miller, William Ian. "Ordeal in Iceland." *Scandinavian Studies* 60 (1988) 189–218.

Mochi Onory, Sergio. *Fonti canonistiche dell'idea moderna dello stato (Imperium spirituale—iurisdictio divisa—sovranità)*. Pubblicazioni dell'Università Cattolica del Sacro Cuore, 38. Milano: 1951.

Mollat, Guillaume. "Guillaume de Montelauzun." DDC 5 (1953) 1078–1079.

Mommsen, Karl. "Oldradus de Ponte als Gutachter für das Kloster Allerheiligen in Schaffhausen." ZRG Kan. Abt. 62 (1976) 173–193.

Monti, Gennaro Maria. "Da Carlo I a Roberto di Angiò." *Archivio storico per le provincie napoletane* 18 (1932) 101–117.

———. *Cino da Pistoia giurista con bibliografia e tre appendici di documenti inediti*. Città del Castello: 1924.

———. "La dottrina anti-imperiale degli Angioini di Napoli: I loro vicariati imperiali e Bartolomeo di Capua." *Studi di storia e diritto in onore di Arrigo Solmi*. Milan: 1941: II, 11–54.

Morandini, F. "Il conflitto tra Lorenzo il Magnifico e Sisto IV dopo la congiura dei Pazzi: Dal carteggio di Lorenzo con Girolamo Morelli, ambasciatore fiorentino a Milano." *Archivio storico italiano* 107 (1949) 113–154.

Mordek, Hubert. "*Proprie auctoritates apostolice sedis*: Ein zweiter Dictatus papae Gregors VII?" DA 28 (1972) 105–132.

Morris, Colin. "*Judicium Dei*: The Social and Political Significance of the Ordeal in the Eleventh Century." *Studies in Church History* 12 (1975) 95–112.

Morrissey, Thomas. "Cardinal Zabarella on Papal and Episcopal Authority." *Proceedings of the Patristic, Medieval and Renaissance Conference*, 1. Villanova: 1976: 39–52.

Muldoon, James. "*Extra ecclesiam non est imperium*: The Canonists and the Legitimacy of Secular Power." SG 9 (1966) 551–580.

———. *Popes, Lawyers, and Infidels: The Church and the Non-Christian World 1250–1550*. Middle Ages. Philadelphia: 1979.

Müller, C. *Der Kampf Ludwigs des Baiern mit der römischen Curie*. Tübingen: 1879.

Munz, Peter. *Frederick Barbarossa: A Study in Medieval Politics*. London: 1969.

———. "Why did Rahewin stop writing the Gesta Friderici? A Further Consideration." EHR 84 (1969) 771–779.

Muratori, L. *Dissertazione sopra le antichità italiane*. Rome: 1755.

Naturrecht oder Rechtspositivismus? Ed. Werner Maihofer. Wege der Forschung, 16. Darmstadt: 1962.

Naz, R. "Jean d'Imola." DDC 6 (1957) 107–110.

Nederman, Cary J. "Conciliarism and Constitutionalism: Jean Gerson and Medieval Political Thought." *History of European Ideas* 12 (1990) 189–209.

———. "A Duty to Kill: John of Salisbury's Theory of Tyrannicide." *The Review of Politics* 50 (1988) 365–389.

Neylon, Lyn Beth.: See Parker, Karen.

Nicolini, Ugo. *La proprietà, il principe e l'espropriazione per pubblica utilità: Studi sulla dottrina giuridica intermedia.* Pubblicazioni dell'Istituto di Diritto Romano dei Diritti dell'Oriente mediterraneo e di Storia del Diritto, 14. Milan: 1940.

Nitschke, August. "Die Reden des Logotheten Bartholomäus von Capua." QF 35 (1955) 226–274.

Nörr, Knut Wolfgang. "Der Apparat des Laurentius zur Compilatio III." *Traditio* 17 (1961) 542–543.

———. *Kirche und Konzil bei Nicolaus de Tudeschis (Panormitanus).* Graz-Cologne: 1964.

———. "Legitimation by Consent: The Medieval Roots." *Viator* 14 (1983) 303–335.

———. "Die Literatur zum gemeinen Zivilprozeß." *Handbuch.* Ed. Coing: 383–397.

———. *Naturrecht und Zivilproceß: Studien zur Geschichte des deutschen Zivilprozeßrechts während der Naturrechtsperiode bis zum beginnenden 19. Jahrhundert.* Tübinger Rechtswissenschaftliche Abhandlungen, 41. Tübingen: 1976.

Nottarp, H. *Gottesurteilstudien.* Munich: 1956.

Oakley, Francis. "The 'Hidden' and 'Revealed' Wills of James I: More Political Theology." *Post Scripta.* Ed. Joseph R. Strayer and Donald E. Queller. SG 15 (1972): 363–375.

———. *Natural Law, Conciliarism and Consent in the Late Middle Ages.* Vaiorum Collected Studies. London: 1984.

———. *Omnipotence, Covenant, and Order: An Excursion in the History of Ideas from Abelard to Leibniz.* Ithaca, N.Y.: 1984.

———. "Pierre d'Ailly and the Absolute Power of God." *Harvard Theological Review* 56 (1963) 59–73. Reprinted in *Natural Law, Conciliarism and Consent.*

Ostreicher, Nancy. *Trial Scenes in Medieval Romance: The Evolution of their Structure and Function.* PhD dissertation, Columbia University, 1980.

Paradisi, Bruno. "Bulgaro." DBI 15 (Rome: 1972) 47–53.

Paravicini Bagliani, Agostino. "Clemente V." DBI 26 (Rome: 1982) 3–16.

Parker, Karen, and Lyn Beth Neylon. "Jus cogens: Compelling the Law of Human Rights." *Hastings International and Comparative Law Review.* 12 (1989) 411–463.

Pennington, Kenneth. "The Authority of the Prince in a Consilium of Baldus de Ubaldis." *Studia in honorem Em.mi Card. Alfons M. Stickler.* Studia et textus historiae iuris canonici, 7. Rome: 1992: 483–515.

———. "Bartolomé de Las Casas and the Tradition of Medieval Law." *Church History* 39 (1970) 149–161.

———. "The Consilia of Baldus de Ubaldis." TRG 56 (1988) 85–92.

———. "An Earlier Recension of Hostiensis's Lectura to the Decretals." BMCL 17 (1987) 77–90.

———. "Enrico da Susa, detto l'Ostiense (Hostiensis)." DBI 42 (1993).

———. "'Epistolae Alexandrinae': A Collection of Pope Alexander III's Letters." *Miscellanea Rolando Bandinelli: Papa Alessandro III.* Ed. Filippo Liotta. Siena: 1986: 337–353.

———. "Gregory IX, Emperor Frederick II, and the Constitutions of Melfi." *Popes, Teachers and Canon Law in the Middle Ages: Festschrift for Brian Tierney.* Ed. Stanley Chodorow and James Ross Sweeney. Ithaca, N.Y.: 1989: 53–61.

———. "Johannes Andreae's Additiones to the Decretals of Gregory IX." ZRG, Kanonistische Abteilung 74 (1988) 328–347.

———. "Johannes Teutonicus." DMA 7 (1986) 121–122.

———. "Law, Legislative Authority, and Theories of Government, 1150–1300." *Cambridge History of Medieval Political Thought.* Ed. J. H. Burns. Cambridge: 1987: 424–453.

———. "Law, Procedure of, 1000–1500." DMA 7 (1986) 502–506.

———. "Lotharius of Cremona." BMCL 20 (1990) 43–50.

———. "Maxims, Legal." DMA 8 (1987) 231–232.

———. "Panormitanus's Lectura on the Decretals of Gregory IX." *Fälschungen im Mittelalter: Internationaler Kongreß der Monumenta Germaniae Historica München, 16.–19. September 1986: Gefälschte Rechtstexte: Der bestrafte Fälscher.* Schriften der Monumenta Germaniae Historica, 33.1–6. Hannover: 1988: II, 363–373.

———. *Pope and Bishops: The Papal Monarchy in the Twelfth and Thirteenth Centuries.* Philadelphia: 1984.

———. "Pope Innocent III's Views on Church and State: A Gloss to *Per venerabilem.*" *Law, Church and Society: Essays in Honor of Stephan Kuttner.* Ed. K. Pennington and Robert Somerville. Philadelphia: 1977: 49–67.

———. "A 'Quaestio' of Henricus de Segusio and the Textual Tradition of his 'Summa super decretalibus.'" BMCL 16 (1986) 91–96.

———. Review of Bartlett, *Trial by Fire and Water: The Medieval Judicial Ordeal.* In *The Journal of Ecclesiastical History* 39 (1988) 263–266.

Pernoud, Mary Anne. "The Theory of the *Potentia Dei* according to Aquinas, Scotus and Ockham." *Antonianum* 47 (1972) 69–95.

Perrin, John W. "Azo, Roman Law, and Sovereign European States." *Post Scripta: Essays on Medieval Law and the Emergence of the European State in Honor of Gaines Post.* Ed. J. R. Strayer and D. E. Queller. SG 15. Rome: 1972: 87–101.

Peters, Edward. *Torture.* Oxford: 1985.

———. "Wounded Names: The Medieval Doctrine of Infamy." *Law in Medieval Life and Thought.* Ed. Edward B. King and Susan J. Ridyard. Sewanee: 1990: 43–120.

Piergiovanni, Vito. "La lesa maestà nella canonistica fino ad Uguccione." *Materiali per una storia della cultura giuridica* 2 (1972) 53–88.

Pignotti, Lorenzo. *Storia della Toscana.* Firenze: 1826.

Pocock, J. G. A. *Machiavellian Moment: Florentine Political Thought and the Atlantic Republican Tradition.* Princeton: 1975.

Pollock, Frederick, and Maitland, Frederic. *The History of English Law before the Time of Edward I.* Ed. S. F. C. Milsom. 2 vols. Cambridge: 1968.

Post, Gaines. *Studies in Medieval Legal Thought: Public Law and the State 1100–1322* (Princeton: 1964).

———. "Vincentius Hispanus, 'Pro ratione voluntas,' and Medieval and Early Modern Theories of Sovereignty." *Traditio* 28 (1972) 159–184.

Prosdocimi, Luigi. "Alberico da Rosciate e la giurisprudenza italiana nel secolo XIV." *Rivista di storia del diritto italiano* 29 (1956) 67–74.

———. "Anguissola, Giovanni." DBI 3 (1961) 317–318.

Prutz, Hans. *Radewins Fortsetzung der Gesta Friderici imperatoris des Otto von Freising, ihre Zusammensetzung und ihr Werth.* Danzig: 1873.

Quaritsch, Helmut. *Souveränität: Entstehung und Entwicklung des Begriffs in Frankreich und Deutschland vom 13. Jh. bis 1806.* Schriften zur Verfassungsgeschichte, 38. Berlin: 1986.

Radding, Charles. "Superstition to Science: Nature, Fortune and the Passing of the Medieval Ordeal." *The American Historical Review* 84 (1979) 945–969.

———. *A World Made by Men: Cognition and Society, 400–1200.* Chapel Hill and London: 1985.

Randi, Eugenio. "Ockham, John XXII and the Absolute Power of God." *Franciscan Studies* 46 (1986) 205–216.

———. "La vergine e il papa: *Potentia Dei absoluta* e *Plenitudo potestatis* papale nel XIV secolo." *History of Political Thought* 5 (1984) 425–445.

Rebuffa, Giorgio. "Jean Bodin e il 'Princeps legibus solutus.'" *Materiali per una storia della cultura giuridica* 2 (1972) 89–123.

Riezler, Sigmund. "Namen und Vaterland des Geschichtsschreibers Rachwin." *Forschungen zur deutschen Geschichte* 18 (1878).

Rivera Damas, Arturo. *Pensamiento politico de Hostiensis: Estudio jurídico-histórico sobre las relaciones entre el Sacerdocio y el Imperio en los escritos de Enrique de Susa.* Studia et textus historiae iuris canonici, 3. Zürich: 1964.

Robinson, I. S. *The Papacy 1073–1198: Continuity and Innovation.* Cambridge Medieval Textbooks. Cambridge-New York: 1990.

Rosen, C. "Notes on an Earlier Version of the 'Quaestiones mercuriales.'" BMCL 5 (1975) 103–114.

Rossi, Guido. "Contributi alla biografia del canonista Giovanni d'Andrea: L'insegnamento di Novella e Bettina, sue figlie, ed i presunti 'responsa' di Milancia, sua moglie." *Rivista trimestale di diritto e procedura civile* 11 (1957) 1451–1502.

Rubinstein, Nicholai. "Political Ideas in Sienese Art: The Frescos by Ambrogio Lorenzetti and Taddeo de Bartolo." *Journal of the Warburg and Courtauld Institutes* 21 (1958) 179–207.

Russell, Frederick H. *The Just War in the Middle Ages.* Cambridge Studies in Medieval Life and Thought (3d series), 8. Cambridge: 1975.

Sabattani, Aurelius. *De vita et operibus Alexandri Tartagni de Imola.* Quaderni di Studi senesi, 27. Milan: 1972.

Sarti, Maurus, and Maurus Fattorini. *De claris Archigymasii bononiensis professoribus a saeculo XI usque ad saec. XIV.* Ed. C. Albicinius and C. Malagola. 2 vols. Bologna: 1888–1896.

Sartore, T. "Un discorso inedito di Francesco Zabarella a Bonifacio IX sull'autorità del papa." *Rivista di storia della chiesa in Italia* 20 (1966) 375–388.

Sartori, Giovanni. "Constitutionalism: A Preliminary Discussion." *American Political Science Review* 56 (1962) 853–864.

Savigny, Friedrich Carl von. *Geschichte des römischen Rechts im Mittelalter.* 2d ed. 7 vols. Berlin: 1834–1851. Reprinted Bad Homburg: 1961.

Schlierer, Richard. *Weltherrschaftsgedanke und altdeutsches Kaisertum: Eine Untersuchung über die Bedeutung des Weltherrschaftsgedankens für die Staatsidee des deutschen Mittelalters vom 10. bis 12. Jahrhundert.* Tübingen: 1934. 2d. ed. 1968.

Schmugge, Ludwig. "*Codicis Iustiniani et Institutionum baiulus*: Eine neue Quelle zu Magister Pepo von Bologna." *Ius commune* 6 (1977) 1–9.

Schneider, Friedrich. *Kaiser Heinrich VII.* 3 vols. Greiz-Leipzig: 1924–1928.

Scholz, Richard. *Unbekannte kirchenpolitische Streitschriften aus der Zeit Ludwigs des Bayern (1327–1354).* 2 vols. Bibliothek des Historischen Instituts in Rom, 9–10. Rome: 1911–1914.

Schubert, Ernst. *König und Reich: Studien zur spätmittelalterlichen deutschen Verfassungsgeschichte.* Göttingen: 1979.

Schwalm, Jacob. *Die Appellationen König Ludwigs des Bayern von 1324.* Weimar: 1906.

Sennif, Dennis P. See Alford, John A.

Sieben, Hermann J. *Traktate und Theorien zum Konzil: Vom Beginn des grossen Schismas bis zum Vorabend der Reformation (1378–1521).* Frankfurter theologische Studien, 30. Frankfurt am Main: 1983.

Simon, Dieter. *Untersuchungen zum Justinianischen Zivilprozeß.* München: 1969.

Simonsfeld, Henry. "Bemerkungen zu Rahewin." *Historische Aufsätze dem Andenken an Georg Waitz gewidmet.* Hannover: 1886: 204–227.

Simson, B. von "Über die verschiedenen Rezensionen von Ottos und Rahewins Gesta Friderici I." *NA* 36 (1911) 681–716.

Skinner, Quentin. *The Foundations of Modern Political Thought.* Vol. 2: *The Age of Reformation.* Cambridge: 1978.

———. *Machiavelli.* New York: 1981.

Sommerfeldt, G. "König Heinrich VII. und die lombardischen Städte in den Jahren 1310–1312." *Deutsche Zeitschrift für Geschichtswissenschaft* 2 (1889) 97–155.

Sorbelli, A. "La scomunica di Lorenzo de' Medici in un raro incunabulo romano." *L'Archiginnasio* 31 (1937) 331–335.

Sorrenti, Lucia. *Testimonianze di Giovanni d'Andrea sulle "quaestiones" civilistiche.* Studi e ricerche dei "Quaderni catanesi," 2. Catania: 1980.

Starr, Joshua. "Jewish Life in Crete under the Rule of Venice." *Proceedings of the American Academy for Jewish Research* 12 (1942) 59–114.

Stein, Peter. "Roman Law." *The Cambridge History of Medieval Political Thought c.350–c.1450.* Ed J. H. Burns. Cambridge: 1988: 37–47.

Steinmetz, David. C. "Calvin and the Absolute Power of God." *The Journal of Medieval and Renaissance Studies* 18 (1988) 65–79.

Stelzer, Winfried. "Zum Scholarenprivileg Friedrich Barbarossas (Authentica 'Habita')." *DA* (1978) 123–165.

Struve, Tilman. "The Importance of the Organism in the Political Theory of

John of Salisbury." *The World of John of Salisbury.* Studies in Church History, Subsidia, 3. Oxford: 1984: 303–317.

Studi sulle "quaestiones" civilistische dispute nelle Università medievali. Studi e ricerche dei "Quaderni catanesi," 1. Catania: 1980.

Stürner, Wolfgang. *Peccatum und Potestas: Der Sündenfall und die Entstehung der herrscherlichen Gewalt im mittelalterlichen Staatsdenken.* Beiträge zur Geschichte und Quellenkunde des Mittelalters, 11. Sigmaringen: 1986.

Tamassia, N. *Odofredo: Studio storico-giuridico.* Atti e Memorie della R. Deputazione di storia per la provincia di Romagna, reprinted in *Scritti di storia giuridica.* Vol. 2. Padua: 1964: 335–464. Reprinted Bologna: 1981.

Tarrant, Jacqueline. "The Life and Works of Jesselin de Cassagnes." BMCL 9 (1979) 37–64.

Tedeschi, John A. "Notes Toward a Genealogy of the Sozzini Family." *Italian Reformation Studies in Honor of Laelius Socinus.* Ed. John A. Tedeschi. Università di Siena, Facoltà di Giurisprudenza Collana di Studi "Pietro Rossi," Nuova Serie, 4. Firenze: 1965: 275–313.

Thieme, Hans. "Le rapport du droit naturel au droit positif." *Ideengeschichte und Rechtsgeschichte: Gesammelte Schriften.* 2 vols. Forschungen zur neueren Privatrechtsgeschichte, 25. Köln-Wien: 1986: II, 940–947.

Thilo, Martin. *Das Recht der Entscheidung über Krieg und Frieden im Streite Kaiser Heinrichs VII. mit der römischen Kurie: Ein Beitrag zur Geschichte des Verhältnisses von sacerdotium und imperium und des Wandels vom Weltimperium zum nationalen Königtum.* Historische Studien, 343. Berlin: 1938.

Tierney, Brian. "Aristotle and the American Indians—Again: Two Critical Discussions." *Cristianesimo nella storia* 12 (1991) 295–322.

———. "Bracton on Government." *Speculum* 38 (1963) 295–317.

———. *Church Law and Constitutional Thought in the Middle Ages.* Variorum Reprints. London: 1979.

———. *Foundations of the Conciliar Theory: The Contribution of the Medieval Canonists from Gratian to the Great Schism.* Cambridge: 1955.

———. "Hostiensis and Collegiality." *Proceedings of the Fourth International Congress of Medieval Canon Law.* Ed. Stephan Kuttner. MIC, Series C, 5. Vatican City: 1976: 401–409.

———. "*Ius dictum est a iure possidendo*: Law and Rights in *Decretales,* 5.40.12." *Church and Sovereignty: Essays in Honour of Michael Wilks.* Ed. D. Wood. Studies in Church History, Subsidia 9. Oxford: Blackwell, 1991: 457–466.

———. "Medieval Canon Law and Western Constitutionalism." *The Catholic Historical Review* 62 (1966) 1–20.

———. "'Natura id est Deus': A Case of Juristic Panthesim?" *Journal of the History of Ideas* 24 (1963) 307–322.

———. "Natural Law and Canon Law in Ockham's *Dialogus.*" *Aspects of Late Medieval Government and Society: Essays Presented to J. R. Lander.* Ed. J. G. Rowe. Toronto: 1986: 3–24.

———. "'Only the Truth has Authority': The Problem of 'Reception' in the Decretists and in Johannes de Turrecremata." *Law, Church and Society: Es-*

says in Honor of Stephan Kuttner. Ed. K. Pennington and R. Somerville. Philadelphia: 1977: 69–96.

———. "Origins of Natural Rights Language: Texts and Contexts, 1150–1250." *History of Political Thought* 10 (1989) 615–646.

———. *Origins of Papal Infallibility 1150–1350: A Study on the Concepts of Infallibility, Sovereignty and Tradition in the Middle Ages.* Studies in the History of Christian Thought, 6. Leiden: 1972.

———. "Pope and Council: Some New Decretist Texts." *Mediaeval Studies* 19 (1957) 197–218.

———. " 'The Prince Is Not Bound by the Laws': Accursius and the Origins of the Modern State." *Comparative Studies in Society and History* 5 (1963) 378–400.

———. "Public Expediency and Natural Law: A Fourteenth-Century Discussion on the Origins of Government and Property." *Authority and Power: Studies on Medieval Law and Government Presented to Walter Ullmann.* Ed. P. Linehan and B. Tierney. Cambridge: 1980: 167–182.

———. *Religion, Law and the Growth of Constitutional Thought, 1150–1650.* Cambridge: 1982.

———. "Some Recent Works on the Political Theories of the Medieval Canonists." *Traditio* 10 (1954) 594–625.

———. "Tuck on Rights: Some Medieval Problems:" *History of Political Thought* 4 (1983) 429–441.

———. "Villey, Ockham and the Origins of Natural Rights Theories." *The Weightier Matters of the Law: Essays on Law and Religion.* Ed. John White, Jr., and F. S. Alexander. American Academy of Religion Studies in Religion, 51. Atlanta: 1988: 1–31.

Tiraboschi, Girolamo. *Storia della letteratura italiana.* 10 vols. Naples: 1777–1786.

Torelli, Pietro. "Note sul tramonto dell'impero universale nel pensiero dei giuristi italiani fino al periodo di Dante." *Studi e memorie per la storia dell'Università di Bologna* 18 (1950) 1–27. Reprinted in *Scritti* (see below): 349–374.

———. "Sulle orme di Guido da Suzzara." *Scritti vari dedicati al prof. E. Masè-Dari.* Modena: 1935: 58–78. Reprinted in his *Scritti di storia del diritto italiano.* Seminario Giuridico della Università di Bologna, 21. Milano: 1959: 293–315.

Torelli, Pietro, and E. P. Vicini. "Documenti su Guido da Suzzara." *Rassegna per la storia della Università di Modena e della cultura superiore modenese.* Appendice all'"Annuario" della R. Università di Modena per l'anno accademico 1928–29. Modena: 1929: 63–89. Reprinted in *Scritti* (see above): 317–348.

Tourtoulon, Pierre de. *Les oeuvres de Jacques de Révigny (Jacobus de Ravanis) d'après deux manuscrits de la Bibliothèque nationale.* Études sur le droit écrit. Paris: 1898.

Ullmann, Walter. "De Bartoli sententia: Concilium repraesentat mentem populi." *Bartolo da Sassoferrato: Studi e documenti per il VI centenario.* Milan: 1962: II, 705–733.

————. "The Development of the Medieval Idea of Sovereignty." *English Historical Review* 64 (1949) 1–33.

————. "Zur Entwicklung des Souveränitätsbegriffs im Spätmittelalter." *Festschrift Nikolaus Grass zum 60. Geburtstag.* 2 vols. Innsbruck: 1974–1975: I, 9–27.

————. *Jurisprudence in the Middle Ages.* Collected Studies. London: 1980.

————. *Law and Politics in the Middle Ages: An Introduction to the Sources of Medieval Political Ideas.* Ithaca, N.Y.: 1975.

————. "The Medieval Interpretation of Frederick I's Authentic 'Habita.'" *L'Europa e il diritto romano: Studi in memoria di Paolo Koschaker.* Milan: 1954: I, 99–136.

————. *Scholarship and Politics in the Middle Ages.* Collected Studies. London: 1978.

Vallone, G. *Iurisdictio Domini: Introduzione a Matteo d'Afflitto ed alla cultura giuridica meridionale tra Quattro e Cinquecento.* Collana di studi storici e giuridici, 1. Lecce: 1985.

Van Caenegem, Raoul. C. *The Birth of English Common Law.* Cambridge: 1973.

————. "Methods of Proof in Western Medieval Law." Trans. J. R. Sweeney and D. A. Flanary. *Mededelingen van de Koninklijke Academie voor Wetenschappen, Letteren en Schone Kunsten van Belgi.* Klasse der Letteren, 45. Brussel: 1983: 85–127.

————. "La preuve dans le droit du moyen âge occidental: Rapport de synthèse." *La preuve: Moyen Age et temps modernes.* Recueils de la Société Jean Bodin, 17.2 Brussels: 1965: 691–753.

Van den Auweele, D. "A propros de la tradition manuscrite du 'De causa immediata ecclesiastice potestatis' de Guillaume de Pierre Godin († 1366)." *Recherches de théologie ancienne et médiévale* 51 (1984) 183–205.

Van Soest-Zuurdeg, Liesbeth Josephina. *La Lectura sur le titre de Actionibus (Inst. 4,6) de Jacques de Révigny.* Leiden: 1989.

Vodola, Elisabeth. *Excommunication in the Middle Ages.* Berkeley–Los Angeles–London: 1986.

————. "Hostiensis (Henry of Susa)." DMA 6 (1985) 298–299.

Waelkens, L. *La théorie de la coutume chez Jacques de Révigny: Edition et analyse de sa répétition sur la loi De quibus (D. 1,3,32).* Rechtshistorische Studies, 10. Leiden: 1984.

Walter, I. See Becker, H. J.

Walther, Helmut G. "Die Gegner Ockhams: Zur Korporationslehre der mittelalterlichen Legisten." *Politische Institutionen im gesellschaftlichen Umbruch: Ideengeschichtliche Beiträge zur Theorie politischer Institutionen.* Ed. Gerhard Göhler, Kurt Lenk, Herfried Münkler, and Manfred Walther. Opladen: 1990: 113–139.

————. *Imperiales Königtum, Konziliarismus und Volkssouveränität: Studien zu den Grenzen des Mittelalterlichen Souveränitätsgedankens.* München: 1976.

Watt, John A. "The Constitutional Law of the College of Cardinals: Hostiensis to Johannes Andreae." *Mediaeval Studies* 23 (1971) 127–157.

———. "Hostiensis on 'Per venerabilem': The Role of the College of Cardinals." *Authority and Power: Studies on Medieval Law and Government Presented to Walter Ullmann.* Ed. P. Linehan and B. Tierney. Cambridge: 1980: 99–113.

———. "Medieval Deposition Theory: A Neglected Canonist *Consultatio.*" *Studies in Church History.* Ed. G. J. Cumming. London: 1965: II, 207–210.

———. *The Theory of Papal Monarchy in the Thirteenth Century: The Contribution of the Canonists.* London: 1965.

———. "The Use of the Term 'Plenitudo potestatis' by Hostiensis." *Proceedings of the Second International Congress of Medieval Canon Law.* Ed. Stephan Kuttner and J. Joseph Ryan. MIC, Series C, 1. Città del Vaticano: 1965: 161–187.

Weigand, Rudolf. *Die bedingte Eheschliessung im kanonischen Recht.* Vol. 1: *Die Entwicklung der bedingten Eheschliessung im kanonischen Recht: Ein Beitrag zur Geschichte der Kanonistik von Gratian bis Gregor IX.* Vol. 2: *Zur weiteren Geschichte.* Münchener Theologische Studien, Kanonistische Abteilung, 16. München: 1963; St. Ottilien: 1980.

———. *Die Naturrechtslehre der Legisten und Dekretisten von Irnerius bis Accursius und von Gratian bis Johannes Teutonicus.* Münchener Theologische Studien, Kanonistische Abteilung, 26. München: 1967.

Weimar, Peter. "Die Erstausgabe der sogenannten Lectura Institutionum des Pierre de Belleperche." *TRG* 35 (1967) 284–290.

———. "Die Handschriften des Liber feudorum und seiner Glossen." *Rivista internazionale di diritto comune* 1 (1990) 31–98.

———. "Die legistische Literatur der Glossatorenzeit." *Handbuch.* Ed. Coing: 129–260.

Wenck, C. R. *Clemens V. und Heinrich VII.: Die Anfänge des französischen Papsttums: Ein Beitrag zur Geschichte des 14. Jahrhunderts.* Halle: 1882.

White, Stephen D. "*Pactum . . . legem vincit amor iudicium*: The Settlement of Disputes by Compromise in Eleventh-Century Western France." *The American Journal of Legal History* 22 (1978) 281–295.

Whitfield, John H. *Machiavelli.* New York: 1975.

Wieruszowski, Helene. *Vom Weltimperium zum nationalen Königtum: Vergleichende Studien über die publizistischen Kämpfe Kaiser Friedrichs II. und König Philipps des Schönen mit der Kurie.* Historische Zeitschrift, Beiheft 30. München-Berlin: 1933.

Wilks, Michael. "Corporation and Representation in the 'Defensor pacis.'" *SG* 15 (1972): 251–292.

———. "John of Salisbury and the Tyranny of Nonsense." *The World of John of Salisbury.* Studies in Church History, Subsidia 3. Oxford: 1984: 263–286.

———. *The Problem of Sovereignty in the Later Middle Ages: The Papal Monarchy with Augustinus Triumphus and the Publicists.* Cambridge Studies in Medieval Life and Thought, N.S. 9. Cambridge: 1964.

Will, Eduard. *Die Gutachten des Oldradus de Ponte zum Prozeß Heinrichs VII. gegen Robert von Neapel: Nebst einer Biographie des Oldradus.* Abhandlungen zur mittleren und neueren Geschichte, 65. Berlin-Leipzig: 1917.

Wolf, Armin. "Die Gesetzgebung der entstehenden Territorialstaaten." *Handbuch*. Ed. Coing: 517–800.

Wołodkiewicz, Witold. "Humanisme juridique et systématisation du droit (à propos d'un ouvrage récent)." [Review of A. London Fell.] *Revue historique de droit français et étranger* 64 (1986) 79–82.

Woolf, C. N. S. *Bartolus of Sassoferrato: His Position in the History of Medieval Political Thought*. Cambridge: 1913.

Wyduckel, Dieter. *Ius publicum: Grundlagen und Entwicklung des öffentlichen Rechts und der deutschen Staatsrechtswissenschaft*. Schriften zum Öffentlichen Recht, 471. Berlin: 1984.

———. *Princeps Legibus Solutus: Eine Untersuchung zur frühmodernen Rechts- und Staatslehre*. Schriften zur Verfassungsgeschichte, 30. Berlin: 1979.

———. *Untersuchungen zu den Grundlagen der frühmodernen Rechts- und Staatslehre*. Unpublished dissertation, Universität Münster, 1977.

York, E. C. "Isolt's Ordeal: English Legal Customs in the Medieval Tristan Legend." *Studies in Philology* 68 (1971) 1–9.

Zacour, N. "Stephanus Hugoneti and his 'Apparatus' on the Clementines." *Traditio* 17 (1961) 527–530.

Zawilla, Ronald J. "Durand, Guillaume." DMA 4 (1984) 314–315.

Zippelius, Reinhold. *Geschichte der Staatsideen*. 3d ed. München: 1976.

———. *Das Wesen des Rechts: Ein Einführung in die Rechtsphilosophie*. 4th ed. München: 1978.

General Index

Index of Manuscripts

Index of Legal Citations

Designer: UC Press Staff
Compositor: Prestige Typography
Text: 10/13 Sabon
Display: Sabon
Printer: Braun-Brumfield, Inc.
Binder: Braun-Brumfield, Inc.